Argument

Language and Its Influence

Argument

Language and Its Influence

J. Michael Sproule

Indiana University Southeast

McGraw-Hill Book Company

New York   St. Louis   San Francisco   Auckland   Bogotá   Hamburg
Johannesburg   London   Madrid   Mexico   Montreal   New Delhi
Panama   Paris   São Paulo   Singapore   Sydney   Tokyo   Toronto

ARGUMENT
Language and Its Influence

1 2 3 4 5 6 7 8 9 0 FGFG 7 8 3 2 1 0 9

This book was set in Times Roman by Black Dot, Inc. (ECU). The editors were Richard R. Wright and James B. Armstrong; the production supervisor was Leroy A. Young. The drawings were done by J & R Services, Inc. The cover was designed by Jo Jones. Fairfield Graphics was printer and binder.

Library of Congress Cataloging in Publication Data

Sproule, J   Michael.
    Argument.

    Bibliography: p.
    Includes index.
    1. Oral communication. 2. Persuasion (Rhetoric)
3. Debates and debating. I. Title.
PN4121.S78   001.54   79-18218
ISBN 0-07-060520-3

To Betty

Contents

Preface

I have written this book for students and teachers in the field of argument. The study of argument is at one time both practical and philosophical. All of us encounter arguments in everyday life as we use language to interact with others. So the principles of argument have immediate relevance and usefulness. But while they possess practical significance, argumentative concepts also raise many philosophical questions. Since classical Greek times, scholars have sought ways to separate good reasons from poor ones. This book is responsive both to the practical and to the philosophical implications of argumentation.

Let me say a few things about the organization of this book. In chapter 1, I begin with a relatively narrow definition of argument as the connecting of two terms in a statement. I then build upon this definition and show how arguments—as message units—fit into the whole environment of human interaction. To illustrate this "anatomy of dispute," actual and hypothetical examples of current-day controversies are cited. In chapter 2, I elaborate on argument as interaction through *language*. The chapter highlights certain characteristics and functions of language. A model is presented to show how argument is a communication phenomenon.

Chapter 3 is the last of what might be called the introductory chapters. It is organized around a triad of key concepts: (l) the relationship of argument to other ways of gaining knowledge (e.g., intuition, emotion); (2) the major forms of argument (descriptions, interpretations, and evaluations); and (3) the key standards for assessing the worth of arguments (validity, ethics, truth, and persuasiveness).

The introductory chapters set the agenda for the rest of the book. Chapters 4, 5, and 6 examine in detail the three forms of argument: chapter 4 centers on descriptive types of argument, such as examples, statistics, and testimony; chapter 5 is concerned with how people use facts as the basis for general interpretations of reality; and chapter 6 looks at arguments based on value premises. The emphasis in these three chapters is on (1) locating the primary and subsidiary issues raised by a claim and (2) judging the validity (soundness) of statements. In each chapter dozens of quoted samples are drawn from present-day controversies. These "specimen arguments" illustrate how the argument forms/types have been used or abused.

Having developed the validity tests for arguments, I devote chapters 7 and 8 to two other important ways of judging the worth of an assertion. Chapter 7 explores certain factors which render a statement persuasive, while chapter 8 examines principles and codes of communication ethics.

The final three chapters are an elaboration of what might be called "argumentative ecology." In chapter 9, I show how arguments are used in a wide variety of environments, such as advertising, law, news reporting, science, interpersonal relations, and literature, and in such nonprint media as stage plays, films, cartoons, and songs. Throughout I encourage students to look about their world—to find arguments operating in everyday life. Chapters 10 and 11 treat policy-oriented argument in the debate context. These final two chapters are practice-oriented. They are designed to teach basic concepts of advocacy.

The chapters of the book are organized to allow a gradual progression from argument theory to argument analysis/criticism to the actual practice of advocacy. This organizational approach follows from the notion that argumentation is both philosophical and practical. However, teachers and students often have particular interests which can better be met if the chapters are read in a different order. If one wishes to study argument as social interaction, for example, chapter 9 might be brought in earlier. If one has strong interests in principles of advocacy (the argument-debate connection), I would suggest going to chapter 10 (and possibly to chapter 11) immediately after reading chapter 1. Likewise, those having strong interests in persuasion or ethics may want to treat these chapters earlier.

One special teaching feature of this text deserves mention at this point. At the conclusion of each chapter there is an applications section. I have included 63 exercises which illustrate various concepts or practices of argument. Most of the exercises are suitable for in-class use as a supplement or an alternative to a straight lecture format. In fact, I teach my own argumentation and debate course around the exercises. I use them either as a focus for discussion in class or as individualized practice out of class. The exercises are designed to give students the chance to work with concepts of argument—to help them develop into better consumers and producers of argument.

In the process of working on this book I have profited from the help and encouragement of many people. I owe thanks to my mentors, colleagues, and students at Ohio State University, the University of Texas of the Permian Basin, and Indiana University Southeast. My contacts with these people—and with others in the speech communication profession—are reflected in every page of this book. The library staffmembers at IUS deserve recognition for their assistance in my obtaining illustrations for the book. Over the last three years I have worked with many highly competent and dedicated persons in the editorial and sales departments of McGraw-Hill, and to them I offer my appreciation. Thanks are due also to Dr. Isabel M. Crouch, New Mexico State University; Dr. Judy Hample, Western Illinois University; and James A. Jaksa, Western Michigan University, who acted as reviewers of the manuscript. I benefited from their criticisms. No roster of recognition would be complete without mention of my family. My thanks for their understanding and support.

To all you good people, then, I offer my heartfelt appreciation.

A final note: My last name is pronounced SpROLL and rhymes with soul.

J. Michael Sproule

Argument
Language and Its Influence

Chapter 1

Working with Some Basic Concepts of Argument

Most people are familiar with the term "argument" and probably most readers of this book would be able to provide a good working definition of what it means "to argue." Although I will refrain for a few pages from giving a formal definition of argument, I will nevertheless maintain throughout this book that anyone who uses language may be called an "arguer." If it is true that all uses of language may be called argument, why, then, should we study concepts of argument? Couldn't we all better spend our time reading about something that we may not already "know"—like how to program a computer, play the piano, or fix a car? My own answer to this question would be to point out that although everyone has a notion of what argument is, all of us benefit from a systematic study of language and its social influence. Knowledge of the functions of argumentative language in particular helps us, at the very least, to be aware communicators. By understanding the use of argument, we may better express our ideas and better interpret others when they use language. Further, I hope to be able to demonstrate that by studying argument we may attain certain specific skills—skills that will better enable us to be consumers and producers of knowledge via language.

In this chapter I will identify for you certain basic concepts relating to

1

argument and, further, suggest applications that will allow you to practice or "process" these concepts. Beginning with a discussion of some misconceptions about argument, I will introduce several fundamental definitions and terms that are central to the process of argument.

COMMON NOTIONS ABOUT ARGUMENT

Before presenting what *I* believe about argument, I would like to take the opportunity to dispel certain common notions about it. I would venture to say that the reader has, at one time or another, encountered one or more of the following statements about argument, each of which I believe to be somewhat misleading.

   1   Argument is elitist: It is used by the powerful in society to increase their wealth and position. The common man is a doer, not a talker.
Comment   It is true that wealthier and/or better-educated people tend to prefer occupations and environments in which word using predominates over physical labor. Thus, the "Man from Marlboro" (the archtypal strong, silent cowboy) is less likely to be a clever manipulator of language than his counterpart in a corporate tax office.
   This dichotomy between the honest, silent rural laborer and the city-bred, slick-talking merchant, lawyer, or politician may be the source of the belief that word users belong to an economic or educational elite. On the contrary, I would support the broader notion of argument as language rather than as polite language used by the educated in formal settings. I would encourage the view that all users of language argue. We argue with ourselves each time that we make a difficult decision. We argue whenever we respond to a request for advice from a friend. We argue when we dress up for a job interview. We argue when we explain to our college professor why an assignment is late. Although my own conception of "where is argument?" is somewhat broader than that of Wayne Brockriede (1975, p. 182), I concur with his basic statement: "So this is my argument about where argument may be discovered: among people, by people, in changing forms, potentially everywhere."

   2   Argument is just politics—like the Kennedy–Nixon debates, the Watergate hearings, or a speech by the President.
Comment   Certainly, politics is a fruitful source of argument. Indeed, most teachers of argument (and I am no exception) are stimulated by political dispute and debate. However, politics is, as I indicated above, only one of many arenas or forums for the using and abusing of argument. Many people who have no interest in politics are nevertheless effective practitioners of argument: the lady next door who is always telling us her theory on the Patricia Hearst case; the taxicab driver who persuades us that X, Y, or Z is really the fastest-growing city; the friend who needs our term paper for a political science class ("Man, everybody does it"). All these nonpolitical persons are arguers: They are people who use language for the purpose of influencing other people.

   3   Argument is basically unfriendly; it creates conflict and produces bad vibrations all around.

Comment Language may create conflict in an intentional or unintentional way. However, one who is skilled in the use of language will be more likely to avoid the needless bad feelings that are created by the things we say. The old saying that "sticks and stones may break my bones, but words will never hurt me" should not blind us to the fact that words can produce deep hurt; but conflict or hurt need not be the source or result of argument.

It is true that we have all observed debater types who are expert at annoying us with their effort to win a point at all cost, but argument may be also used to reconcile conflict and to produce cooperation. Bobby R. Patton and Kim Giffin (1973, pp. 38–39), in their study of group decision making, suggest several ways in which argument may reconcile conflict. Humor or other means may be used to harmonize the discussion. (For those of you who do not believe that humor is argument, I refer you to chapter 5.) An individual may coordinate or reconcile opposing points of view or identify the similarities in what appeared to be diametrically opposed positions. An arguer may identify the source or cause of a dispute and thereby enable the discussants to overcome a seemingly irreconcilable impasse. Indeed, in its function to interpret reality, argument may reduce conflict as well as create it.

Finally, as to whether or not argument is inherently unfriendly, let me point out that ethical argument may be viewed as a kind of love. If we are neutral or refuse to take part in a dispute or a decision, we may do so partly because we do not care whether or not the other person persists in an error or a quandary. When we advise others for their benefit (rather than our own), we are indicating that we care about them—that they and their well-being are a source of concern for us. Argument need not be hostile or impersonal.

4 Argument is a totally or an essentially rational process that involves training in logic and problem solving.

Comment If by "rational" one means "thinking," then argument is probably rational; but one may easily overestimate the extent to which training in argument corresponds to one's ability as an arguer. Rules of Logic and Canons of Argumentative Fallacy notwithstanding, argument may have more to do with common sense than with the rational formulas of decision making and advocacy. Indeed, the philosopher Aristotle (ca. 384 B.C.–322 B.C.), in his work entitled *Rhetoric* (I, 2, 1356a), identified logic as only one of three means of proving conclusions: The other two were feelings (the emotions of the audience) and the speaker's image or credibility.

While I would subscribe to the notion that argument should be based on thinking, I am not sure that the best decisions are always made on rational or logical grounds. Fans of television's "Star Trek" have only to consider the conflict between Mr. Spock and Captain Kirk as to the relative merit of decisions motivated by logic and feeling. Further, a bank might use the logical grounds of ownership and contractual rights to foreclose the mortgage of an unemployed couple, but the dictate of the heart might be a "better" one—to allow them some grace time in which to make the payment. Argument, then, is based on the totality of our humanness, and not merely on our capacity to follow premises to a conclusion.

5 Argument is based on selfishness. The arguer merely manipulates people with words.

Comment   Truly, much political, advertising, and other argument appears to be manipulative in nature; however, argument does not in itself imply selfishness. I have earlier maintained that we may argue because we care about what another person thinks or does. Argument may sometimes be exploitative; but, as we will observe in chapter 8, ethical argument is not.

A BASIC DEFINITION OF ARGUMENT

Thus far I have introduced some opinions about argument without presenting a simple concise statement as to how the term "argument" may be defined. While this temporary lack of a definition may have troubled some readers, it is really less of a problem than might be imagined. Indeed, there exist so many definitions of argument that choosing only one might actually accomplish more harm than good. It is for this reason that I propose two complementary but nevertheless distinct conceptions of argument—a "basic" definition and an "extended" one.

The basic definition that I propose is as follows: An argument is the relationship of two terms via a name-relation-name pattern. In other words, the basic model of an argument is the single declarative sentence in which two concepts (names) are connected via a verb or other connector which establishes the relationship between the two concepts. Given that the basic definition likens an argument to a declarative sentence, it is not difficult to think of examples.

> Smoking is harmful to your health.
> Dr. Shintani is a good teacher.
> The quick brown fox jumped over the lazy dog.

Notice that several of the names in the examples above possess modifiers that give us a more specific idea of the name itself—a *good* teacher, a *quick brown* fox, a *lazy* dog. While the addition of modifiers has the effect of making our simple declaratives more complex, the basic pattern remains: Humans argue when they connect two terms via a relationship word. (It follows, therefore, that questions or exclamations may constitute arguments just as declarative statements do.)

This basic definition of argument is consistent with my point that all users of language may be called arguers. It is not difficult to think of name-relation-name patterns in any field of endeavor:

> "You should vote for Jimmy Carter." (Politics)
> "Darling, would you like to take out the trash?" (Domestic relations)
> "I don't understand this exam question." (Education)
> "Jesus Christ died for our sins." (Religion)
> "We the jury find the defendant guilty. . . ." (Law)
> "We all live in a yellow submarine." (Music)
> "Of course, I can get a job with a liberal arts major." (Personal decision making)

Although some of the above arguments might appear to be trivial, it is nevertheless true that the simple argument readily accomplishes a great deal. Few sentences occur in isolation—we will consider the connection of many basic arguments in the extended definition of argument—but the simple, isolated declarative sentence enables us (1) to provide information ("It will probably rain tomorrow"), (2) to assert conclusions ("Patty Hearst is guilty"), and (3) to show the general relationship among terms ("Forewarning may reduce the persuasive effect of counterarguments"). In short, we can demonstrate the existence, relationship, or truth of terms by using the basic argument. It is for this reason that the sentence is a key unit in the theory of logic (see Brennan, 1961, p. 23), and, as William J. Brandt (1970, p. 24) observes, "the essence of argumentation is the establishment of a convincing connection between two terms."

ASSUMPTIONS: THE SUBSTRATA OF ARGUMENTS

Although the basic definition of argument calls our attention to the relationship of terms via argument, it should be obvious to the reader that single-sentence arguments are uncommon. Sentences are generally to be found in larger language units such as a compound or complex sentence, a paragraph, or a book. Thus, basic arguments depend on and are a part of the wider language experience of individuals in society. The argument that smoking is harmful to your health is understandable and meaningful to a listener only if the communicator and/or listener connect it to other sentences. For example, the term "smoking" would be meaningless unless we, as listeners, saw its relationship to the statement that smoking is the inhaling into the lungs of particulate matter created by the burning of tobacco. Similarly, the expression "harmful to your health" might be explicitly (in the text of a paragraph) or implicitly (in the listener's thought processes) connected to such pertinent statements as these:

> Smoking has X, Y, and Z effect on A, B, and C parts of the body.
> One should avoid unhealthful things because they shorten our lives.
> My friend Joe smoked three packs a day and died of lung cancer.

A Definition of "Assumption"

We may conclude that basic arguments are explicitly or implicitly, consciously or unconsciously, connected to other aspects of our language experience. Sometimes these connections are explicitly made for us by the author of a composition. In such a case the additional sentences that pertain to the basic argument may be called supporting arguments. However, when statements relevant to a particular argument are not explicitly presented, we call them assumptions. We may define the term "assumption," then, to be an unstated subargument that is related to a particular basic argument. Thus, assumptions potentially provide us with additional data enabling us to better interpret a given argument. If we are unaware of an assumption, however, then it has little argumentative value for us. Hence, if a communicator wishes to reinforce an argument, it would be wise for him or her to identify assumptions explicitly (making them into supporting arguments) if these are otherwise unknown to the listener.

On the other hand, in the case of the argument "Smoking is harmful to your health," a communicator might well assume that the audience either knew something about this subject or already agreed with the argument. In such a case the arguer might feel that it was unnecessary to explicitly lay out the relevant supporting arguments and might leave them as unstated assumptions. For example, how many ministers consider it necessary to reiterate the entirety of the Old and New Testaments when making the claim "Jesus died for our sins"? Relevant support remains in the form of unstated assumptions, therefore, when either (1) the author of an argument believes that additional detail is unnecessary or (2) the listener understands and/or agrees with the argument, and thus does not seek out the potential assumptions of the argument.

We have considered assumptions from the point of view of both communicator and listener. However, assumptions are primarily defined from the point of view of the listener, because it is the listener who ultimately decides whether or not to seek out additional details, thereby making the assumptions explicit. If we understand or agree with an argument, we may never perceive a need to probe for assumptions. Yet if the listener does not understand or does not agree with the message of a basic argument, a dialogue of questions and answers like the following may result:

Argument: Smoking is harmful to your health.

Question: Why?

Answer (assumption): Because it does X.

Question: What difference does X make?

Answer (assumption): X causes Y to occur in the lungs.

Question: Is Y bad?

Answer (assumption): Yes, the Y effect shortens life.

Such a dialogue reveals the process by which hidden supporting details—assumptions—are identified by questions posed by a listener.

Assumptions and the Process of Dialectic

The above question-and-answer exchange may be called a dialectic. A dialectic, according to Richard M. Weaver, is a process by which we divide things into classes (1970, p. 16) and identify what belongs in categories of things (1964, p. 64). We may add that the dialectic most often divides and categorizes by the use of questions. Consider another example of an effort by a listener to identify underlying assumptions of an argument:

Argument: The university tuition should be increased by 10 percent.

Question: Since tuition went up 10 percent last year, why does it need to be increased again?

Answer (assumption): Because the university's expenses have gone up 10 percent since the last tuition increase.

Question: OK, but tuition isn't the only source of university funds. Why can't state appropriations or alumni contributions be increased?

Answer (assumption): The governor reports that the state is unable to increase appropriations for education. Further, even if alumni contributions were doubled, this would only cover 20 percent of the university's proposed budget deficit.

This dialogue easily could continue for pages. Observe, nevertheless, that even these few questions were able to elicit many additional arguments that did in fact tend to support the original claim. At this point, the reader might find it interesting to identify an argument and probe for its assumptions by using the question-and-answer dialogue.

The result of this brief discussion of assumptions has been, I hope, to convince the reader that any single declarative statement is really only the visible tip of a potentially large iceberg of hidden assumptions. The connection of visible arguments to hidden assumptions is shown in figure 1-1.

Figure 1-1 shows why assumptions are said to *underlie* argument: Like the tip of an iceberg, the visible arguments are supported by a larger structure of argument that lies beneath the surface of what we are able to see. The diagram also indicates that two arguments that appear unrelated on the surface may actually be connected because they are based on the same set of hidden assumptions. Thus, the arguments that the Louisiana Purchase took place in 1804 and that Andrew Jackson was elected President in 1828 may both rely on an underlying assumption that Brubaker's *History of the United States* is an accurate source of historical information.

AN EXTENDED DEFINITION OF ARGUMENT

Having convinced you, I hope, that any basic argument may be connected to and rely on a host of hidden assumptions, I would like to examine situations in which

Figure 1-1 Arguments and assumptions.

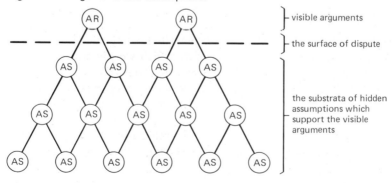

two or more basic arguments are explicitly connected by a communicator in a text of argument. The extended view that argument consists of a set of connected basic arguments is probably a more realistic model for students of controversy as it occurs in the real world. However, throughout this discussion it is well to remember that extended argument may be viewed as but a collection of basic arguments. The basic definition is therefore still valuable because it calls our attention to the origins of extended argumentative compositions.

Argumentation scholars usually suggest that an extended argument consists of two or three identifiable subelements. Rieke and Sillars (1975, p. 48) write that "an argument is a statement with the support for it." Ziegelmueller and Dause (1975, p. 85) hold the opinion that "an argument may be thought of as a complete unit of logical proof. As such, an argument consists of three basic elements . . . the data, the reasoning process, and the conclusion."

Using these quotations as a starting point, I would define the extended argument as two or more basic arguments connected in such a way that one of them is a claim to be proved and the other(s) is (are) data offered in support of the claim. Let us consider an example of an extended argument. In the statement "John must be rich because he drives a Cadillac," the first part ("John must be rich") may be considered to be a claim, and the latter part ("because he drives a Cadillac") seems to fulfill the requirements of data offered in support of the claim. It is important to observe that more than one element of data may be introduced to prove any claim, although the definition of an extended argument requires only that at least one claim be supported by one data element.

The following excerpt from a newspaper opinion column further illustrates the operation of extended arguments. The text is from a James J. Kilpatrick column (*Odessa American,* April 1, 1974, p. 4B) that dealt with the Patricia Hearst case. The column was written shortly after a Symbionese Liberation Army (SLA) tape recording had been given national news coverage. In this tape Patricia Hearst rejected both her parents and conventional society by announcing her conversion to the SLA cause. Kilpatrick attempted in his column to answer the question that was being asked at the time (and indeed ever since): Was Patty Hearst coerced into her SLA activities or was she a willing convert?

> WASHINGTON—The melancholy news, as this is written, is that Patricia Hearst has joined her fanatic kidnappers, taken an underground name and denounced her parents. If true, it is one more wretched chapter in a story without a redeeming feature.
>
> I suspect the purported conversion is not true. To my own untutored ear, her recorded voice was flat and lifeless; it had none of the verve and passion one would expect from a born-again revolutionary. This was the voice, or so it seemed to me, of a drugged child reciting lines. She was almost surely coerced.

These two paragraphs fit well the definition of an extended argument. Kilpatrick's claim in this excerpt appears to be: "I suspect the purported conversion is not true. . . . She was almost surely coerced." The remainder of the two paragraphs is devoted to explaining and/or supporting the claim. We may outline the text as below:

Claim "I suspect the purported conversion is not true. . . . She was almost surely coerced."

Data (1) "The melancholy news, as this is written . . . in a story without a redeeming feature." (2) "To my own untutored ear, her recorded voice was flat . . . revolutionary." (3) "This was the voice . . . child reciting lines."

The first data element provides the context of the situation and orients the reader to the facts of the case. The second and third data elements give evidence to support Kilpatrick's conclusion that as of early April 1974, it appeared to him that Miss Hearst was a coerced rather than a willing convert.

I have presented this real-life example of an extended argument both to illustrate my definition and to suggest that argument normally may be found in its extended form. Indeed, an extended argument on a given subject may consist of tens of claims and hundreds of data elements.

To better acquaint you with the operation of extended arguments, I will present three models of the argumentative situation, each of which broadens our insight into the process by which basic arguments are joined for the purpose of providing data in support of claims. These models are (1) the syllogism, drawn from the study of formal logic; (2) the enthymeme, drawn from the study of rhetoric; and (3) the Toulmin model, devised by the English philosopher Stephen Toulmin as an alternative to the syllogism.

The Syllogism

The syllogism is defined by Brennan (1961, p. 49) as "a form of deductive argument in which, granting the truth of two propositions (called the premises), the truth of a third proposition (the conclusion) necessarily follows." Ignoring for the moment the term "deduction," which I will define later, it is clear that the syllogism is a model of the wider (extended) nature of argument. The conclusion constitutes the claim to be proved, and the premises provide the data.

The syllogism, it must be understood, is a model of formal logic, and for well over 2000 years, logicians have devised rules for its use. Although syllogistic rules are an interesting area of study in themselves, they are far beyond the subject and scope of this book. However, the general structure of the syllogism gives perspective to the operation of extended arguments. Consider the following example of an extended argument modeled via the form of the syllogism:

All cigarette smoking causes cancer.
All cancer causes death.
Therefore, all cigarette smoking causes death.

The example above meets the technical requirements of syllogistic form: Three terms (cigarette smoking, cancer, and death) are related in three propositions.[1] The syllogism constitutes, in my opinion, a good model for gaining insight into the relationship of basic arguments and extended ones. By combining two premises (data) and a conclusion (claim), the example demonstrates the process of inference—that is, the process by which old knowledge (the premises) leads to new knowledge (the conclusion).

Syllogisms such as the example given are organized so that the terms are said to be distributed in the inferential process. When we say that all cigarette smoking causes cancer, we mean that all actions that fall into the category of cigarette smoking (CS) are distributed or placed in the category of cancer (C). (See figure 1-2.)

Note that it does not follow that cigarette smoking (CS) is the only cause of cancer (C). Figure 1-2 indicates that it is possible for there to be members of the set C which are not also members of CS. Because our example syllogism deals with three terms, it is easier to trace the process of distribution with a diagram consisting of three overlapping circles. Therefore, let us follow the directions for distribution that are stated in the two premises and determine whether the conclusion necessarily follows. The first proposition, that all cigarette smoking causes cancer, requires, as we have observed, that all members of the class CS belong also to the class C. Note that in figure 1-3 the shaded area means a set or subset having no members. When we say that all CS belong in class C we are, at

---

[1]Note that this example is a "categorical" syllogism of the first figure with three universal (A) propositions. Centuries ago logicians gave names to various forms of syllogisms to aid students in remembering them. The above is an example of the syllogism "Barbara," so named to remind us that it contains three universal affirmative (A) propositions. I mention these details only to indicate that the above is only one of many forms of the syllogism.

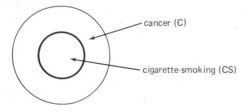

Figure 1-2 Distribution of class CS into class C.

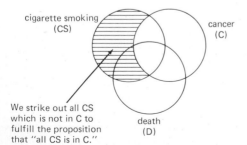

Figure 1-3 Three-circle diagram: distribution of class CS into class C.

the same time, saying that there is no CS which is not also C. Thus, in figure 1-3 we block out a portion of the diagram.

The second proposition distributes the term cancer (C) into the category death (D). Hence, in figure 1-4 we strike out the portion of class C which is not also in D.

As a result of following the directions on distribution for the first two propositions (also called premises or data), we observe in figure 1-4 that the conclusion "all cigarette smoking causes death" is evident, because in the figure it is clear that all remaining members of the set CS are also members of the set D.

This example demonstrates that, in a syllogism, the conclusion is necessarily true if the premises are true. Did the diagrams confuse you? Syllogistic logic and set diagrams are often difficult for readers who are unfamiliar with them. If you like, you might reread the example until you understand the principles of it. However, the purpose of this introduction into the syllogism is not to make the reader an expert in working with the tools of formal logic. Rather, the purpose is to acquaint you with the process by which basic arguments constitute a complete extended argument. In our example of the syllogism, we demonstrated the necessary fact of a claim with only two supporting arguments. Hence, the syllogism may be seen as a model of the skeleton of extended argumentation.

It is necessary, however, to highlight one unrealistic feature of the syllogism. The definition of the syllogism states that if we grant that the two premises are true, then the conclusion (depending on the type of proposition) will be true also. What happens, you may ask, if we do not grant the premises? Simply stated, if we do not concede the 100 percent accuracy of the two premises in the example above, then the conclusion does *not* necessarily follow at all. Let us take another look at the two premises. Has research established the fact that all cigarette smoking causes cancer? Certainly not. We probably all are acquainted with persons who smoke but who do not have cancer. Similarly, does all cancer cause death? Again, no. Evidence suggests that some cancer victims have been cured. Because most arguments such as the above are only partially or generally true, human beings are rarely in a position of dealing with a situation in which we will accept the absolute truth of the data offered in support of a

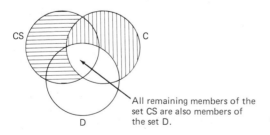

All remaining members of the set CS are also members of the set D.

Figure 1-4 Three-circle diagram: distribution of class C into class D.

claim. Recall the very uncertain data on which James J. Kilpatrick was forced to make his conclusion as to the mental state of Patty Hearst. Such uncertainty is the norm in human argument.

Although the syllogism is somewhat unrealistic (the example "worked" only because we had three basic arguments involving only three terms and because we accepted the absolute truth of the two premises), and although it is complicated, I believe that the syllogism deserves mention in textbook on argument. For one thing, it can be helpful if the premises are simple and straightforward as in this example: Jane is a U.S. Senator; the Constitution requires that a Senator be at least 30 years of age; therefore, Jane is at least 30 years old. Furthermore, as I asserted earlier, the syllogism is a model of the skeleton of the human argumentative process. Like any skeleton a syllogistic demonstration is not the same as the living organism it represents (in this case, a real-world argument such as in the excerpt about Patricia Hearst). Nevertheless, the syllogism gives us insight into the inner workings of the process by which data combine to prove a claim.

The Enthymeme

The philosopher Aristotle developed many of the rules governing the syllogism. However, even Aristotle recognized what we observed earlier—that the syllogism is not a completely realistic model of how people argue. As a result, Aristotle developed the concept of the enthymeme in his effort to make the form of the syllogism apply to real-world situations of argument. The term "enthymeme" may be defined as a syllogism in which stated arguments (visible premises) combine with unstated assumptions ("missing links" supplied by the audience) to produce strong support for a claim (see Aristotle, *Rhetoric*, I, 1–2).

The theory of the enthymeme holds that because the audience probably already knows something about the conclusion, it is unnecessary to present all the relevant supporting information. Aristotle wrote, "If one of the premises is a matter of common knowledge, the speaker need not mention it, since the hearer will himself supply the link" (*Rhetoric*, I, 2, 1357a). In other words, the speaker need present only a few premises, allowing the audience to supply the rest privately.

Let us consider an example of an argument modeled in the form of the enthymeme. Assume that your friend Roger confides in you: "I think Debbie wants to break up with me—she's been acting so standoffish when we're together, and I saw her really playing up to Tom the other day." This statement might be outlined as follows:

Claim   "I think Debbie wants to break up with me."
Data (stated arguments which support the claim)   (1) "She's been acting so standoffish when we're together." (2) "I saw her really playing up to Tom the other day."

Roger's extended argument makes sense because we understand the connection between Roger's data and his claim. Yet in order for us to understand this argument, it was necessary for us to fill in certain missing links—that is, to grant assumptions that Roger made. For example, the connection between "She's been acting so standoffish when we're together" (data) and the claim, "I think Debbie wants to break up with me," requires that we fill in such missing links as these:

- Debbie used to act very friendly toward Roger.
- Acting standoffish is a way of letting a person know that things have changed in the relationship.

The connection between "I saw her really playing up to Tom the other day" and the claim might involve our filling in such links as these:

- When Debbie was interested in Roger she didn't play up to Tom.
- Playing up to someone is a way of letting him know that we are interested in developing an intimate relationship with him.
- People usually have only one special man-woman relationship at one time.

Thus, although Roger presented only three basic arguments (one claim and two elements of data) we may have filled in five (or more) missing links.

This example illustrates the operation of the enthymeme: Stated arguments (data) are combined with unstated assumptions (missing links supplied by the audience) to establish a claim. Of course, many variations of the enthymeme are possible. For instance, if Roger had said, "Debbie has been acting so standoffish when we're together," we might have filled in both additional data elements, such as those cited above, and the conclusion itself—that Roger must be saying that he thinks that Debbie is going to drop him soon.

The enthymeme is an especially valuable model of the extended argument because it enables us to see the relationship between stated data, unstated assumptions, and claims. The theory of the enthymeme recognizes that in normal discourse communicators allow the audience to fill in certain aspects of the wider argument. Thus, if one were to say, "It's raining; therefore, I am not going outside," the listener might fill in several links so as to make the conclusion meaningful. Such missing links might include: (1) people don't like to get wet; (2) rain makes people wet; or (3) the speaker does not have an umbrella. The enthymeme succeeds, then, where the syllogism failed as a model of argument. The enthymeme may be of any length and may comprise any number of terms (as opposed to the syllogistic requirement of three arguments and three terms); the enthymeme consists of stated and unstated parts (as opposed to the syllogistic rule that all premises must be stated); and finally, the enthymeme results in conclusions which are at best only probably true (as opposed to the syllogism, which has conclusions that are usually either absolutely true or absolutely false). The syllogism is an example of deductive reasoning, which may be defined as a process resulting in conclusions that, granting the premises, are necessarily true. The enthymeme is a model of inductive reasoning, a process that results in understandable and probable conclusions but cannot establish necessary truths. Taken together, the syllogism and the enthymeme are models that help us to understand the relationship between data, claims, and assumptions. Lloyd Bitzer (1959, p. 408) testifies to the importance of the enthymeme as a model of interpersonal communication, writing that "its successful construction is accomplished through the joint efforts of speaker and audience, and this is its essential character."

The Toulmin Model

Several years ago, Stephen Toulmin published a book called *The Uses of Argument* in which he proposed an alternative model for looking at extended arguments. Toulmin's layout of argument consists of at least six basic arguments, each of which plays a special functional role in the extended argument. We have already considered two elements of the Toulmin model—data (D), or facts serving as the basis for a claim, and claim (C), a conclusion to be established. However, the model includes four additional elements that clarify the move from data to claim. These elements are: (1) warrant (W), a general authorizing statement that justifies the inductive leap from data to claim; (2) backing (B), specific information that supports the more general warrant statement; (3) reservation (R), a statement of possible exceptions to the warrant and claim; and (4) qualifier (Q), a specific estimate of the certainty attributed to the claim (see Toulmin, 1969, pp. 85–113).

The example in figure 1-5 is a Toulmin diagram containing all six of the elements in their proper order. Notice how the model traces the movement from data (D) to claim (C). Beginning with the specific fact that John has been seen driving a Cadillac, we are introduced to the claim that as a result he may certainly be considered to be rich. These three elements—data, qualifier, and warrant—make up the main line of proof. Indeed, because the qualifier "certainly" is used, we surmise that the author of the argument is fairly convinced of the claim. If the author of the argument had been less confident in the claim, he might have used another qualifier, such as "perhaps" or "possibly."

Figure 1-5 Toulmin model of an extended argument.

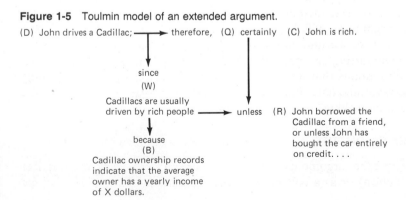

As in the case of both the syllogism and enthymeme, the link between data and claim receives additional attention in the Toulmin model. Specifically, we may ask, how does driving a Cadillac prove that a person is rich? In the example in figure 1-5, the warrant which links data and claim is the statement, "Cadillacs are usually driven by rich people." Notice that if only the data, warrant, and claim are considered, the model is closely akin to the syllogism. However, the Toulmin model presumes a need for specific information to support a general warrant. Thus, a detailed statement of backing (B) is provided to reinforce the general assertion of the warrant. Finally, the model contains a statement of reservation (R) that summarizes possible conditions under which the claim would not follow from the data and warrant. Thus, for instance, if John merely borrowed the Cadillac, then the fact that he drove it would not demonstrate anything about his financial status.

The Toulmin model is valuable because it calls our attention to the different functional roles that basic arguments may play in an extended argument. In particular, I would cite the qualifier and reservation elements of the model as adding to our knowledge about the ways in which arguments work. Whereas the syllogism sought to achieve absolutely certain conclusions (a somewhat hopeless task in human argument), and whereas the enthymeme sought "probable" conclusions, the Toulmin model contains a more specific indication of the degree of probability attributed to a claim. If the data, warrant, and backing establish a strong likelihood that the claim is accurate and if at the same time there exist no major reservations, then we may have cause to possess a high level of confidence in our claim. We might express this confidence by using qualifiers such as "certainly," "undoubtedly," "it is likely," etc. If, on the other hand, the proof (data, warrant, and backing) is weak and/or the reservations are numerous, then qualifiers which indicate less certainty are called for (e.g., "maybe," "possibly," "perhaps"). The model suggests that we make our qualifiers (usually adverbs) compatible with the strength or the weakness of our proof.

The reservations element also marks a departure from the theory and structure of the enthymeme and syllogism. Neither the syllogism nor its cousin the enthymeme left a place for counterevidence (although the enthymeme did not preclude the possibility that the audience might fill in missing links which refuted rather than supported the claim). The reservation thus fulfills an important role in the extended argument. It calls our attention to the fact that few extended arguments will be so strong as to preclude counterevidence. Almost all disputes concerning human affairs are sufficiently complex that one may find both supporting and opposing evidence relative to a particular claim. The reservation requires that we measure the probability of our claim not only on the basis of favorable data, but also on the basis of possible exceptions to the data, warrant, and backing.

THE ANATOMY OF DISPUTE

We have observed that arguments may be found as simple declarative sentences (the basic definition) or as a collection of basic arguments focused on a claim (the extended definition). For the most part we have considered the relationship between favorable evidence and a claim based on that data. However, because few claims go unchallenged, it is appropriate at this point to look at the process by which reservations or counterarguments compete with favorable data.

Situations of dispute are the norm in human language interaction. Although it is possible for everyone to agree that a given piece of data supports a particular claim, it is more frequently true that data and claims are opposed by contradictory data and counterclaims. For those who say, "We don't fall off, so the world must be flat," there will be others who insist that the world is round and gravity keeps us from falling. Dispute occurs, then, when someone disagrees with a claim and/or presents evidence against a claim. The basic elements of dispute are: (1) the agent, the persons or groups involved in dispute; (2) the subject, the topic area in which the dispute takes place; (3) the position, the overall claim (overall goal or general belief) of the agent or agents; (4) the supporting arguments[2] that reinforce the two or more opposed positions; and (5) the end, or resolution, to the dispute.

A Sample Dispute

Let us consider an example of a dispute. In the May 1975 issue of *The Ohio State University Monthly,* differing viewpoints were presented on the subject of faculty-administration collective bargaining on university campuses. Arguing against faculty collective bargaining, Harold L. Enarson, president of Ohio State University (an agent) took the position that "We simply cannot support the proposition that collective negotiations between a university and its faculty and other professional staff are in the best interests of people of Ohio." In supporting this position Enarson advanced several supporting arguments. His major claims were: (1) Collective bargaining cannot function in a setting in which all appropriations come from sources determined by the state legislature; (2) such an adversary relationship between faculty and administration would threaten the university; and (3) a faculty strike would disrupt the university and be harmful to students.

Arguing in opposition to President Enarson, Professor Philip S. Jastram (an opposing agent) took the position that faculty members wanted collective bargaining to cure "a variety of evident deficiencies" in universities. Jastram presented several supporting arguments, including the following major claims: (1) Faculty are today "excluded from participation in decisions affecting

---

[2]Supporting arguments, of course, consist of claims, data, warrants, and backing (to use Toulmin's terminology). However, it is usually not necessary to make such fine distinctions as to the functions of individual supporting arguments. Indeed, a real-world argument may play several of these roles simultaneously. Thus, it would be confusing to use all of Toulmin's distinctions in analyzing real-world disputes. See Willard (1976, pp. 308–319) on the problems of diagramming real arguments according to the Toulmin model (as well as other models). Thus, for the most part, I shall use the term "supporting argument" to denote any type of argument (data, claim, warrant, backing) that supports another argument. Occasionally, I shall distinguish between a claim and the data on which the claim is founded. Only rarely will I identify supporting arguments as warrants or as backing.

compensation and professional matters that crucially affect the performance of their work"; (2) although administrators fear sharing power with the faculty, experience suggests that collective bargaining improves institutional relationships; and (3) faculty do not want to strike, but "if conditions of employment become intolerable, what possible justification can there be for denying the right to withhold services?"

The above dispute highlights the several things that happen whenever claims and data are opposed by counterclaims and opposing data. Two or more agents—in this case, individual advocates—take different positions on the subject of faculty collective bargaining. It is important to observe that just as there may be more than two agents in dispute, there may be innumerable positions on any topic. On the question of collective bargaining, for example, an advocate could argue for complete acceptance or rejection of collective bargaining or for any number of in-between positions. In the dispute cited above, there were only two disputants, and thus only two positions on the subject. Having stated their positions, both agents presented claims and data to support their respective viewpoints. Because the two positions were diametrically opposed, it was no surprise that the supporting claims were in almost total disagreement. For example, whereas Enarson believed that collective bargaining would create an adversarial relationship between faculty and administration, Jastram felt that collective bargaining would promote cooperation. (The two did agree, however, that collective bargaining, if allowed, should be conducted on a campuswide rather than a statewide basis so as to preserve institutional autonomy.)

Possible Outcomes of Dispute

Eisenberg and Ilardo (1972, pp. 72–83) suggest that a dispute may end in one of at least five ways: (1) physical violence; (2) alienation, or the developing of a hostile relationship; (3) stalemate, in which all advocates remain committed to their original positions but the dispute becomes dormant; (4) compromise, in which advocates each adopt a portion of the position maintained by the other disputant(s); and (5) conversion, in which one or more advocates abandon their original position and adopt that of another advocate. In a dispute involving two advocates, it is likely that one of the five ends will result, whereas in a dispute involving more than two agents and two positions, it is possible that more than one end may obtain. In the example above, the dispute seems to have come to a stalemate.

ISSUES

In our brief study of the Enarson-Jastram dispute over faculty collective bargaining, we observed that the opposing claims made by the advocates suggested certain points of disagreement: (1) Would collective bargaining work in the academic setting? (2) Would collective bargaining cause or resolve faculty-administration conflict? (3) Does significant faculty-administration conflict exist now? (4) To what extent should faculty have control over their compensation and conditions of employment? (5) Is it right for faculty to strike? (6) What would be the effects of a faculty strike? Questions such as these, which are raised by opposing arguments in a dispute, are termed "issues." Issues mark the vital points in an area of dispute about which the advocates disagree. An issue arises when one advocate affirms (says yes to) an argument and another advocate negates it (says no to it). From a practical viewpoint, however, we may say that an issue arises when one advocate affirms a statement and that it persists unless or until the opposing agent(s) concur(s).

Types of Issues

You may have observed, in reading over the arguments on faculty collective bargaining, that several differing types of issues appear to have arisen in the dispute. Questions were raised as to the existing state of things in the university community: What faculty-administration actions are presently occurring? Have faculties stated grievances to the administrations of several universities? Further, questions concerning the meaning of collective bargaining were raised: Is collective bargaining inherently foreign to the academic setting? Does collective bargaining mean conflict or cooperation? Another set of issues concerned the general "rightness" of courses of action such as collective bargaining and strikes: Is it right for faculty to strike? Is it right for faculty to have no power to withhold services when intolerable conditions exist? Finally, both the details and desirability of collective bargaining were debated by Enarson and Jastram: Which decision-making system would be more effective in the academic setting, collective bargaining or the present arrangement? Should a plan of collective bargaining involve statewide or campuswide negotiations?

Faced with such apparent differences among issues, argumentation scholars have traditionally classified issues into four types: (1) issues of fact, in which the existence or objective correctness of something is disputed; (2) issues of definition, in which the meaning or proper classification of a thing are disputed (does X fact fit Y definition?); (3) issues of value, in which the goodness and badness of a thing are disputed; and (4) issues of policy, in which the question disputed is what should be done about a thing.

Issues of Fact It is clear that certain of the issues mentioned in the collective bargaining dispute conform to the description of the issue of fact. A fact, according to Perelman and Olbrechts-Tyteca (1969, p. 67), is something about which "we can postulate uncontroverted, universal agreement." In addition to assuming that all human beings may potentially be brought to acknowledge a fact, we may conclude that a fact is capable of independent verification. Hayakawa (1949, pp. 43–48) writes that facts may be distinguished from judgments in that factual language attempts to report events in observational rather than evaluative statements (i.e., there exists a close connection between the word as a "map" and the "territory" of reality that it represents). Questions such as whether there are high or low levels of personal association between faculty and administration in a university or if the rate of employee turnover is great or small would seem to be stated in an essentially factual manner that would allow independent verification of the truth of the matter and would win the agreement of most, if not all, reasonable persons.

Issues of Definition   Issues of definition are not totally distinct from those of fact. However, questions of definition deal more with language that is not strictly observational. In resolving a definitional question, we inquire as to which definition best fits a factual situation or observed thing. Thus, if by examination of the university setting, we have identified numerous examples of faculty refusing to talk to administrators, of high levels of personnel turnover, etc., we might be justified in saying that the facts appear to fit the definition of conflict (sharp disagreement or opposition) rather than that of cooperation (the association of people in harmony). Similarly, when we say that collective bargaining will increase conflict or that it will produce cooperation, we are dealing with issues of definition. Thus, whereas factual issues are stated in language which is more observational, definitional issues are described more in analytic terms.

Issues of Value   Issues of value pertain to the moral goodness and badness of things and require an additional level of analysis. Given that a fact has been identified or that a definition has been applied, does the fact/definition represent something that is morally good or morally bad? Thus, in the situation described above, is conflict morally good or bad? Does cooperation deserve moral applause or censure? Questions of value are crucial for a society and will receive extensive attention in chapters 6 and 8.

Issues of Policy   The final type of issue is made up of questions dealing with actions. The query, "What should we do about this?" is the basic form of the question (issue) of policy. In an issue of policy we decide the merits of various ways of solving problems and attaining good ends. Assume that we have identified an atmosphere of conflict in faculty-administration relations and assume, further, that we have evaluated such a situation to be bad. The general policy issue becomes one of what should be done to dampen conflict and encourage cooperativeness in the university community. Related policy issues might come in the form of questions about the details of a plan to reduce conflict and the effects of each detail.

Observing Issues in a Sample Conversation

Having learned about the four general types of issues, it might be helpful for us to consider how issues arise in another example area of dispute. Assume that three agents are maintaining the following positions on the subject of marijuana use:

  1   The hard-line position: Marijuana production, distribution, sale, use and possession should be considered felony offenses against state law.
  2   The moderate position: Marijuana production, distribution and sale

should be considered felony offenses; the personal use and possession of marijuana should be treated as misdemeanor offenses.

3 The soft-line position: The production, distribution, sale, use, and possession of marijuana by adults should be legal. Sales and other distribution by adults to minors should be treated as felony offenses; production, distribution, sale, use, and possession by minors should be treated as misdemeanor offenses.

Observe how issues emerge in the following dialogue of dispute:

Hard-liner: Marijuana is a social evil—part of the disease that is eroding our society. We must enact strong penalties to prohibit its use and distribution throughout society.

Comment   The hard-line advocate has raised issues of value ("Marijuana is a social evil"), issues of definition ("Marijuana . . . is part of the disease that is eroding our society"), and issues of policy ("We must prohibit its use and distribution"). However, it is possible that the hard-liner believes that he has actually raised issues of fact.

Soft-liner: Wait a minute. Who says marijuana is a "social evil?" How do you know anything about marijuana? Have you ever used it? I used to use marijuana occasionally and found that it didn't have any bad effects.

Comment   The soft-liner has raised an issue of fact (which authorities say that marijuana is a "social evil?"), although this "fact" is probably intended to raise an issue of definition (marijuana's being defined as something that—the soft-liner believes—most authorities do not characterize as an evil). The soft-liner further raises another mixed fact-definition issue when he asks, "Have you ever used it?" In this question he is simultaneously asking for a fact (whether or not the hard-liner has ever used a particular drug) and implying a definition (the hard-liner is presumably ignorant about the drug unless he has used it). Finally, the soft-liner reports a fact ("I used to use marijuana") and what is probably a definition ("I suffered no bad effects").

Hard-liner: You're a pothead, huh?

Comment   Since the interpretative nature of the term "pothead" is so obvious, we may classify this statement as making an issue of definition with some value implications.

Moderate: Hold it. This discussion is getting nowhere. As I see it, the only problem with marijuana is that it is getting into the hands of kids. Let's crack down on people who push drugs on minors and let adults exercise their constitutional rights to do what they please.

Comment   The moderate's arguments raise several issues of definition: "This discussion is getting nowhere" and "the only problem with marijuana is that it is getting into the hands of kids." Further, the moderate raises a value issue about letting "adults exercise their constitutional rights," which one might also call an issue of definition. Finally, the moderate raises questions of policy when he proposes cracking down on pushers who distribute to minors and when he suggests letting adults do as they please.

Soft-liner: (to the hard-liner) Yeah, redneck, don't confuse the issues!

Comment   Two definitional issues are implied here.

Hard-liner: Hold it. Just because I don't use grass doesn't mean that I don't know something about it. According to the "X" study, daily marijuana usage produced conditions described by the researchers as "indicating a general departure from reality in the behavior pattern of the daily-marijuana-use group members." Finally, as to Mr. Moderate's plan, only total prohibition of drug use and possession will rid us of this menace.

Comment   The hard-liner's citation of a quotation from a study raises an issue of fact: Did the researchers in the "X" study in fact make the statement as cited by the hard-liner? However, the researchers' conclusion, itself, raises an issue of definition: Do the behaviors of the daily-marijuana-use group fit the definition of "indicating a general departure from reality?" Finally, of course, in arguing for total prohibition, the hard-line advocate raises an issue of policy.

Moderate: I read the "X" study, too. The daily-marijuana-use group was given a task to complete in thirty minutes, and the researchers pronounced any non–task-related action or statement to be a "departure from reality." Thus, at one point, a marijuana smoker is said to have "departed from reality" when he went over to open a window during the task exercise. Think about that the next time you open a window!

Comment   In raising questions about the legitimacy of the methodology in the "X" study, the moderate is raising issues of definition.

Hard-liner: Well, maybe the window didn't need opening. Besides, that's an atypical example.

Comment   Two issues of definition are suggested.

I am sure you realize that this dialogue could go on almost forever. The important thing to be observed is the way in which issues of fact, definition, value, and policy emerge from a set of arguments in dispute. Also, it is interesting to observe in the dialogue how few issues of fact were raised. Indeed, advocates often believe that they are dealing in the realm of fact when they are actually dealing more with questions of definition, value, or policy. Further, it is interesting to notice how one statement may raise mixed issues—for example, implying issues of fact and definition at the same time. Every argument therefore potentially raises at least one type of issue. The issue may remain hidden on the assumption level, but issues will emerge in the open when one advocate affirms and the other denies (or, at least, chooses not to affirm) a particular argument.

PUBLIC DISPUTES AND AUDIENCE RESPONSE

Thus far I have described the following cycle of dispute. Disputes begin when two or more agents take opposing positions. Disputes end when the agents resolve their conflict—or refuse to do so. Described in this way, disputes center around the behavior of opposing advocates.

You may have noticed that this cycle of dispute excludes consideration of outside audiences. It is well, at this point, to identify the connection between competing advocates and those others who listen to the advocates. In so doing, I will focus on one additional possible feature of a dispute: It can be a public event. The possibility that disputes may become public has important implications for the way in which the arguers conduct the dispute. That is, in public disputes, the agents often communicate less to the other advocates and more to the outside audience.

Sometimes a dispute is a private contest between two or more advocates. A lovers' spat might represent such a situation. Here the agents seek primarily to influence each other. Furthermore, the resolution of the dispute may involve only these two people. In contrast to such private disputes, many situations of argument are public events. Here the advocates make their claims public so as to win support from outside listeners. In public disputes the advocates typically are less concerned about influencing the other advocate(s) and are therefore preoccupied with gaining public support. In such a case the dispute may even be resolved by the outside audience rather than by the competing advocates. A political election is a familiar example of public dispute. The two or more candidates function as opposing advocates: When the candidates address each other, they do so mainly for the purpose of influencing the outside listeners. Most of the time, of course, the advocates address remarks *about* each other directly *to* the outside audience. In the final analysis, the candidates look to the audience—the voters—to resolve the dispute.

Audiences and Persuasion

Public disputes are characterized by the efforts of advocates to influence outside listeners (i.e., persons who are not themselves advocates). For this reason the term "persuasion"—meaning influence through argument—becomes critical. As students of argument we frequently will be asking the question of how effective a given argument (or arguments) was (were) in persuading a given set of listeners.

The effect standard is one of the most popular ways of judging an argument. When looking for effects, the student of argument tries to determine whether an argument influenced the people who listened to it. If an arguer's claim makes listeners more favorable to a certain point of view, then we may say that the arguer and claim were persuasive. If the listeners are uninfluenced by an advocate's point, then we may judge the advocate and argument as unconvincing.

Clearly, the terms "argument" and "persuasion" are closely related: Arguments are a source of persuasive effects; persuasiveness is a way of judging an argument. However, argument and persuasion are not synonymous. Argument, as we have learned in this chapter, concerns the connecting of terms by advocates. Persuasion, in contrast, concerns the effect of the arguments upon receivers. The basic difference between the concepts of argument and persuasion is that argument focuses on language (terms) and persuasion focuses on people (the receivers of argument). For this reason it is clear that the study of persuasion widens our perspective on argument. Argumentation by itself focuses on the question of how advocates construct arguments. When argument and persuasion are studied together, we are drawn to a wider question, that of how advocates construct arguments which successfully influence (persuade) people.

The connection between argument and persuasion will be a major theme throughout this book. I will use persuasiveness—the effect standard—as a way of judging arguments. If you are particularly interested in the argument-persuasion connection, you should consider reading chapter 7 immediately.

Three Additional Ways to Judge an Argument

In the last section I identified persuasiveness—the effect standard—as one way to look at an argument. Students of argument—such as you and I—apply the effect standard when we analyze whether an argument has influenced its target audience.

Although important, persuasiveness is only one way to measure the worth of an argument. Indeed, we have three further ways to judge the merit of an argument: (1) We may determine whether it is a valid statement; (2) we may question whether it is a truthful statement; and (3) we may try to establish whether it is ethical.

Validity   Validity, as I will show in chapter 3, has to do with the logical soundness of an argument. A valid argument is one that makes good sense, given all available information about it. Validity is distinct from persuasiveness: An argument may be persuasive (effective) even though it is unsound (invalid). Also, it is possible that a sensible, valid argument may not be persuasive to a particular group of listeners.

In the next ten chapters, I devote more space to the validity standard than to any of the other standards for judging arguments (effect, truth, ethics). I emphasize validity because of the modern tendency to forget the soundness of arguments and to concentrate on the impression that the arguments make on listeners. In chapters 4, 5, and 6, I will present a wide range of argumentative forms and types. In each chapter I will identify ways by which to judge the validity of the various argument forms/types.

Truth   When we use the truth standard, we seek to learn whether a statement corresponds to "the way things really are." I develop some argumentative truth tests in chapters 3 and 8.

Ethics   The ethics of argument centers around the following question: "Is an argument morally good or bad?" I believe that ethical tests of argument are especially important for an age in which society's morals and values are undergoing challenge. In chapter 3, I identify five ways by which to decide on the moral quality of arguments. In chapter 8, I present a comprehensive treatment of ethical argument and ethical persuasion.

In sum, I will be presenting four ways of answering the question of what constitutes a good argument. This question can be approached by any or all of the following four avenues of investigation: (1) Is the argument persuasive? (2)

Is it valid? (3) Is it truthful? (4) Is it ethical? Throughout the book, I will emphasize that a student of argument should be able to apply these four tests.

Some Further Key Terms of Public Dispute

As the last few pages indicate, this book focuses on the various forms of arguments and the four general ways to judge them. There are, however, three additional key concepts that deserve mention at this time. The concepts of language, situations of argument, and debate will amount to major themes in the book.

Language   Language may be defined as a set of signs to which people attribute meaning. In this way a clenched fist, nervous laughter, the word "handkerchief" and a stop sign all are units of language. They convey meaning. People understand these signs to mean something.

Because meaning is transmitted through language, it follows that language is the vehicle through which arguments are advanced. After all, arguments consist of terms. In order for the argument to function, the terms must be understood; they must be decoded for meaning. Argument and language, then, are closely related. It follows that by knowing more about how language works, we will gain a greater understanding of how arguments operate. This is the focus of chapter 2.

Situations of Argument   Arguments are important in every aspect of life. Principles of argument are relevant to the way that people relate to each other. Principles of argument are involved in facets of life such as business, politics, education, entertainment, the arts, etc. The close connection between argument and "life situations" will become apparent in each chapter as I draw samples of argument from various walks of life.

If you are particularly interested in the various situations of argument, you might want to turn immediately to chapter 9. In chapter 9, I show how arguments operate in a variety of human activities including science, literature, film, song, and interpersonal relations.

Debate   The terms "argument" and "debate" long have been closely associated. This is because debate is a method for presenting arguments in a situation of dispute. In debate, agents defend opposing positions on a specified subject. Here the opposing advocates take turns speaking, so that each agent has the opportunity both to introduce his own points and to respond to his opponent's arguments. By providing for alternating speeches, debate assures that the relevant arguments on a subject will receive full consideration. Thus, debate represents a useful process for studying disputes.

Earlier, I indicated that a dispute consists of two or more agents who amass arguments to support opposing positions on a subject. As a process of argument, debate represents an extension of the general situation of dispute. There are at least three ways that debate can be used in a situation of dispute.

First, debate may be approached informally. In an informal debate two or more advocates agree (explicitly or implicitly) to take turns speaking about a given subject. In this way, informal debate is like a conversation in which two or more views are presented and compared. The earlier three-way discussion of marijuana represents an instance of informal debate, as do (to an extent) the earlier examples of dialectic.

Sometimes, though, it is useful to formalize the debate process of give and take. There are two general ways of doing this. The parliamentary method of debate is useful when the number of agents has become so large that controls need to be placed on speaking. Parliamentary rules provide such controls by limiting the length of speeches and by requiring that all speaking be relevant to some motion. (A motion is a formal suggestion that the group take some action.)

Another method of controlled, formal debate is the academic debate approach. In academic debate the subject is refined into a specifically worded proposition—e.g., "Resolved that the United States should withdraw from membership in the United Nations Organization." The proposition controls the conduct of the dispute as advocates line up on one side or the other—some affirming the proposition and others negating it. In this way formal academic debate amounts to a specialized continuation of the general situation of dispute. The subject is given official wording, the possible positions are limited to two (for or against the proposition), and the order of speeches usually is set.

Debate will be a major theme of this book. Throughout the book, I will be encouraging you both to observe and to engage in informal debates. Chapters 10 and 11, in particular, provide information about the formal procedures for engaging in parliamentary and academic debate. Because these chapters extend the concept of dispute, you may wish to read or to skim these chapters before moving on to chapter 2. In chapters 10 and 11, I also emphasize the usefulness of formal debate as a method to study policy argument.

APPLICATIONS

In this chapter I have introduced notions about and definitions of argument, making distinctions among basic arguments, extended arguments, and hidden arguments (assumptions). I have explained some of the general features of dispute and have considered some of the outcomes of and issues raised in disputes. In the last section of the chapter, the audience element was added to disputes. Here I looked at four ways by which listeners can judge the worth of arguments presented in a dispute: persuasiveness, validity, truth, and ethics. Finally, I identified three key terms of argument—language, situations of argument, and debate—that we will encounter throughout the book.

The time has come for me to give you, the reader, the opportunity to work with some of the concepts and insights pertaining to argument. It is one thing to be able to recognize definitions of concepts, and quite another to be able to use the concepts by applying them to situations of argument in real life. The following applications are based on exercises that I have used in classes throughout the years that I have been teaching. I hope that you will not find any of them merely to be make-work; but, after all, that raises an issue of definition which only you can answer for yourself. Your instructor may wish to do any of the following with the exercises: work with them during the regular class period, assign groups to work on them in class, or assign one or more of them as individual projects.

Exercise 1-1: Modeling an Argument

This exercise is designed to sharpen your understanding of both the elements and organization of arguments. The exercise involves some work with the definitions and models of argument. Specifically, you should do the following:

I   Identify, in writing, a single basic argument (claim) on a subject of your choice or one which is assigned to you.

II Transform the claim into an extended argument by writing it out ("modeling" it) in the form of a syllogism, enthymeme, or Toulmin model.

    A   If you model the argument as a syllogism, remember that you should use only three terms and three propositions and that each of the three propositions should begin with "all" (unless you are familiar with the other forms of syllogistic propositions). You should also use the three-circle diagram, as in figure 1-3, to test the distribution of your terms.

    B   If you use the model of the enthymeme, you should identify at least two stated arguments (data) to support your claim. You should identify at least four unstated missing links that the audience might supply to connect the stated data to the claim. You should, finally, identify certain background characteristics that would explain their ability to supply the missing links you have identified.

    C   If you use the Toulmin model, be sure to identify five basic arguments (plus a qualifier) to correspond to the six elements of the model. You should also diagram the model as indicated in figure 1-5. Finally, you should state your reasons for choosing the qualifier you used by comparing the strength of the favorable data (data, warrant, and backing) to the reservations.

Exercise 1-2: Defining the Anatomy of a Dispute

This exercise is designed to give you experience in defining the elements of a dispute. You should identify each element of a dispute as indicated below:

I   Choose a subject area in which a dispute has taken place, is taking place, or could potentially take place. The subject could involve a personal decision (a dispute with yourself) or a dispute involving you and another person or organization. Also, the dispute could be one that you have heard, such as a national, state, local, city, campus, or other dispute.

Identify your subject area by means of a short phrase—e.g., "crime on campus."

II   Identify at least two agents (persons, groups, or organizations) that have taken positions on the subject. It will be difficult to use more than two or three agents, although you are free to use as many as you desire.

III   State in a single sentence the position of each agent on the subject.

IV   Identify at least five supporting arguments (claims and data) used by the agents to support their respective positions. Write them out in parallel columns, with a number for each column, from one to five (or more).

V   As a result of steps 1 through 4, your anatomy should look something like this:

Subject _____

Agent_____   Agent_____

Position_____   Position_____

_____   _____

             Supporting arguments   Supporting arguments

1. _____   1. _____
2. _____   2. _____
3. _____   3. _____
4. _____   4. _____
5. _____   5. _____

VI   You should identify and explain the outcome of the dispute at this present time or in the past or your prediction of the resolution at a future time. The five possible resolutions mentioned in this chapter were: physical violence, alienation, stalemate, compromise, and conversion.

Exercise 1-3: Identifying Assumptions via Dialectic

Using one or more of the supporting arguments that you identified in exercise 1-2 (or using a claim that you prepare especially for this exercise), you should apply the question-and-answer (dialectic) method to bring hidden assumptions to the surface of a dispute. You should follow these directions:

I   You may make up questions pertaining to the subject, use some of the general questions that are listed below or combine the two. This exercise will give you an opportunity to see how many assumptions may be extracted from a single claim.

II   Remember to use a question-and-answer format such as the one outlined below. Claim: "Smoking is harmful to your health."

    Q   How do you know?

    A   The Surgeon General of the United States has said so.

    Q   Where did you learn this?

    A   In small print on a cigarette package.

    Q   Do you believe that a cigarette package is a reliable source?

    A   It must be, because cigarette advertisements are required by law to carry the warning.

III   In this exercise it is interesting to observe how often we find ourselves having to answer a question with "I don't know." Such an answer usually means that the next question will have a somewhat different focus. Little is to be gained by asking "Why don't you know?"

IV   The following is a list of general questions that you might like to use or to combine with your own specific subject-related questions:

A   Who? Who says so? Who will be affected?

B   What? What difference does it make? What are the causes/effects? What does it mean? What evidence is there? What are the alternatives? What are the exceptions?

C   When? When will it happen? When did it happen before?

D   How? How do you know? How do they know? How will it happen?

E   How much? How many? How likely or reliable is your evidence?

F   How many sources say so? How many sources say otherwise?

G   How unbiased are the sources?

H   Why? Why is it important? Why is it good/bad?

Exercise 1-4: Identifying Issues

Using the supporting arguments for the two or more positions that you identified in exercise 1-2, identify at least two issues each of fact, definition, value, and policy that are raised by the opposing data and claims. Remember that issues are always stated in the form of a question. It is important to realize that many questions may be classified as issues of more than one type. In completing this assignment, you should do the following:

I   Write out the question (i.e., issue).

II   Identify the type or types of issue(s) that the question represents.

III   Briefly write out your reasons for classifying the question as being of one or more particular types.

Chapter 2

Giving and Receiving Messages: Approaches to the Use and Perception of Language

In chapter 1, I described several of the major constituent elements of argumentation. Beginning with notions about and definitions of argument, I presented a framework of dispute in which arguments could be seen to function. In this chapter it is my intention to introduce the reader to an additional aspect of language—the message element—as it functions in human interaction. The result of this inquiry will be a sound perspective from which to study the forms and effects of argument. Beginning with an introduction to the process of meaning, we will study messages from several perspectives: (1) We will look at the different ways in which communicators use messages—the functions that messages perform for their authors; (2) we will study the different ways in which messages may work to prove claims; and (3) we will look at abstracting and outlining as systematic ways for listeners to receive messages. Although this chapter emphasizes the message variable in communication, it is impossible to develop the concept of "message" without reference to "source" and "receiver." Thus, although written from a message perspective, this chapter will lay a groundwork for the subsequent study of persuasive influences on listeners.

A further preliminary is in order concerning terminology. Often, the terms "argument," "language," "evidence," and "message" are treated as relatively synonymous expressions. However, it is important to remember that there are subtle differences among these concepts. Language is the generic (basic) term for the system of communication symbols (stimuli) to which we attach meaning. Argument, according to the extended definition, is the presence of two or more statements, one of which is a claim to be proven, and the other an element of data that is offered to support the claim. Argument, then, differs from language in that argument assumes a more explicit data-claim relationship. From the perspective of the extended definition, idle chatter, for example, is an essentially nonargumentative use of language. Yet, as we will observe in the analysis of literature-as-argument (chapter 9), the differences between language and argument may be so slight as to be almost impossible to detect. Evidence may be defined as a citation taken from an outside source (third party) that is offered as data in support of a claim. Evidence, then, is part of a total argument. Finally, Berlo (1960, p. 30) defines a message as "the translation of ideas, purposes, and intentions into a code, a systematic set of symbols." This definition, of course, is quite similar to that of language. However, a message is usually thought of as being a specific subset of language units chosen by a particular communicator to be presented to an audience. While the four terms—argument, language, evidence and message—possess similarities, the differences are important when the terms are used in a technical discussion.

MEANING

It is appropriate, in a chapter emphasizing the message variable in communication, to begin with a foray into the area of "meaning." Although people intuitively are able to deal with the concept of meaning, language scholars are not entirely in agreement as to how the subject should be defined or studied. As Osgood, Suci, and Tannenbaum (1957, p. 2) observe: "There are at least as many meanings of 'meaning' as there are disciplines which deal with language, and of course, many more than this because exponents within disciplines do not always agree with one another." Although a good case can be made for behavioral theories of meaning such as that described by Skinner (1957, pp. 7–35) and Osgood, Suci, and Tannenbaum (1957, pp. 7–9), I am inclined toward the more traditional semantic theories that originated with Ogden and Richards (1923). Semantic theories of meaning make distinctions among several aspects of the process by which meaning is attributed to things: (1) the interpreter, the person or language user; (2) the symbol, the entity to which meaning is assigned; and (3) the referent, the thing to which the symbol refers. These elements are often combined into what has been called the "triangle of meaning." We may observe, in figure 2-1, the relationship of the three elements.

In figure 2-1 a person (interpreter) uses a symbol (in this case the word "house") to refer to an object (the physical object of a house consisting of four walls, a roof, and contents). The study of meaning therefore can be approached

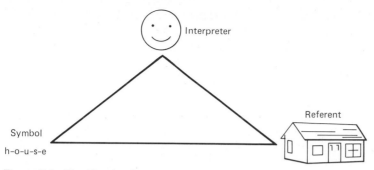

Figure 2-1 The triangle of meaning.

by reference to the binary relationships existing among the elements of the triangle of meaning:

1 The interpreter-symbol connection. In the example above, the interpreter is free to use any of several symbols to represent the physical referent. Thus, a German-speaking person might choose *haus;* a Spaniard, *casa;* or a contemporary of Julius Caesar, *domus.* Further indication of the freedom of communicators to choose symbols is provided by the example of the real estate agent who invariable prefers the symbol "home" over the more impersonal "house." The referent remains the same, although the symbol changes.

2 The symbol-referent connection. Whereas the referent is a part of the real world of objects, the symbol is an artificially created entity that is designed to represent or symbolize the referent. Of course, it is easy to understand that the symbol is not the same as the referent, although a relationship does exist between them. Works on semantics are filled with examples of situations in which the word for something is confused with the thing itself. A student cheats to obtain a good grade (a symbol) but is unconcerned that he lacks that which a good grade represents (knowledge of the subject being the referent). A mother kisses the picture of her child, behaving toward the symbol (the picture) as she would toward the referent (her living, breathing offspring).

It is important to realize that the connection between a symbol and its referent is not a necessary one, and interpreters are free to choose from a range of symbols to designate a particular referent. As Berlo (1960, p. 175) observes, "Meanings are not in messages . . . *meanings are in people.*" In other words, the connection between a symbol and a referent does not exist apart from the viewpoint of an interpreter. A good demonstration of the distinction between a people-centered and a word-centered theory of meaning is made by Barnlund (1962) in his article on a "meaning-centered" philosophy of communication. In Barnlund's view, messages may be generated from the outside by sources, but meanings are created internally—within the symbol user. Thus, a person may be thought of as having communication potentials that, when stimulated by a message (the catalyst), result in a meaning. Meanings are personal, and not objective.

3 The interpreter-referent connection. The personal nature of meaning is further clarified if we consider the relationship between persons and referents. For example, a person who has been raised in the northern part of the United

States is likely to have a particular idea of the referent for the symbol "house." When confronted with this symbol, the Northerner may "think of" an entity that is surfaced with brick and has a basement. However, from the perspective of a Florida homeowner, "house" may represent something entirely without brick or basement. Hence, the word "house" may actually mean something slightly different to the Northerner than to the Floridian. However, one can easily exaggerate the personal nature of meaning. It is clear that once a culture has decided that a particular symbol will stand for a certain referent, it is difficult for one individual to change the commonly used symbol-referent relationship. Hence, we may register our amusement at this dialogue between Alice and Humpty Dumpty taken from Lewis Carroll's *Through the Looking-Glass* (Carroll, 1971, p. 163):

> "I don't know what you mean by 'glory,' " Alice said.
> Humpty Dumpty smiled contemptuously. "Of course you don't—till I tell you. I meant 'there's a nice knock-down argument for you!' "
> "But 'glory' doesn't mean 'a nice knock-down argument,' " Alice objected.
> "When I used a word," Humpty Dumpty said, in rather a scornful tone, "it means just what I choose it to mean—neither more nor less."
> "The question is," said Alice, "whether you *can* make words mean so many different things."
> "The question is," said Humpty Dumpty, "which is to be master—that's all."

Berlo (1960, pp. 190–191) cites this excerpt to reinforce his point that although "meanings are found in people," there exists some social uniformity of meanings, the fact of which makes "meaningful" communication possible. Thus, while the concept of meaning—as indicated in the symbol-interpreter-referent relationship—is something personal, we should remember that meaning is contractual as well. When I say that meaning is contractual I point to the fact that individuals are users of a symbol system that they share with other persons. Although we may theoretically take the Humpty Dumpty approach to meaning, we are likely to be unsuccessful as a word user unless our meanings correspond somewhat to the word usages of other persons. As Weaver (in Johannesen, Strickland, and Eubanks, 1970, p. 136) notes, "Language is a covenant among those who use it." Meaning, although personal, is not entirely relative, for, as Weaver adds, "an effective change [in the meaning of a symbol] cannot be made unless it is endorsed by that part of humanity to which one belongs linguistically" (ibid., p. 122).

The nature of meaning as a contract between and among language users suggests that we may modify the triangle of meaning into an interpersonal triangle of meaning. Figure 2-2 describes meaning as it exists in an interpersonal transaction involving two persons. Whereas the triangle of meaning involved three relationships among the elements, the four elements of the interpersonal triangle of meaning create six binary relationships:

1 The interpreter–other person relationship: their participation in a language community; their past experiences together; the context in which the two communicate, including the time, place, etc.

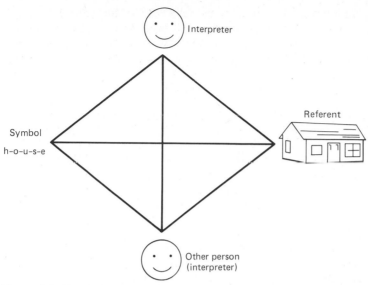

Figure 2-2 The interpersonal triangle of meaning.

2   The interpreter-symbol relationship: the interpreter's use of symbols to represent the world (encoding) and the interpreter's decoding of symbols communicated by the other person.

3   The other person–symbol relationship: the other person's encoding and decoding.

4   The interpreter-referent relationship: the real physical object that the interpreter intends to signify by use of the symbol or which the interpreter "thinks of" when receiving a symbol from the other person.

5   The other person–referent relationship: the intention to communicate and/or to create a picture in the head of the other person.

6   The symbol-referent relationship: the correspondence of the symbol to that which it represents.

The personal and transaction/contractual nature of the meaning process suggests that meaningful communication between individuals is almost miraculous, given the number of opportunities for misunderstanding. Thus, Richards (1965, p. 40) comments that whereas classical theories of language treated ambiguity and misunderstanding as "faults in language," the semantic study of rhetoric views ambiguity and misunderstanding "as an inevitable consequence of the powers of language." The high probability of misunderstanding, which is suggested by the interpersonal triangle of meaning, makes it reasonable for us to give brief consideration to four additional concepts that pertain to the process: dialectical terms, positive terms, abstraction, and ambiguity.

Positive and Dialectical Terms

We have learned that meaning is the representation of a referent by a symbol for an interpreter at a given point in time. Theorists have added several refinements to the concept of meaning. One important distinction is that made between positive and dialectical terms. A positive term is a word with a referent that we can point to—a book, a car, or a coffee cup. A dialectical term is one with a referent that is nebulous—justice, happiness, or independence. One cannot point to justice or happiness. One must carefully construct the meaning of such a term.

Basing his analysis on that of Plato (*Phaedrus,* 262–263), Richard Weaver has given extensive attention to positive and dialectical terms. According to Weaver, anyone may easily perceive the referents of such positive symbols as houses, elephants, doorknobs, and college professors. Dialectical terms, on the other hand, are not something that can be identified by sense perception (seeing, hearing, touching, tasting, or smelling). We do not point to dialectical words; we construct their meaning by the dialectical operation of question and answer (see Weaver in Johannesen, Strickland, and Eubanks, 1970, p. 145).

Recall that in chapter 1 we used a dialectic to identify the assumptions underlying an argument. Consider now how a dialectic may be used to identify the meaning of a dialectical term. Assume that our friend Joan tells us that she thinks that the company's pay scale is unjust. Now, since we can't perceive (see, taste, etc.) a word such as "justice," Joan is clearly speaking in dialectical symbols. We cannot perceive the referent that serves as the focus for Joan's remarks. Only through a dialectic can we get at the meaning of Joan's statement. Assume that Mary is questioning Joan.

Mary: What do you mean by saying that the company's pay scale is unjust?

Joan: I mean it's sexist!

Mary: Do you mean that men make more money for the same work than women do?

Joan: That's right.

Mary: How do you know that the men make more in salary than the women?

Joan: Well, you know Fred who works at the desk next to mine?

Mary: Yes.

Joan: Well, Fred and I were comparing paychecks yesterday, and I found out that he makes $1000 more per year than I do. We've both been with the company since 1969, and we do the same kind of work.

Mary: Do you think that men consistently make more than women throughout the company?

Joan: I don't know. Probably they do. All I know is that Fred makes $1000 more for the same work—and he's a jerk to boot!

Mary: You know, he's also the boss's nephew.

Through this conversation we are able to learn Joan's meaning for the term "justice" as it applies to employee compensation in her company. Joan's answers to Mary's questions indicate that her idea of a just pay scale is one in which comparable employees receive equal payment for their work. Had Mary pursued the point more forcefully, we might have gained an even clearer notion of the elements of justice (according to Joan). Yet even in this informal conversation, we did observe the workings of the dialectical process. Through a series of questions and answers, definitions were expressed and observations were categorized. In this case, prodded by Mary's questions, Joan set up the major categories of "justice" and "sexism" (a particular kind of injustice). Further, she classified certain facts as belonging to the two categories. Thus, given the definition of justice (equal compensation for equal work by comparable employees), the pay differential between Joan and Fred represents an injustice in compensation. Given that Joan knows of only one distinction between herself and Fred (sex), she labels the pay differential as belonging to the category of sexist acts. (At the conclusion of the dialogue, Mary hints that the differential may owe more to nepotism.)

The dialogue thus reveals the essential features of dialectical terms. Such terms do not have easily perceivable referents. We must construct their meaning by defining categories and by placing facts into the appropriate categories. Thus, it would be a simple matter to verify whether Joan's yearly salary is $1000 less than Fred's, but it would be quite difficult to decide whether Joan's salary was unjust. In sum, we may locate positive symbols by simple perception. It requires a dialectic to get at the meaning of a dialectical symbol.

One other feature of dialectic deserves attention at this point. The process of dialectic enables us to connect specific facts (e.g., the yearly salary of a group of employees) to a higher-level ideal (a judgment as to the justice of employee compensation). Recall that Joan used specific facts such as salary figures and observable employee characteristics (sex, work experience) to flesh out her definition of a just pay scale. She connected lower-level positive terms (such as dollars) to a higher-level judgment (which she expressed via a dialectical term). The process of questioning, answering, defining, and categorizing (dialectic) gives us a way to connect positive and dialectical terms. Because dialectical symbols organize positive ones, Weaver believes that the highest level of knowledge involves dialectical terms. Because anyone can know the meaning of a positive term, Weaver feels that knowledge based on positive terms is less sophisticated. Weaver advises us to maintain a dialectical outlook on life. That is, we should seek to use the dialectical process to place facts into categories. According to Weaver, we should not content ourselves with mere factual observations. We should seek to look at the world through dialectical words. (See Weaver, 1948, pp. 12, 59, 130; Weaver, 1970, pp. 49–50; Weaver, 1964, p. 113).

Weaver is correct, I think, in saying that dialectical terms may represent a higher order of knowledge than positive ones. However, it is relevant to note at this point two disadvantages of dialectical terms: (1) They are particularly likely to contain high levels of emotional content; and (2) they may be used thoughtlessly by an advocate who is unwilling to engage in or submit to a dialectic. Let me elaborate briefly on these two problems. Clearly, many words carry favorable or unfavorable emotional overtones. A positive term may carry emotional weight—as in the case of "rat." This word not only designates a particular member of the rodent family, but also creates a feeling of revulsion in many persons. However, the emotional content may be even stronger in dialectical terms than in positive ones: We cannot avoid arousing pleasant sensations when we use the word "freedom," nor can we help but create hurt, outrage, or anger when we call someone a racist. While it is a simple matter to find a neutral substitute (such as "house") for the favorably charged positive term "home," it is difficult to find a neutral synonym for the unfavorable dialectical expression "tyranny."[1] We must be particularly careful in using dialectical symbols, in view of their special emotion-arousing power.

A second problem inherent in dialectical terms is the occasional unwillingness of arguers to define them satisfactorily. The person who calls someone a racist or a commie often does so without creating an adequate definition of racism or communism and without explaining the basis on which a person may be classified as a racist or a communist. When an advocate uses a dialectical term without having engaged in a previous personal dialectic, the term is meaningless: It is just an emotional device that is thoughtlessly bandied about. Misusers of dialectical symbols are often unwilling to be questioned as to their meanings for a particular dialectical word. This is a sign that the arguer is abusing language, because a dialectical word is meaningless unless it is the product of a process that includes questions, answers, definitions, and categorizing. Therefore, we must qualify Weaver's preference for dialectical terms. Such terms may represent the highest level of knowledge, but they may also represent unthinking emotionalism and ignorance.

Abstraction and Ambiguity

Semanticists use two additional terms—"abstraction" and "ambiguity"—to describe the complexities of the symbol-referent connection. Abstraction is the process of leaving out characteristics. Thus, when we say, "Joe Smith bought a car," we are abstracting the nature of his purchase. We are leaving out relevant characteristics about it: whether it is new or used; its manufacturer, style, size, color, etc. Words vary in their level of abstraction—or the extent to which the symbol reveals all the characteristics of the referent. One of the best-known features of Hayakawa's work on semantics is his notion of the "Abstraction Ladder" (1949, p. 169). In figure 2-3 the term "knife" can be made more or less abstract. (Read figure 2-3 from the bottom up.) Using the abstraction ladder we may gain further insight into the relationship between a symbol and its referent. Whereas we previously considered symbols to be either positive or dialectic, the ladder allows us to gain a notion of the degree to which a term is dialectically abstract or positively concrete.

The term "ambiguity" is closely related to that of abstraction and refers to the situation in which the symbol-referent link is obscure—that is, the symbol is

---

[1] The term "denotation" is used popularly to express the neutral or dictionary meaning of a word. "Connotation" is often used to indicate the favorable or unfavorable overtones of emotion pertaining to a word. However, in the field of semantics, "connotation" and "denotation" are used in specialized ways. (See Hayakawa, 1949, pp. 58–60.) Thus, we must be careful in using these words in the popular sense.

high abstraction

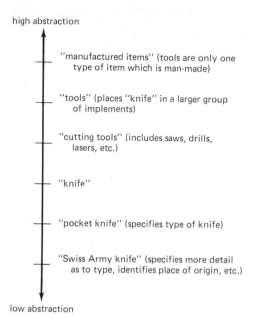

"manufactured items" (tools are only one type of item which is man-made)

"tools" (places "knife" in a larger group of implements)

"cutting tools" (includes saws, drills, lasers, etc.)

"knife"

"pocket knife" (specifies type of knife)

"Swiss Army knife" (specifies more detail as to type, identifies place of origin, etc.)

low abstraction

Figure 2-3 The abstraction ladder.

sufficiently imprecise for more than one referent to be assigned to it by interpreters. Ambiguity, of course, may be corrected or elucidated by dialectic; but often the communication situation does not allow dialectical investigation of the symbol-referent connotative/denotative relationship. In politics, for example, it is more common for candidates to deliver prepared speeches than to allow a single individual to cross-examine them via dialectic. As a result, ambiguities are frequent in political and other forms of human argument.

In the 1968 presidential campaign, for instance, candidate Richard M. Nixon argued against the Lyndon Johnson administration's Vietnam policy in such a manner that both hawks (those who wanted a more aggressive prosecution of the war) and doves (those who wanted a rapid, peaceful settlement of the conflict) had cause to believe that if he were elected Nixon would take to heart their respective (and quite different) opinions as to how the war should be conducted. While hawks applauded the candidate's assertion that "we failed to use our military power effectively," doves could take comfort in Nixon's statements that the Johnson administration had also "failed to use our diplomatic power wisely" (see White, 1970, p. 162). A major Nixon television spot concerning Vietnam found the candidate calling for "an honorable end to the war in Vietnam"; but, of course, this was not responsive to the issue of whether the war should be ended by escalation or by withdrawal (see McGinniss, 1970, p. 89).

To be sure, the example of Nixon on Vietnam is not unique. As Walter Lippmann (1960, p. 197) has observed, ambiguity is a political stock-in-trade: "After all, the art of inducing all sorts of people who think differently to vote alike is practiced in every political campaign."

Because I have introduced so many ideas about meaning, it probably would be helpful for me to summarize this discussion before moving on to other related topics. We may define "meaning" to be the representation or signification of a referent (a real object) by a symbol (a thing to which meaning is assigned) that has significance for an individual interpreter. Meanings are therefore personal. Yet because we share our linguistic heritage with others, we may say that meaning is a sort of contract to abide by given rules that is accepted by members of a language-using group. Thus, meanings are determined by the relationship between communicators and the context of their transaction. Meanings may be expressed in positive or dialectical symbols, but the dialectical process helps to reconcile observable facts and high-level value judgments. Further, the ladder of abstraction allows us to measure the degree to which a symbol's meaning is highly abstract (as in the case of a dialectical term) or quite concrete (as in the case of a positive term). Finally, situations in which a symbol may be interpreted as designating more than one kind of referent are defined as being ambiguous and are quite common in human language interaction.[2]

THE FUNCTIONS OF LANGUAGE

The human use of language is so automatic that we have trouble reacting to the question "What do we use language *for?*" Yet even a moment's reflection reveals, I believe, that language plays several functions for its users. In describing the ways in which language functions, I will be presenting an interpretation of word using from the point of view of the communicator or source of a message. (I will treat the effect of messages on listeners later in this chapter and in succeeding chapters.) Why, then, do communicators use language? Why do people argue? The answer is that they do so for a number of closely connected purposes.

[2] It is relevant at this point to make a parenthetical observation about my use of the term "language." For the most part I have treated language as a verbal phenomenon. For example, this section on meaning has dealt largely with vocal sounds and their written symbolic equivalents, such as in the English, German, French, or Latin languages.

While language usually is thought of as being a system of spoken or written words, I should mention the fact that nonverbal actions also may be considered as language. Gestures, eye contact, facial expressions, distance between persons, general body position, clothing, and other nonverbal phenomena have a linguistic aspect in that interpreters assign meaning to these physical actions. Indeed, "body language" probably is far more ancient than verbal symbols. The clothes we wear, our physical expressions and gestures communicate meaning just as verbal symbols do. A grim-faced, busy person who avoids our glance may be using physical symbols to tell us that he or she doesn't want to talk to us (the intended referent). Teachers soon learn that when students grow restless and begin to collect their belongings (nonverbal symbols), the designated class period is most likely at a close. Indeed, the class bell itself is a symbol to which we assign meaning.

It is important to observe, in this connection, (1) that nonverbal symbols tend to communicate personal feelings more than logical information and (2) that nonverbal symbols do not operate in exactly the same manner as verbal ones. While the matter of nonverbal communication is an important field of study, the succeeding chapters will focus largely on verbal language. However, sections of chapters 9 and 11, in particular, will treat the argumentative and persuasive effects of nonverbal symbols.

The Report Function

Perhaps the most obvious function of word using is that it allows us to report the nature of the world. Because one of the key words in this book is "argument," it seems reasonable to assert that a major function of arguing is the use of symbols to present our version—our descriptive, interpretive, or evaluative report—of how the world is. When people use symbols to identify reality—e.g., "Today is Tuesday," "I need three gallons of gas"—they are relying on the capacity of language to report. Even if one accepts fully the semantic point of view that "meanings are in people not words," it still is true to say that language reports reality when it causes receivers to develop meanings that identify the way they believe that things are. As Watzlawick, Beavin, and Jackson (1967, p. 51) observe, "The report aspect of a message conveys information and is, therefore, synonymous in human communication with the *content* of the message. It may be about anything that is communicable regardless of whether the particular information is true, false, valid, invalid."

The human capacity to report information is a crucial dimension of personal interaction. A basic assumption of human communication is that people generally tell the truth—i.e., they report things accurately. This assumption gives stability to communication. If truth were the exception rather than the rule, the possibilities for meaningful language interaction would be considerably reduced. Because people generally report accurate information—and sophisticated listeners are usually able to detect situations in which deceit is present or likely—the communication process generally works smoothly. In a world in which reports were rarely accurate, much additional effort would need to be expended merely to verify the accuracy of reports. In the preceding section on meaning, I made the statement that, given the number of linkages in the interpersonal triangle of meaning, it was almost miraculous that humans were able to attain common meanings. Common meanings would be even less likely if people did not generally make an effort to report things accurately. The report function of language is an obvious part of the process of argument. When arguers disagree, it is necessary for them to make mutual reports concerning how they see reality. When arguers are basically in agreement, the report aspect of language enables them to add to and refine their mutual understanding of how things are.

The Persuasive Function

The report function is, then, a fairly obvious but nevertheless important aspect of language use. This function is closely related to a second one—persuasion. When we use language we often do so for the purpose of making things happen. The persuasive function is so closely related to the informative role of language that the two are often confused. For example, when a person reports that it is raining, the individual may also be seeking to make something happen—in this case, to cause another person to roll up the car windows. If one reports, "Today is Saturday," he may, at the same time, be suggesting that he should not be required to rise at an early, working-day hour. Granted, persuasive language usually suggests the suasory dimension more overtly than is the case in the two reports just mentioned.

Language need not report to be persuasive. Statements such as the following also have a clear intent to make things occur: "Get up," "Please pass the butter," "Isn't it about time someone mowed the lawn?" Again, however, even messages that sound like reports may act persuasively. The statement "Your dog has fleas"—which is clearly a report—may also have a persuasive function that might convince a person to give his pet a bath. Commands, demands, suggestions, pleas, and the like have clear persuasive functions; but even neutral-sounding, informative statements may possess as strong a persuasive dimension as the drill sergeant's order.

Because this book is devoted to a study of the influence of arguments, you are probably willing to accept the idea that persuasion—making things happen—is a major function of language. However, I would like to highlight another implication of the role of language as a promoter of change. In chapter 1, I asserted that all users of language could rightly be called arguers and persuaders. Having now shown you that even bland, report-type language may have a strong persuasive feature, I believe that my assertion may be considered to be almost a truism. If language has an inherently persuasive flavor, then language users are by definition would-be persuaders. A statement may not actually succeed in changing the world, but insofar as an utterance functions to induce change, it is clearly suasory.

The Attitude-Revealing Function

The third function that I wish to attribute to language is closely related to the report and "make-happen" roles. When we report the world, we are really saying, "This is how *I* see things," and when we use language to persuade, we are telling others, "This is what *I* think should be done." The personal ("I see," "I think") dimension of reports and persuasive efforts suggests that language clearly functions to indicate the relationship between a communicator and the ideas being communicated. Readers may have observed that it is difficult to report a fact or suggest an alternative in a neutral fashion: We normally indicate how we feel about an idea at the same time that we report it or use it in an advisory way.

Language's role to communicate our feelings about what we say is embodied in the term "attitude." There are, to be sure, as many definitions of attitude as there are definers of the term. I would describe an attitude as being a person's positive or negative judgment about a symbol or referent. Our judgments of things may, of course, vary from highly favorable to highly unfavorable. Further, if we have no strong feelings about a symbol, then we may be said to judge it as neutral. Attitudes are often measured by a scale ranging from -3 to $+3$, the extremities indicating highly unfavorable and highly favorable attitudes and the center a judgmental neutrality. Direction of judgment is perhaps the most important aspect of attitude; but the term implies other features as well. Although I will treat the concept in depth in chapter 7, it is useful to cite at this point two additional features of the attitude: (1) salience, or the perceived relevance/importance of the symbol at a particular time; and (2) intensity, or the strength of our feelings about it.

Although some statements are more overtly opinionated than others (due to the style feature of language), the attitudinal function of language is inseparable from the informative and persuasive dimensions. It is important to observe at this point that attitude is often expressed by our nonverbal communication behavior. Thus, our tendency to either look at or avoid looking at an object would reveal our attitude toward it. Physiological changes in heart rate and galvanic skin response (a measure of electrical activity) have been used as indicators of attitude. A behavioral symbol, such as shaking a person's hand (or refusing to do so), would communicate an attitudinal element to the verbal statement "It's so good to see you." We will study the attitudinal dimension of language in greater detail in chapter 7.

The Self-Revelation Function

The attitudinal aspect of language—its function to indicate the relationship between a person and the report being presented—is closely associated with what may be called the self-revealing function of language. However, the self-revealing function of language is more all-encompassing. Whereas language, in its attitudinal role, tells us how a person reacts to the concepts or symbols of the message, the self-revealing function includes all other insights about a communicator that are disclosed by that person's use of language—the feelings of the moment, personality, or feelings toward self. Consider an example of how a statement may disclose information about its author. Assume that we have asked a person for street directions. Let us observe what we may learn about the person from his answer:

Answer #1	Self-revelation
"How do you expect me to know where Wanamaker Street is? Do I look like a map?"	The individual communicates a barely disguised hostility toward the questioner at the same time as a report—"I don't know"—is communicated.

Answer #2	Self-revelation
"No, I don't know; but I have a street map in my briefcase. Let me get it out, and let's see. . . ."	Because the individual is willing to go out of his way to help the questioner, we may infer that the individual has more time, is in a better mood, and is both open and friendly toward the questioner.

Answer #3	Self-revelation
"No, I never know anything. You should ask someone who is 'with it.'"	The individual may be disclosing a general lack of self-esteem in addition to merely reporting the fact of his lack of knowledge.

These sample answers suggest that we may learn about a person even from a single statement. However, because a single utterance reveals only a relatively small amount of information about a person, we must observe a great amount of communication behavior before really gaining insight into an individual. By observing a person's use of language over a long period of time, we may learn that the person is an extrovert or an introvert; has or lacks self-confidence or self-esteem; is strong-willed or weak-willed; is open to new information or is dogmatic; holds liberal or conservative political views; is self-centered or oriented toward others; etc. Weaver (1970, pp. 55–114) makes the point that a communicator's method of arguing reveals much about his basic values—the things he holds sacred, the way he looks at the world. By observing Abraham Lincoln's choice of arguments, Weaver concludes that Lincoln was a man of high principle. Weaver infers from the argumentation of Edmund Burke (an eighteenth-century British politician) that Burke was a man of shallow principle who preferred the easiest or most expedient course of action. A person's use of argument, then, gives the listener insight into his feelings at the moment, his general character, and his philosophy of life. In sum, the self-revelation function of language is as "real" as the report, make-happen, or attitude functions.

The Relationship Function

The role of language as a means of developing the relationship between persons is a final function which I wish to introduce. In the interpersonal triangle of meaning I identified the interpreter–other person relationship as an important determinant of meaning. The function of language to indicate the relationship between two persons is an ever-present and vitally important aspect of human interaction. Watzlawick, Beavin, and Jackson (1967, p. 52) make the following comparison of the report and relationship aspects of a single statement: "Thus, for instance, the messages, 'It is important to release the clutch gradually and smoothly' and 'Just let the clutch go, it'll ruin the transmission in no time' have approximately the same information content (report aspect), but they obviously define very different relationships." In the first message, the relationship appears to be businesslike and based on mutual respect. In the second example cited by Watzlawick, Beavin, and Jackson, the author of the statement appears to have less confidence in and respect for the user of the clutch.

In addition to indicating the status of a relationship, language may be used to change a relationship. A man and a woman may talk about something as mundane as the weather (the report function) and still communicate their feelings about one another. Most readers would probably agree that such relationship signals as "I'd like to see you again" or "I'm totally uninterested in developing an intimate relationship with you" can be communicated clearly no matter what the conversation is ostensibly about. As was the case with the attitudinal dimension of language, the relationship factor is often indicated by nonverbal symbols. Standing close to a person and maintaining frequent eye contact would signify something about a relationship, as would lack of eye contact and nonproximity.

In the past few pages I have identified five functions of language: Language may act to report, persuade, reveal attitude, reveal the self, and finally, reveal and change the interpersonal relationship. The fact that language may play several roles raises at least two questions: (1) Does every statement involve all five functions? and (2) How can we tell which function is most important in a given statement? In response to the first question, I would assert that every communication symbol probably plays each role to some degree. Obviously, however, only one, or perhaps two, functions will predominate. We may use a pie diagram to indicate the mixed-function aspect of any single utterance. Consider figure 2-4, an example of a pie diagram of the statement "No, darling, I am not going to take out the trash now. You know I'm busy when I'm working at my desk." In figure 2-4 I have suggested that the relationship aspect appears to predominate over the report function of the statement. Further, my interpretation of the statement suggests that the report aspect is the least significant because the statement appears to be a command in which the information is already known to both parties. I should point out again that it is difficult to identify the functions of a single statement. We would probably be able to diagnose the functions of an individual's conversation more accurately by analyzing the text of an extended interaction.

The second question that I posed relative to the several functions of language dealt with the mechanics of making a diagram such as figure 2-4. How can we tell what role(s) a given message plays at a given time? I would answer that the context of a message gives us insight into the relative importance of the

Figure 2-4 Pie diagram of the functions of a statement.

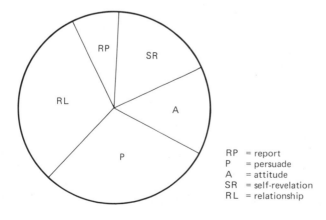

RP = report
P   = persuade
A   = attitude
SR = self-revelation
RL = relationship

several functions. The context of a statement is the set of objects and events that precede, surround, and follow the communication act. Both the discussion of assumptions (in chapter 1) and the interpersonal triangle of meaning (especially the interpreter–other person relationship) suggest that the meaning of a symbol is closely tied to the situation in which it occurs. The situation helps the interpreter to attach an appropriate referent to the symbol. The situation helps us to decide what functions a message fulfills at a particular time. Relevant situational elements might include background information about the communicator, the events that immediately preceded the message, or physical conditions in effect at the time—such as time of day, location, weather, etc. Such factors of a message context would help us to decide the extent to which the statement "How do you expect me to know where Wanamaker Street is? Do I look like a map?" played a report role ("I don't have the information"), a self-disclosure role ("I am a crabby person" or "I am tired and don't want to be bothered") or a relationship role ("I don't want to talk to you").

WAYS OF PROVING

Thus far, I have described ways in which statements may be presented so as to prove claims. Although the language content (the report function) of messages is an important means of proof, it is only one of three general ways in which claims are established to the satisfaction of audiences. In refuting the notion that argument is a totally or an essentially rational process that involved training in logic and problem solving (chapter 1), I quoted Aristotle's remarks that there were three general methods of proving conclusions: (1) the use of logic via argumentative statements; (2) the use of credibility or the reputation of the speaker as a reliable source of information; and (3) the use of emotional appeals directed to the listener's capacity to feel. Aristotle's view of proof is therefore a more organic perspective than that supplied solely by the study of logic. (By "logic" I mean message content as exemplified by the relationship of terms in the syllogism.) Aristotle's notion of argument by message logic, speaker credibility, and audience emotion may be studied via a communication model. In figure 2-5, I present an interactive communication model consisting of four

Figure 2-5   An interactive communication model.

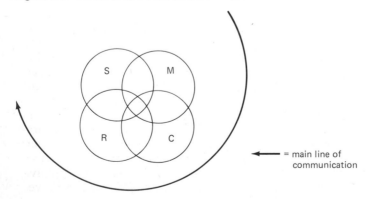

elements: (1) the source, or presenter of language; (2) the message, or set of arguments chosen by the source to prove a claim; (3) the channel, or the vehicle by which the message is presented—verbal or nonverbal signals, direct face-to-face presentation or use of the media, etc.; and (4) the receiver, or the set of listeners who use the message to create personal meanings. The model suggests that the four elements overlap extensively, creating six binary relationships:

1 The source-message relationship. The message depends partly on the personality of the source. No two sources would present the same message in the same way. Although we may hear and or see a message, the message is inseparable from its source because the tone of voice, vocabulary, pronunciation, gestures, and other aspects of the message are also part of the source.

The source-message interaction also gives us greater understanding of what I have called credibility. Credibility is the believability of a message, which depends on its source. Early experimental studies of persuasion confirmed Aristotle's notion that the nature of the source added to or detracted from the persuasiveness of a message. Hovland, Janis, and Kelley (1953, p. 35) concluded: "In summary the research evidence indicates that the reactions to a communication are significantly affected by cues as to the communicator's intentions, expertness, and trustworthiness. The very same presentation tends to be judged more favorably when made by a communicator of high credibility than by one of low credibility."

I will deal with credibility effects more extensively in chapter 7. However, it is important to remember, for now, that the source and message are not entirely distinct and separate entities. There is an interaction between source and message, and the credibility dimension of the interaction modifies the probative value of the "pure" message.

2 The source-channel relationship. As Berlo (1960, p. 63) observes, "No one word in communication theory has been as used and abused as the word 'channel.'" Part of the difficulty in understanding the channel of communication is the fact that the channel overlaps with source, message, and receiver. Thus, the channel includes aspects of the source (our hearing and sight apparatuses, etc.), aspects of the message (print, sound, or body language as the vehicle of the symbols), and the receiver (the hearing and sight, etc., of the listener).

Focusing for the moment on the source-channel relationship, we may conclude that the source exerts a powerful influence on the channel. When a communicator prefers to deliver a speech via videotape rather than in person, we observe the influence of source on channel. When an individual stands nervously before a crowd of listeners, we observe the influence of channel on source (and also that of receiver on source). While we may theoretically conceive of a pure source or pure channel, the two elements overlap in the actual communication event.

3 The source-receiver relationship. Although sources and receivers are separate human beings, they are likely to share a number of cultural, experiential, and linguistic features. Every person is unique, but we possess traits in common with others. Source and receiver overlap in a second way: A source does not exist apart from the perception of a receiver. If a receiver believes a source to be credible, then the source is credible for that receiver, although the same source may be perceived as incompetent or untrustworthy by another receiver. Credibility, then, depends on the source-receiver relationship as well as the source-message link. The perception of an audience by a source is another case of the interaction. During the communication event, a constant reinterpretation of source by receiver (credibility) and receiver by source (feedback) is taking place.

  4 The message-channel relationship. Neither the message nor the channel is a pure concept. The interaction of the message with the channel is well expressed in Marshall McLuhan's (1964, p. 24) frequently quoted statement that " 'the medium is the message' because it is the medium that shapes and controls the scale and form of human association and action." Because some media are more engrossing than others, McLuhan feels able to assert that each channel of communication changes the nature of the message. For example, students typically feel better about a lecture delivered in person (assuming that the professor is a dynamic speaker or personality) than about the same lecture presented via audiotape, videotape, or print.

  5 The message-receiver relationship. When Aristotle differentiated between proof by logic and proof by emotions, he meant that no message is a pure entity existing apart from its audience. The symbols of a message lead to a logical conclusion such as that found in the distribution of syllogistic terms. However, because meanings are at least partially personal, the listener may not actually re-create the meaning intended either by the author of the argument or by the objective rules of the syllogism.

  The interaction of message and receiver also gives us insight into what Aristotle called emotional proof—the persuasive effect of stimulating audience members' feelings. "Persuasion," writes Aristotle (*Rhetoric,* I, 2, 1356a), "is effected through the audience, when they are brought by the speech into a state of emotion; for we give very different decisions under the sway of pain or joy, and liking or hatred." The power of arguments to inspire different emotional states, and the effect of those states on decisions made by the audience, suggest that a message is not an entirely logical set of symbols. In its role as a catalyst, the message is inseparable from its audience.

  6 The channel-receiver relationship. I have already observed the effect of the context or situation on meaning. Because the channel includes the context of a message (the form of presentation, the time, the place, the technology used, etc.), it follows that the meanings created by a receiver will be affected by the channel. The same message delivered in person, by telephone, or by letter would affect us differently. A message presented by an angry speaker in a hot, crowded auditorium would act as a different meaning catalyst than one conveyed by a soft-spoken announcer on television.

The six binary relationships suggested by the interactive communication model assist us in understanding the argumentative process by which language produces effects in listeners. Chapter 7 contains a fuller treatment of the persuasive elements in argument. However, this brief orientation to persuasion should convince readers that the logical content of a message is only part of the province of persuasion. The several relationships among source, message, channel, and receiver demonstrate that credibility and audience emotions combine with logic. The three cooperate to produce proof for claims.

ABSTRACTING AND OUTLINING

Although I described this chapter as being message-centered, readers have probably observed that the receiver is at least as important, if not more so, in communication transactions. Meaning is largely listener-determined and, as we observed in the interactive communication model, the listener is an inseparable part of the source, message, and channel variables. Having described listening in general terms, I now want to emphasize two particular skills of systematic listening: (1) abstracting, or the pulling together of the key terms of a message; and (2) outlining, or the step-by-step recording of the supporting ideas of a message.

Abstracting

When we abstract, we identify the main points of a message and put them together in a much shorter passage. The practice of abstracting is illustrated by a Xerox University Microfilms publication called *Dissertation Abstracts*. To facilitate the dissemination of scholarly research, *Dissertation Abstracts* is made up of short summaries of most doctoral and other dissertations written in the United States: My own doctoral dissertation of 345 pages was condensed into a two-page abstract. The abstract left out considerable detail, needless to say, but it did convey the intent of the full text. Abstracting, then, is a process of identifying the key words and phrases of a message and putting these together in abbreviated form.

The main-idea abstract is a special type of abstract that is particularly important for students of argument and persuasion. By "main idea abstract" I mean an abstract that reduces a message to a single sentence. Consider the following text of a message and see if you can restate the main idea in a single sentence. (Note that the sentence may be a compound or complex one.)

Political communication has always depended on the technology of the society. In the preelectronic era direct communication was bounded only by the strength of the voice, capacity of the hall, or height of the platform. Legal concern for equal opportunity to communicate was only negative, in the form of prohibitions against attempts to forcefully suppress or silence a candidate. Legal safeguards to guarantee equal access to the public eye and ear were unnecessary, for candidates did not differ in their ability to travel and speak—although early-nineteenth-century custom mitigated against extensive stump or "whistle-stop" campaigns. Although newspapers openly backed candidates, such indirect support was also relatively equal. The costs of founding a newspaper were small.

The state of the art of political communication was radically altered by perfection of electronic broadcasting. The development of radio allowed a single communicator to capture and control the attention of millions. However, in the Radio Act of 1927, which regulated the political use of the new medium, no positive provisions were made to guarantee equal radio access to all candidates for a public office. Radio time was treated as a commodity to be sold or given by the radio station owner. The implications of this situation were significant: Ability to pay became a major barrier to many candidates seeking to communicate their views to the public at large. The Radio Act raised the possibility that the better-financed candidate might literally drown out his opponent through legally sanctioned unequal access to the minds of the voting public.

Having read this selection, think about it for a moment (read it again if you need to) and then write out the main idea on a piece of paper in a single sentence.

I would suggest that the main idea of the selection may be summarized as follows: "Whereas before the advent of radio, candidates did not differ significantly in their ability to communicate with the public, the Radio Act of 1927 allowed better-financed candidates to purchase more opportunity to communicate with the public." Your own summary of the main idea may not have been as complete or complex; but the summary should have mentioned the pre- and post-radio era realities of political communication, plus the effect of the Radio Act. Remember that the important factor in identifying the main idea is to make sure that all the critical terms (words) are included in the summary and that the relationship of these variables is made clear.

Outlining

Identifying the supporting ideas of a message is a skill that is closely related to identifying the main idea. However, while the identifying of the main idea is accomplished via an abstract, supporting ideas are recorded via an outline. Also, while an abstract may reorganize the key terms to make them fit into a single sentence, the outline parallels the text of a message and records supporting ideas in the order in which they appear. (It is only in what we may call a "creative outline" that the outline is a rearrangement of the ideas of a message.) We will consider some rules for outlining at a later point. For now, I want you to consider my outline of the selection dealing with the Radio Act of 1927.

I   In the preelectronic era a candidate's direct communication with voters was constrained only by the speaker's voice or the physical setting for the speech.
   A   Legal concern for equal opportunity to communicate was expressed only in prohibitions against the use of force to silence a speaker.
   B   Legal safeguards to guarantee equal access to the public eye and ear were unnecessary, for candidates did not differ in their ability to travel and speak or to found a newspaper.
II   The invention of radio changed this situation.
   A   A communicator could now use the radio to transmit a message to millions of people at one time.
   B   Despite this fact the Radio Act of 1927 made no provision to guarantee equal access to radio communication.
      1   Radio time was treated as a commodity belonging to the station owner that might be given or sold.
      2   As a result, ability to pay became a major barrier to candidates seeking to communicate their views to the public.

In this sample outline, notice that although some of the wording has been changed, the outline presents the ideas in the order in which they appeared in the original selection. Also, while a few minor details have been omitted (the lack of early whistle-stop campaigns, for example) no major ideas have been left out. Indeed, the abstract excludes much more detail than the outline does, because the main-idea abstract is presented in the form of a single sentence.

In my several years of experience as a college teacher, I have observed that students tend to dislike using and making outlines. I defend the study of outlining, however, as an important communication skill. Outlining enables us to identify arguments and the relationships among the single arguments of an extended passage. In chapter 10, I will further suggest that outlining is a necessary skill for one who desires to argue effectively on questions of policy.

The basic rules for outlining may now be summarized as follows:

1 Write out each idea in the outline as either a sentence or a meaningful phrase.

2 Assign to each entry in the outline a symbol, such as "I," "A," "1," "a," etc.

3 Assign only one idea to each symbol.

4 Use a consistent pattern for subordinating the symbols—for example, Roman numerals should precede capital letters, and capital letters should be followed by Arabic numbers and lowercase letters.

5 Attempt to match entries—that is, when you use "A," try to have a "B"; when you have a "1," try to match it with a "2."

6 Don't assign unique symbols to statements that appear to be only embellishment—that is, transitional statements between major and minor points or introductory and conclusionary matter that you consider unimportant. Including the embellishment after a major or minor point does, of course, mean that we may need to deviate slightly and occasionally from rule 3.

Listening Skills

Abstracting and outlining are critically important skills for students of argument. These skills enable us to "get a hold of" the arguments that we are analyzing. Abstracting and outlining are content listening skills—skills that enable us to record accurately what was said or written by an arguer. However, content listening is not the only form of message perception. (See Rice and Ratner, 1967; Duker and Petrie, 1964). Thus, I want to introduce briefly two other approaches to listening: critical listening and empathic listening.

Whereas content listening highlights language's report function, critical listening involves greater emphasis on listener attention to the persuasive and attitude functions. Content listening accepts the message as it is. Critical listening tests the message against certain analytic standards. The critical listener acts as a message tester as well as a message recorder. When we listen as a critic, we add an analytic and an evaluative dimension to the skills of content listening. Critical listening behaviors include: (1) the ability to categorize the supporting ideas of a message as to their type and (2) the ability to state and justify a judgment as to whether a given idea is established as valid, persuasive, ethical, or truthful on the basis of the supporting arguments. One of the major objectives in the study of argument is to become competent in criticizing arguments. Thus, in chapter 3, I will elaborate on critical listening. Throughout the remainder of this book, you will have opportunities to practice critical skills.

Empathic listening is usually thought of as less relevant to the student of argument than content or critical listening. This is because the empathic listener has a different relationship to the arguer. Whereas a content listener is unconcerned with the personal feelings of the message source, and whereas the critical listener seeks to scrutinize the ideas of the message (also ignoring communicator feelings), the emphatic listener has a predominant interest in the personality, well-being, and feelings of the speaker. In the priest-penitent, husband-wife, and counselor-patient situations, the listener would be likely to play an empathic, helping, and caring role. In relationships of this kind, it may be inappropriate for the listener merely to look for content or for weak points in the message. The listener often seeks to maintain what Carl Rogers (1961, pp. 39–40) has called a "helping relationship" with the arguer.

Traditionally, intimate relationships and helping situations have not been studied by argumentation scholars: Such relationships and situations are usually considered to be the province of the counselor or psychologist. I would contend that students of argument should be interested in language as it is used in helping relationships; however, it is true that argumentation normally emphasizes content and critical listening skills. Therefore, when I refer to argument in helping relationships, you should remember that traditional argument theory (which is oriented to content and to criticism) may not be an entirely appropriate vehicle for judging arguments presented in highly personal contexts. To analyze such situations as these, we must be mindful of the particular rules that govern them. I will elaborate on rules in chapter 3.

THE AWARE COMMUNICATOR

This chapter has dealt with factors of message presentation and perception. By understanding something about meaning, language functions, ways of proving, outlining, and abstracting, the reader will become more conscious of the workings of language. The aware communicator is a sender or receiver who realizes that words may lead to misunderstanding. Such a person is less likely than an uninformed arguer to misinterpret a statement by wrongly identifying its major function. Aware communicators understand the relationship of logic, emotion, and credibility in the process of communication. Finally, communicators who are cognizant of their listening orientation (content, critical, or empathic) will be less likely to mistake their own role-influenced expectations for the meaning as intended by the communicator. In sum, the aware communicator is a knowledgeable user and interpreter of language.

As a general introduction to language in the process of human communication, this chapter sets the groundwork for chapters 3, 4, 5, and 6, which deal with characteristic forms and types of argument. As an orientation to creation of meaning, interactive communication, and listening, this chapter may be seen as a prelude to the more detailed study of persuasion theory in chapter 7. My description of outlining and abstracting serves as a foundation for the treatment of case building in chapter 10.

APPLICATIONS

Awareness may be distinguished from skills. While awareness implies "Yes, I know that," skills suggest that the person is also able to do it. In this application section, I present some exercises, suitable for classroom or individual use, that allow students to put their knowledge into practice. Many of the exercises are more suited for in-class use rather than for written assignments.

Exercise 2-1: Word Association and Meaning

Words possess emotional overtones. On the one hand, words inform us by reporting the nature of the world. But, on the other hand, we may substitute emotional terms for report-oriented ones. The emotive word expresses our personal feelings about the thing being discussed. The word association exercise is a way of identifying both the informative and affective connotations pertaining to a particular symbol. This exercise is better for classroom use rather than for a take-home assignment.

I Someone should read aloud (one time) the following list of words (or a list which has been written by the instructor or the class): America; Ford; New York; hippie; girl; black; draft; communism; he-man; state; bird; Russian; car; war; U.N.; politician; cowboy; desk.

II Students should record the first word or phrase which comes into their minds after hearing each word.

III Using the word association lists generated by the class, the following questions may be discussed:

A Which associations are essentially informative (containing agreed-upon details) or affective (containing personal interpretations, feelings or evaluations)?

B Which words in the list tend to attract a majority of informative or affective connotations? Why is this?

C Why did class members respond as they did to the various words? Associations are often made almost automatically when two words are used together commonly. Associations may also be made because of sounds, or opposites, etc.

D Do some of the words have more meanings than others? That is, do connotative associations fall into several distinct groups?

Exercise 2-2: Identifying Positive and Dialectical Terms

To get some experience in differentiating between positive and dialectical terms, you should do the following:

I Select a short message text. A newspaper clipping, advertisement, etc., will do.

II Identify two dialectical and two positive terms in the text. Each of the terms should be a single word.

III For each of your identifications, briefly explain why you believe the term to be dialectical or positive.

Exercise 2-3: Identifying the Meaning of a Dialectical Term

Earlier I noted that certain dialectical terms have referents that cannot be precisely identified. We cannot point to the referent for "freedom" in quite the same way that we can point to the referent for a "thirteen-cent stamp." We use the process of dialectic to get at the meaning of a dialectical term.

In this exercise I would like to give you the opportunity to practice using a dialectic. Follow these steps.

I Identify a dialectical term.

II Write out a set of 20 statements about the term. In writing these statements, you should ask yourself such questions as these: What is included in the term? What does the term exclude? What are some synonyms or antonyms for the term? Who uses the term? How is the term used by others? In what circumstances have you seen the term used? What other words are associated with the term? To what observable events has the term been applied?

III Using your statements, write out a single-sentence definition of the word.

IV Compare your definition to a dictionary definition. What are some of the similarities or differences between your definition and that of the dictionary?

In asking some questions about the meaning of the dialectical term, you have engaged in a small dialectic. That is, you have posed a series of questions and answers. These have helped you to identify some central facts of the meaning of a term.

Exercise 2-4: "I" Am, "You" Are, and "Someone Else" Is

Hayakawa (1949, p. 96) cites an interesting exercise that calls attention to how we may present facts in a favorable or in an unfavorable light. Consider the following two "I," "you" and "he/she" statements:

I am firm, you are obstinate, and she is a pigheaded fool.
I am attractive, you have good features, and he isn't badlooking, if you like the type.

Notice the subtle (and not so subtle) differences in connotative meaning that result when the terms "firm," "obstinate," and "pigheaded" are used to characterize what presumably is the same behavioral referent. The "I" statements put the subject in a favorable light; the "you" statements are somewhat unfavorable; and the "he/she" statements show total bias against the subject.

Using the above examples as models, construct "you" and "he/she" statements to accompany the "I" statements listed below:

I use a little makeup.
I occasionally raise my voice.
It is true that I am losing a little hair.
I usually date more than one person at a time.
I like to take an occasional drink.
I am an average student.
Politically, I am a conservative.
I believe in being friendly with the teacher.
I seem to be gaining a little weight.
I usually need to wear my glasses.
Occasionally, I lose my balance.
I think that premarital sex is OK.
I believe that it is important to save money.

Class members might find it interesting to make up some of their own sets of "I" statements for this exercise.

Exercise 2-5: Ascending and Descending the Ladder of Abstraction

Hayakawa (1949, p. 169) described the ladder of abstraction as a continuum along which symbols were located on the basis of the amount of information about the referent that was omitted. Highly abstract terms omitted almost all reference to a specific object.

I For two of the following terms, identify symbols that are more abstract or less abstract, creating an abstraction ladder for each term: woman; seasickness; cigar; Lake Erie; propeller-driven airplane; the United States of America; paper; things made from petroleum.
II Use figure 2-3 as a guide in building your own ladders of abstraction.
III Be sure to include, in parentheses, some indication as to why you believe the "higher" and "lower" terms to be more or less abstract, as in figure 2-3.

Exercise 2-6: Encoding Ambiguous Communication

Ambiguity occurs when we use symbols in such a way that they may easily be connected to more than one referent. In this exercise you will be given two situations, each of which involves two opposing positions and a question about the issues in dispute.

I Your task is to construct answers (i.e., responses to the questions) that are worded so as to be acceptable to both positions in the dispute.
II If this exercise is done in class, it is helpful to work in groups of five. At least one group member should act as a recorder.
III Situations:

  A   Watergate
     1   Opposing positions:
       a   The so-called obstruction of justice and political conspiracies were nothing but exaggerated phony issues set up by partisan Democrats as a device for forcing our great President Richard M. Nixon from office.
       b   The White House crimes, including illegal campaign spying and obstruction of justice, amount to the most serious scandal in American political history.
     2   Question: What is the meaning of the "Watergate" episode of the 1970s?
  B   Smoking in public places

     1   Opposing positions:
       a   The evidence used to link cigarette smoking and cancer is inconclusive. People should have the freedom to smoke whenever and wherever they want.
       b   Cigarette smoking causes cancer. It is unhealthful both for smokers and for nonsmokers who are in the vicinity of smokers.
     2   Question: Should smoking in public places be banned by law?

IV   For each of the two situations you should identify reasons that your answer is acceptable to both positions—i.e., sufficiently ambiguous to be consistent with the ideas of both sides.

V   Try to make up your own ambiguous message situations by identifying a controversial topic, at least two opposing positions, a question, and an ambiguous answer.

Exercise 2-7: Communication Functions

We have observed that messages may fulfill at least five different functions for the communicator. Although most messages are chiefly oriented to one or two functions, it is possible for any given message to fulfill each of the five functions simultaneously.

I   Identify a short text (under four hundred words) to use in this exercise. The message may have appeared, originally, in written or oral form. It may be real or imagined. However, you should have a written text in front of you to use for this exercise.

II   Identify three statements in the message text.

III   Using a pie diagram, as in figure 2-4, identify the extent to which each of the three statements fulfills any or all of the five language functions described in this chapter.

IV   For each statement, explain your reasons for your interpretation as to the relative importance of the various language functions in the message.

Exercise 2-8: Dimensions of Proof in Messages

In this exercise you will be estimating the extent to which a message is based on logical proof, credibility-centered proof, or emotional proof.

    I   Choose a message for use in this exercise as you did for exercise 2-7 or use the same message as the one that you used in exercise 2-7.

   II   Using a pie diagram, identify the extent to which logical, credibility-centered, and emotional proof are present in three statements taken from the message.

  III   Justify your interpretation as to the relative prevalence of the three forms of proof in the statements. Explain this in a short essay. Be sure to include specific references to and excerpts from the message in justifying your interpretation.

Exercise 2-9: Abstracting and Outlining

Abstracting and outlining are key communication skills. They allow you to take apart and put together the messages you encounter. These skills enable you to see the relationships among aspects of a message.

    I   Identify the text of a short message. A message about four hundred words long would be good.

   II   Write out a one-sentence abstract of the message. Remember to pull together all the main points of the message. You will probably need to use a compound or complex sentence.

  III   Following the directions presented in this chapter, outline the message text.

Chapter 3

An Introduction to the Forms of Argument

As I observed at the outset of chapter 2, it is necessary for students of argument to distinguish carefully between the term "argument" and such kindred expressions as "language," "evidence," and "message." To this I should now add the warning that the distinction between argument and reasoning is an important one. Whereas arguments are visible and audible units of language, reasoning is one of the hidden sources of argument—one of the unobservable ways in which advocates reach conclusions. Nevertheless, several of the hidden ways of knowing—testimony and inference, especially—bear great similarity to certain visible types of argument. As a possible result of this, many authors (see Dick, 1972, pp. 34, 37–38) blur the distinction between argument and reasoning. I believe, on the other hand, that it is important to recognize that arguments possess two characteristics that distinguish them from reasoning: (1) Arguments are perceivable (heard, seen, etc.); and (2) arguments are normally addressed to an audience for the purpose of persuasion. Admittedly, this distinction breaks down when we consider the situation of a person arguing with himself or herself. However, the notion of argument as perceivable and an addressed will normally serve to set it apart from reasoning.

Often, there exists a close connection between a person's private analysis of a subject and his or her public presentation of arguments. However, such is not necessarily the case, and history records many examples of conclusions reached privately on one basis and justified publicly on another. Just such an instance was reported in *Newsweek* magazine (December 20, 1976, p. 76). The article quoted certain critics of the late British psychologist Sir Cyril Burt who alleged that he created fictitious coauthors and manufactured data in many of his scholarly works. In short, Burt was accused of having faked his research. One critic explained that "it is almost as if Burt regarded the actual data as merely an incidental backdrop for the illustration of the theoretical issues." If this statement is to be believed, then Burt reached his conclusions on a basis that necessarily differed from the statistical evidence that he amassed in his published articles: His arguments apparently bore little resemblance to his actual manner of arriving at the conclusions.

The focus of this book is, of course, the analysis of visible statements, or arguments, as they are brought to bear on issues of dispute. However, since the concept of reasoning is often so closely allied to that of argument, it is well to begin this chapter with a consideration of the several ways in which human beings arrive at conclusions. Beginning with a discussion of certain "ways of knowing," I will introduce and define the three basic forms of argument— descriptions, interpretations, and evaluations. I will then present four traditional standards that are used to test the merit of arguments—standards that you, the student, will be using throughout the book. This chapter concludes with a brief discussion of rules for using arguments in various situations of dispute.

WAYS OF KNOWING

Most of the time we take for granted the things we know, forgetting that all our beliefs have some source. It is only when our beliefs are questioned ("How do you know that it is 3:00?" or "How do you know there is a God?") that we experience the need to look for the origin of a belief. Yet when we inventory even a small number of the things we know, it is apparent that our "knowledges" spring from a number of sources. In the next few pages, I will treat several ways of knowing, including experience, revelation, authority, emotions, intuition, inference, and ideology.[1] Although I will consider each of these sources separately, the reader should keep in mind that most of our beliefs may be traced to a combination of sources.

Experience

Conclusions founded on experience are basic to human existence. By "experience" I mean the gathering of knowledge through the senses: sight, hearing,

---

[1]Conclusions reached on the basis of faith, feeling, intuition, and ideology do not, strictly speaking, flow from the careful dissection of ideas that traditionally has been associated with the term "reasoning." This is not to say that conclusions reached only after long deliberation are necessarily better than those rooted in such sources as intuition. Indeed, as Weaver writes (1948, p. 19), "sentiment [emotional liking and disliking] is anterior to reason." On this point, also see Vinacke (1952, p. 74) and Aaron (1971, pp. ix, 143).

touch, taste, and smell. Our sense inputs give us much information about the world at any moment. Thus, as I sit at my desk writing, I am now aware of the background noise of the air conditioner, the clicking of my wife's sandals as she walks down the hall, the piles of notes, books, and clippings on my desk, the hexagonal shape of my "BIC PF-49 Deluxe Fine Point" pen, and the effervescent flavor of the "natural alkaline spa water" that I am drinking. These knowledges are both direct and, seemingly, indisputable. Indeed, as Campbell notes (in Bitzer, 1963, p. 47), "The senses . . . are the original inlets of perception. They inform the mind of the facts." Campbell adds (in ibid., p. 52) that sensory experience is the foundation of our knowledge of real and observable matters. Moreover, it is our memory of past experiences that allows us to function in the world.

It requires only a little reflection for one to realize that experiential knowledge plays an important role in our lives. As infants we enter a world that seems random and inexplicable. Yet it does not take a baby long to realize that there are certain regularities in life. The infant observes that crying leads to attention from others, and gradually the baby is able to focus on objects, discriminating one from another. By the time we have reached adulthood, we have assimilated and organized a great number of experiences about the world. Knowledge based on experience allows us to predict the future. Thus, if I see dark clouds in the sky, I tend to expect rain. If I leave from work at 3:30 P.M. on a weekday in spring, I expect to encounter both schoolbuses and schoolchildren in the neighborhoods as I drive home. Indeed, the eighteenth-century philosopher David Hume (1902, p. 38) observed that predictions founded on experience are in turn based on the assumption that the future will resemble the past. This assumption is very often valid, and it is certainly a necessary part of our being able to get along in the world. If we did not assume the resemblance of the future to the past, we could not even walk normally. We would be forever testing the ground to make sure that it would not give way suddenly under our feet.

Yet from time to time the unexpected does occur; and there are other situations in which past experiences have only a limited value. We may enter a new environment in which our previous experiences give us little help in predicting the future. A transplanted Ohioan, for instance, has less basis for predicting weather in Texas than does a native of that state. Further, as researchers in sensory perception have demonstrated, our senses can be fooled. Both experimenters and teachers have devised ways to impress upon us the fact that our senses may be deceived and our expectations thwarted. The instructor's manual accompanying Pace and Boren's text, *The Human Transaction* (1973, pp. 48–49), contains demonstrations of just this type. In one exercise, the instructor is told to obtain a rubber pencil and place it in his pocket, along with several real pencils. The instructor then removes the rubber pencil, shows it to the class, and asks the class to describe its characteristics. After the students identify such attributes as "hard" or "wooden," the instructor then bends the pencil to demonstrate the point that "our perceptions can yield inaccurate information about the world."

Perhaps the classic study of expectation and sensory perception is Leeper's 1935 study of an ambiguous picture. Leeper began with an ambiguous (composite) drawing, that, depending on how you looked at it, represented either an old woman with a scarf thrown over her head or a young woman wearing a hat with a veil. Leeper commissioned an artist to redraw the ambiguous (composite) picture in two unambiguous (single-phase) versions. One of these emphasized the old woman, and the other the young woman.

In an experiment, a number of subjects first were shown one of the unambiguous (single-phase) versions and then the ambiguous (composite) picture. (See figure 3-1 for a group of pictures similar to those Leeper used.) Leeper reports (1935, p. 66) that "of the group which viewed the single-phase drawing favoring the young woman, not one subject saw the old woman in the composite, even though there are quite a few differences between the single-phase drawing of the young woman and the picture of the young woman in the composite. And of the subjects shown the single-phase drawing of the old woman, only one subject in 31 saw the young woman rather than the old woman in the composite." According to Leeper, these results indicate that the prior experience of the subjects "controlled almost entirely" their organization (perception) of the new experience. This experiment teaches us something about the effect of past experiences in structuring new ones. Just as our previous encounters with wooden pencils may fool our eyes as to the nature of a rubber pencil, we may also use our past perception of an old or young woman to sort out an ambiguous picture.

The importance of experience as a source of belief is evident in contemporary society. A *National Enquirer* report (cited in *Texas AAA Motorist,* April 1976, p. 2) on automobile repair practices gains its strength from the author's firsthand accounts of his experiences at specific service stations and garages. *Newsweek* magazine (July 12, 1976, p. 41) relates the research of investigators who have studied a number of near-death experiences of critically ill and injured

Figure 3-1   An ambiguous figure with two alternative versions.

Picture emphasizing
young woman

Picture emphasizing
old woman

Ambiguous
(composite)
picture

patients. Several psychologists have noted similarities in stories told by patients who, after exhibiting signs of death, later recovered. These experiences have been cited by some as evidence for the existence of life after death. A letter quoted in Jean Adams's nationally syndicated teen advice column, "Teen Forum," (*Odessa American,* September 9, 1975, p. 12B) exemplifies the weight that people often assign to conclusions founded on personal experience:

> I have heard many rumors about pot! I have found out for myself that most of these rumors are not true. I have smoked it since I was in eighth grade and am now a junior in high school. As far as I can tell there has been no physical or mental effect on me—[signed] Freak in New York.

Certainly, there are a number of perfectly sound reasons for advising teenagers to abstain from smoking marijuana. Yet given the letter writer's experiences, it would appear difficult to convince "Freak in New York" to discontinue the practice. The author of the letter appears so confident in his or her experiences that, presumably, only unpleasant sensory perceptions will change his or her mind on the subject.

Sensory experience is, then, a vital source of our knowledge about the world. Yet while persons often place great confidence in sensory perception, our senses may be deceived. Thus, although we cannot function without sensory data, we must be careful not to place excessive confidence in present perceptions or in predictions founded on past experience.

Revelation

Revelation is a source of knowledge that involves a direct inspiration from the deity. Unlike experience, which is generally founded on the uniform experiences of humanity, revelation is a direct communication from God. Skeptics such as Hume (1902, pp. 109–131) allege that no reliable evidence exists to document accounts of divine revelation. Nevertheless, history provides us with accounts by those who claim to have gained knowledge by means of the miraculous intervention of God. For Christians the best-known account is perhaps that given in the Acts of the Apostles (9 :1–6) of the conversion of Paul. Paul (then called Saul) was an active persecutor of the early Christian church. Traveling to Damascus to attack the community of believers there, Paul had a miraculous encounter.

> But Saul, still breathing threats and murder against the disciples of the Lord, went to the high priest and asked him for letters to the synagogues at Damascus, so that if he found any belonging to the Way, men or women, he might bring them bound to Jerusalem. Now as he journeyed he approached Damascus, and suddenly a light from heaven flashed about him. And he fell to the ground and heard a voice saying to him, "Saul, Saul, why do you persecute me?" And he said, "Who are you, Lord?" And he said, "I am Jesus, whom you are persecuting; but rise and enter the city, and you will be told what you are to do."

Of course, 2000 years later we have no way of independently verifying that such an incident took place. Yet it is clear that for Paul the conversion on the road to Damascus became a pivotal point in his life: It marked his transition from an opponent of the Christian church to a missionary for that church. Similar accounts may be found in almost all cultures and times. But the conversion of Paul illustrates the essential aspect of knowledge via revelation: direct contact from the deity.

Authority (Testimony)

Many of our beliefs are based on acceptance of statements made by others. From the beginning of the day to its end, we operate on the basis of testimony from others. Much of our daily information about the world is obtained from the newspapers, television, and radio; yet in the main we have no feasible means of personally verifying the conclusions that we accept from the media or from conversation with acquaintances. For this reason there are probably some who persist in denying that astronauts have successfully walked on the moon. Although we have witnessed live television coverage of moon walks, it is possible for the walks to have been fabricated in studios on Earth. That you and I accept the reality of lunar landings is based on our willingness to accept beliefs originating in testimony. Likewise, the popular success of the *Guinness Book of World Records* is founded on the willingness of readers to accept the testimony of the editors that particular people or objects have existed and events taken place.

As another example of authoritative statements as a source of knowledge, consider the energy crisis. For most of us information about the energy situation comes from testimony. In a survey of people's sources of information on the energy issue taken in spring 1977 by a group of my students, most persons cited radio and television as their primary sources. The two other major sources were print media and personal conversation. All of these information sources are based on acceptance of testimony by others. Indeed, in his initial address on the energy crisis on April 18, 1977, President Carter used his authority as President of the United States to persuade the American people that the energy issue represented a real and significant crisis. Early in the address (quoted by the Associated Press in *The New York Times,* April 19, 1977, p. 24), Carter observed: "I know that some of you may doubt that we face real energy shortages. The 1973 gasoline lines are gone, and our homes are warm again. But our energy problem is worse tonight than it was in 1973 or a few weeks ago in the dead of winter." Carter's energy address was a classic instance of the use of Presidential power to persuade. Speaking from the Oval Office, Carter utilized the authority of his high position as a device to mold opinion on energy matters. For most broadcast listeners the Carter speech would amount to knowledge through testimony.

Scholars differ as to the reliability of testimony as a way of knowing. On the one hand, we tend to assume that most people tell the truth; on the other, most of us have occasionally been told falsehoods. As a result, listeners have developed ways of guarding against the misrepresentations of con artists. As Campbell notes (in Bitzer, 1963, p. 55), "It hath been observed, that from experience we learn to confine our belief in human testimony within the proper bounds." Thus, over the years various ways have been devised to evaluate testimony. I will have more to say about such tests in chapter 4. For the present, we should remember that although testimony is a necessary source of information, it is less personally satisfying than direct experience or revelation.

Emotions (Feelings)

In chapter 1, I cited Aristotle's remarks on the power of feelings in human communication. Our emotions supply us with knowledge just as outside authorities do. As a source of knowledge, emotion is often contrasted to reason or thinking (a source which I will soon examine). Arthur Koestler (1964, p. 57) highlights some of the physical differences between thinking and feeling: "Thinking, in its physiological aspect, is based on electro-chemical activities in the cerebral cortex and related regions of the brain, involving energy transactions which are minute compared to the massive glandular, visceral, and muscular changes that occur when emotions are aroused." In other words, whereas thinking is brain-centered, emotion involves more of the body and is, from an energy point of view, a more powerful way of knowing.

Although Aristotle would have been unable to provide such a clinical description of what it means to feel, he, too, recognized the power of emotions in persuasion. He advised the speaker to conclude speeches with an appeal to the audience's capacity to reach conclusions through feelings (*Rhetoric*, III, 19, 1419b): "Now that the nature of the facts, and their importance, are alike clear, the next thing is to make the audience feel the right emotions—pity, indignation, anger, hatred, envy, emulation, antagonism [etc.]." Indeed, in Book II of the *Rhetoric* (II.1–II.11), Aristotle gives systematic treatment to a large number of emotions which the speaker might seek to create in the audience: anger; mildness; love; hatred; fear; kindness; unkindness; pity; indignation; envy; confidence; shame; shamelessness; emulation; contempt.

We often gain knowledge by directly experiencing a feeling. For instance, an important aspect of my knowledge about the assassination of President John F. Kennedy is derived from the feeling of sorrow and shock that I experienced at the time. However, we may also gain emotional knowledge in an indirect manner through empathy. To empathize is to share another's feelings. In *Gone with the Wind,* Margaret Mitchell (1973, p. 111) provides us with an example of knowledge gained through the empathic sharing of another's feelings. The scene is set at the Wilkes plantation, and a heated discussion about secession is taking place among the men. Objecting to the prevailing sentiment that the South should welcome war as an opportunity to avenge dishonor at the hands of President Lincoln, Ashley Wilkes speaks: "Yes, yes, I know we've been insulted and lied to—but if we'd been in the Yankees' shoes and they were trying to leave the Union, how would we have acted? Pretty much the same. We wouldn't have liked it." Mitchell describes Scarlett O'Hara, the heroine of the story, as being, in contrast, none too prone to empathize with an opponent: " 'There he goes again,' thought Scarlett. 'Always putting himself in the other fellow's shoes.' To her, there was never but one fair side to an argument."

In an article describing techniques of empathic listening, Charles Kelly (1970) identifies concern for the speaker as a central feature of empathy. When we empathize, as I noted in chapter 2, we recognize that the other person is entitled to feelings and we seek to feel as the other person does. Emotional knowledge through empathy is, therefore, a second way of gaining knowledge through feelings.

Intuition

Intuition is the ability of the mind to grasp a conclusion suddenly without seeming to have reference to evidence. Unlike inference, which involves the moving from premises to a conclusion, intuition enables us to gain knowledge without immediate prior consideration of premises. Montague (1936, pp. 55–56) describes intuition as a flash of understanding. He adds that intuitive inspiration is often connected to mysticism or to direct contact with the spiritual world. However, one should not assume that intuition is necessarily mystical or that it is indistinguishable from revelation. In fact, as Koestler observes, many of the great scientific discoveries have come about through intuition. Intuition operates in scientific research through what we may call the eureka principle. *Eureka* is a Greek word meaning "I have found it." This expression has long been connected to one of the great discoveries of the Greek philosopher Archimedes, who, after suddenly finding the solution to a complex problem, ran from the public baths shouting, "Eureka." The eureka effect is the sudden connecting of two previously unrelated ideas, which results in an unexpected flash of insight. The situation of Archimedes (Koestler, 1964, pp. 105–108) illustrates well how sudden imagination can be a source of knowledge.

Archimedes lived in the Greek city-state of Syracuse during the third century before Christ. According to tradition, Hiero, the ruler of Syracuse, became suspicious that an artisan had cheated him by substituting silver for gold in Hiero's crown. However, since the crown weighed the same as did the block of gold given to the artisan, Hiero saw no easy way to prove that the cheaper, lighter metal (silver) had been added. Desiring to learn whether he had been defrauded, but not wanting to melt down the crown, Hiero posed this problem to Archimedes: How can we determine whether silver has been substituted for gold without destroying the crown in the process? Archimedes, of course, knew that gold is heavier than silver per unit of volume (i.e., a cubic inch of gold would weigh more than a cubic inch of silver). Therefore, he knew that if some silver had been substituted, the crown would contain a greater volume of material than if the artisan had used pure gold. But, Archimedes thought, how could one learn the volume of the crown with all of its decorations and irregular shapes? It would be, of course, a simple matter to melt the crown down into a single block and learn its volume by measuring the three dimensions of the block, but Hiero forbade this: How could Archimedes measure the volume of the multifaceted crown? Surely, no ordinary method of measurement would work here. Archimedes had to think of some way to "melt down" Hiero's crown without destroying it.

One day, with these thoughts firmly implanted in his subconscious mind, Archimedes went to visit the public baths. As he stepped into the sunken bath, he observed that the water level rose. To be sure, this was no cause for alarm: Archimedes knew as well as anyone that the water level always rises when one steps into the bath. Suddenly, though, Archimedes put together, for the first time, two things that he already knew but had never before connected: (1) We can learn the specific weight (weight per volume unit) of something by measuring its volume; and (2) the water level in a pool rises when we enter it because a body displaces some of the water. By connecting these two ideas, Archimedes had suddenly found the answer to the problem of Hiero's crown. Because the rise in the water level of a bathtub is equal to the size (volume) of the person taking the bath, it follows that a crown laced with silver would displace a greater amount of water than a crown made solely from gold (which is heavier per unit). In a flash, Archimedes had the answer to a seemingly insolvable problem. All he had to do was alternately place both the crown and the block of gold (like that given to Hiero's artisan) in a tub of water and compare the resulting water levels. If the water level was the same for both, then the artisan was honest. If the water level was higher for the crown, then it meant that the crown was made partly with silver, a lighter metal.

This story illustrates the two essential principles of intuition. First, unlike revelation, intuition involves things that we already know. In this example Archimedes already knew that gold is heavier than silver, per unit of volume, and that bath water rises when we get into the tub. Secondly, intuition requires that we put ideas together in a new way. Archimedes had never before connected these two facts, but he suddenly realized, as he sat pondering the problem in his tub, that the water that he displaced was equal to the volume of

Figure 3-2 The eureka principle.

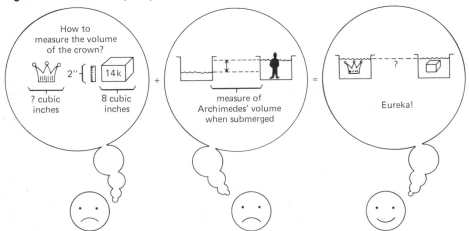

his submerged body. He saw in a flash the answer to the problem of learning volume without melting something into a shape whose volume could be measured with a ruler. As Koestler notes (p. 108), "Discovery often means simply the uncovering of something which has always been there but was hidden from the eye by the blinkers of habit."

Koestler cites a number of further instances in which a scientist had labored unsuccessfully over a problem, only to learn the answer in a sudden, unexpected vision. Using these reports as a guide, he lays out the intuitive process (pp. 118–20). First, the person attacks a problem by using several fixed methods; but because the problem involves new "wrinkles," the old rules fail. Second, in seeking to get past the impasse, the individual becomes frustrated and begins to try random approaches; indeed, the problem becomes so annoying that the individual's unconscious mind keeps working on it, even though the person may be consciously engaged in other pursuits. Finally, two or more previously unrelated ideas come together, and the individual realizes in a moment that the answer has been discovered. The individual has now solved the problem without really being able to explain how he solved it: Because the problem was solved without systematic, conscious thought, it is not possible to lay out the steps taken in arriving at the answer. The solution took place on the subconscious level and cannot be forced into a logical model of premises and conclusion (although the individual may be able to work backward and point out logical connections between the intuitive conclusion and certain premises). Intuitive knowledge is, then, not necessarily mystical or miraculous. Intuition is a sudden, subconscious, creative act that results from recombining things already known.

Inference

As I have earlier observed, inference may be understood as being quite unlike the emotional or intuitive ways of gaining knowledge. Inference, as I defined it in chapter 1, is the conscious process by which old knowledge (the premises) leads to new knowledge (the conclusion). In the words of the philosopher John Dewey (1933, p. 36), "Every inference, just because it goes beyond ascertained and known facts, which are given either by observation or by recollection of prior knowledge, involves a *jump from the known to the unknown.*" When we infer, we consciously and systematically explore concepts as they are expressed in language. Inference is therefore essentially synonymous with reasoning. Unlike the other ways of knowing, inference is a disciplined method of careful thinking. Whereas experience is based on direct sensation, inference is mental. Whereas emotional knowledge is intense, inference is objective, dispassionate, and tentative. Whereas revelation and intuition are flashes of insight, inference is a slow and careful way of arriving at conclusions. Finally, unlike testimony, which requires that we place our trust in the judgment of another, inference is a method based on self-reliance.

The general method of inference involves a systematic study of a problem and is well described in Dewey's reflective thought pattern. Dewey (1933, pp. 106–107) believed that inference began (like intuition) with a feeling of confusion. In response to feelings of perplexity, the reasoner identifies relevant aspects of the problem to be solved. At the same time "the mind leaps forward to a possible solution." These notions of problem and solution may then be refined into hypotheses (predictions or guesses) that "initiate and guide observation and other operations in collection of factual material." Finally, through careful thought and hypothesis testing, a conclusion is reached. Dewey emphasizes (p. 115) that the sequence of these steps is not fixed, but the classic problem-solving sequence—which is derived from Dewey's system—includes these elements: (1) Locate and define the problem, (2) describe and limit the problem, (3) identify possible solutions, (4) evaluate solutions, and (5) choose the best alternative solution. When an individual utilizes inference to reach a conclusion, we may say that he has engaged in reasoning. The person has, in other words, argued with himself. Inference is a systematic and private way to gain knowledge. Yet because we cannot see into a person's head, we have no way of identifying the basis on which the individual has reached the conclusion. We cannot say whether the knowledge was obtained from experience, revelation, testimony, emotions, intuition, or inference. Consequently, our focus in this book must be on the public justification of conclusions—the presentation of arguments to establish claims publicly.

Ideology

The final way of knowing that I wish to treat results from ideology—one's attitude system. In chapter 2, I defined attitude as being a person's positive or negative judgment about something; yet it is important to realize that our attitudes do not exist in isolation from other aspects of our mental processes. Milton Rokeach (1968) has developed a theory of mental organization that is based on the relationship of beliefs, attitudes, and values. In chapter 7 of his book, Rokeach defines an attitude as a collection of related beliefs that are focused on a specific object (person, place, or thing) or situation. These attitudes are supported by underlying values. Rokeach defines values as notions of proper conduct (e.g., telling the truth) or desirable end states of being (e.g., having freedom). This organization is summarized in figure 3-3. Attitudes then are organized to form an ideology.

Figure 3-3   Beliefs, values, and attitudes.

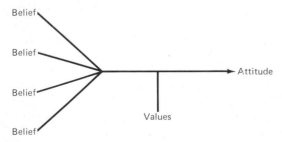

I wish now to examine ideology as another source of human knowledge. Ideologies give us a way of looking at the world: Our world view in turn affects our interpretation of the environment. Perhaps the most familiar ideologies are those political outlooks called liberal and conservative. Contemporary liberals tend to have an ideology which emphasizes both equality with and charity for one's neighbors and which gives less heed to social order. Conservatives tend to emphasize freedom, individualism, and social order. Often, conservatives and liberals view specific issues differently because of their general outlook on life. Liberals, for example, generally support more generous welfare programs and lighter penalties for drug use than conservatives do. This results, presumably, from liberals' liking of charity and a tendency not to make hard moral judgments about individual life-styles. Conservatives, who favor self-reliance in individuals, are less enthusiastic about welfare programs. Also, because conservatives are more concerned than liberals about social order, they take a harder line on drug offenses. Each ideology provides a way of interpreting new situations and issues.

In a survey of attitudes concerning the desirability of weapons research on college campuses, we may observe the operation of ideology as a way of knowing. Ladd and Lipset (*Chronicle of Higher Education,* March 15, 1976, p. 11) surveyed both liberal and conservative college professors on this issue. They reported, "Liberals strongly reject the propriety of classified weapons research on campuses, while conservatives strongly defend it." Of course, liberals and conservatives do not always disagree, but our views are often shaped by political ideology rather than by careful inference on a subject. There are times when ideology may be an important source of knowledge.

There exist many philosophic systems for interpreting the world. Religious faith is an ideology that prescribes many conclusions about the world: e.g., that there is a God, that prayer is likely to be answered, and that murder is bad. Of course, there are many systems of religious thought to which persons may adhere. The role of a particular person's religious system as a source of personal knowledge is reflected in Pat Boone's book, *A Miracle a Day Keeps the Devil Away* (1975). Boone cites a number of unusual occurrences in his life (especially those on pp. 11, 13–14, 49) that he considered miracles because of his faith. For someone else whose religious system did not include belief in frequent miracles, the events would be explained as coincidence. Hume, who was a philosophic skeptic, utterly rejected miracles and asserted that no miracle had ever been sufficiently established (1902, pp. 116–117). Thus, while Boone *knows* that the happenings cited in his book are miracles, Hume would *know* just the opposite. Such knowledge would depend on ideology.

The number of existing ideologies is large. Each of the following attitude systems provides its adherent with a way of knowing the world.

1 Relativism: One idea or opinion is as good as another. Truth is unknowable, and moral judgments depend on the way we feel.

2 Liberitarianism: Individual personal freedom is the ultimate value. The government should not interfere in human choices.

3 Utilitarianism: Whatever creates the most good for the most people is best.

4 Pragmatism: We should judge events on the basis of their practical consequences.

5 Marxist Communism: Society is based on economic principles and class conflict. A worker's dictatorship must be established to root out social evil. When this occurs, then the government can be disassembled.

6 Anti-communism: Communism means a lack of freedom and individual dignity. It must be opposed by whatever means necessary.

7 Natural law: "The Laws of Nature and of Nature's God" (to use Thomas Jefferson's famous phrase) are reflected in the operation of the universe. We should not deviate from the principles of nature.

Of course, I have described each of the above ideologies in extremely general terms. Yet even from these brief descriptions, it is clear that a person espousing pragmatism and utilitarianism might well react differently from one holding to natural law on the issue of birth control. The natural-law advocate might view birth control (via mechanical means) as being a violation of the natural process of procreation. The utilitarian pragmatist might well reply that we must have birth control to curb population growth, or else the quality of life for all will decline. Each would find a different view of truth through his personal ideology.

In the past few pages I have sketched out in general terms several of the sources of human knowledge. Throughout, I have tried to make the point that one's public arguments are not necessarily the same as one's private way of knowing. I am hardly the first to make such an observation. In fact, the point is perhaps better illustrated in comments of Robert F. Kennedy (1967, p. 140) about arguments advanced by Charles de Gaulle (president of France from 1958 to 1968) in support of the idea that France should have an independent nuclear strike force: "De Gaulle's steady and constant drive for nuclear capability has been supported by arguments that have shifted with every turn of events. That so many arguments all have led to the same result may raise at least the possibility that the goal, in fact, determined the reasons." In other words, conclusions may lead to arguments just as arguments may lead to conclusions.

THE FORMS OF ARGUMENT

There are, as we have seen, a large variety of sources of knowledge. In this section I will identify three general means for explaining our conclusions, however derived, to others: (1) description, (2) interpretation, and (3) evaluation. Throughout the book, but especially in chapters 4, 5, and 6, I will make the point that all arguments may be viewed as falling into one or more of these three categories. In chapter 1, I identified the issues of fact, definition, and value as being useful for sorting out arguments in a dispute. I now wish to elaborate on this point and define the three forms of argument as follows:

1   Descriptions are arguments that state or imply first-order issues of fact.
2   Interpretations are arguments that state or imply first-order issues of definition.
3   Evaluations are arguments that state or imply first-order issues of value.

When I say that an evaluation, for instance, raises a first-order issue of value, I am not saying that an evaluation raises only issues of value. Rather, in an evaluation the issue of value is the initial issue, or first order of business. A question of value is emphasized in the evaluative form of argument: It must be examined first.

Consider a real-world situation of evaluative argument. In President Carter's decision in the early part of 1977 to oppose certain water projects, we may observe the operation of issues in an evaluation. Carter (cited in *The New York Times,* April 19, 1977, p. 20) opposed the projects on economic, safety, and environmental grounds. He asserted that public works projects should not benefit only "narrow or special interests," adding that "environmental values must be a primary concern, to insure that irreplaceable natural resources are protected from needless degradation or destruction." The surface issue in this argument is one of value: Are the water projects good or bad, in view of their costs, benefits, and their environmental effects? Hence, the argument may be classified as one that raises first-order issues of value.

Yet it should be clear that issues of definition and fact underlie the basic question of value in Carter's arguments. Recall that an issue of fact involves observable events and things. Factual issues raise such questions as "Did X happen?" or "Does Y exist?" Clearly, the water projects situation involves factual questions concerning the details of each project: location, cost, tons of earth moved, etc. Similarly, certain questions of definition—fitting facts into categories—underlie Carter's evaluative analysis. Do the specific cost figures (facts such as money already spent and budgeted for the future) fall into the category "wasteful" or into the category "cost effective?" Do the figures on total earth moved (facts) mean that the projects may be defined as environmentally damaging or not? In this way, evaluations carry with them deeper questions of definition and fact.

Just as an evaluation contains deeper issues of definition and fact, definition-emphasizing arguments (called interpretations) imply further questions of fact and value. Likewise, although descriptive arguments point to a surface factual question, they allow subsidiary controversies based on definition and value.[2]

---

[2]A separate category of "policy arguments"—to correspond to policy issues—is not needed because arguments are best classified on the basis of *why* they recommend a policy—for reasons of fact, definition or value. There are, however, certain special techniques of policy argument which receive attention in chapters 10 and 11.

The issues raised by the three forms of argument may be summarized as follows:

Evaluations raise (1) first-order issues of value, (2) subsidiary issues of definition, and (3) subsidiary issues of fact.

Interpretations raise (1) first-order issues of definition, (2) subsidiary issues of value, and (3) subsidiary issues of fact.

Descriptions raise (1) first-order issues of fact, (2) subsidiary issues of definition, and (3) subsidiary issues of value.

Having explained the three basic forms of argument, I will devote the next few pages to a specific treatment of each form.

Descriptions

Descriptive arguments deal with questions of fact. In chapter 1, I cited some of the common criteria used to decide whether or not something is a fact. According to my definition, a fact must meet each of the following three tests: (1) It must be something that can be independently verified; (2) it must be capable of being "mapped" (i.e., precisely described); and (3) it must be something that can win the agreement of all reasonable persons. "It is 3:00," "Mars has two moons," and other such statements are based on factual issues that presumably can be resolved to the satisfaction of all. Let me emphasize at this point that factual or descriptive statements are not always true. Many descriptive assertions proved to be false when tested—such as when one states that the day is Tuesday, only to learn, after consulting the calendar that the day is really Wednesday.

Descriptive arguments come in the form of examples, statistics, and testimony, all of which raise first-order issues of fact. When one supports a claim with example argument, the first issue raised is "did the example really happen?" Only later do we ask: (1) what the example means (i.e., how it may be interpreted) or (2) whether the example means that something is good or bad (i.e., the appropriate value). Similarly, when using statistical evidence— numerical summaries—one is using data that point to the existence or nonexistence of things. The descriptive statistical assertion, "The pupil-teacher ratio in the school system is 50 to 1" might be used to support a claim that the system must hire more teachers. A kindred process occurs when we hear testimony: Our first questions should be "Did someone really say that? Did it happen?" Then we can analyze the subsidiary questions raised by the statement itself. Descriptions therefore emphasize what we may call the report function of language. As I noted in chapter 2, when we describe something we use language to identify precisely, in objective terms, the nature of the world.

A news report critical of Richard M. Nixon's first televised interview with British newsman David Frost illustrates well the nature of descriptive argument. The author of the article, David E. Rosenbaum, endeavors to refute Mr. Nixon's assertion that he had not violated the law in limiting the investigation of the Watergate break-in. Rosenbaum cites the following testimonial evidence in support of the claim that Mr. Nixon may have violated the law (*The New York Times,* May 5, 1977, p. 34):

> [Claim] The Watergate prosecutors and the House Judiciary Committee found reason to believe that Mr. Nixon had indeed been part of a conspiracy to obstruct justice.
>
> [Data] In the indictment in which the former President's top aides, including John N. Mitchell, H. R. Haldeman and John D. Ehrlichman, were charged with conspiring to obstruct justice, Mr. Nixon was listed as an unindicted co-conspirator. Leon Jaworski, then the special prosecutor, has said that Mr. Nixon was not indicted because there were questions about whether the Constitution permitted the indictment of a sitting President.
>
> The Judiciary Committee, in its first proposed article of impeachment, charged that Mr. Nixon had engaged in a plan "to delay, impede and obstruct the investigation."

The initial questions raised by the data offered in this news article are ones of fact: Was Mr. Nixon cited as an unindicted co-conspirator? Did Jaworski in fact state that he refrained from indicting Nixon only because he (Nixon) occupied the White House? Did the House Judiciary Committee actually make the charge that Mr. Nixon participated in conspiracy to obstruct justice? Only when these factual issues are resolved can the reader proceed to the definitional question stated in the claim: Did Mr. Nixon commit an illegal act? The key observation to be made here is that while not everyone will accept the interpretive claim that "Mr. Nixon committed an illegal act," they can be brought to agree on the fact that the House committee did allege his guilt.

Descriptive argument consists, therefore, of statements that are factual in nature. The listener may verify descriptive arguments independently; such arguments may be stated with precise language; and all reasonable persons may be brought to accept a truly descriptive assertion. In the situation cited the reader need only refer to various documents and reports in order to ascertain whether the special prosecutor and the House impeachment committee had alleged Nixon's guilt. In chapter 4 I will give detailed consideration to the three forms of descriptive argument—examples, statistics, and testimony—and I will identify some of the methods used to test factual statements. For now you should keep in mind the essential features of descriptive argument.

Interpretations

The surface issue raised by an interpretive argument is one of definition. When we argue definitionally we place things into categories, asking whether fact X fits definition Y. An interpretive argument does not merely identify reality. It relates facts and places them in perspective. Shortly after the 1976 presidential elections, for instance, *Newsweek* (November 22, 1976, p. 4) printed interpretations by a number of readers who sought to explain the reason for Jimmy Carter's victory. Arguing that Carter's win owed something to his lack of specificity on the issues, a New York man wrote: "I liken Jimmy Carter's political victory to Crackerjack—you have to buy the package before you find out what surprise lies inside." Still another correspondent saw union assistance as placing Carter in debt to union leaders: "Carter claims not to owe anything to big business. I wonder what he owes to union bosses." In the opinion of another New York resident, Carter won the Presidency because of a newspaper headline ("Ford to N.Y.: Drop Dead") unfavorable to President Ford's early opposition to New York City financial aid. On the other hand, a Florida letter writer attributed Carter's win to the black vote: "You do not give enough credit to us black voters. We carried the South. Whites gave a majority to Ford in the South, as in several Northern states; without us Carter could not have been elected."

Each of these writers works from the same basis of fact: Jimmy Carter received a majority of electoral and popular votes in the 1976 presidential election. However, each writer uses language to place that fact in a different light. The fact of the victory is said to have come about for a variety of reasons: union help, a New York newspaper headline, and the black vote. Each letter writer seeks not to describe the Carter victory in objective terms but to place it in perspective, thereby giving it meaning. Unlike the descriptive argument, which reports the details of what happened, the interpretation places the details in various categories.

Another instance of defining the meaning of a fact may be found in this letter to "Dear Abby" (*Odessa American,* April 22, 1977, p. 8B):

> Dear Abby: The letter of Paul's wife whose husband had the annoying habit of salting his food before tasting it reminds me of a supposedly true story.
>
>   A personnel director who was responsible for hiring executives would always invite the job applicant out for lunch as part of the interview. If he salted his food before tasting, he [the director] deduced that he made decisions without first investigating.
>
>   Interesting?—[signed] M.E.H.
>
> Dear M.E.H.: Yes. And a reasonable conclusion, too.

M.E.H. identifies a fact (whether or not a person salts food before tasting it) and defines this fact as indicating that the person makes decisions "without first investigating." Abby, in her remarks, makes a second interpretation, calling M.E.H.'s conclusion "reasonable." She places a fact (M.E.H. said such-and-such) into the class of "reasonable statements."

Interpretive arguments are therefore to be distinguished from descriptive arguments. Interpretations draw issues of definition that classify facts. Interpretations thus relate facts and give them perspective. Whereas factual issues are based on the report function of language, definitional issues result from the capacity of language to reveal our attitudes about things. Whereas a descriptive argument identifies reality in neutral terms, an interpretive argument constructs reality by defining the nature of the world in conclusionary terms.

Evaluations

When we evaluate something we raise initial issues concerning its goodness or badness: That is, we draw conclusions about values. Values are those things that people hold as being good or bad. As I noted earlier in the chapter, Rokeach (1968) has divided values into two classes: (1) terminal values, or those that deal with end states such as freedom, equality, etc., and (2) instrumental values, or those dealing with proper conduct such as honesty and morality. We may observe this concern for ends and means in everyday language. In March 1977 I received an offer to subscribe to the *Columbia Journalism Review.* In seeking to motivate me to purchase the subscription, the letter outlined a number of values that I would obtain from the magazine:

> To our way of thinking (and I'm sure to yours), the way you *should* get the news is: accurately, honestly, objectively, and as free from conflicts of interest as possible. Sadly, as the above examples indicate, this is not always the case. . . .
> For thousands of men and women concerned with the quality and integrity of newsreporting and the sanctity of "freedom of the press"—the answer has long been the *Columbia Journalism Review.*

We may observe in these two paragraphs the workings of evaluative argument. The letter identifies both terminal values (quality news, freedom of the press) and instrumental values (honesty and objectivity in reporting) that the *Review* upholds. These evaluations support the claim that one should subscribe to the *Columbia Journalism Review.* Evaluative arguments work by building a conclusion on the goodness or badness of something.

It is frequently the case that the same things are evaluated differently by different people. A good illustration of this phenomenon is supplied by a *Newsweek* article (October 18, 1976, p. 56) on former President Ford's performance as an economic leader. In the resulting "report card" (see figure 3-4 on page 74), six economists provided widely varying evaluations of Ford's economic stewardship. The evaluations of Ford's economic leadership vary from very good (A−) to poor (D). Predictably, liberal Democratic economists rated Ford as less capable than did conservative Republicans. Also, the close connection between evaluations and interpretations is indicated in this excerpt. In the "comments" section each economist supplies interpretations that support the overall evaluation. Thus, the value ratings of Ford are related to subsidiary issues of definition.

In chapters 4, 5, and 6 I will give detailed consideration to the three forms of argument. As I will indicate, there are many subcategories of descriptive, interpretive, and evaluative argument. For now, it is sufficient that you understand that arguments may be classified on the basis of the surface or

REPORT CARD		
Economist	Grade	Comments
Walter Heller University of Minnesota; J.F.K.'s chief adviser	D	Unemployed human beings are used as a defense against inflation. It's just so wasteful, so unnecessary.
Paul McCracken University of Michigan; Nixon's chief adviser	A-	Considering where we were when he came in, the improvement is enormous. At the critical points, Ford made the right decisions and stuck to them.
Arthur Okun Brookings Institution; L.B.J.'s chief adviser	D	If the recession has cured inflation, the grade would be higher. As it is, Ford has turned a sow's ear into a sow's ear.
Beryl Sprinkel Harris Trust and Savings Bank; monetarist conservative	A-	His basic thrust has been dead right. He's avoided the natural but dangerous mistake of overstimulating the economy.
Paul Samuelson M.I.T.: leading Keynesian	C	That's a gentleman's C. He simply listens to his advisers, and he's the kind of President advisers like. An open mind is an empty mind.
Murray Weidenbaum Washington University conservative; former Treasury economist	B+	He's succeeded in getting us out of the recession and into moderate growth, while cutting inflation in half.

Figure 3-4 How six economists rated President Ford's performance. *(Fenga & Freyer, Inc.)*

first-order issue raised: fact, definition, or value. This is not the only system for classifying argument (see other systems in Kahane, 1971, pp. xiii–xiv; Perelman and Olbrechts-Tyteca, 1969, pp. viii–x; O'Neill, Laycock, and Scales, 1917, pp. 170–171), but it is an old system (see Cicero, *De Inventione*, I, viii, 10; Quintilian, *Institutio Oratoria*, III, vi, 1–104) and one that has wide relevance for the modern era.

STANDARDS FOR THE CRITICISM OF ARGUMENT

Throughout this text I will be calling upon you to test the merits of arguments. In separating sound arguments from unsound ones, we must have a yardstick against which the strength of the argument may be measured. As I noted in chapter 2, when we assess the strength of argument, we go beyond the mere perception of language. We both record the content of the message and test that content: We act as a critical listener. It is important to realize that there are several commonly used standards for testing the merits of claims. Arguments are often compared on the basis of their persuasiveness—that is, the effects that they produce in listeners; they may be tested for truthfulness; they may be judged as ethical or unethical; and finally, the validity or logical soundness of an argument may be used as a criterion for judgment. In the following pages, I will examine each of these four criteria.

The Effect Standard

When we probe for the effect of an argument, we are looking for the reaction it produced in those persons who were exposed to the argument. Since the time of the classical Greeks, scholars have evaluated arguments on the basis of persuasive effect. Aristotle's *Rhetoric* was built around the idea that arguers should study the means to win over their listeners. The central place of the effect standard in the field of rhetoric is reflected in Thonssen, Baird, and Braden's text, *Speech Criticism* (1970, p. 19):

> It [rhetorical criticism] seeks an answer to the question: To what extent, and through what resources of rhetorical craftsmanship, did the speaker achieve the end—immediate or delayed—which he sought? By applying appropriate standards which derive from the interaction of subject, speaker, audience, and occasion, the critic assesses the effect of speeches upon particular audiences and, finally, upon society.

Effects, then, deal with changes in listener attitudes or behavior which result from argument. A critic of argument seeks to identify these listener effects.

The effects standard appears at first glance to be a relatively simple approach. It would seem that one merely looks for obvious audience reaction to a given message. Yet the art of identifying effects is more subtle than one might imagine. First of all, what are effects? Applause? Smiles? A later behavior? Unobserved changes in attitude? In short, how can we measure effects of language? How can we know what the members of the audience are thinking?

The problem of identifying effects is a significant one. Often, of course, we are not able to observe the entire audience directly—as, for example, in a nationally televised message. Even when we are able to watch the audience—say, in an auditorium—we have no direct way to peer inside the heads of the listeners. We may infer audience response from clues such as applause, but applause is only a vague indicator as to the audience's reaction to specific arguments in a message. Furthermore, we have few ways to gauge the long-term effect of a message even when the message is considered as a whole. If the audience applauds wildly, but forgets the message twenty-four hours later, can we still judge the message as effective? For these reasons, many studies of audience effect are done in laboratory settings where audience attitude change in response to artificial messages may be carefully measured.

For example, in their study of "The Effects of Three Types of Profane Language in Persuasive Messages," Bostrom, Baseheart, and Rossiter (1973) identified the initial attitude of 128 Ohio University students toward the subject of the legalization of marijuana. The subjects listened to messages that contained either no profanity or one of three types of profanity (religious, excretory, and sexual). After measuring the attitude change which resulted from the different types of messages, the authors concluded (p. 472): "Thus, it would appear that a communicator contemplating the use of profanity can 1) expect to be no more persuasive than if he did not include the profanity, and 2) expect to lose somewhat in terms of whatever positive credibility he may have in the eyes of the receiver." In other words, presenting arguments with profane language does not increase persuasive effect and may actually reduce one's standing with the audience. Such conclusions, of course, are consistent with common sense; but they carry more weight in view of the careful laboratory methodology.

Another approach to the systematic measurement of effect is to survey a random sample of listeners in the field. For instance, most major national polling organizations commissioned studies of viewer reaction to the first David Frost–Richard Nixon televised interview (May 4, 1977), which dealt with the Watergate scandal. A *New York Times* article (May 7, 1977, p. 9) summarized the results of a Harris survey:

> Public opinion surveys made after the interview of Mr. Nixon by David Frost indicated yesterday that most viewers thought the former President had not answered all questions truthfully and that a substantial majority were against his return to a role in public life, the pollsters reported yesterday.
>
> A Harris poll of 1,506 viewers, commissioned by ABC, found an even division over whether Mr. Nixon had been "mostly telling the truth," while 51 percent felt that he had "lied several times" and only 27 said he had not. At the time, a 67-to-25 majority replied that Mr. Nixon had defended himself as well as the circumstances allowed.
>
> Sizeable majorities said that Mr. Nixon "knew he was obstructing justice" and that he had "lied" when he said he had no knowledge about cash payments to Watergate defendants until nine months after the Watergate break-in, the Harris poll reported. It said that viewers, by 71 to 24 percent, declared that Mr. Nixon "could not return to public life."

Certainly the average "man on the street" critic cannot amass the facilities to interview 1506 people, nor can we normally set up a laboratory experiment to test the impact of a statement on a hypothetical audience of subjects. Thus, the experimental and survey approaches are no real answer to the problems I posed earlier: What are the effects of real messages, and how can critics measure them?

Looking for Communicator Purpose   Given the basic problems of effects measurement, critics of argument have identified ways of judging effects in the absence of extensive laboratory and survey facilities. Initially, the critic should seek to identify the communicator's purpose. In so doing, we need first to investigate the context in which the arguments were presented: What was the communicator doing at the time? What forces supported and opposed the communicator? To whom did the communicator speak? What did the audience desire to hear or expect to hear? Such questions help to put the critic in touch with the needs and motivations of the speaker: By searching out the environment in which the communicator functioned, we can glean numerous clues as to purpose. A second source of information on purpose is the message itself. The language of the speech supplies hints as to the intent of its author—what he wants from the audience.

Let us apply these two tests—the external context of the message and the internal language of it—to President Jimmy Carter's speech on energy to a joint session of Congress on April 20, 1977 (as reported in *The New York Times,* April 21, 1977, p. 46). Beginning with the context of the speech, it is clear that Carter desired to implement a comprehensive new energy program. During the 1976 presidential campaign, Carter had criticized the Ford administration for failing to do so, and he promised to have an energy program by April. Carter faced diverse pressure from groups such as consumers and oil industry supporters. Consumers favored low energy prices; industry spokesmen desired the decontrol of oil and gas prices, an act that would increase prices, providing thereby increased incentives for oil exploration. Carter needed to find some way to reconcile such opposing desires. Carter's decision to address a joint session of Congress further suggests both that he believed his speech to be important and that he viewed Congress as needing such a dramatic stimulus. The context of the speech indicates, therefore, that President Carter intended to present a compromise energy package and that he was using the speech to sell his program both to the Congress and to the American people. These are conclusions that one could make without even reading or listening to the speech.

The actual text of the speech confirms these context-bound notions of purpose but also gives us additional clues as to Carter's intentions. In the introduction to the speech, Carter makes several pointed references to his intention to work with the Congress. He refers to the executive and legislative branches as "partners in addressing our nation's problems." He adds that to solve the energy crisis "we must act now, together." He emphasizes to the representatives that in formulating his plan "your advice has been an important influence." When we combine these internal clues to a related factor of context—Congress had felt excluded from earlier Carter energy decisions—we observe that one of Carter's purposes was to win cooperation from the Congress. Relevant to another of Carter's purposes is his emphasis on the details of his plan. He argued that his plan was the fairest method and that it contained necessary actions. Furthermore, he indicated that he desired to win support for each detail of his plan. "This is a carefully balanced program," he asserted, "depending for its fairness on all its major component parts." Carter's attention to identifying the disadvantages of decontrol of oil and gas suggests another purpose: He wished to dampen the sentiment in favor of this proposal. Finally, throughout the speech, Carter indicated that he believed that his proposal was a difficult one—one that would create much opposition. Such statements reinforce the context-bound inferences that Carter intended the speech as a major selling job.

Observing the Entire Communication Situation   Having gained a notion of the speaker's purpose, the effects critic is in a position to take informed observations about the communication situation. The critic should take as many observations about the audience as possible, using opinion polls (when available), sales figures, interviews, and other reports of listener reaction. The critic should look to his or her own reactions to the message and compare personal reactions to responses by others. For historical situations diary accounts or memoirs may be available to show the speaker's thinking. The critic should look also for long-term actions. For instance, how similar to the President's plan is the final program passed by Congress? This would give a notion of Carter's success in convincing the Congress that the plan should be accepted as a whole. Another approach is possible for messages repeated frequently over a long period of time—such as in advertising or political campaigns. In this case the critic may look for subtle changes in the message. One assumes that ineffective arguments will be discarded over a period of time and that effective appeals will be retained. Having taken every possible short- and long-term observation of the communication situation, the critic is now ready to compare speaker intention to the actual results.

The effects standard is an important criterion for the criticism of arguments. Indeed, this standard is commonly viewed as most important in contemporary American society. Effects may be translated into dollars and cents. Thus, more resources are devoted to studying persuasive effects than are devoted to testing arguments by means of the other standards. Whole segments of industry, such as advertising, and fields of study like persuasion are based on the analysis of effects. In chapter 7, I will give further attention to this standard for the criticism of argumentation.

The Truth Standard

Whereas effects deal with observable results, the truth standard requires that we measure a statement against objective reality. To say that something is true is to say that it corresponds exactly with the real world.[3] As Toulmin (1968, p. 74) observed, "According to the 'correspondence' theory of truth, to say that a proposition is 'true' is to say that it 'corresponds to a fact.'" Truth, in this sense, is independent of whether an individual believes a statement to be true. For this reason we may call the truth criterion an objective standard, unlike the effect standard, which measures the subjective opinions of the listeners.

---

[3]The "fact-correspondence" theory of truth is not the only approach to the subject. For example, one could assert that something is true only if it coincides with one's attitudes (i.e., ideology). For a further inquiry into the philosophy of truth, see Brennan (1961, pp. 155–169) and Toulmin (1968, pp. 72–74).

Using the Correspondence Test   The principle of correspondence may be illustrated by the following example. Consider the basic argument "the tree is next to the house." This sentence contains two names ("tree" and "house") and an expression ("is next to") that specifies the relationship between the two names. Toulmin (1968, p. 75) and Hayakawa (1949, pp. 32–33) suggest that we may draw or map such an argument as shown in figure 3-5. One need only compare the sentence to the map to decide that the sentence is true. It corresponds exactly to reality as described by a set of objective structures or positive terms.

This definition of truth as correspondence to a fact would seem to limit the truth standard to the analysis of descriptive arguments. After all, only descriptive arguments deal with mapable facts expressed in positive terms. Interpretations and evaluations involve abstract definitional terms that cannot be reduced to an objective reality. For example, how could one test the correspondence-to-fact of the sentence "The boy is good"? We know the structural equivalent of "house" and "tree"—and "boy," for that matter—but what does goodness look like? Yet, we should remember that interpretations and evaluations both involve subsidiary issues of fact. If an interpretation or evaluation is based upon a falsehood (a disproven fact), then the truth of the interpretation or evaluation would itself be suspect. Therefore, when we apply the truth standard to interpretations and evaluations, we first look for the relationship of definitions and values to an underlying structure of facts. For instance, when we argue that "John's behavior was bad" (an evaluation), we also ask the question "Exactly what did John do?" (an issue of fact; i.e., a description). Yet the correspondence principle is not a completely satisfactory method for analyzing the truth of interpretations and evaluations. This is because a decision about definitional or evaluative truth is a *judgment* rather than an *act of mapping*. When we label an interpretation (e.g., "The woman was polite") as true, we place it into a category—we interpret it.

Because all truth judgments of definitional and value-based issues are interpretive, it follows that such truth judgments are more risky than correspondence tests. Deciding the truth of the statement "Mary is the most responsible person in the senior class" is far more difficult than deciding the truth of the argument "Mary is sitting in the chair." Yet in chapters 1 and 2, I identified the process of dialectic as a means for gaining insight into arguments that involve dialectical terms (terms with meanings that must be constructed—i.e., words that raise definitional and evaluative issues).

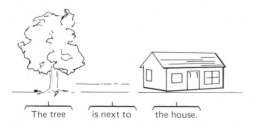

The tree   is next to   the house.

Figure 3-5   Truth as structural correspondence.

Using Dialectic to Test the Truth of Interpretations and Evaluations   Recall that in dialectic we use the question-and-answer method to divide things by classes and identify what belongs in various categories. Consider how one might use dialectic to get at the truth of the statement "Mary is the most responsible person in the senior class." Assume that we are questioning one of Mary's high school teachers.

Q: How do you know that Mary is the most responsible member of the senior class?

A: Well, I've known her for a number of years, and, compared to other students, she seems highly responsible.

Q: What has Mary done that the other students haven't?

A: Well, she either attends class or lets me know when she can't. She does her assignments well and on time. She follows the directions for an assignment and consults with me, in advance, when she doesn't understand a part of an assignment. When she can't take an exam at the scheduled time, she calls in advance to arrange another time. Most students just don't take the time to do these things.

Q: So you are defining "responsible" to mean doing school assignments well, correctly, and on time?

A: Yes, but it goes beyond that. Mary is a reliable person in and out of school. She realizes that she is responsible for what she does or does not do.

Q: OK, so being a responsible person means taking the attitude that "my success and failure is up to me." But what makes you say that Mary is the *most* responsible person in the senior class?

A: Well, you've kind of got me there. I admit that I don't know every senior as well as I know Mary; but I have heard other teachers make the point that she is the most responsible student they have known.

Of course, this dialogue could continue for several pages. However, just in this brief dialectic, we have learned much about the statement "Mary is the most responsible person in the senior class." We have learned from the teacher one definition of responsibility; we have heard about those of Mary's actions that prompt the teacher to classify Mary as responsible; and we have probed the teacher's reasons for calling Mary the most responsible student.

Although our dialectic does not fully tell us whether the statement is true (in the sense of a correspondence definition of truth), it places us in a better position to make an informed judgment (a critic's interpretation) of the truth of the statement. We now have a basis from which to search out several factual questions: Has Mary in fact behaved as the teacher has testified? Have other teachers in fact called Mary the most responsible student? We can inquire about the meaning of the word "responsible" and compare it to the definition provided by the teacher. We can seek to examine the nature of the teacher's relationship with Mary to learn about any possible ulterior motives that the teacher might have in praising Mary.

Although helpful, the dialectical method for investigating the truth of interpretations and evaluations is not as straightforward as the process of dealing with the correspondence of descriptive facts to observable reality. The dialectic does not overcome the need for us to make a subjective judgment in resolving definitional and value-based issues that surround terms like "responsible."

Despite the subjectivism inherent even in a careful dialectic, the philosopher Plato believed that the dialectic would bring us in contact with the truth. In *Phaedrus* Plato writes of the dialectical investigation of truth. Plato composed his works as dialogues involving two or more characters; in the selection below, Plato uses the figure of Socrates to state his (Plato's) opinions. The dialogue opens with Phaedrus questioning Socrates on the issue of truth in communication (*Phaedrus,* 259–60).

Phaedrus: On this point, Socrates, I have heard it said that it's not necessary for the man who plans to be an orator to learn what is really just and true, but only what seems so to the crowd who will pass judgment; and in the same way he may neglect what is really good or beautiful and concentrate on what will seem so; for it is from what seems to be true that persuasion comes, not from the real truth.

In his answer Socrates (speaking for Plato) points out the unfortunate consequences of seeking merely to persuade and not seeking also to advance truth. Socrates then proposes a method—the dialectic—for helping truth to prevail in discourse. Notice in this selection that Plato treats the dual functions of dialectic to establish definitions and to divide things into classes. In this passage Socrates is explaining to Phaedrus two elements of honest communication. Socrates begins by asserting that discourse has value when it includes "two modes of treatment" (*Phaedrus,* 265).

Phaedrus: What are they?

Socrates: The power to organize into a single comprehensive system the unarranged characteristics of a subject. In this way each subject . . . will be perfectly clear through its having been defined. Take, for example, our present discussion of love: the definition of its nature—it doesn't matter for my point whether it is correct or not—has enabled my speech to be clear and self-consistent.

Phaedrus: And what do you mean by the other sort of ability, Socrates?

Socrates: It is the reverse of the other: the ability to divide into species according to natural articulations, avoiding the attempt to shatter the unity of a natural part, as a clumsy butcher might do.

Plato, speaking through Socrates, gives us his answer to the question of attaining truth in communication. When we establish definitions (e.g., the definition of "being responsible") and divide things into classes (e.g., specifying what kinds of behavior indicate responsibility), we come as close as possible to knowing the truth of dialectical terms.

Plato's theory has two implications for the use of the truth standard in judging arguments. First we, as critics, may use dialectic as a means for judging the veracity of interpretations and evaluations. Secondly, if we are judging a communicator who fails in his argument to establish clear definitions and to categorize things appropriately, we may have reason to doubt whether that communicator is seeking the truth. The truth standard therefore consists of the correspondence method and the dialectical process. In judging the truth of an argument, we first look for the issues of fact. We may test the correspondence of a factual statement to an observable structure of reality. Next, we may use dialectic to get at the definitional and value-based questions that are the surface issues in the interpretive and evaluative forms of argument. We may use dialectic in two ways: (1) to see whether the communicator is using dialectic; and (2) to investigate the argument with our own series of questions and answers— our own dialectic.

The Ethics Standard

The field of ethics deals with the principles of right action. Just as we may judge the rightness of a behavior, so, too, may we judge whether or not an argument is ethical. The ethics of argument and persuasion is such an important area of study that I have devoted the entirety of chapter 8 to a consideration of this subject. In it I will explore the general implications of ethics for the process of argument and persuasion. For now, I want to equip you with some tools for judging the ethics of the arguments that you will be meeting in chapters 4, 5, and 6. These tools come in the form of five factors that seem to be involved in making ethical judgments about arguments: (1) the effects or consequences of an argument; (2) the truth of a statement; (3) the values to which an argument appeals; (4) the intent of the communicator; and (5) the means that are characteristic of the communicator's mode of argument.

Effects   The ethics-based critic may begin by examining the observable results of argument. That is, we may try to find out what actually happened (or could happen) because of an argument. As Brembeck and Howell (in Johannesen, 1967, p. 16) note, this question of consequences is an important one for the persuader who seeks to behave ethically. "When we try to take the 'long view,' or estimate effects of our actions on other people, now and later," they write, "we are applying an ethical standard of great importance, a complicated one which might be termed 'social utility.'" By searching for social utility, the authors are asking whether useful (good) consequences result from a unit of communication or whether a message produces socially harmful effects. You will notice that this question causes the critic to make an evaluation by classifying an effect (event X happened as a result of argument Y) as belonging to the categories of "good" or "bad." Thus, the use of the ethics standard is similar to the application of the truth standard to issues of definition and value.

In his book *The Hidden Persuaders* (1958, pp. 225–229), Packard makes a moral judgment about the effects of advertising in creating a materialistic, consumer-oriented society. Packard supplies evidence that advertising may have the effect of making material comfort the ultimate goal of American life. He concludes (p. 227) that "this larger moral problem of working out a spiritually tolerable relationship between a free people and an economy capable of greater and greater productivity may take decades to resolve." Packard is making an ethical judgment about mass communication when he alleges that it may be creating undesirable social goals.

Truth   The relationship of arguments to truth is a second basis often used for ethical scrutiny of communication. Writing of "The Ethics of Controversy," Hook (in Johannesen, 1967, p. 104) sees a close connection between truth and ethics. He comments that "certain methods of controversy, however, poison instead of refreshing the life-blood of democracy. They are characterized by the fact that they do not desire to establish the truth." Flynn (1957, p. 186) takes the position that untruths undermine the very basis of communication and are therefore inherently unethical. He argues that when one "deliberately falsifies, he commits a moral fault because he frustrates the natural purpose of speech, which is to manifest his judgments to other people." The truth standard may therefore sometimes double as an ethical test.

Values   A third method of assessing a communicator's ethics is to identify and make a judgment about the values to which he appeals. Recall that values may be either desirable end states (such as freedom) or approved modes of conduct (such as behaving in an honest way). As I observed in my presentation of evaluative arguments, an arguer may appeal to any one or more of a large number of recognized human values. For example, arguments may appeal to fear, to patriotism, or to our need for sex, freedom of action, equality, prestige, peace of mind, economic well-being, and so on. Thus, the argument "suddenly from Datsun: A sporty car with everything but a sports car price" (*Newsweek,* March 21, 1977, p. 37) seems to appeal to the values of conserving money and of getting a "good buy." The slogan "America, love it or leave it" signifies, depending on one's perspective, patriotism or prejudice. In searching out the values underlying an argument, the overriding ethical question becomes: Are the values to which the argument appeals morally good or morally bad? Presumably, messages that appeal to hate, anger, envy, selfishness, pride, prejudice, and the like are morally bad. Arguments that center on the values of love, charity, equality, fairness, cooperation, forgiveness, hope, and so on are usually accepted as good by society. Value-based notions of ethics seem to depend on the moral sensitivity of the society as a whole. The critic would tend to defer to general public judgments about the morality of various values.

Intent   Throughout the literature on ethics, the concept of communicator intent is often emphasized. One could say, for instance, that a speaker is unethical only when he deliberately seeks to cause harmful effects, knowingly seeks to mislead (lie to) the listeners, and consciously appeals to values that he knows are disparaged by a people as a whole. As Hook (in Johannesen, 1967, p. 106) states, "no *moral* judgment can be passed upon any individual human action without an appraisal of its intent." Under this criterion, harmful acts resulting from a persuasive appeal would not be unethical unless the arguer intended to bring about the bad consequences. The impact of this criterion is usually to make the critic more cautious in branding an argument unethical, for in viewing ethics from the intent perspective, we have a double task: (1) to identify a bad behavior (e.g., causing harmful consequences, lying, or appealing to an immoral value) and (2) to demonstrate that the bad behavior was done deliberately. Yet in order to be fair to the arguer, it is probably advisable for the critic to go to the added trouble of searching out the communicator's intent. This would tend to dampen a hasty criticism.

Means   A final ethical perspective is marked by the attempt to identify types of arguments that by their nature are unethical. Many writers take the position that certain communication strategies are inherently bad. Thus, Minnick (1968, p. 285) identifies four "means of persuasion [that] are generally agreed to be unethical." These include:

1   Falsifying or fabricating evidence
2   Distorting evidence
3   Conscious use of specious reasoning
4   Deceiving the audience about the intent of the communication

Other authors identify name calling as an unethical communication act. Flynn (1957, pp. 186–187) contends that when one calls another by a prejudicial name (e.g., saying to a policeman, "You're a fascist"), the person probably "attaches a false label to the victim." "This evil act is calumny," he writes. The several arguments often identified as inherently unethical do not represent all the strategies held to be immoral, but they illustrate sufficiently the practice of judging ethics on the basis of the means utilized by an arguer.

The five approaches to ethics that I have identified here—consequences, truth, values, intent, and means—in no way exhaust the subject. However, they should provide you with sufficient "ammunition" to make informed ethical judgments about the arguments that you will analyze in the next several chapters.

The Validity Standard

To label a claim as valid is to say that it follows logically, given the relevant arguments. The term "validity" is taken from the study of syllogistic logic and traditionally pertains only to deductive arguments. (Recall the discussion of deductive and inductive arguments presented in chapter 1.) Thus, Irving Copi (1967, p. 4) observes that "a deductive argument is *valid* when its premises and conclusion are so related that it is absolutely impossible for the premises to be true unless the conclusion is true also." He adds that "neither the term 'valid' nor its opposite 'invalid' is properly applied to inductive arguments." "Fallacy" is the term most often applied to disreputable inductive arguments. Fallacies have been defined as "unsound methods of argument" (Brennan, 1961, p. 208), as "deceptive or misleading tactic[s]" (Eisenberg and Ilardo, 1972, p. 55), as "argument[s] which *should not* persuade a rational person" (Kahane, 1971, p. 1), and as "bad reasons" (Crable, 1976, p. 193). The usual approach is to classify certain fallacious types of argument, such as:

- the *ad hominem* (an attack against the person rather than the individual's arguments)
- false dilemma (unfairly reducing a complex situation to two alternatives)
- loaded questions (asking a question in such a way as to get the desired answer)
- begging the question (failing to confront the real issue at hand)
- hasty conclusion (making a claim without presenting sufficient supporting data)
- distortion by omission (suppressing relevant data that opposes your claim)

I believe that the customary approach to fallacy carries with it three disadvantages. First, definitions such as the above tend to have a moral and ethical tone: "unsound," "deceptive," "*should not* persuade a rational person," and "bad." This may make the study of fallacy too subjective and too indistinguishable from the truth and ethics standards. In addition, the attempt to classify all possible fallacies (and everyone has a different list) lends a false air of precision to the analysis of arguments. One gets the idea that when a fallacy has been identified, the critic's job is finished. This is rarely the case, however, since the act of classifying a fallacy is an interpretive act involving dialectical rather than positive terms. That is, one can't really point to a fallacy in quite the same way that one can point to a tree or a house. (Crable, 1976, pp. 193–194, makes a similar point.) Finally, the concept of fallacy often assumes that arguments are either sound or fallacious. This either/or approach differs from two overriding assumptions that I have been making: (1) that all arguments are subject to misuse and (2) that arguments are sound or unsound in varying degrees. Recall that in the discussion of the Toulmin model, we learned that claims possess qualifiers that indicate the degree of certainty attributed to the claim. Further, we saw that the power of the qualifier was related to the evidence that was offered in support of (data, warrant, backing) or in opposition to (reservation) the claim. As I noted then, the Toulmin model suggests that we make our qualifiers compatible with the strength or the weakness of our proof. I believe that in analyzing the objective strength of arguments, a definition of validity (as soundness of a claim, given the relevant evidence) will be more useful than the concept of classified fallacies.

Certainly, some misuses of argument are fairly obvious (e.g., a lie), and some types of argument (e.g., the *ad hominem*) seem to be inherently fallacious. Nevertheless, I believe that we can use the general notion of fallacy to produce a specific definition of rhetorical validity that then may be applied to all claims. The general problem of fallacy seems to involve these factors:

1 Sufficiency of supporting data
2 Relevancy of data to the issues
3 Completeness of perspective: i.e., omitting no significant and relevant data
4 Fairness of interpretation: i.e., making accurate descriptions and realistic interpretations or evaluations
5 Appropriateness of qualifier: i.e., proportioning the certainty of the claim to the nature of the relevant data (both favorable and unfavorable)

I believe that these five general features of fallacy may be refined into a definition of rhetorical validity. I shall use the term "rhetorical validity" to denote a standard of validity that may be applied to all extended inductive arguments. The definition of rhetorical validity[4] that I propose is as follows: An argument is valid when, in an adversarial situation, the degree of certainty attributed to a conclusion by an agent is less than or equal to that established by the relevant (supporting and opposing) proof. In other words, an argument is valid when an advocate confronts both the pros and cons and does not attribute more certainty to a claim than can be established. This definition involves a number of important elements. In the next few pages I will systematically consider these elements.

The Mechanics of Deciding Rhetorical Validity   There are four steps to be followed in applying the definition of rhetorical validity.

1 Identifying an Adversarial Situation   By identifying representative data for and against a claim we set up an adversarial situation. The requirement for an adversarial situation is crucial, for if we used only supporting data to evaluate a claim, every claim having even a single point in its favor would be valid. Common sense tells us that it is possible to find data to support even the most absurd of claims. For instance, in support of the claim "Eugene McCarthy was elected President of the United States in 1976," we may identify the fact that 657,785 people voted for McCarthy in the general election (Delury, 1976, p. 42); but if we restricted our investigation to this single fact, we would be omitting the quite relevant point that two candidates for President received larger numbers of votes than McCarthy—namely, Jimmy Carter (40,276,040) and Gerald Ford

---

[4]From this point forward I generally shall use the term "validity" to denote rhetorical validity, not syllogistic (deductive) validity.

(38,532,630). Thus, in order to test the objective validity of a claim, we must have a context in which a representative sample of relevant pro and con arguments is available. In other words, we can test the validity of only those claims that are located in an adversarial situation.

Some claims, of course, reside in a naturally adversarial situation. Thus, if we were to use a courtroom transcript as a context by which to judge the validity of the claim "George robbed the store," we could be reasonably certain that our judgment would be based on a sample of relevant supporting and opposing data. This is true because in this situation two agents would have the opportunity to present arguments for and against the claim. But suppose we wished to test the validity of a claim taken from a speech in which only one position regarding a dispute was presented. Clearly, the context—the speech—would not be adversarial. In this case, the critic would need to create artificially an adversarial situation, i.e., search out relevant opposing arguments to be analyzed together with the supporting ones.

2 Identifying an Asserted Level of Certainty   To test an advocate's claim for its validity, we need to know how much certainty the advocate is asserting. Does he characterize the claim as "undoubtable" or just "possible"? The asserted level of certainty may be explicitly or implicitly stated by the advocate. That is, an advocate will often make explicit reference to a qualifier, as in the statement "I am *sure* that Gene McCarthy was elected President of the United States in 1976." In other cases, the critic must estimate the level of certainty that the advocate is claiming.

3 Comparing the Pro and Con Arguments   Once we have identified an adversarial context and an asserted qualifier, we are ready to undertake the first of two comparisons that are required by the definition of rhetorical validity: the comparison of the favorable and unfavorable data. This comparison yields the established level of certainty—the level actually established by the data.

In making this first comparison—looking for the relationship of the favorable to the unfavorable data—the critic should begin by reviewing the data. Are the data representative? Are the data relevant both to the claim and to the issues raised by the claim? Are any major supporting or opposing arguments omitted from the context? Do the data contain any factually questionable statements?

Having satisfied the need for representative pro and con arguments, we are ready to compare this pro and con material. Generally speaking, there may exist three relationships between the favorable and unfavorable data.

1   The favorable data may outweigh the unfavorable. In such a case the data would establish a positive level of certainty. The claim would be established as having some affirmative merit. The strength of the established level of certainty would depend on the degree to which the favorable data surpassed the unfavorable. Consider some hypothetical cases. If the favorable data outweighed the unfavorable by a wide margin, the established level of certainty could be expressed by such qualifiers as "certainly," "very likely," "positively," or "surely." If the favorable data surpassed the unfavorable only by a small margin, the established level of certainty would need to be expressed by less positive qualifiers: "probably," "likely," etc.

    2 The favorable data may roughly equal the unfavorable. In this case, the evidence would establish no more than a 50-50 chance that the claim had merit, that it had positive value. The only appropriate qualifiers would be those that reflected this very weak established level of certainty. Such expressions as "possibly," "maybe," "not without some merit," or "within the realm of reason" would reflect the very weak established level of certainty.

    3 The favorable data may be less in weight than the unfavorable data. In this case, the claim would be unlikely. Negative qualifiers such as "unlikely," "some small chance," or "probably not" would correspond to the claim's lack of an established level of positive merit.

The relationships between the data (favorable together with unfavorable) and the established level of certainty are indicated in figure 3-6.

    4 *Comparing the Asserted and Established Levels of Certainty* Through steps 1 to 3, we have identified an adversarial context, an asserted qualifier, and an established qualifier. All that remains is to compare the asserted and established qualifiers. There exist three possible relationships between these two levels of certainty.

    1 The asserted level of certainty may be roughly equal to the established level. In this case, the claim is valid because the advocate has claimed just as much certainty as is established by the data.

Figure 3-6 Comparing favorable and unfavorable data.

If: favorable data outweights the unfavorable data

then: claim is established as: "positively," "certain," "very likely," "sure," probable," "likely," etc.

If: favorable data is roughly equal to the unfavorable data

then: claim is established as: "possible," "within the realm of reason," etc.

If: favorable data is less in weight than unfavorable data

then: claim is established as: "unlikely," "not probable," etc.

2 The asserted level of certainty may be less positive than the established level. In this case, the advocate has *understated* his claim. The claim actually is deserving of a more positive qualifier than that chosen by the advocate. For example, if the advocate asserted that the claim was "possible" but the data established it as "certain," then the claim would be valid as stated, even though the advocate could have asserted more confidence. The situation of an understated claim is rare in actual disputes.

3 The asserted level of certainty may be more positive than the established level. Such a claim is *overstated*. An overstated claim is invalid, because the advocate asserts more confidence than he is able to establish. Rhetorical validity requires, therefore, that we not overstate the amount of confidence which our data legitimately confer on our claim.

The possible relationships between the asserted and established levels of certainty may be summarized as in figure 3-7.

Deciding Rhetorical Validity: An Example Thus far I have discussed rhetorical validity in the abstract. Now let me illustrate how such a measure may be applied to arguments that occur in the real world. In the next few pages, I will apply the definition of rhetorical validity to the "aggression thesis" used by the

Figure 3-7 Comparing the asserted and the established levels of certainty.

If: asserted level of certainty is roughly equal to the established level

then: claim is accurately qualified and, therefore, *valid*

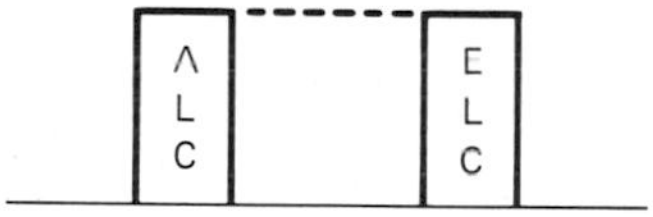

If: asserted level of certainty is less positive than the established level

then: claim is understated and, therefore, *valid*

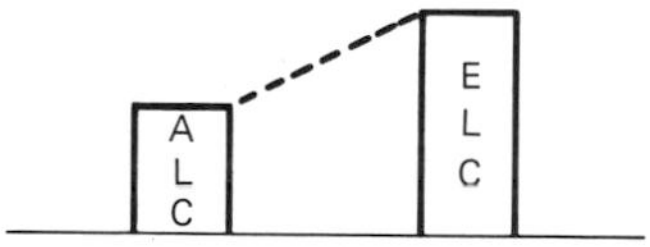

If: asserted level of certainty is more positive than the established level

then: claim is overstated and, therefore, *invalid*

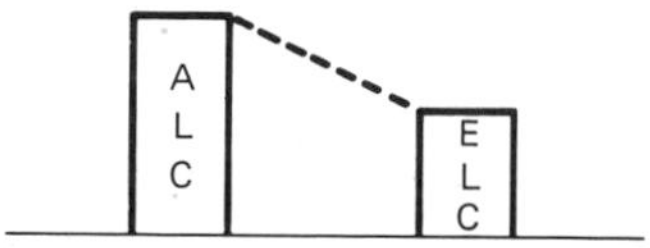

Johnson administration to justify the American military commitment to Vietnam. The administration's case for involvement was supported by a remarkably consistent set of arguments and assumptions; the aggression thesis—the contention that the war amounted to an aggression by North Vietnam against South Vietnam—was a major part of this case. Statements taken from a wide range of documents indicate that the administration used strongly positive qualifiers in putting across the point (italics in the following claims are mine):

Claim "The hard facts and *irrefutable* evidence . . . lead to one *inescapable* conclusion: The Republic of Viet-Nam is the object of aggression unleashed by its neighbor to the north." (Plimpton, 1965, p. 776)

Claim "The record is *conclusive*. It establishes *beyond question* that North Viet-Nam is carrying out a carefully conceived plan of aggression against the South." (U.S. Department of State, 1965, p. 29)

Claim "*Beyond question* this aggression was initiated and is directed by Hanoi." (Rusk, 1964, p. 890)

The question of validity thus becomes the following: Can the data sustain so positive an asserted level of certainty?[5] In support of the aggression thesis, the following data were offered:

1   Under the terms of the Geneva Accords of 1956, South Vietnam and North Vietnam became independent states.

2   The insurgency in South Vietnam is initiated, organized, controlled, and supplied by North Vietnam. Without this aid the insurgency would collapse.

3   There is little native southern support for the insurgency in South Vietnam. What little support that exists results from Communist terrorism.

4   The North Vietnamese government has declared publicly its intention to "liberate" South Vietnam.

These points did not go unchallenged by opponents of United States war policy. Data that opposed the aggression thesis included these arguments:

1   South Vietnam and North Vietnam are really one country and were not divided by the Geneva Accords.

2   The insurgency in South Vietnam began in the south as a result of the oppressive policies of the Saigon government.

3   The insurgency is not controlled by the North Vietnamese, although Hanoi is aiding the southern rebels.

4   Although North Vietnam has violated the Geneva Accords by sending aid to the southern rebels, South Vietnam has also violated the accords on many occasions. In fact, these violations by Saigon helped to cause the present war.

[5]For a comprehensive discussion of arguments surrounding the aggression thesis, see Sproule (1973, pp. 196–203, 216, 285–293).

These opposing arguments raised issues related to the causes of the war, the nature of North and South Vietnam as independent states, the extent of popular support for both the Saigon government and the Communist-led insurgents, and, finally, the extent to which North and South Vietnam had violated the 1956 Geneva agreements.

Having identified representative pro and con arguments in an adversarial situation, we are now in a position to make a critical judgment about the validity of the aggression thesis. Do the data sustain a level of certainty that corresponds to the high level asserted by administration spokesmen? Given that reasonable arguments could be brought against each of the administration's claims, it seems difficult to accept the administration's highly positive tone of certainty. The conflicting evidence doesn't seem to sustain the assertion that the aggression thesis is, for example, "beyond question." A qualifier such as "possibly" seems more appropriate, given the close match between the pro and con data. The administration's claim is therefore overstated and, as a result, must be labeled as invalid. Notice, however, that the invalidity of the aggression thesis does not prove the validity of the opposite view of the war as an internal rebellion. A separate validity judgment would have to be made about the arguments maintained by opponents of the administration. Indeed, given the high tone of certainty in claims by "doves," it is possible that both sides—supporters as well as opponents of United States intervention in Vietnam—used invalid arguments.

The definition of rhetorical validity is applicable to all arguments as long as we test a claim within a context that contains representative pro and con arguments—an adversarial situation. In the example above I created an adversarial situation artificially by comparing speeches, essays, and books representing both sides of the war issue. Validity is therefore a context-bound measure of an argument. The reader will notice, further, that nowhere in this discussion of the elements of validity have I mentioned audience attitude. Validity is a measure of the objective worth of an argument, regardless of whether a particular audience finds it persuasive. (See Toulmin, 1968, p. 71.) Yet, even though the validity standard is an objective one, we must remember that the standard is applied by human critics. Critics tend to become emotionally involved with the arguments they judge. It is usually easier to pick out the weaknesses in arguments with which one does not personally agree. I wish to caution you about the danger of subjectivity that is inherent in applying the validity standard (and, for that matter, the other three standards, as well). Because of our personal beliefs, we may unconsciously overlook faults in favored arguments.

In the last several pages I have identified four ways in which a critic may look at an argument. One may look at the effects, truthfulness, ethical implications, and validity of a claim. Although there are overlaps between and among these standards, we may regard them, nevertheless, as relatively independent measures. For example, one's judgment of effectiveness is independent of an assessment of the truth of an argument. Although each of these four standards is important to the study of language, I will give somewhat more emphasis in succeeding chapters to the validity standard. I will highlight validity because I believe that it is very important to render the reader sensitive to the objective worth of an argument in its context. It would be virtually impossible to give equal emphasis to each of the four standards in a single text, but once you have a good notion of validity, you will have a sound basis from which to assess the truth, ethics, and persuasiveness of arguments.

ARGUMENTS AND DECISION RULES

Before moving on to a detailed treatment of the forms of argument (chapters 4, 5, and 6), I wish to introduce one final point that applies equally to descriptions, interpretations, and evaluations. In the preceding section on standards for judging argument, I identified certain principles which pertained to assessing the effect, truth, ethics, and validity of arguments. Viewed in another way, we could take these principles as rules. For example, in determining the validity of an argument, we follow certain rules such as identifying an adversarial context for our claim and identifying and comparing an established and an asserted level of certainty. These are the procedures or rules that one must follow to make an informed decision about validity. Uses of the effect, truth, and ethics standards imply corresponding rules of procedure. Each of the standards, thus, involves a set of decision rules—rules of procedure governing the use of evidence to make decisions. Decision rules specify the manner in which evidence relates to a claim. Decision rules are context-bound, meaning that a decision about validity, for instance, necessitates a different set of procedures than a decision about ethics.

Thus far I have presented decision rules for four general standards of argument. However, one may identify in society a large number of decision rules that apply to specific situations of dispute. For example, in the field of law there exist certain recognized rules that govern both the presentation and the use of evidence in rendering a legal decision. Just as lawyers know the legal decision rules, so, too, are marriage counselors mindful of those principles of discussion that help marriage partners to reconcile their differences (the rules of argument in counseling). Thus, to evaluate the worth of certain arguments, it may not be enough to apply the four general standards of argument. We may need to consider certain rules that pertain to arguing and making decisions in the field in which the arguments are located. (For a more extended discussion of the field of an argument, see Toulmin, 1969, pp. 11–43.)

As Eisenberg and Ilardo (1972, pp. 5–10) observe, there are both formal and informal rules that govern argument. Formal rules such as those used in academic scholarship, debate, or law are guidelines—usually written ones—that tell us how to arrive at conclusions with evidence. However, there are a host of situations that prescribe informal controls on the use of evidence to obtain conclusions. Consider these two differing views, which result from a military, as opposed to a diplomatic, analysis of an international crisis. (*The New York Times,* May 12, 1977, p. 1.)

> KINSHASA, Zaire—The war in Zaire's Shaba Province has entered its third month and, while the military advances of the combined Zairian and Moroccan forces remain modest and inconclusive, there is no doubt that on the diplomatic front President Mobuto Sese Seko has achieved a spectacular success.

In this example, the reporter uses rules from two fields—the military and the diplomatic. When applied to data about the war in Shaba Province, these rules result in specific conclusions. The evidence, when judged by military criteria, indicated an "inconclusive" situation. However, when viewed from the perspective of international diplomacy, the claim is that President Mobuto won a "spectacular success." The rules for presenting acceptable military and diplomatic conclusions are therefore different. Although the rules for making diplomatic claims are less formal than those for reaching legal conclusions, both contexts contain decision rules. Formal, written rules may be noted for many contexts. More common, however, are the informal rules that seemingly pertain to every context in which language is used: Polite conversation, rap sessions, news conferences, and the like are events that are governed by notions of appropriate language use.

It would be impossible to specify here every potential context of argument and to identify decision rules for each. However, to illustrate the point, I will identify one formal and one informal situation of dispute, with corresponding rules for each.

Decision Rules in Law

In formal legal argument, the concept of presumption is often applied as a decision rule. A presumption of law (which is only one kind of presumption mentioned in legal theory) is "a rule of law that courts and judges shall draw a particular inference from a particular fact, or from particular evidence, unless or until the truth of such inference is disproved" (Black, 1968, p. 1349). Statute law, for instance, provides that certain facts shall serve as presumptive evidence of guilt. Another decision rule in law is the practice of excluding from trial evidence that has been illegally obtained by the authorities. A *New York Times* report of a tax case (May 2, 1977, p. 22) will serve to illustrate the exclusionary rule. The Internal Revenue Service had developed a case against a Cleveland businessman who had sworn on his 1972 income tax return that he owned no foreign bank accounts. To oppose this 1972 declaration, the IRS obtained a document that listed the man as being one of some three hundred American depositors of a bank located in the Bahama Islands. A federal district judge, however, ruled that the document had been obtained illegally and consequently he excluded the evidence from trial.

The presumption of law and the exclusionary principle are only two of the decision rules that govern the use of evidence in law. They illustrate, however, the effect of formal, written rules on legal decision making. In the example of the exclusionary principle, apparently conclusive evidence of guilt was disallowed because illegally gathered evidence is seen to prejudice the rights of defendants.

Decision Rules in Marital Communication

Law represents perhaps the most formalized situation of dispute. Informal discussions, in contrast, represent highly unstructured situations of argument. Yet even these contexts may be seen to involve rules of language use. In their study of intimate communication between marriage partners, Bach and Wyden (1969) have observed certain patterns in how couples fight. Their book is particularly intriguing because they attempt to formalize some norms of good and bad fighting. The authors identify certain undesirable techniques of "untrained" marital fighting such as "gunny-sacking"—when partners keep their grievances bottled up and then, when provoked, let them all loose at once. Many of the bottled-up complaints are irrelevant to the real issue at hand (the immediate provocation) and should be avoided.

These authors have devised a system of "constructive fighting" based on certain rules of arguing. "When our trainees fight according to our flexible system of rules, they find that the natural tensions and frustrations of two people living together can be greatly reduced" (Bach and Wyden, 1969, pp. 1–2). Rules to be followed include the partners' asking one another to specify "what's bugging them" and then mutually negotiating the grievance(s). Whereas untrained fighters might consistently follow certain unstated methods, the trained couple would consciously monitor their fights according to the Bach and Wyden rulebook.

Law and intimate communication are only two of thousands of contexts in which we may discover decision rules. Decision rules are important because they may have a lot to do with the success of our claims in a given field. Both as arguers and as critics of argument, we should be mindful of the rules that govern the field in which a claim is made. The various argumentative situations are like rituals—each with its own set of prescribed behaviors. Conventions may prescribe what is to be said, when it is to be said, and how a statement is to be interpreted. So that we may both argue effectively and judge accurately the claims of others, we must be aware of the rules that regulate language use in the situation at hand.

Chapter 3 has dealt with the various forms, standards, and contexts of argument. My intention in this chapter has been to prepare you to deal with examples of real-world arguments. In chapters 4, 5, and 6, I will build upon the materials of chapter 3, introducing you to samples of descriptive, interpretive, and evaluative arguments. The reader should not assume that the next three chapters contain every possible type of description, interpretation, and evaluation—no roster of arguments, however long, can be complete—but you will have access to many of the more prominent forms and types.

APPLICATIONS

Before proceeding any further into this book, it would be well for you to work with some of the concepts of argument that I have presented in this chapter. The following exercises are designed to give you experience with and insight into the concepts of knowledge source, argumentative form, critical standards, and decision rules.

Exercise 3-1: Sources of Knowledge

I have identified seven general ways for people to arrive at personal knowledge: experience, revelation, authority, emotions, intuition, inference, and ideology. The following exercise gives you an opportunity to search out the basis of certain of your own knowledges. You should complete these steps:

I Identify five things that you know to be true. Write out each thing as a statement as in the statement "I know that my name is George." Be sure to identify only statements that you feel comfortable in revealing to your instructor or to fellow classmates.

II For each statement identify the degree of certainty that you attribute to the knowledge. That is, you might indicate that you are "absolutely certain," "somewhat sure," "not really convinced," "doubtful," etc.

III You should now write a paragraph indicating how (on what basis) you know that each of the five statements is true. What causes you to accept the statement as a truth? For some statements you will have several reasons; for others you may have only one or two reasons. Be sure to number each of your reasons in each paragraph.

IV Having identified one or more reasons for believing each of the five statements, you should classify each reason as representing one (or more) of the following ways of knowing: experience, revelation, authority, emotions, intuition, inference, or ideology. Some reasons will conform to one of these ways of knowing. Others will involve a combination of the ways.

V Having classified each of your reasons for knowing something, write out a final paragraph in which you consider such questions as: What sources of knowledge predominated? What sources of knowledge did you cite for the beliefs about which you are most certain and least certain?

Exercise 3-2: Knowing and Arguing

Earlier, I observed the difference between (1) having a personal knowledge of something and (2) arguing the point so as to cause others to know. As an exercise in knowing and arguing, you should do the following:

I Use the five statements of personal knowledge that you identified in the first part of exercise 3-1 (or construct two statements according to the directions in exercise 3-1).

II Select two of the statements and identify for each arguments that you would use to persuade someone to accept the statement as true.

III For each of the two statements, complete the following analysis of your arguments:
   A Would your arguments be likely to persuade another person? Why or why not?
   B Are your public arguments the same as your personal way of knowing the truth of the statement?
IV Write out a final paragraph in which you respond to this question: Are some beliefs, by their nature, more difficult to "sell" to others?

Exercise 3-3: Changes in Our Knowledges

Sometimes our beliefs undergo a change. This exercise will give you chance to consider why our knowledges change. You should do the following:

I Identify five things that you once knew to be true but that you now believe to be false. As before, write each of these out as statements.
II For each statement identify the reasons that you changed your belief. That is, what caused you not to believe any longer in each of the statements. In doing this, give some thought to the circumstances surrounding your change. Did you change because of something you heard or read? Because of an experience, etc.? Any of the sources of knowledge or forms of argument may have contributed to the changes in your beliefs.
III Having identified some factors of change for each of the five statements, write out a final paragraph or paragraphs in which you generalize on belief changes. Are your belief changes a natural consequence of growing older? Do they represent unique personal experiences? Do you think that others have undergone similar changes? Are the changes in your set of knowledges irreversible—in other words, is it possible for you to return to a formerly held belief?

Exercise 3-4: Creating Examples of the Argumentative Forms

One of the major ideas of this book is that most (if not all) arguments may be classified as descriptions, interpretations, or evaluations. Indeed, the next three chapters are built around these three argumentative forms. This exercise will give you a chance to improve your ability to recognize the argumentative forms. Follow these directions:

I Identify a topic area with which you are familiar—e.g., "Olympic sports," "higher education," etc.
II Identify a claim that might be made about the topic area—e.g., "Olympic sports should receive increased emphasis in the United States" or "higher education faces a troubled future in the United States."
III Identify three descriptive, three interpretive, and three evaluative arguments to support the claim that you formulated in step 2. For each argument, briefly justify your classification of it. For example, why do you label certain statements as descriptions and not as interpretations?

Exercise 3-5: Identifying Argumentative Forms in a Text

This exercise gives you an opportunity to identify, in a real-world context, examples of the three argumentative forms. Observe these directions:

I   Select a short essay (around 400 words) in which the author cites arguments to justify a conclusion. An advertisement or opinion column would be suitable. News stories are probably not as useful, because the author of a news story usually seeks to summarize the opinions of others. This makes it more difficult to identify the opinion of the author (the news reporter), although news reporters certainly function as arguers.

II Having chosen a suitable text, identify in a single sentence the overall conclusion (main idea) that the author seeks to establish. Your sentence may be a verbatim quotation from the essay or a summary in your own words of the author's main point.

III Identify five of the most important statements that the author makes in support of the main idea.

IV Classify each of these five statements as being descriptions, interpretations, or evaluations. Remember that an argument is classified on the basis of the highest order of issue that it raises. Remember also that an argument that raises a first-order issue of value, for instance, may also raise subsidiary issues of definition and fact. Be sure to give reasons for each of your five classifications.

Exercise 3-6: Applying the Effect Standard to a Claim

I have presented four general standards for the criticism of argument: effect, truth, ethics, and validity. This exercise will give you practice in applying the effect standard.

I   As in exercise 3-5, select a short essay of around 400 words for analysis.

II Identify a claim in the essay to serve as the focus for your analysis. You are free to choose the main idea of the essay or one of the major supporting statements. For this exercise the claim chosen for analysis should be a verbatim quotation from the text. If, however, you feel able to paraphrase the advocate's claim accurately, you may do so.

III Identify characteristics of an audience for which the essay was created. Some audiences are very general—e.g., the American people—whereas other audiences are more specific, such as the Cuyahoga County Young Republicans. In some cases you will know characteristics (e.g., sex, age, economic status) of the exact audience selected by the communicator, as in the case of a speech given before a particular group. In other cases—such as a newspaper opinion column—the audience (readers of the column) will not necessarily share any known characteristics. If you don't know the characteristics of the audience (or the audience doesn't really share any), you should identify features of a hypothetical subaudience (e.g., female college students). Remember, the audience that you identify is important to this exercise, because no two audiences will react in quite the same way—even to identical messages.

IV   Identify the initial attitude of the audience toward at least five of the important concepts mentioned in the message. Each of these concepts may be called an opinion (a positive, negative, or neutral judgment). For example, an article on higher education might focus on such concepts as "professors," "students," "contemporary grading practices," etc. The initial attitude of the audience is the audience's attitude toward concepts before exposure to the message. Unless the listeners have never heard a term before, they are likely to have an attitude about the term. When the listener hears or sees the focus, the listener's attitude toward that focus is triggered. Remember that the concept of attitude involves dimensions other than the direction of the judgment. Other dimensions include salience and intensity. In summary, you should make predictions about the initial attitude of the audience toward five focal concepts, using the dimensions of attitude direction, salience, and intensity.

V   Identify the intention of the communicator. What response did this person seek to create in the audience? Review the section on effects criticism, where I presented several internal and external hints to help you assess communicator purpose. Write out as a single sentence your notion of the communicator's purpose.

VI   Identify changes in the audience's initial attitudes that may be attributed to the message. Audience response may take the form of either attitude change or behavior change. That is, you may notice changes in the direction, salience, and intensity of the audience's attitude toward the five focal concepts, or you may find that the audience takes some observable action (behavior) as a result of the message. On the other hand, you may find that no change of any type takes place. Use whatever descriptive information is available to assess message results. Organize your effects analysis around the five focuses. That is, for each focus identify any changes in initial audience attitude that resulted from the persuasive message. In some cases you will be unable to find any information about the actual response of the audience. Certainly, this will be the case when your audience is a hypothetical subgroup that you have created. In this case you will need to make predictions about what you think might have happened (attitude or behavior change) as a result of the message.

VII   You should summarize in a final paragraph a judgment about the effect of the message. Did the communicator achieve the intended purpose? Was the message highly effective in producing desired audience reactions or not? Did audience attitude toward any of the five focuses change? Be sure to justify your overall assessment of effect.

Exercise 3-7: Applying the Truth Standard to a Claim

I   Follow the first two steps of exercise 3-6 in choosing a text and a claim for analysis.

II   Identify descriptions (issues of fact) that pertain to the claim being judged. Insofar as you are able, verify these factual points by checking their correspondence to reality. For instance, if you are dealing with an essay on the costs of higher education, you might encounter statistics on enrollment, appropriations, etc., which could be checked. Testimony could be verified as accurate or inaccurate, and you could research the details of any examples offered.

III Identify interpretations and evaluations that pertain to the claim being judged. You should use the dialectical process to test the interpretations and evaluations.

    A In using a dialectic you should seek to be objective in making your judgments about the author's interpretations and evaluations. The dialectical critic should not act as an advocate or opponent of the arguments being tested.

    B When I say that you will be using a dialectic to get at the issues of definition and value, I do not mean that you will have to write out a question-and-answer dialogue for each issue. Dialectic takes the form of a dialogue when two persons are engaged in conversation. Your dialectic will involve looking for definitions and looking for the placing of facts into definitional and evaluative categories.

    C You should apply dialectic to the important definitions made by the arguer. For instance, the arguer may speak of a "crisis of confidence in higher education financing." As a dialectical critic you should: (1) identify precisely what the arguer means by this; (2) examine the subject further to determine if the interpretation is a good one; and (3) look to see if any other definitions fit the situation better.

    D You should apply dialectic to the evaluative arguments. For instance, the advocate may refer the need to "equalize" school expenditures. This evaluative assertion raises at least three questions that the dialectician must answer: (1) if "equality" is an inherently good value; (2) if this value legitimately applies to the situation; and (3) if there are other values which also apply. The dialectical critic would need to probe each of these questions in order to render an informed judgment about an evaluative argument.

Exercise 3-8: Applying the Ethics Standard to a Claim

I Follow the first two steps of exercise 3-6 in choosing a text and a claim for analysis.

II Identify the consequences that the argument necessitates for the audience and other third parties. Having done so, you are in a position to make a judgment about whether good or bad effects will result. If the results for the audience or others will be bad, then you may have reason to question the claim on ethical grounds. Remember that many hard decisions are necessary ones, but the alternatives in these cases may be worse. Therefore, the consequences principle should not be applied superficially.

III Make a judgment about the truth of the claim. Follow the procedures outlined in exercise 3-7. As I noted earlier, an untruthful claim may be a sign of ethical problems.

IV Identify the values to which the communicator appeals. Often the communicator will not explicitly identify the values to which the argument is appealing. For example, one would be unlikely to say, "I am appealing to the value of revenge." You must often infer the value from hints provided by the communicator. Once you have identified the values that are explicitly or implicitly maintained, you are ready to make a moral judgment about them. Are the values those that society considers morally good or bad? The presence of several morally bad values may suggest ethical problems.

V   Identify the intent of the communicator. In doing this, consult the advice that I gave about estimating speaker purpose earlier, in the section of this chapter that deals with the effects standard. By gaining a notion of intent, you will be in a better position to make a moral judgment about the consequences of the claim, the truthfulness of it, and the values that are implied by it. That is, a communicator who deliberately offers harmful courses of action is more ethically suspect than one who does so unknowingly. Similarly, the deliberate presentation of falsehood and the conscious appeal to bad values is morally questionable to a greater degree.

VI Identify any ethically questionable tactics that the arguer may use. Review the ethically suspect tactics cited by Minnick (1968) and by Flynn (1957). The presence of such strategies may pose ethical problems.

VII Make an overall ethical judgment based on the application of the five tests. If the communicator consistently fails the tests, you may have grounds for a charge of unethical behavior. If there are only a few minor blemishes, then the claim is probably not unethical. This is a judgment that you will need to make and justify.

Exercise 3-9: Applying the Validity Standard to a Claim

I   Follow the first two steps of exercise 3-6 in choosing a text and a claim for analysis.

II Make sure that your claim is located in an adversarial situation. If the text containing the claim includes only supporting arguments, then you will need to identify some representative opposing arguments. In parallel columns list both the supporting and opposing arguments that pertain to the claim chosen for analysis.

III Identify a qualifier that expresses the certainty asserted by the advocate. As I noted earlier, the advocate may explicitly identify such a qualifier, as in the assertion "Without a doubt, the plan will fail," or you may need to estimate the level of certainty being maintained by the agent. If you are estimating the asserted level, justify your choice of a qualifier.

IV Compare the pro and con arguments that pertain to the claim. Estimate a qualifier that reflects the data. That is, if the favorable data outweigh the unfavorable, then a positive qualifier (of some magnitude) may be in order, and so on. This qualifier will be your established level of certainty. Be sure to justify your choice of an established qualifier.

V   Compare the asserted and established levels of certainty. Remember that a claim is valid unless the asserted level of certainty exceeds the established level. This comparison will yield your overall validity judgment. Explain your judgment.

Exercise 3-10: Identifying Decision Rules for Situations

Earlier, I explained some decision rules pertaining to informal and formal situations of argument. Such rules generally prescribe how arguments should be related to claims in an area of dispute. Rules prescribe such things as: What should or should not be said; what is good evidence; how one should use evidence to make a decision; how something should be said; when it should be said; and how a statement should be interpreted.

I To gain a greater familiarity with decision rules, you should identify decision rules for one or more of the following argumentative contexts. Sometimes, students find it difficult to get started on this exercise, so it is probably a good idea to do one or more of these in class. If done as a homework exercise, two or three contexts make a workable number. The contexts are:

- Asking for (or responding to a request for) a favor
- Giving advice to a friend
- Asking for (or giving) street directions
- Arguing with your instructor for a better grade
- Returning an allegedly defective product to a store
- Supporting a claim in a term paper written for a course in your major field of study
- Asking for (accepting or refusing) a date
- Interacting with a door-to-door salesperson
- Selling a product to a person
- Presenting a bill in a parliamentary body such as Congress or a student senate
- Justifying a decision to buy a car
- Making a decision to choose a physician
- Deciding who was the greatest American President

II For each context identify the appropriate rule(s) and explain how the rule pertains to making data and claim statements in the particular context.

III A good variation on this exercise is for students to identify contexts to be used in this exercise. Students may identify contexts that apply to organizations to which they belong or contexts that are based on experiences that they have had.

Chapter 4

Descriptions: Arguments That Draw Issues of Fact

One recurring question posed by today's college students concerns the "relevancy" of their course work in terms of future employment. If I asserted that "studying argument will help you get a job," the thinking student might well respond with questions such as these:

- Give me an example of where a course in argument has helped someone land a job.
- How many argument and persuasion students are so helped by having taken the course?
- Where did you find that information (i.e., who says so)?

In short, the questions would demand descriptive information about my claim. They would seek to find out whether the claim described the real world in an accurate fashion.

As I noted in chapter 3, descriptions—arguments that raise issues of fact—are one of three basic forms of argument. In this chapter I will give detailed attention to the role of descriptive argument in real-world controversy. You may remember that I defined a description as that form of argument that raises a first-order issue of fact. This means that when we hear a descriptive assertion we should first check to see whether the description is realistic before subjecting it to other tests. This holds true for each of the three major types of description—examples, statistics, and testimony—so that when someone offers us an example, our first question should be "did it happen?" Similarly, when an advocate cites statistics or quotes an author's testimony, we have immediate cause to question, "Do the numbers fit the case?" or "Did the author really say that?" Only after having probed the factual basis of the description should we look for its relationship to higher-level interpretations or evaluations.

In general, descriptions serve two functions in situations of dispute. First, almost invariably, a description is intended to serve as the basis for a generalization. That is, advocates cite cases, numbers, and quotations to establish general interpretive or evaluative principles.[1] The second, and related, function of the description is to tie a higher-order statement (interpretation or evaluation) to basic reality. Descriptions justify generalizations by demonstrating that the generalization coincides with the outside world. We tend to believe generalizations that appear to account accurately for events in the real world. On the other hand, if a general statement cannot be supported by specific examples, statistics, or testimony, people tend to lose faith in it.

Let us consider the operation of descriptive argumentation. In the next few pages, I will examine the three types of descriptive argument, paying particular attention to conditions under which the types are effective and valid. The chapter concludes with an overall analysis of the role of description in argument.[2]

THE EXAMPLE

An example is an individual case. It is something that happened at a particular time and place. Synonyms for "example" include "instance," "anecdote," and "illustration."[3] Special subtypes of the example include the hypothetical example and the personal example. In a hypothetical example one invents an imaginary but nevertheless plausible event. When an arguer uses a personal example, the individual relates experiences that actually happened to him.

Examples may be differentiated from interpretive arguments. Unlike the interpretation that constructs reality, the example identifies reality by pointing

---

[1]Because the three types of description establish a body of information pertaining to a claim, they are sometimes termed "evidence" (see Ehninger and Brockriede, 1963, p. 110, and Rieke and Sillars, 1975, p. 97). I believe that a more restricted definition of evidence is necessary to distinguish it from argument. Hence, as I noted in chapter 2, evidence may be considered to be a statement by a third party that is cited by an advocate in support of a claim.

[2]Instances of valid and invalid arguments abound. Readers of this text need look no further than their local newspapers to find excerpts of arguments having local, state, or national significance. Many of the excerpts cited in chapters 4, 5, and 6 are taken from clippings that I have gathered from my local newspapers: the *Odessa* [Texas] *American* and the [Louisville] *Courier-Journal* [Indiana edition]. Other frequently used sources include *The New York Times* [City Edition] and *Newsweek* magazine.

[3]Perelman and Olbrechts-Tyteca (1969, p. 357) distinguish between the example and the illustration. Others, including Brandt (1970, p. 128) do not make as much of the distinction.

to it. An example is not an abstraction. It is concrete. It satisfies the three criteria for a fact: (1) it may be independently verified; (2) it may be described in precise, objective language (i.e., it may be mapped); and (3) it is an event, the occurrence of which all persons may be brought, potentially, to acknowledge. Although it is concrete, the example functions to support a generalization. Hence, it acts to demonstrate the connection between an observable bit of reality and an abstraction.

The Use of Example Argument

The student of argument soon learns that examples are cited in support of many claims. In December 1976, I received a membership advertisement from the American Civil Liberties Union. Seeking to persuade me to renew my membership, the "Dear Member" letter pointed to examples of the organization's civil liberties efforts during the year:

> Dear Member:
>   You have been a member of the ACLU for the past year, and your support has helped win some great victories for civil liberties.
>   • You helped the ACLU stop S.1 [Senate bill 1], the repressive revision of the federal criminal code.
>   • You helped the ACLU beat the proposed new federal wiretapping law which would have legitimized electronic eavesdropping for general intelligence gathering purposes even when there was no allegation of criminal activity.

Each of the "You helped" paragraphs details an example of the association's work. Each of the two instances lends an air of reality to the generalization contained in the opening sentence of the letter (i.e., the claim that the A.C.L.U. had won "some great victories for civil liberties"). This excerpt embodies the essential feature of argument by example. Particular cases are cited in support of a generalization. The cases link the higher-level interpretation to the real world; they may be verified—that is, we may check to see if the A.C.L.U. helped to defeat the measures cited; and, finally, all persons could potentially be brought to acknowledge the results of the A.C.L.U. actions—whether or not everyone agreed with the wisdom of the actions. In other words, one may accept the validity of an example without accepting the legitimacy of the generalization that the example allegedly supports.

The two instances cited in the excerpt conform, essentially, to the requirements of the example. However, the reader may have noticed a problem with one of the above examples: It is not stated entirely in objective reportorial language. In the example of the A.C.L.U.'s stand against S.1, the bill is characterized as "repressive." Such an adjective is conclusional and interpretive. It places S.1 in a value-laden category. The presence of interpretive language in an otherwise descriptive argument is the norm in human controversy. The lines between description and interpretation are ever blurred. It is the task of the critic to separate fact from opinion. Despite the presence of loaded language in the reference to S.1, it would be classified as an example, because it meets the other tests of the descriptive argument.

A very similar instance of example is to be found in a March 1977 letter to members of the American Association of University Professors. The letter solicited contributions to the A.A.U.P. general fund. In support of the general proposition that such a contribution would be in the interests of the members, the letter cited examples of the organization's recent work.

> In a December decision the United States Supreme Court ruled unanimously that it is unconstitutional to prevent a teacher who is not a union representative from offering his views on matters subject to collective bargaining, at a school board meeting open to public participation, solely because the union has an exclusive bargaining relationship with the school board. In so doing, the Court supported the position advocated by AAUP in an *amicus curiae* brief and held that it is a violation of the First Amendment to deny a certain category of teachers the opportunity to speak when that opportunity is provided to all other members of the public. This case, *City of Madison v. Wisconsin Employment Relations Commission,* represents a significant reaffirmation of the First Amendment rights of teachers. Our *amicus* participation demonstrates continued adherence by AAUP to the proposition that its commitments to the First Amendment, to academic freedom, and to collective bargaining are consistent and complementary.

This narrative is descriptive because it cites specific instances that could be verified. However, the final sentence of the quotation reveals the close connection between a descriptive example and an interpretive generalization. The sentence identifies several things that are represented by the example. The A.A.U.P.'s position is said to reveal the consistency of academic freedom and collective bargaining. Once again, an example is cited as the basis for a wider conclusion.

The role of examples in giving the appearance of reality cannot be emphasized enough. Seeking to prove that the 1977 rebellion in Zaire's Shaba Province was supported from the outside, President Mobutu of Zaire showed captured Soviet-made arms. Mobutu was quoted as commenting that "the most important thing is to show the grenades and other Russian weapons" (*The New York Times,* April 28, 1977, p. A4). Tangible physical examples can have a powerful persuasive impact.

Mobutu's examples were in the form of material. One should not think that, to be effective, examples must be physically present. Ronald Reagan used example statements as a major part of his campaign for the Presidency in 1976. A report detailed his strategy: "With his plan to switch $90 billion in federal social programs to the states still a major issue, Ronald Reagan is shifting from the $90 billion figure by 'going on the attack' with a litany of anecdotes on the abuses of those big government programs" (*Odessa American,* January 31, 1976, p. 14B). The Associated Press reported two of the specific illustrations:

> There was a county (in California) with 194 county employees that were drawing welfare in addition to their salaries, and some of them were welfare case workers acting as case workers for each other.
>
> There's a woman in Chicago. She has 80 names, 30 addresses, 12 Social

Security cards and is collecting veterans benefits on four non-existing deceased husbands.

And she's collecting Social Security on her cards, she's got Medicaid, getting food stamps and she is collecting welfare under each of her names. Her tax free cash income alone is over $150,000 a year.

Specific details such as these usually have a greater impact than the more abstract notion of "$90 billion in programs." That the Reagan forces had discovered this is clear from the Associated Press wire release: "Reagan's aides said in interviews here [that] there was a conscientious effort to use the anecdotes more often because they, more than anything else, appear to stir the generally conservative audiences." To this observation I would only add that the power of examples is not limited to conservative audiences. Most listeners regard examples as powerful support for a generalization.

Reagan's citation of several examples should call our attention to the cumulative feature of example argument. That is, several examples are usually more effective than one. Thus, when columnist James J. Kilpatrick asserts that "a hundred such examples could be offered" (*Odessa American,* August 19, 1974, p. 6A) to prove the unfeasibility of a consumer protection agency, the average listener perks up. Kilpatrick cites only three hypothetical examples to illustrate the difficulty in identifying the consumer interest (e.g., is it more in the interest of consumers to have more safety devices or to have lower prices?). His claim that at least ninety-seven more examples could be produced adds an air of reality to his otherwise theoretical argument. Kilpatrick's examples serve to remind us also that even a hypothetical example adds weight to a generalization.

I observed earlier that personal examples may have a particularly impressive effect. Because they are the personal experience of the arguer, the example seems even more real. Also, by citing something that happened to himself, an author boosts his credibility: He evidences direct knowledge of the subject at hand. Consider the emotional power of this personal anecdote revealed by Colorado Lieutenant Governor George L. Brown (*Odessa American,* August 27, 1975, p. 15B):

POINT CLEAR, Ala. (AP)—The black lieutenant governor of Colorado, George L. Brown, says the cordial greeting he received in Alabama this week has erased the "bitter memories" he felt for 32 years over what he described as racial mistreatment during World War II.

In a dramatic, unscheduled speech at the National Lieutenant Governors Conference, the 49-year-old Brown told of being found fettered in chains and the letter "K" burned into his chest after his Army training plane crashed in Alabama in 1943.

The fact that Lieutenant Governor Brown's mistreatment is a personal one makes it more attention-getting than if it were hypothetical or a report of someone else's experience. As an illustration of the general problem of racial discrimination, its force is considerable.

Testing the Validity of Examples

Up to this point I have emphasized the effects of examples in adding persuasive force to generalizations. I would now like to give attention to questions of validity in example argument. In probing the validity of an example, one should apply two tests to the example. First, does the example itself correspond to reality? Second, does the example establish the generalization?

The Correspondence Test for Examples   In chapter 3, I presented a definition of rhetorical validity to be used in testing the legitimacy of inductive claims. However, since descriptive arguments raise factual issues, there is a special test—the correspondence test—for these arguments. Because descriptive arguments use relatively objective language to identify the nature of reality, we may say that a description functions as a "map" of reality (see Hayakawa, 1949, p. 32). In my explanation of the truth standard in chapter 3, I indicated that the truth of descriptive statements could be measured by noting the correspondence between the statement and a picture of reality (see Toulmin, 1968, pp. 74–76). The same procedure may be used as the first test of the validity of a description. Consider how the test may be applied to an example.

In the "My Turn" column of *Newsweek* (May 12, 1975, p. 19), a writer (Margot Hentoff) argued for a return to traditional educational practices. In supporting her thesis she cited examples of statements by youngsters who wanted a return to the basics (the three Rs, grades, discipline, etc.). If we desired to test the validity of any of these examples, we could check to see if the statements had actually been made. That is, we could assess whether Hentoff's examples corresponded to what had actually been said. We could interview the children cited or, if possible, consult tape recordings of their conversations with the author. Much the same could be done with any other of the examples cited in this chapter. Thus, when our interest is to test only the description itself, we may use correspondence as the validity measure.

Testing Whether an Example Proves a Generalization   Unfortunately, however, the correspondence test does not answer all questions that might be asked about an example. Correspondence analysis does not tell us anything about the relationship existing between an example and the generalization that it allegedly supports. A generalization is, by definition, either an interpretation or an evaluation, and thus the validity of generalizations will be fully treated in chapters 5 and 6. However, let me summarize briefly some methods for examining the relationship of an example to a wider abstract conclusion. These tests derive from the definition of rhetorical validity.

I   Compare the example(s) in question to possible counterexamples.
   A   Is the example in question relevant to the generalization? Is the

subject of the example the same as the subject of the generalization?

   B   Is the example typical? Or is it exceptional? Do there exist counterexamples that are unfavorable to the generalization?

   C   If more than one example is cited, do the examples fit together well? (See Perelman and Olbrechts-Tyteca, 1969, p. 357.) That is, are all the instances similar in crucial details?

  II Compare the example in question (together with possible counterexamples) to the qualifier. Do the favorable examples predominate sufficiently to justify the level of certainty claimed for the generalization?

Let us apply the example-generalization tests to a real-world argument. In an article dealing with the indictment for murder of the Watson brothers in Dawson, Georgia, the author (John Margolis) both described the history of the indictment and offered the opinion that the "case and the passions it is beginning to arouse prove that behind the much-heralded new South, the old South still thrives" (*Chicago Tribune,* January 23, 1977, section 1, p. 8).

Assuming that we had verified the facts of the case by means of the correspondence test, our task would be to determine whether the Watson example proved that racism predominates in the new South. First, is the example relevant? Seemingly so, for the example describes some questionable legal procedures. The article gives evidence that the Watsons' race (they are black) may help to account for their apparently unjust treatment. Second, is the example typical? Because the article cites no other instances of alleged legal injustice, the critic has no real basis on which to make a judgment on this matter. To pursue this point, the critic would need to consult other sources to identify other supporting and opposing examples. (The next test—similarity—cannot be applied because there is no second or third example in the article.) Finally, does the example predominate sufficiently to justify the claimed level of certainty? The author asserts that the case *proves* the generalization—that is, a high level of certainty is claimed. However, in the absence of additional examples taken from throughout the South, it would appear that a wholesale condemnation of the South cannot be sustained on the basis of this single article.

Overall, the article provides strong support for the idea that the Watson brothers suffered mistreatment; but no real support is provided to justify a conclusion that pre-1965 conditions again prevail in the Southern states. Hence, even if each detail of the example is correct, the single instance does not contain sufficient weight to validate the high level of certainty asserted in the generalization. As I will explain in chapter 5, a conclusion such as this amounts to an "unfounded interpretation" in view of the lack of supporting evidence.

In sum, examples are a strong type of descriptive argument. Whether actual, hypothetical, or personal, an example adds reality to a dispute. The correspondence test may be used to determine the intrinsic validity of an example. The definition of rhetorical validity suggests further tests for determining whether an example gives sufficient support to a wider generalization.

STATISTICS

Although examples are powerful in adding the color of reality to a general statement, it is difficult to prove a case with only a few examples. This difficulty may be overcome, in theory, by a second type of descriptive argument—statistics. Statistics are numerical summaries of data: They serve to bring together many individual examples which pertain to an issue. By virtue of their ability to group and summarize data, statistics act as a kind of master example.

Statistical arguments confer at least two advantages upon the agent who uses them. First, statistics help to overcome the major weakness of example evidence. When an example is offered, one never really knows how typical the example is. Statistics remedy this problem by putting a single example in perspective. Instead of citing specific examples to prove that the crime rate was serious, an arguer could cite yearly increases in the incidence of various crimes. A related second advantage of statistics is that they allow for standardization and comparison. For instance, a statistical summary of their crime rates would allow two cities to be compared on the basis of number of murders, felony offenses, etc. Comparable standard units (e.g., number of felony offenses per 1000 inhabitants) could be used.

Statistics also carry with them two major disadvantages. For one thing, statistics leave out much detail. The reported results of a football game—yards gained, first downs, etc.—communicate only the bare details of the contest. When details are omitted a certain degree of meaning is lost. Secondly, statistics must be processed. That is, they must be gathered and summarized. Distortion may result from errors made in the preparation of numerical summaries. Such distortion may be accidental or deliberate.

In dealing with statistics, one final preliminary is in order. This relates to the distinction between descriptive and inferential statistics. Descriptive statistics are numerical summaries of an entire population of data. By "population," I mean that each object or event in a particular class is counted. For instance, General Electric Corporation could classify its yearly refrigerator production according to color—e.g., 30 percent white, 25 percent copper, etc. In this case, each refrigerator would be counted—each member of the population. On the other hand, inferential statistics are measures based on a sample of a larger population. Opinion polls perhaps represent the most familiar instance of statistical inference. When the Gallup poll reports that 64 percent of the American people approve of the President's performance in office, you can be sure that the Gallup organization did not survey each of more than 200 million Americans. Rather, the pollsters identified a sample (usually around 1500 to 2000 persons) who represent a cross-section of the entire population of the United States. The sample is then surveyed, and the results are projected onto the entire population. Such an inferential statistic is a projection. It carries with it a certain margin of error, as I will explain later.

In the next few pages, I will consider a great number of instances in which statistical data have been cited to prove a point. The first set of instances reveals some of the uses of statistics. The following set suggests some problems pertaining to statistical statements.

The Use of Statistics

One does not need to search far to identify instances of statistical argument. Consider how statistics give us greater understanding of a situation. In 1975, the editors of *Newsweek* magazine commissioned a poll of voters regarding the strength of Edward M. Kennedy as a candidate for President (*Newsweek,* June 2, 1975, p. 22). Voters' reactions to five questions were tabulated for all adults, by sex (male or female), by party (Democrat, Republican, Independent), and by region (East, Midwest, South, West). We learn, for instance, that while 61 percent of Democrats believe that Kennedy would make a good President, 57 percent of Republicans answered that he would not. Such figures carry more weight than one or two examples of statements by individual voters. They give us much more specific information.

The ability of statistics to put examples in perspective may be seen in other cases as well. A New York Times–CBS news poll (*The New York Times,* April 29, 1977, p. A1) revealed that "64 percent of the public approves in general of the President's performance." One tends to place greater confidence in such a statistic than in an abstract statement such as "most people approve of Mr. Carter's performance." In contrast to a general conclusion that "people have lost faith in American institutions," a 1973 Harris poll found that only two institutions out of twenty-two (medicine and local trash collection) drew expressions of confidence from a majority of persons questioned (*Odessa American,* December 2, 1973, p. 13C).

As these excerpts suggest, statistics are a particularly useful form of descriptive data. Statistics appear to make possible extremely precise descriptions of the world. A news story on the safety of baby carriers (restraints to be used in automobiles) illustrates the use of statistical summaries to gain new insight into human behavior (*Courier-Journal,* November 9, 1977, p. C15). The article reported observations made at a Pittsburgh hospital. Around a thousand new mothers were divided into four groups. One group received pamphlets explaining the dangers faced by children who do not ride in an automobile safety carrier. The group also received a free carrier. Three other groups received, respectively, a 10-minute discussion of the dangers, pamphlets, and no education. The mothers were then observed as they left the hospital. Eighty-seven percent of mothers who received the pamphlets and the free carrier were seen not using the carrier. Ninety-one percent of those who received no education did the same. Thus, the program of education (and free carriers) caused only a very small increase in the tendency of mothers to use the car safety carriers. Such statistical evidence provides a strong indication that the education program was not particularly successful. Seemingly, it offers descriptive information of a definitive sort.

In addition to their ability to bring together individual examples, statistics simultaneously allow for comparison of different members of the same class. By establishing a standard yardstick for judging members of a class, statistics enable us to compare different moving companies, cars, cities, and U.S. Presidents. The May 1975 issue of *Consumer Reports* magazine (p. 282) indicates how moving companies may be statistically compared. The staff of the Consumers Union consulted performance reports required of each interstate mover by the Interstate Commerce Commission. The staff then compared twenty-one moving companies on the basis of five criteria: shipments underestimated, shipments picked up late, shipments delivered late, shipments with damage claim of $50 or more, and average time to settle claim. On the basis of the data, the companies were grouped into three categories: above average, average, and below average. Such statistical information appears far more useful to the consumer than one or two examples provided by friends. Narrations of one or two individual experiences would provide less perspective than the statistical results of thousands of moves.

Once standard units have been established, many things may be compared on the basis of numbers. Thus, *Consumer Reports* (July, 1977, p. 402) summarized the relative desirability of the Chevrolet Chevette, the Dodge Colt M/M, the Subaru DL, and the AMC Gremlin Custom 2-liter. On the basis of around sixty comparisons, the Consumers Union identified the Chevette as the top-rated model among the four. In a manner akin to the comparing of automobiles, the favorability ratings of U.S. Presidents may be contrasted. When indexed on the basis of "voter approval at the end of 100 days in office," the 64 percent approval rating of President Carter (in April, 1977) may be placed beside ratings (after 100 days) of other Presidents: Nixon (61 percent), Johnson, (79 percent), and Kennedy (83 percent) (*The New York Times,* April 29, 1977, p. A16).

Tests of Statistical Argument

Although statistics place examples in perspective and allow for standardized comparisons, they also pose problems. As I noted earlier, two factors detract from the advantages of statistics: (1) statistics omit much information, and (2) statistics must be processed. In view of these limitations, the critic should test statistical argument carefully. In the next few pages I will summarize a number of such tests:

I   What is the source of the statistics?

II   When were the statistics gathered?

III   How were the statistics gathered?
    A   Was the counting procedure fair?
    B   Are the statistics based on adequately and consistently defined units?
    C   Are the statistics based on valid counting assumptions (i.e., estimations)?

IV   If the statistics are a measure of central tendency, is the type of measure specified?

V   If the statistics are inferential, is the method of inference adequate?
   A   Is there an adequate sampling procedure?
   B   Is the method of statistical projection adequate?
VI   Is the conclusion drawn from the statistics a reasonable one?
VII   Are the statistics properly explained when presented?

What Is the Source of the Statistics?   Statistics must be processed by someone. Accordingly, it is well to inquire about the processor. The critic should pose questions such as these: Who gathered and summarized the information? Is the source objective, or did the source gather the statistics so as to prove a point? Questions related to the statistical source are important. As Newman and Newman (1969, pp. 211–214) observe, a desire to prove American success in Vietnam led to exaggerated "body counts" of enemy casualties. In this case, the statistics were compiled partly to prove a point. Apparently, the figures far overstated the number of Viet Cong dead.

When Were the Statistics Gathered?   When the counting is done can also influence the validity of statistical argument. Opinion polls dealing with the popularity of political figures illustrate the importance of the time factor. You may recall the New York Times–CBS poll of April 1977, which identified President Carter's rate of approval at 64 percent. By October 1977 Carter's rating had declined to below 50 percent (*Newsweek,* October 24, 1977, p. 36). Statistics on a President's performance rating are highly variable and are valid for only a certain time. A 6-month-old figure may not represent the current state of the public mind. Opinion ratings for Carter's predecessor, Gerald Ford, also reflect the dangers of dated statistics. Polls reported an apparent drop of 22 percentage points in Ford's standing between May and June 1975 (*Newsweek,* August 4, 1975, p. 27).

How Were the Statistics Gathered?   Although important, questions concerning when and by whom statistics are gathered are less significant than those pertaining to how the numbers are obtained. As I noted above, there are at least three tests related to statistical methodology.

Was the Counting Procedure Fair?   First, one may inquire as to the fairness of the counting procedure. This test causes us to search out the actual method by which numbers were applied to the real world. Many statistics are based on people's responses to survey questions. In such cases the critic must check to make sure that the questions are not biased. In 1975 the National Rifle Association of America sponsored a "National Opinion Survey on Crime Control" that consisted of four questions. Three of the four seemed to be adequately worded, but one of the questions went as follows: "If a new firearms law was enacted in your state banning all ownership of guns, do you believe that hoodlums and organized criminals would volunteer their guns to your local police department?" You may have noticed an interesting feature of this query: It is worded so as to elicit a certain response. Even an avid proponent of banning guns would find it difficult to answer this question in the affirmative. The very idea of criminals marching to turn in their guns is laughable. Because of the bias inherent in this survey item, any inference drawn from it is invalid.

Questions need not be so blatantly misworded to elicit an inaccurate picture of reality. Even a neutrally worded question may cause respondents to feel forced to provide "acceptable" answers. Such a situation may be seen in a survey of illegal aliens conducted by the Immigration and Naturalization Service. The Associated Press reported the agency's plan to pose the following questions: "Interviewers will ask how many illegal aliens live in a home, their age, how they entered the country, how many children they have, what jobs they have held, how much they earn, what taxes they pay and what use they have made of social welfare services" (*Odessa American,* November 10, 1976, p. 9C). Given the aliens' fear of deportation or prosecution, one might expect that the interviewers would receive some false information. Even though the Immigration Service promised not to retain identities of respondents, those surveyed might still be afraid to answer truthfully.

Even when survey questions pose no personal danger, the potential for bias may remain. This phenomenon may be observed in the ratings of professional schools. In 1977 a rating of education, law, and business schools commissioned by the University of California Regents identified the ten top schools in each category (*The Chronicle of Higher Education,* January 31, 1977, p. 7). However, the survey was criticized as being too heavily based on subjective opinions as to faculty quality. Schools with large numbers of alumni would have an advantage over smaller ones, because graduates would tend to rate highly their alma mater. Indeed, any statistics depending on subjective human responses leave open considerable room for error.

Even well-recognized statistical measures may be criticized on this basis. For instance, as economist Milton Friedman notes (*Newsweek,* February 7, 1977, p. 63), the unemployment rate is "not a hard number." He points out that it "depends on the answer, in a sample survey, to the question: 'Has [a member of the household] been looking for work during the past four weeks?'" Moreover, Friedman observes that when unemployment benefits are available, there exists an incentive to report job-seeking efforts; he gives an example of when an extension of unemployment benefits brought an increase in the number of those reporting efforts to find jobs (because such a report was a condition that had to be met before benefits could be received). On the other hand, those who are ineligible for benefits (people who may no longer report job-hunting activities) are removed from the unemployment statistics. Of course, these people may still be without a job.

Before moving on, let me note two additional instances in which the critic needs to look carefully for bias in the counting procedure. Because crime statistics are based on the number of incidents reported by victims, criminologists have always warned that the actual crime rate is probably higher than that indicated in published summaries. These warnings were supported by a survey taken by the Law Enforcement Assistance Administration, which found that actual crime rates are between two and five times the reported rates (*Newsweek,* April 29, 1974, p. 63). A somewhat different form of statistical distortion was indicated by a news story on alleged efforts by Exxon Corporation to artificially reduce its reported profits in the first quarter of 1974 (Associated Press release, *Odessa American,* April 26, 1974, p. 9A). Some securities analysts stated an opinion that Exxon used atypical accounting methods to reduce its profit figures. Of course, 1974 was a year in which oil companies were charged with making windfall profits because of the increase in oil prices, so it would have been to Exxon's advantage to reduce its reported profits. Accordingly, the suspicion.

Are the Statistics Based on Adequately and Consistently Defined Units?   In addition to problems in the counting procedure, the validity of statistics may be reduced by a failure to adequately and consistently define standard units of measure. Hence, a second question may be posed concerning the gathering of numbers: Are units adequately and consistently defined? Frequently, statistics are based on well-recognized units such as yards, inches, or years. However, the unit of measure is often less obvious and objective. For example, the FBI campus crime index is apparently based on the total number of crimes in seven categories reported by university officials. The statistical unit of the survey (total number of crimes in seven categories) has been criticized by Indiana University officials for a number of reasons. For one thing, the index discriminates against schools having large resident populations. These schools naturally report more total crimes on campus. The statistic is not a standard crime rate, since it does not measure the number of crimes per person. Secondly, university officials argue that because it adds together all reported crimes, the index is not sensitive to the seriousness of crimes. The Indiana University–Bloomington police chief argued: "If we had an increase of 50 stolen bikes, it would affect our crime index exactly as if we had an increase of 50 homicides" (*Courier-Journal,* December 7, 1977, p. B1). In sum, Bloomington officials question the adequacy of the statistical unit in the campus crime survey. They seem to argue the need for a unit that differentiates among crimes and that measures the total number of crimes as a function of resident population, as opposed to total crimes committed.

In addition to being adequately defined, statistical units must be consistently defined. This is true in the case of baseball statistics. The number of games played in a season has increased from 154 to 162. Thus, certain new baseball records (those based on totals, as opposed to totals per game) are not entirely comparable to old ones. After all, the earlier players had fewer games in which to accumulate their totals. As a result, the statistical unit "home runs per season" is not completely consistent. It must be adjusted to reflect the advantage enjoyed by more recent players.

Are the Statistics Based on Valid Counting Assumptions?   A third test of counting procedures is to question the extent to which the numbers are based on estimation procedures involving assumptions. Many times, the statistical gatherer cannot just count but must estimate on the basis of a set of assumptions. Kahane (1971, p. 90) cites an instance of questionable counting assumptions. He scrutinizes estimations made by Marvin Kitman in his book *Washington's Expense Account.* Kitman estimated General George Washington's expenses by converting Pennsylvania pounds (the unit in which the records were kept) into Continental dollars (currency issued by the Continental Congress). Kahane argues that the conversion is questionable.

A more recent example of the problem of estimation is to be found in a story dealing with 1975 United States military aid to anticommunist factions in Angola (*Odessa American,* January 20, 1976, p. 1A). A figure of $25 million had been attached to the aid; however, the suggestion was made that the aid was undervalued. If true, then the actual amount of aid was more than the statistics indicated. Similar doubt can be cast on automobile mileage figures published by the Environmental Protection Agency. The E.P.A. figures are based on laboratory studies. Wind resistance, road friction, and individual motorists' driving habits are not taken into account. One could challenge the validity of the figures (i.e., their applicability to real conditions) by arguing that these factors cannot be left out. In other words, the critic could question the assumptions under which the mileage figures were obtained. Note, however, that the E.P.A. method has the advantage of making a better comparison of the relative gas efficiency of the cars themselves by controlling other factors.

Is the Type of Central Tendency Measure Specified?　In the next statistical test, we turn from the method of gathering to the method of summarizing the statistics. Many statistical arguments are based on a measure of central tendency. For instance, if nine students took a college examination, their scores could be averaged as follows:

Percentage scores	Average (sum of scores divided by the number of scores)
100	73.3
90	
90	
90	
70	
60	
60	
50	
50	
660	

The arithmetic average (also called the mean) would be a measure of the central tendency of the scores. However, there are other ways to measure central tendency. The median is that number in a set of scores below which one-half of the scores fall. In the example, above, 70 is the median score, because half of the exam grades fall below 70. Finally, the mode is the number that occurs most often in a collection of scores. A score of 90 is the mode for the column of figures cited. Because a set of scores can have three measures of centrality, the critic of argument must be sure which measure is being claimed as the "average." After all, there is a great difference among 90, 70, and 73.3 as averages.

Is the Method of Statistical Inference Adequate?   As I noted earlier, the difference between descriptive and inferential statistics can be an important one. When dealing with inferential statistics—those that predict results for a population on the basis of a sample—it is well to pay particular attention to the inferential method.

Is There an Adequate Sampling Procedure?   Inferential statistics are valid only when the sample adequately represents the entire population. Hence, an initial test of inferential statistics concerns the sampling procedure—is it adequate? Generally, the larger the sample, the greater the likelihood that it adequately represents the population.[4] Hence, a 1976 Associated Press election survey of thirty Texas voters (*Odessa American,* November 1, 1976, p. 1A) was probably too small a basis for predicting the 1976 Texas Presidential election vote, because some 4 million Texans voted in the Presidential contest of that year.

However, size is not the only factor to be observed in obtaining a representative sample. Basically, the sample must contain the same features or traits as the population. The classic instance of an unrepresentative sample— cited now by almost every argumentation text—is the 1936 *Literary Digest* poll (October 31, 1936, pp. 5–6) of the Presidential election vote of that year. This poll involved a large sample (more than 2 million voters), but the sample was made up of disproportionately well-to-do persons. Apparently, the *Digest* polled voters who were selected from telephone directories and automobile registration lists: The resulting sample was not typical of the voting population in the United States, because many citizens did without these luxuries during the Depression. The poll showed Governor Alfred Landon of Kansas (the Republican) defeating President Franklin D. Roosevelt (the Democratic candidate) by 57 percent of the vote to 43 percent. Actually, Roosevelt received 60 percent of the vote to Landon's 36 percent. In this case, an unrepresentative sample produced an erroneous statistical inference about the upcoming election.

In seeking to assure a representative sample, today's researchers use a random sampling procedure. In a random sample, each member of a population has an equal chance of appearing in the sample. That is, each member is selected independently; the selection process does not systematically influence who or what goes into the sample. There are a great number of specific random sampling procedures. However, the basic goal of each is to avoid the type of systematic bias that invalidated the *Literary Digest* sample.

Is the Method of Statistical Projection Adequate?   In addition to scrutinizing the sample procedure, the critic should pay attention to the method by which findings pertaining to a sample are projected onto the total population. Simply

---

[4]The issue of how large a sample needs to be is unresolved. However, John T. Roscoe offers the general advice (1969, pp. 156–157) that the sample should be around one-tenth as large as the population, up to a maximum sample size of 500.

stated, are the projection methods adequate? One indication of the adequacy of a statistical inference is termed the confidence level. The confidence level is a measure of the arguer's confidence that a statistic computed for a random sample will be a good estimate for the larger population. For example, assume that a soap company is interested in determining the number of days that its product sits on the shelf before being sold. The company might choose a sample of soap boxes and identify the average (mean) length of shelf time for the sample boxes—say, 6 days. The company would be interested in knowing whether the 6-day figure was valid for all boxes of its product (the entire population). The confidence level would measure this probability.

The statistical procedures used to calculate a confidence level are beyond the scope of this text. (The procedure for calculating the level of confidence for a mean involves looking at the relationship among the number of cases in the sample, the standard deviation of the scores from the mean, and the variance from the mean of the sample scores.) A typical confidence level would be like that reported by the New York Times–CBS poll of voter reaction to President Carter (*The New York Times,* April 29, 1977, p. A16): "In theory, one can say with 95 percent certainty that the results based on the entire sample [Carter is approved by 64 percent of the population] differ by no more than 2.5 percentage [points] in either direction from what would have been obtained by interviewing all adult Americans." As this statement suggests, one must be careful in projecting onto the population statistics derived from studying a sample.

Occasionally, the results of a sample are projected hastily onto an entire population. Two instances will serve to illustrate this problem. Newman and Newman (1969, pp. 208–210) relate details pertaining to a questionable statistical estimation that each year financial reasons are primarily responsible for preventing 100,000 high school students from attending college. The Newmans trace the origin of the 100,000 figure (a number which, by the way, acquired quite an aura of authoritativeness) to a survey of a group of high school students who did not attend college (i.e., a sample of a population). Apparently, many of the students cited money as a reason that they decided against going to college. The author of the survey computed the proportion of respondents who mentioned this reason and extended it to the entire population of potential college students. Was this a valid projection? Newman and Newman (1969, p. 209) question whether it was. They reason that we do not know "how many of those who responded to this question were genuinely motivated to go to college, had made an effort to find funds, or would go if funds were dropped in their laps." They conclude: "So we had a statistical sample, projected into a body of 100,000 youths, about whom we know only that they gave a convenient answer to an emotionally charged question." In short, the figure is not a particularly meaningful one.

A second example of questionable statistical projection concerns a subcommittee report of the U.S. House of Representatives that in 1974 there were 2.4 million unnecessary surgeries, costing $3.92 billion dollars and leading to 11,900 deaths. The American Medical Association challenged the subcommittee report on several bases. The key question seems to have been whether the subcommittee was correct in assuming that 17 percent of all surgeries are "unnecessary." Below I summarize a number of the AMA objections as cited by columnist James J. Kilpatrick (in *Odessa American,* June 6, 1976, p. 12D):

1 The 17 percent figure was derived from a study of "elective surgical procedures" recommended to "1,350 New York union members." Needless to say, New York union members are not a representative sample of the U.S. population. For this reason, as well as others, the author of the study specifically cautioned against projecting the results to the wider U.S. surgical population: "The findings presented here cannot be applied to the general population undergoing elective operations."

2 The New York study did not assert that 17 percent of surgery was "unnecessary." Rather the researcher compared surgery which was recommended by one physician to surgery in which a second, confirming, opinion was obtained. So the 17 percent figure referred only to surgery which was "recommended but not confirmed." Such was not necessarily "unnecessary."

Apart from the apparent invalidity of the 17 percent figure, the AMA highlighted other objections to the method by which dollar and death computations were obtained. As before, the key point to be noted is this: When extrapolations are made on the basis of a sample, one must be careful not to rely upon questionable assumptions.

Thus far, I have identified tests relative to who gathered the statistics, when and how they were obtained, whether a measure of central tendency was used, and whether the inferential methods (sample and projection) were adequate. The sixth and seventh tests relate to the way in which the numbers are presented by an arguer. Specifically, is the conclusion drawn from the statistics a reasonable one, and are the statistics properly explained when presented?

Is the Conclusion Drawn from the Statistics a Reasonable One?   In testing the reasonableness of a conclusion drawn from numbers, one is really looking to see whether all relevant explanations of the statistics are considered.[5] In many cases, it is possible to have more than one explanation of the figures. That is, the statistics can be cited to prove more than one conclusion. Consider two instances in which the numbers can be made to support different interpretations.

We are all familiar with the nationally standardized achievement tests that are administered to elementary and secondary students. Many of these tests show that the academic performance of students is declining rapidly. One critic of standardized achievement tests—Dr. W. James Popham—argues that the test

---

[5]Basically, this involves applying to statistical tests derived from the definition of rhetorical validity. Recall that the definition questioned whether "the degree of certainty attributed to a conclusion by an agent is less than or equal to that established by the relevant (supporting and opposing) proof." The supporting proof would be those aspects of the statistics that are consistent with the arguer's explanation. The opposing proof would be those aspects of the statistics that seem to fit another explanation better.

scores do not really prove that students are becoming worse. Writing in the 1976 *IOX Fall Almanac* (IOX stands for Instructional Objectives Exchange), Popham gives two reasons that the tests do not really measure educational attainment. First, he says, the tests do not always match what is taught in a particular school district. For instance, in the area of "reading comprehension," Popham maintains that "there are many legitimate and *different* ways to assess reading comprehension. If a school district is stressing one way [in its teaching methods] and the test is used another way to assess comprehension, the resulting test data will be misleading." In other words, the tests may not match what is taught. Secondly, Popham holds the opinion that the norm-referenced nature of the tests makes them poor measures. He explains this as follows:

1   Standard tests are scored on a percentile basis. A student who scores in the 70th percentile has performed better than 70 percent of those in a previous group who took the test—i.e., the norm group.

2   Percentile scoring requires that test scores be widely spread out. That is, the scores must range from high to low.

3   In order to spread out the scores, test makers choose questions "which are answered correctly by about 50 percent of examinees."

4   Thus, test items that are answered correctly by a high percent of students (say, 80 to 90 percent) are modified or are eventually removed from the test.

5   The questions that are answered correctly most often are "typically" the important items that teachers emphasize. It follows that standardized tests gradually cover material that is less and less significant.

6   Because the tests cover material that the teachers do not emphasize, Popham concludes that standardized achievement tests "fail to detect high quality instruction even when it is present."

In sum, Popham offers an alternative explanation for a decline in test scores. Whereas others argue that the decline measures a trend toward worse instruction (and/or that students are lazier), Popham contends that the tests themselves are becoming worse measures of learning. To be sure, the issues relating to standardized tests are complex. We should not accept Popham's explanation merely because he is functioning as a critic, for the question is far from settled. Rather, the two explanations for declining test scores serve to remind us that statistics require interpretation if they are to be meaningful. Because of the great number of variables relating to any situation, it is often possible to construct more than one plausible explanation for a statistic.

A second example of alternative explanations for statistical findings may be seen in an article on the gap between the salaries of male and female college professors (*The Chronicle of Higher Education,* September 27, 1976, p. 1). The article reported a number of statistics relating to faculty salaries but emphasized the notion that the male-female gap was increasing: "Salary inequalities between men and women faculty members have increased in the past year, the National Center for Education Statistics reported last week." The article pointed out that the gap in salary rose from an average of $2820 to a gap of $3096. (This means that the average female faculty member earned $3096 less than the average male faculty member in 1975–1976; the differential was $2820 in 1974–1975.) The *Chronicle* report went on to assert that the data "confirm the conclusion [that] faculty women in the past year failed to make any overall progress toward job equality." Notice the strong qualifier ("confirm") that the author attributes to the conclusion, in view of the statistical data.

In the weeks that followed the *Chronicle's* salary differential article, several letters to the editor appeared in which alternative explanations of the findings were suggested. Arguments such as the following were advanced in an effort to show that the figures did not prove a lack of progress for women (See *The Chronicle of Higher Education,* October 18, 1976, and November 1, 1976):

1 The number of women holding starting positions (e.g., assistant professor) has increased more than that for men. Therefore, one would expect the average salary for women to decline in the short term.

2 When data for women and men are compared at the rank of full professor, average women's salaries increased more than men's.

3 The statistics on salaries are based on total salary, not purchasing power. Because the value of money has declined (due to inflation), one would expect the nominal salary gap to increase, even if the real gap (in purchasing power) remained the same.

These arguments constitute alternative explanations for the statistical finding that the dollar gap between men and women increased from $2820 to $3096. On the one hand, the increase is said to represent a confirmation that women lost ground; other arguers interpret the figures to prove that no such loss in ground occurred, that in fact, the numbers suggest that women made gains between the 1974–1975 and 1975–1976 academic years. It is difficult to say who is right on this issue, but the controversy over the salary-gap figures shows how intelligent people may differ in interpreting a descriptive statistic. Figures are not as straightforward as they sometimes seem.

Are the Statistics Properly Explained When Presented?   The final test that I offer for statistical argument has to do with the reporting of a statistic. The critic should make sure that all relevant information about the statistic is provided by the advocate. For instance, if it is claimed that WXXX is the "number-one" station, some explanation of the meaning of "number-one" should be provided. Such a claim is probably based on a listenership survey that may be broken down into age categories. Hence, "number-one" may really mean that "when the listening preferences of 21-to-25-year-olds were surveyed, WXXX was mentioned most frequently." Of course, another station might be "number-one" on the basis of the preferences of 16-to-20-year-olds. Therefore, it is important to have the relevant information about the meaning of the statistic. If the critic is to judge the validity of a statistic, it is essential to have sufficient information about the true meaning of the numbers.

Overall, we may say that statistical methods present both advantages and disadvantages for the advocate. Statistics have the advantage of putting examples into perspective and of allowing for comparisons. However, figures leave out details and require processing. These two "howevers" make it necessary for the critic to apply special tests to statistical statements. I have offered seven tests, some of which involve several considerations. Basically, the tests of statistics accomplish two purposes: First, they assess whether a numerical description corresponds to reality (tests 1 through 5, especially). In this connection it is clear that statistics function descriptively—they allegedly point to reality—but the tests help us to determine exactly what is it that the statistics actually describe. Do the numbers identify reality, or do they describe only the biases of their source and/or the biases involved in the counting procedure? The second function of the statistical tests (tests number 6 and 7, especially) is to probe the relationship between statistical data and a higher-level claim (interpretation or evaluation) that may be drawn from it. Here we seek to learn whether all relevant explanations have been considered, whether all variables have been considered. When possible, plausible alternative explanations are available, we must be sure not to overstate our acceptance of any one explanation. That is, we must temper our qualifier. Finally, we must be sure to report all important details of the statistics.

TESTIMONY

The third major type of descriptive argument is testimony. Testimony may be defined as a statement taken from a third party that is cited by an advocate. In using testimony an advocate (the first party) seeks to persuade an audience (the second party) by going outside of the immediate situation. The arguer secures arguments from noninvolved third parties. When we use testimony, then, we specifically cite the words of someone else. We use another's statement as our own argument. In other words, testimony is an attributed argument. It is an argument that we attribute to another source. "Quotation" is a synonym for testimony, for when we cite testimony we quote someone else's words.[6] Testimony may also be called "authoritative proof," for it derives its probative force from our acceptance of the authoritativeness of a witness's statement. As a descriptive type of argument, testimony functions basically to identify reality. It tells us who said what. Remember, however, that a testimonial statement may itself raise subsidiary issues of definition and value.

The Use of Testimony

In some cases an advocate will cite another's statement because the words are put so well. That is, the words do an especially effective job of clarifying the point. Such a use of authoritative argument is to be found in a letter of former Vice President Spiro T. Agnew to Carl Albert, who was then the Speaker of the

---

[6]I should observe that, by its nature, evidence is testimonial. As I noted in chapter 2, evidence is a statement taken from a third party.

U.S. House of Representatives. Agnew wrote to request that the House investigate charges being made against him (i.e., that Agnew had accepted bribes). He cited a similar case of 1826, when Vice President John C. Calhoun requested vindication via a House investigation and quoted Calhoun's words, with this introduction: "On Dec. 29, 1826, he [Calhoun] addressed to your body a communication whose eloquent language I can better quote than rival" (*Odessa American,* September 26, 1973, p. 18A). Agnew cites Calhoun because the latter's words fit Agnew's purpose so well. They explain and clarify the situation in a way that is favorable to Agnew.

In the Agnew example, testimony was cited less for proof than for clarification. However, the basic function of testimony is to prove an argument. In chapter 3, I presented testimony (claims based on authority) as a way of knowing. Because testimony amounts to a major source of human knowledge, it follows that testimony can be a powerful form of argument. Further adding to the power of testimony is its twofold argumentative impact. In addition to the weight of the words themselves (what is said), a testimonial assertion carries a force based on who originated the claim. For this reason academic debate contestants cite innumerable quotations to back up each of their major points. This tendency was reflected in the final round of the 1976 American Forensic Association–sponsored National College Debate Tournament (in Rives, 1976, p. 3). Speeches in this debate were filled with authoritative statements designed both to *clarify* the meaning of the argument and to *prove it.* For instance, in seeking to establish the point that "malnutrition ravages the daily existence of millions of the world's inhabitants," the arguer moved immediately to an authoritative proof. The very next sentence was a reference to an outside source: "The general picture was sadly described in the New York Times in October, 1974." The reality described in *The New York Times* is cited as proof of the advocate's assertion that millions are affected by malnutrition.

Whether designed to clarify or to prove, testimony is a well-recognized form of descriptive argument. Although testimony may contain interpretive or evaluative assertions, testimony is itself a descriptive argument, because the first question it raises is an issue of fact: Did the witness really say that? Did the advocate correctly quote the witness? Only after we have satisfied these queries do we move on to consider whether the statement itself is sensible. In this connection the philosopher George Campbell contends (in Bitzer, 1963, p. 54) that "in what regards single facts, testimony is more adequate evidence than any conclusions from experience." Campbell means that whereas experience can only tell us what was likely, accurate testimony can tell us what actually happened in a particular case.

Tests to Determine the Validity of Testimony

Is testimony always accurate? The strength of a witness's statement depends on the credibility of the witness. Hence, as I noted in chapter 3, we must be careful in accepting the statements of others. The persistent skepticism about testimony has resulted in many systems for evaluating the evidence of witnesses. Two of the earliest were by the philosophers George Campbell (in Bitzer, 1963, pp. 55–56) and David Hume (1902, pp. 116–117). Of the modern frameworks for analyzing testimony, that provided in Newman and Newman (1969, pp. 74–88) is one of the best. In the next few pages I will summarize the major tests of testimony and provide some indications of how the tests may be used. The tests of testimony are designed to help us assess (1) whether the advocate has quoted the witness correctly, (2) whether the witness's testimony is a sensible statement, and (3) whether the testimony really establishes the generalization that it has been alleged to prove.

Has the Advocate Quoted the Witness Correctly?   The first question in dealing with testimony is to decide whether a statement was actually made. When an advocate asserts that X person made Y statement, our first need is to verify that X really said Y. In doing this the critic should assess both whether the quotation itself is accurate and whether it is cited in its proper context. Let us consider the accuracy criterion first.

The Accuracy Test   One of the best studies of accuracy is that by Robert P. Newman and Keith R. Sanders (1965). These authors studied each piece of evidence cited by debaters in the 1964 National College Debate Tournament. The authors studied both a transcript and a tape recording of the debate. They marked each occasion in which a speaker cited testimony in support of an argument. Having determined that the debaters used authoritative proofs, Newman and Sanders systematically compared each citation with the original source from which it allegedly came. In their effort to track down the source of each quotation, the researchers occasionally found it necessary to correspond with the author of the quote (the witness) and with the debater (the advocate) who used it. As a result of this exhaustive study, Newman and Sanders reported that only about one-half of the testimonial statements were accurately cited by the debaters. Their results (p. 8) were as follows:

Types of testimonial citations	Number of citations
Accurate citations	34
Misrepresented citations	23
Harmless inaccuracies	5
Unverified citations	6
Fabricated citations	3
Total testimonial citations	71

Of greatest concern are the twenty-three misrepresentations and three fabrications. Newman and Sanders (1965, p. 8) define a "misrepresentation" as a case in which "the authority has been cited inaccurately in such a fashion as to alter the meaning or force of what he said." Because it distorts the meaning of a statement, a misrepresentation is an invalid use of authoritative proof. Even more invalid, however, are fabrications. Newman and Sanders (p. 8) stipulate that a fabrication is a citation "attributed to an authority who disclaims or does not acknowledge the statement, and whose published works do not contain anything approximating the quoted statement."

The Newman and Sanders study epitomizes the accuracy test of testimony. The accuracy critic scrutinizes the literature, comparing carefully what is alleged to have been said with what was really said (insofar as it is possible to ascertain this).

The Context Test   A second means of determining whether a source has been correctly cited is the context test. In studying the context of testimony, the critic seeks to determine whether an accurately quoted excerpt is cited correctly *in context*. This test is necessary because a quotation may be totally accurate as to what was said, but because the surrounding remarks are omitted, the quote inaccurately reflects what the source meant. An out-of-context quotation can be technically correct but nevertheless misleading.

The out-of-context problem is shown in criticism of former First Lady Betty Ford's 1975 interview on the "60 Minutes" television program. One of the interview questions dealt with the subject of premarital affairs. Mrs. Ford commented that she would not be surprised if her daughter Susan would at some time have an affair. Mrs. Ford's remark drew a certain amount of criticism (see "Letters," *Newsweek,* September 8, 1975, p. 4, and Associated Press reports of August 22, 1975). However, a spokesman for Mrs. Ford—Sheila Weidenfeld— charged the critics with quoting the First Lady's remarks out of context. Columnist Paul Healey (*Odessa American,* August 29, 1975, p. 8A) reported: "As Mrs. Weidenfeld notes, if Mrs. Ford's views are read in their entirety, they establish her as a traditionalist who believes in family togetherness." By focusing on one or two sentences from the interview, Mrs. Ford's critics may have unfairly distorted her meaning.

Is the Witness's Testimony a Sensible Statement   Once the critic has determined that a statement has been quoted accurately and in context, the time has come to apply a second set of tests to the testimony. Does the testimony amount to a sensible statement? A large battery of standards have been developed to help judge the merits of testimony. Methods have been devised for different fields such as journalism, law, and historical writing. However, one may group these tests into three general categories: tests that relate to personal characteristics of the witness, tests that concern the situation in which the testimony took place, and tests that deal with the nature of the statement itself. (Remember that there is considerable overlap among these three categories.) In the following section I identify specific questions that pertain to each of the three major categories. After introducing the tests, I will provide examples of how they may be applied.

Personal Characteristics of the Witness   The first set of tests relates to the person of the witness:

1   Is the source a person of good character? In particular, does the authority have a reputation for past reliability and honesty?

2   Is the source competent to make the statement? Generally speaking, is the source mentally and physically able? If the statement requires a particular expertise, does the source possess this expertise?

3   Is the source unbiased? Does the authority have a motive to tell the truth? To deceive? To distort?

4   Is the source a willing or a reluctant witness? A willing witness is one who has something to gain by testifying in a certain manner. A reluctant witness is one whose testimony works against his apparent best interests.

The Situation in Which the Witness Obtained the Information   Having examined the witness as a person,[7] we turn to the situation of observation—the environment in which the witness obtained the information. The basic issue here can be put as follows: Is the authority speaking from primary or secondary experience? When the witness has obtained the information through direct personal experience, we term the quotation a primary source of information. When a witness obtains the information from a source other than his or her own sense experience, we call the testimony a secondary source. The distinction between primary and secondary sources is an important one, because second-hand (or third- or fourthhand) information is more prone to distortion than that gained through one's own experiences.

An interesting instance of the danger inherent in relying on a secondary source is afforded by a May 1975 column by James J. Kilpatrick (*Odessa American,* May 19, 1975, p. 10A). Kilpatrick apologizes for citing a fictitious, fabricated quotation attributed to A.F.L.-C.I.O.[8] president George Meany. Kilpatrick reported these results in his effort to trace the "counterfeit quotation": "I got the quote from a speech by Sen. Paul Fannin of Arizona, delivered in the Senate on March 6 and carried in the Congressional Record at page S-3184. Senator Fannin advises me that he got it from the National Right to Work Committee. The committee got it from the newsletter of a Southern manufacturers' group." Despite having been widely cited, the quote turns out to have been bogus (although Meany did make remarks similar in tone to the apocryphal quotation). Kilpatrick's inquiry should alert us to the dangers of relying on secondary sources. When we borrow a quotation from another source, we have no direct assurance that our source exercised care in obtaining the quote.

The point to be made here is a simple one. When looking at the environment in which our source obtained the information, we should first determine whether our source (1) witnessed an event personally or (2) relied on the reports of others. Having done this, we may apply tests that have been developed both for primary and for secondary testimony.

I   Primary source tests
    A   Did the witness have access to the event? Was the witness proximate

---

[7]Other factors of credibility are discussed in chapter 7.
[8]American Federation of Labor–Congress of Industrial Organizations.

to what took place? In short, did the authority have a real opportunity to get the information?

  B Was the witness mentally and physically able to make the observation at the occasion (time and place) in which the event allegedly took place?

  C How soon after the event took place did the witness report his observations? Generally, the sooner the report is made, the greater are the chances that it is accurate.

  D Is the testimony given in a time of crisis? Generally speaking, exaggerations and distortions occur more often when the situation is highly tense (see Newman and Newman, 1969, pp. 74–75).

  E What was the attitude of the witness to those who received the testimony? A witness loses objectivity when there seems to be a need to please those receiving the testimony.

  F Was the testimony arranged or spontaneous? The assumption being made here is that when a witness has been coached or hired, the testimony given is less valuable.

  G Do there exist good alternative explanations for the events observed by the witness? Might conditions have fooled the witness, as in the case of a mirage?

II Secondary source tests

  A Does the witness indicate from where the information was obtained? Because a secondary source is not original, its credibility is dependent on the sources from which it sprang.

  B Does the secondary authority cite primary sources or is there also reliance on secondary accounts? Here we inquire as to the quality of the witness's sources.

  C Does the secondary witness quote accurately? This is similar to the test used by Newman and Sanders (1965). We compare a witness's statement to the quotation made by an advocate.

The nature of the statement itself The third general set of witness tests relates to the quotation itself. These tests probe the internal worth of the statement, regardless of who made it and the conditions under which it was obtained.

1 Is the testimony recent or old? The most recent testimony is often the best if we desire to learn the latest developments. However, as I noted earlier, a statement made soon after an event may be superior to a recent account.

2 Is the source careful to qualify remarks properly? The assumption made here is that extreme testimony may be overstated.

3 Is the testimony internally consistent? That is, does it contain contradictory statements or assumptions?

4 Does the testimony raise issues of fact definition or value? A witness may testify as to the existence of fact, or a witness may make interpretive and/or evaluative statements. The critic must carefully segregate the types of issues raised by authoritative statements. Only the factual statements may be independently verified. The others must be assessed or judged.

5 If the witness is testifying to the occurrence of an event, is the event consistent with or contrary to general human experience? Testimony that contradicts the experience of most people must be scrutinized extra carefully. Testimony relating to U.F.O. (Unidentified Flying Object) phenomena, miracles, and the like should, in fairness, be examined more closely than testimony about commonplace happenings.

Tests dealing with the witness, the situation, and the testimony itself all help us to determine whether an authoritative assertion makes sense. If a statement comes from a reliable person, if it meets the situational tests, and if it is in itself a reasonable statement, then we have good reasons to accept it.

Does the Testimony Establish the Generalization? However, even when we vouched for the forcefulness of a testimony, there is another hurdle that it must pass. Testimony is usually cited to establish a conclusion; hence, the third and final measure of testimony is whether it actually establishes the generalization. The following questions help us to assess the relationship of specific testimony to a general conclusion. (Notice that these are essentially the same questions that we applied to example arguments.)

I How does the testimony in question relate to the statements of other witnesses?

   A Is the testimony in question relevant to the generalization? Is the subject of the testimony the same as the subject of the generalization?

   B Is the testimony typical? Is it exceptional? Does there exist opposing testimony which is unfavorable to the generalization? Overall, do favorable or unfavorable testimonies predominate?

   C If more than one witness is cited, do the testimonies fit together well? That is, are all the instances similar in crucial details?

II How does the testimony in question (together with possible opposing statements) compare to the qualifier? Do the favorable testimonies predominate sufficiently to justify the level of certainty claimed for the generalization?

You may well be feeling somewhat overwhelmed at this point. After all, in the last few pages I have introduced some twenty-five separate questions that may be asked about a testimonial argument. Two questions (accuracy and context) related to whether the arguer quoted the witness correctly. Nineteen questions concerned whether the testimony made sense. (These questions were divided into three basic categories: witness, situation, and the testimony itself.) Four questions were posed regarding the extent to which the testimony established an overall generalization. With so many questions to ask, you may well wonder where you should start. I would suggest that you start at the top and work down through all the tests. While some tests will be more fruitful in certain cases, all of the tests are potentially valuable. One should not arbitrarily skip any of them.

Applying the Tests of Testimony

To give you a greater idea of how the tests work, I will apply them to three instances of testimony. In each case, I will show how the testimonial tests help us to judge the credibility of an argument based on authority. The first instance relates to U.F.O. sightings; the second involves scrutiny of psychologists who act as expert witnesses in the legal determination of insanity; the third is an analysis of the Senate Watergate testimony of Nixon counsel John W. Dean III.

U.F.O. Sightings Testimony   Periodically, the subject of U.F.O. sightings draws considerable public attention. Invariably, the testimony about these sightings becomes highly controversial. U.F.O. reports provide us with a good vehicle for assessing the validity of testimony. In January 1978 *Playboy* magazine published a panel discussion involving seven U.F.O. experts (assembled by Murray Fisher, Barbara Cady, and Donald Carroll). The panel included both those who give credence to U.F.O. reports and those who dispute the believability of all U.F.O. claims. The panelists applied most of the tests identified in this chapter. Below, I identify how they analyzed the U.F.O. testimony.

In their discussion the panelists touched briefly on the issue of whether the U.F.O. witnesses were being correctly quoted. Both sets of advocates—U.F.O. proponents and opponents—charged the other camp with distorting the testimony. Advocates supporting the position that U.F.O.s are possible accused the opposition of distorting U.F.O. reports to fit tortured explanations. For instance, Dr. J. Allen Hynek (professor of astronomy at Northwestern University) accused Philip J. Klass (avionics editor of *Aviation Week & Space Technology*) of being unwilling "to consider the evidence except insofar as it can be twisted to fit his preconception that the witnesses *must* have been mistaken" (*Playboy,* January 1978, p. 75). Similarly, Frank B. Salisbury (professor of plant physiology, Utah State University) charged that a well-known U.F.O. skeptic had arrived at alternative explanations for sightings only "by ignoring many key facts" (p. 72). U.F.O. proponents were not the only ones to challenge testimonial citations. Those who denied the reality of U.F.O. sightings also questioned their opponents' use of testimony. Klass charged that James A. Harder (professor of hydraulics at the University of California, Berkeley) had incorrectly reported details of an alleged 1956 U.F.O. sighting in England. Klass argued that "after spending many months investigating this case to determine the facts, I've found that the mystery evaporates" (p. 82). Overall, Klass expressed the opinion that many scientists who accept U.F.O. testimony are guilty of having "an unconscious desire to believe in UFOs" (p. 128). In other words, they overlook weaknesses in U.F.O. testimony. For the most part these exchanges between U.F.O. supporters and detractors raise both the accuracy and context issues.

Beyond the question of whether the panelists were themselves accurately relating the U.F.O. witness testimony, there was also the issue of whether the testimony made sense. Debate centered around the credibility of witnesses—although some arguments were made about the situation of observation and the intrinsic merits of the testimony itself.

As one might expect, the panelists spent much time discussing the believability of those who allege to have observed or encountered U.F.O.s. Regarding the first witness test—overall reputation—the panelists disagreed as to whether most reports came from reliable or unreliable people. U.F.O. detractors contended that sightings often were made by crackpots and that many hoaxes had been discovered. Proponents disagreed: According to Hynek, U.F.O. witnesses were typically "normal, respectable people" (p. 88). In an effort to reinforce this point, Harder argued that unexplained sightings (those that cannot easily be dismissed as being natural or man-made phenomena) tended to be the most reliable reports.

Witness competence was another issue for controversy. One proponent, R. Leo Sprinkle (professor of counseling services, University of Wyoming), argued that "more and more of these stories are coming from expert witnesses—by which I mean policemen, airline pilots, radar operators, astronauts—people professionally trained to be reliable observers" (p. 75). In contrast, skeptics portrayed the witnesses as being easily fooled into making mistaken identifications. Ernest H. Taves (an M.D. with a Ph.D. in psychology) listed over thirty objects that have been mistaken for U.F.O.s. He concluded: "With so many possible stimuli, one isn't surprised at the large number of sightings" (p. 70).

Possible sources of witness bias were also considered. U.F.O. supporters allowed that many people have a subconscious desire to believe in U.F.O.s. Jacques Vallee (who holds a Ph.D. in computer science) noted that belief in U.F.O.s "appeals to a deep need we have for mystery, for irrational belief" (p. 96). This, of course, might supply a motive for deliberately or unconsciously turning in a false U.F.O. report. However, supporters pointed to U.F.O. testimony verified by polygraphs (lie detectors) or given under hypnosis. [Harder contended that it was "impossible to lie under hypnosis" (p. 88).]

You will recall that the final test of the witness's person involved deciding whether the testimony was reluctant or willing. Reluctant testimony worked against the evident interests of the witness, whereas willing testimony was advantageous. Harder argued, in this vein, that "only 13 percent of persons who sight UFOs actually report them" (p. 68). "And no wonder," he added, because witnesses usually obtain only ridicule for their reports. Sprinkle (*Playboy,* p. 90) added that it "took courage" to make a U.F.O. report in view of the resulting personal attacks. In contrast, of course, detractors such as Klass pointed to one U.F.O. witness who "had always wanted to ride on a UFO" (p. 88). Klass implied that by reporting the encounter the witness gained gratification.

As the above paragraphs suggest, the critics clashed over each of the four tests relating to the person of the witness. From the proponents' perspective, U.F.O. reporters were reliable, expert, confirmed by polygraph or hypnosis, and reluctant. From the opposing vantage point, they were unreliable, gullible, credulous, and eager to testify.

U.F.O. witnesses allegedly speak from primary experience. Accordingly, the panelists raised situational points relating to the legitimacy of sightings. The major focus of debate concerned the witness's physical and mental conditions at the time in which the observation was made. Detractors opined that U.F.O. witnesses were often in a poor condition to be observers. Taves, for instance, used this argument to challenge the sighting reported by astronaut McDivitt: "It should be noted that, at the time, McDivitt was suffering from eye irritation because of an accidental urine spill into the cabin atmosphere" (p. 76). In discussing the case of the man from Winnipeg, Taves argued that the witness had been "drunk" (p. 86). Detractors similarly used witness-condition-at-the-time arguments to dispute the close encounter cited by a Barney and Betty Hill. (The Hills reported being taken aboard an alien space craft and being examined.) Klass argued, for example, that Betty Hill's recollections—taken under hypnosis—where recollections of dreams that she had had (p. 88). U.F.O. proponents disputed the "eye irritation" and "dream" explanations of the skeptics.

Three of the other situational tests also received attention from the panelists. Both sides agreed that U.F.O. sightings are stimulated by the news media. In this scenario a few sightings lead to press coverage, which in turn causes other people to look for—and find—U.F.O.s. If the media produce a wave of U.F.O. reports, then one could say that press coverage creates a crisis atmosphere (primary-source situational test four), thereby making the reports less spontaneous (primary-source situational test six). On this point, however, the U.F.O. defenders disputed whether the media accounted for all the sightings.

The final situational text—whether there are good alternative explanations for the events (number seven)—was probably the major point at issue in the panel discussion. Skeptics used "natural phenomena" explanations as their basic argument against sightings: Recall that Taves cited over thirty natural objects or events that had been the source of U.F.O. reports. The basic argument of the defense was to challenge the reasonableness of the non-U.F.O. explanations. In the Coyne helicopter case of October 18, 1973, Klass argued that the crew observed nothing more than a "meteor fireball from the Orionid meteor shower that occurs in mid to late October" (p. 75). Hynek listed several objections to this alternative account, including: (1) The Coyne incident lasted too long to be explained by a meteor shower; (2) bright meteors do not "pace an aircraft"; (3) "they do not look like gray, metal cylinders with a bright light coming from only one end, as he [Captain Coyne] also reported" (pp. 75–76).

In addition to witness and situational tests, the reasonableness of testimony may be assessed by examining the testimonial statement itself. Defenders of U.F.O. testimony made much of this point. Sprinkle suggested that relatively greater attention should be paid to the stories than to the witnesses: "Is it really necessary, or productive, to spend so much time worrying about the credibility of individual witnesses among so many millions? Let's investigate their stories, not them" (p. 90). Yet even here the main thrust of the discussion was to look at individual stories. Applying the internal consistency test, Taves argued that the report of the man from Winnipeg was "found to be riddled with inconsistencies and incongruities." In fact, "he was entirely unable to lead Craig [an investigator] to the site of the occurrence, though they spent hours searching for it" (p. 86). Hynek challenged the idea that the testimony was internally contradictory: "I also investigated this case by going to Winnipeg myself, and I cannot agree that it was a hoax" (p. 86).

Apart from the matter of consistency, the major internal consideration applied to the U.F.O. reports was the question of whether the events are "consistent with or contrary to general human experience." Klass stated his overall opinion that it was "easier to believe in the tooth fairy" than to accept testimony that "there are extraterrestial spaceships in our skies" (p. 68). On the other hand, Hynek supported U.F.O. testimony by reporting his own conversion. "I was, in fact, a complete debunker," he stated. However, he observed, "after years of studying the phenomenon, I'm convinced that it's real" (p. 72). He accused Klass of being too unwilling to accept U.F.O. testimony just because it was unusual. Overall, it seems clear that the panel discussion proved one thing: Reports of the unusual are (and should be) tested more critically than tales of the mundane.

The final category of questions dealt with whether or not testimony could prove the generalization. By maintaining that all U.F.O. sightings could be explained as natural or man-made phenomena, detractors were able to make the testimony appear irrelevant and atypical. Defenders of the testimony generally sought to show that the instances of good testimony outweighed both hoaxes and unreliable statements. Defenders appealed particularly to similarities in multiple reports of the same event. "And what about instances in which separate witnesses report exactly the same effects from a single UFO?" (p. 85). Having posed this question, Hynek cited a 1957 case in Levelland, Texas, "in which seven motorists, in different places at different times on the same night, reported that their cars died and their headlights went out when a UFO appeared. Moreover, all the descriptions of the craft were identical." Detractors argued that similar reports were not surprising if one assumed that a single natural or man-made phenomenon was the cause.

In sum, it is clear that the 1978 *Playboy* panel discussion of U.F.O. phenomena centered on the validity of U.F.O. testimony. The discussants ranged over the whole gamut of tests: They argued about whether the witnesses were correctly quoted; they clashed over the inherent merits of the witnesses, the quality of the situation of observation, and the internal merits of the reports; finally, they disputed whether accounts of U.F.O.s could be taken as viable evidence in establishing the generalization that Earth has been visited by extraterrestial beings.

U.F.O. testimony is only one of many contexts in which tests may be applied to witnesses. In the next few pages, I will comment on two other examples that also illustrate the process of evaluating witness-based evidence: the testimony of expert psychologists and that of John W. Dean III. The use of psychoanalytic testimony in court gives us special insight into the use of expert witnesses in general and hired witnesses in particular. John Dean's testimony before the Senate "Watergate" committee gives us an opportunity to look at both the issue of witness reputation and the question of hearsay—secondary— evidence.

Courtroom Psychoanalytic Testimony   The use of psychoanalytic testimony in court is a practice of long standing. Thousands of times each year courts in the United States look to psychologists and psychiatrists to help determine whether a defendant is legally sane. Recently, however, scholars have taken a harder look at the validity of such expert testimony. Some of the problems with this testimony, according to Robitscher and Williams (1977) include:

1 Psychiatrists may be advocates for their own pet theories of human behavior. In other words, they may be biased.
2 Psychiatrists may feel pressured to supply testimony to support the advocate who hires them—the defense or the prosecution.
3 Psychoanalytic theory is sufficiently vague so that conflicting testimony often is given by different psychiatrists.

Despite these limitations, the authors believe that psychological evidence can be useful in the courtroom. However, they propose some refinements in the use of such testimony. The point to be made here is that experts may disagree or may be biased.

John Dean's Testimony   The case of John Dean's testimony on Watergate and the events related to it supplies us with a vehicle for applying standards dealing with witness credibility and secondary-source testimony. John Dean was the counsel to the President under Richard M. Nixon. According to his own admissions, Dean had become a major go-between during the cover-up phase of the Watergate scandal. Dean acted as liaison between Nixon campaign officials—such as John N. Mitchell, the campaign director—and the White House staff—chiefly, H. R. Haldeman and John D. Ehrlichman. The campaign staff, the White House staff, and Dean maneuvered to cover up the involvement of Nixon officials in the bugging of Democratic campaign headquarters (and other illegal acts). When the intricate web of the cover-up conspiracy began to unravel in March 1973, Dean met with prosecutors and testified about his involvement. However, failing to get full immunity from prosecution in exchange for his testimony (and also fearing that the prosecutors were subject to White House pressure), Dean chose to testify before the Senate Select Committee on Presidential Campaign Activities—the "Watergate" committee. In exchange for "use immunity" (i.e., a deal that nothing Dean said to the senators could be used against him in court), Dean testified from June 25 to June

29, 1973. He outlined the details of the Watergate break-in and cover-up, both admitting his own involvement in the cover-up and implicating a number of powerful figures—including President Nixon. Dean's Watergate testimony is an especially good context for studying the tests relating to the person of a witness: character, competence, bias, and eagerness or reluctance to testify.

Consider the subject of Dean's character. Questions were raised concerning Dean's having been fired from a law firm. Dean (1977, pp. 316–317) explained that he had been exhonorated of any misdeeds by a lawyer's ethics committee. A second line of questioning during the hearings dealt with Dean's overall character. In his prepared remarks, Dean mentioned an occasion on which he "borrowed" $4850 from an amount of money ($15,200) that had been left in his office safe (Staff of *The New York Times,* 1973, p. 273): "I removed a packet of bills amounting to $4,850 and placed my personal check for that amount with the remaining cash." Dean stated that he intended to use the money for his wedding and honeymoon. He was sorely pressed on this point by minority (Republican) counsel Fred Thompson; however, Senator Sam Ervin, Jr. (D., North Carolina) interrupted to point out that Dean had volunteered these details and, had he not done so, no one would have ever known about the matter (Dean, 1977, p. 331). The reader may ask what difference it made if Dean borrowed some money left in his care—what it has to do with Watergate. The answer, of course, is that Dean should not have taken the money and that this indiscretion reflected badly on his character (although his admitting it reflected well on him). Dean was making serious charges against the White House. Hence, his credibility depended partly on his having an unblemished character.

What of Dean's competence? Dean's Watergate testimony involved a great amount of detail: He spoke of the contents of conversations, letters, meetings; he cited specific places, dates, and times. Senator Daniel K. Inouye (D., Hawaii), in particular, commented on the power of detail in Dean's statements. In explaining to the Senator how he (Dean) had assembled his 245-page opening statement, Dean boasted of his memory (Staff of *The New York Times,* 1973, p. 332): "Well, Senator, I think I have a good memory. I think that anyone who recalls my student years knew that I was very fast at recalling information, retaining information." Senator Edward J. Gurney (R., Florida)—the most vocal administration defender on the committee—made a major effort to undermine Dean's reputation for accuracy in detail. Dean had testified that he met with Herbert W. Kalmbach, President Nixon's personal attorney, in the coffee shop of the Mayflower Hotel to discuss cover-up money. Gurney had Dean reiterate the details of the event: It was June 29, in the Mayflower Hotel, Kalmbach was staying at the hotel, and they had later met in Kalmbach's room. Having led Dean through his earlier testimony, Gurney lowered the boom. The committee had subpoenaed the hotel records. It turned out that Kalmbach had not been registered at the Mayflower. He was staying in the Statler Hilton.

Gurney made much of Dean's error in memory. He forced Dean to admit that, despite being a 10-year Washington resident, he had confused the two hotels. Commented the Senator: "Well, I must say I am reminded of your colloquy with the chairman yesterday, Mr. Dean, when you said what an excellent memory you had right from school days" (Staff of *The New York Times,* 1973, p. 358). In his memoirs Dean (1977, p. 328) recalled the significance of his minor error: "I knew that Gurney might demolish my entire testimony because I had made one careless error." However, at this point Dean's attorney handed him a slip of paper. Dean read it and then announced to the committee: "I might go back over one point. The name of the coffee shop at the Statler Hilton is the Mayflower" (Staff of *The New York Times,* 1973, p. 358). This fact seemed to make plausible how Dean had forgotten which hotel had served as the meeting place. He had met Kalmbach in the Mayflower *coffee shop.* The reader may object that, after all, it didn't make much difference which hotel the meeting took place in. However, as Dean noted in his book, if his memory had been proven unreliable, his whole testimony might have been impeached.

Three final lines of questioning were pursued relative to Dean's reliability as a witness. Seeking to explore his motivations for testifying, the senators asked Dean about his efforts to win immunity from prosecution and his pleading the Fifth Amendment before a grand jury. Such actions could be taken as evidence that Dean was both a biased and an eager witness—that he testified only to save himself from prosecution. Such a question is usually asked when one member of a conspiracy testifies against another. A third line of questioning related to the witness's motivation was raised by Senator Inouye. Reading from a statement prepared by J. Fred Buzhardt (Dean's own successor as counsel to the President), Inouye asked whether Dean had initiated the cover-up by himself in order to mask his own involvement in the burglary of the Democratic national headquarters. Dean challenged many of the details of the Buzhardt theory, emphasizing that he was not the main cover-up leader and that he worked under Haldeman and Ehrlichman.

One final test of Dean's credibility needs to be mentioned. In his opening statement, Dean alluded to the possibility that President Nixon had tape-recorded one or more of the Nixon-Dean conversations. Late in the Watergate hearings, the committee learned from Alexander P. Butterfield, former presidential appointments secretary, that Mr. Nixon had installed an elaborate recording system in the Oval Office. Majority (Democratic) committee counsel Samuel Dash informed Dean of this fact and watched for his reactions. Dean recalls that he expressed joy at the thought that tape recordings could corroborate his story. This meant, said Dean, that "my ass is not hanging out there all alone" (Dean, 1977, p. 336). Apparently, Dash had surprised Dean with the information in order to test him. If Dean had indicated that he feared revealing the contents of the tapes, then this would have weakened his credibility. Dean's apparent eagerness to get the tapes was a point in his favor.[9]

[9]I should note in passing that there were other facets to Dean's credibility that I do not have space to consider here. These include (1) Dean's efforts to practice his testimony so as to strike the right image, (2) White House and Senate Republican efforts to discredit Dean by leaking unfavorable (and often untrue) information about him, and (3) Judge John J. Sirica's decision to impose a harsh sentence on Dean—possibly to increase his credibility as a government witness in the trials of Haldeman and Ehrlichman.

I noted earlier that John Dean's testimony illustrates the important difference between primary- and secondary-source material. This difference was especially significant via-à-vis the portions of Dean's testimony that implicated President Nixon. At several points in his remarks, Dean was able to report his conversations with President Nixon. Reports of such personal experiences amount to primary-source information: They are firsthand reports. Consider this exchange between Dash and Dean (Staff of *The New York Times,* 1973, p. 300):

> *Q.:* According to your own statement, in fact, you learned first-hand, did you not, that the President did know about the cover-up when you met with him on Sept. 15, 1972, the day the indictments came down cutting off at the involvement of Liddy. Is that so?
> *A.:* That is correct.

Here Dean testifies from his own personal experience. Notice how much stronger the effect is than when he must rely on secondary information. Dean was able to directly link the President to the cover-up only as early as September 15, 1972.[10] His belief that Nixon knew of the cover-up between June 17 (the day in which the Watergate burglars were arrested) and September 15 was only an inference: "Now, going back to the June 17 time, I believe I have testified to countless occasions in which I reported information to Mr. Haldeman and Mr. Ehrlichman . . . and given the normal reporting channels I worked through it was my assumption, without questioning, that this was going in to the President" (Staff of *The New York Times,* 1973, p. 354).

In the first case Dean was able to testify that he "heard" the President make a statement. In the latter instance Dean only assumed that the President had knowledge. This, then, is the difference between primary- and secondary-source material. In the first case, Dean relied on his own senses. In the latter, he depended on the implied statement of Haldeman (i.e., Haldeman did not deny informing the President, so Dean thought that he must have done so). When one relies on the statements of another, one possesses only a secondary source of information. Because primary and secondary sources are significantly different, there are separate tests for them. Dean's reports of personal conversations would be tested in the same manner as the U.F.O. reports: his proximity to the event, his mental and physical condition, etc. In probing Dean's secondary testimony, we would look to see whether he mentioned his source, whether he relied on primary or secondary sources, and whether he quoted his sources accurately.

These three cases of testimony by U.F.O. witnesses, psychiatrists, and John Dean conclude what I have to say about authoritative proof. Data from witnesses is a common form of proof. It is useful in establishing single facts, and it is necessary because we cannot take the time to personally verify every single thing we know. In short, we need to depend on others. Although testimony is necessary, we have good cause to scrutinize it: People are occasionally mistaken

[10]President Nixon denied any knowledge of the cover-up before March 21, 1973. See Nixon statement of August 15, 1973, in Staff of *The New York Times,* 1973, p. 712.

or untruthful. Hence, I have identified certain tests to which testimony may be subjected: Did the witness actually make the statement? Does the testimony make sense? And does the testimony establish the generalization? We should accept a witness's statements only if they meet these criteria.

ARE FACTS REALLY FACTUAL?

This chapter has dealt with factual arguments. Yet in surveying example, statistical, and testimonial argument, it seems apparent that facts are elusive things. Let me conclude this chapter, therefore, by emphasizing the two basic principles for testing facts. First, factual arguments are the only ones that may—even potentially—be tested by the correspondence principle. When dealing with an example, we may go back and examine each detail in the case. We may ascertain when, where, how, and by whom an act was done. Similarly, we may assess whether numbers accurately present reality. In the case of descriptive statistics, we may verify the counts. In the case of inferential statistics, we may examine the results actually obtained from a real sample. Finally, when an advocate cites the remarks of a witness, we may check to see whether the witness is accurately quoted in context. Because examples, statistics, and testimony may be verified and described to the satisfaction of potentially everyone, they are facts.

However, as this chapter has amply demonstrated, there is a second aspect to factual agreement. Almost invariably, when an advocate describes something, he does so for the purpose of establishing a wider generalization. The relationship between an example (or a statistic or a testimony) to a general conclusion cannot be verified by correspondence. The act of relating a fact to a generalization is an act of judgment. Hence, there is a second, a judgmental, aspect to facts. When a fact is used to support a generalization, it loses part of its objectivity. Accordingly, many of the tests presented in this chapter are designed to assess whether a descriptive argument is able to establish an interpretive or evaluative conclusion.

In answering the question posed above, one must reply that facts are factual—and then again they are not. Facts do describe (point to) reality, but they are also intimately connected to the subjective process by which advocates construct an interpretive or evaluative reality.

APPLICATIONS

This applications section will give you an opportunity to collect samples of descriptive argument and to test these samples via the validity standard.

Exercise 4-1: Identifying Descriptive Claims

As I observed at the outset of this chapter, samples of arguments may be found in periodicals, newspapers, and advertisments, as well as in other print, electronic, and conversational media. The best way to begin is to collect clippings of examples, statistics, and testimony. Over a period of time, as you collect representatives of each descriptive type, be sure to write down the source of each: author, place, date, and page number. (Your instructor may also prefer you to make up your own samples of examples, statistics, and testimony.) As you collect the samples, you may find it necessary or helpful to edit some of them. For instance, if your clipping is long and complicated, it may be useful to write out the argument as a single statement. If your argument is an extended one, it may help to outline major aspects of it. Be sure to look for information about the role of the argument in a particular area of dispute. You might make some notes about this. Your instructor may wish you to bring some of these sample arguments to class for discussion.

Exercise 4-2: Looking at Facts

As I noted above, a descriptive argument usually contains elements of interpretation and evaluation. This is because most descriptions are presented as support for a generalization. This exercise will give you the opportunity to assess descriptions as to their factualness.

I   Take one or more of the descriptions that you collected in exercise 4-1.
II Test the factualness of the description(s) by using the following questions (write out a brief answer to each question):
   A   To what extent may the argument be independently verified? That is, could you, or others, go out and check up on the details contained in the argument?
   B   To what extent is the argument presented in objective, report-oriented language? To what extent is loaded language used in presenting the description?
   C   To what extent could all reasonable persons be brought to accept the descriptive argument?
III State in a sentence an overall judgment about the relative factualness of the description. Is it highly factual? Somewhat factual? Only slightly factual? If you classify the argument as only "slightly factual," did you err in classifying it as a description? Might the argument be more of an interpretation or evaluation? If so, how would you classify the argument now?

Exercise 4-3: Testing the Validity of Examples

The following directions pertain to testing the validity of examples. The tests include assessing the correspondence of the example to reality and assessing whether the example proves a generalization.

I   Use one or more of the examples that you collected in exercise 4-1.
II Apply the correspondence test to the example.
   A   Identify the major details cited in the example. That is, what is alleged to have happened?
   B   Seek to verify whether the events happened as described. Attempt to find sources that corroborate or invalidate the description.

C   Remember that highly loaded language is more difficult to verify than precise, neutral descriptions.

D   State a judgment as to whether the example identifies reality in an adequate or inadequate manner.

III   If the example is used to prove a generalization (conclusion), test the relationship of the example to the conclusion.

A   Judge the extent to which the example is relevant to the generalization.

B   If more than one example is provided to support the generalization, make a judgment as to whether the different examples really fit together. That is, do they all involve the same elements?

C   Look for additional favorable examples. Look also for counterexamples that are unfavorable to the generalization. Summarize the favorable and unfavorable examples and compare them. Determine which examples predominate.

D   Compare the relevant pro and con evidence to the qualifier. Does the evidence (favorable plus unfavorable examples) justify the level of certainty claimed for the generalization? Following the format described in chapter 3 for estimating validity (exercise 3-9), judge the validity of the generalization.

Exercise 4-4: Testing the Validity of Statistics

The following directions explain how the seven tests of statistical argument may be applied. It is possible that not all of the tests apply to your particular argument. However, apply as many of the tests as you can.

I   Use one or more of the statistical arguments that you collected in exercise 4-1.

II   Apply the seven tests of statistical argument.

A   Make a judgment about the reliability of the source of the statistics. To what extent is the source objective? If the source is biased—i.e., it has some motive to make the statistics prove a particular point—does the bias potentially invalidate the statistics? Or does the source appear to cite accurate statistics, despite the bias?

B   Make a judgment about whether the statistics are up-to-date. When were they gathered? If the statistics were obtained long ago, are they still valid? Would any later developments invalidate them?

C   Apply the tests relating to the method by which the statistics were gathered.

1   Are the counting procedures biased or fair? Recall that a biased counting procedure is one that almost forces the numbers into a certain mold. As I noted earlier, sources of bias in survey gathering include poorly worded questions or questions that do not give a total picture (e.g., measuring crime only by reported crimes).

2   Do the statistics involve adequately and consistently defined standard units of measure? Look to determine how reasonable a

statistical unit is. When statistical comparisons are used, make sure that the units are comparable.

  3 Are the statistics based on valid counting assumptions? Look for assumptions that are made in the counting procedure. Evaluate the soundness of these assumptions.

D If your sample argument is based on a measure of central tendency, check to be sure that the measure (mean, median, mode) is clearly specified.

E If your statistical argument is based on inferential statistics, evaluate the method of inference.

  1 Is the sampling procedure adequate?

  a Is the sample large enough? Is the sample at least one-tenth the size of the population (up to a maximum of five hundred in the sample)?

  b Is the sample representative of the larger population? Here you will look for characteristics that the sample and the population do not share—e.g., social status, occupation, attitudes, etc. Remember that a random sample is most often likely to be representative.

  2 Is the method of statistical projection adequate? Here the critic asks the question: Is it reasonable to apply results obtained from a sample to an entire population? Again, we look to see whether the sample represents the population. Remember that a confidence level may be presented regarding the projection.

F Having tested the statistics themselves, the next step is to decide whether the conclusion drawn from the statistics is a reasonable one. (This test is very much like deciding whether an example proves a generalization.)

  1 Basically, we look to see if all possible meanings of the numbers have been considered. The critic looks for alternative explanations that might account for the numerical results.

  2 If you identify some reasonable alternative explanations, you must compare them. Does the explanation favored by the arguer outweigh any possible counterexplanations? Do the two explanations appear equally plausible in accounting for the statistical results, or does the alternative interpretation of the statistics appear the more reasonable one?

  3 Having compared the arguer's interpretation of the statistics to alternative explanations, the critic must now compare the two explanations to the qualifier. Does the explanation maintained by the advocate outweigh the alternative explanations so as to justify the level of confidence attached to the arguer's interpretation? Following the format for estimating validity described in chapter 3 (exercise 3-9), make an overall validity judgment.

G Make a judgment as to whether the statistics are properly explained when presented. If the arguer does not explain the type of statistics involved (descriptive or inferential), the method of counting, etc., then the critic has a basis for reducing the validity of the statistics. Also, if the statistics are presented without a clear explanation, this reduces the validity of any generalization drawn from the numbers.

Exercise 4-5: Testing the Validity of Testimony

Testimonial argument involves many separate validity tests. This is because when we assess testimony we evaluate many separate things. First, we endeavor to decide whether the advocate has quoted the witness properly (a correspondence test). Second, we look to see whether the witness's statement makes sense. Here we look at (1) the person of the witness, (2) the situation in which the witness gained the information (with separate tests for primary- and secondary-source materials), and (3) the quotation itself, regardless of who said it and the environment. Third, and finally, if testimony is offered to support a generalization, we look to see whether the witness's statement establishes the generalization.

Naturally, every test will not apply to every quotation. In evaluating the worth of authoritative proof, the critic applies only those tests that are relevant to the particular argument being evaluated.

I   As before, begin by selecting an argument that you have gathered as part of exercise 4-1.
II Apply the standards for evaluating testimony.
   A   Did the witness actually make the statement as reported by the advocate?
      1   Does the advocate quote accurately?
      2   Does the advocate report the witness correctly in context?
   B   Does the witness's testimony make sense?
      1   Is the witness a believable person?
         a   Is the source a person of good character? Does the authority have a reputation for past reliability and honesty?
         b   Is the source competent to make the statement? Is the source mentally or physically competent? Does she or he possess expertise if expertise is required?
         c   Is the source unbiased? Does the authority have a motive to tell the truth, to deceive, to distort?
         d   Is the source a willing or a reluctant witness?
      2   Did the witness have a good opportunity to obtain the information in the particular situation?
         a   Is the testimony a good primary source?
           (1)   Did the witness have access to the event?
           (2)   Was the witness mentally and physically able to make the observation in the particular time or place?
           (3)   How soon after the event did the witness make a report of his observation?
           (4)   Was the testimony made in a time of crisis?
           (5)   What was the attitude of the witness to those who received the report?
           (6)   Was the testimony arranged or spontaneous?

          (7) Are there any good alternative explanations to account for the observations made by the witness?

       b Is the testimony a good secondary source?

          (1) Does the witness indicate from where the information was obtained–i.e., his own sources?

          (2) Does the witness cite primary or secondary accounts?

          (3) Does the witness quote his sources accurately and in context?

    3 Does the testimony make sense in itself—regardless of who said it and its situational origins?

       a Is the testimony recent or old?

       b Is the witness careful to qualify, properly, his remarks?

       c Is the testimony internally consistent?

       d Does the testimony raise issues of fact, definition, or value?

       e If the witness is testifying to the occurrence of an event, is the event consistent with or contrary to general human experience?

  C If the testimony is used to support a generalization, does it actually establish the generalization?

    1 How does the testimony in question relate to the statements of other witnesses?

       a Is the testimony in question relevant to the generalization?

       b Is the testimony in question typical or atypical?

       c If more than one witness is cited to prove a conclusion, do the two (or more) testimonies fit well together?

    2 How does the testimony in question (together with possible counterstatements) compare to the qualifier? Again, in making this comparison, see exercise 3-9.

III Notice that the last set of tests—those relating to whether a testimony proves a generalization—are based on the definition of rhetorical validity. As in the case of the example and statistics, review the format for establishing validity presented in chapter 3 (exercise 3-9).

Exercise 4-6: Applying Other Standards to Descriptive Arguments

Your instructor may want you to test the effectiveness, truth, or ethics of a descriptive argument. If so, follow the directions for exercise 3-6, 3-7, and 3-8.

Chapter 5

Interpretations: Arguments That Draw Issues of Definition

In chapter 4 we considered arguments that tended to be phrased in descriptive language. The use of example, the summary of data via statistics, and the citation of third parties all tend to raise an initial issue of fact: Did such-and-such occur? Have X number of instances taken place? Did so-and-so make such a statement? It is true that even descriptive arguments are not entirely objective, for the very act of selecting some facts while excluding others can imply an issue of definition: Do the selected facts fairly represent the thing or occurrence? Yet the descriptive use of language, with its emphasis on the report function, can be distinguished from the interpretive. Whereas description seeks to identify what happened—the facts—interpretive statements relate facts and give them meaning. The argument of interpretation both identifies a fact and places that fact in an appropriate category. My first endeavor in this chapter will be to emphasize the difference between description and interpretation. In the remainder of the chapter, I will identify certain recurring types of interpretation that may be seen in disputes on all subjects. (Remember, however, that the types of interpretation share many common attributes.) Throughout the chapter I will identify examples of valid and less valid interpretations.[1] The final section will treat certain forms of interpretation that are generally classed as invalid.

[1] If necessary, the reader should review the definition of "rhetorical validity" presented in chapter 3.

DESCRIPTIONS AND INTERPRETATIONS

Every four years, political attention is focused on the New Hampshire primary, the first test run for aspirants to national office. Each quadrennium the votes are totaled (issues of fact) and at the same time political commentators seek to explain what the numbers really meant (raising issues of interpretation). While almost everyone is in agreement as to the vote totals themselves, vast differences may be seen in the way in which the figures are interpreted. In the 1968 New Hampshire contest, Senator Eugene McCarthy of Minnesota received 42 percent of the Democratic party primary vote and yet was judged to have "defeated" President Lyndon Johnson, who received 49 percent of the vote (see this interpretation in White, 1970, pp. 109–11). On the other hand, in 1976 President Gerald Ford "won" the Republican primary with 51 percent of the vote, compared to 49 percent for Ronald Reagan. Thus, in one case an incumbent President who maintained a lead of seven percentage points in the vote was a "loser," whereas another incumbent President "won" the primary with only a two-percentage-point lead in the totals. If McCarthy won with 42 percent, why did Reagan lose with 49 percent? If McCarthy's 42 percent gave him "momentum," why did Reagan's 49 percent mean that "his candidacy might fall apart if he could not beat Ford next week in Florida" (*Newsweek,* March 8, 1976, p. 20)? To be sure, candidate Reagan raised these same objections, arguing that his was a moral victory (i.e., doing so well against an incumbent President) and that he had done far better than others such as McCarthy who had been rated as victors.

The seemingly arbitrary nature of vote interpreting is also reflected in the 1972 New Hampshire Democratic primary, in which Senator Edmund Muskie's plurality of 46 percent to Senator George McGovern's 37 percent was reported as being a "setback" for Muskie. The reasons for this interpretation are revealed in Timothy Crouse's book on the 1972 contest (1974, pp. 46–47):

> On January 9, 1972, David Broder, the most influential political writer in Washington, wrote from Manchester, New Hampshire: "As the acknowledged front runner and a resident of the neighboring state, Muskie will have to win the support of at least half the New Hampshire Democrats in order to claim a victory. . . ."
>
> Of course, Muskie made no such predictions for himself. All he wanted to do was win, he said, and with all the time he had to spend shuttling back and forth between Florida and New Hampshire, he'd consider himself *lucky* to get fifty percent. Nobody listened to him. And when the returns came in on the night of March 7, leaving Muskie with only 46 percent of the vote, the press started muttering about a Muskie set back.

This quotation provides clues to explain the apparent contradiction between the factual (Muskie got 46 percent of the vote to McGovern's 37 percent) versus the interpretive results (Muskie suffered a "setback") of the 1972 Democratic contest in New Hampshire. For a variety of reasons, Muskie was supposed to do better. His showing, being less than that expected, was viewed as a setback.

Interpretations pertaining to both McCarthy (in 1968) and Reagan (in 1976) involve a similar relationship between expectation and eventuality. McCarthy's 42 percent was much higher than originally predicted, and Reagan's 49 percent was less than expected. Also, because President Ford was appointed rather than elected to office, his failure to overwhelm his challenger was less of a surprise than in the case of LBJ who won the Presidency with a landslide vote in 1964. Thus, interpretations of the vote totals are not entirely based on the totals themselves. The interpretive analysis of the vote puts the totals in perspective— it gives them meaning by relating them to other facts and opinions.

The factual versus definitional issues raised by the New Hampshire primary results can be stated as follows:

Factual issue   What are the vote totals for the various primary candidates?

Definitional issues   (1) Which candidates "won" the primary? (2) Which candidates "did better/worse than expected?" (3) Which candidates "should have done better/worse?" (4) Which candidates "will be helped/hurt by the results?"

Statements that answer the factual issue are descriptions, and those that are responsive to the definitional issues are interpretations. Descriptions identify reality, interpretations construct reality.

Consider another scenario in which differing interpretations were applied to the same set of facts. In 1965 it was agreed by all observers that around 1 million South Vietnamese rural dwellers had moved from the countryside (largely controlled by Communist-led rebels) to urban areas controlled by the Saigon government (which was supported by the United States). Bernard Fall (1967, pp. 350–351), an expert on Vietnamese history, identifies two differing and opposing interpretations that were made of this single fact:

> How differently these effects of the war can be viewed is clearly evidenced by the interpretation of the source of the 1 million South Vietnamese "refugees.". . .
>
> According to Vice-President Hubert H. Humphrey, "nearly a million peasants have fled the regions controlled by the Viet-Cong. . . . All, however, had the choice of whether to come out or withdraw deeper into Viet-Cong territory—and nearly all chose to come out."
>
> That optimistic view is certainly not shared by most observers on the ground. In fact, Roger Hilsman—who, in his former position of Assistant Secretary of State for Far Eastern Affairs, was excellently placed to know the facts—testified in September, 1965, before the Senate Subcommittee on Refugees that, ". . . we must honestly face the fact that it was not Viet Cong terrorism that drove the refugees from their ancestral homes to the cities and towns—though Viet Cong terrorism, impressment of the men, and taxation has increased. It was American and Vietnamese bombing and shelling. We would like to think that the refugees came to the American and Vietnamese held towns rather than deeper into Viet Cong territory because they like us better than the Viet Cong, and there is some grain of fact that they do. But, again being realistic, the greater motive was probably that the only security from bombardment lay in the towns held by the Government, since the Viet Cong have no airpower."

Notice that these two interpretations of the refugee situation have distinctly different meanings. If the refugees fled Viet Cong terrorism, then they were "voting with their feet" in favor of the United States–supported Saigon government. If, on the other hand, they fled from American bombing, then their presence in the cities was an argument against the American war policy. Obviously, therefore, it was in the interest of the United States government to interpret the refugees as anticommunist, just as it was to the advantage of war opponents to picture the flight to the cities as evidence of American brutality in conducting the war. Each of the opposing "realities" had implications for United States policy.

As a final illustration of my point that interpretations draw distinctly different issues than do descriptions, consider this excerpt from "Dear Abby." See if you can differentiate fact from definition (*Odessa American,* May 23, 1975, p. 9A):

> Dear Abby: While standing in the checkout line in a high grade grocery store, I saw the woman directly ahead of me frantically rummaging around in her purse, looking embarrassed. It seems her groceries had already been checked, and she was a dollar short.
>
> I felt sorry for her, so I handed her a dollar. She was very grateful, and insisted on writing my name and address on a loose piece of paper. She stuck it in her purse and said, "I promise I'll mail you the dollar tomorrow."
>
> Well, that was three weeks ago, and I still haven't heard from her!
>
> Abby, I think I'm a fairly good judge of character, and I just didn't peg her as the kind who would beat me out of a dollar.
>
> The small amount of money isn't important, but what it did to my faith in people is.
>
> I'd like your opinion.—[signed] Shy One Buck
>
>
> Dear Shy: Don't assume that she deliberately beat you out of a buck. There are other possibilities:
>
> 1 She may have misaddressed the envelope, and the dollar went astray.
> 2 She may have lost the paper with your name and address on it.
> 3 The incident could have slipped her mind, and the piece of paper may not surface for years.
>
> You bought a dollar's worth of good feeling, so don't feel cheated.

"Shy One Buck" describes the facts of the episode and ventures the opinion that the woman was "the kind who would beat me out of a dollar." Using the same factual base, Abby supplies three different interpretations of it, each of which has an implication as to the "kind of person" the woman in question was. Interpretations therefore place facts in categories, thereby creating definitional meanings.

In the next few pages, I will identify and cite examples of several types of interpretation. Each type represents an identifiable pattern of interpretive thinking, although there is overlap among the various types. Beginning with comparisons, I will present a total of eight major types of interpretation, some of which have recognizable subtypes. Knowledge of the kinds of interpretive language should render you better able to encode and decode the language of definition.

COMPARISONS

Much may be learned from identifying a fact; but often more may be learned by comparing that fact to other aspects of reality. We are all familiar with the use of comparisons, or metaphors, as a means of interpreting the way things are. A successful baseball hitter may be called, "another Babe Ruth," a good pianist may be compared to Van Cliburn, a popular rock group may be described as "the most exciting group since the Beatles." Comparative language allows us to go beyond the identification of information or example—as in the statement "Chicago is a rock group"—by enabling us to relate two phenomena on the basis of certain criteria. For instance: "Chicago is like/unlike the Beatles in the following ways. . . ." Comparative language, then, deals with the similarity and dissimilarity of things. Because "no man is an island" and almost nothing exists in complete isolation, it is reasonable to assume that most persons, places, and things may be compared to other objects.

Comparative arguments enable us to learn about unfamiliar objects by relating them to familiar ones. It is easy to find illustrations of this. Thus, an Ohioan could learn much about Oregon if he were told, "The climate in Oregon is similar to what you have in Ohio." The organist could explain to the pianist, "The organ is the same as the piano, except that. . . ." Comparative argumentation also enables us to refine or clarify our understanding of something by relating the thing to several objects. If you were to inquire about a course taught by Dr. Smith, you might be told, "She's a better lecturer than Professor Jones, her tests are as hard as Mr. Clark's, but she's an easier grader than anyone else in the department."

Scholars have observed the importance of the comparative nature of our speech (Gorrell and Laird, 1967, pp. 376–377): "Metaphor, or comparison in language is more than embellishment; it is part of language itself. We use metaphors constantly in conversation (*He ran like a deer; he is a little devil*). Words develop through metaphors; we speak of the *hands* of the clock, the *foot* of the bed, the *head* of the household, the *legs* of a chair." Gorrell and Laird's point should be taken to heart. Comparison, or metaphor, is often thought of as being mere ornament, such as in the expression "as sweet as sugar." However, metaphor is restricted neither to trite sayings (such as the one mentioned) nor to poetic license, as in "Life is just a bowl of cherries." Comparison has a strong argumentative role in view of its ability to define the nature of reality.

Consider, for example, how the author of this quotation (Oscar Cooley, "Economic Views," *Odessa American,* September 27, 1973, p. 10C) uses comparison to argue against the use of strikes by labor unions: "Union leaders call the strike 'peaceful.' It is in the sense that a hijacking, or a kidnapping, is peaceful. If everyone obeys the orders of the kidnapper or the hijacker, he is only too happy to keep the peace." Cooley argues against the strike by characterizing what seems to him its brutal and evil nature. If a strike is like a hijacking or a kidnapping, shouldn't it be prohibited or at least despised? Of course, another arguer might compare a strike to a "revolution for freedom" of the "little people" against the "captains of industry." Comparing a strike to a revolution against tyranny conjures up quite a different world view than the characterization of a strike as a hijacking or kidnapping. If the author of a claim is able to convince us that a strike may be validly compared to a hijacking (or to a "good" revolution), then we are motivated to behave toward the event or thing as we would toward the event or thing to which it is compared. Because comparisons act to construct reality, they are highly argumentative. There is a close relationship between the data statement that a strike is like a hijacking and the claim that strikes should be abhorred or abolished.

Consider the following instance of comparative reasoning, which defines a particular interpretation of reality (James J. Kilpatrick, "A Conservative View," *Odessa American,* October 23, 1973, p. 4A):

> WASHINGTON—It must have been quite a moment for Dr. Frankenstein when his monster got off the table and walked. Doubtless the young scientist looked upon his creation with pride, gratification, and hope. All of his troubles came later.
>
> The United States Congress may well have put itself in the same fix with the Consumer Product Safety Commission. The CPSC got up and walked last May; and it may turn out to be the dandiest little monster ever devised.

Kilpatrick's comparison of the Consumer Product Safety Commission to Frankenstein's monster is a good example of the use of metaphor as the data base for an argumentative claim. The C.P.S.C. was established in response to disclosures about toys that maimed children and pajamas that exploded into flames when touched by fire. Thus, the commission seemed to have everything going for it—who could argue against protecting children from dangerous toys? Kilpatrick recognizes the apparent desirability of the C.P.S.C. but registers his complaints about it by causing us to recall Dr. Frankenstein's monster, which, like the C.P.S.C., seemed like a good idea yet destroyed its creator. Kilpatrick admits later in his opinion column that he has no examples of C.P.S.C. abuses. Yet via his comparison he is able to argue against the commission by citing certain possibilities concerning it and putting his arguments in a certain perspective. The specific facts in his case against the C.P.S.C.—e.g., his attack on its "comprehensive list of consumer product categories which appear to pose the greatest threat of injury to the American public"—would be weak and isolated were it not for the comparative interpretation.

The argumentative nature of comparison is perhaps best illustrated in cases in which distinctly different comparisons are made about the same object. The different-comparison-of-the-same-thing situation is reflected in the following Associated Press release, which quoted Henry Kissinger, then Secretary of State, on the matter of stationing technicians from the United States in the Middle East to keep the peace between Egypt and Israel. The Associated Press reported (*Odessa American,* September 5, 1975, p. 1A): "Asked about the attitude of Congress, Kissinger said he hopes Congress and the public will understand that the role of the U.S. technicians 'is not comparable to Vietnam. Rather it is comparable to the peacekeeping activities Finland and the other nations on the U.N. force have carried out.'" Kissinger's comment was responsive to the issue of definition pertaining to the entry of American personnel into the troubled Sinai Penninsula: Would the presence of the technicians cause the United States to become involved in another Vietnam-type war, or were the technicians more comparable to routine United Nations peacekeeping forces? The differing implications suggested by the two comparisons were crucial to Kissinger's plan concerning the technicians. If the plan were comparable to "another Vietnam," then it would be less likely to receive Congressional approval than if the plan were comparable to past efforts that resulted in neither war nor loss of life for the peacekeepers.

In scrutinizing the rhetorical validity of comparisons, we must judge whether two or more events (or things) are really equivalent. History suggests that the entry of the United States into the Vietnam war was brought about by a long series of diplomatic and military commitments to preserve an anticommunist government in Saigon. Thus, it would appear that the stationing of American technicians more closely approximates previous United Nations peacekeeping efforts than it does the early stages of United States involvement in Vietnam. The technicians were stationed so as to separate the two sides, not to support one side against the other. For this reason, the Kissinger interpretation appears to be valid. The "another Vietnam" view is probably invalid.

Analogy

The analogy is a particular type of comparison in which four terms are compared, as in the equation "A is to B as C is to D." (See Perelman and Olbrechts-Tyteca, 1969, p. 372.) In arguing for a reformulation of the United States foreign aid program, J. W. Fulbright, then a senator from Arkansas, stated in an Associated Press release (*Odessa American,* February 8, 1974, p. 5A) that the use of foreign aid "has been like trying to treat cancer with morphine; it has served as a narcotic but not a cure." This argument represents the type of comparison called analogy, because it establishes a relationship among four terms: morphine (the pain killer) is to cancer (a disease) as foreign aid is to curing poverty. In other words, foreign aid dulls the pain of poverty in less-developed countries but does not really eliminate (cure) the poverty. An analogy may be diagrammed by means of two ratios (the A:B ratio and the C:D ratio) in which the four terms reside:

A *is to* B (ratio 1) *as* C *is to* D (ratio 2)

or, as in the specific example cited:

Morphine *is to* cancer *as* foreign aid *is to* poverty in less-developed countries

In the ratios just mentioned, the first terms are equivalent to each other and the second ones are also equivalent. Further, in the ratios above, the relation of A to B is said to be like the relationship of C to D.

Many scholars of language have argued that the analogy is neither a strong nor a reliable form of proof. Thus, Brandt (1970, p. 130) asserts that "the analogy is perhaps indispensable to argumentation . . . but it is hard to see how it might ever be a decisive argument and it can be quite misleading." By contrast, Wilcox (1973, pp. 4–7) has argued that the analogy fulfills several critical argumentative functions: (1) to organize and clarify thought by relating terms, (2) to enable us to learn new information by comparing relationships of terms, and (3) to enable us to predict something about one of the ratios by comparing it to the other ratio. I am inclined to accept Wilcox's view that analogy enables arguers to organize, learn, and predict.

Further support for the idea that the analogy is a powerful source of proof comes from the fact that the Johnson administration relied heavily on analogy to justify its Vietnam policy during the period from 1964 to 1967. Relying on a parallel drawn to pre–World War II Europe, the administration reasoned that withdrawal from Vietnam would lead to a wider world conflict, just as appeasement in 1938 of Germany's Führer Adolph Hitler set the stage for World War II. This administration claim came to be known as the Munich analogy, because it was at Munich, Germany, that the leaders of France and Britain gave in to Hitler's demands for a significant portion of Czechoslovakian territory. This gain strengthened Hitler for his later attacks on Poland (in 1939) and on France (in 1940).

Typical of the administration's use of the Munich analogy is this excerpt from a speech by President Lyndon Johnson (*Public Papers of the Presidents of the United States; Lyndon B. Johnson, 1965,* Vol. II, p. 794): "Nor would surrender in Viet-Nam bring peace, because we learned from Hitler at Munich that success only feeds the appetite of aggression. The battle would be renewed in one country and then another country, bringing with it perhaps even larger and crueler conflict, as we have learned from the lessons of history." The administration's analogy may be diagramed as follows:

Munich agreement *was to* World War II *as* withdrawal from Vietnam *would be to* World War III

This example reveals the predictive function of the analogy. Based on the relationship between the Munich agreement and World War II, the claim was advanced that withdrawal from Vietnam would possibly set in motion a third world war. Although the validity of the Munich analogy was and is dubious (as I will shortly demonstrate), it seems clear that the analogy was perceived by the administration as being potentially persuasive. The administration used the argument repeatedly in justifying the expenditure of thousands of lives and billions of dollars in a far-off land.

The validity of an analogy depends upon the equivalence of the four terms and the relationship between and among those terms. In looking at the four terms of the Munich analogy, it appears that there are two key issues of validity: (1) Is the Munich agreement equivalent to plans to withdraw from Vietnam? and (2) Is the relationship between the Munich agreement and World War II equivalent to the predicted relationship between withdrawal from Vietnam and World War III?

Howard Zinn (1967, pp. 86–87) is highly critical of the Munich analogy, writing that "one touches the Munich analogy and it falls apart." Zinn argues that there were "important differences" between the Munich situation of 1938 and that of Vietnam in 1967. Zinn wrote that whereas an outside force (Hitler's Germany) was the main force operating against the Czechs, the main opposition to the government of South Vietnam came from rebels in the south. Further, whereas the Czechoslovakian government was "strong, effective, prosperous, democratic," Saigon was "a hollow shell of a government, unstable, unpopular, corrupt." Finally, it may be observed that the aims of the outside forces (Hitler in 1938; North Vietnam in 1967) differ in important respects: Hitler desired Czechoslovakia not for itself, but as a base for the conquest of Poland and other places; for the North Vietnamese, the conquest of the south (and its reunification to the north) was a goal unto itself. Because the terms and relationships of the Munich analogy are not exactly equivalent, this argument appears invalid. Too much certainty (an overstated qualifier) was ascribed to the analogy, given the amount of unfavorable evidence that opposed it.

Having read my description of comparisons and analogies, you may well have cause to ask what is the difference between a comparison and an analogy? It must be admitted that the distinction is not an easy one to make. However, as Perelman and Olbrechts-Tyteca (1969, p. 399) observe, an analogy involves a clearer distinction between two ratios and four terms. In their view, a comparison or general metaphor is "a condensed analogy, resulting from the fusion of an element from [one of the ratios] with an element from the [other]." Comparisons are, then, a looser or more abstract use of language than are analogies. The assertion "Withdrawal from Vietnam would be the Munich of World War III" is an example of how the precise relationship of terms in the analogy is blurred in the more abstract comparison.

Argument from Precedent

A second major subtype of the comparison is the use of precedent. In the argument of precedent, the agent asserts that in a previous case X was done; therefore, because this present case is similar to the past one, we should do X now also. The argument of precedent is most familiar in the legal setting. Lawyers cite rulings of law from previous cases, asserting that the same ruling should apply in a present situation. Consider this example of the use of precedent taken from prosecutor Vincent Bugliosi's account of the Charles Manson murder trial. Bugliosi relates that he encountered difficulty in persuading the presiding judge that certain details of Charles Manson's philosophy were relevant testimony. Bugliosi writes (1975, pp. 476–477):

> I noted [to Judge Older]: "The prosecution is alleging Mr. Manson *ordered* these murders. It was his philosophy *that led up to* these murders. The motive for these murders was *to ignite Helter Skelter* [a war of blacks versus whites]. I think it is so obviously admissible that I am at a loss for words." . . .
>
> I sweated through that noon hour. Unless I could establish Manson's domination of the other defendants, I wouldn't be able to convince the jury they had killed on his instructions. And if Older foreclosed me from bringing in Manson's beliefs about the black-white war . . . then we were in deep trouble.
>
> I returned to chambers armed with citations of authority as to both the admissibility and the relevance of the testimony.

Bugliosi used precedent as the basis for asserting the admissibility of evidence. If such testimony had been allowed in previous cases, he reasoned, why shouldn't it be accepted in the Manson trial? The argument of precedent is a type of comparison in which an aspect of a previous case is applied to a current situation. One should not assume, however, that precedent operates only in the law courts. Columns of advice to teenagers in newspapers and magazines occasionally contain letters in which the writer maintains the following argument of precedent: "My parents allowed my older sister to date when she was fourteen, but they still don't allow me to date, and I'm sixteen. Is this fair?" As in the case of the analogy, the validity of precedent-based arguments depends on the equivalence of the elements of one case to another.

MINIMIZATION-MAXIMIZATION

In defining "rhetoric," Weaver (in Johannesen, Strickland, and Eubanks, 1970, p. 217) wrote: "But here we must recur to the principle that rhetoric comprehensively considered is an art of emphasis." Weaver meant that in using language to persuade (which is a general definition of rhetoric), we identify and present those details that we wish to emphasize and either ignore or minimize information that is unfavorable to our case. Minimization and maximization are, then, basic to interpretation.

In *Newsweek* (February 24, 1975, p. 68) a typical instance is reported of the use of minimization and maximization. The article reported the debate over off-shore oil drilling. Oil industry spokespersons argued for allowing such drilling as a means of meeting the energy shortage. The industry advocates maximized the economic aspects of the situation and minimized the ecological ones:

> Industry officials at the hearings acknowledged that there were dangers, but they minimized them. In any case, they stressed, America's critical need for energy far overshadowed environmental considerations. . . . Executive vice president Charles

Di Bona of the American Petroleum Institute warned that "the jobs of people up and down the East Coast" would be jeopardized if oil and gas reserves under the Atlantic Ocean were not exploited.

The oil industry position was based on the maximization of data favorable to the question of off-shore drilling. The economy in general, and the workingman in particular, depended on the production, it was argued. The environmental questions were, in this view, secondary. One may identify in the literature at least three subtypes of interpretation via minimization-maximization.

Frequency

One may minimize and/or maximize a detail by asserting that it is typical or atypical. The assertion of frequency allows the agent to allege that something has or has not occurred frequently in the past. Thus, James J. Kilpatrick minimized, on the basis of frequency, when he argued against the extension of the Voting Rights Act of 1965 ("A Conservative View," *Odessa American,* March 14, 1975, p. 12A). This law was enacted primarily to increase the number of blacks registered to vote and extended Federal voting supervision to states on the basis of the percentage of the population registered to vote. Notice how Kilpatrick both acknowledges the examples raised by proponents of the extension and minimizes them at the same time:

> The U.S. Commission on Civil Rights in January released a long report urging that the act be extended for another ten years. In support of that conclusion, the report cited a hundred cases of what it took to be deliberate discrimination against black voters in recent years. But in view of the total number of blacks who freely register and vote, the incidents are unimportant. Some of the incidents are doubtless untrue, and petty discrimination and political manipulation surely are not unique to the South.

While the validity of Kilpatrick's minimization is open to debate—his assumption, for example, that no black citizens have suffered discrimination except those cited in the Civil Rights Commission report—the argumentative force of his assertions are quite favorable to his claim that the Voting Rights Act is unnecessary, despite proven instances of discrimination.

Size

When advocates maximize-minimize by means of size, they assert that the magnitude of something is great or small. Thus, the authors of a *Newsweek* article on "How Clean Is Business?" (September 1, 1975, pp. 50–51) cited examples of business corruption and maximized the importance (size) of these instances.

> Coming as they did after the discovery that American Airlines, Phillips Petroleum and a score of other big companies had contributed huge sums illegally to Richard

Nixon's re-election campaign, the newest revelations [of graft and bribery] have raised serious questions about the pervasiveness of business corruption and illegality. . . .

The answer to [the question of corruption is] important economically as well as ethically; if bribes and kickbacks are viewed as simply another cost of doing business, such costs are inevitably passed along in higher prices to the consumer. Such payoffs may well be minuscule, as businessmen argue, vis-à-vis the total volume of business conducted. But in an economy with a gross national product of nearly $1.5 trillion, graft amounting to as little as, say, 1 per cent of a deal's value can add up to billions of dollars.

This quotation is particularly interesting because its authors both refute a minimization of frequency (that few instances of illegality have occurred) and present their own maximization based on the size of the cost to consumers. This illustrates the role of interpretation in which opposing constructions of reality are presented.

Degree

Emphasis based on degree may be defined as minimizing or maximizing the extent to which something is true now or would be true in the future. As an example of minimization by degree, consider this excerpt concerning the White House's effort to play down Betty Ford's much publicized remarks on the hypothetical situation of her daughter's having an affair. As Paul Healy writes ("Capitol Stuff," *Odessa American,* August 29, 1975, p. 8A), "The White House staff . . . tried to shrug off Mrs. Ford's outburst of publicity, doubting that a first lady's frankness would change votes one way or the other. Privately, they were just as glad, though, that the controversy didn't come two weeks before the 1976 election." The staff in other words, minimized the alleged negative effect of Mrs. Ford's comments.

While I have identified several methods by which arguers maximize or minimize information, it is important to remember that all arguments emphasize some details and, at the same time, omit others. Further, it is true that the differences between minimization-maximization by means of frequency, size, and degree are not substantial. Yet I believe that it is useful to study the methods by which arguers explicitly seek to underscore favorable data and to deemphasize unfavorable evidence. Later in this chapter I will treat distortion by omission (the invalid use of minimization) and distortion by exaggeration (the invalid form of maximization).

CAUSAL ARGUMENT

In causal argument, an advocate attempts to demonstrate that one event brings about (causes) another or that one event is the result (effect) of another. We may argue from cause to effect by asserting that event A is causing or will cause B. We may also argue from effect to cause when we identify a circumstance and allege that it has resulted from another particular circumstance or circumstances. The fundamental question of causal argument may be put as follows: Under what conditions is it reasonable to assert that one event or object is caused by another?

In attempting to respond to this question, we may learn much from the experimental sciences. Experimental methodology has established principles for the analysis of causal relationships. The following discussion of causal principles is taken from Campbell and Stanley's (1966) description of experimental design. These authors use the symbol "X" to designate the exposure of a group of persons to an experimental "treatment." A treatment is some phenomenon that contains the presumed cause of an observable effect. Thus, if one were to study the effect of evidence in persuasion, the treatment might consist of a set of statements (evidence), and subsequently an observation would be made to determine whether the evidence caused attitude change in the listeners. Campbell and Stanley use the symbol "O" to designate the observations that are made about the persons who have been exposed to the treatment.

The most basic form of causal reasoning occurs when we observe (O) an event (X—the treatment) and infer that X was the cause of O.

$$X \rightarrow O$$

Consider an example. Suppose that I am at an airport at 5:00 P.M. on Tuesday and observe (O) a large crowd of people. Subsequently, I learn that the President of the United States was arriving at the same airport at 5:00. I might infer that the President's visit (X) was responsible for the large crowds that I observed (O). I have reached an elementary causal conclusion.

However, suppose that a friend disagrees with my causal analysis by objecting that there are always large crowds at an airport. This objection would tend to suggest that the large crowd was not caused by the President's arrival, but only represented the normal airport traffic. Yet, because I am an inquisitive individual, I place a telephone call to an airport official and learn that on Tuesday the 4:00 P.M. crowd (before the President's visit) was noticeably smaller than the 5:00 crowd (the one that was present during the President's arrival). The result of the new data, when added to my own original observation, may be diagrammed as follows:

4:00		5:00
O_1	X	O_2

Because the crowd at 4:00 was observed to be noticeably smaller (O_1) than the later 5:00 crowd (O_2), I again feel confident that the President's visit—the intervening variable (X)—caused the increase in the crowd that occurred between 4:00 and 5:00 P.M. The normal airport traffic would, in itself, be inadequate to explain the larger 5:00 crowd. However, my friend again objects:

"The fact that the 5:00 crowd was larger than the 4:00 crowd doesn't prove a thing. There are always more people at that airport during the 5:00 rush hour than at 4:00." Again, I am confronted with the need to refine my causal argument. One approach might be to return to the airport the next day for the purpose of making a 4:00 (O_3) and 5:00 (O_4) observation of normal airport traffic:

	4:00		5:00
Tuesday	O_1	X	O_2
Wednesday	O_3		O_4

Assume that I learn that Wednesday's 4:00 crowd (O_3) is the same as Wednesday's 5:00 crowd (O_4) and that both of these are identical to Tuesday's 4:00 crowd (O_1). Further, assume that I confirm that Tuesday's 5:00 crowd (O_2) is significantly larger than any of the other three observed crowds. On the basis of this new data, I again feel justified to infer that the President's visit (X) was the cause of the exceptionally large Tuesday crowd at 5:00 P.M.

The three causal designs that I have presented only scratch the surface of causality in experimental methodology. (In fact, Campbell and Stanley refer to these simple designs as "pre-experimental.") Detailed consideration of experimental principles of causality is beyond the scope of this present discussion. However, argumentation texts often present John Stuart Mill's canons of induction as yet another set of basic rules for causality. They are widely applicable. Mill suggests that we may identify causes in five ways, three of which are particularly useful for our purposes here.

The method of agreement   "If two or more instances of the phenomenon under investigation have only one circumstance in common, the circumstance in which alone all the instances agree is the cause (or effect) of the given phenomenon." (Mill, 1973, p. 390.)

To illustrate the method of agreement, consider this hypothetical case. If, while at work, we left the door to our home unlocked on three occasions and on all these occasions our home was robbed, we might conclude that the unlocked door was the cause of the robberies. While the method of agreement is a common mode of causal reasoning, it is not an easy matter to identify the single circumstance that is common to several instances. In the example cited there are probably many circumstances that are similar in the three instances: absence from home, the fact that the house was painted white, etc. Whether or not a common factor is labeled as a cause is clearly a matter of interpretation: For example, common sense suggests that the color of a house has little to do with its being robbed or not, while absence from home or an unlocked door both appear relevant.

The method of difference   "If an instance in which the phenomenon under investigation occurs, and an instance in which it does not occur, have every circumstance in common save one, that one occurring only in the former; the circumstance in which alone the two instances differ, is the effect, or the cause, or an indispensable part of the cause, of the phenomenon." (Mill, 1973, p. 391.)

The method of difference is illustrated by the previous instance of reasoning about the cause of the larger-than-usual crowd that was present at the airport during the President's arrival. When the Tuesday instance was compared to the Wednesday instance, it appeared that the single item of difference (the President's visit occurred on Tuesday but not on Wednesday) was the cause of the unusually large crowd. However, like the method of agreement, the method of difference is not foolproof. There may have been other differences between airport conditions on Tuesday and Wednesday of which we were not aware. For instance, a famous movie star may have arrived at 5:00 on Tuesday, or the airport windows may have been washed at that same time. Again, causal argument is interpretative, because we infer that the visit of a movie star may have had a causal relationship to the larger crowd (0_2), but the fact that the windows were washed at that time probably had no effect.

The method of concomitant variations "Whatever phenomenon varies in any manner whenever another phenomenon varies in some particular manner is either a cause or an effect of that phenomenon, or is connected with it through some fact of causation." (Mill, 1973, p. 401.)

Suppose that we observe that in classes that we attend regularly, we tend to earn an "A"; but in classes that we often "cut," we earn only a "C." We may have reason to believe that class attendance is causally related to grade performance, yet such an observation of correlation provides only imperfect evidence of causality. It may be that we attend regularly only those courses in which we already know the material, so that our previous knowledge, not attendance, is really the cause of our better grades. Further, the method of concomitant variation again requires that we interpret whether or not the relationship between two simultaneous variations makes sense. For instance, the increasing birth rate between 1946 and 1957 seems causally related to the increase in food sales during the same period. However, one who attempted to argue a causal relationship between increasing church attendance in a particular city and the increasing number of auto accidents in the same city might come into some criticism.

Neither Mill's canons nor experimental methodology have removed the difficulty in precisely identifying causal relationships. The famous skeptic and philosopher David Hume (1902, pp. 28–39) anticipated these difficulties: He argued that "causes and effects are discoverable, not by reason but by experience." Hume meant that there are two reasons that one can never be certain that two events are causally related: (1) We are never in the position of knowing all aspects of any two events and, further, (2) we can never be sure that the future will entirely resemble the past. Thus, we may observe (experience) that two events or circumstances commonly occur together; but we will never be able to positively identify and explain every detail of causality (i.e., use reason to identify the causes).

In the past few pages, I have explained certain theoretical aspects of causal argument and have suggested that it is no easy matter to causally connect two events or things, yet it is clear that arguers frequently use causal arguments. Let me therefore present some examples of causal interpretations so that we may learn how arguers use causality. Consider an example of causal reasoning in scientific investigation (*Odessa American,* June 10, 1976, p. 9B):

> CHICAGO (AP)—Loneliness and estrangement from family may one day be listed with cigarette smoking and environmental chemicals as causes of cancer. Studies have confirmed what medical authorities have been saying for centuries. That is, human emotions can be a factor in the development of cancer, just as they are in peptic ulcer, heart ailments, headache and some other maladies. . . .
>
> At the University of Rochester Medical Center in New York, Dr. William Greene, a psychiatrist, studied more than 100 men and women with leukemia and lymphona, two forms of cancer. In all but a few cases, the victims had suffered loss of a loved one before developing cancer.

This example illustrates Mill's method of agreement as a means of causal argument. Because the researchers were careful, they examined a large number of instances and took pains to identify aspects of each of more than a hundred cases. Thus, the causal conclusions of the researchers are likely to be valid; but, of course, the method of agreement can never yield indisputable causal relations.[2]

The average, "man in the street" user of causal argument is usually less cautious in asserting causal relationships; yet, as is suggested in the following excerpts, causal arguments are widely used outside scholarly (both empirical and historical-critical) circles. Perhaps the clearest understanding of the argumentative role of causal data is to be gained from situations in which advocates identify alternative and competing causes of a single phenomenon. Consider this example of alternative causes for Lyndon Johnson's decision not to campaign for reelection in 1968 (*Odessa American,* August 10, 1975, p. 9C):

> SEATTLE (AP)—Bad health, not bad advice on Viet Nam nor fear of an election loss, made President Lyndon Johnson decide not to run again in 1968, says Sen. Warren Magnuson, D-Wash., a long-time Johnson friend.
>
> "Lyndon talked about it with me," said Magnuson. "He didn't think that he would be able to survive another term because of his health problems."

Why did Johnson "abdicate" in 1968? We will probably never know for sure. Since most events have a multitude of associated causes, we must be careful not to overstate our belief in any particular cause unless we possess overwhelming evidence that the one cause has predominated.

Another example of alternative causes identified by opposing advocates may be seen in the brief period of soul-searching that paralleled the declining

---

[2]In this connection, it is interesting to observe the application of Hume's principle ("causes and effects are discoverable, not by reason but by experience") to this example. The news story on cancer research goes on to report: "Scientists are not sure yet how the emotions might trigger cancer."

fortunes of the South Vietnamese government under pressure from North Vietnamese forces. As *Newsweek* magazine (April 28, 1975, p. 17) reported:

> Ford himself later blamed Congress once again for Vietnam's plight. "The United States did not carry out its commitment in the supplying of military hardware and economic aid," he told the American Society of Newspaper Editors. "If we had, this present tragic situation in South Vietnam would not have occurred."
>
> Even before Ford's criticism, Congress angrily rejected the charge that it was responsible for South Vietnam's collapse. Senate Majority Leader Mike Mansfield snapped that such an accusation was "a distortion so immense that it borders on the irrational."

The argumentative implications of these two causal interpretations were significant. If President Ford had been able to persuade the public of his causal insight—which he was apparently not able to do—then he would have strengthened the notion that his political opponents, who controlled Congress, deserved blame for a failure in American foreign policy. Congressional advocates generally maintained that the fall of South Vietnam was caused by the general ineffectiveness of the Saigon government and by specific military blunders made in 1975 by the South Vietnamese president. Causal argument, then, may be used to explain the past or future relationship of events. Such explanations establish a notion of reality. The validity of causal argument, however, depends upon an advocate's careful attention to potential alternative causal factors.

ARGUMENTS OF SIGN

As is the case with conclusions founded on cause, the argument based on sign asserts that a close relationship exists between two events or things. However, the argument of sign does not presume a casual relationship. Sign-based arguments merely assert that one event or thing is a sign that another event or thing is (was or will be) present. That is, an observed event or thing is considered to be a sign that something unobserved has happened or is present. An Associated Press news story (*Odessa American,* May 9, 1974, p. 8C) on atomic power plants cited this inference of sign by a Vermont resident: "When I see the vapor, I know the plant is operating today."

Another instance of reasoning from sign is demonstrated in a "Dear Abby" column (*Odessa American,* September 9, 1975, p. 6B) in which a New York woman requested a few tips on how to tell if one's husband has been "fooling around." Abby's response: "When a husband suddenly starts wearing his best clothes to work, says he's working 'overtime' but doesn't have the money to show for it, puts extra miles on the car, sometimes gets lost all day Saturday, smiles and whistles a lot and starts telling what a great, understanding wife you are—watch out!" Aside from transforming several wives into amateur detectives, Abby's remarks remind us that a collection of signs is more powerful than a single one.

Tip of the Iceberg

One form of the argument of sign is used often enough to be treated as a specific subtype. This variation of the argument of sign is appropriately named, for it claims that a small, visible thing or event may be taken as but a sign that something larger resides below the surface (as in the case of the iceberg with a visible tip that is only one-seventh of the total ice mass). Consider this example of the tip of the iceberg argument (George Benson, "Looking Ahead," *Odessa American,* February 7, 1974, p. 2D): "The Soviets are developing Cuba into a major naval operating base. [An unidentified Cuban reports that] 'Cienfuegos—the Russian submarine base in the Caribbean—is merely the tip of the Soviet iceberg in the Western Hemisphere. . . .' " This argument seeks to convince us that the danger is greater than it seems by viewing an obvious situation as but the symptom of something more sinister.

The ambiguous nature of signs poses a major problem for those who would use sign-based evidence to justify a claim. For example, in commenting on Senator Edward M. Kennedy's active participation in legislative action relative to a Presidential campaign financing law, columnist Robert S. Allen argued (*Odessa American,* December 13, 1973, p. 8B) that Kennedy's interest in the law could be taken as a sign that he would seek the Presidency in 1976. "On the basis of the dominating role he played in this politics-loaded legislative tug-of-war, it is fair to say that the Massachusetts Democrat is definitely a 1976 White House aspirant." As we now know, Kennedy opposed all efforts in 1976 to place his name in nomination. As a result, his interest in the campaign finance law must have been a sign of something else. Signs may be ambiguous: We may misread them. Thus, the advocate must make sure that an individual sign is clear and representative, as well as consistent with the other evidence.

ARGUMENTS THAT PREDICT FUTURE CONSEQUENCES

We have learned that prediction is often strongly manifested in interpretive arguments. While any interpretation may be based on prediction—e.g., the analogy or causal argument—there are several identifiable types of interpretation in which the predictive element is paramount. These are (1) the argument of direction, (2) the fear appeal, and (3) the *reductio ad absurdum*. Because persuasion often deals with future facts, the predictive role of argument is worthy of considerable study.

The Argument of Direction

The argument of direction seeks to predict the future by asserting that a present act is inherently connected to future acts. The argument seeks to demonstrate that events are not isolated—that once we have done X, there is no stopping until we reach Y and Z. This argument refutes the idea that events can be divided into separate and independent stages. As Perelman and Olbrechts-Tyteca (1969, p. 282) observe: "The argument of direction consists, essentially, in guarding against the use of the device of stages: if you give in this time, you will have to give in a little more next time, and heaven knows where you will stop."

The "domino theory" is perhaps the most famous example of the argument of direction. The domino theory asserts that the fall of one nation to communism would set in motion a chain reaction in which other nations would similarly fall. This argument was used for more than twenty years to justify American aid to the anticommunist forces in South Vietnam. The classic public application of the domino principle to Vietnam was made by President Dwight D. Eisenhower during a news conference in 1954 (The President's News Conference of April 7, 1954, in *Public Papers of the Presidents of the United States, Dwight D. Eisenhower, 1954,* pp. 382–383):

> *Q.* (Robert Richards, Copley Press). Mr. President would you mind commenting on the strategic importance of Indochina to the free world? I think there has been, across the country, some lack of understanding on just what it means to us.
> *A.* (The President). You have, of course, both the specific and the general when you talk about such things.
>
> First of all, you have the specific value of a locality in its production of materials that the world needs.
>
> Then you have the possibility that many human beings pass under a dictatorship that is inimical to the free world.
>
> Finally, you have the broader considerations that might follow what you call the "falling domino" principle. You have a row of dominos set up, you knock over the first one, and what will happen to the last one is the certainty that it will go over very quickly. So you have a beginning of a disintegration that would have the most profound influences.

The Johnson administration continued this line of reasoning well into the 1960s. As President Johnson asserted (*Department of State Bulletin,* April 26, 1965, p. 607): "Let no one think for a moment that retreat from Viet-Nam would bring an end to conflict. The battle would be renewed in one country and then another." The domino theory treated Vietnam as but a transitory stage in an unfolding scenario of war with communism. By increasing the worldwide importance of the Vietnam conflict, the domino theory enabled the administration to argue that our interests in Vietnam justified the vast war expenditures.

The argument of direction is not, of course, confined to foreign policy debate. Opponents of direct federal government intervention in the oil industry have frequently relied on directional argumentation. Thus, the *Odessa American* (February 10, 1974, p. 8B) editorialized against government audits of oil refineries: "But this is one more step toward the takeover of the petroleum industry by political government." And Exxon chairman M. A. Wright (*Happy Motoring News,* July, 1974) characterized plans for federal action in the oil industry as only one stage in a move toward government control of all industry: "And what is more important is that the pattern set against oil can be used against others. For example, why not a U.S. Automobile Corporation? Or a Federal Steel Company?" Whether it is aid to South Vietnam or opposition to controls on oil companies, the pattern of the directional argument remains consistent: An action is not independent, but is part of a sequence that will continue unabated.

To use this argument in a valid manner, the advocate must be able to demonstrate that events will in fact continue unchecked. Thus, during the 1960s and 1970s critics have challenged the assumptions of the domino theory that the fall of one nation would set in motion a chain reaction of communist successes. Even after the collapse of South Vietnam in 1975, the validity of the domino theory was actively debated. President Ford argued (Associated Press release, *Odessa American,* March 18, 1975, p. 4A) that the fall of South Vietnam caused allies of the United States to worry, thus, he said, validating the theory. On the other hand, an Associated Press news analysis concluded in November 5, 1975 (*Odessa American,* p. 8B), that "The fall of Indochina does not appear to have affected U.S. relations with long-time allies." Supporting this latter view, the House of Representatives majority leader, Thomas P. O'Neill, had earlier argued (*Newsweek,* February 10, 1975, p. 25) that rather than having strengthened our position, the American efforts to sustain South Vietnam had actually caused a deterioration in the United States' position around the world. Because of the controversial nature of the domino theory, proponents of the theory would need to guard against overstating its merits. In situations in which the weight of favorable and unfavorable evidence is roughly balanced, qualifiers must be moderated.

The Fear Appeal

Many arguments are characterized by their intent to inspire fear. These arguments emphasize the painful or horrible consequences that will inevitably result from some present action. Many readers will recall viewing driver's education movies such as "The Last Prom" that depicted vividly the effects of excessive speed, drink, and carelessness while driving. Such movies, usually featuring close-up shots of auto accidents, suggested the fearful consequences of certain driving habits. Readers may also recall seeing movies pertaining to venereal disease and smoking that had similar appeals to fear.

An example of fear appeals used in connection with venereal disease is to be found in an advice column by Dr. George W. Crane. Crane argues ("Worry Clinic," *Odessa American,* October 29, 1973, p. 7A): "So America needs to warn youth by vivid movies and lectures which expose the serious medical aftereffects of gonorrhea and syphilis. These may consist of permanent sterility of both male and female victims, plus blindness of newborn babies, gonorrheal arthritis, feeblemindedness and insanity, heart and blood vessel disease, plus many others!" The common theme of venereal disease films and similar treatments of drunk driving, smoking, etc., is an emphasis on the horrible physical effects of certain behaviors.

Although fear appeal arguments are often quite visceral, as in the Crane quotation, many such appeals are more subtle. For instance, Presidents Nixon and Ford, as well as other Republican leaders, used the concept of a "veto-proof

Congress" as a fear appeal during the 1974 midterm Congressional elections. It was argued that a large Democratic majority in Congress would create a "legislative dictatorship" in which the Congress wielded a disproportionate share of federal power. Democratic leaders branded the term "veto-proof Congress" an illegitimate scare tactic (*Odessa American,* June 5, 1974, p. 12B):

> SEATTLE (AP)—The chairman of the nation's Democratic governors has accused Republicans of scare tactics in warning that Democrats could gain a "veto-proof Congress" in the November elections.
>
> "The term 'veto proof Congress' is merely a cynical ploy to detract from the most important issues of 1974," Gov. Wendell H. Ford, D-Ky., said Tuesday as sharp partisanship broke out at the 66th National Governors' Conference. . . .
>
> He [Governor Ford] said he hopes the Democrats attain a two-thirds control of the House and Senate that would give them the numerical strength to override presidential vetoes, but he said he objected to GOP efforts "to use the term to scare people."

Oddly enough, the Democrats did gain virtually their two-thirds control, but President Ford, between August 1974 and May 1976, successfully vetoed more bills than his two predecessors combined.

Although the reality of a veto-proof Congress never materialized, the term was a part of the Republican campaign arsenal in the 1974 elections. The "veto-proof Congress" fear appeal did not predict horrible physical consequences for those pulling the Democratic lever; but the term did tend to suggest that a Democratic victory would bring about a sinister, almost "un-American" result. Fear appeals therefore need not emphasize physical consequences in order to create anxiety in listeners. Nevertheless, in emphasizing future effects the user of the fear appeal must be careful not to overstate his claim: Fear appeals, by their nature, are prone to exaggeration.

The Reductio ad Absurdum

Taking something to its most extreme, and therefore most absurd, consequence is an especially appealing type of predictive argument. This argumentative subtype is often called by its Latin title, *reductio ad absurdum*—i.e., to reduce to the absurd. In the *reductio* the arguer identifies an extreme (or the most extreme) consequence of an idea or proposal and demonstrates that the extreme consequences would easily result from the idea or proposal. The argument of reduction gains its strength by making something appear to be radical. Thus, in editorializing against the present form of the Texas state constitution, William Broyles of *Texas Monthly* (November, 1975, p. 5) identified an extreme or radical aspect of the document: "Unfortunately, far too much of our current constitution made sense in 1876 but has long since lost meaning. The document has had to be amended 220 times and contains enough words (63,000-plus) to fill a short novel. As a result, the entire state has to vote on such questions as whether the people of Lamar County can change the status of their hospital district." Most provisions of the Texas constitution are more conventional than the example of Lamar County's hospital district. But, this *reductio* argument seeks to emphasize the extreme provisions of the constitution.

A similar argument of reduction was maintained by an instructor who fought dismissal from Odessa [Texas] Junior College. Dr. Jaroslav Piskacek was dismissed as a teacher of Spanish largely on the basis that he did not have eighteen graduate hours in Spanish. Piskacek maintained that physicist Albert Einstein would have been barred from teaching math at Odessa College on the same grounds (*Odessa American,* June 11, 1975, p. 14B). Piskacek reduces the eighteen-hour requirement to an absurd state by demonstrating that the requirement would have denied to the junior college the services of a mathematical genius. The image of a world-famous scientist being spurned by a small junior college makes us question what is otherwise a reasonable rule.

In general we may say that the validity of the *reductio* depends on the advocate's success in demonstrating that the extreme effect could likely happen. Dr. Piskacek's reduction concerning the way in which Odessa College rules would preclude the hiring of Einstein succeeds because both the rule and Einstein's educational background are clear-cut. Indeed, the Odessa College administration conceded this point. However, not all reductions are so straightforward. For example, serious problems of validity plague an *Odessa American* editorial (May 31, 1975, p. 10A) against the Zero Population Growth (Z.P.G.) organization's proposals for reducing the problem of illegal (chiefly Mexican) aliens. The plan suggested that to reduce illegal immigration, the United States government should (1) impose fines and jail sentences on employers who knowingly hire illegal aliens and (2) maintain foreign aid to improve living standards in countries from which the aliens come. Seeking to oppose the Z.P.G. plan, the editors develop the following *reductio*: "In a way, the suggested [Z.P.G.] program makes sense. If the 'main impetus for illegal immigration is the poor economic conditions of most countries'—conditions that ZPG proposes to cure by a 'continuing commitment to foreign aid'—then the arithmetic consequence is that this country will go broke and thus cease to be 'the magnet that draws illegal aliens.' " For this reduction to be valid, the editors need to demonstrate the likelihood that foreign aid expenditures will cause our nation to "go broke." Such an outcome is theoretically possible but highly unlikely.

HUMOR

Arguments based on humor are closely related to the *reductio ad absurdum.* Although not all reductions are amusing, humor is akin to the *reductio,* for it also plays on extreme cases or unexpected twists. Such unusual, exaggerated, or extreme interpretations often strike us as being funny. Thus, a *Newsweek* letter to the editor (May 19, 1975, p. 7) pokes fun at a photograph that had been alleged to demonstrate that at least one other assassin assisted Lee Harvey Oswald in the murder of President Kennedy. The author first conceded the point that the picture *might* indicate the presence of a second assassin: "I'm prepared to grant that if one studies the Robert Groden blowup of the Zapruder film long enough he will be able to see what looks like an assassin holding a rifle." Having thus "set up" the joke, the letter writer lowers the boom: "But I was also able to perceive a number of other things, including at least one giant spider, a cheerful giraffe, three French hens, two turtledoves and a partridge in a pear tree."

Humor is clearly interpretive, for it enables us to see the ridiculous in an argument. The quotation just cited acknowledges that the Zapruder film might be viewed as proving the second-assassin theory; but the author of the letter characterizes the picture as proving only very weak support for such an interpretation. However, instead of blandly asserting that "the film is ambiguous," the letter writer ridicules the notion that the film has captured the likeness of a second murderer. We are told that the film might just as well portray a giant spider—or, to drive home the point even further, any other member of the menagerie of the "Twelve Days of Christmas"! How could one ever look at the film again without seeing that smiling giraffe?

In many respects, humorous overtones are more effective in dispatching the alleged proof of the second-assassin theory than a similar argument phrased in a serious vein. Without going into detail as to the persuasive effects of humor, it is clear in this example that humor is more than mere argumentative embellishment: It works to promote good will toward the arguer, to decrease the credibility of one's opponent (nothing is as humiliating as being laughed at), and, finally, it makes the listener less likely to take seriously the argument that has been belittled. Humor is the ulitmate minimization.

As an illustration of the use of humor in an argument, perhaps nothing surpasses the effort by John F. Kennedy in his address (quoted in White, 1967, pp. 337–338) given at the 1960 Alfred E. Smith Memorial Dinner in New York City. (Smith was Governor of New York from 1924 to 1928 and Democratic candidate for President in 1928.) Notice how Kennedy uses the introduction to this speech to simultaneously advance his own credibility, belittle his opponent, and confront the serious religious issue. (Kennedy's Catholicism was a source of concern to some voters.)

"Kennedy was in high form that evening," writes White in his preface to the speech (pp. 337–338),

> and since Kennedy exerts over Nixon the same charm that a snake charmer exerts over a snake, the effect was doubly harmful to Nixon's ego. Kennedy originally, in August, had been reluctant to accept the invitation to this strictly Catholic affair; he felt it would accentuate the religious issue. Evidently he decided finally to speak with a light touch, and for two days before the engagement his aides had been circulating through the press, asking, "Do you know any jokes?" Kennedy began his remarks thus:
>
> I am glad to be here at this notable dinner once again and I am glad that Mr. Nixon is here also [Applause.] Now that Cardinal Spellman has demonstrated the proper spirit, I assume that shortly I will be invited to a Quaker dinner honoring Herbert Hoover [Laughter]. Cardinal Spellman is the only man so widely respected in

American politics that he could bring together amicably, at the same banquet table, for the first time in this campaign, two political leaders who are increasingly apprehensive about the November election—who have long eyed each other suspiciously and who have disagreed so strongly, both publicly and privately—Vice-President Nixon and Governor Rockefeller [Laughter].

Mr. Nixon, like the rest of us, has had his troubles in this campaign. At one point even the *Wall Street Journal* was criticizing his tactics. That is like the *Osservatore Romano* criticizing the Pope.

But I think the worst news for the Republicans this week was the Casey Stengel has been fired [Laughter]. It must show that perhaps experience does not count [Laughter and applause].

On this matter of experience, I had announced earlier this year that if successful I would not consider campaign contributions as a substitute for experience in appointing ambassadors. Ever since I made that statement, I have not received one single cent from my father.

One of the inspiring notes that was struck in the last debate was struck by the Vice-President in his very moving warning to the children of the nation and the candidates against the use of profanity by Presidents and ex-Presidents when they are on the stump. And I know after fourteen years in the Congress with the Vice-President that he was very sincere in his views about the use of profanity. But I am told that a prominent Republican said to him yesterday in Jacksonville, Florida, "Mr. President, that was a damn fine speech" [Laughter]. And the Vice-President said, "I appreciate the compliment but not the language." And the Republican went on, "Yes sir, I liked it so much that I contributed a thousand dollars to your campaign." And Mr. Nixon replied, "The hell you say." [Laughter and applause].

However, I would not want to give the impression that I am taking former President Truman's use of language lightly. I have sent him the following note: "Dear Mr. President: I have noted with interest your suggestion as to where those who vote for my opponent should go. While I understand and sympathize with your deep motivation, I think it is important that our side try to refrain from raising the religious issue." [Laughter and applause].

As an example of the social style of argumentation, Kennedy's speech is possibly an unrivaled effort by a major Presidential candidate during a heated campaign.

Remember the White House effort to minimize the unfavorable reaction to Betty Ford's comments on sex? Consider how Bob Hope handled the argument during an appearance in Midland, Texas (*Odessa American,* August 24, 1975, p. 8D): "She is really candid. She makes Dear Abby sound like Mother Goose." Hope's line, by the way, drew a big laugh from a crowd in one of Texas's most conservative bible-belt communities. Hope's remarks may actually have changed some attitudes in a city in which opinion was running strongly against Mrs. Ford's televised interview. Wouldn't it be hard for those who laughed at the situation to remain so bothered by it?

Sarcasm

The cutting, taunting and caustic use of humor is termed sarcasm. While Kennedy's use of humor at the Al Smith dinner was generally light-hearted, certain of his references to Richard Nixon contained sarcastic undertones—e.g., the reference to *The Wall Street Journal* criticism. Clearly more overtly sarcastic are the remarks of columnist "Injun" Woody Palmer (*Odessa American,* September 27, 1973, p. 7C), regarding a proposal on oil conservation and control advanced by the late Senator Hubert Humphrey: "Hubey also suggests that the consumer should conserve fuel by 'maintaining lower indoor temperatures in winter and resorting to somewhat heavier clothing.' We will eagerly await the first picture showing Hubey sitting around in his house with an overcoat on." Similarly sarcastic was the comment by Oklahoma football coach Barry Switzer (*Odessa American,* August 12, 1975, p. 2B) regarding the musical interests of his former rival at the University of Texas (Austin), Darrell Royal: "Some coaches don't want to coach any more. They would rather sit home and listen to guitar pickers." This snide remark, according to the Associated Press, caused Royal to be "wild-eyed" with anger.

Whereas social-style humor may provoke laughter even among those who are the butt of the joke, sarcastic humor is generally amusing only to those partisans who totally agree with the extreme interpretation. Thus, sarcasm is usually more effective in its role to reinforce the opinions of the already converted. It is less effective as a means to change opinion among opponents and neutrals. Reliance on sarcastic humor may also act to reduce the credibility of an advocate, who gains thereby a reputation for being negative and unfriendly. Sarcasm is often more amusing to the speaker than to the listeners.

Irony

Irony is often defined as a kind of sarcasm in which a word is used to mean the direct opposite of its usual sense. Thus, a person might comment to a friend who slipped on a banana peel: "My, you are *graceful.*" Such irony is often used in argument to call attention to the unexpected effects of something. An ironic interpretation highlights the alleged contradiction among ideas or things. For instance, Tom W. Sigler, a vice president of Continental Oil Company, asserted a contradiction between American principles and proposals to place controls on oil companies (*Odessa American,* May 11, 1975, p. 7D): "The ironic thing is that just 200 years ago we fought a revolution against this kind of thing, to free ourselves from what was regarded as government tyranny." While critics of oil companies would probably prefer to place "Big Oil" in the role of King George III, the mental association of oil company interests with colonial grievances is quite favorable to the view that the petroleum industry should be free of government control.

In sum, humor is argumentative, although it appears to be a more effective vehicle for refutation than a source of positive support. It is difficult to apply standards of rhetorical validity to a type of argument that is seldom entirely serious. If an advocate is not serious, then even his gross exaggerations probably do not deserve to be labeled "invalid." If intended seriously, however, humorous arguments must be tested against the same standards as those that apply for all other interpretive statements.

THE ARGUMENT OF CONSPIRACY

The argument of conspiracy is closely related to the causal, sign, and future-predicting interpretations. Yet because it is a recurring theme in human controversy, it merits consideration as a separate type of argument based on definitional issues. The argument of conspiracy views particular events as part of a wider, secret, and deliberate plan. The conspiratorial outlook minimizes the spontaneous and unique causes of an event (or aspects of a thing), preferring to view a particular happening (thing) as but another manifestation of a general plan. Conspiracy differs from the argument of direction, however. Whereas directional argumentation asserts that one act (e.g., legalized abortion) will set in motion a chain of events leading to an extreme situation (e.g., legalized genocide), the argument of conspiracy asserts that some organized group is working methodically to use the intermediate step as a means of bringing about the extreme situation.

The late H. L. Hunt's analysis of proposals for national "catastrophic" medical insurance (insurance against illnesses requiring long-term, expensive care) illustrates the conspiratorial view. He argued (*Odessa American,* December 18, 1973, p. 10A) that such plans represented "the latest stage in the unending campaign to impose fully socialized, bureaucrat-controlled, tax-financed medicine upon the United States." In this quotation Hunt treats the catastrophic proposals not as an end in themselves, but as merely a stage in a campaign. His argument is characteristically conspiratorial (i.e., not merely directional), because Hunt implies that some group is manipulating the catastrophic-illness controversy as part of an organized plan to achieve a totally government-controlled medical system.

One of the best-known conspiracy theories of recent times has been the interpretation, popular especially between 1973 and 1974, that the Watergate investigation and publicity were part of a conspiracy against President Richard Nixon. James J. Kilpatrick reported that he had encountered the media-liberal conspiracy idea frequently in his mail, citing this sample from a woman in Glenview, Illinois (*Odessa American,* March 11, 1974, p. 8A): "Any clear-thinking person will recognize 'Watergate' for what it is, to wit, a liberal media vendetta against Mr. Nixon, whom they have always hated, because he has done so much to frustrate their mania for one-worldism and a Socialistic America." The other half of the Nixon-as-the-victim-of-a-conspiracy argument is reported in Robert S. Allen's "Inside Washington" column (*Odessa American,* November 26, 1973, p. 14A): "[Representative Harold] Froehlich [R-Wis.] bluntly charged that an impeachment conspiracy was afoot and being pressed from the offices of Speaker Carl Albert."

The interpretation of the prosecution of Watergate-related offences as a conspiracy was (and is) a particularly advantageous position for Nixon defenders. This outlook suggests that opposition to Nixon did not result from legitimate concern over illegality and abuse of power. Rather, the theory suggests that diehard Nixon-haters had merely seized on relatively harmless acts for the purpose of destroying the man. In this scenario Nixon's personal actions are minimized and the past anti-Nixon behavior of his opponents receives emphasis.

Nixon defenders had no monopoly on the conspiracy argument during the period from 1969 to 1974. Consider this claim put forth by Congressman Fortney H. Stark (D., California) (from Associated Press release, *Odessa American,* November 3, 1973, p. 7B) that former President Nixon was likely to resort to a military coup d'état to maintain his Presidency in the face of impeachment. "As the noose of justice draws closer around Nixon," Stark argued, "he is growing more desperate. Considering the President's irrational behavior and the existence of an aristocratic military elite in this country, it is not inconceivable that a military takeover could be attempted." Stark's evidence of Nixon's alleged mental state and his statement concerning a military elite both fail to establish the likelihood of a coup. However, since Stark asserts only a very weak qualifier ("not inconceivable"), this particular argument actually may have been valid.

One should not regard the above examples of conspiratorial reasoning as atypical. The argument has been used frequently in connection with a variety of subjects such as the John F. Kennedy assassination, the 1978 Panama Canal treaties, plans to regulate the oil industry, gun control proposals, and the 1976 allegation by Ugandan President Idi Amin that that United States was in "the total grip of Zionism." Such arguments discredit the motives of an adversary, appeal to people's fear of the unknown, and minimize the particular arguments in favor of any specific course of action. (Richard Hofstadter, 1967, has used the term "paranoid style" to describe certain conspiratorial arguments.)

In general, it appears that the validity of the conspiratorial argument depends on several factors. First, because groups may be found to support or oppose almost anything, we must assure ourselves that the advocate is not using "conspiracy" as merely a name-calling device. When the label of "conspiracy" is applied only for the purpose of discrediting a legitimate undertaking, then its use probably is invalid—e.g., "the conspiracy to elect Gerald Ford as President." Advocates have been known to use the term "conspiracy" as a means of masking the spontaneous, unique, and/or legitimate causes of an event. Finally, for the conspiracy argument to be valid, it must be demonstrated that the secret, organized group of conspirators is a major factor, and not a minor sidelight, of the issue at hand. The lines of the conspiracy should be clearly drawn and not presented as vague innuendo.

DILEMMA ARGUMENT

The final general class of interpretive arguments that I will treat is the argument that identifies two or more alternatives to a situation. The *dilemma* constructs reality by sketching out the possible outcomes or definitions of something. Derived from a Greek root meaning two (di) propositions (lemma), the dilemma usually identifies an either/or, two-sided situation. (It is possible nevertheless, to envision a three- or four-sided dilemma.) Often, the dilemma presents one alternative in a favorable light and contrasts the favored option to one or more alternatives that are rejected. A dilemma may also be cast in the form of two alternatives, both of which are described as being undesirable—such as when one is "between the devil and the deep blue sea." This latter condition also corresponds to the expression "on the horns of a dilemma," which likens the two alternatives to the frontal weaponry of a steer, both sides of which are equally lethal.

The argumentative role of the "this is better than that" form of the dilemma is illustrated by one assertion used to justify the authoritarian policies of Indira Gandhi, the Prime Minister of India from 1965 to 1976. Mrs. Gandhi and her supporters justified her suspension of the constitution, censorship of the press, and jailing of political opponents by means of this dilemma-style argument (*Newsweek,* July 14, 1975, p. 38): "In India, it is more important to be fed than to be free." In other words, it is argued, Mrs. Gandhi's assumption of quasi-dictatorial powers enables her to deal more effectively with India's chronic poverty. Hence, the dilemma becomes: food or freedom. This argument has the advantage of placing Mrs. Gandhi's antidemocratic measures in a favorable light. Although regrettable, her authoritarian policies are said to be preferable to mass starvation. One horn (Mrs. Gandhi's political measures) is described as being less lethal than the other (starvation).

The device of sketching out two equally unfavorable interpretations may be observed in a dilemma-style criticism of the Nixon administration's educational policy that was made in a *Newsweek* letter to the editor (May 13, 1974, p. 6): "The sign reading 'yes your are man Pres. Nixon' that appears in the photograph accompanying your article on 'Nixon's Collision Course' . . . shows one, or both, of two things: the intellectual level of Mr. Nixon's hard-core support or the sorry state of American education under Mr. Nixon's leadership." Both alternatives are, of course, unfavorable to President Nixon. This excerpt offers a foretaste of what I will later describe as the major problem of dilemma-type argumentation which is the difficulty of reducing the complexity of a situation into only two dichotomous, or at least distinct, alternatives. The grammatical deficiencies of the sign may indicate many things, and the authors of the sign may have matriculated and graduated long before Nixon's assumption of the Presidency. It must be remembered, nevertheless, that although the dilemma does force complex reality into but two molds, the dilemma is no different in this respect from other interpretative arguments, many of which construct only one alternative.

It is clear, then, that the validity of a dilemma depends on whether the advocate has identified a truly either/or situation. An opponent need only point out a third possibility to invalidate the dilemma. Consider this example of a false dilemma (editorial, *Odessa American,* September 18, 1975, p. 10B): "People kill other people, sometimes with guns, sometimes with other things. Guns alone are harmless." The problem with this argument is that a strict dichotomy between person and gun cannot be maintained. A gun changes a person. A person with a gun is different from the same person without a gun. A person with a gun is more likely to kill than a person without one.

Another interesting example of a false dilemma was identified in a letter to the editor about the "streaking" fad that was popular in 1974 (*Odessa American*, March 16, 1974, p. 6B): "Will someone please give a good sound reason why streaking should be compared with swallowing goldfish, flagpole sitting, rioting, etc.? We heard several adults say, 'Well, it's better than this or that.' As though it might be the lesser of the evils. Who gave them a choice?" The writer is correct in observing the false dilemma (streaking or "this and that"). College students had and have many potential outlets for their energy, of which streaking and some "greater evil" are only two.

Antithesis

Although it is no easy matter to reduce reality into two parts, the use of dichotomy is quite prevalent in human affairs. The language of antithesis is a form of dilemma that distinguishes a thing from what is said to be its opposite. The rhetoric of the cold war provides numerous examples of the use of antithesis to establish a dilemma-type argument. In his 1951 State of the Union address (see Israel, 1966, III, p. 2980), President Harry S. Truman described the cold war confrontation between the United States and the Soviet Union as "right and justice in the world against oppression and slavery." In his first Inaugural Address, President Dwight D. Eisenhower constructed the conflict in similar terms (Lott, 1961, p. 259): "Freedom is pitted against slavery, lightness against the dark." Succeeding cold war Presidents put the matter in similar symbols. Antithetical language imparts a dramatic flavor, a poetic tone, and a crusading ethos to dilemma argumentation.

STANDARDS OF VALIDITY FOR INTERPRETIVE ARGUMENT

The twenty types and subtypes of interpretive argument presented in this chapter illustrate well the distinction between descriptive argument (that which chiefly raises factual issues) and interpretive argument (that which by its nature emphasizes definitional questions). Close scrutiny of interpretive arguments such as presented in this chapter highlights the difficulty to be encountered in attempting to describe things objectively. Both our definition of and attitude toward something are often clearly reflected in the language we use to present it. Although in chapter 4 we considered arguments that tended to raise chiefly factual issues, it is perhaps more common in popular discourse to find factual issues subsumed under more overtly definitional ones.

The bias inherent in interpretive argument results from at least three common features of this form of argument. First, interpretive argument implies a major effort to select facts that support one's case. Whereas the identification of a fact raises a first-order issue of fact (does X exist, or did Y occur?), the selection of several facts to prove a claim raises an immediate issue of definition: Do the selected facts fairly represent the thing or occurrence, or are they atypical? (This feature also applies to descriptive argument, as we learned in chapter 4.)

Bias is endemic to interpretation for a second reason. The role of interpretive argument to linguistically emphasize favorable data and minimize unfavorable information means that factual issues will always be secondary to definitional questions. The question confronted by the definitional arguer is this: Given that X exists or Y has happened, what does it mean?

Finally, interpretive bias is reflected in the human tendency to present information in such a way as to make disagreement difficult or impossible. Even a strong proponent of gun control would find it difficult, for instance, to answer yes to the following question taken from a 1975 opinion poll sponsored by the National Rifle Association: "If a new firearms law was enacted in your state banning all ownership of guns, do you believe that hoodlums and organized criminals would volunteer their guns to your local police department?" As I noted in chapter 4, this question is stated in such a manner as to almost preclude disagreement. The gun control proponent would find it necessary to restate the question in order to affirm it. For instance, one might be more able to affirm this version of the question which is biased so as to favor gun control: "If a new firearms law were enacted in your state banning all ownership of guns, do you believe that the number of guns involved in accidents, domestic quarrels, murders, and robberies would decrease?"

Although interpretive argument implies bias, it must be remembered that bias may be justified. If, for example, a proposal *is* ineffective, it is not wrong to label it "ineffective." We should not, therefore, reject an argument merely because it is presented in biased language. Rather, in testing the rhetorical validity of interpretation, we should ask this question: Is the biased language justified? In other words, is the amount of favorable data sufficient to support the claim against the unfavorable data, or stated in another way, does the claim assert a level of confidence that can or cannot be established by the relevant reasons? These questions coincide with the definition of rhetorical validity that I presented in chapter 3 and that I applied to descriptive arguments in chapter 4: An argument is valid when, in an adversarial situation, the degree of certainty attributed to a conclusion by an agent is less than or equal to that established by the relevant (supporting and opposing) proof.

As we learned in chapters 3 and 4, the definition of rhetorical validity requires us to identify four aspects of an extended argument: (1) a claim to be tested, (2) a statement of the certainty attributed by an advocate to the claim, (3) favorable data that supports the claim, and (4) unfavorable data that opposes the claim. However, although we will be using the same standard of validity for interpretations as we used to test descriptions, it is apparent that rhetorical validity is more complicated when we are dealing with interpretive language.

Whereas we tested descriptions partially by means of the principle of correspondence (does the description correspond with identifiable reality?), the test of correspondence is not at all useable in resolving issues of definition (see Toulmin, 1968, pp. 74–85). Unlike descriptive argument, which functions somewhat as a "map of reality" (Hayakawa, 1949, p. 32), interpretative argument uses dialectic symbols that cannot be pointed to or mapped. While we may test the correspondence of "John sits in the chair" to a picture of reality, we may not so easily map the sentence "John is an honest and just person." How does one point to or map honesty and justice?

As I asserted in chapter 2, we must construct definitions for such dialectic terms. Thus, to test the validity of an interpretive argument, we must do more than determine its correspondence to a fact existing in the world. We must use our critical abilities to resolve the true relationships among claim, qualifier, favorable data, and unfavorable data. In so doing the critic must: (1) identify and determine the relevancy of both favorable and unfavorable data to a claim; (2) decide whether the arguments contain any factually questionable statements; (3) determine whether or not any relevant information (especially unfavorable data) has been omitted; and (4) judge whether the claim is modified by a valid qualifier (by examining the ratio of favorable to unfavorable argument) or whether the claim is overstated. This latter test will enable critics to decide whether the biased, interpretive language used to present a claim is justified by comparing the relevant claim-supporting and claim-opposing data.

Throughout this chapter I have cited specific factors of validity that pertain to particular types of interpretations. However, by generally applying tests of rhetorical validity, we may identify two basic forms of invalid interpretations: (1) the unfounded interpretation and (2) the distorted interpretation. The unfounded interpretation is invalid because the arguer presents an inadequate amount of favorable support to justify the level of certainty attributed to the claim. The unfounded interpretation is invalid even before the unfavorable information is considered. On the other hand, distorted interpretations attain invalidity either by misrepresenting the favorable or unfavorable data (distortion by commission) or by suppressing unfavorable data (omission).

The Unfounded Interpretation

When one asserts that a claim is unfounded, one means that there exists an inadequate amount of information to support the argument. In judging whether a claim is unfounded, it is especially important to observe the level of certainty attributed to the claim. Thus, were we to assert that "John is certainly rich," we would undertake a larger burden of proof than if we asserted, "The evidence suggests that John may possibly be rich." More evidence (at least more conclusive evidence) is required when we assert a high level of confidence. Identifying a claim as being unfounded does not mean that the claim is impossible to validate. Rather, when we label a claim as unfounded, we mean only that the claim is not sufficiently supported by a particular advocate who presents the claim at a particular place and at a particular time. Rhetorical validity, thus, depends on the context in which an argument is located.

The Unsubstantiated Assertion   To clarify the notion of validity as argumentative context, let me present an example of claims presented without sufficient backing. In 1975 I received a solicitation to join the Conservative Caucus. In a covering letter that accompanied the collection of membership materials, Meldrim Thompson, Jr., Governor of New Hampshire, posed a series of arguments in the form of questions. He asked whether I was "as sick and tired" as he was of "liberal politicians" who did such things as:

1 "force children to be bused"
2 "appoint judges who turn murderers and rapists loose on the public"
3 "force your children to study from school books that are anti-God, anti-American and filled with the most vulgar curse words"
4 "give your money to communists, anarchists and other radical organizations"

The reader will notice that these questions are written in such a form as to indicate that Governor Thompson intended the reader to accept them as truisms—i.e., a high level of certainty was attributed to these claims—although nowhere in the letter was any evidence presented to suggest that the claims were valid.

Yet these assertions require a considerable amount of proof. For example, to establish that "liberal politicians" had "appoint[ed] judges who turn murderers and rapists loose on the public," Governor Thompson would need to present evidence that (1) certain judges had misapplied the law, dismissing charges against persons who should have been jailed; (2) that these persons had in fact committed such additional offenses; (3) that the politicians who appointed the judges knew that the judges were likely to act in such a fashion; and (4) that a large percentage of such politicians could be labeled liberal, as opposed to conservative or moderate. Additionally, evidence would need to be presented to establish that this sequence of events had taken place frequently enough to be regarded as a trend. Finally, it would be helpful to show that judges appointed by conservatives would have acted differently.

The evidence may well be available to establish this series of argumentative links. However, because Governor Thompson presented no support at all, we may consider his assertion to be invalid in view of its unfounded nature. The claim, as presented, is an unsubstantiated assertion.

In addition to the unsubstantiated assertion, we may identify two further types of interpretation that are invalid because of a lack of favorable, supporting evidence: the irrelevant reason and the presentation of an interpretation under the guise of a fact.

The Irrelevant Reason As its name implies, an irrelevant reason is evidence that has no legitimate application to an issue at hand. An irrelevant reason that was frequently heard during the 1973–1974 period was the argument that President Nixon should not be impeached for his "Watergate"-related activities because "everyone has done such things." James J. Kilpatrick quoted one such argument, which he received from a Memphis, Tennessee, letter writer (*Odessa American,* March 11, 1974, p. 8A): "[Nixon's Watergate activities were] not half as bad as what Ted Kennedy was involved in and no one even mentioned removing him from office." The "they did it, too" argument is irrelevant to the issue of whether or not Richard Nixon engaged in impeachable offenses. Nixon's guilt or innocence should be judged on the basis of the rightness or wrongness of *his* behavior. If previous Presidents and/or Edward Kennedy had engaged in similar or worse activities, this would suggest only that they deserved censure, not that Nixon deserved absolution.

A similar irrelevant reason was put forth by a defense witness in the wiretapping trial of Bunker and Herbert Hunt, which took place in Lubbock, Texas, in 1975. These two sons of the late oil billionaire H. L. Hunt were accused of illegally recording the conversation of certain Hunt Oil Company employees. The final witness in their defense was the distinguished Baptist minister, Dr. W. A. Criswell, pastor of the First Baptist Church of Dallas, Texas. Criswell asserted (Associated Press release, *Odessa American,* September 26, 1975, p. 1A): "I have known these two boys a quarter of a century. . . . They are two of the finest boys on this earth." The Hunt brothers' general "goodness," however, was (and is) irrelevant to the issue of whether or not they should have been convicted for wiretapping activities (they were acquitted).

As a related example of irrelevant reason, consider this defense given by a Howard University professor of the behavior of certain black youths who assaulted whites during a "Human Kindness Day" gathering in Washington, D.C. (quoted by Robert S. Allen, "Inside Washington," *Odessa American,* May 27, 1975, p. 8A): "Don't blame it on the children. . . . Those youngsters mauling people were acting out a system of symbolic homicide in an alien force." Such sociological jargon appears irrelevant to the question of blame in this situation. Unless suffering from severe mental illness, the individuals should be held responsible for their behavior; those who assault others deserve blame.

A final instance of irrelevant argument is one advanced by Gerald R. Ford, then Vice President (Associated Press release, *Odessa American,* May 13, 1974, pp. 1A–2A), that President Nixon should remain in office partly because the nation was "a lot better off than if we had elected George McGovern [in 1972]." Even if Nixon was better than McGovern, this would be irrelevant to the issue of Nixon's Watergate-connected misdeeds.

Presentation of an Interpretation under the Guise of "Fact"   The third type of unfounded interpretation concerns the attempt by an advocate to present an interpretation as if it were a fact—that is, an endeavor by the arguer to hide a clearly subjective rendering of the information by disguising it as an objective, agreed-upon fact.

An example of interpretation disguised as fact may be found in an implication by a spokesman of the National Rifle Association of America ("National Opinion Survey," 1975) that gun control proponents generally favor the removal of guns from police officers: "Tell me, what would the crime rate be if the criminals knew our police were unarmed?" Undoubtedly some gun control supporters would react favorably to the idea; but most proposals that I have seen do not prohibit the police from carrying weapons. The N.R.A. spokesman erred by presenting a controversial opinion (gun control means disarmament of police forces) as if it were an acknowledged fact.

Similarly, columnist Tom Rose (*Odessa American,* October 5, 1975, p. 10D) was guilty of an unfounded interpretation when he argued against relinquishing the Panama Canal because, in his words, this act "would give the Communists control over both the Suez and Panama Canals." Rose presents two controversial interpretations ("Egypt is openly under Soviet domination; and the existing government in Panama . . . is also under the thumb of the Communists") under the guise of fact. In the case of Egypt, for example, Soviet influence appeared to be on the wane during the 1974–1978 period—Soviet technicians were expelled and supply agreements abrogated. Mr. Rose erred by treating his controversial interpretations about Soviet control of Egypt and Panama as if no one could or would challenge these assertions. The assertions are unfounded unless or until evidence is supplied to support them.

The Distorted Interpretation

The central deficiency of an unfounded interpretation is its lack of supporting evidence. The distorted interpretation differs somewhat from its cousin the unfounded interpretation in that distortion involves more of a misuse of evidence than an absence of favorable evidence. Distortion may consist of one or both of two misuses of evidence. Distortion by commission occurs when an advocate misrepresents favorable or unfavorable evidence pertaining to a claim. In other words, the advocate does the following: (1) unfairly overstates the significance of favorable evidence, and/or (2) unfairly understates the significance of unfavorable evidence. Distortion by omission, on the other hand, means that an advocate suppresses or omits data unfavorable to the claim.

Distortion by Commission Students of rhetorical argument commonly identify three major types of distortion by commission: exaggeration, equivocation, and the misrepresenting of either an issue or an opponent's position, two variations of a fallacy sometimes termed "straw man." Let us consider briefly each of these forms of distortion.

Exaggeration Exaggeration may be defined as a fallacy resulting from overstating the significance of a particular piece of evidence (or, indeed, of a claim). When one exaggerates, he or she misuses the otherwise legitimate rhetorical technique of maximization. Examples of exaggerated data and claims are not difficult to find. The authors of a *Newsweek* article (May 5, 1975, p. 18) were guilty of an exaggeration when they asserted that "only one conflict in American history—the Civil War—ever divided the United States more brutally than Vietnam or imprinted such an album of nightmarish images on the national psyche." The critic is tempted to remind these authors of the enormous divisions brought about as a result of the bitter Revolutionary War (1775–1781), to say nothing of the Korean action and other conflicts.

Columnist George Benson ("Looking Ahead," *Odessa American,* June 18, 1974, p. 4A) similarly exaggerated the significance of terrorist acts (such as kidnapping and bombing) that were taking place in the United States in 1974. "America," he wrote, "is now in the beginning stages of where South Vietnam was in the early fifties." Even a cursory glance at American and Vietnamese history suggests that the United States is unlikely ever to experience a wave of terrorism such as that which took place in Vietnam. Vietnamese terrorism reached massive proportions because of the strong communist guerilla force that controlled large areas of South Vietnam. No such guerilla force was then in existence or is likely ever to exist in the United States.

As another example of exaggeration, consider columnist "Injun" Woody Palmer's criticism of the 1974 pay increases voted by members of Congress (*Odessa American,* February 21, 1974, p. 3A): "The economy has never recovered from the whopping 40 percent increase given to members of Congress in 1969." Even granting Palmer's evidence that congressional pay raises "trigger salary boosts for almost 10,000 career federal workers and foreign service personnel," and, further, his argument that congressional raises set an "example" for the private sector, it is difficult to accept the notion that such increases—even for over 10,000 people—have a drastic effect in an economy with a gross national produce of over $1 trillion and a work force of nearly 100 million.

Finally, to illustrate the notion of exaggeration, I wish to make reference to two apparent exaggerations made in reference to the alleged effects that would ensue if President Richard M. Nixon were impeached. In arguing against impeachment ("Sensing the News," *Odessa American,* May 25, 1974, p. 10A), columnist Anthony Harrigan voiced the concern that the United States might follow "in the path of the Latin [American] countries whose presidents are ousted on the basis of a political whim." Without proceeding into a detailed examination of this claim, it appears to me that the use of constitutional process of impeachment of a President only twice in more than a hundred years bears little resemblance to the military coups and palace revolts that characterize South American politics. The following anti-impeachment assertion by columnist Jeffrey St. John ("St. John's Journal," *Odessa American,* November 12, 1973, p. 8A) may similarly be classified as an exaggeration: "One can safely predict that if impeachment of Richard Nixon should be successfully carried off, it will imperil our liberties just as the impeachment of Andrew Johnson did." Frankly, it is difficult for me to understand how the constitutionally prescribed process of impeachment could "imperil" the liberties guaranteed all Americans by that same Constitution. Common to the arguments cited here as exaggerations is the tendency to place undue confidence in interpretations that appear to be highly extreme.

Equivocation Distortion by equivocation is a fallacy that is committed when one falsely implies that two words having different meanings are synonyms. That is, the arguer uses words of different meaning as if those words were equivalent. Perhaps the best contemporary example of equivocation may be seen in the tendency of some columnists to equivocate the terms "rated second" and "second-rate." When something or someone is rated second (i.e., in second place), it is meant that the thing or person is rated "number 2" when ranked against other persons or things of the same type. Thus, an Olympic silver medal winner is a person who has finished in second place in some athletic event. "Second-rate," on the other hand, means that someone or something belongs to a category which is identifiably inferior to a comparable "first-rate" category. Thus, when compared to a royal palace, a log cabin is "second-rate" in terms of its size and grandeur (although a palace is a "second-rate" dwelling place when compared to a log cabin, using the criterion of an appropriate birthplace for a character in a Horatio Alger "rags to riches" story).

Having defined the terms "rated second" and "second-rate," it is clear than an Olympic silver medal winner is not a second-rate athlete—unless, of course, the margin between the second-place and first-place performances is an enormous one. Yet although the differences between "rated second" and "second-rate" are obvious, the terms have been frequently equivocated by political commentators. Columnist Anthony Harrigan has put the matter thus (*Odessa American,* May 19, 1975, p. 10A): "Do the American people want the United States to cut back its armed forces and accept second-class status in the world?" Even assuming that defense cutbacks meant that the United States could be classed as the second strongest military power in the world, it does not necessarily follow that America's defense would be "second-class" (unless, of course, the Soviet Union were allowed to attain a vast military advantage). Regardless of minor differences in military power, the United States and the U.S.S.R. would continue to hold the rank as first-class military powers when compared to the other nations of the world. It is quite possible that relinquishing to the U.S.S.R. our traditional first-place ranking in military power would pose dangers by creating conditions that would tempt the Soviets to behave more aggressively. However, the equivocation of the terms "first-rate" and "rated first" detracts from the quality of the debate over military spending.

Straw man   A third form of distortion by commission has been termed the straw man argument. As its name implies, the straw man is a fallacy that occurs when an advocate sets up an artificial issue or opponent. Instead of confronting the real issue or opponent, the advocate attacks the straw man. Like the scarecrow in a corn field, the argumentative straw man appears real and relevant—but it isn't. Straw man argumentation consists of two closely related persuasive techniques: (1) the device of setting up a false issue to confuse the real, important questions at hand and (2) the device of misrepresenting the position of one's opponent and then attacking the misrepresentation rather than the opponent's actual position.

A classic example of setting up a straw man issue occurred in a hearing before the Odessa (Texas) Junior College Board of Trustees on the matter of dismissing Dr. Jaroslav Piskacek from his position as a language teacher at the college (*Odessa American,* June 11, 1975, p. 14B). A college tenure committee had recommended that because of low enrollments in his German classes Dr. Piskacek should be reassigned to teach Spanish at the college. The college administration sought to overrule the tenure committee and thus to dismiss

Piskacek on the grounds that he lacked having eighteen graduate hours in Spanish, the number that is recommended by the Southern Association of Colleges and Schools (an accrediting agency). Piskacek argued that he possessed the recommended graduate hours, and thus the debate centered on the issue of whether Dr. Piskacek did, in fact, possess eighteen graduate hours in Spanish.

At this point in the debate, however, the administration introduced what appears to have been a straw man issue. It was argued that Odessa College had to dismiss Dr. Piskacek in order to maintain its accreditation with the Southern Association. It appears unlikely, however, that the Southern Association would remove accreditation because one faculty member at a particular institution lacked the recommended eighteen hours (especially since a case could be made that the faculty member in question did possess the eighteen credit hours). Thus, the issue of a loss of Odessa Junior College's accreditation acted merely as a straw man diversion.

It requires no special insight to identify similar straw man issues that are periodically introduced into disputes. When the editors of the *Odessa American* argued (November 4, 1973, p. 6D) against a salary increase for members of the Texas State Legislature, they raised a straw man issue that the salary increase "would further the costs of state government." Without going into detail about the merits of the proposed salary hike, it is clear that the increase for a hundred or so legislators would have had a minuscule effect on the Texas state budget.

A second and related strain of straw man argument may be seen in the occasional endeavor by an arguer to misrepresent an opponent's position in order to attack a distorted straw position rather than the opponent's actual position. As a rule, the straw position is considerably less appealing than the real one, a fact that explains why arguers often use straw man misrepresentation.

Such a misrepresentation may be seen in a column by Anthony Harrigan (*Odessa American,* May 25, 1974, p. 10A) in which he argued that many members of Congress desired to impeach President Nixon because of the President's use of profanity (as revealed by the taped Oval Office conversations). "There is a very real danger," he wrote, "that impeachment may proceed on spurious grounds. A President's use of rough language in private talks with his assistants certainly does not constitute a high crime or misdemeanor." Harrigan, of course, is correct in his argument that bad language constitutes an illegitimate reason for impeachment. However, since impeachment supporters were predominantly concerned with matters other than the deleted and undeleted expletives of the Nixon transcripts, it appears that Harrigan is refuting a straw man position that did not represent the real concern of the proimpeachment forces.

Historian Barbara Tuchman (*Newsweek,* February 3, 1975, p. 11) likewise establishes a straw position for her opponents in a column in which she argues against territorial concessions by Israel. "Nevertheless the feeling grows that if only the Jews of Israel would go away and the Jews of America would stop supporting them, the oil problem and the threat of war would vanish. There follows a rising demand upon Israel for concessions: a return of the Mitla and

Gidi passes and Sinai oil fields to Egypt, the Golan Heights to Syria, Jerusalem to satisfy King Faisal, the West Bank to the PLO." Tuchman argues that such concessions would amount to appeasement and would fail to achieve peace, and she implies that calls by the United States government and others for Israeli land concessions are motivated by a desire to ensure supplies of Arab oil. This may be largely a straw position. It appeared that calls for Israeli concessions during 1975 were motivated by a belief that some concessions were fair and that these would be necessary parts of a stable negotiated Middle East peace settlement. Former Secretary of State Henry A. Kissinger's 1975 policy of step-by-step disengagement of Israeli, Egyptian, and Syrian armies seemed to be based on the assumption that land concessions were appropriate and necessary for peace.

Distortion by Omission   Whereas distortion by commission means that an advocate makes a questionable statement, distortion by omission concerns those occasions when an advocate omits known contradictory information that is directly relevant to the issue at hand. It would be unreasonable, of course, to expect advocates to include every possible detail in every argument. However, an advocate lessens the validity of his or her argument by neglecting to cite information that is (1) directly relevant to the issue at hand, (2) sufficiently significant that someone conversant with the issue should be aware of it, and (3) directly contradictory to an important aspect of the argument being advanced.

An interesting example of the omission of relevant information occurred in an advertisement of the "Stadium for Odessa" committee. An October 1974 flyer distributed to voters argued that "Odessa Needs a Stadium" and described the benefits to be gained by voter approval of the 17,000-seat complex. Omitted from the advertisement was the fact that the city already possessed an adequate stadium and that the old stadium could be improved for far less cost than the more than $4 million required for the proposed new edifice. When the omission is compared to the favorable evidence, it is clear that the "Stadium for Odessa" group used an overstated qualifier in claiming a need for a new structure.

As final illustrations of the rhetorical device of omitting contrary information, consider these two instances. The first is reported by *Newsweek* magazine (April 28, 1975, p. 22) and concerns the effort by the U.S. Department of State to document an alleged North Vietnamese campaign of atrocities in conquered South Vietnam:

> Are fears of a Communist blood bath in South Vietnam justified? Yes, argues the American Embassy in Saigon, which is bombarding Washington with cables indicating that a reign of retribution is already under way. . . .
> When the U.S. Embassy in Saigon learned that *Newsweek* was investigating the reports, it suddenly—and for the first time in weeks—offered to make officials available to be interviewed. The embassy, in fact, even showed reporters copies of the classified cables it had sent Washington, setting forth the gruesome details of Communist atrocities. A U.S. official subsequently confided, however, that the

embassy sifted through all the reports it received based on interviews with refugees and culled out only the most extreme cases to send to Washington. And, he added, the embassy did not pass on to [Secretary of State Henry] Kissinger refugee interviews that tended to cast doubt on the blood bath theory.

Because the United States embassy in Saigon hoped to persuade Washington of the need for greater military aid for the collapsing Saigon government, it was only natural to maximize the importance of the alleged bloodbath. However, if the *Newsweek* account is accurate, the embassy may have been guilty of distortion via omission. A similar charge of distortion by omission is leveled by the editors of the *Odessa American,* (February 11, 1974, p. 6A) against "haters" of the oil companies.

> "The oil companies 'windfall' profits," the anti-capitalistic mentality screams. "Why in one year alone, 1973, they doubled their profits of the year before. There oughta be a law! . . ."
> What the haters of the oil industry conveniently neglect to state, is that oil industry profits during 1972, and for several years previously, were extremely low; so low, in fact, that investment capital needed to expand production had fled elsewhere.
> On an average, for example, industry profits during 1972 were in the vicinity of three to three and one half percent. Even doubled, and we know of no oil company reporting a hundred percent profit gain, that would hardly add up to "exorbitant" or "windfall," would it?

While it was clearly in the interest of this conservative oil-country newspaper to promote the petroleum point of view, its observation should be well-taken. When discussing the percentage increase in oil profits, the previous level of profits is relevant information that should not be omitted.

The preceeding discussion of invalid (unfounded and distorted) interpretations should not be taken as evidence that most interpretations are invalid. However, it is clear that the line separating valid from invalid interpretation is a fine one—as in the difficult distinction that must ever be made between legitimate maximization and illegitimate exaggeration. Rhetorical validity depends on the care that is exercised in (1) comparing the favorable and unfavorable arguments and (2) matching the arguments to the qualifier pertaining to a claim. When data are misrepresented or omitted, invalidity is likely to result.

APPLICATIONS

Having completed this chapter on interpretations and interpretive validity, you should be ready to try your hand at identifying and analyzing arguments that are phrased in the language of definition.

Exercise 5-1: Identifying Samples of Interpretive Argument

For those interested in learning to work with interpretive language, the first step is to be able to recognize examples of the interpretive types. Perhaps the best means for demonstrating your knowledge of these types is for you to collect samples of the arguments.

You will encounter most forms of interpretation just in the course of your normal reading and listening. Collect clippings or write down the samples as you encounter them, being sure to identify information about the source (author, place, date, page number) from which you have obtained each example. As I noted in directions for exercise 4-1, you may need to edit your clipping to make it more useable. It may help to abstract or outline it. Be sure to identify a single statement (or paraphrase) from the text to serve as the focus for your analysis.

Your instructor may wish you to bring these examples to class for discussion. It is also possible to construct your own representatives of each of the interpretive arguments. Some students prefer to make up their own arguments rather than to collect them from other sources. You or your instructor may wish to do this in addition to, or instead of, collecting them from others.

Also, as you look for examples, it will become apparent that some argumentative statements may simultaneously exemplify more than one pattern of interpretive thought.

Exercise 5-2: Testing the Validity of Interpretive Arguments

One of the key words in this textbook has been "validity," and thus it is important to be able to judge the extent to which our sample arguments are valid. In completing this exercise on validity, you should review both the definition of rhetorical validity presented in chapter 3 and the section "Standards of Validity for Interpretive Argument" presented in this chapter. Be sure to reread the directions for exercise 3-9. These guidelines describe the overall process of validity analysis. The specific directions for analyzing the validity of definitional arguments are as follows:

I   Use one or more of the sample arguments you gathered in exercise 5-1.

II   Select a single sentence statement to serve as the focus for your validity analysis. You may take a statement, verbatim, from your clipping. Or you may abstract the argument into a single claim.

III   Identify a qualifier that expresses the certainty asserted by the advocate. You may be able to take a qualifier directly from the text, or you may need to estimate a qualifier. If you make an estimate, explain how you arrived at it.

IV   Place your sample argument in an adversarial context. That is, identify at least five arguments that support and five that oppose the claim. Some of the arguments may be contained in the clippings that you have collected; otherwise, you will need to rely on your general knowledge about the dispute. Your comparison of the favorable and unfavorable information is criticial to the assessment of validity. Once you have identified the relevant data (including significant, relevant data that may have been omitted), you will need to decide whether the favorable data is greater than, equal to, or less than the weight of the unfavorable data.

V On the basis of step 4, judge whether or not the information favoring the claim outweighs the unfavorable information. If the favorable outweighs the unfavorable, a positive level of certainty is established. If not, then a neutral or negative level of certainty has been justified. Explain your judgment.

VI Compare the asserted and established levels of certainty. The claim will be valid unless you think that the asserted level exceeds the established. Make (and justify) a judgment as to whether the asserted level of certainty is less than, equal to, or greater than the established level. This comparison will yield your overall validity judgment. Explain your judgment. If, for example, the advocate has used the qualifier "certainly," then the favorable evidence must outweigh the unfavorable evidence to a great extent. If the advocate has asserted the qualifier "possibly," then the favorable evidence need not outweigh the unfavorable by a great margin. Finally, if the advocate has qualified his claim as being "possible, but not likely," then the claim may be valid even if the favorable data are *less* in weight to the unfavorable! That is, if the advocate uses an extremely weak qualifier (as was the case in the conspiracy-type argument by Fortney H. Stark), then only slight supporting evidence is needed.

VII In analyzing interpretive validity, you should remember that each pattern of interpretive argument has a specific feature that relates to the testing of its validity. For instance, to invalidate a dilemma one need only identify a third reasonable alternative. Your validity analysis may enable you to classify individual arguments as belonging to one of the general types of invalid interpretation. Thus, a dilemma argument that ignores one or more reasonable alternatives may represent a distortion by omission.

VIII In the course of completing this exercise you may observe that it is usually easier to recognize weaknesses in arguments with which we ourselves disagree than in those that we support and believe to be true.

Exercise 5-3: Applying Other Standards to Interpretive Arguments

Your instructor may want you to test the effectiveness, truth, or ethics of an interpretive argument. If so, follow the directions for exercises 3-6, 3-7, and 3-8.

Chapter 6

Evaluations: Arguments That Draw Issues of Value

Chapter 4 dealt with arguments whose basis was fact. In chapter 5 we explored the dimensions of definition that can exist when claims are made. In this chapter I will complete my presentation of the trilogy of argument. Here I will treat the third form of argument—claims that raise initial issues of value. The introductory section of the chapter will explain the basic workings of value argument. In the next three sections, I present a number of values that are commonly used as the basis of arguments. Finally, I will introduce some methods for assessing the validity of evaluations.

LANGUAGE IS EVALUATIVE

Arguments reveal the way we look at the world. When an advocate contends that something is good or bad, we learn more about that person's vision of the ideal world. Because our language invariably suggests our preferences, Weaver calls language a "value-laden vehicle" (in Johannesen, Strickland, and Eubanks, 1970, p. 223). Weaver is making the point that words carry value judgments: When we discuss something as being "effective," we reveal a preference for it. Similarly, a "successful" plan is a good one—in contrast to a "failure," which is bad. Even a single word—"progressive" or "oppressive"—amounts to a value judgment. As a result, when we attach words to things—e.g., a "new car"—we impute a value to the thing.

One should not carry Weaver's point to extremes, however. It is often possible to use language with some degree of objectivity. As I noted in chapter 2, language has the capacity to report as well as to reveal our preferences. "The frog is sitting on the log" is a sentence that reports more than it evaluates. Nevertheless, because some claims involve words that carry a high degree of evaluation, it is necessary to give careful study to arguments in which evaluation is paramount. This brings us to the subject of evaluative claims—arguments that raise a first-order issue of value.

The basic question concerning value arguments deals with the meaning of "value." Exactly what is a value? In chapter 3, I noted that values have to do with the moral goodness and badness of things. I also cited Rokeach's distinction between terminal and instrumental values. Further insight into the phenomenon of value may be gained by reference to Rokeach's full definition of a value (1973, p. 5): "A *value* is an enduring belief that a specific mode of conduct or end-state of existence is personally or socially preferable to an opposite or converse mode of conduct or end-state of existence." In other words, values are a person's notion of what is to be preferred. When we evaluate, we make a decision as to what is best.

It is difficult to discuss "the preferable" or "the best" in the abstract. The meaning of value may be clarified by listing some examples of things held as being preferable. Below is a list of values that I have obtained from many clippings collected over the years. Each of the following concepts has served as the basis of a value argument. That is, each of the concepts has been identified as something preferable:

academic freedom	exclusivity
academic integrity	fairness
Americanism	family
balanced budget	federalism
beauty	freedom (of choice)
charity	free enterprise
collective action	free market
commitment	freedom of the press
compromise	God
conservation	health
democracy	honesty
dignity	honor (pride)
distinction	individualism
economic growth	jobs
economic stability	legality
efficiency	life
energy	love
environment	loyalty
equality	military strength

money

moral behavior

national security

prestige

property

protection

punishment

religion

responsibility

rights

sacrifice

safety

self-defense

self-help

self-interest

sex

sovereignty

states' rights

strength

success

truth

two-party system

This list is not intended to be comprehensive. Everyone could probably add ten or more values to the roster without much effort. The list is also not particularly systematic. As you read through the values, you may have noticed that these values are a pretty mixed bag. Well-recognized values such as freedom are lumped together with terms such as "environment." Certainly, the list is a rather miscellaneous set of things held as preferable. Rokeach's notion of terminal versus instrumental values gives us some help in sorting out the above terms. For instance, "freedom" would be a desirable end-state, whereas "honesty" is a preferable mode of conduct. However, this distinction does not tell us all we need to know about the functioning of values. Thus, before examining any of the above values in detail, let us try to bring some further order to the concept of value itself.

Values as Ultimate Terms

Rokeach's definition of value suggests that values require a discovery of the preferable. It follows, then, that evaluation requires choice. After all, one can identify the preferable only by comparing it to what is not preferable. Hence, every evaluation is a conscious effort to identify what is best in a particular time or place. Values, then, function as ultimate terms. When we choose one value (e.g., "safety") over another value (e.g., "freedom"), we are saying that in a particular situation safety is the ultimate or highest term. It takes precedence over freedom and over all other values which might apply. Weaver (1970, pp. 211–212) describes ultimate terms as being words that "carry the greatest potency" for people: They are the most forceful or powerful words. Ultimate terms are concepts held as preeminent in a given context.[1]

Let me cite some examples. A few sentences ago, I presented safety as a value that might sometimes take precedence over freedom. In this connection, traffic laws are instances in which we give up freedom in order to achieve safety. Adherence to stop signs requires us to give up some of our freedom to move, but such adherence presumably enhances our safety. In many driving situations, therefore, safety is the ultimate term and freedom is a subordinate one. The same process of identifying the ultimate term can be found in all value

---

[1]For some persons, an ultimate term would predominate in every case.

arguments. In the March 1976 edition of *Happy Motoring News* (a publication of Exxon Corporation), the editors included an essay on divestiture (the process of forcing corporations to sell off some of their holdings). Next to the article on divestiture appeared a short feature treating the rural tradition of raising a barn (a group of neighbors would work together to build a barn for a family). The barn-raising article was entitled "The Right to Own Property." These two articles, when taken as a whole, revealed the use of "property" as an ultimate term. Once the reader of these articles accepted property as ultimate, then divestiture—for whatever reason—could not be sanctioned.

The important thing to be noted about ultimate terms is that they may vary from situation to situation. In the article dealing with divestiture, property was ultimate. But in other contexts, different terms often come to the fore. Thus, an Indianapolis judge appealed to "separation of church and state" as being the ultimate basis for rejecting a textbook that favored the Biblical account of creation (*The New York Times,* April 18, 1977, p. 21). The judge explained that the Constitution prohibited teaching religious doctrine in public schools. Thus, in this instance, "religion" was held as subordinate to "separation of church and state." In other contexts, of course, "religion" is treated as the key term.

Thus far, I have discussed ultimate terms as being things treated in a favorable light. However, for every positive ultimate term, there exists a negative one. Weaver (1970, pp. 212, 223) calls the positive terms "god terms" and uses the expression "devil terms" to denote things held as being the worst. Weaver's own list of positive and negative ultimate terms includes the following:

god terms	devil terms
progress	tory (a nineteenth-century term)
fact	rebel (during the civil war)
science	Nazi
modern	fascist
efficient	communist
American	un-American
allies	prejudice

In Weaver's view, an advocate could win favor for a concept by connecting it to one of the god terms. For instance, "an efficient engine" would be a favorable evaluation. Conversely, a "communist plan" would be a bad one; a "prejudiced person" would deserve censure.

Weaver's concept of god terms and devil terms suggests that one may find value arguments based both on positive and negative concepts. This theory is borne out in practice. Recent calls by college presidents for less federal government interference in higher education will illustrate the point. *The Chronicle of Higher Education* (April 19, 1977, p. 5) contained a one-page "1976 Declaration of Independence" signed by the presidents of four metropolitan Washington, D.C., private universities. The presidents contended that the increasing volume of federal regulations threatened to undermine higher education. Although supporting the general social goals that underlay federal policies, the presidents argued that the regulatory practices were unnecessarily high-handed, disorganized, and consuming of resources. Throughout the article, "institutional independence" functioned as the god term, and "governmental interference" operated as the opposing devil concept.

The essential flavor of ultimate terms used in advertising is captured by Erma Bombeck in her nationally syndicated column (*Odessa American,* February 20, 1977, p. 4E).

> Mayva popped into my utility room the other morning and said, "So you've switched to the new laundry detergent ALL NEW SCUM FIGHTER?"
>
> "No, it's the one I've been using for 20 years. It's just had sparkle added to the second rinse."
>
> "I thought they added sparkle last year?"
>
> "No, last year it was Improved with the bleach built in and before that they added an Advanced Formula so I could see the difference."
>
> "Wasn't that the year my detergent was called Revolutionary Clean?"
>
> "No, yours was Power Boosted to eliminate the odor. Remember? People were fainting a lot."
>
> "I remember, but I liked it better when it was Reborn."
>
> "That was the year mine was Streamlined, but then the ecologists screamed and they came out with a low sudser called Perfected."
>
> "Remember the year HMQ was added?" smiled Mayva.
>
> "I certainly do. Incidently, what was HMQ?"
>
> "I don't know, but their advertising campaign had a fuzzy monster coming out of the washer and grabbing the clothes right off your back."
>
> "You've used your detergent a long time too, haven't you?"
>
> "Yep," said Mayva. "I've stuck with it through Renovated, Futurized, Upgraded and Reinforced to fight grease."
>
> "Me too," I said. "I've hung in there through Newly-Developed, Renewed, Revised and Enriched."
>
> "I was going to buy mine when it was All Modern, but before I could buy a box, it had changed to Advanced."
>
> "You've got to move fast or you miss a step," I said, opening the dryer.
>
> "Was yours ever All Purpose?"
>
> "Oh sure, at one time my laundry detergent was so powerful it could clean without water and would take the liver spots off your hands."
>
> "I wonder where they go from here," asked Mayva. "I mean where do you go after Better! Better! All New! and Ultimate Perfection?"
>
> "Funny you should say that. I just got a new box of my detergent in the cupboard. It reads, "The Original Scum Fighter!"
>
> "We've been had," said Mayva.
>
> "I know."

As a result of hours of advertising, consumers have come to accept expressions like "new" and "improved" as conferring an ultimate seal of approval. These have become ultimate positive expressions in advertising.

Values as Sources of Motivation

In addition to playing the role of ultimate terms, values may be seen to function as motivating concepts. A motive is an internal intent, need, desire, or goal (see

Bormann et al., 1969, pp. 263–264). Motivating concepts are terms that may stimulate us to be interested in something, need something, desire something, or set up something as a goal. Many of the values presented in my original list have a motivational element. Concepts such as beauty, health, and prestige are things that are desired by most persons. If an object is described as giving beauty, health, or prestige, we are likely to desire it. If something produces pain or anxiety, we are persuaded to avoid it. When advocates cite the value of something, they cause us to desire it. In this sense, values are labels for things people need—or, in the case of negative values, things people want to avoid.

One does not have to look far afield to find countless examples of values used as motivating concepts. The value of prestige is very frequently used in advertisements for memberships or credit cards. Consider the appeals to prestige and exclusivity that are contained in this opening paragraph from a letter (March 1976) offering to consider me for a Diners Club card:

> Dear Mr. Sproule,
>   A person of your position certainly knows distinction. That's precisely why I'm sending you this invitation to apply for membership in Diners Club.

Clearly, this paragraph is directed to my ego and desire for prestige. The persuasive intent is evident: If I want to obtain prestige, I should apply for the card. The letter went on to assure me that the membership standards were quite strict: "We often turn down people other cards would accept!" However, lest I fear rejection, the letter assured me that mine was a special invitation and that I had been chosen to receive it by the "membership committee."

The close connection of positive and negative motivating values can be seen in an advertisement (fall 1976) for an executive's self-training course. As a promotion for its "Executive's Workshop," the Bureau of Business Practice offered to send subscribers an examination copy of their "The Executive's Complete Portfolio of Letters." The book was described as having "crisp, concise, expertly-written" letters for every business situation. Appeals to both positive and negative values were used to highlight the merits of the letter portfolio. The following values were cited:
Positive motivating concepts (1) Monetary gain: The letters would help in "pulling in overdue accounts." (2) Convenience: "You'll save hours of work."
Negative motivating concepts (1) Avoidance of anxiety: "You'll never work and worry over a business letter again!" (2) Avoidance of embarrassment: "You'll be spared the risk of embarrassing errors."

This message neatly integrates both positive and negative motivations. By appealing to human needs, the advertiser increases the likelihood that the consumer will be persuaded to act.

It is important to realize how widespread is the motivational use of values. One quick way to gain experience in dissecting the motive use of values is to pay close attention to television commercials. In a span of but a few hours, you will see messages that connect a product to one or more values. Commercials purport to show us how to gain desirable outcomes and avoid painful ones. The television viewer has but to purchase a given product to become:

popular	healthy
sexy	comfortable
beautiful	intelligent
admired	noticed

By the same token, the consumer is told that certain purchases will enable one to avoid undesirable states of being. Deodorants will preclude embarrassment. Soaps will prevent disease. Drugs will cure pain.

In short, Americans are daily bombarded with a host of motivational value arguments. These appeals focus on values that are closely connected to human needs. By appealing to these values, advocates seek to stimulate a response from the listener.

Values and Interpretations

In the last few paragraphs I have explained how values may be manifested both as ultimate and as motivating concepts. Now is probably a good time to mention something about the difference between evaluations and interpretations. You will recall from chapter 5 that an interpretive argument classifies something. It defines something in terms of something else. For instance, "Joe Gonzalez is another Babe Ruth" (a comparison). If language is truly evaluative, then it follows that many classes will be value-laden. Thus, when Joe Gonzalez is compared to Babe Ruth, the listener knows that Joe is being evaluated as "good." In fact, because Babe Ruth was one of the all-time baseball greats, Joe is probably being called "great."

The hypothetical argument about Joe Gonzalez has an important implication for the meaning of evaluative argument. This hypothetical argument might lead one to believe that interpretations are the same as evaluations. After all, the Gonazlez argument was an interpretation that possessed an evaluative dimension. To avoid confusing interpretive and evaluative arguments, it is necessary to return to the original definition of evaluation: Evaluations are arguments that state or imply first-order issues of value. This means that in an evaluation the quality (good/bad) dimension is so strong that it becomes our primary interest in investigating the argument. In other words, the question of definition (does X thing belong in Y category?) becomes subsidiary to the value issue: Is X good or bad (in view of its connection to Y)?

An illustration will serve to highlight the difference between evaluation and interpretation. In an article entitled "Kill the Metric," Lisa Schillinger (*Newsweek,* November 8, 1976, p. 9) disputed the advantages claimed for converting the United States to the metric system of measure. Her thesis statement represents an evaluative (as opposed to an interpretive) conclusion: "Conversion to the metric system in this country is simply an exorbitantly expensive experiment in inconvenience." To be sure, the statement contains an element of definition—metric system conversion is placed into the categories of "expensive" and "inconvenient." However, one will notice that the terms "expensive" and "inconvenient" are extremely value-laden. In the context of the article, both mean "bad." Hence, the argument is much more of an evaluation than it is an interpretation. The first-order issue requires that we resolve the goodness or badness, the rightness or wrongness of metric conversion. Definition is a subsidiary question—although still an important one. In sum, evaluations involve terms that are intimately related to goodness or badness. Definition-based arguments are those in which more conventional terms are used.

Values as Associations with the Good (or Bad)

There is one more thing to be said about value argument. Value statements are often very subtle arguments. In the example immediately above, the value claim was explicit and unsubtle. The metric conversion plan was termed "expensive" and "inconvenient." The connection was explicitly made by the arguer. Often, however, value arguments take more of the form of implications. The value connection is implicitly suggested more than it is flatly asserted.

One facet of celebrity advertising serves to illustrate value arguments that are based on subtle associations. Consider the use of football star O. J. Simpson in Hertz car-rental commercials. James J. Jordan, president of Batten, Barton, Durstine and Osborn, the agency that developed the ads, explained the economic advantages of associating Simpson and Hertz (*Newsweek*, January 10, 1977, p. 61): "Simpson stands for superstardom, speed, durability, all the points Hertz is trying to make about itself."

Another prominent instance of value associations is to be found in the monthly telephone and auto gasoline bills received by many consumers. The billing envelopes of such large corporations often contain a chatty newsletter-type publication. For instance, Exxon's *Happy Motoring News* usually contains a feature picture and article dealing with some contribution that Exxon has made to the environment. The May 1976 issue emphasized that the Escambia river is "alive and well," despite proximity to Exxon's Jay oilfield, and described the company as "deeply concerned with preserving the area's ecology." September's lead picture dealt with the bald eagle; in December the emphasis was on "Petroleum and the American Indians"; the February 1977 issue detailed a land donation by an Exxon geologist. The *Happy Motoring News* pictures and stories helped to connect Exxon with ecological and environmental values: Given the apparent unpopularity of large corporations in general and oil companies in particular, such articles help to build a positive corporate image. Everyone knows that petroleum companies are not organized to promote a positive ecology and environment; yet such value associations make effective arguments as to the social consciousness of business.

In this introductory section I have sketched out some of the basic workings of value arguments. Values are things held to be preferable. Values function both as ultimate terms and as sources of motivation. Value arguments resemble interpretations but involve a more explicit focus on goodness or badness. Finally, value arguments can be subtle. They are present when advocates associate their cause with the good (or their opponent's with the bad).

To give you a greater feel for the operation of value arguments, I will devote the next three sections of the chapter to samples of value arguments. The section that immediately follows will contain representative samples of some of the most frequently used value arguments, including arguments based on freedom or equality. The section that comes next is devoted to situations of value conflict—when one value is held as supreme over another. The final substantive section of the chapter concerns value arguments that apply to advocates. Such arguments as inconsistency and *ad hominem* will be explored here.

SOME IMPORTANT SOURCES OF VALUE ARGUMENT

In reviewing modern writings one cannot escape the conclusion that certain values are used almost incessantly as the basis for evaluations. Values such as freedom, equality, morality, safety, and privacy have become extremely prominent both as ultimate terms and as motivational concepts.[2]

Freedom

Being free of controls imposed by others is a particularly important value for Americans. Comparative surveys taken of college men in the United States, Australia, Israel, and Canada (Rokeach, 1973, p. 89) suggest that Americans may value freedom as being somewhat more important than other national groups do. This value was rated as most important by the American (and the Canadian) men: Australian and Israeli men rated freedom, respectively, as third and fourth in importance.

In view of its high ranking in the American value system, it is not surprising to find that freedom is a major source of value argument: Appeals to freedom appear frequently in contemporary argumentation. New Hampshire citizens George and Maxine Maynard cited freedom as the basis for their claim that they should be allowed to tape over the state motto—"Live Free or Die"—which is printed on automobile license plates. In a 7–2 decision, the U.S. Supreme Court upheld the Maynards' challenge of the state law which forbade obscuring any part of the license plate (*The New York Times,* April 21, 1977, p. A18). The court cited the First Amendment's freedom of speech provision as the basis for its decision.

Freedom has been used as the basis for opposing other laws and regulations. A 1975 release (*Odessa American,* June 30, 1975, p. 8A) reported that "about 2,500 bare-headed motorcyclists rallied at the [Wisconsin] state Capitol to protest a law which requires them to wear safety helmets." In addition to challenging the safety value of the helmets, the protesters alleged that the law

---

[2]Indeed, according to Rokeach (1973, pp. 165–188) the first two of these values—freedom and equality—serve as the turning points along which political ideologies differ.

violated their constitutional rights. Court rules that prohibit advertisements by lawyers have also been challenged as contrary to the principles of freedom. In 1976 a Seattle attorney, Richard Sanders, tested the prohibition by running an ad (*Odessa American,* February 11, 1976, p. 6B). Sanders used the value of freedom as a basis for denying that he had done wrong: "I believe I do have freedom of speech, the freedom to communicate my ideas to the public."

One common denominator of these three situations is the use of freedom as a value premise for argument. In each case the advocate asserted a right to be exempted from some form of control.

Equality

Equality is another value that is seemingly built into the traditional American value system. Gaining sanction in Thomas Jefferson's bold assertion in the Declaration of Independence that "all men are created equal," this value has long been used as a source for argument. In recent years the value of equality has gained greater argumentative status in view of new laws and legal decisions that have given greater significance to the value. Examples of recent equality-based legislation include:

- The Equal Pay Act of 1963: prohibits pay differences for men and women doing the same work.
- Title VI of the Civil Rights Act of 1964: prohibits discrimination based on race, religion, or national origin in educational programs receiving federal funds.
- Title VII of the Civil Rights Act of 1964: prohibits employment discrimination based on race, religion, national origin, or sex.
- Title IX of the Educational Amendments of 1972: prohibits discrimination on the basis of sex in federally supported educational programs.

Laws such as these have led to the establishment of programs, commissions, reports, and court cases dealing with alleged deprivations of equality. "Equality" has become a modern god term, with corresponding devil expressions like "discrimination" and "bias."

Value appeals based on equality have become common in arguments dealing with government expenditures. For instance, limits on federally funded abortions have been opposed on the basis of equality. The November 1976 issue of *Civil Liberties* (publication of the American Civil Liberties Union) cited court cases to argue that "such restrictions violate the rights of poor women to equal protection of the law" (p. 8). Writing in the "My Turn" column of *Newsweek* (June 9, 1975, p. 11), Lucy Komisar argued that limitations on federal abortion funding had the effect of "selling out the poor."

School financing is another area in which the equality argument has gained in popularity. *The New York Times* (April 20, 1977, p. 45) reported a ruling by the Connecticut Supreme Court that dealt with equality in education: "The Connecticut Supreme Court ruled yesterday that the existing system of financing schools largely through local property taxes provided unequal education and was therefore unconstitutional." What the court referred to was the greater ability of some school districts to raise funds in view of higher local property values. In a 1971 ruling by the California Supreme Court, the court argued that such funding "discriminates against the poor because it makes the quality of a child's education a function of the wealth of his parents and neighbors" (*Newsweek,* November 8, 1976, p. 64). In rulings such as these, the court has appealed to equality as a value justification for its actions.

Equality arguments have recently proliferated in administrative circles, legislatures, and law courts. Yet the use of the argument is not confined to governmental action. Consider an instance taken from the field of sports. A 1976 news story reported that tennis star Chris Evert and others threatened to boycott the Wimbledon tennis tournament because of the higher prizes for men than for women. Evert was said to have called for equal prize money (*Odessa American,* June 26, 1976, p. 4B).

Morality

Morality is a term that denotes an approved manner of behavior. When a society approves of conduct, it is said to be moral. Correspondingly, immoral acts are those considered as wrong by most people. Notions of morality may also result from codes, such as the Ten Commandments. Feelings of moral rightness and wrongness can be the source of value arguments. Indeed, because moral claims often deal with deep-seated personal beliefs, they can be quite emphatically argued. Let us consider some examples of morally based value arguments.

A letter to the editor (*Courier-Journal,* December 27, 1977, p. A6) dealing with a change in the Catholic Communion rite illustrates morality as a source of argument. The writer objected to the practice of receiving the Communion bread in the hand and used morality as a basis for evaluating the practice: "The forces of evil that have infiltrated the Catholic Church have succeeded in promoting further irreverence to the Blessed Sacrament by the reinstitution of Communion in the hand." Words such as "evil" and "irreverence" indicate that the claim is not merely interpretive—that it is evaluative.

Religious practices have strong moral connotations. However, contemporary sexual behavior is perhaps the most common field for moral arguments. My clippings file is loaded to the brim with moral evaluations of sexual conduct. Let me enumerate just a few.

1   The image of "Barbie" dolls: A newspaper feature story (*Odessa American,* May 6, 1976, p. 5A) quoted Bill Barton—designer of the original "Barbie" doll—as having doubts about the current product. Barton objected to Barbie's increasing bosom and her "too sexy" clothes. He concluded: "It has become an immoral situation where money and the selling of a product have become the most important thing."

2   The appropriateness of "Man, a Course of Study": "Man, a Course of Study" is an educational program dealing with human behavior that is taught in

many elementary schools. A part of the course involves study of other cultures. One of the cultures is that of the Netsilik Eskimos, who live in the Canadian Artic. In the unit on the Netsilik, students are introduced to practices such as trial marriage, wife swapping, infanticide, and even cannibalism. In an article on the course *Newsweek* (June 30, 1975, p. 62) summarized the arguments of those who question the inclusion of such items in the elementary school curriculum: "Presenting scenes of the Eskimos' primitive life-style without critical comment, the critics contend, undermines Western moral values."

   3   A homosexual character in "Doonesbury": "Doonesbury" is a current-events comic strip written by Gary Trudeau. Since his early days as a cartoonist for the Yale University student newspaper, "Doonesbury's" Trudeau has dealt with controversial subjects. In fact, many newspapers carry the cartoon on the editorial page. In early 1976 Trudeau briefly introduced a homosexual male character into the strip. Several newspapers suspended the comic strip for the week during which this character appeared. Charles Egger, editor of the *Columbus Citizen Journal* explained his paper's decision to suspend (*Journal Herald* [Dayton], February 13, 1976, p. 6): "We felt the subject matter was not appropriate for the comic page."

Each of these excerpts contains a moral evaluation. In each case, an advocate uses the value of socially approved (moral) behavior as the basis for a claim.

Safety

Being safe and secure is a condition that most persons value highly. Most readers have probably noticed safety used as a motivating value in advertisements. For instance, an ad for the "General Electric Home Sentry Smoke Alarm" cited safety as the major advantage of the product (*Newsweek,* September 27, 1976, p. 22): "It could help you save your family's lives." An ad for Pace citizen's band radio (*Newsweek,* August 30, 1976, p. 76) similarly used safety as the principle value term. The ad contained two photographs that illustrated the safety feature. The first showed a woman standing by her smoking car on a lonely country road. She was shown using her CB radio. The next scene resembled a parking lot. The stranded woman's lone vehicle was surrounded by a tractor, two pickup trucks, four sedans, one jeep, one van, and a Mack truck. All of the vehicles sported prominently displayed CB antennas. Piling out of these conveyances were about a dozen helpful-looking men. The point was clear: A CB provides security.

   Food additives have provided a recent forum for claims based on the value of safety. During the 1970s a host of products have been labeled as cancer-causing: cyclamates, hexachlorophene, red dye no. 2, certain hair dyes, etc. The controversy over saccharin represented a particularly heated discussion center-ing on safety claims. In early 1977 the Food and Drug Administration released the results of studies on the artificial, low-calorie sweetener saccharin. The Canadian government's research had suggested that saccharin was responsible for causing bladder cancer in laboratory rats. As a result of the "Delaney Amendment" to the 1938 Food, Drug, and Cosmetic Act, the F.D.A. announced its intention to ban the production and sale of saccharin. The value of safety is clearly the pivotal terms in the Delaney Amendment (quoted in *Newsweek,* March 21, 1977, p. 65): "No additive shall be deemed to be safe . . . if it is found, after tests which are appropriate for the evaluation of the safety of food additives, to induce cancer in man or animal."

An interesting facet of the saccharin controversy was the use of the safety value by both supporters and opponents of a ban on saccharin. The F.D.A. position was simple: Saccharin had been shown to cause cancer; therefore it is unsafe; therefore, it should be banned. However, opponents also used safety as a value premise in support of the continued sale of saccharin. They argued as follows:

1   The Canadian government tests were based on massive doses of saccharin. Limited use of the artificial sweetener might still be safe.
2   Because sugar is hazardous to the health of diabetics and overweight persons, banning it might harm the health of these individuals.

The saccharin dispute suggests that value arguments share an important feature of inductive arguments: Plausible claims may be advanced on an issue by more than one side.

Privacy

I have chosen the value of privacy as a fifth general illustration of the workings of value argumentation. I chose to consider privacy because this concept has recently gained in popularity as a premise for evaluations. The growing potency of this value term is reflected in a March 1976 issue of the *Bicentennial Times.* The *Times* reported a Massachusetts Bar Association program that dealt with the right to privacy (cosponsored by Boston 200—the city Bicentennial agency). The bar association explained that "although the Constitution did not mention the term 'privacy,' a Constitutional right to privacy has long been implicity accepted" (p. 16). The association and Boston 200 coproduced a series of radio and television spots that examined situations in which personal privacy had been invaded. As the bar association program suggests, privacy is being used increasingly as a means for evaluating human action.

In 1975, for example, the Alaska Supreme Court used the value of privacy to support a position that people have a right to use and possess marijuana in their own homes. The court argued that government had no power to prohibit private marijuana usage, notwithstanding its possible unhealthfulness. The court stated (*Odessa American,* May 28. 1975, p. 1A) that "this right to privacy would encompass the possession and ingestion of substances such as marijuana in a purely personal, noncommercial context in the home."

The most prevalent contemporary use of privacy arguments seems to be in the area of information gathering. Privacy has been used as a basis for challenging a Pennsylvania "Educational Quality Assessment" test. Much of this test measures students' attitudes toward peers, authority, human relations, and the like and seeks to assess qualities such as honesty and citizenship. Opponents of the test claim that many of the questions are an invasion of privacy. Many argue that the test requires self-incriminating answers. Such objections—and the possibility of court action—were sufficient to persuade the Pennsylvania State Board of Education to make some changes in the testing procedure. The board agreed to make the test completely anonymous and to inform students of their right not to take the test (*Newsweek,* September 1, 1975, p. 41). A similar concern for privacy has led IBM Corporation to strictly limit the amount of information it gathers about employees. The new IBM application form omits such traditional employee information as date of birth, martial status, and previous addresses (*Newsweek,* November 10, 1975, p. 96).

As in the case of equality, the privacy value is becoming a major basis for legislative action. For instance, the Family Educational Rights and Privacy Act of 1974 has significantly curtailed the practice of posting college grades. According to the Ohio State University ombudsman, Walt Craig (*The Lantern,* October 28, 1977, p. 5), "The use of social security numbers to post grades is also a violation of the student's right to privacy." A similar use of the value of privacy may be seen in efforts to legally limit automatic telephone dialers. These devices were first marketed in the summer of 1977. Even though only a few were sold, the whole idea of automatic, taped telephone calls generated many arguments against the devices. Legislation to limit the machines followed immediately. Congressman Les Aspin (D., Wisconsin) termed them "the ultimate invasion of privacy by advertisers" (*Courier-Journal,* November 18, 1977, p. B10).

Freedom, equality, morality, safety, and privacy are certainly not the only values held in esteem today. Numerous other terminal and instrumental principles are highly held. However, examination of just these five value terms illustrates the basic operation of evaluative arguments. Objects as diverse as "Barbie" dolls and CB radios are placed into value-laden categories. They are evaluated as good or bad. Common to all value arguments is the notion that a certain value principle gives ultimate sanction to an argument.

THE CONFLICT OF VALUES

What if more than one value applies to a situation? If value arguments are based on that which is preferable, then might not some situations involve a choice between or among values? Don't advocates have to select which value to emphasize and which to subordinate? The suggestion that values may conflict brings us to an important facet of evaluative argumentation. In most of the examples above, I cited only one of the values that allegedly applied. Thus, the telephone machines were said to violate privacy. Oversexed "Barbie" dolls represented an alleged affront to morality. However, careful review of these value situations would reveal, I think, that more than one value applied. For instance, in using privacy as a basis for legalizing home consumption of marijuana, the Alaska Supreme Court subordinated the values of safety and moral behavior. The court passed over arguments that marijuana smoking may be unhealthful and that many regard it as wrong. Similarly, in banning saccharin, the F.D.A. chose safety over freedom. The agency evaluated the sweetener as cancer-causing. This was cited as a justification for limiting consumers' freedom to purchase the product.

The point to be made here is that evaluations are inherently controversial. In almost every situation, it is possible to identify more than one value that applies. Hence, when an advocate evaluates something, he invariably chooses to emphasize one value and deemphasize another.

Freedom versus Morality

Possibly the most frequent value conflict is that between freedom and morality. One can find many instances in which one advocate has used freedom to oppose the morally based arguments of another. Morality is a basis used to challenge the freedom of advertisers on childrens' television programming. Opponents of advertising to children argue that advertising exploits children, induces them to desire harmful products (such as candied cereals), and ultimately makes them cynical of all statements. Professor Thomas Bever of Columbia University asserted (*Newsweek,* February 21, 1977, p. 69) that the advertisements may be "permanently distorting children's views of morality, society and business." Such arguments are used to support limitations on the freedom of advertisers to promote their products.

Periodic disputes over sexually oriented literature is another occasion for the freedom-morality conflict. In 1977 the publisher of *Hustler* magazine, Larry Flynt, was found guilty of publishing an obscene work. The case marked a classic struggle between morality-based arguments and freedom-oriented arguments. Clearly, Flynt's magazine was vulnerable to charges of immorality. As *Newsweek* magazine noted (February 21, 1977, p. 34): "To say that the content of Hustler is in bad taste is a gargantuan understatement, and even civil-libertarians are openly uncomfortable about defending its gynecologically crude nudes, articles about dismemberment and cartoons dwelling on bestiality." On the other hand, prohibiting Flynt's magazine infringes on his freedom to publish and infringes on his readers' freedom to purchase.

Further examples of the freedom-versus-morality conflict may be found in arguments for and against laws on personal conduct. A news story put the issue succinctly in describing opposing evaluations of new California sex and marijuana laws (*Odessa American,* January 1, 1976, p. 8C): "Supporters say the new laws are long overdue reforms that remove draconian penalties for victimless crimes. Critics contend that they will erode moral standards and encourage marijuana use and 'unnatural' sex acts." Each side uses a recognized value as the basis for argument. The laws are evaluated differently on the basis of differing ultimate terms.

As a final instance of disputes based on competition between freedom and morality, consider the argument over contemporary sports salaries. Recent court decisions and arbitration agreements have given sports stars the freedom to play out their contracts and select other teams. Previously, players had been limited in their ability to leave a ball club. As a result of their greater freedom, a number of stars have been hired by competing teams at extremely high salaries. Baseball team owner Charlie Finley argued (*Newsweek,* June 28, 1976, p. 65) that "there's no way we can operate with astronomical, unjustified salaries." Does the players' freedom outweigh the allegedly immoral effects of high sports salaries? Previous practice was to limit freedom for the "good of the game." Now, freedom seems to have gained greater status as the highest value term in sports employment.

Other Sources of Value Conflict

As the number of recognized values is large, so, too, is the potential for value conflicts. Below, I list a number of disputes in which differing values may be used as the basis for opposing positions on an issue.

1 Property versus safety (cited in *The New York Times,* April 19, 1977, p. 26): In 1977 the U.S. Supreme Court agreed to hear arguments on the constitutionality of provisions in the Occupational Safety and Health Act of 1970. The act permits O.S.H.A. inspectors to visit factories without a search warrant and to levy fines. A lower court ruled that this section of the law amounted to an unreasonable search and seizure—which is prohibited by the Fourth Amendment. The lower court thus affirmed the right to property as more important than the value of safety. The executive branch appealed the lower court decision, arguing that the safety legislation depended on the inspection provision.

2 Safety versus freedom: In a letter to "Dear Abby" (*Odessa American,* June 8, 1975, p. 10B) an airport security worker complained of the "dirty looks" and "snide remarks" she received from travelers who objected to the screening process. "Abby" sympathized with the worker and supported the antihijacking program: "I think the inconvenience of being searched is a small price to pay for a safe flight, don't YOU?"

3 Property versus morality: In June 1976, *The Ohio State University Monthly* (p. 15) reported on a university action against "ticket scalpers." The Ohio State University trustees adopted a resolution that prohibited the resale of athletic tickets for more than their original price. The trustees' action amounted to a limitation on the property rights of ticket purchasers. Many view the selling of tickets for profit—scalping—as wrong. Clearly, the trustees felt this way: They placed morality on a higher plane than property in this issue. Remember, however, that notions of morality differ. Citing results of a poll of students at Ohio State, *The Ohio State University Monthly* reported (September 1975, p. 9) that "more than two-thirds of the student body does not regard selling tickets for a profit as wrong."

4 Privacy versus freedom (of the press): In 1975 the U.S. Supreme Court overturned a Georgia statute that prohibited the publication of a rape victim's name. Because the victim's name had been mentioned in a criminal indictment, the Court ruled that the press could not be legally restrained from publishing it. The Court argued that "the freedom of the press to publish that information" outweighed the "interests in privacy" (*Newsweek,* March 17, 1975, p. 66).

5   Property versus life: In July 1967 Marvin Katko was injured by a shotgun booby trap set by farmer Ed Briney. The trap had been placed in a vacant house owned by Briney. Katko pleaded guilty to petty larceny for entering the house. However, he also brought a personal injury suit against Briney and was awarded damages of $30,000. Briney was forced to sell eighty acres of his farm to pay the damages. This incident is an illustration of a value conflict between property and life. Briney claimed the right to protect his property. Arguing that Katko would not have been injured had he not trespassed, Briney contends that "Katko was awarded for stealing" (*Odessa American,* February 8, 1976, p. 13C); Katko, on the other hand, admits his own guilt but argues that Briney was more at fault for crippling him. In other words, whereas Briney looks to property as the key term, Katko argues that human life has a value priority in this case.

6   Life versus women's rights: In 1974 Mrs. Inez Garcia was convicted for the murder of Miguel Jiminez, who, she said, had stood guard over her while another man raped her. In 1977 the case was retried and Mrs. Garcia was found innocent. The case is an interesting one, because it has been used as a basis for placing women's rights on a higher plane than life. A feminist activist was quoted (*Odessa American,* March 6, 1977, p. 10C) as arguing that the acquittal represented a breakthrough in overcoming the "whole problem of violence against women."

In each of the cases, above, the same object was evaluated differently. If one focuses on safety, inspections conducted under the terms of the Occupational and Health Safety Act are good. If one identifies property as the ultimate value, then the no-warrant inspections and fines are bad. The cases cited above by no means exhaust the range of possible value conflicts. However, they illustrate the need for arguers to consider their value choices carefully.

Conflicts Based on the Same Value

In the examples above, advocates used different values to produce opposing evaluations of the same set of facts. However, the student of argument will often encounter disputes in which opponents look to the same value. In these cases the arguers disagree over how the value should be applied. The sides each invoke the value differently. An opinion column by John D. Rockefeller III (*Newsweek,* June 21, 1976, p. 11) illustrates conflicts based on the same value. Rockefeller defends legalized abortion. He recognizes that "abortion is against the moral principles defended by the Roman Catholic Church, and some non-Catholics share this viewpoint." However, Rockefeller contends that proponents of abortion have a strong moral argument as well and argues that the anti-abortion position restricts "the religious freedom of others and their right to make a free moral choice." He concludes: "Where abortion is legal, everyone is free to live by her or his religious and moral principles." Rockefeller's moral argument for abortion illustrates how advocates may differ as to how a value applies to a situation.

Consider a related example of conflict over the meaning of equality. In 1977 and 1978 the U.S. Supreme Court heard arguments pursuant to the case of Allan Bakke. Mr. Bakke argued that he had been discriminated against because he was a white male. Bakke was one of hundreds rejected by the University of California for Davis Medical School. However, sixteen minority applicants gained admission, despite their having lower academic credentials. Bakke contended that the use of racial criteria to reserve places for certain candidates denied him equal treatment. The university defended its policies as being efforts to bring about general social equality for minority groups who had traditionally suffered discrimination. Hence, the racial criteria were said to be necessary to achieve racial equality. The value dilemma that is inherent in this dispute is well summarized by an October 26, 1977, editorial printed in *The Times* of London (reprinted in *The Chronicle of Higher Education,* November 28, 1977, p. 15).

> The issue raises a genuine dilemma, not least among Americans of enlightened and liberal views, who are divided over it. Two desirable social objectives are in irreconcilable conflict. On the one hand, there is the principle of non-discrimination and equality between men, irrespective of race. On that basis Bakke has a justified grievance that, because of the colour of his skin, and not because of any lack of merit, he has been given inferior treatment to someone of lesser attainment but, in the context, privileged racial group. On the other hand, and especially in the longer term, the narrowing of the economic, educational, cultural, social gap between whites and blacks is an objective which has for a long time been a cornerstone of government policy.

The point of the abortion and Bakke disputes is a simple one. Advocates may sometimes evaluate a situation differently by using the same value term. Thus, both sides of the abortion dispute have called their position "moral"; Bakke's case is bad if one takes a certain view of equality and good if one takes another.

These cases of value conflict are indications that evaluations require that choices be made. In most of the above situations, advocates took opposing positions on an issue—and used different values as the basis for the positions. However, in some the same value was applied differently to the two positions in a single situation. Indeed, the dimension of choice is an important feature of value argumentation. This has an important implication for judging the validity of evaluations. As I will indicate in the section on "validity," one's value preferences must be explained and justified.

VALUES APPLIED TO ADVOCATES

Values are terms that are applied to objects. The values that we have considered in this chapter may be used equally well as modifiers for persons, places, and things. However, there are a certain number of values that seem to apply best to persons—advocates of a position. In this section of the chapter, I will present five value terms that are most often used to evaluate the worth of arguers.

"Character" is a term used to denote the qualities possessed by a person. To say that a person has a good character is to say that he possesses qualities esteemed as good. "Character" is thus a kind of catchall term that is used to describe the value characteristics of a person. Each culture and subculture possess a notion of what constitutes esteemed personal characteristics. Strength may be considered desirable by one culture, whereas another accords primacy to gentleness. Honor may be more important than honesty—or vice-versa. Lack of universal agreement on what characteristics are good makes it difficult to define the expression "good character" precisely. Nevertheless, it is possible to find arguments based on notions of good character. These include: adhering to socially approved modes of conduct (i.e., having good morals), being competent, having good motives, being consistent, and not being simply expedient.

Morals

The person who behaves in a socially approved manner is thought of as being moral. As I noted, above, it is difficult to identify a mode of conduct that would be acceptable to all persons, but it is quite a simple matter to find examples of instances in which advocates have been evaluated on a moral basis. Let us consider some of these.

Opinion polls show that in general people have a high degree of respect for the late President John F. Kennedy. For instance, a 1976 Louis Harris poll (cited in Wallechinsky, Wallace, and Wallace, 1977, p. 31) ranked Kennedy second (to Roosevelt) in "overall performance" among the last seven American Presidents. Kennedy was rated highest among Presidents who "most inspired confidence" and who were "most personally appealing." On two occasions, however, *Newsweek* magazine has reported negative assessments made about the Kennedy Presidency. These reports list certain Watergate-like practices sanctioned by Kennedy (e.g., wiretapping) and his reputation with women (*Newsweek*, January 19, 1976, p. 31; December 29, 1975, pp. 14–16). In one report (January 19, 1976, p. 31), it was suggested that a tide of unfavorable stories "seems bound to shake the country's perception of its prince-President." In other words, the article predicted a less favorable future moral evaluation of Kennedy.

A particularly interesting case of moral evaluation took place during the 1976 Presidential campaign. Democratic candidate Jimmy Carter granted an interview to representatives of *Playboy* magazine. Most of the interview amounted to little more than the standard meet-the-candidate exchange. The discussion ranged over the familiar issues and personalities. However, in response to a final question about whether he had "reassured . . . people who are uneasy about your religious beliefs," Carter launched into a long soliloquy. He spoke of Baptist beliefs; he made references to Scripture. Carter then spoke of the "almost impossible standards" that Christ had set for his followers. Mentioning Christ's injunction that anyone who looks at a woman with lust has already committed adultery in his heart, Carter revealed that "I've looked at a lot of women with lust." Carter added that although he had committed adultery only in his heart, he did not condemn the person who "leaves his wife and shacks up with somebody out of wedlock." In his view, the person who was loyal to his wife should not feel superior to one who "screws a whole bunch of women." Carter then made a summary statement about sin and religion. He closed by relating his religious views to the job of the Presidency: "But I don't think I would *ever* take on the same frame of mind that Nixon or Johnson did—lying, cheating and distorting the truth." Carter expressed the hope that his "religious beliefs alone would prevent that from happening to me." (*Playboy,* November, 1976, p. 86.)

This interview turned out to have a powerful effect on the public. *Playboy* released an advanced text of the interview in mid-October. It was immediately sensationalized by the media. Initial emphasis was given to the "I've looked at a lot of women with lust" statement. CBS television news not only reported the statement orally, but flashed the words onto the screen, line by line. As in the case of Betty Ford's remarks on sex and her daughter, the networks and wire services reported innumerable expressions of "shock," "outrage," and the like from the public. Then came the word from Carter supporters: They praised him for his deep beliefs and candor. After a few days, attention shifted to Carter's use of the words "shack up" and "screw." Next, the focus was on his remarks about ex-President Lyndon B. Johnson. Finally, comment centered on the wisdom of granting *any* interview to *Playboy,* regardless of what he said.

Supporters of President Ford did not overlook the potential implications of Carter's interview. Carter had connected himself to a magazine that has been criticized as having an essentially hedonistic outlook on life; he used "dirty words"; he admitted to moral failings; and he insulted former President Johnson—thereby risking the ire of Texans. Ford campaign forces sponsored a national newspaper advertisment that showed the *Playboy* cover—bearing Carter's name—together with the front cover of *Newsweek* (October 18), which bore Ford's picture.

Carter's *Playboy* interview is a classic illustration of how moral values may be applied to an advocate. By connecting himself to *Playboy,* adultery, and "dirty words," Carter gave his opponents the opportunity to attack him as a person.

The Kennedy and Carter examples have centered on the issue of sex as a focus for moral claims. Before moving on to other sources of evaluation, I should emphasize that there are other bases for the moral evaluation of advocates. For instance, former Secretary of State Henry Kissinger has been plagued by charges that his Vietnam policies were immoral. For instance, certain students protested against his appointment to the faculty of Columbia University. As *The New York Times* reported (April 23, 1977, p. 23), "critics claim that Dr. Kissinger should not be allowed to teach because of his 'immoral' involvement in [the] Vietnam war." Similarly, Ohio State University football coach, Woody Hayes's attack on a sidelines cameraman was the source of a debate over his character. Opinion was divided between those who objected to his "repulsive actions" and those who believed that he was justified in defending his privacy (*Ohio State Lantern,* November 23, 1977, p. 4, and *Columbus Citizen-Journal,* November 25, 1977, p. 6). In both the Kissinger and the Hayes situations, conduct has been used as the basis for a moral evaluation of a person.

Competence

Like morals, competence is a standard value that may be used to assess the merits of a person. Since the time of Aristotle, advocates have realized the importance of being thought competent (*Rhetoric,* II. 1. 1378a).

The desire to be considered competent is reflected well in an August 1976 campaign advertisement for the Carter-Mondale presidential ticket (*Newsweek,* August 30, 1976, pp. 2–3). The advertisement emphasized that "there's nothing wrong with our country that strong, competent, compassionate leadership can't change." The text of the message emphasized the governmental experience of the ticket and and described some of Carter's goals; it asserted that "he's already proved that he can accomplish these reforms as Governor of Georgia." Carter was presented as having the "vision, experience, competence and vigor" to do an effective job as President.

The competence issue was a centerpiece of the Carter campaign. However, the issue is a traditional means of reinforcing the image of an advocate. Richard Nixon, for instance, campaigned hard in 1972 on the basis of a good foreign policy. Indeed, this point was so effectively stressed that, despite Watergate, Nixon is still regarded as having been a competent foreign policy leader. A 1976 Harris poll (in Wallechinsky, Wallace, and Wallace, 1977, p. 31) rated Nixon as being the recent President who was "Best in Foreign Affairs." (He was rated last in domestic affairs.)

Motives

I have defined motives as internal causes of action. Motives refer to one's reasons for doing something. Arguments about advocates are frequently keyed to the advocates' supposed motives.

The sports scene provides one example of an evaluation based on motive. In 1975, Oklahoma football coach Barry Switzer charged that Texas coach Darrell Royal had ulterior motives in favoring limitations on college recruiting. Switzer argued that Royal favored the cutbacks only because they would work to the advantage of Texas; he said that if he were limited to visiting a Texas prospect only twice in seventy days, then "I have to think Darrell Royal has a better chance to sign him than I have" (*Odessa American,* August 12, 1975, p. 2B). This argument makes Royal's position appear to be self-serving. In reality, University of Texas coach Royal maintained, his support of restrictions was unrelated to the University of Oklahoma's reputation for successful recruiting in Texas.

Another interesting charge of ulterior motives came in a letter to the editor of *Newsweek* (*Newsweek,* September 22, 1975, p. 5). It concerned an opinion column written by Tom Paine, senior vice president of General Electric, on the subject of interplanetary space travel (*Newsweek,* August 25, 1975, p. 11). Paine argued that mankind could gain great advantage from space travel and that space travel could represent a solution to the population problem on earth. Reacting to this theory, the letter writer suggested that Paine's motive was to drum up business for General Electric.

As is evident from the two cases above, the basic issue in assessing motives is to determine whether an advocate is sincere in his proposal. Those who charge ulterior motives are arguing that the advocate is really motivated by a hidden, private concern. Thus, an official of the U.S. Department of the Interior used a motives challenge when he questioned efforts to halt the sale of off-shore oil leases. Certain state officials had argued that the sales should be postponed because the Department had not prepared an adequate environmental impact statement. The unnamed official was quoted as identifying another possible motive of the state officials (*Newsweek,* February 24, 1975, p. 68): "A lot [of them] are using environmental opposition as a bargaining chip. They are holding out for a bigger share of the action."

Consistency

One frequently used test of an advocate is consistency. To pass the consistency test, an advocate must demonstrate that he has neither (1) changed his position on an issue nor (2) taken a contradictory stance. In looking around, the critic will observe numerous instances in which opponents have charged an arguer with being inconsistent. Seemingly, this is a critical value check for an advocate (although one wonders why changing one's mind is perceived as being so devastating a fault).

As I said, examples abound. Consider the following report (*Odessa American,* August 29, 1974, p. 3A) of a rock music festival held in Windsor Great Park, England. The reporter observed that "the festival claimed to have an ecological theme. But some of the campers were reported to have ripped branches from the park's ancient oak trees to fuel their campfires." Here the fans' pro-ecology beliefs are said to be inconsistent with their behavior. A very similar inconsistency argument in the area of human rights was reported in 1977. A news release (*Odessa American,* March 10, 1977, p. 12B) cited a statement by the *People's Evening News* (an independent Ghanaian paper): "One cannot imagine how we Africans condemn the brutal killings and racial repression of white-minority regimes in southern Africa only to keep quiet over equally inhuman atrocities such as [those] occurring in Uganda." In this case, the lack of protest about Ugandan dictator Idi Amin is said to contradict the concern for oppression in South Africa. The Soviet news agency, Tass, echoed the *People's Evening News* argument, in an effort to discredit President Carter's statements on human rights in the U.S.S.R. Tass cited two North Carolina cases against blacks as a basis for alleging a discrepancy in Carter's concern for human freedom (*Odessa American,* March 12, 1977, p. 4A): "One would like to ascertain what the new administration is doing . . . to safeguard such rights and freedoms inside the United States." Tass uses the argument of inconsistency in an effort to undermine Carter's position on Soviet mistreatment of dissenters.

The charge of inconsistency has a great deal of intuitive appeal. It is used frequently to question the credibility of an advocate: If an advocate's position is internally inconsistent, then each of the advocate's arguments loses force. However, it is important to recognize two limitations on the validity of arguments premised on consistency. For two reasons a charge of inconsistency may itself be invalid. First, advocates may change their positions over a period of time. There is nothing inherently wrong with changing one's opinion. Opinion changes are frequently necessary, because new information is always becoming available. Opinion changes often indicate thoughtfulness and a willingness to receive new information. In such a case the statement "I've changed my opinion" may be a healthy sign. In a July 4, 1976, opinion column (*Newsweek*, p. 108), Meg Greenfield wrote of the potential advantages of opinion changes. Further, she cited an occasion in which an advocate had effectively defended his change of opinion:

> The only adequate defense I ever saw made against the bloodchilling (to politicians) charge of inconsistency occurred at the test-ban-treaty hearings in the Senate back in 1963. Sen. Frank Church was working over the nuclear scientist Edward Teller, who opposed the treaty, and at one point he unloaded an imposing series of past Teller statements that contradicted the opinions Teller was giving now. "How do you explain that?" the senator demanded with an air of understandable triumph.
>
> "It's easy, Senator," Teller replied—"*I have changed my mind.*" It was an awesome moment; since no one had ever said that in the hearing room before, no one knew what the answer was.

Greenfield cited this instance in support of the proposition that consistency may not be a universal good. Accordingly, some charges of contradiction may not amount to much.

There is a second limitation to the charge of inconsistency. Sometimes an alleged inconsistency does not really exist. Such is the case with a charge levied against Jimmy Carter early in the 1976 presidential campaign. *Newsweek* (September 6, 1976, p. 15) relates the incident: "In a stop at the Iowa State Fairgrounds, Carter promised to stop the Ford Administration's grain embargoes 'once and for all.' But Carter then told the *DesMoines Register* that he would *support* grain embargoes in extreme situations—a U.S. food shortage, for example." The next day Republican vice presidential candidate Senator Robert Dole made political capital by trumpeting a Carter contradiction. But was it really so? Carter's argument against embargoes was that they limited farmers' ability to effectively market their goods overseas. But policies usually involve some degree of complexity: Carter's support for embargoes in extreme emergencies—such as domestic food shortages—was hardly inconsistent to his general opposition to embargoes (just as his desire for peace would not preclude his calling for war in an extreme occasion). Hence, the alleged contradiction was more apparent than real: It owed more to political heat than to logical light.

In sum, consistency is a value applied to the statements and actions of advocates. We have good reason to doubt advocates who seem to vacillate from one position to the other. However, charges of contradiction are often invalid. The complexities of an issue may require an advocate to change his mind.

Similarly, false contradictions may be manufactured by distorting the distinctions in an essentially consistant stance.

Expediency

That which is expedient is easy to do. To charge that an advocate is expedient is to say that he is weak—that he takes the course of least resistance rather than that of principle. An expedient position is one that is chosen for its ease rather than for its objective rightness. When advocates seek to discredit their opponents, the charge of expediency is useful. Such a charge has a dual impact. First, it makes the opponent's position appear illegitimate. Secondly, it makes the advocate appear weak and unprincipled.

A *New York Times* editorial (quoted in *Academe,* March 1977, p. 1) used the charge of expediency in an effort to discredit the Internal Revenue Service (IRS) plan to tax tuition rebates for the children of college faculty. As the editorial explained, "the IRS wants to start collecting income tax on the value of the free or reduced tuition traditionally given children of college faculty members." This plan was opposed by the American Association of University Professors. The A.A.U.P. contended that teachers were being singled out, because the IRS was not proposing to tax similar benefits given to other groups. For instance, discounts to department store employees and free airfare for airline workers were unaffected. *The New York Times* concurred with the A.A.U.P. charge of expediency. The *Times* supported the general notion of closing tax "loopholes" but noted that "a proper agenda for such reforms ought to start with the economically and ethically least defensible exemptions rather than with those that are merely most vulnerable for the lack of politically powerful support." In short, the IRS plan was branded as "expedient." The plan was said to originate not in the application of ethical and economic principles, but in the comparative political weakness of professors.

Further illustrations of the expediency charge may be observed in periodical literature. Thus, in 1971 columnist Stewart Alsop used this value to criticize a plan to cut off American military aid to South Vietnam. Alsop singled out several of those who voted for the plan. He attacked them with these words (*Newsweek,* November 8, 1971, p. 122): "It is hard to believe that men of the stature of Edmund Muskie and Edward Kennedy and Hubert Humphrey and Walter Mondale could vote for such an act, however politically expedient such a vote may be." Four years later a letter-to-the-editor writer (*Newsweek,* February 24, 1975, p. 4) complained that much opposition to Israeli policy resulted from "the sweet smell of [Arab] oil money."

The sample arguments of expediency cited above have a similar ring. An advocate's position is said to be convenient rather than correct. The advocate is characterized as being a person of weakness rather than of principle.

The five values portrayed in this section of the chapter are certainly not the only bases for evaluating a communicator. The reader should expect to encounter other values that are commonly applied to agents in situations of dispute. The main point to be remembered, however, is this: Advocates may be evaluated as well as positions.

TESTING THE RHETORICAL VALIDITY OF EVALUATIONS

In my introductory remarks about values, I suggested that an evaluation is a particular person's way of looking at the world. I also suggested that values may conflict and that competing positions may each be supported by a recognized good. These two observations raise an important question about testing the validity of values. Can we really assess the logical correctness of an evaluation? Specifically, since values are notions of the good, are they not inherently personal? Further, is it possible to make an objective analysis of value statements? These questions highlight a legitimate problem in using validity to test evaluations. Values *are* personal and subjective. Yet, if values are entirely subjective, then it follows that all evaluations are equally good. By this criterion Hitler's decision to exterminate those whom he considered *Untermenschen* (inferior people) would be as good as Jesus' injunction to love one's neighbor as oneself. Clearly, mankind has opted for a view of values as being both subjective and objective. Values are personal; but most critics would support the belief that personal decisions can be rationally examined. Individual value judgments may be compared to the value sensitivity of a society as a whole.

In the next few pages, I will suggest some ways that values may be tested for their validity. The reader will notice that these validity tests bear a great similarity to the tests of ethics that I presented in chapter 3. Truly, in assessing the validity of evaluations, the critic makes ethics-related decisions. Below, I explain three tests of value validity: (1) whether the value cited by the advocate is one that people generally recognize as being a good; (2) whether the advocate gives sufficient reason for his or her value choice (i.e., the emphasis of one value over another); and (3) whether the value is adequately applied to the situation of dispute. The results of these three tests, when used in conjunction with the definition of rhetorical validity, enable the critic to make an informed judgment about value validity.

Is the Value Truly a Good?

Is the value cited by the agent one that people generally recognize as being a good? This brings us back to the definition of value: notions of what is socially preferable, that is, things that most people regard as preferable to others. At the outset of chapter 6 I cited a list of recognized goods. The opposite of each value would be considered an evil, something not to be preferred, and would be called a "bad value." Corresponding to the good of Americanism would be un-Americanism. The opposite of patriotism is treason. Discrimination exists as a challenge to equality. Slavery is the converse of freedom. To reinforce the notion of bad values, let me explain three bad values that frequently serve as the basis for claims. These are "two wrongs make a right," "provincialism," and the *ad hominem.*

The two-wrongs argument is a perversion of the value of justice. The user of this argument asserts that a bad act is really all right, because others have done the same. A 1974 feature story on Holdrege, Nebraska, contains a good illustration of the two-wrongs argument (*The New York Times,* June 6, 1974, p.

24). The correspondent questioned a number of Nixon supporters about Watergate. The article quoted a Miss Nellie Johnston as having strong opinions about the charges against President Nixon. She expressed complete confidence in the former President: "I can't believe there's one dirty thing wrong with Richard Nixon." She doubted that Nixon had knowledge of any of the Watergate-related events. Finally, she put the issue in perspective. Referring to "dishonesty," she asked about "all those votes the Democrats always steal in Chicago." She also cited Presidents Wilson and Johnson, who went to war after "talking about their going to keep us out of war." Finally, Miss Johnston discussed "immorality": "What about Wilson running around with another woman until his wife died of a broken heart? And L.B.J. took the same tax deductions for his papers." In short, the charges of wrongdoing against Nixon lose importance in her eyes because of what she views as parallel wrongs by other American Presidents and by Democrats.

Although appealing, the two-wrongs argument is invalid because it is inherently irrelevant. Questions about Lyndon Johnson's honesty and morality are not germane to Nixon's guilt or innocence in the events surrounding the Watergate break-in. Each would have to be evaluated separately. Yet, although most people would accept in the abstract the notion that two wrongs do not make a right, the argument appears and reappears. Three *Newsweek* writers unwittingly relied on this invalid value premise in an article on black-white relations in Africa. The article referred to discrimination against whites by certain black-majority African governments. The actions were evaluated as follows (*Newsweek,* June 2, 1975, p. 43): "Given the legacy of a long and bitter colonial history, it is hardly surprising that Black Africans have adopted their own brand of racial discrimination." It might not be surprising, but it is still wrong. Even the massive wrong of colonialism cannot justify a favorable evaluation of present-day discrimination. The wrongs of each must be tabulated separately.

Provincialism, a distorted form of loyalty, is another perverse value. The provincial view is one that considers familiar things as necessarily better than others—although the unfamiliar has not been investigated. The provincial view takes for granted that the local high school is better than the one across the river—without really comparing the two. An editorial in the *Odessa American* (June 17, 1975, p. 4A) criticized the Soviet Union for exaggerating its contribution to World War II victory. The editors accused the Soviets of provincialism, explaining that "according to speeches made in the Soviet Union recently, it was the Russians who beat the Germans single-handedly and then scared the Japanese into surrender." The editors make a good point relative to the Japanese surrender. Truly, the United States was the principal contributor to victory in the Pacific. But in minimizing the role of the U.S.S.R. in the European theater, the editors may also be victims of a provincial world view. History records that the Russians bore the brunt of German power for three years (from 1941 to 1944) before the Allied landings in France.

Everyone, of course, is subject to provincialism. Thus, a news report cited an apparent case of provincialism in Japanese textbooks (*Odessa American,* January 21, 1977, p. 8A). The Japanese teachers union was quoted as complaining that their texts have deliberately played down Japan's "responsibility in the start of the war in the Pacific." The educators were said to feel that the books unfairly minimized the Japanese attack on Pearl Harbor.

As a final example of a bad value, consider the *ad hominem* argument. *Ad hominem* is a Latin term which means "to the man." The *ad hominem* argument is one that focuses on alleged faults of an advocate while ignoring the arguments advanced by the advocate. In other words, the *ad hominem* argument is invalid because it is not responsive to the issues in dispute. Although it is an irrelevant argument, it is quite easy to fall into making evaluations that are premised on *ad hominem.* Consider three examples.

In late 1975, the city of New York was faced with financial bankruptcy. The city appealed for federal loan guarantees to assist it in borrowing needed funds. President Ford was publicly unsympathetic to New York's plight. Ford's comments prompted former Mayor of New York City (1966–1973) John Lindsay to write a column "Speaking Up for New York" (*Newsweek,* October 27, 1975, p. 13). Lindsay mentioned the President's "attack" on New York. He responded with these words: "Mr. Ford talks sweepingly of New York's mismanagement, as if he had a history of competence in the field of management." Lindsay then cited a host of Ford's inadequacies as a leader: He never faced "a diverse constituency" because he ran from a "safe and homogeneous Congressional district"; he was isolated for 25 years in the "marbled cocoon of the House of Representatives"; he had never "met a payroll." Although Lindsay's remarks made for interesting reading, they were irrelevant to the issue: Had New York leaders mismanaged the city's finances? Ford had a perfect right to raise such questions, regardless of his own alleged failings as a leader.

Similar *ad hominem* arguments may be found in any large sample of modern periodical literature. For instance, the argument appeared in a response to economist Milton Friedman's case against national health insurance. In addition to refuting Friedman's claims against national health insurance, Leonard Woodcock, then the president of the United Auto Workers, also argued against Friedman the man (*Newsweek,* May 26, 1975, p. 4): "Since University of Chicago professors receive free health insurance, they may not be fully aware that the costs of premiums today usually exceed $1,000 a year for family coverage that is less than fully comprehensive." But Woodcock's attack on Friedman pales before a description of former member of Congress Bella Abzug as a "bulky New York radical, rancorously strident woman libber, incessant dove (except when it comes to Israel), and militant gadfly on virtually everything." (Robert S. Allen, "Inside Washington," *Odessa American,* June 7, 1975, p. 10A.) The excerpt makes for eye-catching prose, but it is a poor substitute for substantive argument.

Like the other bad values, the *ad hominem* represents a misuse of a recognized value. As I noted earlier, it is all right to apply moral tests to an advocate, but one should not assume that such tests substitute for refutation of the arguer's claims. In short, the two-wrongs argument, provincialism, and the *ad hominem* amount to misuses of value argumentation. Yet one should not think that these three are the only inherently invalid value premises. Each of the positive values that were originally cited may be twisted into a socially disapproved quality. Patriotism may be a guise for prejudice. Irresponsibility may be disguised as freedom. The good of saving money may serve as a convenient mask for greed. Justice may be used as a euphemistic term for revenge.

Because any recognized value may be distorted, the critic must look behind the label, must judge whether the advocate is really using a socially acceptable value or whether the advocate appeals to unacceptable terms.

Is the Value Emphasis Acceptable?

Having examined the value claimed by the advocate, the critic's task is to look at the value emphasis. As I noted earlier, most situations involve a conflict of values. Thus, the critic should scrutinize the advocate's emphasis of one value over others. The critic searches to make sure that the arguer has truly relied on the most preferable concept.

The situations that I presented earlier provide a basis for analyzing value emphasis. Recall the trial of *Hustler's* publisher, Larry Flynt. Flynt's case represented a conflict between morality and freedom. In judging this case, the critic would need to examine the situation and decide which value was most deserving of status as the ultimate term. In doing this, it would be necessary to identify the important factual and interpretive issues in the dispute. Factual information would clarify what really happened: the nature of Flynt's publication, the relevant Ohio laws. Interpretive analysis would help the critic in understanding the implications of the dispute. For instance, is *Hustler* a "corrupting influence?" Would jailing Flynt establish a basis for government censorship of the media? Such an investigation would help the critic to sort out the information that supports one or the other of the competing values.

However, in the final analysis the critic's own outlook on life will determine that person's viewpoint about the importance of the alternative value terms. Persons who are highly religious and who are conservative in matters of sex will probably favor making "morality" the key term. Those who are more liberal on sex, or who are highly concerned about censorship, will probably opt for "freedom." In sum, the critic's own biases will influence critical judgments about the advocate's value choices. However, the critic has an obligation to investigate the various positions: A fair hearing must be given to the two (or more) sides. Further, the critic must justify and explain any critical analysis and conclusions reached. The requirement to investigate and explain will serve as a check on hasty, unthinking criticism.

One final thing needs to be said about testing the validity of an arguer's value emphasis. I noted earlier that some situations involve a conflict between positions supported by the same value. The examples that I cited were (1) the dispute over abortion and (2) the Bakke case on equality. If various agents in a dispute may invoke the same value, how can we compare the value emphasis? The answer, of course, is that we cannot. The critic, however, *can* examine the way in which the two sides use the value. It is quite likely that different applications of the same value will not be equally valid. The value in question will probably support one side's position better than it supports the opposing position. This brings us to the third validity test of evaluative claims.

Is the Value Adequately Applied?

Values have an abstract element to them. We can talk about "freedom" in the abstract without giving examples of free people. However, a dispute is a specific context of agents, sides, positions, issues, and arguments. Consequently, when an advocate uses a value argument, it must be applied to an identifiable set of circumstances. This being the case, we may ask whether or not the value has been adequately applied to the details of the situation. In other words, does the value really fit the circumstances of the particular case? I will give some samples of the "goodness of fit" test for values.

Some pages ago, in my description of the equality value, I cited tennis player Chris Evert's demand for equal prize money for the women players at Wimbledon. The news report that described Miss Evert's demand also contained a response by Sir Brian Burnett, chairman of the Wimbledon All-England Club. Burnett maintained that the women spent only about one-half as much time on the court as the men and that the women's quality of play was not equal to that of the men. "Therefore," Burnett argued (*Odessa American,* June 26, 1976, p. 4B), "on a strict basis of equal pay for equal amount of work, the women players should get approximate 50 per cent of the men's prize money." Burnett pointed out that the women actually got more than fifty percent and hence they were being treated fairly. One would have to investigate the matter further in order to decide firmly in favor of Evert's or Burnett's evaluation. However, the anecdote does illustrate clearly the problem of using a general value to give meaning to specific details of a situation.

The equal-pay-for-equal-work question takes us into the realm of the value that we call "justice." As the philosopher Perelman (1963) notes, justice is a particularly difficult value to apply. Perelman puts the point nicely. Speaking of the use of "justice" by advocates, Perelman (1963, p. 6) observes that "each will defend a conception of justice that puts him in the right and his opponent in the wrong." He goes on to explain a general rule of formal justice. Formal justice is "a principle of action in which beings of one and the same essential category must be treated in the same way" (p. 16).[3] Even this rule of justice is not easy to apply to a specific set of happenings. Consider the dispute over a Miami, Florida, ordinance on beach attire. The Miami city council defeated a proposal to allow "bare breasted bathing" for women. A news report (*Odessa American,* February 17, 1977, p. 10D) cited the argument of justice through equal

---

[3]Perelman recognizes that this rule does not solve all problems associated with justice. For one thing, it is no easy matter to establish and apply the categories. Perelman recognizes the impossibility of a "perfect system of justice" (p. 56).

treatment that was raised by supporters of the measure. It was argued that the current ordinance requiring women to cover their chests "was discriminatory because it required that only women cover their chests." In this situation, the argument of justice depends on the categories that one establishes. If one views the ordinance as requiring persons to cover parts of the body associated with intimate activities, then the ordinance could be viewed as nondiscriminatory. After all, women and men are built differently. On the other hand, if the ordinance is seen as requiring only women to cover their chests, then it would treat women differently than men. Whether or not the law treats members of the same class in the same way is a matter of conjecture. In such a dispute, the critic would need to make a decision about whether a value was well applied.

The Evert and Miami Beach examples demonstrate the problems encountered when one applies a value. The critic must carefully assess whether the advocate has used a value that really fits the situation. Consider a final case in which the applicability of "freedom" may be challenged on validity grounds. In their "Commentary" column (*Odessa American,* August 27, 1974, p. 8A), writers Edward Rowe and Howard Kershner defended the internal policies of the South African government. Rowe and Kershner characterized South Africa's policy of creating independent black homelands as a "very encouraging development in freedom." Unfortunately, an investigation of the South African policy would not seem to bear out the columnists' use of the freedom value. The independent homelands policy has thus far given the majority blacks only a relatively small portion of South African territory, and it is being imposed on the black tribes. Further, the existence of the small, poor homelands may be used as a basis for abrogating the citizenship rights of blacks who live outside their assigned "homelands." It seems apparent that freedom cannot really be used as a basis for favorably evaluating this South African policy.

There is a final aspect of value applicability that must be mentioned. In explaining the second test for evaluations—is the value emphasis acceptable?—I noted that this rule does not really apply to situations in which two advocates claim the same value premise. For example, if two opponents both use the value "freedom," there is no basis for deciding which side is using the most ultimate value. As I have noted, in such a case the critic must examine the way in which the two sides use the single value. In all probability the critic will find that the value fits one agent's position better than it fits the other's.

To illustrate this point, let us return briefly to the Bakke case. Recall that Bakke claimed that he had suffered "reverse discrimination," because minority candidates with lesser academic credentials had been admitted to the Davis medical school at the University of California. He challenged the policy of reserving space for members of minority groups. In contrast, the university defended its policy as a justifiable means for removing the effects of past discrimination against minority groups. Here we have two competing conceptions of equality. Which of the two is the more valid? Strict application of the rule of justice—equal treatment to members of the same category—would seem to favor Bakke's position. In this view all members of the category "applicants" should be treated in the same way. Selecting some candidates on the basis of their belonging to a minority group would appear to be unjust to candidates in other groups.

However, as the earlier-cited editorial of *The Times* (London) noted, abolition of the minority places would probably result in fewer minority admissions. This would represent a setback in efforts to improve the lot of a group of people who have suffered discrimination for so long. In this sense, equal opportunity for applicants would almost guarantee unequal outcomes for different groups in society.

Perelman (1963, pp. 32–35) presents the value of "equity" as a device for tempering the strict application of equality that is required in the rule of formal justice. Equity provides that we treat members of the same class with not excessive inequality. That is, we bend the role of equality only slightly. According to this formula, if the reserved places policy resulted in a major social good, then we could tolerate a certain inequality to other (nonminority) applicants.[4]

Because the University of California special admissions program is based on the value of *equity,* it follows that this program deviates somewhat from strict equality. Hence, it would seem that Bakke's position on equality is the more valid, since he argues for the firm application of the value.

We began this discussion with the assumption that both the University of California and Bakke were arguing from the same value premise. However, the present analysis would suggest that the dispute is more of a value conflict situation. Equity opposes equality. If so, then we would need to return to the second validity test in order to resolve the merits of the case: That is, we would need to decide whether equity or equality were the most important value term in the dispute over medical school admissions.

Applying the Definition of Rhetorical Validity

Once the critic has used the three tests, an overall judgment can be made about the validity of the evaluation(s) in question. This judgment requires use of the definition of rhetorical validity. The results of the three tests, when used in conjunction with the definition, make possible an informed critical decision. The critic would use information supplied by the three value tests to answer these questions:

1   Overall, does the information that supports an advocate's evaluation outweigh the information that opposes the advocate's evaluation? For instance, if the arguer claimed that his plan created freedom, does it really do this, or does the evidence suggest that another value term better fits the agent's plan? In short, the critic first decides whether the relevant information favors or opposes

---

[4]This, of course, is a theoretical discussion of equality. Specific cases such as Bakke's are decided on the basis of law as expressed in the Constitution and in court decisions. However, even in law cases, the juries and justices often fall back on their personally held value outlooks.

the advocate's particular evaluation. This decision would provide an established level of certainty.

   2   Does the favorable evidence outweigh the unfavorable evidence enough to justify the qualifier? (Recall that the qualifier is the asserted level of certainty.) Thus, in this question we are seeking to compare the established and asserted levels of certainty. Recall that claims are valid only if the asserted level is less than or equal to the established level. If the asserted level is greater than the established level, then the claim is overstated.

We may briefly review the process of testing the validity of evaluations. First, we assess the evaluation according to three tests: Is the claimed value socially accepted as a good? Is the value emphasis acceptable? Is the value adequately applied to the situation? These tests give us the necessary information for applying the definition of rhetorical validity. The critic first decides whether the data favoring the arguer's evaluation exceed the data opposing it. This provides a measure of the established certainty level. Finally, the critic compares the established level to the qualifier (asserted level of certainty). If the asserted level is less than or equal to the established level, then the evaluation is a valid one.

Validity and Associations

In my introductory discussion of value argumentation, I made mention of value associations. I explained that implicit suggestion is often used to connect a concept to a recognized value. One does not have to state that "X is good" in order to make a value argument. The connection may be made subtly. Thus, the Hertz auto rental company benefited from the favorable qualities of O. J. Simpson by featuring him in their ads. On an intellectual level everyone knows that a car rental company is different from an athlete; but by using Simpson in its commercials, Hertz hoped that his attributes of excellence would be associated with them.

   Ultimately, the validity of value associations must be judged in the same manner as explicit value connections. However, when values are applied via vague associations, the critic's job is more difficult. The critic must seek out the value claim(s) that may be camouflaged in the details of a message and then must make explicit the outline of the otherwise diffuse argument.

   There is another significant facet to value claims presented as associations. Almost by definition, such a claim will carry with it only meager argumentative support. Because an association provides only the outline of a claim, it follows that the supporting data may be equally obscure. Validity is a measure of the extent to which favorable data (compared to the unfavorable) sustain an asserted level of confidence. If the favorable information is obscure, then this information is less effective in justifying the claim. As a rule, therefore, value associations would appear to be less likely valid than explicit value assertions.

   This brings me to one final type of value argument: guilt by association. Guilt by association is a type of argument in which an object is associated with things held as bad. Guilt by association is an implicit negative evaluation. Such arguments are used frequently against persons. A report in *Newsweek's* "Periscope" section (June 21, 1976, p. 13) provides an illustration of guilt by association. The report quoted evangelist Billy Graham's opinion that the White House Sunday services, which were popular during the Nixon years, should be discontinued. The news report cited one of Graham's probable reasons for favoring an end to the services: "Graham's role as White House spiritual adviser goes back to the Eisenhower years, but in the view of critics—and even of supporters—his close association with Richard Nixon did not add luster to his ministry." In other words, although Graham had nothing to do with the scandals connected with Watergate, he suffered from association with a President plagued by scandal.

As I noted above, guilt by association is a form of argument in which a person or thing is implicitly connected to the negative attributes of another object. To make the strategy clearer, consider some other examples of this argument in action.

    1 A story in the news (The Chronicle of Higher Education, April 18, 1977, p. 2) stated, "Graduate students in the department of government at Cornell University have denounced the involvement of students and faculty members with the Central Intelligence Agency and the Federal Bureau of Investigation." The news story indicates that the graduate students' resolution was broadly worded, indicating that guilt was assigned somewhat vaguely.

    2 In a column opposing the impeachment of President Richard M. Nixon (*Odessa American,* May 25, 1974, p. 10A), Anthony Harrigan emphasized the "radical factor in the drive for impeachment." Among other things, he called attention to the "active interest of the Communist Party in the establishment of the impeachment precedent."

    3 Former United Nations Ambassador Daniel P. Moynihan contended that it was "no accident" that Ugandan dictator Idi Amin was the 1975 head of the Organization of African Unity. Moynihan's critics contended that, "by seeming to associate all Africans with Amin's misdeeds," Moynihan had needlessly offended African leaders. (*Newsweek,* October 20, 1975, p. 50.)

In each of the disputes above, guilt is assigned more by implication than by direct argumentation. As I have noted, such obscure claims have greater-than-average validity problems.

It is no simple matter to assess the validity of value claims. Because evaluations deal with personal notions of goodness and badness, they are not as straightforward as descriptions. Evaluations are frequently made by implicit association. This further complicates the critic's task. Finally, in assessing the validity of evaluations, the analyst must eventually make his or her own value judgments. However, validity judgments must and can be made. They *must* be made, because society needs the thoughtful analysis of and application of value principles. They *can* be made because an argument critic is not merely one who judges, but also one who explains. The key to assessing value validity is to provide a justification for one's decisions: When the analyst supports a validity judgment about an evaluation, it becomes possible to present an intelligent discussion of value issues. Such a discussion may lead to widespread agreement about the goodness or badness of an object.

APPLICATIONS

In this chapter I have presented a great number of evaluative arguments. Did any of these examples arouse your feelings? Such feelings are an important aspect of value argumentation. For one thing, feelings are a way of knowing. Further, as I noted in the section on validity, a critic's decision ultimately depends on the critic's own world view. Nevertheless it is important to remember evaluations are more than feelings: There is a logical aspect to such claims. The practitioner and student of argument should go beyond merely emotional reactions; reasons and explanations should be an integral part of evaluative arguing.

In the applications section, I have included a few exercises to give you the opportunity to work with evaluations. In these exercises be aware of your feelings but also discipline them. Explore your reasons for feeling as you do.

Exercise 6-1: Constructing a Value List

You have read about values in this chapter. Reflect a bit over the range of values that you have encountered here or elsewhere.

  I   Write out a number of values that you think are important.
 II   Revise your list and rank the values on a Scale of 1 to 10, so that "1" is your highest-ranked value.
III   Your instructor may wish to elaborate on this exercise or use it as the basis for a class discussion.

Exercise 6-2: Applying Values to a Dispute

  I   Identify a situation of dispute that interests you and/or one that you know something about. The dispute should concern something about which most of your classmates would have some knowledge. Local, state, national, or international situations are all viable for this exercise.
 II   Identify at least two positions that have been taken on the dispute. Summarize the arguments of each position in a sentence (or two).
III   Identify values that underlie the arguments of at least two of the opposing positions. That is, list ultimate terms, motivating concepts, or "good associations" that seem to pertain to each position. Often, the value terms will be specifically cited by an arguer; however, the critic usually has to infer some of the values. For each position list the values in order of their importance.
 IV   Identify the position that you favor. Did your review of values change your opinion about the dispute?

V Reconsider the most important value for each position. Write out a short
essay justifying one of these two values as ultimate over the other.
   A In doing this, review the three tests of value validity.
   B Remember that if both sides rely on the same value, it is necessary to
   explain which side does a better job of applying the value. That is,
   which position does the value "fit" best?

Exercise 6-3: Identifying Values in a Text

I Choose a message text of around four hundred words in length. The text
must be one in which the arguer states and supports a position.
II List the values that the advocate cites or implies in making a case. Cite the
text to justify your identifications.
III Review the list and rank-order the values so that "1" is the value given
greatest emphasis by the agent.

Exercise 6-4: Constructing Your Own Evaluation

I Identify a situation of dispute as you did in direction 1 for exercise 6-2.
II In a single sentence write out an evaluation that pertains to the dispute. In
doing this you should take some facet of the dispute and connect it to a
value (positive or negative). For instance, "the plan to do X will be an
injustice for Y people."
III In a short essay justify your evaluation. Identify specific reasons that
support your value argument.

Exercise 6-5: Identifying Samples of Value Argument

I Over a period of a week or two, collect representative arguments that
illustrate one or more of the types of evaluative argument. A good way to
do this is to cut out a news story or to write out the details of an argument
that you encounter.
II In completing this exercise consider the large number of value terms that I
have listed or illustrated.
III Your instructor may prefer that you make up your own samples of
evaluative argument.

Exercise 6-6: Testing the Validity of Evaluative Arguments

Reread the directions for exercise 3-9. These guidelines describe the overall
process of applying the validity standard. The specific directions for assessing
value validity are as follows:
   I Use one or more of the arguments that you gathered in exercise 6-5.

  II Construct a single-sentence statement that reflects the argument being advanced in your sample. For instance, "The actions of X seriously invaded the privacy of Y." Be sure that your statement makes clear which value (or values) the advocate is using.

 III Identify a qualifier that expresses the certainty asserted by the advocate. You may need to estimate a qualifier. If so, explain your estimate.

 IV Place your sample argument in an adversarial context. That is, identify at least five arguments that support and five that oppose the claim. Some of the arguments may be contained in the clipping that your have chosen. Otherwise, you will need to rely on your general knowledge about the dispute.

  V Apply the three tests of evaluative validity. Judge whether the claimed value is a recognized good, whether the value emphasis is adequate and whether the value is adequately applied (i.e., if it fits).

 VI On the basis of steps four and five, judge whether or not the information favoring the claim outweighs the unfavorable information. If the favorable outweighs the unfavorable, a positive level of certainty is established. If not, then a neutral or negative level of certainty has been justified. Explain your judgment.

 VII Compare the asserted and established levels of certainty. The claim will be valid unless you think that the asserted level exceeds the established level. Make (and justify) a judgment as to whether the asserted level of certainty is less than, is equal to, or is greater than the established level. This comparison will yield your overall validity judgment. Explain your judgment.

Exercise 6-7: Applying Other Standards to Evaluative Arguments

Your instructor may want you to test the effectiveness, truth, or ethics of an evaluative argument. If so, follow the directions for exercises 3-6, 3-7, and 3-8.

Chapter 7

The Process of Persuasion

Persuasion refers to a change in listener opinion brought about by a message. Persuasion deals with the effects of language on receivers. One cannot discuss "argument" without implicit or explicit consideration of the term "persuasion." Argument denotes statements made by arguers and persuasion measures the effects of statements on listeners. To be meaningful, the terms require each other. When arguments are addressed to listeners, they enter into the realm of persuasion. When persuasive outcomes result, arguments may be seen as the source.

In chapter 3, I explained that arguments could be judged on the basis of their effects, truth, ethics, and validity. The effects standard conforms easily to the above definition of persuasion: Effects are the mark of persuasion. But you may have noticed that the other three standards involved persuasion as well. To illustrate: When a critic judges an argument as true or false, ethical or unethical, valid or invalid, the critic is acting as a persuader. He seeks to convince reasonable people that a given argument possesses certain characteristics.

However, the critic-as-persuader is a special case. The primary job of the critic is to apply objectively certain criteria for judging arguments. The critic then explains his judgment in such a way that any rational person would accept it. In contrast, this chapter deals more with arguers who (1) have a strong personal point of view on the subject matter; (2) allow that subjective point of view to influence their analysis of the question; and (3) use arguments to persuade a given target audience. Unlike the critic, the typical arguer does not seek objectivity and does not seek to convince all rational people. The typical arguer has a strong personal point of view and desires to impose it upon an identified target group.[1]

My definition of persuasion emphasizes the impact of "messages" in producing "changes in listener opinion." However, one should not exaggerate the role of messages. After all, listeners interpret the messages; meaning requires listener decoding. Further, the new messages must compete with old beliefs. The human mind is not a blank slate on which arguers may write whatever they wish. The new data interact with previously existing knowledge. Because messages require decoding, and because new data coexist with the old, it would be a mistake to overestimate the influence of individual persuasive messages on receivers.

The overemphasis on messages in persuasion has been termed the hypodermic notion of persuasion. Fotheringham (1966, p. 12) summarizes this viewpoint: "Each audience member is individually and directly 'injected' with the message. Once it has been 'injected,' the message may or may not affect him, depending on whether it is potent enough to 'take.' " The hypodermic approach, which Fotheringham critiques, looks at the message as the active element in persuasion. The listener is seen as passive. The hypodermic notion views persuasive effects as a result of message potency rather than as a message-receiver interaction.

Certainly, the message is a powerful variable in persuasion; but after all, message is only one of the key elements in the process. The interactive model of communication (figure 2-5) viewed message as inseparable from source, channel, and receiver. The force of the symbols was seen to depend on the personality and credibility of the source, on the medium of transmission, and on the feelings of the audience. In this sense there is no "pure" message. Persuasive effects are produced when communication symbols interact with other facets of a situation.

Because persuasion is measured by listener effect, it is appropriate for me to give renewed attention to the receiver variable. Thus, the first section of this chapter deals with people: I explain how people function in a world of language symbols and I present a theory of the human image system. In the next sections I consider these aspects of persuasion: (1) the outcomes of persuasive attempts (that is, the range of effects that may occur when new messages combine with existing receiver beliefs, attitudes, and values); (2) the results of research into factors that make successful persuasion more likely; (3) certain theories that have been offered to account for "how persuasion happens"; and (4) a

---

[1]Perelman and Olbrechts-Tyteca (1969, p. 28) use the term "convincing" to denote "argumentation that presumes to gain the adherence of every rational being." They reserve the expression "persuasive" for communication that "only claims validity for a particular audience."

"synthetic" model of persuasion containing some of the shared elements of other persuasive theories.

THE HUMAN IMAGE SYSTEM

An image, according to Boulding (1956, pp. 5–6) is a person's "subjective knowledge" of something. In chapter 3, I identified a number of ways that people can know something. Our knowledge can spring from experience, revelation, authority, emotions, intuition, inference, and ideology.

No matter what its source, the important thing about knowledge is the personal element—that fact that it is *our* knowledge. Our knowledge will differ from someone else's knowledge. Hence, an image is subjective. Different individuals have different images of the same thing.

Let me clarify the notion of image by giving an example. Suppose that you and I were discussing Athens, Greece. Each one of us would have an image of Athens based on our knowledge about it. For instance, one might know such things as these:

> Athens is the capital of Greece.
> The Acropolis and many famous classical ruins are located in Athens.
> Athens was a great city in classical times.
> Athens is a nice place to visit.
> Athens has a warm climate.
> Many tourists visit Athens.
> Today, Athens is a modern city.

Yet if I asked each reader to "list twenty things that you know about Athens," I would expect to have thousands of different lists. A single object–Athens–would be "pictured" somewhat differently by each of us. Someone who has visited Athens might "know" that

> It would be enjoyable to return there soon.
> Greek food is good (or bad).
> Most Greeks have dark hair.
> X hotel is a good (or bad) place to stay.
> The highway from Athens to Delphi is narrow and winding.

A person planning to take a trip there might have knowledge of a different sort.

> Air fare to Athens is expensive.
> The tourist book recommends . . .
> The Greek alphabet is different from ours.
> The trip will be a good educational experience.
> Compared to Rome, Athens looks . . .

Among those who had visited Athens, images would vary according to when the visit took place, what the visitor saw while there, and so on. The varying images of nonvisitors might result from books read, travelogs seen, stories heard. In short, there are so many possible ways for our images to differ that it would be unlikely for two persons to have exactly the same image of the same object. The key word for the moment is "exactly." Images may be similar, as in the case of two persons who visited a city together, but even in this case, one would be surprised to find an exact correspondence between the two travelers' images. By their nature, images are individual, personal, and subjective.

The Organization of an Image System

You may have noticed that there are differences among certain of the elements of one's image of Athens. Some of the statements about Athens tended to be factual in nature—e.g., "Athens is the capital of Greece." Others, such as "Air fare to Athens is expensive," were more judgmental. Finally, some of the statements were evaluative, as in the case of "Greek food is good (or bad)." Earlier, we used the terms "description," "interpretation," and "evaluation" to label different kinds of public statements (arguments). However, students of persuasion prefer to use another set of words to label elements of our images. The terms "belief," "attitude," and "value" are most often employed. Let me define each of these expressions.

Beliefs   A belief is a cognition (thought) about the nature of something. Beliefs tend to be relatively factual cognitions. But one needs to be very careful in using "factual statement" as a synonym for "belief." For one thing, beliefs are not really statements in the same sense that an argument is a statement. By definition, a belief is an internal thought. A belief may be written down as in the case of the Apostles' Creed ("I believe in God the Father. . . ."), but few people write down all their beliefs about a thing. (In fact, some beliefs may be subconscious.) There is a second danger in equating facts and beliefs. A fact is something that may be independently verified, whereas although some beliefs seem to possess verifiability ("Athens is the capital of Greece" would seem to be one of these), other beliefs are not so verifiable. We "believe" that the sun will rise tomorrow, that "an object continues to exist when we are not looking at it" (Bem, 1970, p. 5), that our senses generally provide accurate information, and that physical laws will be the same tomorrow as they are today. Yet none of these beliefs can be verified; therefore, beliefs are not quite the same as descriptive arguments. However, when written down, many beliefs assume the form of descriptions.

This discussion suggests that there may be two distinct types of beliefs.[2] One type appears straightforward and closely related to the descriptive argument. We may call these "verifiable beliefs." Verifiable beliefs tend to originate from

[2]Rokeach, 1968, chapter 1, identifies five types of belief.

authority or inference (although they may come from other knowledge sources as well). For instance, one's belief that "John Wayne was born in 1907" might begin with a reading from *The World Almanac and Book of Facts*. A belief that Kabul is the capital of Afganistan might have its source in this inference:

> Athens is the capital of Greece.
> Athens is marked on the map by a big star.
> The map locates Kabul in Afganistan.
> Kabul is marked by a big star.
> Therefore, Kabul is the capital of Afganistan.

By their nature, verifiable beliefs may be challenged. In fact, people tend to expect that some of their verifiable beliefs will be proven wrong. This is not to say that people like to have their verifiable beliefs upset. It is just that frequently we find it necessary to abandon a verifiable belief.

The other type of belief may be called "primitive" belief. A primitive belief possesses several characteristics that differentiate it from the verifiable. First, it cannot be proven or disproven. Secondly, such a belief tends to originate from experience, revelation, emotions, or ideology (although it may spring from authority or inference). Thirdly, people expect their primitive beliefs to be unchanging. Finally, primitive beliefs are so basic that one rarely gives them any specific thought.

Take, for instance, our belief that the sun will rise tomorrow. Such a cognition results from experience: The sun has always risen to date. However, one cannot prove that the sun will behave tomorrow as it has in the past; we just assume that it will. Moreover, we rarely give the matter much thought because we take it for granted. Some primitive beliefs are closely akin to values, as in the belief that, generally, one should not call someone on the phone when one expects the individual to be asleep or eating a meal.

Attitudes In chapter 2, I defined "attitude" as a person's positive or negative judgment about a symbol or referent. However, Rokeach's definition of attitude as an organization of several beliefs focused on a specific object or situation (1968, pp. 159–160; 1973, p. 18) is valuable at this point. Rokeach's definition enables us to relate attitudes to beliefs. Attitudes are overall judgments of an object; but these global assessments are based on the beliefs that we hold about the thing in question.

For many years, "attitude" has been the key term in persuasion theory. "Attitude change" has become synonymous with "persuasion." In chapter 2, I pointed out that the concept of attitude includes the importance of an object and the intensity of our judgment about it. However, the element of attitude direction seems to be primarily responsible for its popularity in persuasion research. Researchers can study persuasion by looking at changes in the direction of an attitude (on a scale of negative to positive) that result from a stimulus (message). Assume that you are given the following scale on which to indicate your judgment about an object:

unfavorable -3 -2 -1 0 1 2 3 favorable

By circling one of the numbers, you would have expressed your overall attitude about the focal concept.

The typical attitude scale is far more complex than the single unfavorable-favorable continuum above. It is probable that at some point in your college career you will have the opportunity to fill out a "course reaction" or "instructional evaluation" form. This form will consist of a number of statements such as "The exams were graded fairly." You will be instructed to indicate your agreement or disagreement with each of the several items. You may be given the choice to respond, "strongly agree," "agree," "neutral/no opinion," "disagree," and "strongly disagree." When summarized, the form will measure your attitude toward a particular college course. Such a form is an attitude scale: It amounts to a scalar measure of your attitude about one of your classes.

An attitude scale is a verbal measure of an attitude. When using a scale of verbal statements, the researcher assumes that persons will reveal accurately their personal attitudes by reacting to the set of statements. However, attitudes have been measured nonverbally as well as verbally. Three types of nonverbal attitude measures are galvanic skin response (G.S.R.), pupil dilation, and heart rate. These measures are physiological in nature. That is, they are sensitive to changes in bodily function that result from a stimulus. These nonverbal measures have been used to assess "stage fright," emotional responses, and other conditions such as interest and attention.

Values   I have dealt extensively with the concept of value. In chapter 6, I explained that values were notions of the preferable and I provided some examples of value terms. At this point, the key question related to value is this: What is the difference between values and beliefs or attitudes? The basic difference is one of position. A value is a deeper-seated tendency that serves as the basis for beliefs and attitudes. Values are underlying notions of goodness and badness, general principles that support specific belief and attitude-type cognitions.

Rokeach (1968, pp. 159ff.) explains two other differences. First, he distinguishes between value and attitude. A value is a cognition that transcends specific situations and objects. On the other hand, an attitude is a judgment about an individual object. Attitudes, then, are focused on objects, whereas values exist in the abstract. Differentiating between values and beliefs, Rokeach observes the element of action in values. Values are not merely beliefs about the preferable. They are an actual preference. Values suggest and guide analysis, action, and choices.

The Belief-Attitude-Value System   The preceeding discussion of beliefs, attitudes, and values suggests that these cognitive elements are organized into a kind of system. Values are the basic element, and they provide stable notions of good and bad. Beliefs and attitudes function within the overall value framework. Hence, values are the basis of our image of the world. Beliefs add a data element to the image. They provide specific information that fills out the image. Attitudes organize our cognitions about specific objects; they are a collection of beliefs focused on a specific object. An attitude is a judgment about something—a judgment that results from the totality of our beliefs about it. (I summarized this system earlier in figure 3-3.)

The preceding discussion also suggests that the term "image system" should be distinguished from that of image. Our image system would represent the total set of things we know. This system would be our subjective knowledge of the world in general. It would consist of all our belief, attitude, and value cognitions. An image, on the other hand, can be described as a subjective knowledge of some particular thing. We might have an image of Athens, or of the University of California or of Alabama. This image would amount to the total set of beliefs, attitudes, and values that we associated with the individual city, university, or state.

In sum, our subjective knowledge of the world—our image system—is an organized collection of images. When we receive a new message, that is, when we hear an argument, the new data must find a place in our existing store of information. As I shall soon suggest, the image system determines our reaction to arguments: It accounts for whether or not new data persuade us. But before we examine this idea, we should say a few more things about the images themselves.

Dimensions of Images

The image system consists of thousands of separate pictures of reality. That is to say, it is made up of many separate beliefs, attitudes, and values. Are all of these images alike in nature? Probably not. There are many ways in which images may differ. Our image of Athens may be less distinct than the image of our hometown. For us, the image of Florence Nightingale may be more vague than that of "The Bionic Woman." Let us consider some of these ways in which images can differ. (My discussion of image dimensions is indebted, particularly, to Boulding, 1956, pp. 47–63, and Clevenger, 1966, pp. 81–87.)

Clarity   Some of our images are clearer than others. A clear image is one that contains a richness of specific detail. We know much about the thing; we are aware of its overall composition–its "shape." Some images, however, are not particularly clear. We have only a vague awareness of the object. Its outlines seem murky and fuzzy.

Consider a personal example. My image of Odessa, Texas, is a fairly clear one. I lived in Odessa from 1973 to 1977 and had an opportunity to learn much about the place. I have a good feel for its size. I know most of its major streets, its major buildings, its industries. In general I am familiar with the people who live there, with the climate of the place as well as the geography.

Contrast this to my image of Columbus, Ohio. Although I lived for a longer time in Columbus (from 1967 to 1973), I never got thoroughly acquainted with it. Most of my knowledge is of the university and downtown areas. There are many gaps in my image of the city, and I am unclear on many details. I would not be very helpful as a source of information on what there is of interest in this city.

Certainty   Images may differ along a continuum from certain to uncertain. For instance, I am certain of my image of what it means to be a college professor. If someone were to ask me to "describe college professors," I am sure that I could do so. Granted, I have not met every possible professor. Still, I would feel comfortable discussing the interests, habits, values, etc., of college faculty. But if you asked me to explain the workings of an automobile, I would be on shakier ground. I know the overall idea of how a car operates and I can do certain (limited) things under the hood, but I am less confident about my material than I am when describing something that I know.

Salience   Some images are more prominent in our total picture of things. A salient image is one that comes easily to mind; it is important to us. Other images, though, are deeply buried. We refer to them infrequently. They reside below the surface as relatively hidden items. They are latent.

Every semester that I teach public speaking, I am reacquainted as to the salience-latency of certain images for today's college students. Rock music and getting a job are quite salient for most of my students; political subjects such as foreign policy and the defense budget are relatively more latent. Yet only a few years ago, politics was the hot topic of conversation. It was "relevant." Getting a job was a lower priority item for students.

"Involvement" has sometimes been used as a synonym for salience. This is illustrated in an experimental study by Miller (1965; reprinted in Himmelfarb and Eagly, 1974, p. 254). Miller increased the saliency of a message by stressing to the participants how important the issue was for them in their lives. Emphasizing the life-relevance of fluoridation, Miller believed, made the subjects involved in it.

Consistency   Images may differ as to their internal consistency. Some of our knowledges fit well together; others are contradictory. Remember than an image is a collection of belief, attitude, and value impressions that are focused on an object. In some cases our knowledges of an object add up to a unified picture of the thing; in other cases, our total picture of the thing includes elements that clash.

What is your image of your university? Many of your beliefs, attitudes, and values probably are favorable: You may like many of your courses; you may feel positively toward the physical layout of the place; you may value higher education. On the other hand, you may feel that the university parking situation is bad, the bookstore unreasonable, and the student activity fee excessive. You may be troubled by friends who say that a college education today is a "waste of time." An image consisting of such conflicting impressions would be dissonant: The pieces of the picture would be out of order. On the other hand, probably many of your images are consonant. Here the individual pieces add up to a coherent, consistent view of the thing.

Persuasion theory tends to suggest that consistent images are the more stable of the two. Consistent images are said to be more resistant to change. I will examine this proposition further in a later section of the chapter.

Consciousness   Many things reside at the level of our consciousness. We are conscious of events happening in the immediate present. To illustrate: I have a clear image of "today." It is very cold outside; the driveway is blocked by a snow drift; and I am aware that the gas bill is likely to be high this month. I am less conscious of what's on the television or what my wife is doing right now. It could be said that these latter two are unconscious images. Although many images are relatively unconscious, we can bring them to the level of our consciousness by simply giving them some thought. If you were to write down a list of ten subjects, you would become aware of a host of previously unconscious images.

In addition to the conscious-unconscious dimension, psychotherapy has revealed that people possess subconscious images. Boulding (1956, p. 53) defines subconscious images as those that "cannot be brought into conscious view by any simple act of will." They may be largely forgotten or even suppressed.

Reality   I know that the pen that I am holding is real. I know that the "tooth fairy" is not. The reality dimension deals with our notion of whether things actually exist(ed) or are(were) "make believe." Legends, ghost stories, and fairy tales are usually thought of as less real than our images of familiar persons, places, and objects.

The recent controversy over televised violence illustrates the reality-unreality facet of images. Researchers, parents, and politicians have been grappling with the question "Do children perceive T.V. violence as 'real?'" If children are able to draw a clear line between the real world and television drama, then exposure to violence on television may be largely harmless; but if the childrens' image of television places violence in their sphere of things that are real, then the violence is likely to have a greater influence on their social behavior.

Commitment   Commitment to image results from our decision to closely associate ourselves with it. If we spend a lot of time thinking about something, we become more committed to it. If we express our opinion publicly, we further increase the commitment. If we take action on the matter, we become even more attached to our image of it. Miller and Burgoon (1973, pp. 28–31) use the terms "private belief," "public endorsement," and "behavioral commitment" as labels for the possible levels of one's commitment to an image. They also identify a fourth way that one can become attached: If someone tells us that we are committed to something, then we have a commitment of sorts. They call this an "external" commitment.

Consider an example of how a person may become committed to a particular belief, attitude, or value. Assume that the student government of your institution takes a position in favor of having a student representative on the university's board of trustees. Many students will never care one way or the other on this issue. However, some may give a lot of thought to it. As a result of this internal analysis, these individuals would be expected to have a degree of personal involvement with their image of the issue. Other students may sign a petition on student representation or participate in a rally. Such public and behavioral acts would amount to even higher levels of commitment. Finally, there will be a few students who become committed without their having given any real thought or without having taken any action. Their commitment may result from being told that "this is how 'the students' feel on this issue."

Integration   Some images are closely associated with others. For instance, my image of "Gone with the Wind" is closely connected to my image of Clark Gable. My image of the moon is connected to that of the space program, Neil Armstrong, and John Glenn. But I don't associate the planet Pluto with anything in particular. This image is relatively isolated.

In chapter 6, I spent a great deal of time explaining how values operate by association. I cited the example of Hertz, which sought to win favor by association with the talents of O. J. Simpson. Hertz sought to connect our images of Hertz and Simpson.

Shared Public Images

I have made the point that images are personal, that no two people have exactly the same image of the same thing. Your image of the Empire State Building would differ slightly from mine. It would differ because you and I likely have a different collection of beliefs, attitudes, and values relative to this building. Also, our two images might vary because our mental pictures possessed different degrees of clarity, certainty, salience, consistency, reality, commitment, or integration.

However, it is best not to overdo the point. Obviously, many people have almost identical images of the Empire State Building. We would expect that two young accountants sharing an office on the sixty-first floor would have essentially the same image of the building. Also, because the Empire State Building is an observable thing, a new accountant from Beatrice, Nebraska, could gradually shape a fuzzy image of the structure. Upon entering New York City, her image of the building would differ quite sharply from that of the other two accountants. But after joining the firm, after working on that sixty-first-floor office, her image would gradually come to be more like that of her coworkers. The point of all this is simple: Although images are personal, they can also be shared and public.

What causes image to be the same or to differ? To answer this question we only need to go back to the section on "Ways of Knowing" in chapter 3. Images are composed of knowledges. These knowledges arise from sources such as experience, revelation, authority, emotion, intuition, inference, and ideology. If two people have a common source of knowledge about something, it is likely that their image of it will be similar. Consider an example. If two people have stayed in room 503 of the Hotel Monteleone (New Orleans), and if they have both used the same hotel guest facilities, then it is probable that their images of the hotel will be similar. Because the two have had like experiences, we would expect their images to be congruent.

There is a second principle at work in making congruent images—*feedback*. (See Boulding, 1956, pp. 67–68, 166–167.) If two persons have a different picture of a thing they may "compare notes." Suppose that you are listening to an individual who has a clear and certain image of the "Bermuda Triangle." Assume that your image is unclear and not at all certain. You could adjust your image by asking questions. The feedback between sources and receivers allows discordant images to become harmonious. In short, images can be shared and public. This is because of similar knowledge sources and because of interactive feedback.

Why have I spent so much time discussing the human image system? I have done so in order to "set up" my treatment of persuasion. My definition of persuasion takes persuasive effects as being the product of an interaction between messages and listeners. In earlier chapters I presented much information about the message variable—types of arguments. But messages do not produce persuasion: Persuasion results from messages that have been filtered through a human image system. In this interactive process, the message affects the image (e.g., producing new beliefs) and the image affects the message (e.g., a person will pay more attention to something that he values highly). In succeeding sections I will examine this interaction further.

THE OUTCOMES OF ARGUMENT

When I use the expression "outcomes of argument," I mean the effects that arguments can have on a person's image or image system. A "persuasive effect" might involve the addition, deletion, or modification of a belief. Effect might come in the form of an alteration in the direction of an attitude. It is also possible that one's value premises might undergo a transformation. Further, any image element (belief, attitude, or value) might take a turn with respect to its clarity, certainty, salience, consistency, consciousness, reality, commitment, or integration. So when I use the term "effect," I mean effects on people—that is to say, on people's images.

As I observed earlier, persuasive effects have become almost synonymous with attitude change, and much of the study of attitude has dealt with the success or failure of messages to modify the direction (on a scale of favorable to unfavorable) of an individual's attitude. Of course, attitude is only one element of the image system that I have sketched out above, but there is some merit in the use of attitude direction as the focal point in discussions of persuasive effect. Direction of judgment is a person's overall assessment of a thing. Direction refers to whether we react positively, negatively, or neutrally to something, and the concept of attitude direction implicitly includes the belief and value components of image. An impact on the direction of our judgment might result from a belief or value transformation; therefore, the concept of attitude is useful because it gives focus to the discussion of effects.

The Range of Effects

Although a case can be made for treating persuasive effects solely as attitude effects, I will nevertheless give explicit attention to belief and value outcomes. Given my presentation of the image system as a complex of beliefs, attitudes, and values, it is logical to consider the impact of argument on each of the components. However, the reader should bear two things in mind: first, that a transformation of any one component of an image—say, a belief—will have a corresponding implication for the other elements as well; secondly, that persuasion theory emphasizes attitude effects relatively more than belief and value outcomes.

Belief Effects   Messages may add to our store of beliefs. Messages may also subtract from our beliefs or modify our beliefs. Recently, I read a *National Geographic* article on the Panama Canal (February 1978). The article contained an elaborate map of the Canal Zone (pp. 282–283). Before reading the map, I had only the vaguest of notions as to the configuration of the canal. I had seen pictures of the locks before, and I had a general idea that the canal crossed a lake. However, the *National Geographic* article added to my store of beliefs about the canal. I now understand more about the geography of the waterway. I can visualize better the relationship of the locks and the lake to other features of the canal system.

Of course, by adding to my beliefs about the Panama Canal, the article had the additional effect of subtracting from and modifying my beliefs. My notion that the canal consisted mostly of locks was replaced by a view that relative to total length the locks are only a small part of the waterway. The article also modified my canal-related beliefs. My beliefs became clearer; I became more certain and more conscious of them; and they took on an increased salience. (The consistency, reality, commitment, and integration aspects of my beliefs remained essentially unaffected.) As a reader, the major belief effect of the "Panama Canal" article was one of belief addition. The newly added beliefs also led to deletions and modifications of my previous canal-related beliefs.

One should not think that new information always has mainly a belief-adding impact. Another article in the February 1978 *National Geographic* worked primarily to modify my beliefs. This second piece dealt with the Minoan and Mycenaean civilizations of ancient Greece (ca. 3000 to 1000 B.C.). The article did not particularly add to or subtract from my beliefs about the Minoans and the Mycenaeans because I had previously read a great deal about these people. (In fact, raised on books about "lost worlds," I entered college with thoughts of becoming an archeologist.) Yet the article on "Greece's Brilliant Bronze Age" did not leave my beliefs unaffected. The article got me interested again in getting more information about the classical past: It increased for me the salience of the Minoan and Mycenanean times and it made me conscious of things that I had not thought of in years. However, the article did not affect, to any great degree, the clarity of certainty of my beliefs about ancient Greece. This is probably because its major implication was to remind me of things that I had read or seen earlier. Nor did this essay on the Greek past do much to the consistency, reality, commitment, or integration of my belief cognitions.[3]

Attitude Effects New data may have the effect of changing the direction of our attitude toward something. It may make us favorable to something that we have heretofore opposed (or it may do the opposite). It is also possible that a message will leave the direction of our attitude unaffected. Finally, it is within the realm of possibility that the attitude effect will be one of modification in one of the dimensions of our judgment about a thing (clarity, salience, etc.).

Attitude Change One possible effect of an argument is to change the direction of our judgment about something. Chapters 4, 5, and 6 contained a host of messages about a range of concepts. In most cases the messages were designed with the hope that the symbols would prompt a change in people's thinking and action.

A study of a political rally for Democratic Presidential candidate Senator Edmund S. Muskie (D., Maine) illustrates effects on the attitudinal component of images. Two researchers, Lynda Kaid and Robert Hirsch, distributed questionnaires about Muskie to persons attending a Muskie rally in 1972 in order to collect reactions to Muskie both before and after his appearance. The attitude scale measured the participant's judgments of Muskie's trustworthiness and his general demeanor. The researchers (Kaid and Hirsch, 1973, p. 50) reported a "significant positive shift" in Muskie's image as a result of his appearance. In other words, the Muskie rally had favorably altered the direction of the participant's judgments: The candidate's trustworthiness and demeanor were moved further along the positive end of the scale.

The Kaid and Hirsch study describes a situation of "successful persuasion." The attitudes of the listeners were changed in the direction desired by the message source. Although successful persuasion is the intent behind most arguments, today's scholars in persuasion remind us that attitude change effects are not easily obtained. This wariness about effects may be traced to early studies of voting behavior. These studies suggested that campaign communication converts few listeners. (See Lazarsfeld, Berelson, and Gaudet, 1944, p. 94.)

---

[3]Observe that my discussion of belief effects has dealt with verifiable, as opposed to primitive, beliefs.

Accordingly, researchers place two qualifications on findings that indicate that attitude change has occurred. First, they often question the duration of change. That is, how long does the change remain in effect? Secondly, researchers question whether or not the listeners had a predisposition to change. They try to determine whether the listeners were ready to change and thus sought out the message.

Kelman and Hovland (1953; reprinted in Himmelfarb and Eagly, 1974, p. 138) summarize the problem of persistance in persuasive effects. "[A]n individual," they write, "may be exposed to a communication, and accept the communicator's point of view, but after a period of time he may revert to his previous attitude." The individual may revert because the novelty of the new information wears off. The information supporting attitude change also may be overwhelmed by data already existing in the image system, or the new information may be forgotten gradually over time.

Kaid and Hirsch (1973, p. 49) specifically addressed themselves to the issue of duration of change. They requested the rally attenders to participate in a later follow-up study. These subjects filled out a questionnaire about Muskie that was mailed to them two or three weeks after the speech. Although the listener's judgments about Muskie had changed somewhat, Kaid and Hirsch found that the overall favorable shift to Muskie persisted.

But were the rally attenders ready to change their opinion of Muskie? That is, did they deliberately attend the rally as a means of changing their attitude? The issue of predisposition to change is an interesting one. Klapper (1963; reprinted in Mortensen, 1973, p. 188) reports an instance in which an existing predisposition to change was more significant in producing change than the message itself. The study dealt with the musical preferences of radio listeners. The researcher looked at persons who had acquired a taste for classical music. Fifteen percent of these individuals reported that the classical music programs "had initiated their liking for classical music." The programs were said to have caused a change in attitude toward classical music. However, Klapper reports, closer investigation of these radio listeners revealed that "most of these people were predisposed to develop a liking for such music before they began listening to the programs." In some cases the persons had friends who were classical music lovers, and they desired to emulate these friends. Others entered a socioeconomic environment that caused them to feel that liking classical music was expected. In these cases the music (the message) had indeed caused the change, but the listeners were ready to change. They tuned in for that purpose.

Kaid and Hirsch argue that audience members at the Muskie rally were not all predisposed to favor Muskie. In support of this they offer data to show that only 52.3 percent of those surveyed identified themselves as Democrats, members of Muskie's political party. However, it is possible that even the non-Democrats attended partly because they wanted to change. They may have been ready to become more favorable to Muskie.

It is evident from all this that even when messages seem to be responsible for change, the student of persuasion must be careful. One must avoid the hypodermic view, which overstates the single influence of the message variable. It may prove to be the case that audience attitude is altered for only a short time, or it may be that the audience changed mostly because the members felt ready to do so.

There is one further key point to be made about attitude change effects. In the Muskie example, we saw that the listeners changed attitude in a way desired by the message source. However, sometimes a message backfires: The communication actually makes the listeners less favorable to the arguer's point. This is termed the "boomerang effect." Persons who have very extreme attitudes may well respond to a call for attitude change by moving in a direction opposite to that desired by the communicator. Cronkhite (1969, p. 140) cautions us that in dealing with individuals possessing extreme attitudes, the arguer "must be careful not to ask for too much attitude change lest the listeners respond by changing attitude in the opposite direction."

Attitude Maintenance The second general attitude effect is maintenance. In such a case the listener maintains the original position as measured by points on an attitude scale. There are three possible types of maintenance effects: (1) the original attitude direction is reinforced or strengthened, (2) the listener maintains the attitude by benign avoidance—i.e., by simply missing the significance of the message, and (3) the listener is upset by the message and actively resists it.

To reinforce is to strengthen something already existing, to augment it. The reinforcement effect takes place when a message further enhances one's original attitude. Many messages designed to change attitudes have the effect of reinforcing them. For instance, if I am favorable to using seat belts in automobiles, a television "spot" on seat belts ("Buckle up for Safety") may only remind me that I favor the belts without making my attitude more positive. The television spot might not contain enough data to change the direction of attitude, so that if I filled out "before" and "after" attitude scales, a researcher would conclude that the message had "not changed" my attitude.

Recall that attitudes are made up of many beliefs focused on a concept. The reinforcement effect of a message might be to supply additional beliefs that provide a firmer support for an overall attitudinal judgment. Klapper (1960, chapter 2) takes the position that the major effect of messages transmitted by the mass media is to reinforce existing predispositions rather than to change them.

A second maintenance effect is unintentional avoidance. In this situation the listener does not recognize the implications of a message; hence, it does not change the original attitude. The listener does not consciously avoid the information; rather, the listener's inattention is unintended. Unintentional avoidance may spring from several roots. For one thing the listener may not understand the message. Were this the case, its lack of effect would be expected. Secondly, the listener may not understand the significance of the message. That is, he or she may miss its relationship to the original attitude. In this connection an arguer might make a vague reference to the "Czechoslovakia situation" as a basis for arguing against the foreign policy of the U.S.S.R. If one did not know that Soviet forces had intervened in 1968 to topple the government of Czechoslovakia, then the example would not have much impact on one's attitude toward Soviet foreign policy. Finally, a listener may accidentally miss part of a message. A juror in a courtroom might miss a key point while suddenly remembering that the car lights had been left on. In this case, the message force would be lost unintentionally.

The third source of attitude maintenance may be termed active resistance to the message. By "active resistance" I mean that the listener perceives the data, understands and appreciates the implications, and is bothered by them. Because the communication is upsetting, the receiver seeks to resist it—to reject the new information and maintain the old attitude.

The active resistance effect assumes that people desire to avoid attitude change. As Boulding (1956, p. 8) asserts, "our image is in itself resistant to change." He adds, "when it receives messages which conflict with it, its first impulse is to reject them as in some sense untrue." It is not difficult to understand why images—or individual belief, attitude, or value components—are resistant to change. Our images give meaning to the world; they make it possible for us to define ourselves in relation to other objects. Image changes require that we reassess our knowledge of the world. This can be inconvenient, embarrassing, or even painful. Katz (1960; reprinted in Beisecker and Parson, 1972) observes that attitudes play several functions for human beings. One of these functions is ego defense. As Katz notes (p. 23), "Many of our attitudes have the function of defending our self image." For instance, a person could overcome personal feelings of inferiority by holding another racial group as inferior. The individual would resist arguments favoring racial equality because such data would undermine part of the person's self concept—"at least I'm not one of *them!*"

In addition to this internal cognitive benefit, others have pointed to the social advantages to be gained by maintaining an attitude. Lazarsfeld, Berelson, and Gaudet (1944, p. xx) argue that by "maintaining their attitudes intact," persons are "able to avoid or minimize conflict with the persons in their social environments who share these attitudes." Here keeping an attitude enhances our feelings of security in social relationships.

At least two factors, then, seem to contribute to resistance to changing one's attitude. First, an attitude may be a crucial part of our image of ourselves. Secondly, if we adopt a position that differs from that of our friends, we may receive a degree of social punishment. Active resistance may be the easiest course. Further, because a new attitude may contradict an old one, a convert may be criticized for inconsistency. This marks a third advantage of resistance.

Attitude Modification   Attitude change and maintenance both primarily involve the direction of our judgment about something. However, a message may affect certain facets of our attitude other than its direction. As a result of new data, an attitude may take on increased relevance (salience). A message could make us more conscious of a concept. The attitude focus could also become more real for us. Attitude modification effects deal more with the organization of an attitude—its place in our image—than with direction of judgment.

The concept of attitude differentiation represents another class of modification effects. (See Cronkhite, 1969, pp. 60–61, 158.) Attitudes pertain to our assessment of objects. When confronted with new information that is inconsistent with an old attitude, we may "divide our attitude." We may differentiate it into two or more parts. Consider an example. Assume that a person has an unfavorable attitude toward policemen in general. Assume, further, that the person has a favorable encounter with a policeman. We might expect attitude change to result. There is a basis for such an expectation. The individual's attitude toward "cops" might move toward the positive end of the scale. It is possible, though, that the individual will regard the nice policeman as merely an exception to the rule. If so, the individual could divide or differentiate his attitude toward the police. He could keep his unfavorable attitude toward police as a whole and form a new, favorable attitude toward "policeman X." In this case, the attitude focus is altered rather than the attitude itself.

Value Effects Messages may affect our values as well as our beliefs or attitudes. However, because values are more stable factors of our image, value effects are not quite the same as belief and attitude transformations. It is unlikely that a single message will cause us to embrace a new value or to reject an old one. However, messages can have value implications for people. It would seem that even single messages can alter a person's particular value emphasis—i.e., cause one to revise the way she or he applies values to a situation. Further, repeated messages seem able to alter our value system itself. A set of messages could change the way we look at life in general.

The first class of value effects concerns the impact of arguments on value application. In chapter 6, I explained that many values potentially apply to an event or object. Different persons may evaluate the same thing differently because they emphasize one value over another. Consider an example. In early 1978 baseball commissioner Bowie Kuhn vetoed the sale of pitcher Vida Blue to the Cincinnati Reds. The Reds' management had agreed to pay the owner of the Oakland Athletics $1.75 million (plus a minor league player) for the services of Blue. Kuhn justified his decision by arguing that skyrocketing player salaries would cause wealthy teams to dominate the game by unfairly pricing out the other ballclubs. The Athletics' owner, Charles O. Finley, on the other hand, argued that the commissioner was depriving him of the full market value of his players.

The Kuhn-Finley controversy represents a conflict of values—fairness versus property, among others. One's evaluation of Kuhn's act would depend on whether dampening "money baseball" was a higher-order value than depriving "property rights." Persuasive messages on this subject could affect listener values by altering one's value hierarchy with respect to the ill-fated Athletics-Reds deal. Assume that a sports fan who favored Kuhn's decision is reading the evening paper. Because the reader initially approved of the commissioner's act, it is likely that she held "purity of the game" to be more important in this case than the "baseball free market." However, what if the reader encounters a pro-Finley sports column? The new information might convince the fan that the "free market" was more important than "money baseball." By causing the fan to switch her ordering of the values, the message would be altering the reader's value emphasis. Of course, it is equally possible that despite the message the reader would persist in her original value perception.

The second type of value effect that I mentioned was an effect on a person's entire value outlook. Again, the sports world affords us an illustration. Goldstein and Bredemeier (1977) argue that televised sports have altered the viewers' notions of sports and, subsequently, the viewers' value systems. The authors' case is as follows. As presented on television the outcome of a sports contest (winning or losing) is treated as the primary goal of sport. The process of play—the act of engaging in sport—is treated as less important. The authors contend that, as presented, televised sports convey the idea that to have participated in a losing venture is bad. One must search for the causes of one's failure. It is not enough just to have participated.

By shaping viewer perceptions of athletic contests, Goldstein and Bredemeier (1977, p. 158) allege that the professional model (winning is everything) has become transferred, widely, to the American public: "Broadcast sports . . . impart values, especially to the young, and influence spectators' views on the purpose and nature of participation in competitive athletics." They view these value effects as socially harmful. By making victory the motivation for sport, the players are deprived of the inherent pleasure of sport. Further, the "win" mentality enhances a tendency to treat opponents as enemies. Losing becomes a humiliation. The Goldstein and Bredemeier article treats the effect on value systems of repeated media messages.

What, then, are the possible effects when an argument is addressed to an individual's image system? A message may add to, subtract from, or modify our beliefs. A message may change the direction of our judgment about something—our attitude. Such a change may be in the direction hoped for by the communicator, or it may boomerang. Messages may also leave one's attitude direction unaffected. This is the "no-change," or attitude modification situation. A no-change effect may exist because the individual's attitude is reinforced, or the individual may maintain an attitude by unintentionally avoiding or actively resisting a message. Messages may also modify attitudes by altering the organization of the attitude as opposed to the direction. Finally, arguments may succeed or fail in altering a specific value emphasis or in altering a value system.

Remember, though, that the image system is an organized whole. It is possible—even likely—that several of the above effects will take place simultaneously when an argument is perceived by the image system. After all, arguments deal with two or more concepts. They provide information that may have fact, interpretation, or value implications or a combination of any of them. Thus, the range of effects is not a set of mutually exclusive categories. One might expect several effects to result from even a single argument.

Messages, Images, and Selectivity

The foregoing survey of possible belief, attitude, and value effects suggests that the range of persuasive outcomes is a wide one. It must be remembered, however, that some outcomes are more likely than others. In this connection, an earlier observation by Boulding (1956, p. 8) is worth repeating: "[O]ur image is in itself resistant to change." Boulding's assertion suggests that (all other things being equal) belief, attitude, and value change or modification may be less likely than belief/attitude/value maintenance. Indeed, the demise of the hypodermic notion of persuasion came about as scholars observed the ability of receivers to ignore arguments inconsistent with the listeners' existing image. Research has identified four general ways that receivers "ignore" messages. Listeners may be selective in exposing themselves to arguments; in paying attention to arguments; in interpreting arguments; and in remembering arguments. Below, I examine each of the selective processes.

Selective Exposure   Selective exposure denotes a tendency of some persons to avoid information that is inconsistent with their image of reality—and consequently to seek out information favorable to the existing image. Since the classic study by Lazarsfeld, Berelson, and Gaudet (1944), scholars have held the view that message receivers do choose arguments that are favorable to their existing images. These three researchers studied responses by voters in Erie County, Ohio, to the Presidential election campaign of 1940. They reported (p. 89) that two thirds of those who maintained a pro-Republican or pro-Democratic orientation from May to November "managed to see and hear more of their own side's propaganda than the opposition's." Furthermore, the researchers learned that "the more strongly partisan the person, the more likely he is to insulate himself from contrary points of view."

The findings reported by Lazarsfeld et al. are reflected in many everyday contexts. Liberals are more likely to read *The New Republic,* conservatives, *The National Review.* Smokers are less likely than nonsmokers to read articles that highlight the relationship between smoking and lung cancer. Even informal conversations seem to be affected by the principle of exposure selectivity. In a study by Deutschmann (in Kraus, 1977, p. 236) it was reported that only 11 percent of the 1960 Kennedy-Nixon debates viewers discussed the debates "with a person (or persons) of views contrary to their own." Viewers tended to selectively avoid situations where they would encounter conversations with persons having opposing views. Most (47 percent) preferred to talk with "persons of the same views as themselves." Others (42 percent) participated in conversations among persons of "mixed views."

Most observers agree that the selective exposure effect is widespread. However, scholars have not come to an agreement as to why persons are selective. Is the listener in fact making a conscious or an unconscious decision to avoid image change? Is image protection less important than the receiver's personal interest in the chosen message? Does the potential personal utility of the message have to do with selectivity? Indeed, factors such as message interest and message utility may account for some listener selectivity; yet there remains evidence that persons select messages because the message supports (or does not threaten) the individual's existing image.

Selective Attention   Even when one is exposed to a message containing undesired arguments, one can be selective. It is possible, in this situation, to focus attention only on those aspects of the message that are favorable to our point of view. This is selective attention. It is possible that this took place in the 1960 Kennedy-Nixon debates. Of course, one of the features of these debates was their ability to overcome the selective exposure syndrome: Democratic and Republican partisans were forced to watch "the other guy"; but it would still have been possible for viewers to have paid more attention to the arguments advanced by the candidate they already favored.

A study dealing with selective exposure by Atkin (1971) provides insight into selective attention. Atkin studied reactions to newspaper stories about the 1968 Presidential candidates—Richard M. Nixon, Hubert H. Humphrey, and George C. Wallace. He created a number of newspaper "front pages" in which stories about the various candidates were placed. Some front pages contained a large "Nixon" story, together with smaller "Humphrey" or "Wallace" articles; others featured Humphrey, and so on. Atkin found that readers tended to select campaign stories about their favorite candidate—even when the article was considerably shorter and less prominent than an article about the opposing candidate.

The Atkin study illustrates both selective exposure and selective attention at work. If the front page is viewed as a collection of separate articles, then the study demonstrates the tendency of subjects to expose themselves to favorable information. Alternatively, if the front page is considered to be a whole message unit, then the study supports the view that one pays relatively greater attention to the supportative parts of a communication.

Like the exposure phenomenon, selective attention is prevalent in our everyday life. Buyers of a particular model car are often surprised to find that the highways seem suddenly filled with cars like their own. Of course, the cars were always there. It is just that the owner is now more aware of them. He is giving them more attention.

Selective Interpretation   Selective interpretation (also called selective perception) occurs when we structure the meaning of a message to suit our own needs and preferences. In chapter 2, I described meaning as largely listener determined. Receivers were seen as the ultimate judges of what a message means for them. This personal nature of the meaning process is what makes selective interpretation possible. If a message is potentially threatening to our image, we can misperceive it. If we desire to reinforce a preconception, we may interpret unfavorable arguments in such a way that they actually support our position.

Voting studies supplied early evidence of a selective process of interpretation. Berelson, Lazarsfeld, and McPhee (1954), in their study of the 1948 Presidential election, concluded that an election really involves two campaigns (pp. 231–232): "One is the objective campaign that is carried on in the 'real world,' and the other is the campaign that exists in the voter's mind, that is, the 'real' campaign as perceived." In describing the latter, the perceived campaign, the authors found that voters may exaggerate the differences between the two parties so as to make their choice of one party more rational. If a favored candidate takes an undesirable position, the voter may misperceive the candidate's position so as to remove the conflict. Similarly, in the Kennedy-Nixon debates, Nixon supporters were able to reinterpret unfavorable data about their candidate as positive in nature. Lang and Lang (in Kraus, 1977, p. 327) provide an example: "One of his supporters remarked on Nixon's 'not smiling at all, being ill at ease, and on the defensive' but then went on to interpret this as being 'more careful, more subtle, and thinking over a problem.' " In this case, derogatory nonverbal cues were recast to fit the person's existing favorable image of Nixon.

Other examples of selective interpretation are not difficult to find. Klapper (in Mortensen, 1973, p. 185) mentions two. He points out that "communications condemning racial discrimination, for example, have been interpreted by prejudiced persons as favoring such discrimination." Similarly, smokers are "much less likely [than nonsmokers] to become convinced that smoking actually caused cancer" after reading an article on the subject.

Selective Recall   People have been found to be selective in what they remember about a message. Selective recall (or selective retention) is the forgetting of information unfavorable to an image and the remembering of favorable information. Probably most of us have engaged in some selective recall. Like the story that grows funnier in the retelling, our memories are often loaded in our favor.

Studies of reaction to the Kennedy-Nixon debates provide data relevant to the question of selective recall. Katz and Feldman (in Kraus, 1977, p. 201) surveyed a number of these studies. They reported evidence to suggest that, measured in terms of recalling "who said what," Democratic viewers retained no more information about Kennedy than Nixon. The same was true for Republicans, so in at least one respect there was no selective recall of information. However, when the viewers' attitude toward the information was considered, a tendency toward selective recall was uncovered. It was learned that those surveyed "tended to recall those of their own candidate's statements with which they personally agreed and statements of the opposition candidate with which they disagreed." In order to maintain their original image of the candidates, the viewers remembered "positive" things said by their favorite and "negative" things said by the opponent.

The selective-recall studies mentioned underscore an important finding about selectivity. This is that the selective processes do not always operate. Likewise, in several experimental studies of selective exposure, the results did not support the theory that people generally select supportive rather than anxiety-producing information. Sears and Freedman (1967; reprinted in Beisecker and Parson, 1972, p. 171) cite two studies in which "neither smokers nor nonsmokers had any significant preference between an article suggesting that smoking causes lung cancer and one arguing that smoking does not cause lung cancer."

In short, the findings about message selectivity are not uniform. Sometimes, people do not seem to seek, pay greater attention to, perceive, and remember favorable information. All of us can think of cases in which we looked at the other side's case, talked with someone we knew would disagree with us, or remembered things that were bothersome. Yet there remains a consensus that message selectivity is an important facet of persuasion. Selectivity in exposure, attention, interpretation, and recall are considered crucial factors in explaining the outcomes of argument. The selective processes clarify why belief/attitude/value change occurs less frequently than image maintenance.

Images and Behavior

Thus far I have treated persuasive outcomes as being effects on human images of things. However, persuasion often is connected to human behavior. Advertisers, for instance, desire to influence viewers to purchase products. They are not satisfied merely to improve the consumers' image of the product. Hence, it is well to give some thought to the relationship between human images and human behavior.

Boulding (1956, p. 6) argues that "behavior depends on the image." What he means is that our conception of the world determines our behavior toward it. This is a perfectly understandable proposition: We brush our teeth (or do not do so) according to our image of dental care; we go to a place of worship (or do not do so) on the basis of our views of the relationship between mankind and a Supreme Being; and so on. In every sphere of human endeavor our actions are related to our images.

Here is another example taken from a study of mass media effects. Drabman and Thomas (1975) conducted three studies into the behavioral impact of television violence. Groups of youngsters in the third- and fifth-grades were exposed to various "violent" television programs (a western and a detective series). Other groups were exposed to "nonviolent" programming. Control groups were exposed either to no program or to an "exciting" program. After exposure to the programs the children were studied to determine how long they would take to summon "appropriate adult help" when a fight began between two kindergarten children. The authors learned (p. 87) that the third and fifth graders who "saw the aggressive film took significantly longer to seek appropriate adult help than children who did not see the film." Viewing the aggressive programs seemed to have made the children less sensitive to real-world violence. This lessened concern for violence was apparently reflected in their behavior when confronted with what they believed to be a real-life fight.

It seems clear that behavior is related to our image of things. Our behavior toward our teeth is conditioned by the beliefs, attitudes, and values that we possess regarding teeth; our reaction to a fight is dependent upon our image of violence. Yet the exact connection between images and behavior remains unclear. This lack of clarity is reflected in attitude change research. Recall that most attitudes are measured by "paper and pencil" texts—e.g., an "instructional assessment" form. These tests have been criticized as unrelated to behavior. For instance, if you rated your instructor "70" on a scale of 1 to 100, does this mean that you would or would not take another course with that person? Research suggests that this question is a difficult one.

In a study by Leventhal, Singer, and Jones (1965; reprinted in Himmelfarb and Eagly, 1974), the researchers showed subjects various messages designed to persuade them of the advantages of tetanus innoculations. After receiving the messages the subjects (seniors at Yale University) filled out a questionnaire. This measured their attitude toward receiving innoculations. The researchers then checked the records of the Yale medical center to see how many of the subjects actually obtained the shots. The results showed a generally "positive relationship between attitudes and behavior" (p. 327). However, the link was not a perfect one, for "more action did not occur in that condition where the attitude change was greatest" (p. 328).

The lack of a perfect connection between attitudes and behavior has troubled many persuasion theorists, and many explanations have been offered for this finding. But should we really expect attitudes and behavior to be congruent, to be "the same?" Perhaps not. Behaviors tend to be public acts, but attitudes are largely internal—although the act of marking a questionnaire is a behavior. Further, attitude tests emphasize direction of judgment, whereas a person's image consists of many interrelated beliefs, attitudes, and values. Cronkhite (in Kibler and Barker, 1969, p. 118) summarizes this point. He writes that attitude measures "may not correlate with behavior" because the tests "may fail to reflect the *importance, intensity,* or *motivational strength* of an 'attitude' and may give no indication of the amount of *knowledge* upon which the 'attitude' is based." If this is true, one should not expect attitude direction to represent fully the motives for human behavior; but when the whole of a person's image is taken into account, the connection between internal analysis and external behavior should be closer.

Yet the image-action relationship is still a tricky problem. One would not expect that a person's decision to buy a car would result only from his image of the car. The behavior would spring from a whole range of images that were focused on the car. The person's image of other cars, of ecology, of himself, etc., would be relevant. Thus, while we may rely upon Boulding's proposition that "behavior depends on the image," we must add a caveat: Neither images nor behavior are easy to measure—nor are they easily correlated.

Shared Images and Audience Characteristics

In my description of the image system I noted that, although personal, images could be shared. Because of common experiences (or commonalities in other knowledge sources) one person's image can approximate another's. Because of feedback, two persons can compare and merge their images. The shared nature of images has a significant implication for would-be persuaders. Because images are not entirely personal, arguers can deal with listeners as a group. That is, the arguer can construct messages for a whole audience of people, not merely for individual audience members.

Of course, many times we do construct messages for a single hearer, as in the case of a one-to-one conversation. In other situations, though, we must deal with groups of people. Tonight, for instance, I have been asked to address a sorority group on the subject of parliamentary procedure. While I know some of the audience members personally, I do not know them all. Yet my task as a communicator is not a hopeless one; I can make some predictions about the general images of my subject that are likely to be held by the group. In short, I can analyze the audience as a whole: I can consider the age, sex, level of education, etc., of the listeners; I can take note of the nature of the organization. To recapitulate: An audience is a collection of persons who are exposed to a message (or who are likely to be so exposed). Audience analysis is the examination of the audience by a communicator.

Let me say some further things about audience analysis, because the concept is so important in persuasion theory. First of all, it is important to identify audience characteristics such as age, sex, level of education, and group membership. Audience characteristics such as these are significant because those who share characteristics will likely share an image. When a group of persons possesses similar characteristics, they also are likely to possess a similar image of something. Further, the more characteristics are shared, the greater are the chances that the audience possesses the same image. Hence, a group of 20-year-old female college sophomores who want to use parliamentary procedure in their meetings will probably possess a similar image of parliamentary procedure. What is more, their image of it will differ systematically from that held by a group of 50-year-old war veterans who have been victimized by a "parliamentary whiz" at the last post meeting.

Audience analysis may clue us in to the overall image held by a group. Because the listener's image determines the effect of a message, it follows that persuaders often devote considerable effort to identifying or predicting the features of the potential audience. Many audience traits are demographic in nature. That is, they are observable and are essentially stable. Sex, age, level of education, income, religious affiliation, and the like are examples of demographic traits. Characteristics of this type can shape the audience's perception of arguments. Women, for example, were shown in one study to be somewhat more persuasible than men (see Cronkhite, 1969, pp. 136–137). However, the fact that many readers will frown when coming upon this statement may indicate that this general finding is less true today than when the studies were completed.

Hosts of studies have given insight into the implications of audience demography. The general impact is put well by Lazarsfeld, Berelson, and Gaudet (1944, p. xii) in their report of the relationship between voting behavior and audience characteristics. From their analysis of "crystalizers"—those who had "no definite vote intention" in October but who cast ballots in November—the researchers were able to predict the crystalizers' decisions on the basis of demographic traits. In the final analysis, crystalizers generally "would decide finally to vote in the same way as did people with similar social characteristics who had made up their minds earlier in the campaign."

Beyond demography, researchers have studied other audience features that influence persuasion. Among these are personality traits (e.g., dogmatism, anxiety, hostility, self-esteem). Also it has been found that persuaders gain a great advantage if they are able to identify in advance aspects of the audience's image toward concepts which are to be treated in a persuasive message. If I want to persuade you against smoking, my task becomes easier if I know something of your existing image of smoking, health, cancer, etc.

Overall, then, persuasion theory treats the effect of arguments on audience groups as well as the effects on individual images. Image effects remain the basic outcome of argument and groups of people may share an image. This means that they may be expected to react similarly to a set of arguments. Hence, argumentative effect may be studied vis-à-vis audiences as well as with respect to single persons.

Persuasion as Image Building

In the last few pages I have introduced many ideas about "the outcomes of argument." I have identified the range of belief, attitude, and value effects that arguments may cause. I have investigated the "selective processes" and used them as a basis for explaining why image maintenance is a more likely outcome than image change. The relationship between images and behavior has been considered, as has the relationship between persuasion as an individual image effect and persuasion as an influence on a whole audience of people.

It is now appropriate for me to draw together the strains of this discussion of persuasive outcomes and to set the direction for the remainder of the chapter. What can be said about persuasion thus far? To begin with, because meaning is personal and messages must be interpreted by each individual, it would seem that persuasion is a subjective, personal process. Messages are received into the human image system. The effect of the message is not merely a function of the objective "strength" of the message. Effects result from the interaction of argument and image.

Because a new message is integrated into an existing image system, it follows that image change will occur less frequently than image maintenance. Because the elements of the image system are organized into a whole, it is difficult for a single message to produce a change. A new argument may well put pressure on an old attitude, but the old attitude is strengthened by its connection to other beliefs, attitudes, and values. Each element of the system is anchored to others, and if a persuader seeks to change a well-integrated, strongly anchored image element, the task is all the more difficult.

Changes in the image do occur, nevertheless. Messages do work effects. But these image alterations more often take the form of gradual evolution rather than sudden conversion. New images tend to be built up over time. The image-building effect of communication is well reflected in an article on "The Scary World of TV's Heavy Viewer." Gerbner and Gross (1976, p. 45) compared the image of the world held by those who viewed television for an average of two hours or less per day (light viewers) versus the image held by those who watched for four or more hours (heavy viewers). They concluded that "violence on television leads viewers to perceive the real world as more dangerous than it really is." Heavy viewers expressed less trust in other people and overestimated the chances that they would be "involved in some type of violence during any given week." The authors underscore the point that I made just a moment ago that persuasive effects may be gradual and evolutionary. The prevalence of violence on television—where "about 20 percent" of identifiable characters are shown as having law enforcement occupations (as opposed to less than 1 percent in the real world)—gradually induces viewers to adopt an image of life as more dangerous.

Argumentative outcomes are effects on beliefs, attitudes, and values. Images are resistant to but not immune from change. Image change may be immediate, but it is more likely to be gradual. Images are related to behavior, but the relationship is a difficult one. Finally, image effects are personal, but when a group of people—an audience—shares demographic, personality, or image characteristics, the members of the group are prone to react similarly to a message.

In the final sections of the chapter, I will build upon these conclusions about persuasion. I will cite some features of argument that have been found to enhance successful persuasion. I will summarize several theories as to how and why persuasion operates. All of this will lay the groundwork for a final section in which I present a synthetic model of persuasion.

ARGUMENTS AND PERSUASIVE EFFECTS

The previous section dealt with encounters between messages and the image system. Arguments were seen to have a dual relationship to the human image system. On the one hand, arguments may prompt changes or modifications in one's image of something. On the other hand, the image system exerts a counterinfluence on the incoming arguments. Therefore, although arguments are a necessary factor in image change or modification, they are not sufficient to produce effects. Receivers may act selectively to avoid changing their image.

Even though argumentation cannot always produce an image change, scholars have identified ways to maximize the impact of arguments. These pertain to the whole range of verbal and nonverbal message construction techniques. In the next few pages, I will explore certain factors of argument that tend to improve an arguer's chances for success.

Credibility Effects

I have written about credibility as the receiver's perception of the believability of the source. This was a theme in chapter 2. Since the time of Aristotle, students of persuasion have been aware of the persuasive implications of credibility. When an audience perceives an advocate as credible, it generally follows that the audience is more prone to be persuaded by a message presented by the advocate. Aristotle himself attested (*Rhetoric,* I. 2. 1356a) to the power of credibility in his assertion that the nature of the speaker was "the most potent of all the means to persuasion." Although most modern researchers would hesitate to label credibility as the most important element in persuasion, all recognize its influencing role. The more credible the source, the greater the likelihood that an argument will bring about image changes.

As I pointed out earlier, credibility is produced via the interaction of source, message, and receiver. Credibility is an interactive variable. It is the perception of a source by a receiver. Furthermore, the existence of credibility is influenced by the message and by the general situation in which the message is presented. Let us consider how credibility becomes a factor in a situation of dispute.

Credibility has been found to result from characteristics of a message source. Early experimental research identified the impact of source-centered credibility. In these studies the same message was attributed to different sources. For instance, in a study by Hovland and Weiss (1951), messages were attributed alternately to "high-credibility" sources (e.g., the *New England Journal of Biology and Medicine*) and "low-credibility" sources such as "a mass circulation monthly pictorial magazine." Overall, greater attitude change occurred when the messages were attributed to the high-credibility source. The Hovland and Weiss study seems to have measured general reputation. A medical journal has a better reputation for accuracy on a medical topic than does a popular mass magazine. Similarly, we would expect a professor of astronomy to be more credible than an undergraduate physics student when the subject was eclipses of the sun. In such cases the audience's favorable perception of the source interacts with the message. The source lends believability to the statements being made. The "who" adds to the "what."

Many times, however, credibility results primarily from the message itself. This is usually the case when we know little about a speaker in advance. For instance, I once attended a program on U.F.O.s in which the speaker was introduced as having worked in the aerospace industry and as having earned a master's degree in physics. Being from the academic world, I was not particularly impressed by the speaker's qualifications. After all, he didn't have a Ph.D. Yet this particular speaker gained credibility in my eyes as a result of his presentation. He readily admitted that many U.F.O. stories are hoaxes and that no conclusive evidence exists to prove that Earth has been visited by extraterrestrial beings. He debunked many U.F.O. theories as far-fetched—e.g., that the Bermuda Triangle is a base for U.F.O. ships. On the other hand, the speaker emphasized that the best U.F.O. reports are from people who were reluctant to report the experience. He also spent considerable time developing the theoretical possibility of intergalactic space travel. His calm, reasoned approach to the subject made me more favorable to his point of view. His presentation (i.e., the message, verbal and nonverbal) enhanced his believability. This in turn added to the force of his pro-U.F.O. position. Aristotle (*Rhetoric*, I. 2. 1356a) believed that "internal" credibility—i.e., credibility created by the speech—was a more proper cause of persuasion than prior reputation.

Characteristics of the audience seem to be related to speaker credibility. Apparently, some people are more responsive to credibility cues than are others. Some are more "credibility prone," in other words. They are more sensitive to differences between high- and low-credibility sources (Siegel, Miller, and Wotring, 1969, p. 124). Rosenfeld and Plax (1975, p. 278) argue that listeners who are "lacking in self-esteem" are "likely to perceive a speaker as dynamic." McGuckin (1967) has proposed that when the advocate and listener possess a similar "cognitive style," the advocate is perceived as more credible. This study provides some evidence that advocates who "think like us" are held in greater esteem. This point can easily be extended to include other similarities between source and receiver. Likeness in dialect and clothing, as I will indicate later, can enhance believability.

Credibility also arises from the situation. We may define "situation" as a context of events in which a message is presented. Situational factors of credibility include the topic under consideration. After all, it is the topic that determines whether attributes of a source are relevant to an argument. For instance, the reader might perceive me as more believable on the subject of argumentation than on the subject of nuclear warfare. My teaching and research background would be relevant to the former subject but not to the latter. Audience stress at a particular moment also has been found to exert an influence on the perception of credibility. Sigall and Helmreich (1969; reprinted in Beisecker and Parson, 1972, p. 268) found that "when the audience is under high stress," variations in communicator credibility have less impact "with regard to opinion change."

In addition to the topic and stress features of a situation, if circumstances cause the audience to doubt a speaker's motives, the arguer becomes less credible. This common-sense principle was illustrated in an experiment by Walster, Aronson, and Abrahams (1966; reprinted in Himmelfarb and Eagly, 1974). Experimental subjects listened to messages advocating either more power for criminal prosecutors or less power. The messages were attributed alternately to a "prosecutor" or a convicted "criminal." The experimenters assumed that the audience would realize that regardless of the stated reasons for the changes, a prosecutor's interests are served when his powers are increased. It makes his job easier. Similarly, it is to the advantage of a criminal to weaken the prosecutor, because this lessens the chances that the accused will be convicted. The researchers hypothesized that when a prosecutor argued for increasing his powers, the audience would recognize the "ulterior motives" and rate him as less credible. The same would prevail for the criminal who spoke for decreasing prosecutor power. Further, they predicted, a source arguing against self-interest (e.g., a criminal favoring more prosecutor power) would be thought of as more credible. They believed that this would be the case because of the absence of ulterior, self-serving motives. The results favored the hypotheses: "[W]hen the communicator advocated changes opposed to his own self-interest he was perceived as more expert, more honest, and more influential than when he advocated changes in his own self-interest" (p. 163).

In sum, credibility arises from the interaction of source, message, receiver, and situation. Sources confer believability on messages, and vice-versa. Further, the extent to which a receiver is impressed by a source may depend on an interaction of source attributes, audience attributes, and audience preferences. Finally, the general situation may influence the perception of credibility by an audience.

Two final things need to be said about the operation of credibility. One of these concerns the factors of credibility, and the other, the persistence of credibility effects. The first point relates to how audiences apply credibility to advocates. In chapter 6, I suggested that listeners evaluate communicators by using standards such as morals, competence, motives, consistency, and expediency. Aristotle (*Rhetoric*, II. 1. 1378a) mentioned three dimensions of credibility (three "sources of trust"): character (virtue), intelligence (competence), and good will (good motives). Statistical studies have confirmed these Aristotelian dimensions but have provided evidence for the existence of other factors such as "dynamism" and "sociability." (See Cronkhite and Liska, 1976, for a review of these studies.)

Persistence of credibility effects is a final subject that deserves mention. When persons accept new information, they are likely to be highly conscious of the source of that information. This explains why the credibility of the source makes us more (or less) willing to accept new information. However, as the new data is integrated into our image system, we may lose track of "who said what." That is, we may forget that X argument came from Y source. As a result, credibility effects may deteriorate as time passes. A study by Kelman and Hovland (1953; reprinted in Himmelfarb and Eagly, 1974) indicated that over time arguments made by highly credible sources tend to lose favor. Correspondingly, an argument gains favor as the listener forgets that it originated from an untrustworthy source. This latter effect—the gaining of strength by an initially rejected argument—has been termed the "sleeper effect" in persuasion. Another of the Kelman and Hovland findings is of interest here. The authors learned that by reminding the listeners of "who said what," they could maintain much of the original credibility effect.

Language Effects

Language style denotes an arguer's choice of words. When a communicator selects opinionated or unbiased words, uses or eschews profanity, and speaks in either short or long sentences, the choices are an exercise of freedom of style.

Style choices have been found to influence both a persuader's credibility and the chances of successful persuasion. Below, I introduce some factors of style that appear to make a difference in suasory impact.

Clarity   Traditionally, language scholars have advised the use of a simple, clear speech style. Clarity is necessary for audience understanding: Communicators must remember that the audience needs help in following a line of argument. Clarity has to do with the use of meaningful but simple words. The clear speaker avoids vague expressions such as "The university's synchronized incremental projections" in favor of simpler statements such as "Let's take a look at the expected future budgets of the three colleges during the next five years." Obscure words are hard to listen to, as are long, drawn-out sentences. As a rule, audiences are less impressed with people who make listening difficult (Carbone, 1975).

One exception to the general rule about clarity should be noted, however. When an arguer is presenting a point of view that differs from that of the listeners, it is sometimes advantageous to speak in vague terms. In chapter 2, I cited the example of Richard Nixon, who sought to please both "hawks" and "doves" by presenting his Vietnam policy in an ambiguous fashion. Ambiguity allowed both sides to interpret the message as favoring their respective solutions to the war. Ambiguity enhances the opportunities for selective interpretation. The listener perceives the message to mean what he or she wants it to mean. Goss and Williams (1973) have found evidence that equivocation (i.e., deliberate vagueness) can prevent a loss in credibility when a communicator is advocating a position with which the listeners disagree.

Concreteness   Because concrete language is specific, concreteness is closely related to clarity. However, concreteness involves an added dimension of elaboration. A concrete style is one that includes plenty of explanation and support for each idea that is introduced. Ample use of descriptions and comparisons enables the listener to "get a hold" on a claim. For instance, a statement that "we must put an end to consumer rip-offs in America" will have a hollow ring to it unless it is brought to earth. Examples, statistics, and testimony can put descriptive flesh on the skeleton of such a statement. By explaining that W, X, and Y practices have cost consumers Z dollars, the arguer reduces an abstract claim to terms that are more meaningful, and a high-level statement is made concrete. Carbone (1975) has found evidence that descriptive language increases a speaker's perceived credibility.

Similarly, the use of interpretive language can impart greater force to an argument. In chapter 5, I identified a number of sample arguments in which comparisons helped to make the point: A strike was like a hijacking, the Consumer Product Safety Commission was like Frankenstein's monster, and so on. Because comparison adds to the meaning of an argument, it imparts greater force to the claim. Hence, arguers may expect that comparisons will add to their opportunity for success with an audience. (On this point, see McCroskey and Combs, 1969.)

Concrete language also helps to win attention. Often, a descriptive assertion will perk the audience up. Most teachers realize that including an anecdote or story can help maintain the class's interest in a theoretical subject. In addition, most of the interpretive arguments mentioned in chapter 5 have attention-getting power. Listeners usually respond well to humor. The use of antithesis adds interest by suggesting conflict—e.g., "us versus them." Fear appeals have been found to bring about emotional arousal in listeners (Leventhal, Singer, and Jones, 1965; reprinted in Himmelfarb and Eagly, 1974, pp. 321–328). By arousing the listeners, concrete statements establish the conditions for image change.

Variety   Variety means diversity and change. Arguers should be aware of the favorable effects of variety in language. Variety can take many forms. A quotation adds variety when it follows a string of the arguer's own declarative assertions. Short, simple sentences create a feeling of variety when they follow a series of longer ones. In fact, just about anything that breaks up a pattern imparts variety to a message. Occasional variations in sentence length, quoted material, and humor or seriousness can help to keep the audience's attention. Carbone (1975) has found some support for the idea that diversity in vocabulary—when one uses a greater range of words—adds to a speaker's credibility. By increasing attention, boosting source credibility, and winning greater attention, linguistic variety assists in bringing about persuasive effects.

Appropriateness to Situation   Appropriate language fits the occasion at hand. Inappropriate speech stands out as being odd. We are all familiar with the dimension of language appropriateness. Most college students use a slightly different language in talking with friends, professors, parents, and ministers. Bernstein (in Williams, 1970, p. 29) observes that when talking to children adults "use a form of speech in which both the syntax and vocabulary are relatively simple." This is not necessarily the same style that they use for other adults. Bernstein cites another case in which "the speech used by members of an army combat unit on maneuvers will clearly be different from the same members' speech with the unit's chaplain."

Profanity is a good example of language that is related to situation. In locker-room talk, profane expressions usually are considered legitimate. Speakers gain credibility by using them. In polite speech, the same words are considered out of place. Recall the punishment meted out to Jimmy Carter for his use of "screw" and "shack up" in a published interview. Mulac's article (1976) on the credibility effects of obscene language suggests that some of the old taboos on "dirty words" may be breaking down—especially among women. But one would still expect to find a listener's reception of obscenity to be closely related to the situation of communication. Arguers should be careful about using language that may be considered out of place.

Intensity   Language intensity is a term introduced by Bowers (1963). It refers to the arguer's use of loaded language—language that has the effect of indicating the speaker's attitude about a concept. Highly intense language indicates that the speaker's attitude deviates greatly from the neutral portion of the attitude scale. Feezel's research (1974) into listener perception of qualifiers suggests that an audience is highly sensitive to the degree of force attributed to a conclusion.

Intense language and strong qualifiers can be effective. This is especially true when the audience shares the speaker's attitude and/or holds the speaker as being highly credible. However, when the audience is not particularly favorable to the speaker or the speaker's position, then care must be exercised. Intense language may offend and produce a boomerang effect.

The Rhetorical Faux Pas   "Faux pas" is a French expression meaning, literally, "false step" (blunder). In argumentation a faux pas is a word or phrase that gains notoriety. The word or phrase becomes controversial and reflects poorly on the communicator.

A good illustration of the effects of faux pas is to be found in former Michigan Governor George Romney's 1968 campaign for the Republican presidential nomination. During an interview Romney commented that while visiting Vietnam he had "just had the greatest brainwashing that anybody can get" (quoted in White, 1970, pp. 71–72). Romney expressed the opinion that the diplomatic corps and the military had presented a one-sided picture of the Vietnam situation. Romney declared that since his return he had studied Vietnamese history and as a result no longer felt that it was "necessary for us to get involved in South Vietnam to stop Communist aggression."

Romney did not emphasize the "brainwashing" metaphor. It was just a single interpretive term that he tossed in to clarify his point about the one-sidedness of the United States government's pronouncements on Vietnam; but, as in the case of Betty Ford's and Jimmy Carter's comments on sex, the press picked up the "brainwashing" remark and sensationalized it. Romney's opponents used the incident as an opportunity to attack the Governor's credibility. Romney was accused of being easily influenced and therefore incompetent. I can still remember letters to the editor dealing with the possibility that Romney would be "brainwashed" by the Russians if he should ever negotiate with them. Of course, all of this was unfair to Governor Romney: He made only a passing reference to the word in question. But the episode shows that arguers must guard against slips of the tongue that can be distorted by others and made into a major credibility liability. "Brainwashing" became a focal point, a symbol of Romney's alleged incompetence.

The language factors mentioned here—clarity, concreteness, variety, appropriateness, intensity, and the faux pas—illustrate how word choices can affect both communicator credibility and persuasive outcome. Our language reveals what kind of person each of us is. It can make audiences more likely or less likely to go along with what we advocate.

Evidence Effects

In chapter 2, I defined evidence as the citation by an advocate of a statement taken from a third party. This definition raises a basic question relative to the use of evidence by persuaders. First, why would a statement attributed to a third party be more persuasive than one that originated with the speaker? In other words, why should we expect to gain an advantage by quoting someone else when we could just as well make the statement ourselves? Clearly, Aristotle posed much the same query. In the *Rhetoric* (I. 2. 1355b–1356b and I. 15. 1375a–1377a) he treats proof by witnesses and documents as less significant in the argumentative process than the speaker's own actions.

Times have changed. In our modern world we see life as involving a mass of details. Things are complicated. We are forced to rely on the expertise of others in almost every sphere of endeavor. Because our world is so dependent on specialization and detail, quotations from experts and "facts" have gained prominence. We take it as a mark of knowledge when someone cites evidence; and because our world is one based on facts, we regard a quotation as shedding the light of reality onto a generalization. As I noted in chapter 4, testimony adds the color of reality to an argument by connecting an abstraction to the real world. Hence, in answer to the basic question about evidence, I would say that we give credence to evidence because our world is based on the acceptance of statements (oral and written) from others.

There is experimental support for the idea that evidence adds some persuasive force to speaker assertions, although, as McCroskey (1969, pp. 169–170) notes, "No firm generalization can be drawn concerning the effect of evidence on attitude change." The effect of evidence is not a massive, overwhelming one, nor would we expect it to be. After all, one could just as well make a point in one's own words instead of citing a quotation.

The main value of experimental work on evidence is that it gives us further insight into the conditions under which outside evidence adds persuasive weight to assertions made by an arguer. McCroskey (1966, p. 124) found that citing evidence is more helpful for a communicator possessing moderate to low credibility than to one of high credibility. Arguers would be most advised to cite evidence when the evidence source possesses higher credibility than the arguer himself. Anderson (1970, p. 84) found support for the idea that evidence is most believable when the quotations "do not reflect the self-interest of the evidence source." According to this finding, advocates are advised to cite quotations that come from sources who do not appear to have ulterior motives for making the statement.

In sum, arguers can add reality to their cases by citing evidence. Evidence can be particularly helpful for the low-credibility arguer—provided the evidence is from a source held as more credible than the arguer. Finally, it seems that advocates are best served by quotations that come from sources who do not appear to be making a self-serving statement.

Organizational Effects

The organization of a message refers to the placement of arguments; it involves questions about the order of elements—introductions, internal summaries, conclusions, and the like. "Arrangement" is a synonym for organization.

Since classical times argumentation theorists have advised that the speaker pay close attention to organization. A good organization is one that places the arguments into a coherent whole. Good organization is said to consist of arranging one's data and claims so as to (1) make clear their meaning and (2) make clear their relationship to the position being advanced. Much of what I said about outlining (chapter 2) flows from traditional norms of quality organization.

Baird (1974) has found support for the idea that good organization aids listeners in comprehending a message. He constructed two sample speeches. In one of these speeches the ideas were carefully arranged; in the other, the paragraphs and sentences (within paragraphs) were arranged randomly. Baird found (p. 124) that "speeches of high organizational quality . . . produce significantly greater amounts of comprehension than low quality speeches."

In addition to aiding listener understanding, research suggests that good organization increases audience recall of information along with speaker credibility. McCroskey and Mehrley (1969) found that speakers having both low and high initial (prespeech) credibility lost credibility when using poor organization. Darnell (1963) studied the effects on retention of various sentence arrangements. Differences in sentence order were related to differences in the audience's ability to recall details of a message.

Having seen that organizational quality can benefit an arguer, let us examine some arrangement strategies that appear to improve a persuader's chances for success.

Repetition of Information   Wilson and Miller (1968; reprinted in Himmelfarb and Eagly, 1974) cite findings that repeating an argument aids the listener in remembering it. Translating this general finding into specific advice is not difficult. Advocates would do well to present each major argument in the form of a succinct statement, then go on to elaborate, explain, and support the argument. The capsule statement can be used when the argument is first presented, when the argument is concluded, and when a general summary is made. This approach seems all the more advantageous because Wilson and Miller have found evidence that repeated arguments are sometimes more persuasive.

Use of Summaries (and Previews)   Classical scholars such as Aristotle (*Rhetoric,* III. 19. 1419b) and Cicero (*De Inventione,* I. lii. 99) suggest that the final section of a speech should contain a summary of the major arguments of one's case. Baird (1974, p. 125) has found some experimental support for the idea that summary reviews aid listener understanding of a message. He also cites data that demonstrate that previews (introductory orientations) help the audience to comprehend more information about a message.

Stating the Position   One's position is one's overall conclusion or thesis on the subject at hand. Generally, research suggests that both greater understanding and greater attitude change occur when an advocate explicitly states his overall position. (See Cronkhite, 1969, pp. 194–195.)

This finding makes sense because such a position statement helps the listeners to mentally organize the arguer's entire presentation. The advocate must be careful, however, about where in the speech he makes the overall position statement. If the audience disagrees with the speaker's thesis, it may be better to state the position later in the speech rather than at the outset. However, if the audience is in agreement with the communicator initially—that is, favors the position being advanced—then it may be advantageous to state it earlier.

Should the Advocate Cite the Positions of Others?   As we all know, there are a wide variety of positions that may be taken on an issue. Persuasion theory suggests that in some situations it is probably advantageous to support one's own position and not to mention other alternative ones. Such a strategy results in what is termed a one-sided message. Correspondingly, a two-sided message is one that is arranged to include both the arguments that support the arguer's own position and arguments favoring another position(s).

Lumsdaine and Janis (1953; reprinted in Himmelfarb and Eagly, 1974) compared the effects of a one-sided "radio program" versus a two-sided one. The one-sided program mentioned only those arguments that supported the communicator's position that "Russia would be unable to produce large numbers of atomic bombs for at least the next five years" (p. 367). In the two-sided program, the communicator sought to establish this same position, but in addition to containing the arguments that supported it, his presentation included mention of "opposing arguments," which were "interwoven" into the message. The authors report that in some instances the opposing arguments were merely presented and not refuted by the communicator. The results of the study suggest that a one-sided message produces greater opinion change among "members of the audience who were already favorably disposed toward the communicator's position." However, for those persons who, before hearing the message, disagreed with the communicator, the two-sided presentation produced more gains for the arguer. This makes sense. Those who were already committed might not expect to hear the other side of an argument, whereas an unfavorable audience might demand this of a speaker.

The Lumsdaine and Janis study contained another instance in which a two-sided strategy worked better. The researchers exposed some audience members to a message that took the position contrary to that of the original one (to wit, that Russia would be able to produce many atomic bombs within two years). This allowed the researchers to test which type of message (one- or two-sided) was better in protecting listeners against later counterarguments. The two-sided message was found to be more effective when the listeners were later exposed to an opposing argument.

We may posit these conclusions vis-á-vis the one-sided and two-sided strategies. One-sided argument is better when (1) the audience initially agrees with your position and/or when (2) you desire only immediate attitude change (i.e., the possibility that listeners will later reverse their attitude is of no concern to you). A two-sided presentation is better when (1) the audience initially disagrees with your position and/or (2) you desire sustained attitude change (i.e., you want the listeners to remain "with" you even after they are exposed, later, to opposing positions).

Forewarning   In the normal course of events an arguer can expect that an audience will be exposed to arguments that oppose his position. This is a reasonable assumption that flows from the fact that controversy is a way of life in our society. If this is true, then a salient question for arguers may be put as follows: Should I warn my audience about the counterarguments that they may later encounter? Research indicates that such a forewarning does induce resistance to subsequent attitude change.

Freedman and Sears (1965; reprinted in Himmelfarb and Eagly, 1974) arranged for speakers to address a group of high school seniors on the subject of teenage driving. The speakers took the position that teenagers should not drive—a position that "virtually all" of the audience opposed. Some of the students were warned 10 minutes before the talk that they were going to hear a speech that opposed teenage driving; some received this warning 2 minutes before; others received no warning. The researchers found that students who were forewarned became significantly less likely to be persuaded by the message. In other words, those who were forewarned were more resistant to attitude change (as measured immediately after the speech). Furthermore, those who received a 10-minute warning changed less than those who were warned 2 minutes before being exposed to the message. This suggests that when listeners are forewarned of an upcoming message that will challenge their opinion, they begin to construct arguments in defense of their original attitude. Those who have more time to construct image defenses are more successful in warding off arguments that oppose their attitude.

Where Should Your Strongest Arguments Be Placed?   One of the earliest questions posed by attitude change researchers dealt with whether an arguer's first or last arguments were more effective. Some studies suggested that a primacy effect operated. That is, all other things equal, one's earliest arguments (in a message or in a dispute) were better remembered and more persuasive than those that came later. Other experiments seemed to point to a recency effect. In these findings, all other things equal, the last arguments (in a message or in a dispute) were better remembered and more persuasive.

The findings on primacy versus recency are not entirely consistent. For example, some research suggests that the primacy effect is likely to occur when a listener is unfamiliar with the subject matter. On the other hand, certain studies suggest that primacy operates when the topic is a familiar one. However, one fairly consistent finding (Miller and Campbell, 1959; reprinted in Himmelfarb and Eagly, 1974, p. 284) is that the recency effect is weaker when two messages follow each other in rapid succession and stronger when there is a "long delay between the first and second communication coupled with immediate measurement [of the listeners' attitudes] after the second communication."

Finally, there is consensus on this bit of advice on placing arguments. Arguments placed either at the beginning or end of a message are better remembered than those placed in the middle.

What General Organizational Patterns Are Best?   Rhetorical theory has identified a large number of general approaches to organization. One may organize a message according to time, space, cause and effect, and so on. Research findings suggest that two patterns in particular may bring advantages to the persuader. These are the need-solution and refutation patterns. One cannot really say that these two patterns are best. It is just that they seem to involve some advantages.

The need-solution pattern is one in which the arguer identifies a need or problem and then presents a solution to the problem. Cohen (1957; cited in Cronkhite, 1969, pp. 196–197) found evidence that it is best to arouse the audience's feeling of need before presenting a solution (rather than the other way around). Subjects exposed to a problem-solution organization changed attitude more than with a solution-problem format.

A refutation method of organization is one in which the arguer explicitly identifies and refutes opposing arguments. Given the findings related to two-sided messages (it is sometimes persuasive to identify opposing arguments) and forewarning (listeners who are warned of upcoming opposing arguments are more resistant to them), it would seem logical that refutation is a good arrangement strategy. It is.

McGuire (1962; reprinted in Himmelfarb and Eagly, 1974) found additional support for the advantages of including a refutation section in one's speech. He constructed and tested "defensive messages" of two types. In one type, claims were supported by data. In the other, claims were supported and counterarguments were mentioned and refuted. In both cases the subjects were later exposed to an "attacking message." The attacking message contained arguments that opposed the original claims. McGuire found (p. 379) that the supportive strategy (claims supported by data) "conferred less resistance to the attack than did the refutational defenses." Furthermore, he learned that the refutational approach was superior even when the original defensive messages refuted counterarguments different from those actually presented in the subsequent attacking message. It would seem, then, that a refutation section puts the listener "on guard." When the receiver is later exposed to counterarguments, there is a motivation for discounting them.

Nonverbal Effects

Argumentation is not merely a verbal phenomenon. It is well that I reiterate this point. Traditionally, verbal language and verbal argument strategies receive the greatest attention in works on argumentation. The reason for this is not difficult to understand. Written arguments are more available; written arguments are, in general, more permanent than spoken ones. They are more likely to be available for purposes of subsequent analysis. Also, written arguments are easier to deal with. When presented as a written statement, a claim is an essentially verbal thing. It consists of words and sentences that may be cataloged, compared, and diagrammed. But when an argument is presented in an oral setting, it becomes more complex. We have to take into account the speaker's voice, his gestures, mannerisms, body movement, etc. We must pay attention to factors such as voice tone and body movement because they give us clues as to how the words—the verbal symbols—are to be interpreted. An arguer might state, "My opponent has raised a good point." Yet suppose that while making the assertion, the arguer raises her eyebrows, smiles, shakes her head, and draws out the word "good" (e:g., g-o-o-o-o-d). These nonverbal cues would suggest that the arguer does not really mean for us to take her verbal statement seriously. She is being facetious. She is just kidding.

Nonverbal factors of argument have been studied since classical times. The term "delivery" has been used to denote the study of voice, body movement, and related subjects in argumentation. Recently, the term "nonverbal communication" has gained stature as a label for such language study. Nonverbal studies seek to explain how communication occurs even when words are not present or are held constant. Space considerations prohibit a full survey of the nonverbal features of argument, but the following information should serve to reinforce my reminder that argumentation is not an exclusively verbal phenomenon. It does not begin and end with words.

Vocal Effects   Anthropological evidence indicates that vocal communication originated long before written symbols were evolved. "Speech" is a more ancient form of communication than is writing. Today, of course, with advances in print media, our communication world is no longer exclusively oral. Yet for most of us the spoken word may be more familiar than the written. In conversation and through the electronic media, speech retains its significance for modern persons.

Because we encounter speech daily, we are aware of its variations. Human speech may differ along several lines: (1) rate (words per minute), (2) articulation (the clear or unclear production of speech sounds), (3) volume (loudness versus softness), (4) pitch (high versus low on a scale, as in the musical scale), (5) spacing (how the words are grouped together), and (6) pronunciation (the choice of vowel or consonant sounds together with the accenting of syllables). Scholars have found that the nature of a person's voice may affect an audience's perception of the speaker and its reception of the message.

Pearce and Brommel (1972) studied the effect of vocal delivery on a speaker's credibility. They compared a "conversational" versus a "dynamic" style of vocal delivery. The conversational mode, they indicated (p. 303), "was characterized by generally lower pitch, less volume, less use of pauses or variations in loudness for emphasis and less fluctuation in pitch and rate than the dynamic style." Their experimental results indicated that when the conversational style was used, the speaker was rated as significantly more trustworthy and personable. In other words, the conversational delivery mode seems to build certain factors of credibility. Next, the authors examined voice and attitude change. They found that a dynamic delivery produced the most attitude change when used by a speaker introduced as Undersecretary of Health, Education, and Welfare (a high-credibility introduction) and the least attitude change when the speaker was described as an undergraduate student (low credibility). When, at the outset of the speech, the audience expects the speaker to be credible, the dynamic delivery may work best; but it may work to the detriment of a speaker initially considered to be unauthoritative.

In addition to affecting attitude change and credibility, vocal cues have been found to influence many other judgments that receivers make about speakers. Hopper and Williams (1973) found that employers used vocal characteristics to judge the competence, agreeableness, and self-assurance of interviewees. Moe (1972) found that listeners are able to detect accurately the degree of a speaker's social status by listening to tape recordings. In another study of "vocal characteristics," Hart and Brown (1974) obtained three samples of speech from twelve male speakers: (1) a recording of the speaker reciting a passage, (2) a recorded extemporaneous response to a question, and (3) a typewritten copy of the extemporaneous response. These samples were rated by judges. The researchers found that judgments about the speaker's "social attractiveness" were based mainly on voice. Finally, a whole series of studies have shown that people are sensitive to vocal dialect. Miller (1975) established that English-speaking Canadians react more favorably to a message when it is read by another English-speaking Canadian than by a Canadian having a French accent. Giles (1973) found similar results in England, noting that messages presented in regional accents may be more persuasive to receivers who speak with a regional accent.

Overall Delivery Effects   A number of studies have looked at the simultaneous impact of several nonverbal factors. For instance, Mulac and Sherman (1975) examined "speech skill," which they defined as involving six factors: content, intelligibility, bodily action, personality, language, and voice. They found (p. 310) that "speakers appraised as demonstrating a higher degree of speech skill were also perceived as more credible." Gunderson and Hopper

(1976) also examined the effect of a number of delivery elements including voice volume, speech rate, voice quality, posture, gesture, and body movement. Their major finding was that good speech content (organization and evidence) can make up for weaknesses in delivery. A speaker with poor delivery habits is not automatically doomed to failure. Yet unpublished studies by McCroskey (cited in McCroskey, 1972, pp. 243–244) suggest that delivery should not be ignored by speakers. McCroskey reports that when the message content is uniformly strong, good delivery produces more attitude change than does poor delivery. This indicates that speakers should not neglect delivery in the belief that evidence and organization are the only things that matter. By itself, delivery does not appear to have as great an effect (in terms of credibility and attitude change) as does organization or evidence; but it does have a role to play and should not be discounted in accounting for the effects of arguments.

The studies of overall delivery seem to show that bodily action (gestures and movement) interact with both message content and voice in conveying an overall impression of speaker and arguments. Other research findings support a notion that factors such as mode of dress and speaker-receiver eye contact are important in delivery. Knapp (1972, pp. 79–86) synthesizes a number of inquiries into the effects of attire. Clearly, our perceptions of a previously unknown speaker are affected by the clothing worn. Receivers are prone to use mode of dress as the basis for judgments about the communicator's attitudes and personality. Receivers associate less conventional clothing with more liberal attitudes. Speakers should be aware of this. Furthermore, as Arnold (1973) indicates, objects carried by a speaker can increase credibility in certain cases. He found that when speaking on the topic of hearing loss, the same speaker was judged as significantly more authoritative when wearing a hearing aid than when not wearing it. The hearing aid did not add credibility when the topic was "women." Generalizing from this finding, speakers can expect listeners to be sensitive to objects that indicate that the speaker is knowledgeable about the topic at hand.

Eye contact has also been related to credibility. The results of an experiment by Beebe (1974, p. 24) suggests that "an increase in the amount of eye contact generated by a speaker in a live public-speaking situation enhances the listener's perception of the speaker's credibility." An extensive set of experiments by Mehrabian and Williams (1969) established eye contact (along with voice, facial activity, and gestures) as related to the "perceived persuasiveness" of communication.

Argument and Persuasion Operate Interactively

In the last several pages, I have reviewed certain findings on the persuasive effects of argument. This survey has identified a host of communication factors that are associated with successful argument outcomes. Certain overall generalizations are possible.

I   Increases in speaker credibility enhance the likelihood that a message will persuade receivers. However, credibility-induced persuasiveness may diminish over time as the audience forgets "who said what."

    A   Credibility can result from reputation, the message (content plus delivery), the nature of the audience, or the situation at hand.

    B   The audience's perception of credibility involves a number of judgments about the communicator. These include character, competence, motives, dynamism, and likeability.

II   Clear, concrete, and diverse language enhances both speaker credibility and audience understanding. To the extent that language adds to credibility and comprehension, it should increase the persuasiveness of a message. However, findings are less certain in this regard.

III   Speakers should use certain language options (e.g., profanity and intense language) only when conditions are favorable.

    A   It may be best to avoid intense statements unless the audience is highly favorable to the speaker or to the message.

    B   Speakers must be careful to avoid a faux pas.

IV   Evidence appears to add to the credibility of moderate- to low-credibility speakers.

    A   High-credibility speakers appear to have less to gain from evidence citations.

    B   Evidence is most believable when it originates from sources with no suspected ulterior motives.

V   Good organization can enhance the audience's ability to understand and recall a message. At the same time, it can increase the speaker's credibility.

    A   Speech summaries increase understanding.

    B   Repetition of main points increases recall.

    C   Stating one's overall position in a clear fashion increases both an audience's understanding and the amount of attitude change.

    D   A one-sided message seems best when the arguer is interested only in immediate attitude change and/or the audience already agrees with the message.

    E   A two-sided message seems best when the arguer desires long-term attitude change (i.e., desires to "innoculate" the audience against later counterarguments) and/or the audience initially disagrees with the message.

    F   Forewarning the audience about possible counterarguments helps to maintain attitude change.

    G   More audience retention results when the strongest arguments are presented either at the beginning or at the end of a message rather than in the middle.

    H   The need-solution and refutation patterns of organization appear to increase the likelihood of audience attitude change.

VI   Vocal characteristics lead to audience perceptions about the credibility, status, and attractiveness of a speaker.

    A   A "conversational" mode of delivery seems to enhance the speaker's perceived trustworthiness.

    B Similarity in dialect between speaker and listener can enhance the persuasiveness of an arguer's communication.

VII A dynamic style of delivery produces increased attitude change when the speaker initially possesses a favorable reputation.

VIII Overall delivery (voice, body, face, clothes, and objects) can affect speaker credibility. In particular, when two messages are well organized and are well supported, good delivery can make the difference between them.

In reading over these conclusions about argumentative effects, you may have noticed that argument and persuasion are interactive. We have seen that audiences are influenced by statements, organization, evidence, language style, speaker reputation, and other features of the speaker including voice, bodily action, clothes, and objects. The process of argument and persuasion therefore is not merely a function of the message. The process involves a close integration of source, message, channel, and receiver variables. For instance, credibility is the receiver's perception of a speaker, which can be enhanced by message (e.g., organization and evidence) and channel (e.g., voice). Furthermore, attitude change is an influence on part of a receiver's image that may be brought about by perceptions of messages, channels, and speakers. Overall, then, the effect standard deals with the persuasiveness of arguments, but "argument effects" are part of an interrelated process involving all facets of a communication situation.

THEORIES OF PERSUASION

Thus far in chapter 7, I have examined the effects that arguments bring about in receivers. Basically, we can say that receiver effects are image effects. "Effects" refer to the change, maintenance, or modification of a listener's interpretation of the world. For the most part, I have surveyed the range of possible belief, attitude, and value outcomes and I have identified some reasons that these effects occur. I have not as yet provided much in the way of an overall theory of persuasion.

Since the beginning of persuasion research, scholars have sought a universal theory to explain why arguments sometimes produce one outcome and at other times create a second effect. A theory of persuasion would be a set of principles that specified the relationships among the elements of the process. (See Kerlinger, 1964, p. 11, for a general definition of "theory.") A theory of persuasion would specify how source, message, channel, and receiver intermingle to produce argument effects. Such a general set of principles would seek to account for a host of research findings cited in this chapter. These principles would go below the surface to identify the subtle connections among source, message, channel, and receiver. In addition to explaining the various findings about persuasion, a theory of persuasion would allow for predictions. It would tell us to expect X effect when source W presented message Y through channel Z to receiver Q.

The reader may already suspect that there exists no single theory of persuasion. The subject has been studied by many scholars during many historical ages with no final result. No one, to my knowledge, is able to predict with absolute accuracy the effects that will result from a given argumentative situation. Even though the final chapter in the book of persuasion has yet to be written, there have been several insightful systems advanced over the centuries. None of these sets of principles contains all the answers: None will enable us to explain or predict everything. Yet by examining some of these systems, we will gain a greater understanding of the persuasive process.

Two further preliminaries are in order. First, I have elected to present only a sample of the many possible theories. Secondly, my purpose is only to outline the theories—not to say all that could be said about each. Notwithstanding these limitations, the three types of theories that I have chosen to examine should help to make the subject of persuasion more meaningful. Further, these three groups will serve as the basis for the final section of this chapter—a synthetic model of persuasion.

Rhetorical Theories

Many approaches to persuasion may be brought together under the heading of rhetoric. In its popular sense, rhetoric means ornate, overblown, or propagandistic communication. However, as this term is used in communication research, it means the analysis of arguments. In one sense, then, all theories of persuasion are rhetorical, because all involve the analysis of how arguments function. The term "rhetoric," however, has been used as a label for a particular *kind* of persuasion theory.

Rhetorical theories of persuasion possess these general attributes: (1) they are rooted in a tradition which first flourished in classical Greek times; (2) they look at arguments not only according to the effect standard, but also according to the truth, ethics, validity, and quality standards; and (3) they are based on a mixture of historical, critical, philosophical, and empirical research approaches. Thus, although countless works of rhetoric have been produced in the centuries since Aristotle, the works generally can be distinguished from others on the basis of these three characteristics. In the next few paragraphs, I will elaborate on these three characteristics, showing how rhetorical theories contribute to our understanding of persuasion.

Rhetorical theories are rooted in the classical tradition of rhetoric. "Classical rhetoric" refers chiefly to the scholarship of Greek and Roman philosophers, linguists, and orators during the period from 500 B.C. to A.D. 100. The earliest works are attributed to a group of teachers called the sophists. Interest in rhetoric increased in the fourth century before Christ as major philosophers such as Plato (ca. 428–348 B.C.) and Aristotle (ca. 384–322 B.C.) wrote treatises on it. In the years after Aristotle, lesser works were produced in Greece. Later, the Romans took up rhetorical studies. Representative writers include Cicero (ca. 106–43 B.C.) and Quintilian (ca. A.D. 35–95).

Rhetorical works continued to be produced through the Middle Ages and medieval periods. In the Renaissance the older Greek and Roman works were rediscovered and studied. The Renaissance marked a period in which new approaches to rhetoric were begun, and the post-Renaissance tradition of many approaches has continued to the present day. Writers such as Richard Weaver represent contemporary rhetorical theorists.

Apart from its pedigree the second distinguishing feature of rhetorical theory is its approach to the subject of argument. As I noted above, theories of rhetoric generally assume that arguments can be studied on the basis of their truth, ethics, validity, and quality as well as on the basis of their effect. At the outset of this chapter, I identified persuasion as a process of effects. Rhetorical theories therefore interpret this definition liberally: They look at the truth, ethics, validity, and quality of messages constructed for the purpose of generating effects. Throughout this book I have cited the works of Plato, Aristotle, Cicero, Quintilian, and Weaver. I now want to take a moment to generalize on their way of looking at persuasion.

Plato defined persuasion as the winning of the soul through speech (*Phaedrus,* 271). Plato points out that in order to persuade, the speaker must know something about the nature (souls) of people. However, Plato did not elaborate on the techniques for dealing with people—i.e., the techniques of persuasion. He felt that the strategies for effects (winning souls) were less important than the question of whether or not the orator sought truth. This takes us back to Plato's discussion of the truth standard, which was explained in chapter 3.

Plato's pupil Aristotle was influenced by but differed from his famous master. Unlike Plato, Aristotle gave considerable attention to the techniques of the effect standard. In the *Rhetoric* Aristotle identified ways to analyze audiences. Further, he gave advice to the would-be persuader. Aristotle explained how arguments could be discovered through analysis of a subject; how arguments were arranged in a speech; how we should choose a language style for arguments; and how one could best deliver arguments to an audience. Aristotle made additional points, as I noted in chapter 1, about the "logical," emotional, and credibility-centered means of persuasion.

Aristotle's *Rhetoric* teaches the orator how to deal with the emotions and biases of real people, yet Aristotle inherited his teacher Plato's concern for a truthful rhetoric. In reading carefully through the *Rhetoric,* one becomes aware of Aristotle's interest in making truth and reason prevail. Aristotle realized that emotional bias sometimes makes it difficult for people to accept truth, so he taught the techniques of dealing with emotions, not as ends in themselves, but as tools that would help the moral orator to make truth prevail. Aristotle hoped that rhetoric could make the truth supreme in several ways: (1) by encouraging the speaker to study and know his subject; (2) by reminding the speaker that unethical speaking originates not in technique but in bad intentions; and (3) by giving the well-intentioned speaker a means for making the best possible case for his perception of truth. (See *Rhetoric,* I. 1. 1354a–1356a.)

Overall, Aristotle's rhetorical theory is marked by his concern for the triumph of truth and for well-intentioned (ethical) speaking. His theory also is characterized by the belief that the best rhetoric is one based in careful, reasoned judgment. Aristotle did not discount the importance of human emotions, nor did he condemn them as a whole, but he seems to have believed that man's capacity to make judgments differentiated him from animals. Therefore, although he recognized the probative power of *pathos* (emotions) and *ethos* (credibility), he believed that *logos* (proof through speech or reasoning) was especially fitting for man's nature. (See Aristotle, *Nichomachean Ethics,* X. 7. 1178a4–8). Aristotle's interest in reasoned judgment means that his rhetoric is closely connected to the validity standard of argument. Recall that in assessing validity the critic makes a careful judgment about the argument based on all possible information about it. Judgments of validity are distinct from an audience's subjective (I like it/I dislike it) reaction to a persuasive appeal.

The rhetorical theories of Plato and Aristotle illustrate the relationship between effects and such other argument standards as truth, ethics, and validity. Simply stated, rhetorical approaches recognize that persuasion depends on an orator's ability to win favor from and stimulate the emotions of people. Nevertheless, rhetorical theory gives equal, if not greater, weight to the truth, ethics, and validity of communcation: The substance of rhetorical theory is its concern for elements of a moral suasion.

You may recall that I mentioned the quality standard as being important in rhetorical theory. Quality deals with aesthetics (rules of art) in communication. Language quality is a basis for evaluating literature and drama as well as prose argumentation. Because quality is comprehensively treated in literary theory, I will not elaborate on it here.

A final distinguishing feature of rhetorical theories is the method of research used by rhetorical scholars. Aristotle and his Greek and Roman followers used observations and analysis as their research tools. They observed speakers, messages, and audiences and the interactions among them. They also reflected over their observations, seeking to draw general principles. Modern rhetorical theorists use observation and philosophical analysis (reflection) also. Besides these tools, contemporary theorists use historical and critical methods. They analyze the effect, truth, ethics, and validity of messages presented in contemporary and historical contexts. These methods of inquiry set the rhetorical researcher apart from other persuasion scholars. The rhetorical approach can be distinguished from the experimental-empirical method. Most of the studies cited in the section on "Arguments and Persuasive Effects" were based on experimentation with human subjects. People who identify rhetoric as their field of study are less prone to use experimentation and statistical analysis than are the theorists whom I will mention below.

In sum, rhetorical theories mark a distinct approach to persuasion. The study of rhetoric is a tradition begun in classical times. It treats effect but gives major weight to standards other than effect, and it is an approach based more on philosophical, critical, and historical research than on the experimental-empirical approach.

Cognitive Consistency Theories

In recent years the social sciences have contributed a number of theories to the field of persuasion. Many of these may be classified as "cognitive consistency" theories, because they are based on the tendency of people to desire and achieve a consistent image system. Earlier in the chapter I identified the image system as consisting of collected beliefs, attitudes, and values. "Cognition" is a general term for these three image elements. The word "cognition" means "thought," and therefore our image system consists of many belief, attitude, and value cognitions.

In my presentation of the image system I suggested that on the whole people desire to keep their beliefs, attitudes, and values—their cognitions—consistent. Cognitive consistency theories seek to explain how new information affects an existing image system. The theories endeavor to explain why new arguments sometimes cause the image maintenance, image change, or image alteration effect. In short, the cognitive consistency approach is designed to clarify the range of possible persuasive outcomes. Below, I examine two of the many formulations of cognitive consistency.

Dissonance Theory   One of the earliest consistency theories was that put forth by Festinger (1957). Festinger sought to provide an explanatory principle (theory) that could account for the many individual findings of persuasion research. He postulated that when two relevant cognitions are joined, they can have a consonant or a dissonant relationship. Consider an illustration. Suppose I know that "I am smoking" (a belief) and, further, that "smoking is harmful to my health" (an attitude or value). According to Festinger's theory (p. 12), my two cognitions would be in a dissonant relationship—that is, "they do not fit together." Considering the two cognitions alone, if I really felt that smoking was harmful, then I "should" not be smoking. Festinger (p. 13) argues that "x ["I am smoking"] and y ["smoking is harmful"] are dissonant if not-x ["I am/should *not* be smoking"] follows from y." A dissonant relationship results when we realize that two cognitions are inconsistent and that one must change in order for consistency to exist.

Consonant relationships, on the other hand, are those in which one cognition logically follows from the other as in the case of "tomorrow I have a big exam" and "I am studying for it." To repeat: (1) Two cognitions are in a dissonant relationship when a person perceives that they do not fit together, and (2) two cognitions are in a consonant relationship when the person thinks that one follows consistently from the other.

The theory of cognitive dissonance is based on Festinger's assumption (p. 18) that *"the presence of dissonance gives rise to pressures to reduce or eliminate the dissonance."* Festinger sought to use this principle as a basis to account for findings about persuasion. For instance, he cited it (p. 123) as a means for understanding situations in which "persons will actively seek out information." These are occasions of deliberate selective exposure. Recall that earlier in the chapter I indicated that scholars have not come to agreement as to why persons are selective in exposure. Festinger's dissonance principle was an early effort to explain this phenomenon of selectivity. Festinger theorized that if the dissonance were large (i.e., the two cognitions were important or involved many subsidiary cognitions), then selective exposure might be a device to reduce dissonance. In this view, people would seek out only the information that would assist them in reducing dissonance—and would avoid the opposite kind of information. Hence, in the face of antismoking messages, dissonance would predict that "smokers would evade the impact of this possibility [cancer] which tends to produce [a] cognition which is quite dissonant with the knowledge that they continue to smoke" (Festinger, 1957, p. 155). Throughout his book Festinger identified dissonance-provoking situations and strategies (such as selective exposure) that could lead to dissonance reduction.

Congruity Theory   Congruity theory originated in the work of psychologists Osgood, Suci, and Tannenbaum (1957). As I indicated in chapter 2, these authors have done considerable work on the concept of "meaning." Their congruity principle marks an attempt to relate meaning and persuasion. The authors postulate that our attitude toward something is a major component of what the term means to us. Accordingly, they sought to identify the attitude effects that result when two symbols are connected. Their congruity principle holds that when two symbols are connected by an assertion, there is a tendency for a person's evaluations of the two symbols to shift to a congruent position.

An example will help to clarify the congruity principle. Suppose that I have an attitude of +3 toward classical rhetoric (on a scale of −3 to +3). Suppose, further, that I read a journal article that suggests that classical rhetoric is useless—an idea that I rate as −2. The congruity principle would predict that when "classical rhetoric" is connected to "useless," for that moment my attitude toward each "shifts." I become somewhat less favorable to classical rhetoric and somewhat more favorable to the idea that it is useless. My two attitudes shift in such a way that they become closer together on the attitude rating scale of −3 to +3. They become more congruent. (The more extreme term shifts less.)

The congruity principle involves a set of mathematical formulas in which the shift toward congruity (or equilibrium) is calculated. These formulas measure how much each term will shift. The simplified congruity formula would predict that after "classical rhetoric" was called "useless" in the article, my attitude toward rhetoric would be +1 on the −3 to +3 scale. Congruity theory predicts, further, that some attitude change will persist, despite the proclivity for "classical rhetoric" to return to its original +3 position.

Osgood, Suci, and Tannenbaum presented the congruity principle as a general explanation for changes in attitude direction that result from the association of symbols. In particular, they cited the theory as being useful in predicting the outcome of situations in which a source (i.e., a person) is connected to a concept. The connection of Jimmy Carter and *Playboy* magazine would be such a case. Congruity theory therefore is useful in explaining how value arguments such as guilt by association operate.

Cognitive consistency theories such as dissonance and congruity have added to our understanding of persuasion. These theories allow us to apply my original basic definition of argument (a relationship of two terms) to the image system. The theories help to explain how the connecting of two terms—such as "smoking" and "harmful to health"—can affect a person's image system. Specifically, they help to sort out the reasons that selective exposure occurs and how guilt by association operates. The approach of cognitive consistency is more "scientific" (experimental and statistical) than are rhetorical theories; but because they focus only on effects, they also are more limited. Moreover, these two theories have been criticized as being inadequate even for the explanation or prediction of effects. Certainly, they do not supply the final answers to questions about effects; but they add to our understanding of the effects-generating process.

Interpersonal Theories

Rhetorical and consistency theories are based primarily on observations of public communication situations in which messages are presented by a speaker to a large collection of people. Aristotle's *Rhetoric,* for instance, dealt mainly with public speaking. The cognitive theories derive essentially from experiments in which subjects are exposed to written or recorded messages. In contrast, interpersonal theories look at the influence of people upon other people. They treat persuasion as something that may occur informally as individuals are influenced by the people with whom they converse. I want to consider two major contributions to the theory of persuasion as person-to-person contact.

The Two-Step Flow of Communication   In their study of Erie County voters, Lazarsfeld, Berelson, and Gaudet (1944) sought to identify how people settled on a candidate. Naturally, they found that many voters obtained political information from the mass media, yet they found that more people tended to identify personal contacts as the basis for their voting decisions. Following up on this, the researchers identified certain individuals as "opinion leaders." These persons possessed an above-average interest in the 1940 presidential campaign and they tended to decide early about a candidate and stick to that decision. Opinion leaders reported that the "formal media were more effective as sources of influence than personal relationships" (p. 151). In contrast to the opinion leaders, "people who made up their minds later in the campaign were more likely to mention personal influences in explaining how they formed their final vote decision."

The researchers used the term "two-step flow of communication" to denote the process by which the media influenced opinion leaders and these leaders in turn affected others through political discussion. They suggested that "ideas often flow *from* radio and print *to* opinion leaders and *from* them to the less active segments of the population" (p. 151). On the basis of their entire study, they concluded (p. xiii) that "face-to-face contacts turned out to be the most important influences stimulating opinion change."

Later studies have refined and elaborated on the original two-step hypothesis. As Kraus and Davis (1976) note, the Erie County study served as a foundation for a "social influence" theory of mass-media persuasion. Later works on social influence tended to reject the strict two-step view of mass media influence, and emphasis on an opinion leader elite has declined. However, the two-step social influence theory has made a lasting contribution. It has provided a vehicle for explaining the impact of personal contact—a channel variable—in persuasion.

Balance Theory   Balance theory attempts to explain how people's ideas are influenced by interpersonal contact with others. Developed by theorists Heider (1946) and Newcomb (1953), balance is well applied to interpersonal communication by Miller and Steinberg (1975). In any conversation or continuing relationship, two people will have occasion to talk about many subjects. Each topic or concept that is discussed can lead to a balanced or out-of-balance interaction. Figure 7-1 illustrates balance in a two-person interaction. Assume that Sally is discussing the school bond issue with her husband, Fred. Assume, further, that Sally and Fred have positive attitudes toward each other. In such a situation the interaction will be balanced only if the two parties' attitudes toward the bond issue are the same. Figure 7-1 represents a balanced communication interaction. Sally and Fred both favor the bond issue. But suppose Fred does not favor the issue. In this case, we would substitute a "minus" sign for the "plus" sign that marks the arrow leading from Fred to the school bond issue. If this were the case, then Sally and Fred probably would have a dispute over the issue: It could become a source of conflict between them.

Because an unbalanced situation is less satisfying than a balanced one, balance theory predicts that the two parties will be pressured to balance their attitudes toward the topic. This would amount to a pressure similar to that described in congruity theory. Sally and Fred could balance the situation in one of several ways. For one thing, either one might change his or her attitude toward the bond issue in such a way that both agreed. They may create a quasi balance by ignoring the topic or by misinterpreting the other person's attitude. It is even possible that balance might be restored by the two parties changing their

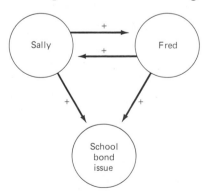

Figure 7-1   A balanced communication interaction.

attitude toward each other. Of course, one would not expect a marriage to dissolve over one disagreement; but this alternative points up the fact that when two persons don't like each other, they probably are less bothered by a disagreement over something like a bond issue. After all, we expect to disagree with the people whom we do not like.

In sum, balance theory seeks to explain how attitudes change through interpersonal interaction. Communication is more pleasant when we can agree with our associates: Lack of agreement creates a pressure toward balance. Serious or repeated disagreement may change the nature of the relationship itself.

Other Theories

I have cited three theoretical approaches to persuasion—rhetorical, cognitive consistency, and interpersonal. I have mentioned at least two contributions in each category. The reader should be aware, however, that there exist many other theories of persuasion. For instance, one could turn to a whole set of information processing theories of communication. These formulations seek to explain persuasion by analyzing how people deal with new information—and old. Skinner (1957), whom I cited in chapter 2, has developed a distinctive "behavioral" approach based on conditioning. His theory looks at communication as being a response-reward process in which people communicate in ways that bring rewards. In mass communication a whole area of "diffusion" research has emerged. This theoretical method looks at how new information is transmitted from person to person.

Certainly, then, my list of theories of persuasion is not a complete one. Nevertheless, this survey has allowed me the opportunity to make two key points. First, persuasion theories are general principles that seek to explain and organize the many findings of persuasion research. Second, by becoming more knowledgeable about persuasion principles, we gain a greater ability to understand and predict the outcomes of argument.

A SYNTHETIC MODEL OF PERSUASION

In this chapter I have presented an overview of the human image system as a collection of beliefs, attitudes, and values. I used this as a basis for identifying the possible image change, maintenance, and modification effects of argument. I then identified a range of credibility, language, evidence, arrangement, and nonverbal factors that have influence. Thirdly, I outlined certain theories. My purpose in this final section of the chapter is to synthesize, or join together, the preceeding material into an organized whole. I will call this synthesis a "model of persuasion." A model is a physical representation that is designed to clarify the operation of some organized process. Hence, my synthesis will take the form of a diagram in which I relate the image system, arguments, and persuasive outcomes.

In order to build a model of an ongoing system, we may begin at any point in the process. The explanation of my "interactive model of communication" in chapter 2 began with the message source, so it seems fitting to begin here again. Accordingly, we may postulate that persuasion involves a source—a communicator who wishes to influence others. In an effort to influence receivers, the communicator uses arguments. This brings us back to my basic definition, cited in chapter 1, which looked at arguments as connected concepts. These arguments are perceived by receivers, who must integrate them into an existing image system. Hence, the final aspect of the model is an "influence process" in which new arguments are perceived by receivers and have some kind of effect (image change, maintenance, or modification). You may recall that "no effect" is a maintenance outcome.

Figure 7-2 represents this conception of persuasion. Beginning with a source, statements are directed to a receiver. The statements consist of at least some connection between two terms but may involve a whole set of data-claim assertions. If presented orally, nonverbal factors constitute a part of the argument. The statements interact with the receiver's image system—together with other information available to the receiver. The result of this integration is an influence process, in which the new arguments first are perceived (accurately

Figure 7-2 A synthetic model of persuasion.

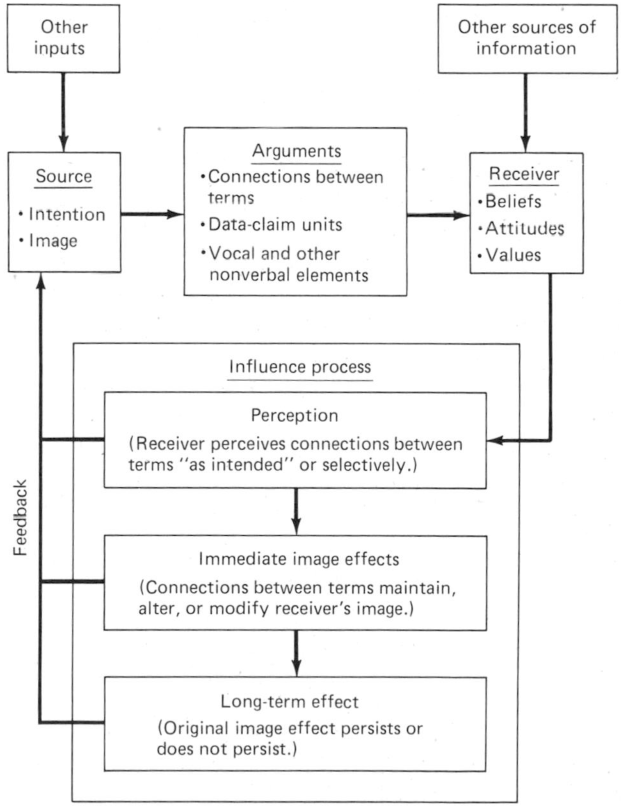

or selectively) and then affect the image system. The immediate effects may have long-term implications. Finally, the results of the argument are returned to the communicator in the form of feedback.

Of course, the model presented in figure 7-2 outlines only a process by which arguments produce effects. However, as I noted in my description of rhetorical theories, it is possible to take a broader view of persuasion. This would involve judgments made about the truth, ethics, validity, and quality of the arguments presented in a given situation. It is possible to develop a conception persuasion based solely on effects, but I would encourage the reader to take the broader view and to become concerned with other standards by which arguments may be judged.

APPLICATIONS

In the following exercises I want to stress the concepts of image system and image alteration. In chapter 3 and elsewhere, we have looked at the effectiveness of messages on audiences. However, in these exercises you will be able to deal more specifically with the effect standard.

Exercise 7-1: Constructing Your Image of an Object

In the first section of the chapter, I identified an image system as a person's total set of beliefs, attitudes, and values. An image, on the other hand, is an organization of several beliefs, attitudes, and values that are focused on a specific object. This exercise calls for you to plot your image of some "thing."

I   Identify the concept—person, place or object—that will serve as the image focus. "Disneyland," or "the Mississippi River" would be examples of what I mean here.

II   Write out ten beliefs and five value statements that you associate with the focal concept. Be sure to indicate and explain the overall direction of your attitude on a scale of −3 to +3.

III Having outlined certain belief, attitude, and value aspects of your image, you should consider the dimensions of your image of the object. Discuss the following dimensions: clarity, certainty, salience, consistency, consciousness, reality, commitment, and integration. Devote at least one paragraph to each dimension.

Exercise 7-2: Predicting the Image Effects of Arguments

In the following exercise your task will be to predict the image effect of a message. Because this is an exercise in prediction, there is no right or wrong answer. However, be sure that your predictions are clearly presented and justified.

I   Select a message that you have encountered recently. The message should be in a form that will allow you to refer to it frequently. This requirement probably will limit you to written messages, although a recorded message will also work nicely. It would also be possible to use a message that you have heard or seen previously but that is not recorded or written. In this case you should outline the message, including as many details about it as you can remember.

II Identify a hypothetical audience of people who were exposed to the message. This audience could be a group of people or a single listener—for instance, you. If you choose a group of people as your audience, be sure to indicate some characteristics of the audience—e.g., age, occupation, and so on.

III Identify one or two main concepts of the message.

IV Describe the audience's image of the concepts that you selected in step 3.

    A For each concept write out some of the audience's beliefs and values. In describing the audience's attitude, be sure to identify the overall direction of attitude on a scale of -3 to $+3$.

    B Also discuss at least three dimensions of the audience's image of each object, choosing from among clarity, certainty, salience, consistency, consciousness, reality, commitment, and integration.

    C Remember that if your audience is a group of people, the image will be a generalized "shared public image." As I noted earlier, when a group of people shares certain characteristics (e.g., age or occupation), they are more likely to possess a common image of something.

V Having identified an audience image about relevant message concepts, you are ready to predict the image effects of the communication. (If you are using your own image for this exercise, you will be able to describe and explain actual effects.)

    A Make an overall judgment as to the effect of the message—that is, state whether the major effect was one of image maintenance, change, or modification.

    B Predict the specific effects that you believe might have taken place. Before doing this, reread the sections on effects. Be sure to justify your predictions in each case.

        1 Describe any resulting belief effects.

        2 Explain whether the message produced a shift in attitude direction.

        3 Describe any resulting value effects.

        4 Describe any resulting modifications on the three dimensions of the audience's attitude.

        5 In justifying your predictions, be sure to make specific references to aspects of the message and characteristics of the audience's prior image of the concepts.

Chapter 8

The Ethics of Argument and Persuasion

The Equal Rights Amendment will destroy the family.
Teachers who work for the C.I.A. are contaminated.
Nazis should be prohibited from marching in Skokie, Illinois.
Advertising on children's programs exploits the kids.
There is too much sex on T.V.

We have all heard or seen evaluative claims such as the above. One has only to look around a bit to find a host of arguments dealing with the rightness and wrongness of things.

In chapter 6, I introduced the notion of value argumentation. I defined value statements as arguments that state or imply that something is good or bad. In this chapter I want to emphasize a special feature of value argument. I want to look at the ethics of argumentation.

I have already given some attention to ethical matters in argument: I identified ethics, in chapter 3, as one of four standards that a person could use to judge an assertion; I identified five factors or principles of ethics and promised that chapter 8 would explore the general implications of ethics for the process of argument and persuasion. Now it is time to take a systematic look at the ethics of communication.

Arguments are claims made by an advocate. Thus, when one examines the ethics of argument, one is looking to see whether a statement should be judged as morally good or bad. Because the term "morals" refers to the rightness or wrongness of an act, the ethics of argument can be stated as a simple question: "Is it right or wrong of me to say X?" But one does not judge the ethics of communication by focusing only on the message aspect—the language: Communication is a process in which a source, message, channel, and receiver interact. Hence, the ethics of communication involves many aspects of the effect standard. We have to take a look at speaker purpose and audience reaction. Judgments of ethical argumentation require a further analysis of the entire situation of communication as reflected in this wider question: "Is it right or wrong of me to make argument W for purpose X to audience Y with result Z?" In the process of communication, then, "ethical persuasion" becomes a synonym for "ethical argument."

I call the first section of the chapter "the ethical imperative." I want to get across the idea that communication ethics is extremely important. Continuing, I take the position that persuasion is not necessarily immoral but that it is not amoral either. Language is not just a tool—like a wrench: By its nature language is used for good or evil. In this section of the chapter, I explore some conditions that seem to render communication as good or bad. In the third section of the chapter, I identify some theories of ethics. These are different perspectives that writers have used as a basis for making ethical judgments. I think that we can gain insight from the systems of ethics that have been developed over the centuries. Next, I give some advice concerning how both persuaders and listeners may judge communication acts. In the final section I give some examples of ethical judgments.

THE ETHICAL IMPERATIVE

At the opening of this chapter I included five examples of statements having ethical implications. You may have noticed that each of the arguments deals with the ethics of communication. To say that the Equal Rights Amendment will destroy the family is to allege both that this set of words (a proposed constitutional amendment) is evil and that it is wrong (unethical) to advocate it. Similarly, in the other arguments, such communication acts as making reports to the Central Intelligence Agency (C.I.A.), marching in Nazi uniforms, advertising to children, and broadcasting sexually oriented programing are deemed wrong.

One could easily find many more such assertions centering on the ethics of communication. Partially for this reason the subject of ethics is receiving greater attention in books on argument and persuasion. Another reason for the revival of ethical studies in persuasion may be the lingering effects of the Vietnam war and the Watergate scandal. During the heyday of these two controversies (Vietnam, from 1965 to 1973, and Watergate, from 1972 to 1976), the American public was exposed to repeated reminders that government officials may make misleading or self-serving statements. Similarly, the civil rights movement and war protest movements of the 1960s caused Americans to evaluate the morality of such symbolic acts as mass protests and violence. Therefore, although the connection between argument and ethics is an old one—Aristotle (*Rhetoric,* I. 2. 1356a25) wrote that rhetoric was an offshoot of ethical studies—the 1970s have brought renewed interest in the argument-ethics relationship.

Viewed in one way, the renaissance of ethics is a remarkable development. After all, the period since World War II has seen a vast increase in research about persuasive *effects*. The advent of "scientific studies" in persuasion elevated the effects standard and minimized the truth, validity, and ethics approaches. Persuasion researchers viewed language as a value-free tool: They tended to emphasize the results of arguments, leaving ethical questions for philosophers. Yet it is possible that the very dominance of the effect standard has become another cause of the resurgence of ethical studies, for many questions posed about the ethics of communication relate to the use of modern persuasive techniques: advertising methods, mass media, etc. Viewed from this perspective, the reemergence of ethics in an age of persuasion may not be so surprising after all. The ethics of persuasion might have resurfaced even without the tumult of the 1960s.

Arguments and Ethics Are Inseparable

I have alluded to the notion that arguments are in themselves value-free. This means that they are ethically neutral or amoral. A plausible case can be made in support of the proposition that "the means of persuasion themselves are ethically neutral" (McCroskey, 1972, p. 269). McCroskey bases this position on the idea that language cannot be misused unless there is an intention to do so. In this view the techniques of argument are neither moral nor immoral unless deliberately used for moral or immoral purposes. Notwithstanding McCroskey's observation, I am more inclined to accept Nilsen's (1966) philosophy of the inherently ethical nature of language. He argues (p. 12) that "every act of speech is essentially a social act . . . having an ethical component," that language seeks to influence the attitudes and behavior of listeners. Accordingly, he believes that an act of speech brings with it a moral obligation: When using arguments the communicator undertakes ethical obligations toward his listeners.

This idea of ethical obligations is based on two assumptions about language. When one makes a statement, the nature of language forces the listener to take for granted that (1) the speaker knows what he is talking about and (2) the speaker is endeavoring to tell the truth. Of course, we all know that people sometimes speak ignorantly or deceitfully. All of us develop methods to recognize these bad features of communication. Yet if ignorance and deceit were the rule—rather than the exception—then language as we know it could not function. The acceptance of communication involves an act of faith. This places an obligation on the speaker. The ethics of communication hold that arguers should not break faith with listeners.

Because the speaker-listener relationship necessarily involves the ethical assumption of good faith, I contend that arguments are not really value-free. Arguments (unless spoken in jest) link the source and receiver in a contractual bond requiring that both respect the communication ethic—that both speak in an informed and straightforward manner.

There is another way of demonstrating the essentially ethical character of language. Every act of speech involves a choice. Confronting a situation of dispute, the arguer has a wide range of argumentative choices. One may be to emphasize facts A and B to the exclusion of C and D: The speaker constructs particular interpretations that give the desired meaning to the facts. Finally, the arguer chooses to highlight some values rather than others. In other words, the "facts" don't speak for themselves: It is the arguer who gives voice to information. Just as the arguer must keep faith with the audience, it is also essential to remain mindful of the "facts." Language gives one the power to create reality. Having the power to establish the "way things are," the advocate has the duty to represent things as he or she really sees them. Again, language users undertake ethical obligations.

Some Representative Ethical Controversies

Because of the ever-present ethic of communication, ethics is a root issue in every argument; yet it is obvious that ethical issues are more evident in certain disputes than in others. An arguer seems to undertake fewer ethical responsibilities in contending that the sun will rise tomorrow (because everyone assumes that this will take place) than in advising us to buy X brand of paint (because not everyone would ordinarily assume that X was best). If ethics truly is an essential part of argument, it follows that we should be able to find many disputes pivoting on communication ethics. This does seem to be the case; one can easily spot many ethics-based controversies in today's world. In the next few pages, I identify some of these.

The Controversy over the Equal Rights Amendment   Article V of the Constitution specifies a number of alternatives whereby constitutional amendments may be proposed and ratified. The customary method has been for Congress to propose amendments for ratification by the legislatures of three-fourths of the states. Accordingly, in 1972 Congress sent the proposed Equal Rights Amendment to the states for ratification. This amendment provided that no citizen should be denied rights on the basis of sex and that the federal government should have the power to ensure that discrimination did not take place.

Despite initial wide public acceptance, the E.R.A. became a fixture in the American political landscape. In every legislature across the land, the measure has been debated and redebated, and it has become a controversy in which the two sides have each accused the other of unethical behavior.

Opponents of the amendment have focused on the E.R.A.'s grant of power to the federal government. They have alleged that the broad term "equality" would lead to homosexual marriages, coeducational high school gym classes, etc. In short, opponents emphasize the possible role of the E.R.A. in bringing about a government-imposed moral and social revolution. Branding many of the changes as undesirable, they view the amendment as evil; they connect the amendment to possible radical changes in the American way of life. By associating the E.R.A. with generally unpopular causes, detractors have challenged the ethics of proamendment forces.

Supporters of the E.R.A. also have used ethics-based assertions. Eleanor C. Smeal, president of the National Organization for Women (quoted in *Courier-Journal*, March 12, 1978, p. G15), has charged the opposition with using "myths and distortions" by saying that E.R.A. would bring about "coed bathrooms, homosexual marriages, women in the trenches." In addition to attacking the ethics of the opposition's tactics, E.R.A. proponents have questioned the overall morality of the anti-E.R.A. position. This argument was evident in the debate that preceded the Kentucky legislature's 1978 rescission of the E.R.A. Amendment supporters claimed that the antiamendment forces sought to make women second-class citizens.

The Campaign against Children's Advertising   In recent years much debate has focused on the advertising that accompanies children's television programs. Critics have identified a number of faults in this advertising. For one thing, they argue that the advertisers often peddle undesirable products—such as candy and sugar-coated cereal. *Newsweek* (February 21, 1977, p. 69) cited the conclusions of critics who take the position that the ads "hook children on poor eating habits long before they develop the mental defenses to resist." Furthermore, according to psychologist Thomas Bever, television ads distort children's views of the world: They become aware that advertising claims often are exaggerated, and consequently, according to Bever, "they become ready to believe that, like advertising, business and other institutions are riddled with hypocrisy" (p. 69).

Over the past few years, a major campaign has been waged against television advertising on children's programs. The organization Action for Children's Television has endeavored to reduce the amount of advertising time on shows for children. Also, because vitamin overdoses are a major cause of poisoning in youngsters under 5 years of age, the A.C.T. fought to remove commercials for vitamins and medicines from children's shows. The ultimate goal of the organization has been to eliminate children's advertising altogether. Peggy Charren, A.C.T. president, argues (*Newsweek,* February 21, 1977, p. 70): "We feel it is wise to separate children from the marketplace until they are ready to deal with it."

The Argument against Subliminal Advertising   In his book, *The Hidden Persuaders*, Vance Packard (1958, pp. 35–36) called the public's attention to what he termed "subthreshold" persuasive techniques. Packard cited a *London Sunday Times* news story that reported on a device that could flash "split-second" ads on a movie screen. Supposedly, a New Jersey movie theater was using the technique to sell ice cream. As Packard explained, the flashes of message were "too short for people in the audience to recognize them consciously but still long enough to be absorbed unconsciously" (p. 35). Packard reported that the subthreshold technique seemed to boost ice cream sales.

Subliminal persuasion is the customary term for verbal and nonverbal stimuli that are received by the unconscious mind. Subliminal messages take the form of words or pictures that, because of their small size, camouflage, or fast projection, are not consciously perceived yet are picked up by the subconscious mind.

As Wilson Bryan Key (1973) notes, Packard's exposé of subliminal persuasion prompted wide consternation. Laws were proposed—although apparently none was enacted—to ban the technique; and newspapers and magazines editorialized against the practice. The controversy died down until the early 1970s, when at least two events again helped to bring subliminal persuasion into the public eye. One of these was the publication in 1973 of Key's book *Subliminal Seduction.* In it Key identified and analyzed an alleged widespread use of subliminal techniques in contemporary advertising. The second was the publicity during 1973 and 1974 which surrounded the film *The Exorcist.* The news media carried reports of the intense reactions that the movie produced in many viewers. There were reports that Warner Brothers had spliced pictures of the devil into the film. The debate about subliminal techniques was on again.

Let us consider the reasons for the fuss. Key's two books on subliminal argument contain the most comprehensive treatment of this method of communication. In his 1973 work Key analyzed a number of what he termed "subliminal" advertisements. One of these was for Gilbey's London Dry Gin.

Figure 8-1   Ice cube sex?

Ostensibly, this advertisement pictures a bottle of gin with a glass of gin and tonic. However, upon closer examination, Key argues, "most people" can find buried, hidden symbols. Key focuses on the ice cubes in the glass, contending that one can find the word "sex" spelled out in the cubes. You don't see it? Well, consider Key's advice (1973, pp. 4–5) on how to decode this subliminal stimulus:

1 Start with the third ice cube from the top. Keep looking until you see the E formed in the cube.
2 Now focus on the second ice cube until you can make out the S, which is traced by the bright reflection.
3 Finally, hold the picture at arm's length and read downward to the last cube. Do you see the X?

Key reports that when it is called to their attention, over 90 percent of people can perceive the subliminal symbol "sex."

Key's 1973 book includes over thirty pictures illustrating the use of subliminal symbols and treats several alleged subliminal techniques. Subliminal persuasion takes the form of both nonverbal pictures and words. Key's 1976 book contains further illustrations, including examples of where words (e.g., "sex") and pictures (e.g., a penis) have been drawn into advertisements. He uses these many examples to raise basic questions about the ethics of subliminal ads and offers these arguments against the techniques: (1) they tend to decrease the consumer's free choice by unfairly attacking the subconscious, and (2) techniques that work on the subconscious mind may have undesirable health effects by stimulating unconscious fear reactions (Key, 1973, pp. 8–9). He calls for increased attention to ethics in courses in mass communication and journalism (p. 190).

Key's analysis of subliminal persuasion in general and of the Gilbey's gin ad (figure 8-1) in particular is challenged by Emil A. Pavone, vice president of public relations for National Distillers Products Company—the authors of the Gibley's ad. Pavone's argument is as follows:

> Despite the notoriety of the "subliminal sex" thesis, we who market Gilbey's Gin and Vodka, and Sauza Tequila, among many other famous brands, believe the allegations are nothing more than a clever ploy to peddle paperbacks to impressionable youngsters and unsophisticated teachers. That sex is an element in many ads, we do not deny. But, all of the elements in our ads are straightforward; nothing in them is intended to have a "subliminal" effect. This applies with equal emphasis to both our past and our present advertising. We believe these comments would also apply to the ads of virtually all major American advertisers. It is worthy of note that messages which assertedly can be sensed by the unconscious mind are in a class with "the emperor's new clothes."[1]

Reflected in the E.R.A., children's advertising, and subliminal advertising controversies is a concern for the integrity of the speaker-listener relationship.

[1]Personal communication. May 1979.

The pro- and anti-E.R.A. factions accuse each other of advocating, knowingly or unknowingly, a bogus, evil position. Children's advertising opponents criticize advertisers for selling products that promote tooth decay and foster bad nutrition. Overall, the charge is made that certain messages are unethical because they promote unsound, morally wrong positions. The authors of these messages are viewed as having chosen to emphasize morally bad arguments over morally sound ones.

These three areas of dispute may be classified as having ethical implications for another reason. In addition to selling a "bad bill of goods," the advocates are said to have used practices that take unfair advantage of the listeners. The warring pro- and anti-E.R.A. camps attack each other for relying upon lies. Critics of television advertisements directed at children assail sponsors for their endeavor to win young minds through misleading cartoon messages. Subliminal persuasion is said to violate the listener's right to make a free, conscious choice.

Some Additional Ethics-Based Controversies   Although I have focused on three examples of ethics-centered argumentation, let me emphasize that I could present many more illustrations of this kind. Some further examples may help to demonstrate the point that ethical disputes are common.

1   Network television shows (*Courier-Journal,* February 16, 1978, p. A8): The national Parent-Teacher Association (PTA) released a survey of network television shows. The network offerings were rated "good" to "bad" on the basis of the amount of violence portrayed, the overall quality, and the lack of "offensive" content.

2   Defending the American Nazi Party (*Courier-Journal,* February 3, 1978, p. A11): The American Civil Liberties Union has been attacked for defending the right of the American Nazi Party to demonstrate in Skokie, Illinois, a Chicago suburb. The A.C.L.U. opposed ordinances that limited protest demonstrations in Skokie, a community containing many Jewish residents. Aryeh Neier, executive director of the A.C.L.U. indicated that 15 percent of the group's members have "not renewed their memberships" because "they don't like what we're doing."

3   Advertising Indiana liquor in Ohio (*Courier-Journal,* December 31, 1977, p. B4): A Hamilton (Ohio) County judge has accused Tri-State Discount Liquors of Lawrenceburg, Indiana, of unethical advertising behavior. According to the Associated Press, the company advertises "that its prices are 25 per cent lower than those offered" in Ohio and Kentucky. Judge Robert Blackmore commented that "he thought Tri-State had violated 'the sense of fair play' by not telling customers it's illegal to carry purchased liquor across state lines."

As in the earlier examples, the situations represent cases in which someone's communication is judged wrong in a moral sense.

Ethical Issues Are Important

I would be the first to admit that the whole subject of ethics has an ivory tower sound to it. Often we associate ethics with academic or religious types who issue moral statements about "the real world" as they write from the isolated comfort of a book-lined office. The ethics of argument, or of anything for that matter, is a subject that may appear to lack practical importance. Persuasion, on the other hand, is today thought of as very practical indeed. Persuasion—in the form of advertising—sells products and makes the economy run. In contrast, what does ethics do?

I would like to argue against the view that ethics is only an academic matter having no significance for ordinary people. In fact, I take the position that the ethics of argument may be more socially important than persuasive effects. In making this point I shall return to the basic premise of ethical argument—maintaining the integrity of the speaker-listener relationship.

Ethically questionable arguments, I believe, have a tendency to create distrust in listeners. Hence, if speakers seek only "effective arguments"— thereby neglecting ethical judgments—the society becomes a less trusting one. The greater the concern for mere persuasive effect, therefore, the more cynical listeners may become. The result would be a society in which people assume that all sources are liars.

One does not have to look hard to find examples of just this situation. As a result of the Watergate scandals, people as a whole are less likely to accept at face value statements by the President of the United States. Although it is probably a good thing for people to scrutinize carefully the arguments of national leaders, the post-Watergate assumption that all government officials are liars probably will hamper the effectiveness of the government itself. For instance, the ability of the President to marshal public support for needed reforms may be reduced by the public's skepticism. Perhaps this is the reason that President Carter was unable to create rapid support for his energy legislation in 1977 and 1978.

On April 18, 1977, President Carter addressed the nation on the subject of energy. He characterized the increasing supply/demand imbalance as a crisis. Carter used the expression "moral equivalent of war" to impress people with the seriousness of the subject. He reiterated this phrase in his address to a joint session of Congress on April 20. Despite the urgency of Carter's energy messages, his proposals became stalled in Congress. When a year had passed with no congressional enactment of a national energy program, a cartoonist parodied the President's "*moral equivalent of war*" address as "M*E*O*W," a sad commentary, indeed, on the apparently declining power of the President to rally the nation to important causes.

Of course, it is really too early to tell whether recent political history is the cause of Carter's inability to win quick approval of new energy measures. However, there is a clear historical example in which the discovery of exaggerated government communication subsequently led to a partial loss of faith in official statements. In the period 1914 to 1917, the American public was exposed to many arguments put forth by the Allies (Britain and France, chiefly), who sought to win United States support. The Allied cause in World War I was portrayed as noble and good; their opponent—Germany—was characterized as

Figure 8-2 President Carter's declining power to persuade. (© 1978 *The Courier-Journal*, Louisville, and Hugh Haynie.)

warlike and evil. This anti-German advertising campaign accelerated when the United States entered the war in 1917.

After the war, as journalists and scholars evaluated the First World War more objectively, it became obvious that much of the prowar, anti-German advertising was exaggerated. Articles and books appeared that suggested that the Germans were not solely responsible for the war. Accounts appeared to the effect that German's conduct of the war had not been as bad as portrayed in Allied advertising. More important in casting doubts on the earlier prowar campaign were a number of books that analyzed propaganda used by the Allies in drumming up American support for their side of the conflict. One of these was Lasswell's 1927 work on *Propaganda Technique in the World War* (reprinted in 1971). Lasswell traced the Allied effort to blame the war on Germany and the endeavor to picture the Germans in satanic terms. Books of this sort gradually created a notion in many people that the 1914–1918 war arguments were not objective truth. Many now saw the arguments as conscious attempts to maximize certain ideas in such a way as to exaggerate the truth.

Because of the post–World War I propaganda analysis movement, many people in the 1930s were afraid that the United States could again be drawn into European war through foreign propaganda. An organization called the Institute for Propaganda Analysis was formed to prevent this from happening again, but it went out of business after the United States actually joined World War II. Although the Second World War enjoyed popular support, some remained skeptical about the anti-Nazi advertising campaign by the United States government. They reasoned that because the facts had been exaggerated in the World War I period, the same might be true of what was said against the Nazis. Therefore, both before and during the war, there was a reluctance to believe what turned out to be a true representation of Nazi-imposed horror. This excerpt from a book by Wayne Booth (1974, p. 6), professor of English at the University of Chicago, illustrates this tendency.

> I can remember how doggedly, during the years just preceding World War II, I held to my "critical" refusal to believe the atrocity stories about the Nazis. I had been taught that Americans had been gullible in World War I when they believed atrocity propaganda put out by the Allies. I knew better than to believe that the Nazis were persecuting Jews. . . .

Booth's self-analysis is a good illustration of the significant social consequences of unethical communication. The Allied interest in mere persuasive effects during the 1914–1918 war produced a breakdown in source-receiver trust. Having been falsely led to believe in the Kaiser's total wickedness, some Americans assumed that Nazi atrocity reports were part of a new prowar, anti-German advertising campaign. Hence, true stories were rejected in the 1930s because of false ones perpetrated twenty years before. A lack of concern for ethics had a significant delayed impact.

The point of the example cited is that when people are misled they distrust the sources that have deceived them. If the majority of a society's information sources behave without concern for honest communication, then all communication is weakened. Trust in sources is a necessary condition for verbal communication. Insofar as this trust is lost, language itself is undermined. Without willingness to believe on the part of the receiver, the source's language loses its integrity, and people become divided and alienated.

In sum, the ethics of argument not only is a matter of interest to academics and theologians. All of us should be interested in the maintenance of ethical standards: When ethics is ignored, trust is lost; when trust is lost, communication as a whole loses its vital force.

WHEN IS IT ETHICAL TO PERSUADE?

Communication always contains an ethical dimension. This is because all communication depends on the existence of a relationship of trust between source and receiver. If communication necessarily implies ethical choices and responsibilities, then the question of when it is ethical to persuade becomes crucial. Unless we can separate ethical and unethical arguments, we will distrust all arguments.

"Persuasion" Is a Controversial Term

Some people, in fact, do seem to take a position that *all* persuasion is unethical. They reason that persuasion implies an effort to influence someone excessively—rather than letting the person make an independent decision. "Let the facts speak for themselves" is the rallying call for these individuals. This school of thought finds intellectual support in the writings of Plato. Plato was troubled by the way in which persuasion was taught in ancient Greece. He attacked the sophists for their emphasis on the *techniques* of persuasion (see chapter 7). Plato believed that when one concerned himself primarily with effective technique, one overlooked truth in argument. Effects-oriented argument was, for Plato, a device for making bad things appear good, and vice-versa. Seemingly, he had a point: Illustrations of ethical problems in sophistic teaching are apparent. For instance, in the *Rhetoric to Alexander* (III. 1425b36–38), the author (an unknown sophist) suggests that if one is praising a person, one can attribute to the person "qualities that do not exist." When one is speaking about a person who is unworthy of praise, this may be effective advice; but it hardly seems ethical.

Plato's condemnations of sophistical rhetoric, expressed in his *Gorgias* and *Phaedrus,* have been influential in associating "rhetoric" and "persuasion" with "exaggerated, untruthful argument." Clearly, this suspicion of persuasion has persisted in some quarters. A contemporary philosopher, B. J. Diggs, notes (1964; reprinted in Ehninger, 1972, p. 139) that because "misuse of 'the persuasive arts' has been so common, [many people] have regarded persuasion as inherently evil, something which by its nature 'ought to be avoided,' like a lie."

Yet to assert that persuasion is evil by its nature is, I think, to miss some of Plato's real argument about rhetoric. In chapter 3, I described his notion that one could attain truth through dialectic (the systematic question-answer method of investigation). This suggests that Plato views a rhetoric based on dialectical analysis as being an ethical rhetoric. Writing in *Phaedrus,* Plato identifies three closely-related characteristics of the "good rhetoric":

1 It should seek truth rather than mere probability (*Phaedrus,* 262).
2 It should use the dialectical, question-answer format (*Phaedrus,* 265).
3 It should define terms clearly (*Phaedrus,* 265).

Plato's good rhetoric involves careful analysis and presentation of the subject. The good persuader would seek truth through dialectic and would avoid ambiguity by carefully defining terms. I think that Plato did not condemn *all* persuasive (rhetorical) communication. Rather, he seems to have objected to many rhetorical practices of the time, such as using ambiguous terms or making statements known (by the arguer) to be false.

In addition to Plato's truth-seeking and ambiguity-avoiding criteria, Weaver (1964, pp. 63–65) has identified another Platonic requirement for a "good rhetoric." Generalizing on the philosophies of Plato and Aristotle, Weaver identifies communicator motive as a related requirement for honest persuasion. Weaver argues that the moral communicator is one who understands the need of the audience and who has its best interests at heart. The good *rhetor* has a good intention in desiring to persuade an audience. Briefly said, the good persuader cares about his audience.

The preceding paragraphs support the view that persuasion in itself is all right. Persuasion, according to this interpretation, becomes unethical only when (1) the source acts selfishly (caring nothing for the best interests of the listeners), (2) the source is unconcerned about the truth of the subject, or (3) the source misleads the audience by using bad tactics such as ambiguous terms.

This threefold description of unethical persuasion is quite consistent with the earlier examples of ethical controversies. Some of the examples identified *techniques* of persuasion that could be considered wrong in themselves. Thus, critics of subliminal advertising charged that this method unfairly attacked the unconscious mind. In other of the controversies, the ethics of a message were questioned because of the message's *effect*. In this connection, advertising of certain products on television programs for children allegedly encouraged poor nutrition. Still other ethical arguments centered on the issue of the communicator's selfish *intention* to mislead. A relevant example was the liquor advertisements that failed to mention to Ohio residents the illegality of transporting their purchases from an Indiana discount store—an act that the ads encouraged.

Both the theory and the examples of ethics take us back to the original five tests that I identified in chapter 3:

1   Does an argument bring about good or bad effects?
2   Is a statement truthful?
3   Does an argument appeal to good values?
4   Does the communicator have a good intention?
5   Does the communicator use acceptable techniques (means) of persuasion?

In a sense this discussion of ethics has come full circle. Yet we have gained some ground in this present chapter: In chapter 3, I merely presented the five ethical tests; in this chapter, I have explained some of the intellectual origin of the tests.

Are the Five Principles of Ethics Enough?

The five tests of ethics amount to principles of ethics. A principle is a settled rule that serves as the basis for a system. It follows that the five tests of communication ethics could serve as the foundation for a system of persuasion ethics. However, these five principles do not provide us with all the equipment that we need to make ethical judgments about communication: There is yet a missing ingredient. What is missing is a way in which to tell which of the five principles is the most important. If two of the principles are in conflict, then how do we make an ethical judgment? Which would have priority?

Let us take note of a hypothetical example. Suppose that you are planning a surprise birthday party for a friend. Suppose, further, that one day your friend asks you if you knew that his birthday was coming up, and you answer no. It is evident that you have violated principle 2 of our ethical system: You have told a lie. Yet you might object if someone were to charge you with unethical communication behavior. You might protest that if you hadn't lied you would have spoiled the surprise. Simply stated, you might claim that your lie was for a good cause and that by lying you had his best interests at heart. You would be claiming ethical vindication by reference to principles 1 and 4 of the ethical system. In this situation we have ethical principle 2 ranged against principles 1 and 4.

What we need now is a basis for choosing between or among ethical principles when they are in conflict. The five ethical tests do not answer all the questions that we need to ask about the ethics of communication. We require a basis for preferring one principle over another. What we need is a *code* of ethics.

CODES OF ETHICS

A code is an organized body of laws or principles; an ethical code would organize the five ethical principles. The code would tell us which principle was the most important in a given dispute. To return to the earlier hypothetical example, an ethical code would tell us whether our desire to have a successful surprise party justified our telling a lie in order to maintain the surprise. The code would specify whether principle 2 was superior to or subordinate to principles 1 and 4. A code, then, is an overall conception of how ethical judgments should be made. It is a framework for applying general ethical principles to specific ethical disputes.

It would be convenient if there existed only one universally accepted code of communication ethics. If this were the case, then we would have a reliable guide for choosing the appropriate ethical principle. It would then be a simple matter to tell when principle X was more important than principle Z. We would feel confident in making an ethical judgment based on one princple rather than another. Unfortunately, there exists no universal code of ethics. Instead, we are faced with several alternative codes that have been developed over the years.

In the next few pages, I will identify some general ethical codes. These codes have been developed as an aid to making ethical judgments. Each has its strengths and weaknesses. As you read through the ethical codes, work to identify the similarities and differences among them.

Objective Codes of Ethics

An objective code is one that enumerates good and bad actions. In an objective code, a "bad act" is always bad and a "good act" is always good—no matter why, where, when, how, or by whom it is done. In some respects the Ten Commandments are a good example of an objective code of ethics. Taking

God's name in vain or sleeping with your neighbor's husband are bad acts—no matter what excuse one might have.

Like the Ten Commandments, codes of communication ethics tend to be enumerative. Such codes list bad and (sometimes) good argumentative tactics. Many books on persuasion attempt to gather the undesirable practices into objectively codified systems. One example is Minnick's (1968) list of generally accepted unethical practices, which I cited in chapter 3. Minnick argued that it was unethical to falsify evidence, distort the meaning of evidence, use bad reasoning, and deceive the audience about the intent of your communication.

One of the most ambitious attempts to establish an objective code of communication ethics is reported by Klopf and McCroskey (1964, p. 13). They endeavored to identify a list of debate practices that were "unethical or questionable *in spite of the variables*" (such as communicator intent or the circumstances surrounding the act). These authors surveyed the literature on ethics and communication, constructing a questionnaire containing forty descriptions of possible practices in debate—e.g., "citing opinion or facts out of [the] context in which they were written." They then surveyed debate teachers to learn the extent to which the practices were judged as ethical or unethical.

Naturally, opinions differed in a survey of this type. However, a number of practices were rated as "unethical" or "ethically questionable" by more than half of the 244 respondents. Some of the unethical practices related to general argument strategy. These included:

- "Breaching normal courtesy, such as heckling, grimacing, or loud whispering while opponent is speaking"
- "Citing opinion or facts out of [the] context in which they were written"
- "Fabricating evidence"
- "Injecting personalities into the debate"

Other commonly cited unethical practices pertained to particular decision rules of the debate situation. Ninety-five percent of the respondents believed that a debate ethic was violated when the judge decided the debate "on the basis of his personal opinions on the topic."

In an objective code one has merely to note the presence of a given communication behavior in order to justify a conclusion that the speaker has acted unethically. A critic using the Klopf and McCroskey formula would need only to point to an occurrence of fabricated evidence to demonstrate an ethical failing by the speaker. The formula for an objective ethical judgment is as follows:

X speaker committed Y act.
Y act is found on the list of unethical practices.
Therefore, X speaker committed an unethical act.

This formula aspect provides both advantages and disadvantages. Let me mention some of the advantages first. Objective codes are helpful because they often represent the basic ethical thinking of a group of people. For instance, in the Klopf and McCroskey (1964) code of debate ethics, judgment was based on the opinions of a majority of debate teachers. In this case an objective code helps us to know what people in general view as good or bad. Such codes represent a "master judgment"—that is, a judgment based on the wisdom of people as a whole. Objective codes of communication ethics are useful for a second reason. These codes establish a basic standard for judgment. The mechanics for making objective ethical judgments are straightforward. Such standards take much of the guesswork and subjectivity out of ethical analysis.

Viewed from another perspective, of course, the advantages of objective ethical codes become disadvantages. Basing ethical judgments on the majority opinion may have the effect of reducing ethics to a question of popularity. That is, whatever is unpopular is unethical; that which is popular becomes ethical. To avoid this shortcoming, an objective ethical code must be careful to select the "right" majority. A code based on the ethical judgments of persons of good sense is superior to the moral preferences of a lynch mob.

There is a second problem relating to the use of objective codes as a standard of judgment. Return, for a moment, to the second premise of the objective formula: "Y act is found on the list of unethical practices." There is a danger that such a premise may represent an evasion. As stated, this premise leaves out the justification of *why* action Y belongs on the unethical practices list. Hence, an objective code may become a substitute for reasoning. Instead of explaining why a tactic is unethical, we may rely upon an objective code as an easy way out. Instead of analyzing the communication practice, we merely say, "See, it's on the list." This second objection to an objective code is frequently raised. Toulmin (1968, p. 28) argues that "the objective doctrine is, therefore, not just unhelpful to us: it is a positive hindrance, diverting . . . [our attention from] the question of ethical reasoning."

I think that there is a tendency in our modern age to be too quick in rejecting objective codes. Such codes do have weaknesses, as I have observed. Yet objective guidelines are a help: They make us sensitive to the opinions of others, and they facilitate judgment by giving us a formula that, despite its imperfections, may have substantial validity. In sum, the objective approach is defensible so long as we avoid two pitfalls: (1) equating the judgment of the majority with mob prejudice and (2) allowing the code to substitute for thinking.

In my introduction to the subject of ethical codes, I observed that the codes enable us to decide which ethical principle is the most important in a given dispute. Let me now demonstrate how the objective code does this. Recall my hypothetical example of an ethical controversy: Is it all right to tell your friend that you didn't know that he was going to have a birthday when, in fact, you are preparing to surprise him with a party? Assuming that the particular objective code that you are using identifies lying as unethical, the judgment would be rendered in this manner:

You lied to your friend.
Lying is an unethical communication practice.
Therefore, you acted in an unethical manner.

In this objective system, your good intention to protect the surprise effect would be considered irrelevant. Because lying is an "objective wrong," your act would be seen as unethical, regardless of its having been motivated by your love for your friend.

Relativistic Codes of Ethics

The objective code is only one of five general ethical approaches that I want to consider. I presented the objective code first because it probably is closest to the notion of traditional morality. Traditional morality usually is associated with lists of prohibitions: do not steal, do not fornicate, etc. Because humans are contrary people, there has always been a tendency to reject objective codes. "Who says that stealing is wrong?" becomes the retort.

Consider an instance of this modern challenge to objective morality. Today, we witness a movement away from customary standards of sexual ethics. The "old (objective) morality" included rules against adultery, masturbation, fornication, premarital sex, etc. However, many now reject such rules as "moralistic guilt feelings" based on "prudish Victorian beliefs."

This example of changing sexual ethics reflects the central premise of what can be called the relativistic code of ethics. Relativism is an ideology that holds that all things are equally good. In the field of ethics the doctrine of relativism teaches that one ethical judgment cannot be justified as better than another. "Everything ethical is relative." Because judgments are equally good, we cannot *reason* in ethical matters. So "if it feels good, do it"—and don't feel guilty, since there's no use in reasoning or arguing about ethics.

The reader will notice that the relativistic code represents an opposite approach to the objective code. If all judgments are equally good, then there would be no point in establishing a list of good and bad acts. Lists constructed at random would be as valid as the majority opinion or divine revelation (as in the case of the Ten Commandments).

As treated in philosophical works, the theory of relativism is somewhat more complicated than I have indicated here; yet even this brief exposition of the assumptions of relativism is enough to suggest why many philosophers disapprove of it. Relativism suggests that there is no way to rationally decide questions of ethics. In other words, reason cannot be used in ethics. Accordingly, we can say that the relativistic code fails to meet the basic criteria for an ethical code. It does not allow for reconciliation of different viewpoints on or principles of ethics. A code of ethics should allow us to decide between two ethical positions. To return to the "surprise party" example, the code should enable us to settle this ethical question one way or the other. However, the relativistic approach considers all ethical opinions to be equally legitimate. As a result, it allows for no such settlement of differing points of view. A "code" of this kind is usually rejected because it is no code at all. Further, it seems to contradict the basic assumption that man is a rational being: If humans can both argue and agree, then why base society on the premise that there can be no analysis of behavior? In fact, can a society be based on such complete relativism? Would not it just disintegrate?

Individual Codes of Ethics

The basic tenet of the individual code can be put in these words: "What *I* judge as being ethical *is* ethical." This theory has the advantage of stressing the need for each of us to make our own individual ethical judgments. However, like relativism, the individual code seems to involve more problems than promise.

To be sure, the individual code does meet the basic test of a code. It enables a person to decide which ethical principles are most important; it provides that whatever principle you think to be most important is most important. However, by making each person's own opinion into the standard of ethics, the individual code leads to some problems.

First of all, the individual code carries with it most of the disadvantages of the relativistic "code." It permits no solution of ethical disputes in which two individuals take opposing positions. Indeed, one finds it difficult to imagine that a workable society could be based on the premise that there exist as many valid notions of ethics as there are people.

In addition to the association with problems of relativism, Hartwig (1973) identifies a particular flaw of the individual code: No individual can be fully neutral and reflective when judging his own behavior. Hence, the term "individual judgment" is partially contradictory. No human being is detached and unfeeling enough to function completely as a judge in the matter of his or her own actions. Hartwig's point makes a lot of sense. We cannot detach ourselves from ourselves. Because judgment requires a detached, analytic decision, it follows that no one is fully competent to be his or her own judge. We like (or dislike) ourselves too much for this to be the case.

Hartwig's objection to an individual code of ethics is a limited one. His analysis applies only to a situation in which we are judging the ethics of our own behavior—not someone else's. However, the point is a significant one—one that I will return to later when I develop a set of "ethical self-checks." For now, however, it is interesting to note that Hartwig offers the dialectical method as a correction for the pitfalls of individual self-judgment. He takes the position that an individual's own judgment is adequate until challenged; but, he says, an individual's self-judgment is validated only when analyzed and agreed to by others.

In short, the individual code of ethics is only slightly more useful than the relativistic. In the case of our surprise-party organizer, it has the advantage of forcing each of us to confront the question: Which do *I* think is more important, ends (keeping the party a surprise) or means (lying)? Indeed the fact that one chooses to lie in order to preserve a surprise suggests that the person's own code favors ends over means. Pure "ethical individualism" allows no final settlement between two individual judgments.

Situational Codes of Ethics

The situational notion of ethics holds that no two situations are entirely the same. On this basis situationalists argue against the use of universal standards of ethical practice. Because every case is different, the situationalist argues for making case-by-case judgments rather than applying universal principles.

Consider how a situationalist would deal with our five ethical principles—the effects of an act, truthfulness, appeal to good or bad values, communicator intent, and persuasive technique. The situationalist would prefer not to make a *general* choice among the five. Rather, it would be a question of which principle is most important in the situation at hand. The situation-based code is one in which particular details determine the relative importance of principles. This differs from the objective code, in which principles determined the relative importance of details (i.e., lying is bad, regardless of intent).

Let us consider how a situational code might be used to make an ethical decision in the case of the hypothetical surprise party. The situationalist would probably desire to analyze a lie-to-keep-a-surprise by means of each of the five ethical principles. First, there is no question that in this case the person lied when she pretended not to know about the upcoming birthday. This would amount to an application of both the truthfulness and techniques principles. Second, what was the effect of the lie? Presumably, it was that the party was kept secret—resulting in happiness for the "victim" of the lie. Third, it seems that the communicator intended by the lie to benefit the "victim" by denying knowledge of the birthdate. This would be the test of intent. The fifth test—appeal to *good or bad values*—does not appear to be highly applicable to the situation according to this code.

In a quantitative sense the ethical scales are balanced. Our liar "failed" two tests—truthfulness and means (lying is a bad technique), but she "passed" the effects and intent tests. The situationalist might make an ethical judgment of the following sort.

1 The speaker lied for the purpose of bringing about a good result for the listener.
2 Thus, in this situation the intent and effect principles are more important than the truthfulness and means test.
3 It follows, that a decision to lie was morally better than a decision to jeopardize the surprise party.
4 Hence, the speaker behaved in an ethical manner.

The essence of a situational judgment is captured by the phrase "in this situation." In different circumstances truthfulness and means could be more important than the intent and effect. Let us consider how this might be the case.

Suppose that person A hates surprise parties—a fact that is known to person B but not to persons C, D, E, F, and G (all of whom like surprise parties). Person B decides to give a surprise birthday party for A and invites the others. B does so from a desire to win favor from C, D, E, F, and G and thinks, "Well, A won't mind that much." One day, A asks B if B is aware of A's upcoming birthday. B lies and says "no." How do you think a situationalist would judge B's decision to lie to A? The reasoning might be something like this:

1 B lied to A. Lying is a bad communication practice.

2 B lied for a selfish purpose. Hence, the lie cannot be justified by good intent toward the victim of the lie.

3 B's lie worked against the interests of A. Hence, the lie cannot be justified as bringing about good results for A.

4 It follows that B's lie is unethical. It cannot be justified by good intent or good effects.

What we have in these examples is two different applications of the same ethical principles. In the first case the critic gives intention and effect more weight than untruthfulness. A lie is said to be justified by the speaker's intent to benefit the receiver of the lie. In the second example speaker intention and the effects test are not seen as justifying an untruth.

In short, the situationalist does not apply a fixed objective code. The situation approach provides for analyzing each act on the basis of the surrounding events. The situationalist will not be committed in advance to any organized set of ethical principles. The relative importance of the principles is said to depend on the particular characteristics of the circumstances at hand.

Situationalism has been offered in recent years as a "new morality"—in contrast to the "old morality", which was based on objective rules. However, as Fagothey (1972, pp. 149–154) points out, even the "old" morality of "objective" rules has involved considerations of the context of an act. He cites the position of St. Thomas Aquinas that moral judgments are based on an act, the motive (intent) of the act, and the circumstances (when, where, how) of the act. In short, situationalism is not totally distinct from the objective approach. The old moralists realized the rules have to be applied to different circumstances. What is different about situationalism is its tendency to make ethical principles secondary to the particular details at hand. Overall, then, situationalism's major feature is its on-the-spot method of organizing ethical principles. An objective code would specify that good intent always justifies a lie or that good intent never justifies a bad tactic. Situationalism would hold that good intent may or may not justify a bad act.

Like the objective approach, situationalism can be a defensible method for making ethical judgments. Situationalism's strength is its realization that ethical judgments must take into account the particular features that surround each human act. Moreover, the situational view is on strong ground in asserting that no two situations are ever exactly alike. On the other hand, a major shortcoming of situationalism is its proclivity to deny the existence of principles of ethics. When one scrutinizes a large number of situational ethical judgments, it appears that situationalists do hold to some general principles: They place great weight on having a good intent toward one's fellow man. Situationalism is not entirely situational.

Utilitarian Codes of Ethics

Utilitarianism is a code that gives most weight to the effects of a particular act. Utilitarianism holds that acts should be judged on the basis of their consequences. In this view, actions that bring about good for the most people are ethical. Actions that cause less good are less ethical.

The English philosophers Jeremy Bentham (1748–1832) and John Stuart Mill (1806–1873) are commonly cited as the intellectual founders of modern utilitarianism. Of course, as Mill himself notes (1951, p. 7), utilitarianism has existed as a school of thought for thousands of years.

At the root of utilitarianism is the assumption that man's basic motivation is both the pursuit of pleasure and the avoidance of pain. Furthermore, utilitarianism views pleasure as a measurable concept. Certainly, the ability to calculate pleasure is necessary if utility (pleasure for the most people) is to be the standard of ethics. Consider how ethical judgments might be made according to a utilitarian code. In the case of our surprise-party example, a utilitarian thinker probably would vindicate the lie using a set of arguments such as this:

1   The lie brought about pleasure both for the liar (she enjoyed giving the party) and the victim (he enjoyed the party in his honor).
2   Thus, the lie added to the total amount of pleasure in the world.
3   The lie caused no suffering or unhappiness.
4   A truthful statement might have reduced the pleasure for the two individuals.
5   Hence, the lie was ethical.

As you can see, a utilitarian code elevates the effects, or consequences, principle of ethics. It makes effects the ultimate sanction for an act.

Utilitarianism has considerable appeal as a basis for making ethical judgments. However, this code has received wide criticism. For one thing, as Frankena (1973, p. 35) notes, it may be difficult to calculate precisely the pleasure that will result from one act versus another. Precisely how does one measure, compare, and balance the various goods and bads that may result from two opposing choices? Indeed, the whole matter of constructing an "ethical impact statement" is quite a problem.

Utilitarianism has been attacked on other grounds as well. Equating morality with quantity of pleasure bothers many people. Such an equation seems to elevate sensual pursuits—it has a godless sound to it. Furthermore, utilitarians are criticized for preferring "the easy way" to "the right way." They are viewed as being willing to sacrifice principle in pursuit of pleasure.

In response to these criticisms, different systems of utilitarianism have been developed. Essays have been written defending the doctrine against charges from all comers. Mill's own essay on utilitarianiam (1951) contains several sections in which he attempts to answer some of the objections. In response to the claim that utilitarianism elevates mere bodily feeling, Mill argues that utility need not be based on "low" pleasures. Like Aristotle, who argued that the life of reason is the most pleasant, Mill prefers "mental" to "bodily" pleasure. He emphasizes that "it is better to be a human being dissatisfied than a pig satisfied" (p. 12). Mill claims that true utility would motivate "nobleness of character." In like manner, he defends his code of ethics against the charge that it is godless. "In the golden rule of Jesus of Nazareth, we read the complete spirit of the ethics of utility," he writes (p. 21).

In the form proposed by Bentham and Mill, utilitarianism has won few converts among philosophers; yet utilitarianism can be seen as the foundation for several modern systems of ethics. For instance, the underlying spirit of utility can be seen in Toulmin's definition (1968, p. 137) of the overall "function" of ethics: "to correlate our feelings and behavior in such a way as to make the fulfillment of everyone's aims and desires as far as possible compatible." In this view a system of ethics should make it possible for all to attain happiness. It should make sure that the happiness of the majority is not at the expense of the minority. Similarly, Frankena's theory of ethics as moral obligation (1973, pp. 43–60) relies partly on the notion of utility (together with "equal treatment" or justice).

What Toulmin and Frankena are trying to tell us, I think, is that certain features of traditional utilitarianism must be controlled if it is to be a defensible ethical system. Hence, they dilute pure utilitarianism (which emphasizes total effects) with doses of "good intentions toward others."

A Final Note on Codes

It is time to draw this discussion of ethical codes to a close. My purpose in treating this subject was to introduce you to several different approaches to the subject of ethics. In chapter 3 and in the early part of this chapter, I derived five principles of communication ethics. Unfortunately, any set of ethical principles is likely to produce conflict when actually applied to a real context of events. Such was the case with my set of five principles. It is not difficult to imagine situations in which a bad technique (e.g., an *ad hominem* attack) is used with a good intent in mind. Similarly, the truthfulness standard may at times come into conflict with the "good effect" principle, and so on, down the line.

What is needed, therefore, is a method for weighing the relative importance of ethical principles. Over the years several codes of ethics have been developed to help with this need. The codes emphasize one principle or another. An objective code, for example, makes intent and consequences subordinate to the question of whether a given act is found on a list of prohibited (or approved) behaviors. Situational codes emphasize different principles at different times. Utilitarian codes elevate the question of whether an act brings about good or bad effects for people. Overall, then, ethical codes supply a perspective for making ethical judgments.

Although I have identified five codes of ethics, it is important to realize that the five overlap in many ways. For example, an objective code may be established partly on the basis of utilitarian ideals. In such an instance, a rule against fabricated evidence may produce, in the long run, the most good. Also, I want to make the related point that many persons have developed personal codes of ethics—codes that involve a mixture of the five general types above. Toulmin and Frankena have put forth their own codes by synthesizing previous philosophical work on ethics. You might want to read more about their theories.

A final word about ethical codes is needed. As a source and as a receiver of messages, you should be aware of your own ethical code. You may want to use this chapter as the basis for your own further reading and thinking about ethics. I hope that you will do so.

APPLYING ETHICAL STANDARDS TO COMMUNICATION

In the previous section of the chapter, I suggested that choosing or developing an ethical code is a prerequisite to making ethical judgments. Admittedly, however, this advice is not of much help to the person who is confronted with an ethical decision. Indeed, the real problem in ethics is applying principles and codes of ethics. Developing them is comparatively easy.

At this point I want to give more attention to the process of making and justifying ethical judgments. In treating this subject I will outline a method for making ethical decisions from the point of view of a receiver of communication and from that of a source.

Ethics as a Receiver or Critic Judgment

Many times we are called upon to evaluate the ethics of someone else's arguments. For instance, while watching a television commercial we may have need to reflect over the morality of our buying that product; or if we are debating someone, we may wish to use the ethics standard as a basis for refuting an opponent's argument. At any rate, when judging the ethical implications of someone else's arguments, it may help to follow these steps.

1 Identify a message to be judged. You might decide to evaluate the ethics of the speaker's overall main argument, or you might prefer to make one or more ethical decisions about supporting arguments in the message.

2 Obtain as much information as possible about the communication situation. Look for clues as to the speaker's intention and the effects of the message. Pay attention to details of the message itself. What is the main idea? What are the supporting ideas? What evidence is used? What argumentative tactics does the source employ?

3 Choose an overall perspective from which to make an ethical judgment. That is, choose or develop an ethical code. When I say to "choose" a code I mean that you may select one of the five general codes that I presented in this chapter. To "develop" an ethical code means to construct your own system by selecting aspects of other codes.

4 State a judgment about the ethics of the argument that you have chosen for analysis. To what extent is it ethical or not?

5 Justify your judgment. This step involves the application of reason to ethics. Here you identify arguments to support your ethical analysis. Basically, this requires the relating of details of the situation to wider ethical principles and codes. Your justification might take the form of my examples earlier in the chapter. Review exercise 3-8, in which I explained how to apply ethical principles. In preparing to explain your ethical judgment, you should prepare to defend it against possible challenges. Also, do not forget that you may be called upon to justify your choice of an ethical code.

In the next section of the chapter, I will illustrate the use of this method. I will use it to judge one of the ethical controversies presented at the outset of this chapter.

Ethics as a Communicator Judgment

Probably all readers of this book will have occasion to wonder whether they are communicating ethically. As communicators we make choices of what ideas to maximize and what notions to minimize. Whenever such choices are made, ethics are involved.

Toulmin's Steps in Making Ethical Choices Toulmin (1968, pp. 144–157) has identified a general method for making and justifying personal ethical decisions. The first step of this method is deciding whether a choice is based on an established rule of action. For instance, one may reason that (1) you should not say X because (2) you know X to be untrue and (3) being truthful is a recognized rule of communication. In this scenario one has searched for a general rule of society to guide one's specific personal choice. One chooses to reject an untruthful statement because of a socially accepted rule. In sum, we can justify a choice by referring to our obligation to follow a rule (pp. 145–146).

Toulmin recognizes, however, that not all accepted social rules are just and right. Hence, the moral reasoner should give thought to the rightness of the particular social rule he is applying (pp. 150–152). To continue with the example given, the arguer could reason that "it is a good thing that society rejects lying because communication would be hopeless, otherwise."[2] In this case examination of the rule itself strengthens the person's intent to choose the truthful alternative. On the other hand, however, our examination might cast doubt on the wisdom of a social rule. This eventuality might prompt us to start over and look for another rule.

As I have demonstrated, a first step in making a personal ethical decision is to search for and examine social rules that might apply. Unfortunately, there

---

[2]Truth is seen to harmonize the communication relationship of source and receiver. Hence, the rule of truthfulness fits Toulmin's definition (1968, p. 137) of the function of ethics: "to correlate our feelings and behavior in such a way as to make the fulfillment of everyone's aims and desires as far as possible compatible."

may be more than one rule that applies, and the two or more rules may conflict. This creates an ambiguous situation. Because ambiguous situations are not uncommon, Toulmin (1968, p. 147) proposes a second step in deciding upon an ethical choice: If the situation is ambiguous, it may be necessary to base our choice on an estimation of the likely consequences of our act. Which choice would bring greater good? And for whom? Here Toulmin is not speaking in strictly utilitarian terms. His idea of "consequences" entails duty and obligation to other persons. (Remember his theory of the function of ethics—to harmonize the relations between people.)

Toulmin's third step (1968, p. 157) in justifying an ethical choice is designed for cases in which the first and second steps do not make any particular choice seem better than the other(s). The following statement summarizes the gist of his point: When steps 1 and 2 do not point clearly to a choice, then we must rely on a personal ethic. Toulmin calls this our "rule of life," which we form through personal experiences and contact with others.

Throughout this discussion of ethical choices, Toulmin emphasizes the need for justifying our choices. The three steps are a set of procedures for working through the features of a particular choice.

An Ethical Self-Check for Persuaders   It may help you to understand personal ethical choices better if I enumerate a checklist for would-be persuaders. The following is a classified list of questions that a persuader might use to check whether a communication was ethical. You will recognize these questions as relating to ideas presented earlier in the chapter. The first set of questions calls for a persuader to consider his tactics and purpose.

1   Do I believe that "it" (a communication act) is right in general and/or in this situation? (The "it" in the previous sentence could denote a main argument, supporting argument, or a particular argumentative tactic used in a message.)

2   Do I believe that my argument is valid? To what extent am I certain of this?

3   Do I care about my listeners? That is, do I have their best interests in mind, or am I advocating a course of action that is against the audience's welfare?

The next self-check questions focus the communicator's attention to society's collective ethics.

4   Does the society in which I live hold "it" to be right in general and/or in this situation? Does a recognized social rule apply to what I am proposing to do?

5   Does my communication act (argument or tactic) appeal to values that the society holds to be morally good or morally bad?

6   Would I be proud for others to know my real motives or thoughts on the subject?

7   What social consequences would result if my act were to become a general practice? Put another way, how would I react to the practice if done by another person—particularly, an opponent?

These seven questions would help an advocate to decide whether a proposed message was ethical. The questions call for the persuader to reflect about both the message and his or her own conscience, to look for social rules, and to examine the interests of the audience (as well as other situational details).

In this section of the chapter I have presented methods for using ethical theory to make ethical judgments and choices. As I said above, however, the real problem in ethics is applying theory to real-world disputes: the methods I have identified are only a partial solution. Let me now make some ethical judgments about actual situations.

JUSTIFYING ETHICAL JUDGMENTS: SOME EXAMPLES

At the outset of the chapter, I cited six examples of contemporary disputes that seemed to center on communication ethics. To illustrate ethical judgments I will now take some of the ethical theories and methods and apply them to sample disputes.

Making a Receiver Judgment about
Advertising Ethics: A Case Study

Because of its prevalence, advertising provides ample opportunities for making ethical judgments as a receiver. In the next few paragraphs I will explain how one might analyze the ethics of an advertising message. Follow along as I apply the step-by-step method for making ethical judgments as a message receiver.

First, we have to gather a message. Let us select a typical Saturday morning television advertisement for a brand of candy bar. For purposes of analysis, let us assume (1) that the advertisement is animated so as to appeal to children and (2) that it is based on the activity of a popular cartoon character, who encourages children to buy the candy product.

We have now identified the general message (a cartoon advertisement for candy) and the specific persuasive technique used (the attention-getting effects of animation plus the cartoon character's popularity with children). Now we are ready for the third step: choosing/developing an ethical perspective (code) as a basis for judgment. Rather than adopting one of the five general codes of ethics, it may be useful to develop an individually tailored code. Accordingly, I have set up the following code: (1) To be ethical a message must pass all five general ethical tests. In other words, the effects, truth, values, communicator intention, and persuasive techniques of the message must all be good. (2) But if a message passes at least one of the tests, it may be reevaluated. In this reevaluation, the message *may* be judged ethical *if* the tests it passes clearly are more important and relevant than the ones it fails.

Notice that this specially developed code has elements of the objective code: the message must pass standard objective rules, e.g., "Thou shalt not lie." But the second provision of this code is situational in nature: in some cases (i.e., under some circumstances), a message may fail one or more of the five tests—*if* the tests which the message is judged to have failed clearly are less weighty than the ones the message has passed.

Now I am ready to state and justify a critic's judgment about the ethics of the Saturday morning cartoon advertisement for candy.

Judgment

The advertisement is at least somewhat unethical.

Justification

I   The advertisement probably fails three of the general ethical tests.

    A   Intent: The advertisement seeks to increase consumption of a nutritionally poor food, which contributes to tooth decay.

    B   Effect: Candy contains large amounts of sugar, which contributes only slightly to nutrition but much to dental problems.

    C   Values: The advertisement encourages poor rather than good nutrition.

II   The advertisement poses problems with respect to the final two general ethical tests.

    A   Persuasive techniques: It is ethically questionable to use a cartoon figure to sell a product to children. This use of a popular fantasy authority takes advantage of children who are less able than adults to separate a television program from a real commercial product.

    B   Truth: We will assume that the advertisement contains no false statements (i.e., no distortion by commission). However, the advertisement may distort reality if it *omits* the bad-health effects of too much candy.

III   Since the advertisement poses problems with respect to all the ethical tests, there is no reason to go any further—it is at least somewhat unethical. The *extent* of the message's ethical failings could be estimated by more detailed application of each ethical test.

Making Ethical Choices as a Communicator

As human beings we all function both as givers and receivers of communication. As I have noted, communication involves choice—the decision to include or exclude and minimize or maximize certain arguments. I also suggested a method—actually, two methods—for judging the ethics of our choices. I cited Toulmin's steps and presented my own "ethical self-check for persuaders." Now I want to apply the ethical checklist to a communication decision that I had to make several years ago.

The summer after my freshman year in college, I got a temporary job selling encyclopedias for a company that shall remain nameless. I went through the sales training course, which consisted largely of memorizing a *spiel* that had allegedly been developed by a "famous psychologist at the cost of millions of dollars." After some training sessions the trainees were put under the supervision of an experienced salesperson. We observed the veteran as he "placed" the encyclopedias with buyers (we were told to avoid the word "sell").

As the training sessions progressed, I became increasingly uneasy about what I was learning to do. For one thing, the training leaders misled the trainees on several points. When we were accepted into the sales program, we were told that the job involved contacting persons who had expressed an interest in learning more about the encyclopedias. Later, as we were ready to begin the observation phase, the leaders admitted that the sales were strictly of the random door-to-door variety. It is clear why the leaders misled us. Door-to-door salesmanship is a hard, frustrating process. Many of the trainees would never have begun the sales course if they had known that it was geared to door-to-door sales. However, after one had spent a week in training, one was more likely to stick with it, despite the door-to-door drawback.

Some other things bothered me, too. It was clear that we were selling encyclopedias, but the sales talk did not make this clear to the prospective customer. In fact, it contained an "opener" to the effect that the salesman was only "checking on the effectiveness of our advertising." We were taught to show the person a picture and ask if he "had seen this ad in a magazine." We were taught to gain entry to the home under the guise of finding out more about the success of X Company's advertising.

Furthermore, the deceit did not stop here. Once inside, the trainees were told to use a disguised sales method. This involved telling the customer that we were "placing" a few "demonstration sets" because the company had found that "word of mouth good will" was the best way to sell sets. We then were to tell the customer that we had not yet "placed" a set in this neighborhood and that if he were interested, we might arrange for him or her to get a demonstration set.

The next step in the sales pitch was designed to break the news that the "demonstration set" had to be paid for by the consumer. The "famous psychologist" had devised a marvelous method for doing this: We were to tell the customer that in order to defray certain incidental costs, it was necessary to charge "a dime per day" for the set. We then drew an analogy to the paperboy, who collected such a sum for the daily newspaper. In explaining the "dime a day" feature, the salesperson implied that the company actually had persons who "collected" for the sets. This, as you might imagine, was another falsehood. The company had no such persons. The company desired the customer to pay for the sets directly. Hence, the pitch included another strategy for getting this hard fact across.

The salesperson explained that the collecting process was itself expensive; therefore the company would be willing to "give" the customer a set of bookcases for the encyclopedias. All the customer had to do was to "help" by just paying the "fee" in a few installments. The final aspects of the sales approach involved getting the customer to sign the contract, collecting a down payment, and getting away before the customer had time to think.

The training leaders never really admitted to us that the sales pitch was based on rampant falsehoods and misrepresentations. Rather, they attempted to rationalize the deceit as simply using methods for overcoming the natural prejudice against door-to-door sales. In fact, they maintained, the devices "helped" the customer not to miss out on a good deal.

To an 18-year-old this all sounded somewhat plausible, so I put aside my increasing misgivings and went into the field with an experienced salesperson. Unfortunately, the field experience only worsened my impressions about the sleazy ethics of the sales pitch. It was one thing to read and study the sales talk, but it was quite another to see it actually used on gullible customers. There were also some incidents in the field that aroused my consciousness of the shoddy enterprise that I was apparently entering into. One of the sales teams (salesperson plus trainee) "placed" a set with a customer who changed his mind after signing the contract. I was told by the novice half of the team that this individual followed them around town with a shotgun! There were also certain "tricks of the trade" that gave me pause. For example, a backyard swing set might suggest that parents could be wheedled into buying "for the sake of the children." All of this made me wonder if our slick pitch was really to "aid" the customer in overcoming an irrational prejudice against the door-to-door sale of our product or simply to sell encyclopedias by any possible means.

The magic day finally came when the trainees were turned loose on their own. By this time I was thoroughly demoralized; only my earlier inability to get a summer job had kept me in the field for a final two days. I have to admit that the fee for placing a set was a large one; however, my two field days were hardly "field days." After a few halfhearted efforts, I spent both days sitting in the shade of a park reading the demonstration volume of our encyclopedia, which was a good one, despite the company's selling techniques.

I remember vividly the second day of reading and reflection. I sat by the river of a small Ohio town thinking over the whole matter. Eventually, I came to a number of conclusions. First, I decided that the sales tactics were clearly unethical: The sales pitch involved innumerable misrepresentations; we were taught to disguise our sales effort as an advertising survey; and, carrying the "advertising" lie another step, we were told to sell encyclopedias under the guise of "placing" one demonstration set in a particular neighborhood. In fact, of course, the company would have placed "demonstration models" in every house in town, if possible. Furthermore, the sales pitch used the "dime a day" phrase to obscure the fact that the consumer was buying a set of books that would cost more than $400 in the end (and in 1968 this sum was worth much more than it is today).

Beyond the fact of the obviously unethical tactics was the utter disregard for the consumer's interest. Our teachers of sales techniques instructed us that the poorest people were often the most likely to buy—"accept placement of"—the sets. In other words, we were encouraged to market the sets to people who probably could not afford them. Hence, at the very least, the salespersons acted selfishly, but in many cases they persuaded listeners to adopt a course of action that was against the listener's best interest.

That day on the riverbank was my last as a novice encyclopedia salesperson.

I chalked up the two wasted weeks to experience and secured a lower-paying but more honorable job.

Let me now relate this narrative to the seven ethical self-check questions that I presented earlier.

1 Did I believe that selling the encyclopedias (using the prescribed pitch) was right in general and/or in this situation? The answer is a simple one—no, I did not. I felt that the distortions were wrong in general. Furthermore, I believed that none of the circumstances mitigated the wrongness of the unethical tactics. The fact that the product was of high quality was no defense for selling it under false pretenses to people who might not be able to afford it. The argument that the distortions were devised only to overcome the prejudice against door-to-door sales was no more than a rationalization. Clearly, it seemed to me, the falsehoods in the sales pitch were not designed to help the consumers, but rather to fool them. Although I did not know it at the time, I had decided that continued participation in the sales campaign was ethically wrong according to the first self-check question.

2 Did I believe the sales arguments were valid? Except for arguments that the encyclopedias were of high quality, almost every claim that we were taught was invalid.

3 As a seller, would I care about my listeners? The whole premise of the sales pitch was to mislead the consumer so as to facilitate a sale. Clearly, such persuasion represented an uncaring attitude of the persuader toward the listener.

4 Does society hold such tactics to be right in general and/or in the specific situation? The tactics used in the sales pitch represented sales misrepresentations. These kinds of falsehoods are prohibited in many codes of fair trade. I noted with some satisfaction a report (*Courier-Journal,* December 31, 1977, p. B9) about a December 1977 ruling by the Federal Trade Commission that reaffirmed the prohibition against sales disguised as market research. In other words, this tactic—called "come-on selling"—clearly fails another ethical test. It violates recognized social rules.

5 Did the sales approach (argument or tactic) appeal to values that society holds to be morally good or morally bad? The arguments of the pitch did not appeal, in themselves, to bad values. In our dialogue with the consumer, we were taught to stress the values of a good education, reading, and helping one's children with their studies. However, the sales tactics were founded on the unethical value of "selfishness."

6 Would sellers have been proud for others to have known their real motives or thoughts on the subject? In the course of the training process, I heard both the training leaders and veteran salespersons make many disparaging comments about the gullibility and stupidity of consumers. Given the effort to disguise this contempt from the customers, I believe that it is obvious that the sales force would not want its real motives or thoughts revealed.

7 What social consequences would result if this act were to become a general practice? The Federal Trade Commission and other organizations endeavor to stamp our practices such as those employed in this encyclopedia pitch. I think that this is based on the notion that such tactics poison the marketplace.

It seems evident that my decision to leave the sales campaign was the ethically correct choice. I arrived at my conclusions without benefit of the "ethical self-check for persuaders." However, I believe that the persuasion role for which I was being trained did violate every one of the seven tests.

ON THE DIFFICULTY OF USING REASON IN ETHICS

In the last two sections of this chapter, I have stressed a philosophy of ethics that involves justifying ethical judgments. Toulmin uses the expression "reason in ethics" to denote the justifying of ethical decisions by means of argument. For him (as well as for me) the ethical standard of argument is an exercise in reason-giving. However, in observing ethical controversies—such as the six mentioned earlier in the chapter—it seems to me that most people do not espouse the philosophy of reason in ethics. Many take the following twofold ethical position: (1) ethics involve questions of value, and (2) one cannot argue matters of value. We may call this the "ethics as intuitive feelings" school of thought. By "intuitive," I mean something that is personally obvious and does not require—indeed, does not allow—argument. Let me give two illustrations of the "ethics as intuitive feelings" position.

I have already mentioned the February, 1978 National Parent-Teacher Association (P.T.A.) criticism of the quality of network television programming. The P.T.A. rated many shows as objectionable because of violence and other offensive content, and it also examined the shows in terms of overall excellence and portrayal of the quality of life in the United States.

The news story (*Courier-Journal,* February 16, 1978, p. A8) that reported this P.T.A. critique contained some information about the response of the networks. A spokesman for the National Broadcasting Company (N.B.C.) was quoted as making the following assessment of the P.T.A. study: "[It] appears to be based not on objective or scientific criteria but rather on subjective value judgments, not necessarily reflecting those of the country as a whole."

This quotation is interesting. Notice that it elevates descriptive argument and denigrates evaluative argument. In fact, the quotation assumes that the P.T.A. position is suspect simply because it is based on value judgments. The assumption is made—though not justified—that value arguments are by their nature invalid. The spokesman seems to assert that all he has to do is call attention to the presence of value arguments in the P.T.A. position. He implies that value arguments require no response once they have been identified as such.

I flatly reject this assumption. In support of my rejection, I offer chapter 3, chapter 6, and chapter 8 of this book. In my view, all arguments raise the issue of value—although in some the value assumptions are less prominent than the factual or definitional ones. If this is the case, then value-emphasizing arguments must be treated in the same manner as fact or definition-emphasizing arguments. Value arguments would require a specific, sensible response—just as do the other forms of argument.

Consider a second illustration of the "ethics as intuitive feelings" perspective. In March 1978 the American Association for Higher Education voted to refuse to hold conventions in Chicago until the Equal Rights Amendment to the Constitution is ratified by the State of Illinois. During the debate on this resolution, it was pointed out that such a decision would be in conflict with contracts previously signed by the organization. Hence, the argument went, the association might be sued for breach of contract. It was suggested, further, that a suit of this type would have serious financial effects on the organization. Its existence might be jeopardized.

The news report of the debate (*The Chronicle of Higher Education,* March 27, 1978, p. 9) contained the following response to the argument that the boycott of Chicago was risky. A delegate is described as being " 'embarrassed' that the association would consider finances when faced with 'a basic moral issue.' "

This argument is noteworthy because it assumes that only one side in a dispute can have moral (i.e., value) issues in its favor. Hence, if the morality rests on one side, there can be no argument of the moral issues of the proposed Chicago boycott.

Given my definition of value ("the moral goodness and badness of things") in chapters 3 and 6, it is easy to see why I am unimpressed with the delegate's view of value argumentation. The very argument that the boycott violated contracts raised a value (i.e., moral) issue. Similarly, the assertion that a lawsuit could jeopardize the existence of the organization is one based partly on values. In my view it was invalid to assert that the "finances" of the organization did not have value implications. It follows, then, that both sides raised moral arguments. For this reason, the "moral issue" (the rightness versus the wrongness of the boycott) required debate. The tendency to take the "feelings" versus "reason-giving" approach to ethics in the E.R.A.-related boycott issue is reflected, further, in a comment by the president-elect of the American Psychological Association. Supporting the boycott, Nicholas Cummings asserted (*Psychology Today,* February, 1978, p. 95) that "rednecks may not understand ERA, but they do understand money." Here name-calling (presumably based on moral outrage) is substituted for analysis of the moral issues. There were good arguments in favor of the boycott—as well as against it—but this excerpt leaves them unstated. In fact, it seems to go along with the view that argument is inappropriate in value-tinged questions.

I am bothered by the prevalence of the view that argument is inappropriate for value issues. I think that this view has fundamental intellectual problems in assuming that one can make a rigid separation between factual and definitional arguments and value-based ones. Certainly, the value implications of some claims are more obvious than are others. It is possible, further, that simple factual assertions (e.g., "the sky is blue") may contain almost nothing in the way of moral content. But in the case of complicated ethical debates such as I have presented in this chapter, it is unacceptable to argue that moral issues are clearly separate from factual ones. Moreover, I find it disturbing when one side asserts (with no justification) that all the rightness is on its side, and none on the opponent's. Surely this claim—which may well be true—requires an extended set of supporting reasons.

Wayne Booth (1974, pp. 24–25), a professor of English at the University of Chicago, shares my concern over the apparent popularity of the "intuitive feelings" view of ethics and its implications. For if one cannot *argue* about moral matters, what is left? Indeed, there is a certain irony here. Given that factual questions are more straightforward than value ones, why is argument appropriate to the former but not to the latter? It would seem that value questions require even more careful thought and public debate than do descriptive ones. Would not descriptions require only minimal argument (except for the definition and value issues that they inevitably raise)? "Resolved that the sky is blue" seems to be a rather unpromising proposition for debate.

At the outset of this chapter, I introduced a basic premise of this chapter—that ethics is an important subject. In the next section, I presented six ethical controversies so that you could see real-world instances of ethical dispute. In the next two sections, I presented some of the philosophy that underlies the subject of ethics. This was the rationale for the five ethical principles. Afterwards, I introduced a set of five ethical codes, showing how the principles were not enough. Next came my method for making ethical judgments, together with two examples of its use.

The only job remaining is to put some of this chapter into practice.

APPLICATIONS

Basically, I think that the best way to apply this chapter is to discuss it in class. However, as always, I think it is good to apply the concepts to actual situations of dispute.

Exercise 8-1: Preparing for a General Class Discussion of Communication Ethics

Ethics is often a complicated subject. I hope that this chapter has clarified the subject for you, but there is always the danger that it has not. For this reason, you or your instructor may want to treat the subject in a general class discussion. If so, you should prepare for the discussion by doing the following:

I   Write out a brief answer to each of these questions:
  A   What is the author's definition of "the ethics of argument?"
  B   Why does the author say that ethics is an important field of study?
  C   The author lists several disputes that he labels "ethical." Why does he label them as such?

    D Why does the author say we need a code of ethics? (Hint: What does a code do to the principles of ethics?)

II Write out a brief definition and/or explanation for each of these terms or expressions:

    A Principle of ethics

    B Code of ethics

    C "The method for judging ethics as a receiver of communication"

    D "An ethical self-check for persuaders"

    E "Reason in ethics"

Exercise 8-2: Deriving an Objective Code of Communication Ethics

This is another exercise that seems especially appropriate for a general class discussion.

  I Identify at least ten communication acts that seem to be unethical. This list could include types of argument, persuasive strategies, etc.

 II For each, briefly explain why you believe the communication act to be unethical.

III Your instructor may wish you to bring your list to class. Perhaps your class can derive a master list from everyone's individual responses.

 IV If your class attempts to develop a list of "unethical communication practices," it might be interesting to attempt to classify these as follows:

    A Practices that are highly unethical under most circumstances.

    B Practices that are unethical under some circumstances.

    C Practices that are only occasionally or mildly unethical.

Exercise 8-3: "Situationalizing" an Objective Code of Communication Ethics

  I Review the list of unethical practices that you developed in exercise 8-2.

 II Select two of the unethical communication acts for further analysis.

III For each, state a judgment as to whether or not surrounding circumstances could ever make such an act ethical. By "surrounding circumstances" I mean (a) the intent of the communicator, (b) the effects of the act, and (c) other factors such as who, when, where, how and to what degree.

 IV Explain each judgment.

Exercise 8-4: Identifying a Dispute about Communication Ethics

In doing this exercise you may take one of two general approaches: (1) Collect a clipping that contains information about what you believe to be an ethical controversy or (2) use your general knowledge of a controversy to describe it. In any event, you should do the following:

I   Identify in a word or phrase the subject of the dispute. For instance, "sex on T.V.," "protest rallies," "sports interviews," "rock concerts," etc., would be suitable.

II Identify at least two positions that have been taken on the subject. These should be ethical positions. Write out each position as a full sentence. For example, "Subliminal advertising does not hurt anyone and should be allowed" versus "Subliminal advertising attempts to deny the consumer free choice and therefore should be prohibited."

III Explain why your subject is an instance of a dispute about communication ethics.

Exercise 8-5: Making and Justifying an Ethical Judgment as a Receiver (Critic)

I   Use the ethical dispute that you identified in exercise 8-4 or develop one now for this exercise, following the directions in exercise 8-4.

II Use the five-step method for making an ethical judgment about someone else's ethics.

III In doing this exercise, be sure to review the example of how to apply the five-step method.

Chapter 9

Communication Strategies in Contemporary Society

The theme of this book is the influence of language in our daily lives. Throughout I have tried to illustrate the principles of argument by use of examples. This was especially true for chapters 4, 5, and 6. These contained numerous samples of the forms and types of argument.

In chapter 9, I want to take a slightly different approach in demonstrating how argumentation theory applies to the outside world. In this chapter I will treat a number of contexts in which one can see the workings of argument. For instance, I will show how arguments are involved in our relationships with other people. I will show how cartoons argue. Overall, I will mention eleven situations—from advertising to popular films. In each case I will show how the agent (advertiser, filmmaker, etc.) uses symbols to communicate a position. This chapter, in short, reinforces my basic idea that argument appears in many places.

One of the functions of this chapter will be to demonstrate that argument does play an important role in many facets of life. But I have yet a second general objective for this chapter: I want to demonstrate that there are many ways to argue. A person desiring to support a position on some subject is not limited to making a speech or writing an essay. Persons may also argue through artistic means such as music, literature, drama, film, and cartoon. This chapter reinforces the notion—which I have emphasized throughout the book—that argument may be found in many shapes. Let us consider now some of the various places and shapes of argument.

I shall begin the chapter by treating three relatively obvious contexts for arguing: advertising, politics, and law. The next two argument contexts are less obvious. Sometimes we assume that newspeople and scientists just report the facts. However, such individuals use language for the purpose of communicating a point of view (a position). For this reason they clearly function as arguers. Argument in literature, on the stage, and in film are the focuses of the next chapter sections. Here I examine the use of devices such as personification (allowing characters to represent ideas). Pictures (cartoons) and songs represent two more ways in which advocates may advance their position. Finally, by isolating the role of argument in interpersonal relations, I "round out" the discussion of argumentative places and shapes.

ADVERTISING: PERSUADING CONSUMERS

Many of the examples presented earlier in this book have been taken from the field of advertising. Let us look at a few more. Try a little experiment. Sit down at the television set and watch an hour or so of advertisements. Really pay attention to them and watch for a number of things: the product, the "value" of the product, and the causal connection between product and value. You might see something like this:

Time	Product	Value	Causal link
7:05 P.M.	Close-Up toothpaste	Social or sexual popularity	If you use the product you will have bright teeth and fresh breath. This will make you more successful with the opposite sex.

Back up a bit and take a look at what happened in this illustration. The advertisement probably caught your attention by showing someone in a state of deprivation. In this case it is probably some individual lacking a date for the evening. Next, our attention shifts to a friend. The friend advises the individual to use Close-Up toothpaste instead of buying a new dress, suit, or car. The succeeding scene shows the person now successful in his or her social life.

A Cornucopia of Values

"Cornucopia" means horn of plenty. Advertising can be likened to a cornucopia because it shows us a seemingly numberless list of good things to be had. This cornucopia feature of ads should call attention to a basic function of advertising—the use of values as motivating concepts.

Let us continue our television monitoring just a bit more to see how commercials hold out values as a motivational carrot.

Time	Product	Value	Causal link
7:07 P.M.	Cadillac	Prestige; luxury; sexual success	Commercial depicts the luxury of the automobile. Driver uses vehicle to transport well-dressed woman to "high society" event.
7:08 P.M.	Geritol	Health; beauty	Attractive and healthy woman describes her use of the product in glowing terms.
7:17 P.M.	American Express Travelers Cheques	Safety; convenience; freedom from from anxiety	In serious tones, actor Karl Malden describes how American Express Travelers Cheques can be replaced if stolen.

The examples are only three of the many that appear each day. Each commercial tells that our life will be materially improved through use of a product.

Advertising reveals an interesting picture of the American public. In the main, we are a handsome people (the models commonly are quite attractive), and, as depicted in advertisements, we are a fortunate people. All of our problems are minor and require only a simple, material solution. We have drugs to mitigate any possible discomfort: headaches, constipation, backache, burns, insomnia, and the like. Even our social discomforts may be removed quickly by the application of certain cosmetics, soaps, sprays, and pastes.

The above is part of a generalized picture of Americans that may be drawn from modern advertising. Upon closer inspection it even becomes possible to detect "subpictures." That is, advertisers seem to have different images of different subaudiences. Compare, if you will, the advertisements shown during the CBS Evening News to those of a popular variety show. Advertisers seem to view news watchers as being more in need of products such as laxatives and sleeping aids.

The values touted in advertisements amount to goals that the advertiser desires to promote. Viewed in this way, the advertising world undertakes an obligation to justify the ethics of the material-centered values it promotes. The notion that material consumption represents the American way of life is an interesting one—but one that should not be passively accepted.

It is evident that there is a general ethical question raised by advertising's emphasis on material consumerism. Beyond this, there are questions related to the use of particular values in advertising. In chapter 8, I discussed the implications of subliminal sexually oriented advertising. However, the prevalence of overt sexually based advertising raises ethical questions as well.

Surely, it is obvious that sex is one of the basic value motives used in advertising. Open any mass circulation magazine and look at the advertisements for cosmetics, cars, vacations, liquor, cigarettes, etc. Let me highlight a liquor ad that appeared in *Newsweek* (November 8, 1976, p. 5). (See figure 9-1.)

If Key were to take a look at the advertisement, he might emphasize the presence of possible subliminal devices. (Hint: What favorite three-letter word is suggested in the name Sauza Extra?) Beyond this, however, there is the use of

Figure 9-1   Sex as a motive in advertising.

an attractive female model in the marketing of a Mexican liquor and a suggestive text: "Who knows where it will all lead?" Is sex a justifiable motive for use in the marketing of liquor, or cars, or cigarettes? If so, why?

The Technique of Suggestion

An advertising agency's choice of motivational appeals (values) brings us to the question of advertising's argumentative and persuasive tactics. Seemingly, suggestion is the basic device of advertising. By "suggestion" I mean the use of verbal and nonverbal symbols to associate one thing (the product) with another (the value). Suggestion is present when we see a person obtaining something good through use of a product. As in the case of the ad for Close-Up toothpaste, suggestion does not explain how a toothpaste can radically improve one's sex life. The advertisement only suggests that this will be the case by associating, in the viewer's mind, the product and the value. Advertisements include values as motivating concepts: they do not advance a full-fledged value justification, but merely hint at a connection, leaving the explanation unstated.

Some examples may illuminate the technique of suggestion. Consider a television ad for Atlas tires. The announcer asserts that the tires "hold on water," meaning that they give good traction on wet roads. This is verbal suggestion. The next scene shows a car driving through a puddle of water. Here we have nonverbal suggestion. In this illustration the ad only *suggests* that the tires provide good traction. No verbal explanation is given to advance the claim that the tires actually do "hold on water." A verbal connection *is* made, but in the absence of supporting arguments, it remains only an assertion. Similarly, the visual argument remains at the level of suggestion. All that we see is a side view of a tire entering a pool of water. For all we know, the tire could be hydroplaning (i.e., riding on a thin film of water).

The Validity of Advertising Techniques

Once we realize that suggestion is the basic technique of advertising, we can better understand both the ads themselves and the widespread criticism of advertising. Kahane (1976) has done a particularly good job of summarizing the intellectual defects of advertising messages. In a section entitled "How Advertisements Con" (1976, pp. 144–153), he provides a stinging criticism. Basically, Kahane objects to these features of modern advertising: (1) Ads are one-sided, (2) ads imply falsehoods, (3) ads often "play on our fears or desires" without actually giving proof that they will satisfy our needs, and (4) ads use meaningless statements, jingles, slogans, and pictures.

Ads Are One-Sided Ads "never tell what is wrong with the product," complains Kahane (1976, p. 144). This truism raises a major validity problem for ads. Except in the rare instance of one ad refuting another, the advertisements are not found in an adversarial situation. The consumer lacks the advantage of a "marketplace of ideas" in which informed choices and comparisons can be made.

Ads Imply Falsehoods   This is a basic problem that springs from the technique of suggestion. Obviously, something like Lifebuoy soap is not, by itself, going to make a person popular. However, Lifebuoy advertisements imply that this will be the case. Consider an example of just such an ad. The commercial begins by showing another of advertising's poor souls at a party. It is clear that the poor soul cannot get anyone to notice him. It seems that everyone else is standing on a higher level—two or three feet above the floor. We see our poor soul looking up at the others. But wait In the next scene, our friend is shown using Lifebuoy soap. Magically, we see him rising in the shower. He is now on the "higher level." The final scene shows him as a success at the next party.

This commercial suggests that Lifebuoy soap will, by itself, make a person socially successful. Taken literally, the ad implies something that is probably false. If the commercial actually stated that "X soap will make users more socially successful," then the Federal Trade Commission (and others) might demand proof. However, because the argument is by suggestion, the ad is permissible. Nevertheless, it is still misleading.

Ads Often Play On Our Fears or Desires   Again, we may trace this problem back to the nature of suggestion. Advertisements hold out "solutions" for us without giving proof that the product will achieve the desired result. Advertising does not deal in reasons. Furthermore, many of advertising's value appeals are irrelevant. Hygienic products are not relevant to the basic issues in interpersonal relations. By suggesting that pastes and soaps will lead to success in dealing with people, the ads trade in the superfluous.

Ads Use Meaningless Statements, Jingles, Slogans, and Pictures   Again, the criticism goes to the nature of suggestion. If advertisements avoid reasons and explanations, something has to take their place; so we have interesting but irrelevant substitutes:

Statements: A bank commercial emphasizing "friendliness."
Jingles: A toothpaste asserting that it gives one's mouth "sex appeal."
Slogans: An appliance manufacturer calling on consumers to "come home" to its products.
Pictures: A homely man surrounded by beautiful women after having used a particular aftershave.

Overall, advertising does have major validity problems. Each ad would have to be analyzed on its own merits, of course; but as a class of messages, ads have major deficiencies. They appeal to values that are often irrelevant to the purpose or quality of a product, and they use suggestion to connect a value and a product. However, this causal connection usually is made in the absence of reasons to establish the connection. Let the consumer beware.

ARGUMENT IN POLITICS: A DEBATE ON
THE PANAMA CANAL TREATIES

"Politics" is a word derived from the classical Greek expression for city—*polis*. In ancient Greece, politics meant the governing of the city state; it referred to the process by which public policies were made—a "policy" being a course of action. Each society or nation has its own system of public policy making. Ours, which is based on the universal right of adult citizens to vote for representatives, is usually called a democracy or a republic.

The question of how to argue public policy is one that has interested people for centuries. Much of Aristotle's *Rhetoric*, for example, is taken up with his explanation of how to show that a policy brings about "good things." Chapters 10 and 11 of this book deal with the subject of arguing for and against policies.

Many of the examples in earlier chapters have been drawn from the general field labeled "politics." Nevertheless, I think it would be helpful for me to examine a single instance of political argument. This single case will give me the chance to show how advocates develop positions for and against a course of action.

I have chosen for my case study a 1978 debate on whether or not the Senate should ratify the proposed Panama Canal treaties. This debate was held on January 13, 1978, at the University of South Carolina. It pitted columnist William F. Buckley, Jr., against former California Governor Ronald Reagan and was moderated by former U.S. Senator Sam J. Ervin, Jr. Buckley supported the resolution. That is, he took the position that the U.S. Senate should ratify the treaties. Reagan argued that the Senate should not. Each speaker was supported by a panel of experts and a panel of examiners.

The resolution itself dealt with a particular policy issue that faced the Senate and the people of the United States during late 1977 and early 1978. Long-standing negotiations between Panama and the United States had led to two treaties: One provided for gradually turning over canal operation to Panama; the other was for the neutrality of the canal. The question became: Should the U.S. Senate accept or reject the treaties? As we now know, the treaties were accepted, with reservations, by the Senate. The debate between Buckley and Reagan will help you to understand what this decision was all about.

The debate consisted of two introductory speeches—one by each of the debaters. Next, each speaker was questioned by "examiners" and by each other. Finally, the debaters each made a concluding statement. My analysis will be focused on the opening two speeches, in which the speakers outlined their basic positions.[1]

---

[1] I have consulted a transcript of the debate prepared by the Southern Educational Communications Association.

Buckley for the Affirmative

The debate began with Buckley's opening address in support of the resolution—his *affirmative* speech. In the first section of his presentation, Buckley established his personal credibility. Let me indicate why it was necessary for him to do so. First of all, Buckley is a prominent spokesman for political conservatism in the United States. He favors the Republican party over the Democratic party. These two observations are important, because the conservative community generally opposed ratification of the treaties. Furthermore, President Jimmy Carter made ratification a major goal of his administration. In supporting the treaties, Buckley both deviated from the conservative mainstream and supported President Carter.

There is yet another reason for Buckley's credibility establishing introduction. Although Buckley favored ratification of the treaties, he opposed many of the arguments used by treaty supporters. Hence, he used the introduction to indicate his own reasons for ratification—as distinct from those advanced by more liberal treaty supporters.

Let me now describe Buckley's introduction. His initial remarks represent an effective use of humor.

> *Mr. Buckley:* Thank you, Mr. Chairman. Ladies and gentlemen. If Lloyds of London had been asked to give odds that I would be disagreeing with Ronald Reagan on a matter of public policy laughter I doubt they could have flogged a quotation out of their swingingest betting man because judging from Governor Reagan's impeccable record, the statisticians would have reasoned that it was inconceivable that he should make a mistake. [laughter] But, of course, it happens to everyone. I fully expect that someday I'll be wrong about something. [laughter] Ronald Reagan told me over the telephone last Sunday that he would treat me very kindly tonight as he would any friend of his suffering temporarily from a minor aberration. He does not, in other words, plan to send the Marines after me. Perhaps he is saving them to dispatch to Panama. [laughter] (p. 2)

Notice how Buckley used this passage to suggest that Reagan—who usually agrees with Buckley—was wrong in this instance. Furthermore, Buckley got the audience in the right frame of mind: He got them to laugh with him by mildly poking fun at himself—someday, maybe he'll be wrong Buckley demonstrated by this means that he is a "good guy"—someone likeable. Finally, Buckley got in a subtle dig at his opponent: Perhaps opposition to the treaties *would* require sending in the Marines.

In the next paragraph Buckley continued to establish his own credibility. He reminded that audience of his conservative credentials: his hawkish position on the Vietnam war, his general anticommunism. He showed solidarity with his conservative opponents, namely Reagan and the pro-Reagan examiners and advisers.

Having reinforced his personal credibility, Buckley next used the device of "prior refutation" to separate his position from that of other treaty supporters.

"Prior refutation" means to preempt an opponent's argument. Buckley does this by enumerating several pro-treaty arguments that he would *not* be using. By doing this he narrowed the range of protreaty arguments that Reagan might attack during this particular debate. In essence, he denied Reagan certain favorite arguments that the former governor used against liberal treaty supporters. Buckley stipulated that his protreaty stance did not represent, among other things, any general support for President Carter's foreign policy. Most importantly, however, Buckley disavowed the argument that our presence in Panama is a "last vestige of colonialism" (p. 3). In fact, said Buckley, colonialism is not such a bad thing. Finally, Buckley emphasized that he harbored no illusions about Panama or its dictator—both were unstable.

Having put considerable distance between himself and other more liberal treaty supporters, Buckley outlined his conservative case for ratification. He argued that "the United States, by signing these treaties, is better off militarily, is better off economically, and is better off spiritually" (p. 3). Buckley thus identified three areas of advantage to be gained through ratification. Each area amounted to a value and each was supported by a number of arguments.

In developing the question of military advantage, Buckley reasoned that American access to the canal would be enhanced if we were to have "the cooperation of the local population." Buckley argued that ownership of the canal was a matter of Panamanian pride. He then cited the example of Egypt, which closed the Suez Canal in 1967. He used this as a basis for the idea that if Panama continued to lack sovereignty over the canal, it might prefer to sabotage the canal—despite the economic loss.

Buckley's argument of economic advantage was based on the notion that the United States would still retain considerable revenue from tolls. He then specifically refuted the idea that the United States would be somehow paying Panama to take the canal off our hands. Buckley then examined American economic and military aid commitments totaling $60 million per year. These, he said, were small, compared to the billions in aid that we channel to Spain, Turkey, and the Philippines for the right to maintain military bases in those countries.

Making his final major point, Buckley argued a spiritual advantage—that by recognizing the need for sovereignty felt by a small nation, the people of the United States would gain satisfaction. This satisfaction would be based on the realization that we acted generously and in a manner consistent with our ideals. Buckley again coupled his positive point with a refutation. He disassociated himself from the claim—used by many treaty supporters—that the measure would gain us worldwide favor: "I happen to believe that the surest road to international prestige is to pay absolutely no heed whatsoever to foreign opinion" (p. 5).

Let me take a moment to comment upon Mr. Buckley's use of argument. His basic strategy was to connect a policy (ratification of the treaties) to values: military, economic, and spiritual gains. In so doing he employed a number of descriptive arguments: statistics to support his argument of economic advantage;

an example (Egypt) to support his military one. Buckley also used interpretive claims. This form of argument was particularly important in his effort to minimize, by means of comparison, the $60 million per year in aid to Panama. Buckley's three areas of advantage to be gained by the United States amounted to points that centered on the subject of dispute—as opposed to his opening, credibility-focused remarks.

Reagan for the Negative

Former Governor Reagan used his speech introduction to outline his twofold position in opposition to the treaties. First, he redefined the debate. Reagan argued that the question was not one of accepting or rejecting the treaties. Rather, he said, the available options included sending the treaties back for renegotiation. Secondly, Reagan contended that the treaties were "fatally flawed." The governor only touched on the first part of this position, spending almost all his time in listing defects in the two canal treaties.

Reagan initially elaborated his objections to the treaty giving Panama, by 1999, full ownership of and sovereignty over the canal. He observed that this treaty would replace the old 1903 treaty, having the effect of removing all special power for the United States in the Canal Zone. As a result, Reagan continued, Panama would be free to expropriate the canal immediately. Reagan noted the provisions against using force to recover expropriated property—provisions made in the United Nations charter. In this connection, he cited the examples of the unsuccessful British and French invasion of Egypt after President Nasser nationalized the Suez Canal.

Reagan next scrutinized the "second treaty"—i.e., the one guaranteeing the canal's neutrality after the year 2000. He contended that it was excessively ambiguous. For instance, he said, the treaty did not contain the word "guarantee." As a result, the United States would be forced to accept Panama's good faith. In this connection, Reagan noted that the treaty allowed other nations—e.g., the Soviet Union or Cuba—to become parties to the neutrality agreement. This, he maintained, would dilute America's power to use force or guarantee the canal's neutrality, because any party to the treaty could claim the same right.

Having outlined some theoretical ambiguities in the neutrality accord, the governor presented some testimony to illustrate the point. He compared explanations of the treaty made, on the one hand, by the American government to those made by Panama's chief treaty negotiator, Dr. Romulo Escobar Bethancourt. Reagan identified what he said were contradictions in the American and Panamanian interpretations of the treaty:

United States interpretation	Panama's interpretation
1 The United States can guarantee the neutrality of the canal.	1 The United States has no guarantee over Panama.
2 United States vessels have "head of the line" privileges in an emergency.	2 The United States is allowed "expeditious passage"—but no more than that.

Reagan's final major indictment of the treaty concerned the provision for joint Panamanian-American defense of the canal until 1999. To support his contention that there would be little cooperation, he cited a marching chant of the Panamanian National Guard: *Que muera gringo. Gringo abajo. Gringo al paredon.* (Death to the gringo. Down with the gringo. Gringo to the wall.)

Having examined the treaties, one by one, the governor next presented a narrative of the canal's history. He used this as a vehicle for refuting certain protreaty arguments.

Contending that history was being "rewritten by the State Department" (p. 7), Reagan hinted that banking interests supported the treaties for economic gain. He rejected the notion that the canal had lost its value, mentioning statistics to show that almost all the world's shipping could use it. Continuing, he presented a large set of additional observations, including these:

1 The canal is vital to national defense. Most high-ranking retired military officers opposed the treaties. Reagan suggested that retired officers are not subject to White House pressure and thus are "free to speak their minds" (p. 8).

2 The canal has never been sabotaged during four wars. True, he said, the canal cannot be defended *absolutely* against sabotage, but neither can the United States Capitol building be so defended.

3 The Canal Zone was not taken by force. Panama benefited from American intervention: We helped Panama to win independence from Colombia, and the building of the canal brought many economic and health advantages to Panama.

4 It is not true, as treaty supporters suggest, that "no Panamanian signed the 1903 treaty" (p. 8). Panama appointed a French citizen to be its representative, and the Panamanian government subsequently ratified the treaty.

Reagan concluded by offering alternatives to the treaties—such as giving more representation and land to Panama. He ended with the statement that the United States should have "no more yielding to threats of blackmail" (p. 10).

Overall, Reagan's approach differed from that of Buckley. The governor spent less time in developing his own credibility. He presented a far larger number of arguments, developing them less than Buckley did. Finally, unlike his opponent, who organized arguments around three advantages, Reagan's address was more loosely put together. The final section, in particular, consisted of an almost miscellaneous string of claims.

While the overall structure of his speech differed from Buckley's, Reagan used the same type of political arguments. He cited descriptive evidence— notably, the comparative statements of the American and Panamanian governments. In stressing the economic value of the canal, Reagan cited statistical confirmation about world shipping. As reflected in "additional observations" 3 and 4, Reagan's final historical narrative provides us with a clear illustration of the use of interpretation. Finally, by stressing the "dictatorial" nature of the Panamanian government and its use of "blackmail," the governor connected the treaty to values that are disapproved of by most Americans.

The Debate as an Exercise in Political Argument

I have described only the first two speeches of the Buckley-Reagan debate. Actually, the contest also involved a long period of cross-examination followed by two summary speeches. Taken by themselves, however, the two opening speeches reveal much about the nature of political argument.

First, as the debate makes clear, political argument concerns public policy. It deals with matters on which the public as a whole must make a decision. "What to do about the Panama Canal" was a question requiring an answer by the American people, acting through their elected representatives. In the debate at hand, ratification and nonratification amounted to alternative courses of action—alternative policy proposals. Each side used argument as a basis for winning support for its policy choice. Politics thus requires that an advocate stake out a clear position on an issue.[2] Both the debaters did this: Buckley argued for total ratification of the treaties; Reagan opted for total rejection, with the possibility of later minor concessions to Panama.

A second salient feature of policy argument is its emphasis on the future. Both debaters sought to predict the future implications of their policies. Buckley argued that by giving canal ownership and control to Panama, we would enhance American access to the canal. Continued operation of the canal would become a source of pride to Panama—rather than a source of humiliation. Reagan took the opposite tack. He contended that we had full access *now*. The treaty would make us dependent on something less certain—the good will of Panama. In this connection, both debaters made different assessments of the post–year 2000 neutrality treaty. Buckley contended that it gave us enough leverage to assure access; Reagan dissented from this view. As we can see, then, policy argument comes down to a matter of prediction: What will happen if we do X rather than Y?

In making predictions about the future, policy advocates rely on notions of what is probable, that is, likely to occur. In seeking to make their predictions seem likely, political arguers rely heavily on past precedent. It is not surprising, in this connection, that both Buckley and Reagan mentioned the history of Egypt's Suez Canal. Both used the history of the Egyptian waterway as a basis for predicting what the Panamanians would or would not do.

This probability feature of political argument is closely related to a fourth characteristic—that policy argument rests on a set of characteristic premises. These concern power, human nature, public good, and human rights. The whole debate, it is clear, turned on issues dealing with power. The ability of the United States to defend the canal and the power of Panama to deny access to the United States were both central questions. Human nature was used to make predictions of what would probably happen. The public good and human rights, together with other such premises, amount to the ultimate value of a policy.

---

[2]There is an exception to this requirement, of course. During campaigns for political office, candidates usually remain vague as to the policies they will pursue. This is because the major function of campaign rhetoric is that of establishing personal credibility.

Does it enhance good and right? Exactly whose goods and rights are enhanced?

Like advertising, public policy argument is a particular context in which claims are advanced. Political arguers draw from the same general stock of arguments as do other advocates; but political argument possesses characteristic features, owing to its focus on projection and its reliance on particular value premises.

ARGUMENT IN LAW: THE HOROWITZ CASE

Charlotte A. Horowitz was enrolled for two years as a medical student at the University of Missouri Medical School in Kansas City. In 1973 she was dismissed from the school for reasons of poor clinical practice, interpersonal relations, attendance, and hygiene, together with an alleged inability to accept criticism. Horowitz sued the school, contending that her Fourteenth Amendment rights to due process of law had been violated. She argued that she had been dismissed without a formal hearing on the matter of her alleged academic weaknesses. The school maintained that it had acted reasonably.

The Horowitz case made its way gradually through the federal court system. Finally, in 1978, the U.S. Supreme Court decided the issue in favor of the medical school. The Court's decision was justified in a majority opinion written by Justice William Rehnquist. This opinion represents an instance of legal argumentation. In the next few pages, I want to take a closer look at it.[3]

The Descriptive Roots of a Legal Opinion

The first section of the Supreme Court opinion amounts to a recitation of the events in question. *Board of Curators of the University of Missouri v. Charlotte Horowitz* begins with factual statements—claims that could be independently verified.

Justice Rehnquist chose the chronological method of organization in detailing the facts of the case. He began with the medical school's requirement for clinical work in areas such as pediatrics. He noted that the student's work is "evaluated on a periodic basis by the Council on Evaluation." This group was composed of faculty and students. It had power to "recommend various actions including probation and dismissal." Rehnquist further explained that the council's recommendations were reviewed by a faculty coordinating committee, with the final decision resting with the dean of the college. Rehnquist observed that a student was not usually allowed to appear before the council or the committee.

Having outlined the medical school's procedures, Rehnquist turned to the history of Horowitz's particular dismissal. It seems that she had received some bad marks in clinical practice during her first year in school. She was advanced to

---

[3] I will be relying on the transcript of the majority opinion as reprinted in *The Chronicle of Higher Education*, March 6, 1978, pp. 13–14.

the second year by the evaluation council—although only on a "probationary basis." Rehnquist noted that faculty dissatisfaction with Horowitz's clinical skills "continued during the following year." He cited a midyear review of Horowitz. The evaluation council recommended that she not be graduated and, further, that she be dismissed altogether, barring "radical improvement."

In the final paragraphs of his factual case review, Rehnquist enumerated the review and appeals procedures that followed this unfavorable assessment:

1 Horowitz was allowed to work with seven practicing physicians, who were to make assessments of her clinical performance. Two recommended that she be graduated on schedule, two said that she should be dropped from the school immediately, and three suggested a further probationary period.

2 In mid-May the evaluation council met again. On the basis of continued unfavorable clinical reports, the Council decided not to permit Horowitz to reenroll.

3 The faculty coordinating committee and dean approved this recommendation.

4 After an appeal by Horowitz, the university provost for health sciences "sustained the School's actions."

The Court's Judicial Reasoning

Having established the series of events leading up to Charlotte Horowitz's dismissal, Rehnquist now sought to justify the Court's decision in favor of the medical school.

The crux of Horowitz's suit was her contention that the school's actions had violated the rights given to her by the Fourteenth Amendment to the Constitution: "nor shall any State deprive any person of life, liberty, or property, without due process of law." Mr. Rehnquist moved immediately to outline the crucial issues raised by Horowitz's claim and the school's defense.

First of all, Rehnquist pointed out that for two reasons the Court had no need to decide whether Horowitz had been deprived of property by the medical school:

1 "Respondent [Horowitz] has never alleged that she was deprived of a property interest."

2 Rehnquist cited a 1972 Supreme Court decision holding that "property interests are creatures of state law." In other words, the state government is the agency with power to decide whether a place in a medical school constitutes a property interest. Hence, Horowitz would have to demonstrate that the state had so acted.

Rehnquist next confronted the issue of whether or not Horowitz had been deprived of liberty. He cited several cases in which the Supreme Court had considered similar claims. In these cases the Court held that job dismissals did not constitute a deprivation of liberty. The Court reasoned here that the dismissed employee was free to seek other employment and, unless the reasons for dismissal were publicized, the dismissal would not impede a person from obtaining another job. Rehnquist noted the medical school's claim that it had not publicized Horowitz's academic weaknesses.

At this point Rehnquist redefined the dispute. He turned from the question of whether Horowitz had been denied liberty, focusing now on whether or not the deprivation had been in accordance with due process. Here Rehnquist stated a judgment that Horowitz "has been awarded at least as much due process as the Fourteenth Amendment requires." Rehnquist identified due process as the central issue in dispute. The remainder of the Court's opinion is an effort to justify the conclusion that if any deprivation occurred, it took place with sufficient due process.

In the next page or so, I will outline some of Rehnquist's due process contentions. Notice how his arguments involve a mixture of past precedents and general principles.

I   The school informed Horowitz as to the "faculty's dissatisfaction with her clinical progress and the danger that this posed to timely graduation and continued enrollment."

II   Horowitz received procedural due process.

   A   The school exceeded due process requirements by allowing Horowitz to be observed by seven outside physicians.

   B   In *Gross v. Lopez* the Supreme Court held that in disciplinary matters due process requires a school to give a student an "opportunity to present his side of the story."

      1   The Federal Appeals Court (which ruled in favor of Horowitz) incorrectly interpreted *Gross v. Lopez* to require a formal hearing.

      2   Actually, due process would require only an "informal give-and-take" between the administration and the student.

      3   In *Cafeteria Workers v. McElroy,* the Supreme Court held that to require a hearing in all such cases would impose an inflexible procedure.

   C   There is a significant difference between a disciplinary dismissal and dismissal for academic reasons. Therefore, an academic dismissal would call for "far less stringent procedural requirements" than removal for reasons of discipline.

      1   State and lower federal courts have recognized the difference between academic and disciplinary dismissal. This is evidenced in numerous judgments.

      2   "Reason, furthermore, clearly supports the perception of these decisions."

         a   "A school is an academic institution, not a courtroom or administrative hearing room."

         b   In *Gross v. Lopez* the Supreme Court recognized the similarity between school discipline and other legal proceedings. Hence, the Court required that a student be given an opportunity to state his or her own side of the matter.

    (1) "Even in the context of a school disciplinary proceeding, however, the Court stopped short of requiring a *formal* hearing."

    (2) This is because such a hearing may be too costly and disruptive in the educational setting.

  c In contrast to a hearing for misconduct, an academic evaluation bears "little resemblance to the judicial and administrative factfinding procedures to which we [Supreme Court] have traditionally attached a full hearing requirement."

    (1) In *Gross v. Lopez,* fact finding was useful in answering such questions as whether or not the student did disrupt class, attack a policeman, and so on.

    (2) An academic evaluation is more of a subjective, expert judgment. It is more like "the decision of an individual professor" in awarding the proper course grade.

III "Under such circumstances, we [the Court] decline to ignore the historic judgment of educators and thereby formalize the academic dismissal process by requiring a hearing."

  A "The educational process is not by nature adversarial; instead it centers around a continuing relationship between faculty and students."

  B In *Gross v. Lopez* the Supreme Court held "that the value of some form of hearing in a disciplinary context outweighs any resulting harm to the academic environment."

  C The Court stated that to require a hearing in academic matters would "risk deterioration of many beneficial aspects of the faculty-student relationship."

  D The Court cited two additional points.

    1 As the Massachusetts Supreme Court stated, such a hearing may be useless in learning about scholarship.

    2 Our nation is committed to the notion that the public school system should be locally controlled.

The Use of Argument in the Decision

As I have observed, the interesting feature of the Court's opinion is the mixture of precedent-based and principle-based argument. Rehnquist cited relevant portions of previous cases to establish several of his arguments. For instance, the precedents of several judgments were cited to establish the distinction between a dismissal based on academic grounds as opposed to one reached on disciplinary grounds. Testimony—in the form of past court decisions—is a major basis of legal argument.

    However, Rehnquist did not simply rely on past rulings; he made every effort to justify the rulings. After citing precedents to establish the academic dismissal versus disciplinary dismissal distinction, he sought to use reason to support this traditional legal interpretation. Rehnquist's reasons included both interpretations and evaluations:

Interpretations

   1   "A school is an academic institution, not a courtroom or administrative hearing room."

   2   Academic evaluation "bears little resemblance to . . . judicial and administrative factfinding procedures."

   3   An academic evaluation is like a professor's expert decision about a course grade.

Evaluations

   1   In *Gross v. Lopez* the Supreme Court decided "that the value of some form of hearing outweighs any resulting harm to the academic environment."

   2   To require a hearing in academic matters would "risk deterioration of many beneficial aspects of the faculty-student relationship."

Here we can see the use of comparisons, analogies, and cause-effect–based assertions. It is apparent that Rehnquist devoted considerable effort in making the decision against Horowitz appear sensible and, indeed, inevitable. He strove to make understandable the distinction between an academic and a discipline-based dismissal. Legal argument is not, then, simply the application of law (statutes and rulings) to the circumstances of each case. It also involves the use of argument to justify a decision as being reasonable. Interpretations and evaluations are key elements of judicial justifying.

   In sum, we can see that the Supreme Court majority opinion was based on the whole range of argumentative forms. Descriptive arguments were cited to provide the factual basis. Further descriptive argument included testimony in the form of court precedent. However, legal argument is more than the automatic application of law to facts of a case: Legal decisions require interpretive and evaluative claims.

ARGUMENT IN NEWS REPORTING:
PERSUADING THE "INFORMED" PUBLIC

How do you react when you pick up your newspaper or tune in the evening news? Do you rant about the biased, stupid media, or do you consult them to see "what the news is"?

   I pose this question because today's news readers and watchers react in a variety of ways to "the media." Some people look at news reports as being relatively factual accounts of the world. Others see the media as biased. Still others—and I am included—view news reporting as a simultaneous exercise in informing and persuading. No matter what your orientation toward the media, I think that you will find it helpful to look at the role of argument in reporting. To view the reporter's job as inherently persuasive is to develop an understanding of what is going on in the media.

News Is an Exercise in Persuasion

In a few minutes I will retire to the family room and tune in the C.B.S. Evening News. I will listen and watch while Walter Cronkite, or someone else, reads "the news"; I will watch as pictures are flashed on the screen; and I will turn my gaze to a magazine, from time to time, as the usual run of commercials appears. This scenario of news watching probably is familiar to most readers. But let's back up a bit and "replay" this situation from the newscaster's point of view.

During the day wire service reports have passed over news editors' desks. Film crews have sent in clips of certain of the day's (and previous day's) happenings. There is more news available than can possibly be shown in the approximately 24 minutes available (after commercials). Beyond this, the commentator may desire to air a feature story that has been in the works for some time.

You probably realize what I am leading up to. Managing editor Walter Cronkite needs to *select* what will be aired and what will not be aired. This editorial selection is the first reason that news reporting is an inherently argumentative enterprise. Like any other persuader, the editor includes some information and excludes other. This decision will have consequences for the viewer. It will shape the viewer's image of reality.

There is a second and closely related factor that renders news reporting persuasive. In addition to including or excluding events, news editors and reporters maximize certain happenings and minimize others. In short, they communicate a point of view about the day's events. Let me give you an example. In January 1978 President Carter visited several foreign countries. His trip began in Poland. During Mr. Carter's arrival there, the State Department–supplied translator made a number of miscues. For instance, he used a Polish word having the connotation of "lust" in translating the President's statement that he was happy to be visiting Poland. These slips received considerable media attention. A couple of days later, during the visit to India, Mr. Carter was caught off guard by a news microphone. He was heard to remark privately to an aide that after returning to Washington he would have to compose a very "cold" and "blunt" letter to the Indian prime minister on the matter of American uranium shipments. (Carter was unhappy about India's reluctance to accept inspection of its nuclear plants.) Again, the faux pas became the centerpiece of reports on Carter's India stop.

The editorial choice to feature incidents such as the above had an effect in shaping perceptions of the Carter trip. In this way, it had a persuasive impact. Reports of this kind reduced the extent to which the trip was favorably received. Insofar as they imparted a comic flavor to the trip, the decision to feature the miscues was relevant to public attitudes.

Consider a third reason that news reporting is a persuasive act. Reporters tend to use credibility-boosting devices to enhance their message. In chapter 7, I emphasized that credibility-enhancement was a major persuasive tool. Indeed, in my earlier description of William Buckley's speech for ratification of the

Panama Canal treaty, I noted his use of credibility-centered appeals. I noted that such arguments helped to advance Buckley's overall argumentative position.

It is not difficult to detect credibility devices in news reports. An observation about print journalism will illustrate the point. You may notice that news magazines add an air of authority by the use of "you-are-there" realism. This lead-in from *Newsweek* (May 1, 1978, p. 33) shows what I mean.

> The trial was in its third day in the ornate high-ceiling courtroom in Macon, Ga., when U.S. District Judge Wilbur Owens ordered the lights turned off. A technician switched on seven television monitors placed on tables around the courtroom, and the videotaped testimony of the star witness began. Attorneys for the prosecution began the questioning.
> "Would you please, sir, state for the record your full name?"
> "James Earl Carter, Jr."
> "And you are now the sitting President of the United States?"
> "I am."

The story dealt with Carter's testimony in a Georgia political conspiracy trial. This passage, however, reads like something out of a novel. It communicates a feeling that the reporter is completely knowledgeable about the subject. Kahane (1976, pp. 195–196) notes the rhetorical effect of such linguistic realism. The use of minute detail adds believability to the reporters' overall conclusions. If the authors are able to report the exact number and placement of television monitors, then surely they must be right when they assert (*Newsweek*, May 1, 1978, p. 33) that "for Jimmy Carter, the proceedings turned out to be something of an embarrassment." (Despite Carter's testimony that the defendant, a state official, had attempted to bribe him, the official was acquitted.) Notice that the interpretation about what the testimony meant to Carter is stated with a certainty equal to that used in describing the "ornate ceiling." The realism used to present the physical setting thus imparts an aura of force to the wider generalizations; yet from the standpoint of validity, accuracy about television facilities does not strengthen a claim about the overall implications of the testimony.

In sum, it becomes clear that news reporters argue—just as anyone else does. They do not merely report incidents; they interpret and evaluate them for us. This is made clear in almost any news report that one collects. A report on the kidnapping and assassination of Italian former Premier Aldo Moro (*Courier-Journal*, May 10, 1978, p. A16) contained both factual news and argument. The reporter referred to the "dark gray suit" worn by the victim but also advanced a particular—and quite bold—interpretation of the Moro incident: "Before it was clear that Moro had been killed, the kidnapping itself united Italians more than at any time since the end of World War II." The reporter must have viewed his interpretive claim as having the same intuitive validity as his description of the victim's suit, because no supporting arguments are given. Does so sweeping an assessment of the kidnapping amount to "news," or is it simply argument?

The Media Make News as well as Report It

Despite the inherently persuasive nature of news reporting, the media do make an effort to be objective. This is a laudable aim. Journalistic objectivity is an effort to set oneself apart from the events one observes. This act of setting oneself apart is a necessary ingredient of judgment, as I have noted elsewhere. But there is a problem here: Reporters are not separate from the events they relate. Objectivity, then, is a goal, not a reality of new reporting. The journalist and the news are closely connected; this overlap of reporter and reported occurs both subtly and blatantly.

The subtle overlap of news reporter and news events is unavoidable. This is because a news reporter becomes part of "what is going on." In late 1977 and early 1978, there was a nationwide coal strike. A settlement was reached between management and the United Mine Workers. This was duly reported. However, news reporters like to predict news as well as to relate it, so many interviews were conducted on television to determine whether or not the coal miners would ratify the contract. Most of those interviewed expressed sentiments against the contract. Once these interviews were telecast, they became a part of the coal strike event. The interviews contributed to a growing image that the contract would be rejected (which it was). In this situation, the news reports did not merely reflect what was happening; the reports helped to shape what was happening.

I am not the first person to realize that news reports contribute to ongoing events. This has been known for some time. For this reason people who want to make a point use the media to communicate that point: Stories are "planted" with reporters. An interesting case in point is related by Craig Smith (1977). Smith describes the effort by an in-law of Edward M. Kennedy to start a "Teddy Boomlet" at the 1968 Democratic convention. Apparently, the in-law "fed" the media a story to the effect that Kennedy would consider accepting the nomination. The story goes that Kennedy actually had not made this decision. According to Smith (1977, p. 155), the in-law "used the reporter to start the 'boom' in hopes that the movement would persuade Kennedy to seek the nomination." In this situation false information was leaked for the purpose of influencing events. Smith comments, "It was a case of news in reverse: a source using a reporter to create a news event."

Instances such as this mark the transition point between the subtle and blatant mixing of news and news reports. The overlap becomes even more blatant when the media simulate news. In the 1950s there was a program called "You Are There." In it correspondents interviewed famous persons during reenactments of past events. My memories of the show are vague, but I recall persons such as George Washington, who was "interviewed" during a Revolutionary War battle.

Everyone realized, of course, that such "interviews" were only dramatic reenactments. However, there is evidence that some of today's news programs use film that also records simulated happenings—reenactments passed off as legitimate, spontaneous occurrences. The Advisory Commission on Civil

Disorders (*Report of the National Advisory Commission on Civil Disorders,* 1968, p. 377) related one such incident. The commission alleged that "a New York newspaper photographer covering the Newark riot repeatedly urged and finally convinced a Negro boy to throw a rock for the camera." The "Walker Report" on violence associated with the Democrats' 1968 Chicago convention alleged similar press reenactments. One of these was reported by former U.S. Senator Gale McGee (*Rights in Conflict,* 1968, p. 303), who saw a television crew lead two girls over to some National Guard troops. The girls then began to shout "Don't beat me" as the cameras rolled.

One does not know how prevalent these reenactments are. However, I believe that simulated news is more common than we think. Many of us have witnessed events that have been restaged by a public relations director because the original didn't get on film. I can imagine that the Newark and Chicago reenactments were similarly easy to rationalize. The reporter had only to say to himself: "Things *like* this *are* happening; but I didn't get any on film; so it's not really a distortion to reenact such a scene." Thus, the distinction between opinion and fact, between fact and fiction, is broken down. Considering what we know, it is not so surprising that some people believe that the moon walks were simulated in a television studio.

Some General Problems of Media Rhetoric

In the last two sections, my intent was to establish the point that news reporting is an exercise in persuasion. In this connection, let me make two comments in defense of the press: (1) the media's self-imposed effort to "tell it like it is" represents a laudable response to the innate subjectivity of the business, and (2) it is clear that today's news reports are, on the whole, better than they used to be. Nevertheless, real problems remain. In this discussion I have already alluded to certain validity debits in media-based news argument. These include sham credibility devices and faked testimony (i.e., simulated film events).

In the past twenty years, numerous additional criticisms have been launched against the argumentative techniques of news reporting. I do not have the space here to do justice to these analyses, so I will simply list a few of the major objections, in the hope that you may pursue the question further.

	Objection	Possible implication
1	News reporting is a business.	Television news is "jazzed up" to attract high ratings. Print news is influenced by the desires of the advertisers.
2	News reports are quite brief.	Space limitations may lead to superficiality and to distortion.
3	Presently, there is no good definition of "news."	The extreme and controversial gets relatively more coverage than the commonplace. Today's happenings are featured to the exclusion of historical perspective.
4	The media desire to identify and maintain a theme in the news.	The news may be shaped to fit a viewpoint that is hastily imposed upon events.

ARGUMENT IN SCIENCE: B. F. SKINNER
ON FREEDOM AND DIGNITY

Weaver (1970) has called "science" a "god term." In doing this Weaver is attesting to the public's favorable attitude toward the enterprise of science. Of course, there are some individual scientists and sciences that each of us do not like. But "science," per se, is well regarded.

Public reverence for science is built in part upon a notion of the nature of science and in part upon a view of scientists themselves. For most people the term "science" connotes "collected knowledge." Perhaps it also suggests the pursuit of knowledge and the application of new knowledge to human problems. Scientists accordingly are those who do the collecting and pursuing and applying. They are intelligent, objective, articulate, and open-minded.

Such utopian views of science are diminishing, as is the notion of scientist-as-superman. One does not need to read heavily in the philosophy of science to detect this movement. One can trace these developments in popular periodicals such as *Psychology Today*. The May 1978 issue of this magazine contained a review of the controversy over "sociobiology" (Pines, 1978, pp. 23–24). Those who favor the view of sociobiology contended that many human traits are built into our genes: Some bad traits may be inborn. Some liberal-left groups attack this approach because it suggests that social problems cannot be removed by changing people's environment. This view is also vulnerable because of its close association to Nazi race theories. Hence, sociobiology has been called "racist" and "sexist," among other things.

What of scientists? They are not immune from attack, either. The April 1976 issue of *Psychology Today* contains an article (Mahoney, 1976) that casts doubt on the popular reverence toward the women and men of science. Mahoney cited findings to the effect that scientists score no better than others in tests designed to measure reasoning. Further, he reported his own test of scientific objectivity. He sent out variations of a psychological article for review. The results showed that "our scientific reviewers tended to recommend the article [for publication] only when it supported their positions" (p. 65). He then went on to cite interviews and anecdotes that cast doubt on the open-mindedness and humility of research professionals.

What we have here is a growing awareness that science is an exercise in argument, coupled with a view of the scientist as an advocate for a certain position. I will now sketch out a few more reasons that science is persuasive, and I will cite B. F. Skinner's defense of "behaviorism" as a case in point.

Science as a Context for Argument

My introduction to the preceding section of this chapter has already set the tone for this one. I view science not so much as a collection of knowledge but as a body of arguments. Seen from this perspective the people of science become arguers. Before I launch into a case analysis of Skinner's scientific argument, I believe that it is necessary for me to elaborate a bit on the notion of science as a context for argument. It would be presumptious for me to claim the "science is argument" view as being my own, because this is an increasingly widespread view. However, let me lay out for you some of the tenets of this view.

Weizenbaum (1976) contends that scientific proofs and explanations constitute arguments. He makes his point as follows: (1) a scientist must believe in what he is doing; hence, (2) he assumes a position with respect to his subject matter; (3) he then seeks to convince others of the truth of what he has found; and therefore, (4) scientific statements are not infallible—only things accepted by scientists, for the time being, on the basis of argument. Weizenbaum (1976, p. 15) is deliberate in his choice of the term "argument" to describe the scientific enterprise: "I choose the word 'argument' thoughtfully, for scientific demonstrations, even mathematical proofs, are fundamentally acts of persuasion." Weizenbaum's thesis is illustrated in an essay on Charles Darwin (1809–1882), one of the founders of the theory of evolution. (See Campbell, 1975.) Darwin's theory of evolution, in its original form, was based, partly, on extended analogies drawn between animal breeding and natural selection.

If we accept Weizenbaum's statement, then, despite its complexity, science comes down to a particular kind of argument. This view is supported by another notion of argument, which can be drawn from chapter 1. In chapter 1, I pointed out that arguments rest on assumptions (subarguments) that are accepted by the audience. This is also true in the case of science. Any specific science—such as biology—rests on a set of assumptions that are accepted by biological researchers.

Take another example: sociology. In 1976, Alfred McClung, president of the American Sociological Association (*The Chronicle of Higher Education,* September 7, 1976, p. ?), pointed out that sociologists are "socialized" as graduate students into the profession. They learn what is accepted and not accepted by their professors. Over a period of time, through interpersonal influence, graduate students are induced to accept their teachers' view of things. (You will recall from chapter 7 that interpersonal influence is one of the basic ways of looking at persuasion.) Therefore, we can say that young sociologists gradually are persuaded to accept the main assumptions (arguments) of their field.

This process of scientific persuasion continues throughout the career of any scientist. Scientists engage in research, which is then published. How do you suppose a scientist's work is selected for publication? In the main, it is selected after review by a panel of fellow scientists: To be accepted, a scholarly article must win favor from its audience; strong arguments are necessary. Once published, a piece of research is read by members of the scientific community. This marks a second reason why scientists must complete their research with an audience in mind. If a scientist deviates too much from the prevailing assumptions of his field, he risks loss of respectability. Hence, scientific work is published only when the scientist persuades the reviewers. The work is accepted as legitimate only when it persuades the general audience of readers.

Science, then, meets all the tests for an argumentative enterprise. It is a process by which advocates take positions on a subject and present arguments to justify the position. These arguments are presented with a view toward winning acceptance from the audience. The audience possesses a set of preexisting assumptions and uses these assumptions as a basis for evaluating a scientific message.

At this point it is necessary for me to add one qualification to this interpretation of science. Let us back up a bit and take a further look at scientific assumptions. What are they, anyway? Kuhn (1970, pp. 10–11) uses the term "paradigm" to denote basic assumptions made by scientists. A paradigm is a body of theory that defines (1) the important research questions and (2) the appropriate research methods to be used in a field of science. Paradigms are "traditions of scientific research" that attract "an enduring group of adherents" and allow supporters to pursue further research.

Kuhn's notion of the paradigm is useful in understanding the upcoming discussion of B. F. Skinner's argumentation. Skinner is a psychologist who was instrumental in beginning a "tradition of scientific research" in psychology. This tradition, called "behaviorism," is not the only way of looking at people. There are other, competing schools of psychological thought. Skinner's 1971 book, *Beyond Freedom and Dignity,* can be seen partly as an effort to justify the behavioral paradigm of psychology. His audience is one of scientists and the educated general public. His purpose is to persuade us to accept behaviorism and reject the alternative ways of looking at psychological man.

Exactly what Skinner means by "behaviorism" will become clearer as I proceed. My purpose is to lay out his argument—not to expound on Skinner's overall philosophy. Consequently, I will confine my presentation to the first chapter of *Beyond Freedom and Dignity.*

Skinner's Case for Behaviorism

What follows is an outline of Skinner's basic case (1971, pp. 1–23). I want you to look for two things as you read over the outline: (1) what the arguments mean and (2) the argumentative strategies used by Skinner. I will comment upon them shortly.

I Mankind has made little progress in understanding the actions of people—human behavior. In the last 2500 years, however, the fields of physics and biology have made great progress.
  A Modern physics and biology have gone far beyond the primitive theories of the classical Greeks.
  B "[B]ut the dialogues of Plato are still assigned to students as if they threw light on human behavior" (Skinner, 1971, p. 3).
  C In fact, Plato would have no trouble understanding most discussions of human affairs, but the classical Greeks could not comprehend a page of modern physics or biology.
II All of this suggests that Greek notions of human behavior had a "fatal flaw."
  A Greek physics and biology have led to modern science.

B But "Greek theories of human behavior led nowhere" (p. 4). This suggests not that "they possessed some kind of eternal verity," but that Greek psychology "did not contain the seeds of anything better."

III To understand human behavior, we need to apply to it the modern methods of science.

  A The early Greeks explained physical movement in a prescientific way. They believed that an object—e.g., a rock—moved because it "wanted" to move. "According to Butterfield, Aristotle argued that a falling body accelerated because it grew more jubilant as it found itself nearer home" (p. 6).

  B Today, physics and biology have "abandoned explanations of this sort" (p. 5).

  C But in the field of human action, we still cling to notions of internal purpose. "Almost everyone attributes human behavior to intentions, purposes, aims, and goals" (p. 6).

  D If the notion of purpose does not really explain the movement of objects, there is reason to question whether it explains human movement.

IV The prescientific view holds that a mental state (e.g., attitudes toward children) is the cause of a person's behavior (e.g., large families).

  A But the mental view does not explain how the mind controls the body.

  B A second more significant disadvantage of mentalism is that it makes behavior secondary. Behavior is viewed as being only a symptom of an inner mental state. In other words, some people use "inner man" as an explanation for "outer man."

   1 People tend to do this because we assume that there are no understandable physical antecedents for many human actions.

   2 But offering "inner man" as an explanation is no real explanation. It makes behavior something "miraculous" (p. 12).

V Let us reject this path of "ignorance" and "follow the path taken by physics and biology" (p. 12). Let us avoid internal mediating states (such as "feelings") and look "directly to the relation between behavior and the environment" (p. 12). It is environment, not feelings, that produces the tendency to act.

VI There are reasons that it has taken mankind "so long to reach this point" (p. 13).

  A The fact that people behave differently from objects has made us look to "inner man" rather than physical causes.

  B The fact that people think that they experience feelings is another reason.

  C "There is a much more important reason why we have been so slow in discarding mentalistic explanations: it has been hard to find alternatives. . . . The effect of the environment on behavior remained obscure" for a long time (p. 14).

VII Now the science of "behaviorism" has emerged.

  A Its central principle is this: "Behavior is shaped and maintained by its consequences" (p. 16). That is, we behave to gain a reward. When rewarded for a behavior we tend to repeat it.

  B Behaviorism has two important results.

1 In the laboratory we can study behavior systematically by arranging experiments in which a behavior has some type of result.

2 In society people have the power to manipulate the environment to produce changes in human behavior.

VIII Admittedly, the use of behavioral technology to modify society raises objections.

The rest of Skinner's book represents an effort to answer those objections.

What can we learn about scientific argument from Skinner's case? Initially, let us take a look at Skinner's method of argument. Probably, you noticed that Skinner's argument (contentions 1 through 3) is based heavily on analogy. His position goes something like this:

> Greek physics was based on the internal feelings of objects.
> We have rejected Greek physics.
> Greek psychology was based on the internal feelings of people.
> Therefore, we should reject Greek psychology.

Central to the validity of this analogy is his assertion (in contention II, subpoint B) that the tenacity of Greek-based "mentalism" does not result from its continued validity. This argument in turn falls back upon the Greek physics–Greek psychology analogy (i.e., modern physics has gone beyond Greek physics, but modern psychology has not advanced much beyond the Greeks).

Skinner continues his case in contention IVB by examining alleged bad effects of mentalism: (1) It subordinates behavior, and (2) it relies on "miracles." Skinner then equates mentalism to "ignorance," thus raising a value issue (contention V). Finally, in contention VI Skinner refutes three objections to behaviorism. In the remainder of the book he deals with others.

Skinner's position in favor of behaviorism is a classic model of scientific argumentation. He believes in his position. He amasses descriptive, interpretive, and evaluative arguments. He presents his arguments, seeking to win over an audience: the community of scholars interested in human beings, together with the educated general public. Like any paradigm, behaviorism is not a certainty. Skinner's position can be and has been challenged. Opponents defend the contributions of "mentalistic" approaches and point to problems in Skinner's system. In sum, behaviorism's validity rests on the extent to which its supporters and opponents qualify their claims in view of the arguments. The discussion on this matter continues today.

ARGUMENT IN LITERATURE:
THE RHETORICAL ROOTS OF *ROOTS*

In book form and as a television special, Alex Haley's *Roots* was a high point of the 1976–1977 reading and viewing season. *Roots,* which depicted the experience in slavery of Haley's family, touched a deep emotional chord in many viewers.

Most Americans were aware of the institution of slavery as a fact; but in portraying slavery as part of a family's real background, *Roots* acted persuasively. Through minimization and maximization, it modified the viewers' image of black history.

Roots is an historical novel. Many of its characters actually existed. Furthermore, Haley made an effort to make his work consistent with the known history of the period. Yet in presenting his family story, Haley used a literary format, employing characterization, dialogue, and narration to tell the story.

Works of fiction[4] do not merely entertain. The author of a novel or other fictional work seeks, as well, to teach the audience. *Roots* is a good example of the use of literature to persuade. The argument of a literary work is somewhat more subtle than that of a speech or essay. In a speech the arguer states a position and presents specific arguments to support it: "1, 2, 3. . . ." Literary devices of argument are less explicit. However, as Corbett (1969, p. xx) notes, the literary author labors to make a point. The author works "behind the scenes manipulating various elements in order to influence our reactions to events, emotions, thoughts, and characters in the work."

The "elements" of argument in *Roots* are many. Perhaps the most important of these is point of view. In *Roots* we see racial relations from the perspective of blacks. Both in narration and dialogue, the reader sees events through the eyes of Kunta Kinte (Haley's African ancestor) and Kunta's descendants. Haley is fully aware of the significance of point of view, for on the concluding page of *Roots* (1976, p. 688), he expresses the hope that "this story of our people can help to alleviate the legacies of the fact that preponderantly the histories have been written by the winners."

In addition to point of view, Haley advances his position by the use of characterization, dialogue, and narration. Haley's black characters represent dignity and strength. Their white opposites are either deliberately brutal or are unknowingly guilty of participation in a corrupt system. Both dialogue and narration allow Haley to tell black history the way *he* sees it.

Let me now touch on the story of *Roots,* making clear both Haley's position and how he argues it.

Kunta Kinte's Life in Africa

Traditionally, Americans have viewed Africa as a "dark continent" inhabited by savage peoples. Haley's first major effort in *Roots* is to revise this view of black America's African antecedents. In the first 150 pages of the book, Haley describes life in the village of Juffure near the Gambia River. Through the eyes of Kunta Kinte, we see the Mandinka people as having a high civilization. We

---

[4]There is some difficulty in categorizing *Roots.* Because the story is based on historical research, there is a basis for assigning it to the province of nonfiction. On the other hand, most of the details and dialogue are Haley's own creation. Haley terms the work "faction." He notes (1976, p. 686) that "since I wasn't yet around when most of the story occurred, by far most of the dialogue and most of the incidents are of necessity a novelized amalgam of what I *know* took place together with what my research led me to plausibly *feel* took place."

see the villagers as a happy people, despite their many hardships. More importantly, however, narration and dialogue reveal them to be a noble people worthy of respect and admiration.

In the first part of the book, Haley focuses on the training that the Mandinka youth received. Time and time again, Haley, the narrator, writes of the good "Mandinka home training." Haley tells us that home training produced in the young such admirable traits as honesty, dignity, respect for others, and, overall, good manners. Haley gives even more emphasis to the manhood training received by boys. Kunta Kinte's society gave important hunting and protection roles to men. Through manhood training boys were given additional necessary lessons in strength, courage, and wisdom.

Kunta Kinte's upbringing gives the reader much insight into Mandinka ways. Further, through Kunta Kinte's eyes we view the whole fabric of a well-developed culture. Clearly, this description is at considerable variance with the stereotype of savage Africa. The Mandinka people are seen as a religious people. They are Moslem, and Haley intersperses references to the village's religious customs. Juffure also possessed a well-fashioned system of government. We observe the village council as it does its administrative and legal work. Through Kunta we see that the Mandinka are a people of fair laws. Widening his perspective, Haley tells us (1976, p. 53) of the "great Mandinka Empire" of which Kunta's village is but a part. The Mandinka people revere education as well. Haley describes the educational system. Reading and writing are taught to the children, beginning at age 5. Haley reinforces the significance of education for the Mandinka through anecdotes. For instance, during a visit to a village founded by his uncles, Kunta sees the honor paid to the *marabout*—the holy teacher.

Haley's vision of the Mandinka of Kunta's time is coupled with favorable references to their past. During the manhood training, the students are treated to a visit by a *griot*—an oral historian. The *griot* relates to the boys stories of the great black empires in Benin, Ghana, and Mali. All of this happened, the *griot* emphasized, "long before the toubob [white man] ever put his foot in Africa" (Haley, 1976, p. 102). Apart from general African history, we learn specific details about Kunta Kinte's own noble ancestry: his grandfather, the holy man; his well-known uncles; his respected father.

In the opening thirty-two chapters of *Roots,* Haley supplies us with a vision of a sophisticated and orderly society. Kunta's people have a proud history. Through strong family and tribal institutions, the Mandinkas acquire and pass on noble traits. This description of Juffure accords fully with Haley's argumentative purpose. His intent is to emphasize the quality of early black Africa—to create, in his words, "a hypothetical Eden" (*Newsweek,* April 25, 1977, p. 87).

It seems to me that Haley has at least two additional purposes in the opening chapters of *Roots:* (1) to minimize the fact that the Mandinkas themselves held slaves and (2) to picture the white man from the African blacks' point of view.

Haley uses a number of scenes to point out differences between Mandinka slavery and the white man's brand of enslavement. The most important of these (p. 52) occurs when the young Kunta asks his father, "Fa, what are slaves?" Kunta's father, Omoro, begins by explaining that "slaves aren't always easy to tell from those who aren't slaves." In the dialogue that follows, Haley identifies some of the salient features of slavery in The Gambia. Slaves are "all respected persons." Except for those enslaved because of a criminal act, they could not be beaten, nor could the slaves be sold unless they "approved of the intended master" (p. 53). Other features of Mandinka slave life included their ability to marry into the owner's family, together with their ability to buy freedom. Lest the reader miss the point of all this, Haley has Omoro later emphasize (p. 59) that there exists a "difference between slaves among ourselves and those whom toubob takes away to be slaves for him." According to Omoro this difference lay in the horrible treatment accorded the captives of the whites.

Haley's use of a literary point of view to portray the white man is another striking feature of the early passages in *Roots*—and one that continues throughout the book. We listen and watch with Kunta as he learns about the "hairy, red-faced, strange-looking white man whose big canoes stole people away from their homes" (p. 21). Kunta first encounters the white man in his mother's stories. Be good, she says, or "I will bring the toubob" Later references picture the whites as ugly, smelly, soft, easily fooled, quarrelsome, cruel, deceitful, sexually immoral, and generally disrespectful. Of course, Haley is presenting a stereotype of the slave trader; but the description seems plausible as we watch with Kunta and perceive the white man from afar.

There is another, related theme in black-white relations that Haley introduces via his early overall characterization of whites. With Kunta we overhear deliberations of the village council of elders as they consider the marauding white slavers. Someone raises the point about how traitorous blacks have aided the toubob. The senior elder adds (p. 121): "Greed and treason— these are the things toubob has given us in exchange for those he has stolen away." Thus, the theme of whites' corruption of blacks is introduced.

The rhetorical function of this first part of the book seems evident. Haley counteracts traditional unfavorable views of Africa; he pictures the black homeland as an Eden whose only fault is the unwarranted intrusion of the white slaver; he sets up further contrasts, which will appear later—Mandinka versus toubob slavery and the character of blacks versus whites.

Kunta Kinte Enslaved

The bulk of *Roots* is taken up with Kunta Kinte's life as a slave in the United States. This section begins with his capture and the horrible voyage across the ocean, during which many perished. Plucked from his beloved Gambia, Kunta Kinte is subjected to incredible brutality during the capture and slave voyage. The slave voyage, in particular, contains some of Haley's most graphic descriptions. The crowded conditions, the filth, the disease, and the beatings are presented in full detail.

Haley uses Kunta's capture and voyage experiences as a means for continuing the comparison of blacks and whites. He pictures the captives as brave and well organized. They use strategy to fool the easily duped whites. Though of different tribes, the captives develop a growing sense of brotherhood as they plan an uprising. Overall, they resist the indignities in every manner possible. That the uprising never takes place cannot be credited to the wisdom of the white sailors. Disease finally overcomes the prisoners. The reader comes to wonder whether Kunta and his friends might not actually have succeeded, despite the odds, for the sailors are just as we saw them earlier: weak, quarrelsome, sexually perverted, and deceitful.

Next, we see Virginia slavery through Kunta's eyes. We observe the blacks' reaction to slavery and read Haley's continuation of the black-white moral contrast. Once in Virginia, Kunta Kinte cannot understand why it is that the blacks accept their status as slaves. He himself resolves to escape as soon as possible. He does so four times, only to be stopped when two slave catchers chop off his foot. This act of physical violence is not the only evil that we see wreaked on the captive blacks. Nevertheless, Haley does not emphasize the physical aspects of Kunta's life as a slave. Through Haley's account, the reader comes to see that the psychological brutality of slavery was far more demeaning than the bodily harm done.

From the start, we see slavery as an institution that deprives men and women of their heritage. Early on, Kunta Kinte is robbed of his name. Named for his illustrious grandfather, this Mandinka freeman becomes the slave "Toby." Having seen the importance that the Mandinka place on names, we come to understand the inhumanity of this forced name change. We see other dehumanizing aspects of slavery as well: the effort to stamp out all African customs; the breaking up of families; the fear brought through slavery. We see slaves parroting the white's distorted views of African culture. It becomes clear that even well-intentioned kindness by whites ultimately harms the slave. For instance, Kunta's daughter Kizzy becomes the favorite playmate of the owner's niece. Superficially, this is to Kizzy's advantage. However, from Kunta's point of view, it is not. His daughter has become the "pet" of Missy Anne. Kizzy has been "stolen" from her father and is further separated from her heritage. Moreover, this seemingly innocent friendship ultimately proves both heart-breaking and disastrous for Kizzy: heartbreaking because Missy Anne inevitably deserts Kizzy for white friends; disastrous because Kizzy, having been taught to read in secret by Missy Anne, is caught having forged a pass for an escaping slave. The point is clear: Healthy black-white relationships are not possible under slavery.

The inherent perversity of slavery is made clear in another of Haley's major theme arguments: There is no such thing as a "good slaveowner." Massa Waller, Kunte's second owner, represents perhaps the best that the south had to offer as a slaveholder. He opposes physical violence. As a medical doctor he even attends at the birth of Kunta's daughter. For all his enlightenment, however, Waller is a party to a corruption. Although opposed to breaking up slave families, he adheres to the code of selling slaves who attempt escape. He sells Kizzy for this reason. Through the voice of Kunta's slave friend Fiddler, we hear

Haley's summary judgment of such "good" owners: "Niggers here say Mass William [Waller] a good master, an' I seen worse. But ain't none of 'em no good. Dey all lives off us niggers. Niggers is the biggest thing dey got" (p. 259).

Overall, then, Haley's account supports the position that slavery is irredeemably evil. Regardless of the way that the slaves are treated physically, the psychological debasement is total. This focus on the nonphysical abuse is especially persuasive: It renders Haley's account largely immune to comparisons drawn between black slavery and the "wage slavery" of northern workers. Perhaps the workers did not have significantly more creature comforts, but they possessed a world of spiritual dignity that men like Kunta Kinte, the slave, could not have.

What of the blacks' response to slavery? On this score Haley clearly labors to turn aside visions of the slaves as peaceful and content. When Kunta arrives at the farm of his first master, he (and, therefore, we) see that blacks resist slavery in all possible ways. Haley relates Kunta's initial observations on slave tactics (p. 226):

It occurred to Kunta that these blacks masked their true feelings for the toubob. . . . He had by now many times witnessed the blacks' grinning faces turn to bitterness the instant a toubob turned his head away. He had seen them break their working tools on purpose, and then act totally unaware of how it happened as the "oberseer" bitterly cursed them for their clumsiness. And he had seen how blacks in the field, for all their show of rushing about whenever the toubob was nearby, were really taking twice as much time as they needed to do whatever they were doing.

Beyond this, Kunta notices how the slaves laugh at and fool the master. He hears tales of other, more gruesome hidden retaliations by the enslaved—including poisoned food.

Further enhancing Haley's descriptions of black discontentment and resistance are his repeated references to slave escapes and rebellions. Occasionally, Haley uses dialogue to make this point, as when he has the old gardener say (p. 257): "Ain't hardly nobody ain't thought about runnin'. De grinnin'est niggers thinks about it." Further, along these lines Haley works in many narrative references both to escapes and to rebellions.

Haley's arguments about psychological degradation and black resistance are closely related to another of his key claims: Many of the stereotyped "black traits" were the product of white misperception or black strategy. In the excerpt just cited, for example, we read of how the overseer mistakes resistance (breaking a tool) for clumsiness. In other places we perceive how slavery drives blacks to play a role. Again, the old gardener makes this clear to Kunta (p. 257): "Reckon since you been born I been actin' like de no-good, lazy, shiftless, head-scratchin' nigger white folks say us is." The reader realizes the double injury here: By definition slavery robs the enslaved of self respect; in order to resist, the slaves are forced to act clumsy and "no good."

Thus far I have noted several of Haley's arguments about slavery: (1) the unavoidable psychological brutality—apart from the physical; (2) the inherent evil of the slave owner; (3) the existence of active black resistance; and (4) the effect of black resistance and white misperception of it in creating negative black stereotypes. At the same time that he makes these points, Haley continues his contrast of blacks versus whites. Despite their chains we see the blacks as having a basic nobility. Unlike the whites, who divide themselves according to wealth, the blacks remain as brothers. Freed blacks, for instance, often work to purchase the freedom of others. In contrast to the poor "white trash" who take out their resentment of other whites through violence against blacks, we later see Kunta's great-grandson's family help a starving white.

A final theme in Haley's position on slavery deserves mention. Into his account Haley intersperses favorable interpretations of black history. He works in many references to the contributions of blacks. A case in point is Haley's mention of black contributions to the Revolutionary War. He uses a dialogue to refute the white-imposed notion that light-skinned blacks are smarter than darker-skinned blacks because of their white blood. He includes anecdotes to bolster the black man against the old stereotype of the more-aggressive black woman.

What, then, is the meaning of *Roots?* I would say that it is more than an epic story: It is an epic argument. Through the eyes of the enslaved, we see emphasized certain aspects of slavery that have been largely forgotten and poorly understood. Overall, a favorable image of black history, character, and culture emerges. Through the format of the novel, Haley achieves what 10,000 speeches possibly could not.

ARGUMENT ON STAGE: *THE NIGHT THOREAU SPENT IN JAIL*

Having read the section on *Roots,* you have a good notion of what I mean when I say that literature argues. I intend by this to say that the author of a literary work is able to shape an audience's image of something. In *Roots* Haley shaped our image of slavery in particular and the black experience in general. In this section of the chapter, I want to look at how two authors used a dramatic play to shape an image of war.

Henry David Thoreau became a folk hero to many in the turbulent 1965–1974 period. His *Walden* and *Civil Disobedience* fitted perfectly into the protest spirit and ecological awareness of the times. Thoreau's personal protest against the Mexican-American War (1845–1848)—he refused to pay his taxes—was in tune with the anti–Vietnam war movement. Thoreau's tax rebellion earned him a night in jail, and this became the title of Jerome Lawrence and Robert E. Lee's play (1972).

Clearly, Lawrence and Lee structure their scenes and characters to make a point.[5] *The Night Thoreau Spent in Jail* is an antiwar play, and it is a play that

---

[5]Lawrence and Lee's antiwar, antimaterialist, pro-protest position is made clear in their short essay "The Now Thoreau," on pp. 91–93 of the actor's scriptbook, which I have used for my analysis.

defends protest as a valid response to social ills. Because *Thoreau* is a stage play, Lawrence and Lee were limited to using scene, character, and dialogue as persuasive tools. There is no narrator. Such a format requires even more audience imagination than does a book like *Roots*. But, as we shall see, the dramatic form is one that can be made to work for an arguer.

Thoreau's Philosophy of Nonconformism

In the chapter introduction, I defined personification as a literary device whereby characters are used to represent ideas. Just as point of view was critical to *Roots*, so is personification the major argumentative tool of *Thoreau*. In the first act of the play, there is a development of Thoreau's philosophy of life. We are also introduced to the other characters. The first act is an interplay of Thoreau's past and present life. Scenes of Thoreau in jail (the present) are juxtaposed with flashbacks to his early life (the past).

The first series of short scenes establishes the young Thoreau's philosophy of nonconformism and traces its origins to the influence of Ralph Waldo Emerson, the scholar and philosopher. Short exchanges between Thoreau and his mother merge with a view of Thoreau listening to an address by Emerson. "Cast conformity behind you," intones Emerson (Lawrence and Lee, 1972, p. 13); "Cast . . . Conformity . . . Behind You . . . " repeats the young Thoreau, as he gazes up to his idol in admiration.

A word about the general construction of the play is appropriate at this point. As one can see from the short, overlapping introductory scenes, this play is made up of brief, fast-paced, closely connected dialogues. In their "Notes from the Playwrights," Lawrence and Lee explain (p. 6) that "scenes should *leap-frog* from one to another, like quick cuts in a motion picture." This movie-style format allows the authors to show the relationship of one piece of dialogue to another. For example, Henry's offbeat approach to life—illustrated in dialogue with his mother—is seen to originate in Thoreau's worship of the older Emerson.

After this initial introduction to Thoreau and Emerson, the scene shifts to Thoreau's present. Thoreau is in jail. We hear him explain his war protest position to the other prisoner. He complains of the American war against Mexico (p. 18): "But we've got a President who went out and boomed up a war all by himself—with no help from Congress and less help from me." Through Thoreau the authors are making a point about the questionable origins of the Mexican War, which President Polk is alleged to have provoked. The audience, of course, immediately realizes that the Mexican War symbolizes the Vietnam conflict. The whole play becomes an argument-by-analogy against the Vietnam war. Thoreau continues, clarifying to his cellmate how he (Thoreau) happens to be in jail (p. 18): "No. I refuse to commit murder. That's why I'm here." Now the audience sees that the play is to be about war protest. Thoreau's action against the Mexican War justifies, by analogy, the Vietnam protests.

This initial jail scene also contains Thoreau's first explanation of his antiestablishment point of view. He opposes government and conformity to the majority opinion. He supports individual insight and personal conviction. The succeeding flashbacks reinforce this. We are transported back to Thoreau's days as a public school teacher. We look on as Henry has his first conflict with the "establishment"—represented by Deacon Nehemiah Ball, chairman of the Concord School Committee. Ball speaks for rigid adherence to authority and discipline. Thoreau prefers imagination, analysis, and reason. This is brought out in a number of exchanges. We see the different reactions of the two men to a child's question about God. Ball calls the youngster a "young heathen" (p. 23) and admonishes him that "matters of theology, boy, are discussable with your spiritual leader." Thoreau, on the other hand, respects the boy's curiosity and launches into an explanation. Later, when the class is unruly, Thoreau announces, "I shall lecture them" (p. 26). Ball, in contrast, insists that "You will flog them—for showing irreverence to authority." Thus, we have laid out for us the contrast between Thoreau and the establishment. Thoreau is for open inquiry through rational discussion; Ball supports blind adherence to authority enforced by physical power. Clearly, the authors make Thoreau's philosophy appear the more attractive.

The scene returns to the jail, and we see Thoreau manifest his humor and intelligence. This is quickly followed by a series of flashback scenes. Henry confronts the establishment again, this time as the teacher of a "free school" and as an unsuccessful suitor to Ellen, the older sister of one of his pupils. In a number of dialogues, Henry reveals his philosophy. He supports an unstructured, free-wheeling brand of study. He emphasizes the individualist point of view. He rages against the kind of "progress" that maltreats Nature. He explains the Emerson-Thoreau notion of "transcendentalism," in which one's imagination can go beyond (transcend) present physical reality. Finally, there is a flash to a scene of Emerson—Henry's mentor—upstaging the Reverend Ball (p. 41).

> *Deacon Ball:* Tell me, Doctor Emerson. What is the feeling of a clergyman when he hears another pastor in the pulpit?
> *Waldo:* Relief.
> *Deacon Ball:* That you don't have to give the sermon?
> *Waldo: (Drily.)* That it's over.

Emerson then defends Thoreau's preference for worshiping God through Nature rather than in church.

The next few scenes show Thoreau in turmoil. His brother John dies. We see the beginnings of Thoreau's conflict with Emerson—a conflict that marks the climax of the play. Gradually, Lawrence and Lee reveal some of the differences between Thoreau and Emerson. This becomes apparent in the scene in which Thoreau agrees to work for Emerson in exchange for permission to build a cabin on Walden Pond. Emerson, it seems, is detached from the world. He has little time either for his son or for his estate. Thoreau, in contrast, is well attuned to people and life.

Act I ends with the arrest scene. Coming in from Walden, Henry is met by

Constable Sam Staples, who must serve Henry with a court order for back taxes. Unlike Deacon Ball, who represents the high-handed, authoritarian face of society, Sam is symbolic of the bumbling tool of the establishment. Unlike Ball, Sam does not like to use force. He does not want to arrest Thoreau. But Sam is a conformist: For him following "the law" is the course of least resistance. For Sam the law is the law, and there is no point in reasoning about it. Henry, as ever the thorn in the establishment's side, will not hear of compromise. He spurns Sam's offer to loan him the tax money. He demands to be arrested. He will not pay the taxes to support "the government" when "the government" is prosecuting an unjust war. By now a crowd has gathered, and he uses the opportunity to speak out on civil disobedience (p. 57):

> *Henry:* "If *one* honest man in this state of Massachusetts had the conviction and the courage to withdraw from this unholy partnership, resist—*peacefully*—and take the consequences, it'd be the start of more true freedom than we've seen since a few farmers had the guts to block the British by the bridge up the road."

Horrified by the turn of events, Emerson visits Thoreau (pp. 61–62):

> *Waldo:* Henry! *Henry!* What are you doing in jail???
> *Henry: (Turns, faces front, responding to the challenge. Defiantly, pointing accusingly across Concord Square.)* Waldo! What are you doing *out* of jail???

Thoreau versus Emerson on Social Protest

Act I has established several things for the audience. We hear of Thoreau's philosophy and we see it in action. We watch Henry contend with the establishment's world of blind obedience and physical discipline. We see a conflict developing between Thoreau and Emerson regarding how a thinking person should react to an unjust majority. As Act II begins we wonder whether Emerson will support Thoreau's protest—or not.

Act II takes us by surprise as the authors turn from Henry's tax protest in favor or more flashback insights into the origins of Thoreau's split from Emerson. We learn that Emerson is in the process of returning from a trip to Europe, and it becomes evident that Thoreau's activism is superior to Emerson's philosophizing. Two scenes make this point. In one, Emerson's young son identifies his philosopher-father's essential weakness—detachment from real life (pp. 66–67).

> *Edward:* And, Mama. I've asked Henry to be my father. (Lydian *and* Henry *look at each other.* Henry *shrugs, a bit embarrassed.*)
> *Lydian:* Oh? What about your real father?
> *Edward:* He's never here. He's always 'way on the other side of the ocean, or out somewhere making speeches, or up in his room where I can't disturb him. But Henry—*(A pause.)*
> *Henry:*—is here.

The author's decision in favor of Thoreau's philosophical activism is reinforced after Emerson's return. Thoreau has become incensed about the Fugitive Slave Law, under which escaped blacks were captured or killed in the North. He demands that Emerson speak out (p. 75).

> *Waldo:* I have cast my vote. I put it in the ballot-box. What more do you expect me to do?
> *Henry: (Moves into the scene. Aflame with indignation.)* Cast your whole vote. Not just a strip of paper! Your whole *influence*
> *Waldo: (Turning.)* We have to go along with the majority—!
> *Henry: (Exasperated.)* "Go Along!!!"

With this exchange, the audience is led to see that Emerson's well-intentioned moderation contains a fatal flaw: By going along with the majority, one abandons the possibility of rapid change.

As the dialogue continues we hear Thoreau make the point that some things—like slavery—must be changed immediately. The conversation between Thoreau and Emerson becomes more intense. Finally, Thoreau connects the slavery and war issues, putting a blunt question to Emerson (p. 78): "Are you aware of the reasons [for the war]—slave-holders grasping for more slave territory? *More* slavery and less freedom, is that what you want?" Finally, overpowered by Thoreau's conviction, Emerson relents. He agrees to address an antiwar message to the people of Concord. Thoreau rushes off to gather the crowd. However, Emerson does not appear. He sends his wife to offer lame apologies—he "wants more time to meditate on these matters" (p. 80).

The final moments of the play include Henry's dream about war. In the dream sequence the Reverend Ball and Constable Staples are transformed, respectively, into a general and a sergeant. Thoreau's bumpkin cellmate, Bailey, becomes a raw recruit being taught to hate and kill. In this fevered scene Emerson acts out the part of the President, who will "appoint a committee" to study the war. Emerson's son Edward, dressed as a drummer boy, becomes an innocent victim of the purposeless war. Finally, all action freezes as the voice of young Congressman Abraham Lincoln is heard protesting and demanding (p. 86): "Stop the war, Mr. President! For the love of God, *stop this war!*" Thoreau praises Lincoln for refusing to go along with the warmongers, but the fighting resumes. Now we see Thoreau's brother John fall in combat. Thoreau rushes to him. Then suddenly it is light again. Henry is awakened by Sam, who brings breakfast. Sam informs Henry that he is free to go. Aunt Louisa has paid the two years' back taxes.

Thoreau is a powerful play. Much of its force derives from the effort of Lawrence and Lee to tackle such hard concepts as war, social injustice, and the citizen's dual duty to society and to individual conscience. As with Haley's *Roots,* the authors of *Thoreau* use the literary form to persuade as well as to entertain. They use the characters to represent argumentative positions, presenting claims by means of dialogue. They instruct the audience by permitting one position to win out over the other. *Thoreau* teaches us (1) that individual conscience and reason are preferable to adherence to authority and discipline and (2) that active protest is superior to passive moderation in matters of social evil.

ARGUMENT IN FILM: *PATTON* VERSUS *M*A*S*H*

After reading the section on *Thoreau,* you should have an inkling of how an author uses scenes, characters, and dialogue to advocate a position. The medium of film is quite similar to that of the stage play. It follows that one argues through film in much the same manner as in a live drama. In fact, modern plays such as *Thoreau* have even borrowed film techniques—for instance, cutting immediately from one scene to another.

Notwithstanding the similarity between stage and film arguments, I want to take a moment here to show how movies can be persuasive. Furthermore, the two films I have selected—*M*A*S*H* and *Patton*—treat the theme of war, as did *Thoreau*. This is a second reason that my treatment of film can be brief. Let us see the message of war in these two cinematic efforts.

Patton: The Theme of "Purposeful War"

Among the many themes in *Patton* is the notion that war can be purposeful. This basic position is connected to several subsidiary, supporting themes: discipline is good, General Patton's hard-driving approach to war is the correct one, etc. Let us consider how these arguments are advanced through the medium of film.

Patton begins with an enormous shot of the American flag. Moments later, General George Patton strides into view—strong, confident, and bemedaled. He makes a short, tough speech in which "winning" emerges as a god term. "Real" Americans, it seems, love the sting of battle and love to win. Patton explains that this sentiment is the reason that Americans have never lost a war. If victory is the purpose of war, however, one might ask: "What is the purpose of winning?" The remainder of the movie seeks to give insight into the meaning of war.

The next scene, in fact, gives us a graphic demonstration of the meaning of defeat. We see the scattered remains of an American military force defeated by Germany's General Rommel at Kasserine, in North Africa. We see that defeat—the opposite of winning—means death. The next two scenes clarify the cause of the defeat: The American troops are not yet good enough to beat the Germans. As if to further make this point, we next see that the U.S. Army headquarters building is a disorganized, disorderly mess: The duty officer is not on duty; another solider is asleep. Moments later, inside, Patton finally verbalizes a major argument that the film has been working up to: The Kasserine defeat happened because the Americans didn't act or look like soldiers. Patton's second-in-command, General Omar Bradley, agrees.

Thus far, the movie has established the following chain of thought: (1) the purpose of war is winning; (2) winning is necessary to avoid death; and (3) an army loses when it does not act and look like an army. It follows, therefore, that the only viable course of action is to "shape up" the American Army. This is what Patton proceeds to do. We see him immediately institute tighter discipline. He enforces the dress code, institutes firm hours for the mess: open at 6:00 A.M.—no one admitted after 6:15. He tears down a pin-up photograph, and insists that no "yellow-bellies" or battle fatigue will be allowed. Two scenes later the wisdom of Patton's actions are given independent confirmation by the enemy. We witness a conversation in the German Army headquarters. Rommel comments that the Americans are bad soldiers and that their leadership is bad. The audience knows, of course, that because of Patton's actions, this is no longer true.

The next scenes further develop the character of Patton: his bravery (shooting at an attacking German aircraft); his strange belief in reincarnation; and his attention to military detail (we see him reading a book on Rommel). The American-German rematch now occurs, with victory to Patton. During the battle, one of Patton's aides is killed. We see the general grieving over the brave young soldier.

By now it is clear to the viewer that Patton symbolizes a rugged, disciplined approach to winning wars. The audience begins to suspect that Patton's approach will be vindicated. However, the makers of the movie do not want to establish Patton as a one-sided, plaster hero. Thus, during a portrayal of the Sicily campaign both Patton's strengths and weaknesses receive attention. Among the general's strengths is his apparent strategic insight. His invasion plans seem superior to those of the British. Further, we observe Patton's tactical genius. We watch as he does his own reconnaissance at the front line—and beyond it.

At this point, however, the authors of the movie include some of Patton's weaknesses. In a visit to a hospital, Patton slaps a soldier who is crying that he cannot "take it" any more. Patton calls him a "yellow coward." Still later, Patton admits to his own vanity, protesting that he realizes that he is a prima donna. Even later, Patton smiles when an aide tells him that people cannot determine when he (Patton) is acting and when he is not. But despite his tendency toward display and theatrics, the movie ultimately vindicates even his excesses. We see that the slapping incident was motivated by concern for the soldier. It was an effort to help him recover his nerve. Patton's personal flamboyance is partly an effort to inspire and give confidence to the troops. As all of this is revealed, we feel sorry for Patton because he is passed over for command of the U.S. Army in Europe. His blunt, honest nature—exemplified by the slap—has ruined his chances.

As the war progresses from Italy to France, we see further evidence that Patton is a noble figure and that his approach to war is the correct one. He is unconcerned about politics and publicly insults our Russian allies. Patton is given a new command and sets records in the reconquest of France. After running the Germans out of France, Patton pleads for permission to invade Hitler's Reich immediately. He predicts that Berlin could fall in ten days. Unfortunately, his counsel is ignored. Subsequently, the now-reinforced Germans begin a counterattack—the Battle of the Bulge.

Patton's actions during the "Bulge" campaign further vindicate his views. He looks on proudly as his well-trained and disciplined troops advance to stem the tide. "God, I'm proud," he says. After the crisis has passed, we watch as the Allies resume a rapid advance. The camera focuses on a truck. It bears the banner "Home Alive in '45." The soldiers on the truck happily greet Patton. "Hi, general," they exclaim. Thus is driven home the point: Patton's method of war produces victory with the fewest casualties. His toughness has a humane effect. Three scenes later Patton's Third Army has linked up with the Russians, but Patton is not fooled by our eastern allies. He calls the Russian general an "S.O.B." In the very next scene, he advocates fighting the Russians right away—since we will have to, eventually. These concluding minutes of *Patton* confirm his vision of war as something purposeful. War is used to defeat evil, as represented by the Third Reich and Stalin's Russia.

What is the argument in *Patton?* The movie vindicates Patton as a person. Despite his faults he is well intentioned and brings about good. Patton's view of war is made to ring true. Through war, good triumphs over evil. Victory comes about when hard discipline is coupled with hard training. Finally, Patton's hardheaded, even brutal, approach ultimately results in the quickest victory with the fewest casualties.

As in the case of *Roots, Patton* is designed to refute certain notions. Just as *Roots* refutes many unfavorable black stereotypes, *Patton* undermines many antiwar arguments. The movie justifies war as a way to defeat evil. It vindicates military discipline against permissiveness. In short, the overall position of *Patton* is quite removed from that of *Thoreau,* in which discipline is disparaged. As we shall see, it also stands in stark contrast to the image of war developed in *M*A*S*H.*

*M*A*S*H:* The Theme of "Purposeless War"

Carpenter and Seltzer (1974) contend that the movie *Patton* lent general support to Vietnam war proponents. In particular, they cite evidence that *Patton* helped President Nixon to decide to invade Cambodia in 1970. Apparently, Nixon watched the film several times shortly before authorizing the attack. Of course, such a claim can never be established conclusively. It is likely, though, that had Nixon watched *M*A*S*H,* his enthusiasm for widening the Indochina war might have received less of a boost.

What is the vision of war that emerges from *M*A*S*H?* It is not a particularly favorable one, to be sure. For one thing, *M*A*S*H* emphasizes the human suffering caused by war. We see the doctors doing their best amid the blood and tension of an operating room. In both the movie and the television series, the unglamorous aspects of war predominate. There are no flags flying or bands playing, nor are we treated to excited advances and triumphal marches. War, as portrayed in *M*A*S*H,* is not an adventure.

It is possible, many people recognize, to justify the human sacrifices of war if the sacrifices lead to a greater good, a greater *purpose. M*A*S*H* casts doubt on whether this can be the case. If the army wins a battle or two, there will always be more. If we defeat the North Koreans and the Chinese, there will be other wars. In fact, war just doesn't accomplish much: One's allies in the past war become the enemy in the next contest. $M^*A^*S^*H$ communicates the feeling that war doesn't make any sense. In this way, $M^*A^*S^*H$ opposes the major premise of *Patton:* From the perspective of the field hospital we learn that war does not achieve anything of value.

The vision of war in $M^*A^*S^*H$ opposes that of *Patton* in other ways. In *Patton* discipline is closely connected to training, and both are shown to produce the quickest victory with the fewest casualties. In $M^*A^*S^*H$ army-style discipline is made to seem un-American. The best doctors are those who adhere the least to dress codes and the like. Army values such as obedience, uniforms, rank, and rules appeal, it appears, predominantly to "un-American" types like Major Frank Burns: "Discipline" is personified by this semicompetent, narrow-minded, hypocritical officer; moral goodness is represented by figures such as Captain B. F. Pierce. In $M^*A^*S^*H$ the best surgeon of the unit conforms least to military-type regulations.

The idea that discipline saves lives is shown to be a fraud in $M^*A^*S^*H$. Those who have watched the television series realize that the Pattonesque commanders are the ones who always produce the highest casualties.

Patton was a hit movie. $M^*A^*S^*H$ has been a top-rated movie and television series. But are they just entertainment? Hardly, I think. Both articulate a position on war; both defend that position through cinematic devices of argument. Is war necessary and purposeful? Or is it not? The camera can be used to make either point.

ARGUMENT IN CARTOONS: PICTURES THAT PERSUADE

In the last section I looked at the argumentative force of "moving pictures." Pictures, however, need not move to persuade: Photographs and drawings can be used to advance a cause. Let us look at the use of modern political cartoons with this in mind.

When I say "political" cartoon, you probably think of a funny drawing on the editorial page of your newspaper. You are halfway there, for this kind of cartoon, also termed an "editorial cartoon," *is* a political cartoon. However, although I will emphasize editorial drawings, I want to observe, now, that your newspaper's "funnies" can also argue eloquently. "Dick Tracy," for instance, takes a "law and order" stance against liberal judges and politicians; "Brenda Starr" seems often to be a symbol of the successful woman in a "man's profession"; and the antics of Gary Trudeau's characters in "Doonesbury" take a "political" stance as well. See if you can detect any overall themes in your newspaper's funnies. For now, however, let us confine our attention to the cartoons of the editorial page.

Cartoons as a Persuasive Force

Since the beginnings of American history, cartoons have been used to advance positions on questions of public policy. Nevins and Weitenkampf (1944) have collected many representatives of the early American political cartoon. Figure 9-2, an etching of 1800, is one. Nevins and Weitenkampf (1944, p. 20) explain the drawing.

> In this rather well drawn caricature all the venom of the opponents of Jefferson is concentrated. The Republican leader is kneeling before the snake-encircled "Altar of Gallic Despotism," dropping the letter to Mazzei which proved very damaging to

Figure 9-2 A cartoon attack on Thomas Jefferson. (Reprinted with the permission of Charles Scribner's Sons from *A Century of Political Cartoons* by Allan Nevins and Frank Weitenkampf. Copyright 1944 Charles Scribner's Sons.)

its writer. In a burst of indiscretion, in 1796, Jefferson had written his Italian friend, Philip Mazzei, that while the mass of the American people were democratic, the government was reactionary. A vigorous fight would have to be waged, he declared, to preserve the liberties of the republic. The letter was printed in a Paris newspaper in 1798. Naturally, its attack on Washington as unfriendly to "republican principles" aroused resentment, and a great ado was made over the unhappy missive.

In this etching we have an example of drawings as a persuasive tool. The cartoon expresses an overall unfavorable opinion of Thomas Jefferson. The opinion is furthered through various facets of the picture. Jefferson is connected to the worst excesses of the French Revolution. We see that he is ready to add the Constitution and American independence to the list of things already consumed by French radicalism. Notice that the "age of reason" and the works of Rousseau and Voltaire are already burning. Fortunately, however, Jefferson is stopped by the American eagle, dispatched by a watchful Providence.

As weekly and daily newspapers increased in number, cartoons became an established part of the political scene. Cartoonist Thomas Nast's campaign against "Boss" Tweed is an early instance of the persuasive effect of cartoons in their relatively modern form. William M. Tweed was the leader of the Democratic political machine in New York City. Tweed and his associates— called "the Ring" or "Tammany Hall"—controlled the offices of New York City government. They used this control for economic gain. From his position at *Harper's Weekly,* Nast vilified Tweed in cartoon after cartoon. Paine (1904, p. 179) identifies one particular cartoon (see in figure 9-3) as doing "more to terrify the Ring than any previous attack." This drawing pictures several members of Tweed's ring—including the dishonest city contractors who profited through corrupt public works projects. In response to the question "Who stole the people's money?" each answers, "Twas him" and points to the person to his right (*Harper's Weekly,* August 19, 1871, p. 764). According to Paine this cartoon prompted Tweed to attempt silencing Nast (Paine, 1904, p. 179). "Let's stop them d——d pictures," Tweed is said to have exclaimed. "I don't care so much what the papers write about me—my constituents can't read; but, d——n it, they can see pictures!"

In both examples of political cartoons cited above, it was necessary for me to include much explanatory material to make plain the meaning of the picture. This points up the fact that editorial cartoons are predominantly things of the moment. Years—or even months—later a cartoon may be impossible to decipher. As a form of argument, cartoons rely heavily on the audience's existing knowledge and assumptions. Unless one knows that the fat man in figure 9-3 is Tweed, the cartoon loses some of its sting.

There is another feature of cartoons that deserves mention at this time. This is the inherent ambiguity of pictoral symbols. In chapter 2, I noted that ambiguity was an unavoidable feature of written words (verbal symbols). However, nonverbal symbols are even more vague as a guide to a person's meaning. For instance, if you are speaking and someone smiles, what does the

"WHO STOLE THE PEOPLE'S MONEY?" — DO TELL . N.Y.TIMES.   'TWAS HIM.

Figure 9-3 "Them d——d pictures."

smile signify? Support? Amusement at your wit? Or does it mean that the listener thinks your statement and/or you are laughable? Turn back for a minute to the Jefferson cartoon in figure 9-2. I think that the eagle has seized the paper away from Jefferson. On the other hand, however, the author of the picture could be using the paper marked "Constitution & Independence, U.S.A." to mean that the eagle represents these forces and thus is holding the paper.

Carl's (1967) study of pictoral cartoons supports this notion of the ambiguous nature of pictoral symbols. Carl selected a number of editorial cartoons taken from major American newspapers. He contacted the authors of the cartoons in an effort to ascertain the "real," or intended, meaning of each pictoral message. Carl then showed the cartoons to groups of people, asking them to identify the meaning of each cartoon. His findings indicate that, more often than not, readers do not "get the meaning" intended by the cartoon artist. Only about one-third of the people surveyed came up with an interpretation congruent (wholly or partially) with that of the author. Pictoral symbols *are* ambiguous.

Cartoons and "The Issues": Some Recent Examples

Elsewhere in the book I have used President Jimmy Carter's 1977 energy proposals as an example of a public controversy. I have mentioned the snail's pace at which the energy "package" went through Congress. Suppose you wanted to advance the following argument: "The slow progress of Carter's energy proposal is due in part to a major shortcoming of his plan: It does much to stimulate conservation but offers little stimulus for increased energy production." You could develop your argument in a speech or essay; or you could prepare a cartoon. Cartoonist artist Hugh Haynie made just this point in figure 9-4. Haynie portrays Carter as driving a truck labeled "energy bill" along a snowy road. The truck is stuck on the road, and the caption suggests that Carter cannot understand why. What do we notice about the truck? The front tires—labeled "conservation"—are rugged and large. The back ones, which symbolize the "production" part of Carter's proposal, are small. Hence, the moral of the story: Perhaps Carter's energy bill would not be stuck in Congress if it did as much to promote production as it does to enhance conservation.

Let us take a look at another area of dispute in which cartoon arguments have been made. In November 1977 President Anwar el-Sadat of Egypt visited Israel. This act began a "peace initiative" that led many observers to believe that grievances between Israel, Egypt, and other parties in the Middle East might be resolved through negotiations. It soon became apparent that the Egyptian-Israeli peace talks would not proceed quickly. One sticky point emerged as Israel demanded that its settlements on captured Egyptian territory be retained. The Egyptians objected. The issue emerged: Should Israel retain control of its settlements on the Sinai Peninsula after the peninsula was returned to Egyptian

Figure 9-4 A cartoon argument against President Carter's energy plan. (© 1977 *The Courier-Journal,* Louisville, and Hugh Haynie.)

"Durn . . . stuck again! I just don't understand it."

sovereignty? In figure 9-5 we see how cartoonist Oliphant used a picture to support Egypt's position on the settlements question.

This picture shows President Sadat standing beside two pyramids. Sadat is angry: His fists are clenched. In front of him is a sign stating, "Leaving Cairo City Limits: Welcome to Greater Israel." On the other side of the sign are three figures who represent Israeli soldiers or settlers. They are planting a garden. The soldiers are avoiding Sadat's gaze. What do you think the cartoonist is trying to say? I believe that the cartoon advances the following argument:

Israel has established settlements on territory captured from Egypt.
The settlements are on land that Egypt regards as belonging to Egypt and other Arab nations.
Therefore, the Egyptians rightly are angry about this.

Notice that much of the cartoon's force comes from its use of exaggeration. The Israelis are shown settling in right next to Cairo (the capital of Egypt) and the pyramids (Egypt's most famous landmark). As I noted, this is an exaggeration. None of the settlements in question were even remotely close to Cairo; yet the exaggeration helps make the cartoonist's point that the Egyptians regard the land on which the settlements are located as being an integral part of Arab land—just as Cairo is.

Consider a final example. In April 1978 Soviet leader Leonid I. Brezhnev offered not to produce a Russian neutron bomb if the United States also would refrain from producing one. A neutron bomb is one that kills people by emitting high levels of radiation but does little damage to property. Western military strategists argue that this bomb would be useful in the defense of Europe. They

Figure 9-5 Pictorial support for Egypt. (*Oliphant,* © 1978, *The Washington Star.* Reprinted with permission, Los Angeles Times Syndicate.)

say that it would allow N.A.T.O. (North Atlantic Treaty Organization) forces to use nuclear weapons against a Soviet invasion force while limiting damage to Western Europe.

There were other points at issue in the neutron bomb controversy. For one thing, officials did not believe that the U.S.S.R. had yet developed a neutron weapon. The United States, on the other hand, had perfected the bomb and was ready to begin production. If this was the case, then Brezhnev's offer was more to Russia's advantage than it was to the advantage of the Western nations. This is the point made by Haynie in figure 9-6.

Editorial cartoons may be found relating to many controversies now occurring. Look for them in your newspaper or in magazines. Try to interpret them. If you do not understand a cartoon, investigate the subject and consult others until you do.

ARGUMENT IN SONG: THE LYRICS AND CADENCE OF COMMUNICATION

It has been said that music has the power to sooth savage impulses. But music does more than this: Through its power to capture our attention, music carries considerable influence. We encounter this influence daily. On television and in

Figure 9-6 A cartoonist's view of Chairman Leonid Brezhnev's arms-limitation deal. (© 1978 *The Courier-Journal,* Louisville, and Hugh Haynie.)

"I'll make you a deal...I won't build any more of these things if you won't."

movies, music is used to set a mood. Music complements the dramatic dialogue or action on the screen. A chase scene calls for different musical treatment than a love scene. In addition to musical melody, the musical lyrics—the words—carry a suasory force. Popular songs and commercial jingles both tend to have a "catch phrase." Lines such as "It's the real thing," or "I'd like to buy the world a Coke" become a focal point for listener interest during a Coca-Cola commercial. The same holds true for almost any other song.

Let's look at some of the implications of music's power to control interest and attention.

Music as a Vehicle for Argument

In order for arguments to be effective, the advocate must get the listeners into the proper frame of mind. This can be done through argumentative statements (see chapter 2). For example, an audience can be made angry by examples of injustice. Similarly, a speaker may induce the listeners to like him by using arguments that show he is one of them or has their interests at heart. Feelings of anger and liking also can be developed through song. Indeed, there exist songs which are able to express almost any human emotion. We have songs for sadness, songs for joy, songs for patriotism, songs for love, songs for worship, and so on. Mood setting is, then, a basic rhetorical aspect of songs. Music communicates a feeling and unites the audience in that mood. During a single day we may go to our place of worship, where solemn music readies us for a dignified worship service. Later, we may attend a concert where popular songs unite the listeners in excitement expressed through clapping. Different music, different moods.

Beyond the mood-setting function of songs, we should be aware of music's capacity to communicate a general outlook on life. For instance, country and western music, as a whole, reflects certain values and assumptions about life. The world of country music is one in which tragic love predominates. The instruments often paint a picture of sadness as the lyrics speak of sweethearts divided by infidelity or other interpersonal conflict. In this connection, the theme of revenge is not uncommon and tends to be portrayed in a favorable light. Expressions of deep, emotional religious faith are frequent (country-gospel music), as are expressions of pride in family, region, and nation. Corny humor is frequently in evidence. In short, country music tends to present life in a characteristic way.

In the 1960s and early 1970s, popular rock music emphasized a life style and outlook distinct from that of country and western songs. Robinson, Pilskaln, and Hirsch (1976) observe the change in rock music's "story line" during this period. Concern with "romantic love and courtship" (a staple during the 1950s and early 1960s) diminished as more attention was given to "different sides of controversial social issues, such as Vietnam and alternative life styles" (p. 125). Before 1965, the radios were tuned to tales of teenage romance and surfing. Later in the decade pop hits celebrated antiwar ("where have all the flowers gone?") and counterculture themes ("I get high with a little help from my friends"). As youth became more concerned with social issues and alternative life styles, their music changed to reflect and enhance this new emphasis. The songs of the period became a part of a change in outlook. Summarizing the implications of the late 1960s rock music, Robinson, Pilskaln, and Hirsch conclude (1976, p. 135): "Protest rock constituted a cultural revolution insofar as it was aligned with and helped shape the youth culture of that period."

Country music and 1960s rock illustrate how songs both reflect and, at the same time, help solidify an approach to life. It is not difficult to search out other examples of the outlook-setting, value effects of song. In World War II, for instance, the popular song functioned to build morale. Mohrmann and Scott (1976) have classified a host of early 1940s war-theme songs. They found that the most popular "war songs" were not the most militant in nature. Rather those with humor or having "catchy" lyrics and/or melody prevailed. Mohrmann and Scott (1976, p. 156) argue that by its nature the popular song is not suitable as a vehicle for "complex persuasive appeals." Rather, like the country and rock examples above, the war songs tended to reflect and solidify the general wartime mood.

Most writers, it seems, tend to credit song with powers of attitude reinforcement rather than attitude change. However, one should not be led to believe that this attitude reinforcement effect is of no real significance. In a social movement cohesion, group identity, and morale are essential. The rhetoric of song helps to supply these needed aspects of a mass persuasive effort. Thomas (1974) contends that songs such as "We Shall Overcome" materially strengthened the civil rights movement. Singer John Denver argues (*Playboy,* December 1977, p. 135) that his "Rocky Mountain High" had "a great deal to do with stopping the Winter Olympics in Colorado in 1972." This relationship of songs to causes is frequent in American history. Most popular movements have had some form of musical accompaniment.

How Music Influences

I have observed that music is influential. It is now appropriate to give some thought as to *how* songs build the mood and solidify the outlook of a group in society.

At the outset of this discussion, it is important to keep in mind that a primary function of music is entertainment. During World War II, as Morhmann and Scott (1976) noted, many war songs lacked popularity because they were not entertaining. They were so argumentative, and they taught so much, that they did not capture and hold listener interest. We may assume, therefore, that unless a song entertains, it will not persuade very much.

This connection between entertainment and persuasion may be difficult to achieve. John Denver gives us an example of the problem faced by an entertainer who desires to support a cause. Denver can sell out a concert hall; but when he and some other popular performers gave a performance as part of a solar-energy fair, event, only a few people showed up. Denver believes that the concert's connection with a cause made people leary of attending it. Perhaps these people feared that the concert would teach too much. The concert may have drawn chiefly those who were already committed to an anti–nuclear power position. How, then, does a song writer reach the neutral public so as to change attitudes? Denver reports that he is writing a tune on nuclear power. "And the song will say it," he notes (*Playboy,* December 1977, p. 135). We can predict, however, that the ultimate persuasive impact of Denver's anti–nuclear power song will rest on its ability to entertain.

The notion that a song writer may function as an advocate suggests a starting point in our effort to answer the question concerning "how does music influence?" We should begin by taking a look at the musical source—the writer or singer. Since the public often identifies a song with the singer rather than the writer, we have cause to emphasize the recording artist. All others being equal, a "name" singer should have an easier time drawing an audience. The reputation of the artist probably would enhance the chances that a song will become popular. There is another factor of singer reputation, however. Artists become known for particular types of songs: Audiences would tend to expect certain melodic styles and lyrical themes from a given performer.

One may justly question, however, the extent to which the credibility of an artist may enhance the audience's liking of a piece. Artist reputation might help gain the tune an initial hearing, but the melody and lyrics would seem more important in the utlimate success of a song. First of all, there is melody. Irvine and Kirkpatrick (1972, p. 276) cite findings that musical melody stimulates many parts of the body—not just the ears. As one succumbs to the sway of the music, a person may experience an "almost instant light hypnosis."

In addition to musical sound, the lyrics or words contribute significantly to the total impact. Some songs, of course, are narrative in nature. They tell a complete story. Others contain one or more lines with persuasive punch. Lewis (1976) describes certain unwritten rules of the trade in country music lyric writing. He reports some findings gathered through interviews with veteran song writers. These writers emphasize the importance of having a catchy phrase that will please the majority of listeners. A 1977–1978 country and western hit illustrates the role of the "hook line." "Take this job and shove it," went the refrain. Apparently, the sentiment struck home, because the song—recorded by a then-little-known artist, Johnny Paycheck—rose on both the popular and country music charts.

Through melody and lyrics a song captures the physical and mental attention of the audience. As I noted earlier, the major effect seems to be one of unifying the listeners, bringing them into a common group experience. The feeling of togetherness can be enhanced by having the group sing along. Rock musicians and revival preachers have known this for years. But even when the audience is not overtly singing, the listeners can be covertly captured. Have you ever caught yourself humming or singing along by yourself? Irvine and Kirkpatrick (1972) report that listeners may subvocalize a song. That is, even if the persons are not making audible sounds, their larynxs may be following the tune.

Overall, though, we should remember that a song may be only part of a total situation. Heard within the context of a rock concert or protest rally, a song would strike us differently from the same piece heard over the car radio. Music may be most effective when combined with group singing, speeches, chants, and banners. At a rally advocates may capitalize on music's power as part of a persuasive combination for winning interest and unifying the mind and body of the crowd.

Like any form of art, then, music works to entertain: It pleases the audience. However, while giving pleasure, song can also reinforce the attitudes of the listening public.

ARGUMENT IN INTERPERSONAL RELATIONS: "INFORMAL" PERSUASION

Perhaps the most prevalent source of argument is everyday conversation. Many of the examples of argument in this book have been taken from the hypothetical dialogues of two persons. One of the major theoretical areas of persuasion presented in chapter 7 was that of interpersonal influence. Interpersonal persuasion can be quite subtle. Through it we adopt the opinions of those with whom we associate. We become a member of a group that possesses shared beliefs, attitudes, and values.

Interpersonal influence is a universal phenomenon. Daily, we measure and compare our opinions and behaviors against the opinions and behaviors of our associates. For the most part, our ways probably conform to theirs. You can check this for yourself. Identify some of your important beliefs or preferences or behaviors. For instance, what do you think about premarital sex, what music do you like, and what kinds of clothes do you wear? How do your ways compare to the beliefs, likes, and actions of your circle of friends?

Interpersonal Transactions and Relationships

There are many perspectives for describing informal, interpersonal influence. One way is to focus on single transactions between persons. Suppose that you wish to discuss your progress with the instructor of one of your courses. You might visit your professor and converse with her or him. This conversation would amount to a transaction: It would be a related set of interactions between people at a particular time and place. Over the course of the semester, you might have many such transactions with your instructor consisting of one interaction or many.

It is easy to see that life is full of transactions between people. In its simplest form a transaction could take the form of a single-interaction greeting exchange between two people: "Hi, how are you?" "Fine, and you?" On the other hand, a transaction could amount to a lengthy debate between two people that involved many interactions. It could involve an exchange of letters. In short, we have transactions daily with many individuals.

As I noted, transactions can be used as a basis for examining our interpersonal communication. In recent years, a number of books have appeared on subjects such as "assertiveness." Training in assertiveness is designed to make people better able to express their intentions to others. All of us, of course, hate to make trouble or to "look funny." Sometimes we allow our reluctance to raise uncomfortable issues to get the better of us. We refrain from returning a defective radio. We do a favor for a friend when we don't really have the time. One function of assertiveness training is to make us better at handling such potentially unpleasant transactions. It is supposed to make us more able to communicate information that we think will upset the other person.

Assertiveness training represents the transactional approach to interpersonal communication. Such training would make us more able to state our intention to anyone in any kind of situation. Overall, then, a transactions-based approach to communication is one in which we focus on the speaker's intention. We emphasize the connection between intention and message rather than the relationship between the two parties. In the case of assertiveness training, one is taught to create more assertive messages and thereby to achieve one's purposes. We all know, however, that our communication depends on whom we are talking to—in addition to our intention. So the relationship perspective is a useful complement to the transactional viewpoint.

We may define "relationship" as a continuing pattern of interaction between two persons. People treat friends differently from the way they do a tennis coach. There are different relationships with these two individuals. One treats an employer differently from one's child. Again, we have communication action depending on the type of relationship. The one (employee-boss) is a subordinate-superior type. The other is a family-type pattern of interaction (also involving superior-subordinate aspects, however).

The concept of relationship is useful in dealing with interpersonal influence. Various relationships carry with them different influence strategies. One may set out to influence a child in a manner that probably differs from one's approach to "the boss." Similarly, our hypothetical tennis star may be quite reluctant to upbraid the coach for lateness but may scold a friend, without hesitation, for such an oversight. As before, a different relationship seems to call for a distinct form of communication behavior.

These hypothetical examples illustrate the influence of power and status in a relationship. In an organization a subordinate has less power and status than the boss. The employee is less able to cause the boss to do something. Further, the employee doubtless has fewer trappings of prestige than the boss—such "status" items as a large desk, private secretary, reserved parking spot, etc. Because the employee has less power and status, compared to the boss, this subordinate is more timid than the employer is in raising issues. However, as a parent this same person may have the upper hand in the relationship with the child. The parent uses less formality in dealing with the child than in communicating with an employer.

There are many other factors besides power and status that explain why a person's behavior will change to fit the requirements of a relationship, so in discussing interpersonal influence one must consider the type of relationship that the parties share.

I have introduced the concept of relationship because I want to focus on argument as it operates in a certain kind of relationship. I want to look at intimate man-woman relationships. In particular, I want to focus on how relationship partners manage conflict—how they deal with occasional disagreements over issues.

Language and Intimate Communication

An intimate relationship, as I will use the term here, refers to the kind of relationship that exists between married partners or lovers. The notion that intimate communication is an exercise in argument takes us back to chapter 3. In the section on arguments on decision rules, I cited Bach and Wyden's (1969) attempt to specify rules for fighting in marriage. Bach and Wyden's book is one of many recent works on communication in marriage. By looking at some of these, it is possible to get ideas about how to deal with issues in an intimate relationship.

But before getting into the details, it might be worthwhile to consider a preliminary question. Specifically, what do rules have to do with communication in marriage? Admittedly, it does sound somewhat mechanistic to suggest that one use rules and guidelines in communicating with a spouse or loved one, but consider the alternative. Most marriages and affairs begin in a romantic glow; the two parties are caught up in the joy of sharing with another in an intimate way. Although love of this kind persists, there comes a time when the romantic fires are transformed into the steady warmth of a continuing relationship. By this time the two persons may be living together, and their love bond is strained by the inevitable conflicts that emerge when two live as one.

Intimate conflict is inevitable; but so is conflict in work and other relationships. There is something, though, that sets intimate conflict apart: Probably, it is more deeply felt than any other form of disagreement. Conflict in the work situation may bring bad feelings, but the capacity of intimates to hurt each other is unrivaled. As the social and religious prohibitions against divorce have declined, intimates feel even freer to terminate a conflict-ridden relationship. The divorce rate in America has risen to unprecedented heights. Books on marriage conflict are written and sell well.

I want to take a look at a few of the insights provided by two books on marital arguing. Miller, Nunnally, and Wackman (1975) begin their book by treating the subject of self-awareness. They identify five factors of one's self-awareness:

    1 Sense impressions
    2 Thoughts
    3 Feelings
    4 Intentions
    5 Behaviors

In their view any one or more of these factors could be a source of motivation. A woman standing in line at the bank might *sense* that the other lines are moving faster. She might *think,* "This always happens." She might *feel* angry. *Wanting* to be served more quickly, she might move (a *behavior*) to the next line.

The statements that we make to others tend to express one or more of the five factors of self-awareness. This is another of Miller, Nunnally, and Wackman's key points. Our hypothetical bank customer might remark to the cashier: "Why don't you people do something about the slow lines? I'll bet it doesn't take this long at other banks." These two sentences seem to express a basic feeling of anger, coupled with the interpretation that the bank in question is the slowest. There is a behavioral component in this message too. The woman may be suggesting that she will go elsewhere if things do not change.

Miller, Nunnally, and Wackman (1975) believe that practice in recognizing self-awareness can improve the communication between intimates. Let us consider a hypothetical conversation between a wife and husband.

Wife: Are you finally home? It's about time. I guess you just don't care about me!

Husband: I can see you are being your usual sweet self.

Wife: What do you expect me to do when you're late all the time?

Husband: Of course, *you're* always on time!

As you can see, the marriage partners are getting nowhere in resolving the grievance, which seems to involve being on time. Let us see how some self-awareness practice might help things out.

The wife's opening statement seems to reveal anger or disappointment. However, instead of telling her husband how she feels, she launches into an attack ("it's about time") and interprets her husband's reasons for being late (you're late because you don't care). The wife might have improved the lines of communication by revealing that her husband's lateness hurt her: "It's eight o'clock, and I feel hurt that you are late for dinner on our anniversary." Such a response would reveal the major source of the wife's behavior (hurt and anger). It would be easier for the husband to confront this issue rather than dealing with the charge about his not caring.

What of the husband's first statement? It is a sarcastic interpretation that was probably prompted by anger. Were the husband to focus on his wife's probable feelings, he might say something like this: "I sense that you are angry about my being late." He could then report his own feelings: "I am surprised that you are angry, because I thought we had agreed to go out for a late dinner." A response such as this does much to enhance continued, sane discussion of the problem.

These examples illustrate the authors' point about self-awareness skills in marriage. It helps to recognize one's own and one's partner's self-awareness. It helps when a person explicitly refers to the various self-awareness elements.

Bach and Wyden (1969), too, offer a host of suggestions about how to use language to identify and solve conflicts in marriage. They present some "bad" strategies for marital arguing together with suggestions about how to "fight fair."

"Facing the issues" is at the heart of the Bach and Wyden system. They present anecdote after anecdote to illustrate the unhappy consequences of evading conflict. When ignored, relationship conflict and relationship issues only fester and become more difficult to deal with.

The corollary of evasive fighting is nonspecific fighting. The nonspecific fights center around personal attacks. Feelings are expressed, but the issues remain untouched. Bad fighting can take other forms. The authors describe a "kitchen sink" fight as one in which the partners throw in every possible grievance. "Gunnysack" fighting is a closely related phenomenon. The partners hold in their grievances until, when a fight has begun, all the pent-up issues emerge.

As an answer to poor marital communication, the authors offer some suggestions for effective conflict resolution. They suggest that the parties explicitly identify the issue that is bugging them. They even suggest making an appointment to fight, drawing an analogy to labor negotiations. They provide charts and diagrams to assist partners in evaluating their fights. For instance, their "fight elements profile" includes nine criteria for judgment (Bach and Wyden, 1969, pp. 162–165):

1   Reality: Is the fight based on real grievances or imaginary, non-authentic ones?

2   Injury: Do the partners make unnecessary efforts to hurt one another?

3   Involvement: Is there a give and take between the parties? Or does one or the other act uninvolved?

4   Responsibility: Do the partners take responsibility for their feelings by saying "*I* think or feel?"

5   Humor: Is humor used to bring relief or to ridicule/hurt the other?

6   Expression: Do the fighters express their grievances in a straightforward manner? Or do they behave manipulatively?

7   Communication: Do the intimates make clear statements and listen well?

8   Directness: Do the fighters emphasize the present grievance? Or do they dredge up old or irrelevant issues?

9   Specificity: Do the fighters respond to what their partner actually did/said? Or do the partners spend most of their time analyzing the other?

Marital communication books seek to improve the resolution of relationship issues. Most of the advice centers on what to say and what not to say. By focusing on issues and statements, marital communication books bring traditional standards of argument (e.g., relevance of argument to issue) to a new field of language interaction.

APPLICATIONS

This chapter has consisted of eleven short case studies. In some my purpose was to highlight one of the "places" in which we may find argument. In others my chief aim was to demonstrate that speeches and essays are not the only means by which claims can be advanced.

One way to apply the contents of this chapter is to do further reading into one or more of the subjects I have introduced. I hope that this chapter will stimulate you to do this. However, there is also another way. This chapter has focused on argument in nontraditional places and in nontraditional forms. I offer two exercises that will encourage you to explore further the wide-ranging role of argument in our daily lives.

Exercise 9-1: Widening Your Perspective on Argument

I   See if you can identify additional forms or places of argument. List as many as you can think of. For instance, religion, door-to-door sales, and textbooks seem to involve factors of argument and persuasion.

II   Choose two of the additional contexts of argument that you identified in direction 1. For each, write a paragraph describing, in general, how principles of argument and persuasion apply to the context.

Exercise 9-2: Analyzing Nontraditional Argument Forms

The traditional form of an argument is a verbal statement delivered in a speech or essay. In this chapter and elsewhere, I have highlighted some alternatives that are available to the advocate. These include nonverbal movement, songs, films, literature, stage plays, and cartoons.

I   Choose one of the nontraditional mentioned forms—or identify one of your own (e.g., architecture).

II   Find an example of where this form has been used to make a point. For example, if you want to analyze film as a vehicle for argument, select a particular film that you have recently seen.

III   Apply the effect, validity, truth, or ethics standards to your sample message. Consult exercises 3-6, 3-7, 3-8, and 3-9, in particular.

Chapter 10

Policy Analysis Skills

Up to now we have looked at how arguments work—or should work. Now it is time to get some practice in using arguments. In the preceding chapters I have presented various forms, types, and contexts of argument and I have identified principles for judging arguments according to standards of validity, persuasiveness (effect), ethics, and truth. In chapters 10 and 11, I wish to concentrate on the process by which arguments are gathered and delivered in support of or opposition to policy questions. It is well to be able to judge arguments. It seems to me, though, that it is better to be both a critic and a creator of argument. Chapters 10 and 11 treat the creative process of analysis and advocacy. In these two chapters I will give you an opportunity to apply your knowledge of argument and persuasion to questions of policy.

I have presented sample arguments taken from various persuasive messages. Often, these examples were responsive to the policy issue: "What should be done about X?" However, for the most part we have been dealing, thus far, with questions of fact, definition, or value. In chapters 10 and 11, however, we will focus specifically on the "what should be done" aspect of argument—the use of argument to establish or refute a policy position.

Policy questions afford us a good opportunity to observe the entire argumentative process. This is because policy questions involve a range of descriptive, interpretive, and evaluative claims. When we advocate a policy, we must identify what is happening now (description and interpretation), we must establish whether or not the present situation is desirable (interpretation and evaluation), and, finally, we must present a new policy that is better than the old one (description, interpretation, and evaluation). Thus, policy questions deal with problems and solutions and ends and means as well as causes and effects. When we amass arguments to advocate a policy position, we deal first with the nature of things as they are now. We ask such questions as: What is happening now? Why is it happening? How does the present state of affairs compare to an ideal world? The policy advocate also confronts the future and asks these questions: How may we solve problems that exist today so as to make for a better tomorrow? What will be the result of new policies?

Policy argument traditionally has been presented in the form of oral speeches and written compositions. Of course, in chapter 9, we learned that policy positions could be expressed in nontraditional ways such as in songs. Indeed, if one desired to advance the cause of nuclear power plants, one would not be restricted to essay writing or speech making. A person could produce a film, write a poem, stage a skit, or draw a cartoon to get the point across. Thus, a chapter on policy argument could well deal with film making, poetry, drama, or art. I have chosen, nevertheless, to limit this chapter to a discussion of the principles of oral and written composition. There are a number of purely pragmatic reasons for this. For one thing, I am a teacher of speech, not of music or art. Further, the treating of nontraditional policy advocacy would add a great deal of length to this book. And, after all, the subjects are presented competently elsewhere. However, my real reasons for confining policy argument to speech or essay making are twofold: (1) composition is the customary vehicle for policy argument, and (2) having learned the process of argumentative composition, those who possess other kinds of artistic talent may easily translate the process into aesthetic terms.

Policy argument frequently is associated with the process of debate, in which two or more agents give speeches to support opposing positions on a given subject. In the speech communication field, debate is the usual model for studying situations of dispute. Although one can argue without formally debating, debate is an especially good framework for studying policy argument. The system of debate involves the discovery of arguments and the organization of arguments into a coherent case in support of a position. Debate theory further treats the methods for refuting opposing arguments and for defending your own arguments against attack. The debate technique therefore is an excellent laboratory setting that enables us to follow the development of arguments in a situation of dispute. Through debate we observe the discovery, organization, delivery, refutation, and resubstantiation of arguments.

Generations of speech communication teachers have refined the practice of debate into a procedure that involves carefully stated and applied formal decision rules. *Forensic debate* is customarily defined as a situation of dispute in which two sides argue the merits of a stated proposition: one side supporting the proposition; the other opposing it.[1] While not all contexts of dispute correspond to the rules of forensic debate, the forensic debate method is still a good vehicle for learning about policy argument in all settings. Once we have learned the forensic format, we may modify it to fit the needs of other situations of dispute—such as marital communication. The formal rules of forensic debate will help you to learn methods of analysis, organization, delivery, refutation, and resubstantiation. These general skills may be modified to fit the decision rules involved in other contexts.

In chapter 10, I will treat the related skills of policy analysis and case organization as they usually are practiced in forensic debate. Our dual concerns will be the discovery of arguments through analysis and research, together with the organization of the arguments we find. Later, in chapter 11, I will present the final aspects of policy debate: delivery, refutation, and resubstantiation of arguments.

BASIC TERMS OF FORENSIC DEBATE

As I noted earlier, forensic debate is a field of argument for which many formal decision rules have been developed. By their nature decision rules are particular to a situation. It follows that many of the rules of forensic debate will not apply easily to other contexts. Yet if we view forensic debate as a model of argument—just as the syllogism is a model—then we may learn much by studying the debate situation.[2]

The Proposition

The basic term in debate is "proposition." In debate the general subject matter under consideration (the subject of dispute) is refined into a formally stated proposition.[3] For instance, on the general subject of medical care, the proposition may be formulated in the question "Resolved: That the federal government should establish a compulsory program of comprehensive medical care for all United States citizens." A proposition, as you can see, is an asserted conclusion pertaining to a general subject matter. The proposition serves as the starting point for the debate. It sets the arguers on a particular course and restricts them to that course. Thus, on the proposition cited above, the advocates must argue for and against programs of medical care. They are precluded from debating about veterinary medicine, the Cincinnati Reds, or

---

[1]As taught in speech communication departments, debate generally may be called academic debate or contest debate. Most often, debate uses the forensic debate model. The term "forensic" is derived from the Greek word for legal oratory. Thus, the forensic debate model is akin to argument in law courts. Occasionally, academic debate is presented in the parliamentary style, which is modeled after the rules of parliamentary procedure.

[2]Hereafter, I generally will use the term "debate" to denote "forensic debate." The names of other forms of debate, such as "parliamentary debate," generally will be cited in full.

[3]The proposition sometimes is referred to as the "resolution," because propositions begin with the word, "resolved." Propositions also are sometimes called "questions," as in the parliamentary expression, "putting the question [resolution] to a vote."

contemporary rock music. According to the rules of debate, such extraneous matters would not be given any argumentative weight.

Notice that the above proposition is a proposition of policy. A proposition of policy—which is the normal starting point in debate—may be defined as a proposition that advocates that some specific action be taken with respect to a subject matter. In the above instance the proposition specifies that a compulsory program of comprehensive medical care be established for United States citizens by the federal government. Of course, this is not the only action that could be taken on the subject of medical care. A voluntary program could be established; it could be implemented by state governments or by the private sector of the economy; and many other variations are possible as well. Thus, it is possible that several propositions could be created for a given subject area. However, in debate only one proposition is selected and debate proceeds on the basis of this single asserted conclusion.[4]

Although the proposition limits the debate on policy to a yes or no decision on a particular approach to the subject, it also raises a host of subsidiary questions. In the resolution on medical care, we may identify several underlying issues pertaining to a federal, compulsory, comprehensive program. These include: (1) How many people today are covered by private and public programs of medical care (fact); (2) the relative advantages of public medical care as compared to private insurance policies (definition); and (3) whether or not present medical care programs are doing a good or a bad job in meeting the needs of United States citizens (value). Inasmuch as a policy question encompasses further questions of fact, definition, and value, debate theorists suggest that propositions of policy are particularly fruitful for study.

Because the proposition governs the conduct of a debate, it follows that special concern is given to the careful wording of the proposition. Generally, the proposition should be worded so as to avoid ambiguous or emotional terms. The proposition should deal with a single subject in a declarative statement. Specifically, the proposition should indicate the exact act (change) and agent (implementer of the change). Let us consider further these specific act and agent requirements.

Debate theory holds that the proposition must be worded so as to specify an act—a change that will be implemented.[5] The change can be constructive or destructive. That is, the act specified by the resolution may establish something

[4]Other types of propositions—those of fact, definition, and value—also may serve as the starting point for a debate. However, in actual contest practice this occurs less often.

A proposition of fact asserts a factual conclusion about a subject matter—e.g., "Resolved: That today is Tuesday." A proposition of definition asserts an interpretive conclusion—e.g., "Resolved: That the United Nations Organization is an effective body for promoting human rights." A proposition of value asserts a conclusion in which a value judgment is expressed, as in the case of "Resolved: That capital punishment is a just punishment for certain criminal offenses." However, because propositions of policy also involve subsidiary questions of fact, definition, and value, the traditional practice in contest debate has been to consider the merits of policy resolutions.

[5]When I later define the debate concepts of presumption and burden of proof, it will become clear why propositions must be worded to advocate a new change—a departure from the present way of doing business.

new or eliminate something now existing. The proposition "Resolved: That the federal government should place a heavy tax on new cars with gas mileage of less than 30 miles per gallon" is one that establishes a new course of action. It calls for a policy not now being enforced. Propositions also may take the approach of eliminating a present policy as in the proposition "Resolved: That federal price controls on natural gas should be eliminated." Many acts, of course, involve a combination of establishing and abolishing. Thus, in the medical care resolution cited earlier, the compulsory program would establish new actions but replace (eliminate) old policy approaches.

Although it is necessary for a proposition to specify a new act, there is no real requirement as to the amount of detail needed to describe the proposed change. Some resolutions describe the policy change in very general terms: "Resolved: That the United States should significantly curtail its foreign policy commitments." Here the resolution does not specify which commitments (foreign aid, military alliances, etc.) should be reduced, nor does it indicate exactly how much they should be reduced. A great deal of freedom is given to the advocates, who may take a large number of positions on the proposition. For example, arguers could support (i.e., affirm) the withdrawal of American bases from the Philippines; the affirmative could advocate withdrawal of the United States from the United Nations Organization. On the other hand, the resolution could be reworded to reduce the range of acceptable affirmative policy positions, as in the question "Resolved: That the United States should significantly curtail its military commitment to Taiwan." In this case the debate would be restricted only to military policy and only the military policy toward one country.

In addition to specifying an act, the proposition should identify the agency responsible for implementing the change. The resolutions cited up to this point have specified the "federal government" or "the United States." This is because the actions required by the propositions were either in the sphere of national domestic policy (controlled by the federal government) or in the area of foreign policy (a subject area that applies to the United States as a whole). In general, then, the resolution should place responsibility for change on the agency that exercises control (or could exercise control) in the area in which the action is to be taken. Thus, a resolution on capital punishment, the Equal Rights Amendment, or abortion laws might require action by state governments. This is because both criminal offenses and the ratification of constitutional amendments are largely (though not entirely) in the province of state government. Likewise, because international affairs are controlled either by international agencies or by treaties between specific governments, a resolution on international policy would specify action by an international organization (e.g., "Resolved: That nuclear weapons . . . controlled by an international organization") or by a group of national governments (e.g., "Resolved: That the Latin American nations should . . .").

In sum, the proposition specifies the act to be undertaken and the agency that should oversee the change in policy. The role of the proposition as a limiting factor is important and necessary for a coherent debate. The proposition specifies both what must be argued and what must not be argued. Topical arguments are those that legitimately belong to a debate on the given resolution. Extratopical or extrapropositional arguments are those that, under the provisions of the resolution, cannot legitimately be argued. The constraints on act and agency imposed by the proposition become an important element of debate analysis, as I will indicate later.

The Affirmative and Negative Sides

Debate rules specify that two sides, called affirmative and negative, will argue opposing positions on the proposition. As you might guess, the affirmative side (or advocate or team) supports (affirms) the conclusion stated in the proposition, while the negative opposes (or negates) that conclusion.

Each side usually is composed of two speakers, and the two sides alternate turns speaking, so that an affirmative speech is followed by a negative one. (I will explain the exact order of speeches, later.) The affirmative begins the debate when the first affirmative speaker presents a case to justify the conclusion asserted in the proposition. A case consists of arguments that support the affirmative position. However, a case is not a random collection of miscellaneous supporting arguments. It is an organized set of related arguments that establish systematically the affirmative (or negative) position on the proposition.

In the course of the debate, the affirmative and negative teams present, explain, and defend their respective cases. Both teams also spend an extensive amount of time refuting the opposition's case. Much of this chapter will be devoted to explaining how the affirmative and negative discover good arguments and organize them into a case. Case presentation, refutation, and resubstantiation will be explained in chapter 11.

Presumption and Burden of Proof

Given that the affirmative and negative both present positions (expressed as cases) on the resolution, it would seem logical that each has an equal opportunity to win the debate. However, because debate follows a legal model, this is not quite the way things operate. In actual practice the negative enjoys a slight advantage, because the negative side defends the present method of doing business—i.e., the present system (sometimes called the status quo). Since the time of Aristotle, the assumption frequently has been made that change involves risk and therefore that it is probably better to preserve the existing order (see *Rhetoric*, I. 8. 1365b25).

Because change is thought to imply risk, debate theory grants a presumption[6] to the present system. The present system exists—it occupies the ground—and, accordingly, it is given the benefit of the doubt when contrasted to new, untried, and hypothetical alternatives. As defenders of the present system (i.e., as opponents of the change required by the proposition), the negative side

---

[6]A presumption is an argumentative advantage that is given to some object or concept because it is thought to be likely or normal (see Perelman and Olbrechts-Tyteca, 1969, p. 71).

benefits from presumption. The negative side possesses a favoritism that persists unless or until good reasons are supplied to show otherwise.

Presumption perhaps is better understood, as a decision rule, when it is contrasted to its opposite—the burden of proof. Generally speaking, a burden of proof is a requirement to prove one's assertion. The necessity to prove one's argument is reflected in the saying "He who asserts must prove." This means that people must take the responsibility to justify their claims. Because the affirmative is the side which advocates a departure from the present system, it follows that the affirmative has a responsibility to prove the assertion of the proposition—that is, to demonstrate the superiority of the change proposed by the proposition. The affirmative must not only show that the policy change is good; it has, in debate, a burden of proof to show that the new system is better. After all, why should one take the trouble to change if the new way of doing things is no better than the old?

In debate, therefore, burden of proof may be viewed as the corollary of presumption. In other words, given that the negative position enjoys a presumption, the affirmative speakers (advocates of a new system) incur a burden to show the superiority of their proposed change. It is important to observe that the burden of proof continues to rest on the affirmative team throughout the debate. This is because a decision to keep the present system or to accept the new changes is made at the end of the debate. When the final tally is made, the affirmative must prevail (overcome presumption by successfully carrying the burden of proof) on all crucial points. If the affirmative fails to meet its burden on a major issue, then the affirmative side has failed to overcome the presumption on that issue. Who would accept a new policy approach (plan) that had a major flaw?

In sum, presumption is an advantage conferred on the present system. The burden of proof is the requirement to overcome the presumption by demonstrating the superiority of a new system. (See Ziegelmueller and Dause, 1975, pp. 19–20, for a justification of the general theory of presumption and burden of proof in debate.)

It is difficult to talk about presumption and burden of proof in the abstract. Let me now relate these two terms to a hypothetical set of arguments. (In so doing I will introduce two additional key terms of academic debate: the prima facie case and stock issues.)

Prima Facie Case   Assume that two teams have been assigned to debate the proposition "Resolved: That the federal government should establish a compulsory program of comprehensive medical care for all United States citizens." At the outset of the debate—before any speeches are given—the negative speakers enjoy a presumption. If for some reason the debate were to be cancelled, the present system would have a right to continue in force, because it had not been shown to be inadequate.

Because no change is required unless or until there is reason to make one, it is logical for the affirmative side to begin the debate. As I noted earlier, the affirmative and negative teams present cases to justify their opposing positions on the resolution. It follows that the affirmative would need to present a good case to justify a totally federal system of medical care as being better than the present mixed system of private and public medical care. When I say that the affirmative must present a good case, I am really saying that the affirmative side's burden of proof requires that it identify a case that reasonable people would accept as being a legitimate justification for change. This justification consists not only of a set of arguments to support change but also a specific program of action (plan) to implement the changes required by the proposition. Let us investigate the meaning of "legitimate justification."

Suppose that the affirmative team presented a case that consisted of three arguments in support of a plan:

Arguments (affirmative case)

1 We the affirmative speakers do not like the present system of medical care.
2 Yesterday, our friend Joe needed to wait in the emergency room for two hours to get treatment for a broken arm.
3 Our friend, Sally, recently had an appendectomy that was very expensive.

Plan (program of action)
Because of the problems of contemporary medical care, we believe that the following plan should be adopted:

1 All hospitals and other major medical facilities will be nationalized as part of a national health program.
2 All citizens will be guaranteed free medical care—to be paid for by tax revenues.
3 All physicians will be paid on a fee scale set by the national health program.

Would the three arguments, as presented, constitute a legitimate justification that reasonable people would accept as sufficient reason to adopt this particular plan? I hope that you are shaking your head, or otherwise indicating that they don't justify the proposed change, because I don't think that the above case is a good one. The present system of health care consists chiefly of private insurance and certain public programs such as Medicare (for the elderly) and Medicaid (for the indigent poor). Nowhere in the affirmative case is there any argument that demonstrates that for the vast majority of citizens, the present system of health care is inadequate. Even granting that Joe had to sit two hours in an emergency room and that Sally had an expensive operation, the affirmative team has failed to show that there is any reason to nationalize hospitals, pay the medical bills of all citizens, and make physicians federal employees. A reasonable person might well say, "So what?" to this affirmative case. On the face of it, the case fails to justify the change required in the proposition. The affirmative therefore has failed to overcome the presumption favoring the present system. The affirmative side's arguments have not met the burden of demonstrating a real reason to change the medical system for *all* United States citizens. Under these circumstances, the negative is under no responsibility to refute the affirmative case. It falls on its own merits (i.e., lack of merit).

It is clear that some affirmative cases will be insufficient to overcome presumption. Thus, to meet the burden of proof, the affirmative speakers must present a special sort of case. We call this case a prima facie case. "Prima facie" is a Latin expression meaning "on the face of it." A prima facie case is one that, in the estimation of reasonable people, is sufficient to establish the merits of a proposition unless or until arguments are brought against it. The case that we considered regarding a universal health care system for Americans was obviously—on the face of it—insufficient to prove much of anything. In contrast, a prima facie case is one that almost anyone can accept as establishing the merits of the proposition. A prima facie case stands on its own merits: It is sufficient to establish the proposition unless or until the negative side is able to refute it. A prima facie case is the only set of arguments that enables the affirmative side to meet its burden of proof. It is the only set of arguments that is sufficient to overcome the general presumption in favor of the present system.

Let me give you an example of a prima facie set of reasons to adopt a plan of comprehensive medical care. Suppose that the affirmative speakers, having seen the prima facie weaknesses of their earlier case, have reexamined the topic area. Assume that they have organized the following new case as a justification for the proposition.

  I The present system of medical care allows many thousands of persons to receive inadequate medical care.
     A Private insurance is inadequate.
        1 Private insurance is voluntary.
        2 Comprehensive coverage is expensive.
        3 As a result few people have comprehensive medical coverage.
     B Public programs are inadequate.
        1 They aid only a small segment of the population.
        2 They do not provide for all the needs of the recipients.
        3 They place burdens on recipients.
  II Only a compulsory and comprehensive program financed by general tax revenues will enable all citizens to receive adequate care, regardless of ability to pay.

Of course, this skeleton of a case leaves out many specific details. Assuming, however, that the affirmative debaters were able to substantiate the major claims of their case, the case would be prima facie in nature. It would establish that many citizens lacked adequate care and that present programs were responsible for the lack of care. These arguments would remove the presumption that the present system was the best method of medical care.

Clearly, the case just presented could be structured more effectively. For one thing, it would be good to mention some of the public programs that allegedly have failed. Nevertheless, unlike the first medical care case constructed by our hypothetical affirmative team, this second case would stand on its own merits. It would stand unless or until the negative side was able to demonstrate the superiority of the present system by either (1) refuting the details of the affirmative case or (2) showing that there exist weaknesses in the affirmative plan.[7] Unlike the previous affirmative case, which did not even require refutation (because it was not prima facie), this affirmative case at least requires the negative side to actively work to reestablish presumption. Notwithstanding its imperfections, it will stand until it is successfully opposed.

Stock Issues Close examination of prima facie cases reveals that they characteristically do several things. First, a prima facie case identifies a disparity between the reality of the present system and an ideal. In the second example case the ideal is "adequate medical care for all United States citizens" and the alleged reality is a lack of such care. The affirmative speakers may illustrate the disparity by identifying an unmet need, by identifying an area in which improvement is possible, or by pointing out an unmet goal.

A second feature of a prima facie case is that it proves the disparity between reality and the ideal to be significant. In the example above, the affirmative speakers demonstrate that many people lack adequate medical care—not just a few. The disparity is shown to be of wide and serious scope.

Thirdly, a prima facie case shows that the disparity between the real and the ideal is inherent. An inherent disparity is one that will not go away of its own accord or through natural processes. Unlike a mild cold, which we know will last only a day or so, an inherent problem will persist until some major new effort is made to eliminate it. In demonstrating that a disparity is inherent, the affirmative team must prove (1) that the present system cannot eliminate the disparity (even with minor changes in the system) and (2) that in the final analysis the best way to solve the disparity is to adopt the change prescribed in the resolution.

In the second sample case the affirmative speakers attempt to meet these two requirements of inherency. They argue that by its nature (voluntary and expensive) private insurance will leave many without comprehensive coverage. Further, they allege that the limited coverage and associated costs and/or inconveniences of public programs render them insufficient to meet the needs of all citizens. In short, the affirmative speakers are saying: "By its nature [its inherent quality as a federal, compulsory and comprehensive plan] our plan will be a better way to solve the disparity than the present system could ever be."

---

[7]Because the affirmative case establishes the affirmative's position on the resolution, it follows that the affirmative plan is technically an inseparable part of the affirmative case. However, the two terms—"case" and "plan"—are often discussed separately.

The final three features of a prima facie case are these: It must justify and culminate in a plan that solves the disparity (e.g., gives all citizens adequate, comprehensive care); it must be workable (i.e., shown to involve no infeasible details); and it must be free from serious disadvantages or drawbacks (i.e., it should cause far more good than ill).

These six necessary characteristics of the prima facie case are termed the stock issues.[8] Stock issues are those that normally arise in a proposition of policy. They are questions that any reasonable person would ask in seeking to decide between the present system and the change prescribed by a debate resolution. No one would accept a change unless it solved a significant and inherent disparity with a plan that more closely approximated the ideal (in a workable and advantageous way). The stock issues are so vital to the outcome of a debate that the affirmative side must amass a preponderance of proof on each stock issue. If the affirmative failed to establish even one stock issue, then no reasonable person would accept the affirmative position.

The Debate Judge   The rules of presumption and burden of proof are especially important in the determination of which team—the affirmative or the negative—has won a given debate. In chapter 1, I observed that all disputes come to some end or resolution. This is true in policy debate. However, the decision in debate (a judgment in favor of one side) is rendered not by a general audience, but by a judge. A debate judge is an impartial observer (often a teacher) who enforces decision rules and awards a victory to the affirmative or negative on the basis of who did the better job of debating.

The judge is a special audience. This is because the debate is not decided according to the judge's own opinion—as would be true in the case of a regular audience member. Rather, the judge seeks to separate the assessment of the debaters' skill in handling arguments from a personal attitude (the judge's) toward the arguments. Unlike some situations of argument, debate is a context in which the advocates do not themselves determine the outcome. They await the decision of the critic/judge. Occasionally, however, contest debates are held before general audiences. In this situation the advocates seek to persuade—that is, to change, maintain, or otherwise affect the attitudes of the listeners. However, because "lay audiences" are not attuned to the decision rules of debate, the common practice is to have debates decided by expert judges.

A Summary of the Rules

In the last few pages, I have introduced a great number of terms and decision rules that apply to the situation of forensic debate. The concepts of proposition, affirmative side, negative side, case, present system, presumption, burden of proof, prima facie case, stock issues, and judge really are quite straightforward. However, they can be difficult for the beginner. For this reason it probably will

---

[8]Although the six stock issues all are necessary features of a prima facie case, they may not always be sufficient. For instance, if a case contains irrelevant or untrue arguments, then it would not be prima facie in nature, even though it might, on the surface, pass the six stock issue tests.

be helpful for me to summarize the terms and their relationships before moving on to other subjects. Read over the following summary of the key terms of forensic debate. Make sure that you understand these important postulates of policy argumentation before you move on to the rest of the chapter.

I   Forensic policy debate begins with a proposition that specifies the subject and scope of the debate.
  A   The proposition asserts a conclusion on the subject chosen for debate.
  B   The proposition is worded so as to avoid ambiguous or emotional terms.
  C   The proposition must deal with only a single subject.
  D   The proposition specifies the specific act (new policy) that is to be taken.
  E   The proposition specifies the agency that is responsible for implementing the change.
  F   The proposition limits the arguments that legitimately may be presented by advocates.
     1   Topical arguments are those that are appropriate to the debate.
     2   Extratopical or extrapropositional arguments lie outside the sphere of allowable argumentation.
II   In forensic debate two sides—the affirmative and the negative—maintain opposing positions on the proposition.
  A   The affirmative side supports the change required by the proposition.
  B   The negative side opposes the change required by the proposition.
III   The opposing positions of the affirmative and negative sides are presented in a case. A case is an organized set of related arguments that systematically establishes the affirmative or negative position on the proposition. The affirmative case includes a specific plan that implements the change required by the proposition.
IV   Since the affirmative side advocates a policy that challenges the existing order, the affirmative is required to overthrow an existing presumption (favoritism) that the present system is the preferable way of doing business. This requirement to overthrow the favoritism given to the present system is termed the burden of proof.
V   In meeting this burden of proof, the affirmative side is required to establish a prima facie case.
  A   A prima facie case is one that, in the estimation of reasonable people, is sufficient to establish the merits of a proposition unless or until the negative side is able to refute it.
  B   Sufficiency of proof is the criterion for the prima facie case.
     1   A case with sufficient support cannot fall unless refuted by the negative.
     2   A case without sufficient support does not require refutation. It falls on its own merits. It can be dismissed.
  C   Sufficiency of proof may be more specifically understood by examining six necessary attributes of a prima facie case. A prima facie case must amass a preponderance of proof on each of the six stock issues. The stock issues are necessary (but not the only) requirements for a

prima facie case. A case could meet the six stock issue tests but lack prima facie status because of untrue or invalid argumentation.

VI Stock issues are those that normally occur in a proposition of policy. They are questions that any reasonable person would ask in seeking to decide between the present system and the policy change prescribed by the resolution.

   A A prima facie case must establish that a disparity exists between the reality of the present system and some ideal. The case may demonstrate that there is a need to change, that change will produce advantages, and/or that change will better meet a goal.

   B A prima facie case must establish that the disparity is significant—i.e., that it is of wide and serious scope.

   C A prima facie case must establish that the disparity is inherent to the present system.

      1 An inherent disparity will not go away of its own accord or through natural processes.

      2 An inherent disparity will persist until some major new effort is made to eliminate it.

      3 An inherent disparity can best be eliminated by implementing (via the affirmative plan) the change required by the resolution.

      4 If a disparity is truly inherent, the present system—even with minor improvements—will be inferior to the affirmative plan as a means of eliminating the disparity.

   D A prima facie case must support and culminate in a plan that is able to remove the disparity—i.e., to solve a problem, accrue an advantage, or meet a goal.

   E A prima facie case must support and culminate in a plan that is workable. In order to be workable, the details of the plan clearly must be functional.

   F A prima facie case must support and culminate in a plan that is free from serious disadvantages or drawbacks. This means that the plan must cause far more good than ill.

VII The affirmative side must carry its burden of proof (involving, especially, its obligation to present a prima facie case) throughout the debate by maintaining a preponderance of proof on all crucial issues.

   A At the end of the debate, the affirmative side must prevail on all stock issues.

   B At the end of the debate, the affirmative must prevail on all other vital issues which have arisen in the debate.

VIII The judge impartially applies the decision rules of debate to the cases presented by the affirmative and negative sides.

   A When a preponderance of proof has been established by the affirmative team on all crucial issues, then the affirmative has undertaken successfully its burden to supplant negative presumption. In this event, the judge awards the decision to the affirmative side.

   B If the negative side is able to carry any crucial issue, then the negative has identified a fatal flaw in the case or plan proposed by the affirmative side. In this situation, the negative has upheld the presumption favoring the present system and is awarded the decision by the judge.

These eight postulates of forensic policy debate represent a general consensus on the part of debate theorists. However, while some disagreement persists as to the meaning of debate terminology (see Brock et al., 1973, pp. 146–163), the set of definitions and rules outlined constitutes a good starting point for learning policy debate skills, Having learned some of the basic terminology and procedures, you are ready to move on to the more important matters of analysis, organization, and case building.

ANALYZING DEBATE PROPOSITIONS

As I have observed several times, the debate begins with a formally stated proposition. Because the proposition controls the range of acceptable arguments, positions, cases, and plans, it follows that debate preparation starts with an overall analysis of the proposition. Generally speaking, this initial analysis of the proposition—which is completed by both the affirmative and negative sides—consists of two interrelated steps: (1) analysis of the meaning of the proposition and (2) analysis of the nature of the present system. Having accomplished the steps of this preliminary inquiry, the affirmative and negative are ready to begin gathering evidence and building cases.

In the next few pages I will describe the two steps involved in the initial analysis of the proposition. In explaining this dual process of analysis—and for the remainder of the chapter—I will be using the hypothetical proposition "Resolved: That the federal government should place greater controls on the content of entertainment programs broadcast by national television networks."

Analyzing the Terms of the Proposition

Confronted with the above proposition—or any proposition—the logical first question becomes: What does the proposition mean? Understanding the proposition requires that the debater examine the major terms (words) of the resolution. Let us observe how a debater might interpret the above resolution that I have chosen for illustration. This proposition appears to involve five major collections of terms. The debater would seek to determine the meaning of each of them.

"The Federal Government" Clearly, the resolution specifies that action should be taken by the highest level of national government. However, to designate the "federal government" as the agent does not answer all questions about exactly who should implement the change. This is because the government in Washington is composed of the executive branch, which includes many regulatory offices and agencies, plus the legislative and judicial branches. Indeed, the resolution assumes that if the affirmative side can justify change,

Congress will enact the needed change, the courts will find it constitutional, and the executive branch will sign and administer it.

Who actually will be in charge of the affirmative plan? Given the complexity of modern government, it usually is the case that some existing administrative department or regulatory agency currently has a concern with the debate topic area. In this present proposition the Federal Communications Commission (F.C.C.) has a degree of control in the broadcast communication area through its power to issue licenses to local stations. However, the commission exercises little control over the television networks. Also, the Federal Trade Commission (F.T.C.) plays a role in the regulation of television advertising. It is important to note, however, that the debaters are not required to increase the powers of the F.C.C. or F.T.C. The debaters are free to construct a plan that restructures the national control of the network television industry—provided that the control still is exercised by the "federal government."

"Should"   Debate propositions usually are worded to specify that a given change should be made. The addition of "should" to a resolution means that the debate centers around whether or not a change ought to be made—not that it will or will not be made. The distinction between "should" and "will" is an important one. In the real world of policy analysis, an advocate must be concerned not only with proving that something should be done, but also with the question of the government's (or some other group's) willingness to approve the change. In politics, one can have a perfectly cogent case to prove that some national action should be taken, only to find that the Congress will not so act.

Fortunately, the debater's task is more limited. Because debate is a laboratory exercise, the common practice is to exclude considerations of "will" and to concentrate on issues of "should." It is considered sufficient that a team demonstrate that an action should or should not be taken. If the team proves that some action "should" be taken, the assumption is granted that the relevant agency "will" do so. Hence, in debate "should" is commonly defined as "ought to but not necessarily will," meaning that the debater must prove only that something should be done, not that it will be done.

The distinction between whether something should or will take place has significant implications in determining the range of acceptable arguments in a policy debate. Assume that an affirmative team has proven that increased controls should be placed on network television entertainment programming—and that the team has expanded the power of the F.C.C. to exercise this control. Assume, further, that the negative team is able to prove that the F.C.C. members presently are opposed to such controls. Because of the term "should," the negative side cannot legitimately use its argument that the F.C.C. will refuse to act as the affirmative desires it to act. Under the normal rules of debate, once the affirmative has demonstrated that greater controls should be placed on the content of television programs (by the F.C.C., acting as the "federal government"), the affirmative need not prove that the F.C.C. actually will impose the

greater controls. Hence, the question of whether the presently constituted
F.C.C. desires to implement a plan of "greater control" is irrelevant.

There is one exception to the general understanding of "should." If an
affirmative side bases its case on the contention that the main difficulty with the
present system is its inherent unwillingness to take action on a problem, then the
negative team is justified in demanding that the affirmative prove that the agent
of change (specified in the proposition or plan), in fact, will act as it should. This
line of argument is termed the "should-would" or "attitudinal inherency" issue
in debate.

"Place Greater Controls"   This phrase provides the first major hint of the
act that the proposition requires. To determine the meaning of "greater
controls," the debater would need to identify the nature of controls presently in
force. The resolution would demand that the affirmative plan contain controls
that were significantly more stringent than those currently being applied.

"On the Content of Entertainment Programs"   This phrase further qualifies the nature of the act. The term "content" would require the debate to center
on the words and pictures actually broadcast. The term "entertainment
programs" would seem to exclude from debate those programs that were
devoted to news, sports, weather, advertising, and information (documentary
and public service programs). However, the line between entertainment and
information, for example, is a fine one—as is the distinction between entertainment and several other of the program categories.

To take another example of the difficulty in defining "content of entertainment programs," it is clear that advertising is presented during certain
entertainment programs; it could be argued by some that the proposition
requires advertising to be controlled, because advertising may be a part of the
content of an entertainment program as actually seen by people. Granted, it
seems to be stretching the point to argue that the proposition requires a greater
control of advertising; but "unusual" interpretations of terms always are
possible when a proposition must be deciphered by competing advocates, each
of whom seeks to gain an advantage by a particular construction of the
resolution.

"Broadcast by National Television Networks"   This final phrase places
additional limits on the act being debated. The term "television" apparently
excludes radio. The specification that controls be placed on "national television
networks" also reduces considerably the scope of the resolution. Two points
seem clear: First, entertainment programming originated by local television
stations would seem to be excluded from control; secondly, the greater controls
would definitely apply to entertainment programs marketed by the major
television networks—the American Broadcasting Company, the National
Broadcasting Company, and the Columbia Broadcasting System.

Yet, there are sources of entertainment programming other than the "big three" networks. Some shows are produced and circulated to local stations by independent syndicates. Other syndicates circulate programs such as "I Love Lucy" which long ago were broadcast by the networks. There also exist independent networks that broadcast sports, religious programming, and so on. Finally, in recent years, cable companies have begun to produce their own programs in addition to transmitting shows originated elsewhere. Overall, the debater would be forced to judge whether syndicated programs and entertainment offerings by small networks and cable companies were subject to control under the terms of the proposition.

Taken individually and together, the terms (words) of the resolution require considerable interpretation. Ideally, the affirmative and negative sides would come to agreement on the case and plan requirements of the proposition. However, because language carries with it a certain degree of ambiguity, there exists considerable potential for conflict on the meaning of the resolution itself.

Analysis of the Present System

Once the general meaning of the proposition has been ascertained to the satisfaction of the debaters, the focus of attention shifts to the nature of the present system. As I noted earlier, both sides in debate must come to some understanding of what the present system entails. For the affirmative the present marks a jumping-off point, because the affirmative team must advocate a change that goes far beyond the scope of the current manner of operation. The negative, too, is interested in the present state of affairs, because one major negative strategy is to contend that the present system is superior to the affirmative plan. There is no such thing as the one right way to analyze the nature of the present system. Thus, I will introduce several ways to gain an understanding of present conditions in the topic area of debate. Let us continue to study the broadcasting resolution as an illustration of subject analysis.

Elements of the System   A good starting point in the analysis of the present system is to gain a notion as to how the elements of the system fit together. In the hypothetical "greater control" resolution, one major question concerns the present relationship of the federal government to the broadcast industry. Because the resolution requires greater government controls to be placed in television programming, it is appropriate to identify the present status of government controls.

As I noted before, two government agencies—the F.C.C. and the F.T.C.—exercise federal authority over aspects of television broadcasting. The F.C.C. grants multiyear licenses to corporations, permitting the corporation to use a particular frequency in a particular location. The F.C.C. measures the performance of licensees against legal requirements (expressed in the Communications Act of 1934, as amended) and F.C.C. standards. During the license granting and renewal period, the F.C.C. listens to presentations by the license holder, by groups competing for the license, and by other interested parties.

The nature of F.C.C. control of network programming would be of particular concern to debaters. Although networks originate a great deal of entertainment fare, the F.C.C. does not grant a license to the network itself, but only to the local affiliates of the national network. As a result of this the resolution would require an extensive change in the direct relationship of the government to the national television networks.

Other units of the federal government—the F.T.C. and the White House Office of Telecommunications Policy—exert some influence on network policy and thus would need to be investigated. Some attention would also have to be given to the Public Broadcasting System and its relationship to the demands of the resolution.

The question of the relationship existing between the government and the networks is not the only means of probing the nature of the present broadcasting system. Because the resolution that we are considering deals with programming content, it would be appropriate for the debaters to study the present method by which entertainment programs reach the television screen. This question would draw the advocates' attention the the production of television shows and the process by which the networks acquire shows. This would lead logically to a study of the connection between the national networks and their affiliated local stations. Arguers would examine the degree to which the station and the network controlled the scheduling of entertainment shows. Because all programming goes through the local station, and because the affirmative team could control local stations only by working through the networks, the station-network relationship would be critical. By posing and answering broad questions such as those dealing with the government-network relationship, television production, and the station-network connection debaters would be able to isolate elements of the present system. The advocates would become aware of the interaction among elements of the entertainment broadcasting system.

Historical Background   A second general method of learning about the present system is to study the historical background of that system. Arguers would ask such questions as: How did things get the way they are now? What differences exist between now and then? One should not assume that a chronological survey of the subject area is only of historical interest. The debater can gain useful information about the present system and possible future systems by studying past operations.

Consider an example of how historical inquiry may be of benefit to the debater. If an advocate were researching a resolution on governmentally imposed wage-price controls (such as those imposed by President Nixon in 1971), the advocate could gain much useful information by studying both Nixon's system and the method of price controls that operated during World War II. Information about World War II controls possibly could be directly relevant to the topic at hand—allowing the debater to argue comparatively. If, for instance, the World War II plan had been hard to enforce, then the debater would have a good precedent for challenging the feasibility of a new plan of controls.

The same comparative principle holds true for research into the history of broadcast programming and government regulation of broadcasting. By studying the legal history of government broadcast regulation, as expressed in the Radio Act of 1927, the Communications Act of 1934, and rulings by the F.C.C., the debater would have both a good notion of the present structure of regulation and a sound basis from which to predict the direction of future government action.

Disparity Analysis   Ultimately, analysis of the present system is evaluative in addition to being descriptive and interpretive. This means that both sides will be making value judgments about the status quo. The affirmative will look for undesirable aspects of the system and will argue for change in these areas. Generally speaking, the negative will evaluate the present system more favorably. Both teams will compare the present state of affairs to some notion of an ideal. The affirmative will seek to identify a disparity between the present and an ideal future. In contrast, the negative normally will attempt to deny or minimize the disparity. The affirmation and denial of the stock issue of disparity is therefore a third general method for probing the nature of the existing order.

In pursuing a disparity analysis, the debater compares present conditions to future possibilities. Traditionally, three approaches have been used to affirm that a disparity exists. First, it may be argued that one or more problems exist that create a need to change the present system. Second, an affirmative team may identify goals or ideals in the topic area (e.g., goals for entertainment broadcasting or an ideal situation of entertainment programming). The affirmative can argue that the goals and/or ideals are presently not being met. Finally, the affirmative side may look to the future and identify the possible advantages to be gained by implementing a new system. These alternative approaches— need, goal, and advantage—constitute the three most common types of affirmative cases. I will consider each in detail later.

Applying these three case approaches to the resolution on government control of entertainment broadcasting, the arguer would be on the alert for several things. One thing to watch for would be possible problems: Excessive portrayal of violence on television might be fruitful, here. The advocate would search for certain potential unmet goals. Through reading the debater might come to feel that there presently existed a lack of public interest considerations in broadcasting as networks sought to maximize profits. The area of advantages to be gained might stimulate the debater's interest in a requirement for more variety in television programming, so as to better reflect diverse public preferences. Violence, public interest, and variety would be only three of many approaches to the disparity question.

Debaters on the negative side would duplicate the affirmative's interest in all possible sources of disparity. Of course, the negative side generally would seek information to deny the alleged need, unmet goal, or advantage.

For both sides, then, disparity analysis would be a helpful starting point for work on the debate proposition.

Stock Issues Analysis A fourth general method for analyzing the present system—the stock issues approach—is one that builds upon disparity analysis. Disparity, of course, is the first or most basic stock issue. It calls the debater's attention to possible needs (problems), potential deviations from goals, and attainable advantages of new policy. However, in following the stock issues method of inquiry, the advocate would go beyond the identifying of one or more discrepancies. The advocate would probe to learn about the significance or importance of the disparity, together with the inherency of it. Furthermore, the arguer would work to ascertain the extent to which a plan could eliminate the disparity. In this connection the workability of the plan and the overall balance of the advantages compared to the disadvantages would be of interest. In short, stock issues analysis would involve testing the present system by means of all six of the stock policy questions. Let us look to see how an advocate might undertake such a testing procedure.

The Disparity Issue As I have noted the approaches of need, unmet goal, and advantages of a new plan are the three most common means of isolating a discrepancy between a real present system and an ideal future. An advocate's exploration of violence levels could lead to a claimed need. Alternatively, as we saw earlier, an advocate could allege that the networks pursued profit to the detriment of public interest and could use this as a basis for contending that the present system did not meet the goal of public interest broadcasting. I used the value of variety in programming as a possible advantage of a new plan.

Claims about violence, public interest (versus profit), and program variety would require close investigation of many questions. What, for example, *is* "violent programming," and why does it require control? Similarly, what is the "public interest"? Why does the network profit system work against the public interest? Finally, how would a system of "program variety" differ from today's television offerings? Why would variety be better?

The identification of disparities is only a starting point in a stock issues investigation of a proposition. In this method of analysis, attention shifts quickly to the significance and inherency of the alleged deviations from the ideal.

Significance of Disparity To say that a disparity is significant means that it is of such importance as to require a major policy change. In analyzing the present system, advocates must not content themselves with finding a problem, unmet goal, or new-plan advantages. The advocate must search for a *compelling* need, goal, or advantage.

In determining the significance of a disparity, the debater must take a hard look at the alleged need, goal, or advantage-based disparity. Earlier, I cited the portrayal of violence on television as a hypothetical need. In assessing the significance of this problem, the debater would search to see whether demonstrable harms resulted from violence-oriented programming. The would-be affirmative advocate would have to go beyond merely explaining the meaning of the problem: It would be necessary to document that the problem brought about such harms as to positively demand the affirmative plan (which outlined the nonviolent alternatives that greater government control would bring).

In attempting to isolate a compelling need, the affirmative-oriented arguer might allege that violent program content caused widespread undesirable social effects (e.g., crime). Alternatively, the advocate could seek to emphasize possible psychological damage that violence produced in the viewing public.

Once the significance arguments had been identified, the debaters (especially those interested in the negative side) would look for ways to deny the importance of the harms. Because the issue of significance places a burden of proof on the affirmative to prove a great magnitude of harm, the negative would need only to demonstrate that the harms were not widespread or serious. The negative side would not be required to show that violent programming was totally harmless. In using the significance test as a basis for analysis, the negative would ask such questions as these: How many people are affected? How serious are the effects? What evidence exists to causally connect televised violence to prevailing social conditions?

Affirmative and negative team strategy would be similar for debates centering on unmet goals or potential future advantages. As in the case of needs analysis, the burden would rest on the affirmative to show that a significant goal was largely unmet or that a major advantage could be won by means of the plan. The negative side would look for ways to minimize the extent to which a goal was significant or unmet and to downplay the importance of a possible new advantage.

Inherency of Disparity   Analysis of the present system by means of the stock issue of inherency requires advocates to consider the ability of the present system to bridge the disparity without resorting to the affirmative plan. This stock issue draws our attention to all the various disparity-reduction possibilities existing in the present system. As I noted in my explanation of basic terms, the stock issue of inherency places four burdens on the affirmative side: (1) to prove that the disparity will not go away of its own accord due to natural evolution; (2) to prove that the disparity will persist until some new effort is undertaken to eliminate it; (3) to prove that the disparity can best be eliminated by implementing (via the affirmative plan) the change required by the resolution; and (4) to prove that even with minor improvements, the present system will be inferior to the affirmative plan as a means of ending the disparity.

In using the inherency issue as a guide to analysis, both sides must examine carefully the causes of the alleged disparity. If, for example, the affirmative desired to prove the inherent harm of violence on television, these advocates would need to consider why violence would persist in the present system, despite possible present efforts to reduce it or to modify its effect. To this end the affirmative might argue that violence attracted large audiences and, because of profit competition, the networks would be unable to reduce the level of violence unless all were expressly required to do so by the affirmative plan. This set of arguments would establish a "line of inherency"—i.e., a line of reasoning that explained why the present system could not eliminate violence, whereas the affirmative plan could do so.

The negative side would need to seek out arguments to challenge the affirmative team's line(s) of inherency. In this connection the negative could claim that networks were presently cooperating in efforts both to reduce the level of violence and to portray violence in a more socially responsible way (i.e., not glorifying violence). With arguments of this sort, the negative side would be asserting that the problem of violence was already going away. The negative team could develop other inherency arguments such as the assertion that additional voluntary restraints on violence were possible. The negative could cite the possibility of broadcaster self-regulation through the National Association of Broadcasters. To qualify as inherency arguments, however, these additional restraints would need to be far short of the change required by the resolution.

There is a key point to be remembered in analyzing the present system by means of the inherency issue. This is that inherency deals with permanence of harm—not with the existence or significance of the harm.

As a final postscript, remember that the inherency issue is not restricted to "needs" cases. This test of permanence would apply, in similar fashion, to disparity claims based on unmet goals or future new advantages. The ability of the present system to better attain the goal or to more fully realize the advantage would be at issue.

Removal of the Disparity by the Plan   The stock issue of solving the disparity draws our attention to the ability of an affirmative plan to do what it is supposed to do—namely, remove a problem, meet a goal, or realize an advantage. Like the other stock issues, the solvency issue is a hunting place where the advocate can expect to find good arguments for and against the proposition. However, analysis of the solvency question does mark a slight shift of attention. The three disparity issues (the disparity itself, the significance of disparity, and the inherency of disparity) look chiefly to the nature of the present system. The solvency issue, on the other hand, changes the focus of analysis from the status quo (the way that things are) to the change required by the proposition (the way that things could be).

By again using the topic of federal control of broadcast content, we may observe the usefulness of the solvency stock issue as a guide to analysis. In the past few pages, we have considered a hypothetical affirmative indictment of violence in television programming. Specifically, we assumed that the affirmative team maintained two contentions: (1) that the portrayal of violence caused undesirable social effects (such as crime) and (2) that it led to psychological damage in viewers. Given these need indictments, the affirmative side would be required to construct a plan of government control that would be able to eliminate the disparity between the real present system and an ideal future one. In short, the affirmative would need to construct a plan capable of solving the problems. Having constructed such a plan, the affirmative team would be required to explain how the plan actually did away with the evils of the present system.

The first step for the proposition-supporting speakers would be to look for possible government controls capable of solving the problem of violence. Hypothetical alternatives might include (1) a monitoring agency that would assess the level of violence on network programs, (2) a legally imposed ceiling on total violent acts broadcast per day, and so on. Certainly these are not the only possible elements of a plan; but these two do illustrate the use of solvency as a guide to thinking about a new broadcast system based on greater government control.

Having written out a number of possible plan provisions, the affirmative side would then consider the potential beneficial effects of the provisions. Would the plan "planks" eliminate the harms? In answering this question, the affirmative team would seek to make predictions about a new system based on the plan. Given the affirmative argument that exposure to violence is harmful, it would seem to follow that a plan that significantly reduced the exposure would solve the problems caused by that exposure. However, the affirmative would need to establish that the monitoring agency could accurately rate levels of violence and that their ceiling would exclude enough violence to make a difference.

The negative team, too, would be interested in identifying the range of possible plans and effects of those plans. In studying the solvency potential of affirmative plans, the negative would look for reasons why a plan of government control, taken as a whole, would fail to eliminate the disparity—in this case, eliminate the harmful effects of television violence. The negative would look for exceptions that could doom a plan of government controls on network shows. The negative speakers might identify exceptions such as the following:

   1   The affirmative plan can control only television shows that are broadcast by the networks. Violent television programs originating from other sources— e.g., syndicated reruns, syndicated shows, local shows, cable television shows, etc.—could continue. Hence, the plan could not solve problems caused by exposure of viewers to violence.
   2   If violence on network television were reduced, the level of violence in movies, radio, comic books, etc., might increase. The public would seek exposure to desired violence by turning to other media.

These two lines of argument are only representative of the whole range of possible reasons that a plan of control on network shows might fail to eliminate the harmful effects of exposure to violence in television. Nevertheless, these two lines are typical of the "plan attack" arguments that one can generate when using the solvency issue as a guide to debate topic analysis.

In sum, the solvency issue draws our attention to the effect of a plan as a whole. Under the provisions of the resolution, the affirmative plan must place controls on *entertainment* programs broadcast by *national television networks*. The affirmative side would be limited to constructing a plan having these overall features. The affirmative would identify how such a plan eliminated evils (or, alternatively, met goals or accrued advantages). The negative would look for exceptions of such a plan *taken as a whole*. In the two samples of negative solvency arguments just presented, the negative side focused on the nature of the affirmative plan as a control on *national networks* (violence originates elsewhere) and as a control on *television programs* (people would turn elsewhere for violence). Hence, exposure to violence—and the alleged harmful effects thereof—could continue, despite the affirmative plan.

Plan Workability   In the previous section on the solvency issue, I emphasized that solvency deals with the ability of a plan, taken as a whole, to resolve a disparity. The stock issue of workability, on the other hand, causes debaters to analyze the details of possible affirmative plans. (Some theorists prefer not to separate the solvency and workability issues.)

The hypothetical affirmative plan that we have been examining included two provisions: (1) that a monitoring agency be established to assess the level of violence on network programs and (2) that a ceiling on total violent acts be imposed. Analysis of workability would involve consideration of the effectiveness of such details in eliminating the disparity. Both the affirmative and negative sides would consider the feasibility of measuring or indexing the violence level of all network shows. Both sides would consider such questions as (1) the possibility of measuring accurately the occurrence of violent acts; (2) whether a violence index would take into account the circumstances in which violence was portrayed; (3) whether the violence index rate would act on the basis of the degree of violence portrayed; and (4) how high or low the ceiling on violence should be.

The affirmative speakers would seek to answer these questions in such a way as to prove the feasibility of the plan. The speakers would need to demonstrate that their violence index was accurate enough and their ceiling was low enough to do away with the evils that they had identified.

The negative side would look for weaknesses in the mechanism of the plan. For instance, the negative side could claim that levels of violence could not be measured accurately or fairly. This argument could be used to prove that the plan was not workable—i.e., that it could not provide a machinery capable of stopping the problems caused by violence on television.

Plan Disadvantages   The stock issue of disadvantages causes the advocates to study the total effect of the affirmative plan. In analyzing a plan according to the disadvantages issue, the debaters confront the question "Does the plan do more good or ill?" The affirmative side seeks to prove that in addition to solving the disparity, the plan will be reasonably free of undesirable side effects. The negative side seeks to identify as many harmful side effects of the plan as possible.

Let us take a look at some possible disadvantages of the plan and, further, scrutinize some ways for the affirmative speakers to defend their plan against these disadvantages. Inasmuch as the affirmative plan gives the federal government new powers to control program content, the negative could raise the issue of government censorship. The negative might argue that giving the government the power to control the content of entertainment programs would lead to government control of the content of news programs. By using this argument of direction, the negative could argue that the plan undermined a free press. A second disadvantage that the negative team might pose would be that to a certain extent violence is a natural part of life. Thus, the negative speakers might claim that the affirmative plan would make television unrealistic and bland. Along this same line the negative team could further argue that a low ceiling on violence would preclude the showing of many classic programs on television—e.g., *Tom Sawyer* or *The Ten Commandments*.

In analyzing the plan from the standpoint of possible disadvantages, the affirmative side would need to prepare defenses against such disadvantage arguments as those that have been put forth. For instance, the censorship argument is a claim based on direction. Thus, in defending against this charge, the affirmative speakers would need to find arguments showing that control of violent entertainment programs would not lead to other controls on program content—especially news programs. The affirmative side might argue by analogy in this connection, citing F.C.C. controls on obscenity. The affirmative could argue that just as controls on obscenity have not led to news censorship, neither would controls on violence lead to such censorship. The disadvantage issue also would cause the affirmative side to search out reasons that the plan would not lead to unrealistic, bland programming. Here the affirmative might contend that the ceiling would allow some small amounts of violence. By taking this tack, however, the affirmative side would need to be careful not to give the negative a basis for arguing that because the plan still allowed some violence, it would not do away with the evils of violence on television.

As I noted earlier, the stock issues serve as a storehouse of potential arguments. Each of the six issues calls the debater's attention to important aspects of the proposition. In preparing for a policy debate, both the affirmative and negative sides will benefit from using the stock issues method of inquiry. The affirmative speakers can use the stock issues as a means for constructing and testing the strength of their case and plan. They also can use stock issues as a basis for anticipating negative arguments. In a like manner, those opposing the proposition can use the stock issues in inventing arguments. The negative can anticipate possible affirmative cases and plans. On this basis, the negative speakers can prepare arguments against various affirmative case and plan approaches.

In concluding this section on analyzing debate propositions, I wish to emphasize that I have not treated every possible system for inventing arguments. Related methods of invention are presented in Young, Becker, and Pike (1970), Monroe and Ehninger (1974), and McCroskey (1972). However, the analytic methods described here should be sufficient to get you started in working with your particular debate resolution.

GATHERING EVIDENCE

As I explained in chapter 2, the term "evidence" denotes descriptive, interpretive, or evaluative statements taken from others that reinforce an advocate's own arguments. In other words, "evidence" often refers to statements from third parties, as opposed to statements made by the debater.

Because it refers to the recorded observations and opinions of others, evidence is closely connected to research. "Evidence gathering"—as opposed to "analysis"—usually refers to consulting other sources for information that bolsters one's own arguments. Of course, analysis and evidence gathering are inseparable means of preparing claims on a proposition. Thinking through a proposition—analyzing it—suggests possible sources of evidence, and research—the gathering of evidence—suggests, in turn, new arguments.

Writers on debate traditionally identify a number of advantages to be gained by gathering and using evidence. As I have noted, research (evidence gathering) normally helps the debater to identify new arguments on the proposition. In this way evidence gathering helps the debater to compensate for a lack of personal experience in the topic area treated by the proposition. A second advantage of the gathering and utilization of evidence is that through evidence we give legitimate recognition to others for stimulating our thinking on the topic; we give credit where credit is due. Thirdly, the obtaining and using of evidence increases the explicit connection between our own arguments and the real world. When debaters are able to cite others who have made similar observations, interpretations, and evaluations, they add credibility to their own personal conclusions. Evidence helps us to make a personal conclusion more "real" by showing that it is not just the product of one fevered brain.

Library Research

My main purpose in this section on evidence will be to identify various alternatives for gathering and recording evidence. Because the rules of academic debate require teams to use evidence obtained from the public sector (i.e., evidence that is available to all who look for it), it follows that most evidence gathering occurs in the library. Of course, the best way to become familiar with your library is to consult the library guide, which most institutions provide or, when necessary, to consult the reference librarian. Nevertheless, I would like to mention briefly five general categories of material that are available to the library researcher: books, periodicals, newspapers, government documents, and other miscellaneous reference works.

Books   Traditionally, the main business of a library has been to acquire and catalogue books. Although this is less true today—because libraries have expanded the information retrieval process—it remains the case that most library space is devoted to books.

Books generally are indexed according to author, title, and subject matter.

Cards containing this information are filed in the library's card catalogue. Most libraries also possess other lists such as the *Library of Congress Catalogue of Printed Books.* This may be of help in your research when your library is weak in the area that you are studying.

For the debater books have the advantage of containing extended treatments of a subject, but it is important to remember that by the time a book is published, the material usually is several years old.

Periodicals   Periodicals, including journals, magazines, and newsletters, are another fruitful source for research on any subject of debate. Most libraries maintain current subscriptions to hundreds of publications. For most debate topics there will be a number of publications that specialize in the subject under consideration. For instance, in the area of the government control of entertainment programming, such periodicals as the following would be sure to contain helpful information: *Journal of Broadcasting, Journalism Quarterly, Television Quarterly, Broadcasting,* and the *Educational Broadcasting Review.* Other topic areas would be similarly served by a set of specialized periodicals.

Of particular help in locating serialized material are the many periodical indexes. Your reference librarian will be able to help you to locate the most useful index for your subject. Some indexes are references for general literature. One of these, *The Reader's Guide to Periodical Literature,* probably is familiar to you. Others are semispecialized, as in the case of the *Public Affairs Information Service,* which indexes journals and magazines dealing with government, politics, and the economy. Still other indexes deal with a relatively small number of subject-related publications: The *Guide to Legal Periodicals* is one of these. Generally speaking, a periodical index will supply references for articles by author and subject.

Newspapers   Newspapers can be valuable for debate work because they present up-to-date accounts of events on a daily basis. Newspapers are most useful when the researcher has access to an index to the paper. Not all newspapers have indexes. *The New York Times Index* may be found in most college libraries. A number of the other major papers, such as *The Wall Street Journal* or the *Chicago Tribune,* also have their own indexes.

Government Documents   In recent years debate resolutions often have dealt with some form of government action. This fact, plus the wide range of regulatory and investigative roles of the government, make official documents particularly useful. Government documents are considered to have desirable qualities: They can be quite up-to-date; they often contain both pro and con material on a resolution; and they are available in many of the larger libraries.

From the U.S. Government in Washington, D.C., comes a host of congressional hearings and reports. Administrative agencies issue bulletins and publish their rulings. Government documents may be located either through the *Monthly Catalogue of United States Government Publications* or through the indexes of the *Congressional Information Service.* Publications by state and local governments vary both as to their comprehensiveness and their indexing format. Because each state and locality maintains its own format, your reference librarian is the best source of information on these materials.

Reference Works   A final set of materials for the debater includes a variety of general reference works. Almanacs, statistical collections, encyclopedias, dictionaries, and biographical collections are to be found in the reference section of the library. Normally, these materials will not contain a great deal of specific information on your particular subject. However, certain reference items can prove helpful. *Blacks Law Dictionary* is an invaluable source of data on the meaning of legal terms. Fact collections such as *Facts on File* or *Kessings Contemporary Archives* provide weekly summaries of national and world events. These can be of immense help when you are researching specific examples or happenings. Statistical collections, too, can aid you in getting a grasp on the basics of a topic. The Bureau of the Census publication, *Statistical Abstract of the United States,* is highly recommended in this connection.

Ultimately, experience is the best teacher in matters of library research, so expose yourself as much as possible to the many kinds of reference works. There is also another bonus inherent in library research: The skills that you develop in researching a debate subject will help you in your other studies as well.

As I noted earlier, a general rule of contest debate is that evidence should be available to all—it should rest in the public domain. As a result, evidence gathered by personal letters, surveys, interviews, and the like may not always be acceptable for debate; however, these materials can be very helpful in gaining perspective on the proposition of debate. Further, these unpublished sources will very likely alert you to other published information.

Finding sources of evidence is only the first step in gathering evidence. Even when you have identified collections of information pertaining to your subject, you are still left with the problem of deciding what to record. The major tests of argument that I presented in chapters 4 through 6 will help you to separate good evidence from bad. Beyond this, your analysis of the proposition will suggest areas in which the descriptions, interpretations, and evaluations of others can be a useful adjunct to your own arguments.

We have been studying a hypothetical affirmative indictment of televised violence. The affirmative side's case ideas would suggest areas in which research was necessary. The affirmative would consult library material to obtain evidence to the effect that: (1) the amount of violence is significant, (2) televised violence is not decreasing, and (3) media violence directly brings about undesirable social effects. Here the requirements of the developing affirmative case would suggest a number of points needing the support of evidence.

Similarly, the negative side would seek outside support for its contention that broadcasters are voluntarily decreasing the amount of violence on television, that the networks are not the only source of violent programming, and that a program of government control would damage the free press.

Just as the developing case structure will suggest needed evidence, so, too, will research aid in the refining of the case. Analysis and research go hand in hand, as I noted earlier. Thus, as you research you should jot down ideas for cases and/or plans and for case and plan attacks. Further, after you work out your best lines of argument, you can search for evidence to strengthen these conclusions.

Recording Evidence

Recording the evidence is the next step in the process of collecting supporting materials for debate. Perhaps the most commonly used format is the index card method. Because debaters handle so much information on a variety of subjects, they usually find it convenient to record evidence on 4×6 inch index cards (or cards of some other size) and file the cards by means of guide cards with tabs. Using this format a debater can store a great amount of material, add to the material when necessary, and gain access to the material quickly.

Guidelines for Index Cards   In recording the results of his research, the debater should follow these four basic rules:

1   Prepare each file card as an independent unit of data. Because the card system allows you to access each card individually, you should attempt to limit each card to a single idea. Occasionally, it is necessary to deviate from this rule, but it usually is confusing to record more than one point per card.

2   Keep each card as brief as possible. You should seek to record just the key points made by an evidence source. Shorter quotations are easier to use and can be read verbatim during the debate.

3   Edit the quotation fairly and accurately. Rules 1 and 2 often call for the debater to edit a longer quotation into a more manageable and useable format. Remember, though, that editing is a dangerous business: The debater is forever tempted to edit the quotation in such a manner as to improve its usefulness. Hence, the general rule of editing may be stated as follows: Edit only to facilitate communication of the author's real meaning. Sometimes, a quotation is not meaningful by itself and explanatory material must be added. Such information should be enclosed in brackets [ ] to set it off from the text being quoted verbatim. On the other hand, it is often necessary to condense a quotation. When words are eliminated, ellipses (. . .) should be placed at the point where the deletions occur. This will remind you that the quotation does not correspond exactly to the original. Overall, the editing should insure that the quoted excerpt is representative of the larger context from which it is taken.

4   Seek to record reasons, and not merely conclusions. In the course of your investigation, you will encounter many conclusional statements that support your position. One would expect to find, for example, many statements to the effect that televised violence is harmful or that televised violence is not harmful. Remember that unless the debater records the *reasons* that violence is thought to be harmful or not harmful, the quotation will be of little real value. The researcher should therefore seek to record the "why" or the "because" statements that precede or follow the author's conclusion.

Some Sample Index Cards   Having identified the exact statement to be recorded, the debater should use the following format in preparing the index cards for use. At the very top of the card, an explanatory heading should be included. This heading should explain in a few words the contents of the card. Next, the card should contain a complete identification of the information source, including the author's name, the author's qualifications, the title of the book or document (give the title plus the name of the periodical in the case of an article), date of publication, and page number. Finally, the quotation itself should be written out. Figures 10-1 through 10-3 are sample index cards prepared according to this format. The first quotation, shown in figure 10-1, reports a conclusion by the Surgeon General of the United States. However, the quotation is not "just" a conclusion: The first sentence indicates that the conclusion is based on a vast amount of study and reflection. For this reason, the first part of the quotation is significant to the total value of this piece of evidence. The heading of the quotation summarizes the essential point made by the Surgeon General. The source information specifies the author, his qualifications, and data about the document from which the excerpt is drawn—including the specific Senate committee, the date that evidence was given and the page of the transcript.

It is important to observe that the source information mentioned on the index card is only an abbreviated version of the full bibliographic citation. If cited fully, the above document would be identified as follows: "*Surgeon General's Report by the Scientific Advisory Committee on Television and Social Behavior, Hearings* before the Subcommittee on Communications of the Committee on Commerce, U.S. Senate, 92d Cong., 2d Sess., March 21, 22, 23 and 24, 1972." Although technically incomplete, the abbreviated source heading below does contain the essential details of who, what, when, and where. Abbreviations are all right so long as they contain the essential information.

Figure 10-1   A sample evidence card.

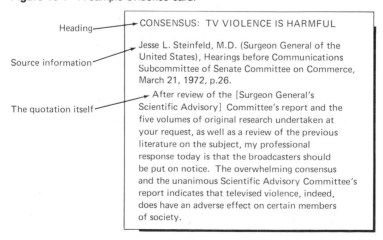

Figure 10-2 is another sample quotation of evidence on the subject of televised violence. This quotation, which presents a description and conclusion, could be used in helping to establish the idea that the networks desired to reduce levels of violence. Such a quotation would assist in supporting a negative team's inherency argument that the present system could control the portrayal of violence without the affirmative plan. As before, the heading captures the flavor of the quotation, and the source information identifies clearly, although in abbreviated form, the origin of the statement.

In figure 10-3, I present a third example of the format for recording evidence. This quotation illustrates the frequent need to gather secondary evidence. It would be better to quote directly from the original survey cited by Skornia. However, given the reliability of the source, who is a well-known authority on broadcasting, this "quotation of a quotation" would be acceptable evidence.

A statement such as Skornia's might have a number of uses in a debate on government control of broadcasting. The negative side, for example, might use this piece of evidence to prove that consumer boycotts could reduce television violence. If proven, this point might be seen as removing part of the need for a plan of government control. Hence, in figure 10-3 the debater has chosen to head the quotation "Viewers will boycott sponsors of violent T.V."

Organizing Evidence Cards

Collecting evidence cards is the second of the steps in preparing evidence for debate. Because the typical debater collects numerous file cards, the need arises to index the cards in a useful manner.

Figure 10-2   A sample evidence card.

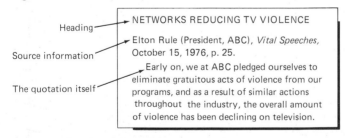

Figure 10-3   A sample evidence card.

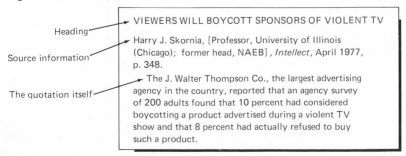

The Card File The typical indexing method is to file the cards under categories marked with tabbed guide cards. Figure 10-4 shows what a typical card file looks like. An effective filing system will enable the debater to secure appropriate evidence when it is needed in debate. The filing system should be specific enough so that the debater can quickly locate an indiviudal card when it is needed. On the other hand, the card file should be general enough so that several evidence cards may be indexed under a single tab card.

It is difficult to lay down hard-and-fast rules about the card file. However, three common guidelines apply to the organizing of a file card system. First, your system should reflect the subject under consideration. In the previous sections on analysis, we observed that the broadcast system consisted of television production, national networks, local stations, cable companies, syndicated program companies, government regulation, and so on. These topics—and their related subtopics—would suggest file headings. Secondly, your file system should reflect your analysis of the debate topic. Your affirmative case and plan will be particularly helpful in suggesting needed divisions. Finally, your file should be responsive to your opponent's potential analysis. You should anticipate possible cases and plans, and possible case and plan attacks, filing evidence to support or refute these.

Blocs In addition to the card file, many debaters find it helpful to prepare analysis blocs. An analysis bloc is a collection of arguments and/or evidence relating to a single point of controversy. Blocs are especially useful in two situations: (1) when the debater desires to organize corresponding arguments into a single line of argument and (2) when a certain issue recurs and the same arguments or pieces of evidence are being used over and over again. In both cases it is helpful to organize the related arguments (together with supporting evidence) into a single bloc of information. The bloc, then, is a collection of possible responses to a certain point that is likely to be raised by the opposition. The debater need not always present each and every argument contained in the bloc, but the bloc makes available a range of strong, related responses.

Generally speaking, one does not prepare blocs until one has some experience with the topic area. Blocs prepared too early may prove to be weak—they may not contain the best possible responses; "Early-bird" blocs may be irrelevant—they may fail to treat the most frequently argued issues.

Figure 10-4 A basic card file.

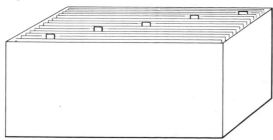

Nevertheless, when you have identified a set of strong claims pertaining to a critical issue, it may be useful to organize this material into an analysis bloc.

Figure 10-5 is an example of an analysis bloc. The bloc contains a general heading (like the evidence card) and specific subheadings, and the arguments are

Figure 10-5   An evidence bloc.

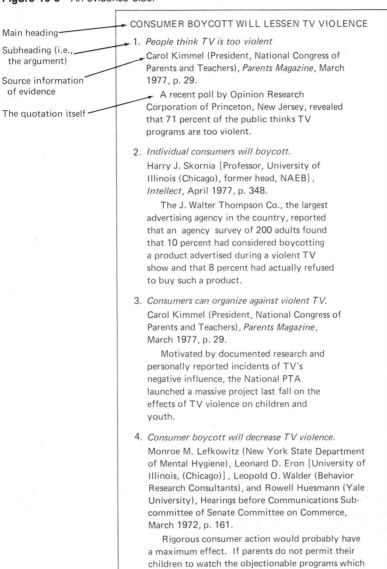

Main heading

Subheading (i.e., the argument)

Source information of evidence

The quotation itself

CONSUMER BOYCOTT WILL LESSEN TV VIOLENCE

1. *People think TV is too violent*

   Carol Kimmel (President, National Congress of Parents and Teachers), *Parents Magazine*, March 1977, p. 29.

   A recent poll by Opinion Research Corporation of Princeton, New Jersey, revealed that 71 percent of the public thinks TV programs are too violent.

2. *Individual consumers will boycott.*

   Harry J. Skornia [Professor, University of Illinois (Chicago), former head, NAEB], *Intellect*, April 1977, p. 348.

   The J. Walter Thompson Co., the largest advertising agency in the country, reported that an agency survey of 200 adults found that 10 percent had considered boycotting a product advertised during a violent TV show and that 8 percent had actually refused to buy such a product.

3. *Consumers can organize against violent TV.*

   Carol Kimmel (President, National Congress of Parents and Teachers), *Parents Magazine*, March 1977, p. 29.

   Motivated by documented research and personally reported incidents of TV's negative influence, the National PTA launched a massive project last fall on the effects of TV violence on children and youth.

4. *Consumer boycott will decrease TV violence.*

   Monroe M. Lefkowitz (New York State Department of Mental Hygiene), Leonard D. Eron [University of Illinois, (Chicago)], Leopold O. Walder (Behavior Research Consultants), and Rowell Huesmann (Yale University), Hearings before Communications Subcommittee of Senate Committee on Commerce, March 1972, p. 161.

   Rigorous consumer action would probably have a maximum effect. If parents do not permit their children to watch the objectionable programs which portray unnecessary violence and refuse to buy products advertised by such programs, the networks will quickly receive this message and develop programs which are more acceptable.

followed by supporting evidence. In this sample bloc, a number of arguments and pieces of evidence are organized to prove the single point that, through consumer boycotts, the present system can reduce televised violence. Potentially, this bloc would be valuable in supporting a negative line on inherency.

The strength of this bloc derives from the cumulative effect of the arguments-plus-evidence combination. The first argument establishes a motive for consumer action: People think that television is too violent.[9] The second argument demonstrates that people already have used the boycott method and that many more have considered using it. The negative team would want to argue that, given publicity, even more consumers would participate in an organized boycott. This is the thrust of the third bloc argument concerning the ability of consumers to organize. Even though the national P.T.A.'s antiviolence campaign is not a boycott of program sponsors, it does indicate a willingness of groups to campaign against violence. The logical extension of this argument would be to suggest that a boycott campaign was possible. Finally, the fourth argument of the bloc helps to prove that the boycott would work—that it would force a reduction in violent programming.

I have noted that it is not necessary for each point in the bloc to be supported by evidence. However, when relevant quotations are available, it is wise to include them in the bloc.

I have presented the index card, card file, and bloc methods of arranging information as being useful in organizing material for debate. These are not the only methods for gathering, recording, and organizing evidence. Indeed, if you have only a short time in which to prepare, if you have completed only a small amount of research, or if the topic is not a highly "factual" one, then the techniques that have been presented may not be helpful. In such a case you may prefer to make rough notes, to collect clippings and file them in folders, or to mark certain magazines and books. In any event, whenever evidence is appropriate and desirable, you will need to have a system for recording and indexing it. I have emphasized the card file and bloc methods because they are desirable in the extreme situation when relatively large amounts of information must be stored and retrieved. Furthermore, they are good research methods to acquire for later use in other situations.

BUILDING THE AFFIRMATIVE CASE

I have presented the topics of analysis and evidence before that of case building. You should not take this to mean that these two steps always precede case building. Indeed, all three steps are somewhat simultaneous and overlapping. Rather, I have treated analysis and evidence first because they are steps that both the affirmative and negative sides complete. Once the basic analysis is completed and evidence gathered, however, the affirmative and negative sides

[9]The negative side would need to be careful in making such a point. This might support the affirmative's need analysis. The negative speakers could maintain that violence was not *harmful* but that is *unpopularity* would serve as a check on the level of violence.

go their own separate ways, to a certain extent. I mean by this that affirmative case building and negative case preparation are somewhat distinct processes (although many debaters will prepare both sides of the question). Accordingly, I will devote the next two major sections of this chapter to a discussion of case construction strategies for the affirmative and negative positions.

You will remember that I described the affirmative case as being an organized set of arguments that establishes the affirmative team's position on the resolution. The affirmative case thus plays three major roles in getting the debate started. First, it provides the affirmative team's interpretation of the proposition. Because the proposition limits the range of legitimate argumentation, the affirmative case provides an explicit or implicit indication of what the affirmative side understands the proposition to mean. Second, the affirmative case justifies the change required by the resolution. You may recall that in order to overthrow presumption, the affirmative case must supply a prima facie case for changing the present system. Finally, in the broad sense the affirmative case includes the affirmative plan (although "case" and "plan" often are discussed separately). This case-plan relationship establishes a "third-and-a-half" function of the affirmative case—to specify the exact nature of the change that is demanded by the resolution.

Having reemphasized the basic function and scope of the affirmative case, I want to provide you with some suggestions for constructing affirmative cases. Also, I want to give you some case examples. Taken in its simplest form, case construction can be reduced to four steps:

1   Look for a disparity between the reality of the present system and some ideal situation. As I have observed earlier—the point bears repeating—affirmative teams generally take one of three approaches to the identifying of a disparity. Some look for a "problem" or "need" to be solved; others focus on an unattained goal. Finally, the affirmative side may seek to obtain advantages by substituting a new plan in favor of the present system.

The disparity analysis is only a first step in case construction. At best, this step fulfills only the affirmative duty in connection with the first two stock issues (disparity and significance of disparity). The affirmative team has four additional stock burdens yet to be shouldered.

2   Find the causes of the disparity. The notion of cause is a necessary part of an affirmative team's disparity analysis. If the affirmative team only proves that a disparity exists, they are vulnerable to the argument that the disparity is not inherent—i.e., that it may go away of its own accord, atrophy because of natural processes, or be eliminated by some existing feature of the status quo.

In seeking to find the causes of a disparity, the affirmative searches for material to support the notion that the disparity can best be bridged by the affirmative plan—that it cannot really be solved by the present system. To illustrate: If the cause of violence on television is the public's demand for violence, then it follows that only a government regulation can reduce violence. Because the networks compete for viewers, inherently they would cater to the public's desires—unless the desires were made illegal. This scenario would represent a potential affirmative line of inherency.

3 Identify a way of solving the disparity. The affirmative team has the responsibility to solve the disparity it finds. This burden coincides with the requirement that the affirmative team work out the details of the change required by the proposition. These burdens merge in the affirmative plan. The plan must explain how the disparity is to be removed and, in so doing, be consistent with the guidelines for change established in the resolution.

Basically, the affirmative plan must meet the three stock tests of solvency: the plan, as a whole must be able to remove the disparity, the plan must be functional (workable) in its specific details, and the plan must, on balance, do more good than ill (it must be advantageous, overall).

4 Organize the ideas gathered in steps 1 to 3 into a structure having three elements: contentions, subpoints and causal case links. Contentions are the major ideas in the affirmative case—the major themes in the affirmative's position. Contentions would be written as major points on an outline. Subpoints are subsidiary arguments that support a contention. Causal links are implicit or explicit statements that indicate (1) the relationship of the disparity to an element of the present system and (2) how that element (and hence the disparity itself) is to be removed by the affirmative plan. The final case organization should be something that can be outlined according to the format explained in chapter 2.

To be sure, the four elements of affirmative case construction are abstract and difficult for the beginner. It may be helpful, therefore, for me to work out examples of affirmative case structure. In the next few pages, I will present three hypothetical case outlines to illustrate the affirmative "needs," "goals," and "advantages" cases. (Recall that these are the three most common methods of presenting a disparity.) As before, my examples will focus on the proposition "Resolved: That the federal government should place greater controls on the content of entertainment programs broadcast by national television networks."

The Needs Case

Perhaps the most straightforward way to approach a given resolution is to organize affirmative arguments into a needs case. Recall that in a needs case the affirmative side identifies one or more problems (areas in which harm is occurring) and presents a plan to remedy the problems. In essence, the affirmative demonstrates a need to change the present system and then details a program (plan) of change.

In my description of the analysis and evidence-gathering processes, I have already given many hints as to how one might go about constructing a needs case. I have cited the subject of violence as a possible area of harm. Next we shall consider how a case might be built around the harmful effects of television violence. As you read through this case, see if you can follow how it relates to the four rules of case construction that I have emphasized.

I A significant amount of television programming is oriented to violence.
   A Network shows emphasize violence to attract the largest possible audience.

    1 Violence is popular.

    2 The networks control 80 percent of total daily programming.

  B Present controls are inadequate to deal with the problem of violence.

    1 The television industry's self-regulation has failed consistently.

    2 Because of provisions against censorship, government regulation presently is unable to curtail violence.

II Children are exposed to a great amount of television violence.

  A The nation's children watch a vast amount of television.

    1 Ninety-seven percent of American homes have at least one television set.

    2 Only 30 to 40 percent of a child's viewing time is spent watching programs designed for children.

  B It is impossible to prevent children from exposure to violent shows.

    1 Parents often are unable to monitor the child's viewing habits.

    2 Parents often are unwilling to monitor the child's viewing habits.

III Television violence is harmful to children.

  A The number of children harmed is in the millions.

    1 All children are affected to some extent.

    2 Many children suffer serious harms.

  B There are numerous harms.

    1 Television violence creates antisocial *attitudes*.

    2 Television violence reinforces tendencies toward antisocial *behavior*.

Plan

I An independent, seven-member monitoring commission will be established under the Department of Health, Education, and Welfare.

  A Members will be appointed by the President, subject to approval by the U.S. Senate, for terms of 7 years.

  B The commission may secure whatever staff and facilities are needed.

II The commission will impose the following controls:

  A Programming after 5:00 A.M. and before 9:00 P.M. must:

    1 Not depict more than two acts of serious violence (with or without a weapon) per hour against a person.

    2 Not depict more than four acts of serious violence per hour against property.

    3 Portray all violence in an unfavorable light, either by showing it as unjustified or by demonstrating its harmful consequences.

    4 Portray all violence in as brief a time frame as possible.

  B The limits set forth in statement IIA may be doubled for programs shown after 9:00 P.M. and before 5:00 A.M.

III Network programs will not be prescreened. The commission will call for an explanation if it determines that the limits have been violated.

IV Special advance permission to exceed the above limits may be granted when a particular program meets these tests:

  A It has a plot that requires more violence than the allowable level.

  B It is a "classic" program or possesses other positive social merit.

V A schedule of fines will be prepared and will be assessed against a network for violations determined by the commission to be deliberate, significant, or harmful. Fines may be appealed through the federal court system.

Let us take a look at the workings of this hypothetical case and plan. In the needs case outline, the three contentions are stated separately and denoted by numerals. Each contention is buttressed by two subpoints, with each subpoint in turn possessing two subpoints. The case is based on the notion that exposure to violence is significantly harmful to children (IIIA and IIIB). In contentions I and II, this harm is causally connected to the nature of network television programming. Contention I, subpoint A establishes that because of competition the networks seek violence as a means of gratifying the public's desires. This establishes, therefore, a line of inherency—suggesting that *by its nature* the present system is biased toward violence. In contention I, subpoint B, the affirmative team seems to establish additional lines of inherency by contending that neither industry self-regulation nor present government policy is capable of reducing the high level of violence.

Contention II, subpoint A is included in order to establish the necessary link between television violence and children. The affirmative debaters prove that children actually are exposed to the violent programming. Finally, in II, subpoint B, the affirmative team develops another line of inherency, suggesting that parental control will not be successful in preventing the exposure of children to violence.

It is important to observe that the above case outline does not include all the details that the affirmative would present in a speech based on the outline. For example, in explaining subpoint IIB1, the affirmative might provide two reasons that parents often are unable to monitor their children's television watching: (1) many parents work, and (2) many families own more than one television set. In the actual presentation of the case, these relevant details—plus appropriate evidence—would be given.

One final note on the basic case structure: Many teachers advise that an affirmative case should possess parallel structure. This means that if contention I has two major subpoints (A and B), each of which has, in turn, two subpoints (1 and 2), then contention II should be similarly structured. The sample needs case that I have outlined does possess parallel structure. In my view, however, this is more of an aesthetic criterion than one of paramount importance.

Having sought to establish the stock issues of disparity, significance of disparity, and inherency of disparity, the affirmative team presents a plan to solve the harms that they have identified. Notice that the plan acts directly on the cause of the alleged harms: the presence of violent acts on television programs. The plan sets a limit on such acts. Further, it is important to observe that the affirmative plan is consistent with the guidelines provided in the wording of the resolution. That is, the plan establishes control by the federal government on the content of network television programs. The plan fulfills each term dealing with the nature of the policy change. Furthermore, the plan's details are neither contrary to, nor do they go beyond, the intent of the resolution. The affirmative team has added only necessary details pertaining to the nature of the commission, provisions of the controls, and method of enforcement.

In sum, the above needs case is prima facie in nature. It meets the affirmative side's burden of proof on each of the stock issues. It supplies a rationale and method for change that would be accepted by reasonable persons unless or until refuted. I should emphasize, however, that this case is vulnerable to many lines of attack—as I will show in the following section on negative case approaches. Nevertheless, the case does fulfill its initial duties: It provides a definition of the terms of the resolution; it identifies cogent reasons for change; and it explains the nature of that change.

The Goals Case

The goals case—sometimes called a criteria case—identifies a disparity by (1) asserting that a given goal exists with respect to something (e.g., the broadcasting industry), (2) arguing that the goal is not presently being met, and (3) arguing that the goal can be best met by the affirmative plan. Consider the following example of a goals case.

I   Under the provisions of the Communications Act of 1934, the broadcast media are held accountable to a high standard of practice.
  A   Because the airwaves are public property, the medium of television should operate in the interest of the public as a whole.
  B   Because the medium of television is influential, it should operate in a responsible manner.
  C   Because the medium of television is pervasive, it should be accountable to the public.
II   In the present system these goals are not being adequately met.
  A   Network entertainment programs cater to the interests of only a segment of the population.
    1   Networks compete to achieve the maximum audience at each viewing hour.
    2   As a result, only those programs appealing to the largest audience segment are shown.
  B   Network entertainment programs reveal a lack of responsibility.
    1   Violence is prevalent in network shows.
    2   Violent programming is harmful to children and youth.
  C   The content of network entertainment programs is not presently scrutinized by the public through its elected/appointed representatives.
    1   The Federal Communications Commission denies that it has the power to supervise the content of entertainment programs.
    2   The public desires greater governmental controls on program content.

Plan

I   The powers of the Federal Communications Commission should be extended to cover the content of network television entertainment programming.

II The F.C.C. will require a more diversified schedule of entertainment programming.[10]

III The F.C.C. will require a reduction in the number and duration of violent acts broadcast on network television programs.

IV Network adherence to the above guidelines will be monitored, and a schedule of fines will be developed for noncompliance. Fines may be appealed through the federal court system.

The criteria case just outlined has the same essential features as the previously presented needs case: contentions, subpoints, and causal case links. As before, the affirmative side seeks to prove the existence of a significant disparity. In this case they are arguing that major goals are being largely unmet. Further, the affirmative endeavors to develop lines of inherency. This would be a major function of contention II, subpoint A, subpoint 1 as well as IIB1 and IIC1. Finally, in the plan the affirmative speakers present what they hope will be a solution having workable details—one that is reasonably free of undesirable side effects (i.e., disadvantages).

The goals or criteria case approach is used far less frequently than the traditional needs case. One likely reason for this is that the concept of unmet goals often does not have the same dramatic effect as that of harmful effects in persuading audiences to believe that a significant disparity exists. Because a goals establishment contention (e.g., contention I) has less dramatic power, affirmative teams often cite the goals in an introduction and spend a relatively greater amount of time demonstrating that the goals are not being met.

The Comparative Advantages Case

The comparative advantages case is another affirmative mainstay. It is quite frequently used—at times, even more than the traditional needs approach. Like the needs and goals cases, the advantages format is another strategy for proving that a disparity exists between the present and the possible. However, unlike the other case forms, the comparative advantages case begins with a plan and culminates in stated advantages to be gained through the plan. Theorists prefer this plan-before-advantages approach because it allows the audience to compare immediately the structure of the present system and that of the affirmative plan.

Here is a hypothetical example of the comparative advantages case.

---

[10]As in the previous plan for a needs case, specific guidelines would be presented in this connection. This applies also to step III of the plan.

Plan

I The Federal Communications Commission will be empowered to do the following:
  A Limit the frequency of violent acts shown in entertainment programs televised by national networks. (Appropriate details would be provided.)
  B Prohibit the broadcasting of advertisements for drug products during and between entertainment programs televised by national networks. (Appropriate details would follow.)
II Network adherence to the above guidelines will be monitored, and a schedule of fines will be developed for noncompliance. Fines may be appealed through the federal court system.

Advantages

I The plan will decrease the exposure of children to televised violence.
  A Network entertainment programs are oriented to violence as a means of capturing large audiences.
  B Children are exposed to large amounts of violence on television.
  C Violence is harmful to children.
  D The affirmative plan will strictly control the level of violence, in contrast to the inactivity of the present system.
II The plan will reduce the exposure of viewers to drug advertising.
  A Drug advertising is prevalent in entertainment programming.
  B Drug advertising creates a climate in which drug use is seen to be necessary even for minor discomfort.
  C Drug advertising contributes to drug abuse.
  D The affirmative plan will eliminate drug advertising during the peak viewing hours, in contrast to the inactivity of the present system.

You will observe that the two advantages have really nothing in common, except that they both follow from government controls of some type. Indeed, the comparative advantages format is particularly useful when the debater has identified a number of unrelated disparities that nevertheless have a common source (in this case, a lack of government control).

As before, the various stock issues are covered in the structure of the affirmative case. For each advantage the affirmative seeks to demonstrate a significant disparity. For each the affirmative seeks to demonstrate a line of inherency by suggesting that the plan accrues the advantages more effectively than can the present system. Also, as with the other cases, the comparative advantages plan is designed to shoulder the solvency, workability, and disadvantages burdens.

Although the comparative advantages case has many things in common with the case formats described earlier, debate theorists have not yet come to a consensus as to the relationship between the advantages approach and the more traditional needs case. (Cf. Dick, 1972, pp. 49–52, and Ziegelmueller and Dause, 1975, pp. 164–166.)

There is one final point worth raising about the specific advantages case just presented. As I noted in the earlier section on analysis, it is possible that advertising does not fit under the category "content of entertainment programs." Hence, the negative side may have cause to question whether the affirmative plan goes beyond the limits of the proposition in controlling advertising. I will raise this same point again in the following section on negative case strategy.

The three case formats described here should meet the requirements of most debate situations. However, because there is no single way to present a prima facie justification for change, the affirmative side is free to structure a case in any way that it pleases, so long as the case overthrows presumption. One may identify in debate literature references to other formats for organizing and presenting the affirmative's side of the policy question. These include the principles and preventative cases (Dick, 1972, pp. 46, 47, 52), the effect-oriented and on-balance cases (Ziegelmueller and Dause, 1975, pp. 166–168), the chain of reasoning, residues, systems, public interest and opinion cases (Rieke and Sillars, 1975, pp. 176–181), and the inverted-needs case (Smith and Hunsaker, 1972, pp. 136–137). In sum, the debater need not feel tied to a rigid format of case construction. A compelling rationale may be presented in many ways.

NEGATIVE CASE ALTERNATIVES

It is often difficult to talk in specific terms about the negative "case," because the negative side traditionally spends more time in refutation than in constructive case building. Yet, given the definition of "case,"—an organized set of arguments that establishes an advocate's position on the proposition—it is clear that in order to be successful, the negative team must also have a case. Part of the reason that the term "case" does not seem to fit the negative team's role in debate is that the negative speakers can prepare only a portion of their case in advance. Much of what the negative side does is a response to affirmative initiatives. The negative speakers must remain flexible. They must stand ready to adapt to the structure of the affirmative case and plan. The nature of the negative case, therefore, is one that requires careful attention.

In general, one can say that the negative case really consists of two elements: (1) constructive arguments (new ideas) initiated by the negative speakers, and (2) refutation of the case advanced by the affirmative side. Sometimes, the difference between the negative's constructive and refutation arguments is quite pronounced. For instance, the first negative speaker in a debate[11] often presents an initial "philosophy" of the negative side before attacking the specific points made by the first affirmative speaker. The philosophy is an overall construct initiated by the negative side, whereas the

---

[11]I will give detailed consideration to speaker duties in chapter 11.

point-by-point attack is an adaptation to a case structure established by the affirmative side. For this reason many debate texts speak of "straight refutation" (i.e., a point-by-point analysis of the affirmative case in which little attention is given to establishing a central negative position) as a negative strategy of advocacy.

Overall, though, the dichotomy between the negative team's constructive and refutation arguments is a difficult one to maintain. The negative's constructive arguments have the effect of refuting the affirmative case by showing its weakness on an issue. Similarly, the negative's refutation arguments establish a difference between the affirmative and negative sides. In other words, the refutation arguments help to define or construct the negative position. For these reasons it may be more helpful to view the negative's options against the background of the present system. Just as the present system exists as a starting point for the affirmative team, so, too, is it a starting point for the negative. Basically, the negative side has the option to defend the present system as it is,[12] to maintain a modified defense of the present system, or to abandon the present system in favor of another position.

Defense of the Present System

Defense of the present system has been the traditional position selected by negative speakers in debate. In taking such a position, the speakers deny the existence of a significant and inherent disparity. Consider how a negative team might use defense of the present system as a position from which to challenge contention III of the affirmative needs case presented earlier. The affirmative argued that millions of children were harmed by television violence and listed two basic harms: (1) the creation of antisocial attitudes and (2) the reinforcing of tendencies toward antisocial behavior. Consider how the negative might develop an opposing position by defending the present system of broadcasting:

Negative position: Televised violence is not harmful to children

I   Basically, there is no clearcut evidence as to the effects of television violence on children.
  A   Contrary findings exist: Some studies show that violence is harmful, but others do not show this to be true.
  B   Long-term studies are needed: Most studies deal only with short-term effects immediately after children are exposed to a violent program.
  C   In sum, more research is needed on the relationship of violence to attitudes and/or behavior.
  D   The affirmative side must show clear evidence of long-term harm.

[12]Brock et al. (1973, p. 88) make the useful point that in one sense there is no such thing as the status quo. They argue that the present system is not a "thing" at rest but, rather, is a living, breathing, constantly changing organism. However, it is still possible to define the present system as the "way things generally are now" and use this as a position in debate.

II Violence exists in many forms in society.

   A Children experience many forms of violence: at home, in peer relationships, etc.

   B Television violence may help children to adapt to a violent world.

III Merely exposing children to a certain number of violent acts does not necessarily harm them.

   A The context in which violence is portrayed is a significant factor that is relevant to the effect of the violence.

   B Television today is increasingly portraying the harmful effects of violence—teaching children that violence is undesirable.

IV One should not assume that children view television violence as real. Even at an early age, they realize the difference between real violence and television violence.

V It is possible that violence on television harmfully affects the small number of children who are potentially violent.

   A However, given the unfavorable home influences on these children, it is unfair to cite television as a major cause of their violent behavior.

   B Most of these children would turn to violence, anyway.

VI Critics consider only the number of violent acts portrayed. What about the thousands of acts that benefit society and thus counterbalance the violent acts?

By denying that the harmful effects of violence on television exist, the negative side is contending that the present broadcast setup is acceptable. The negative does concede two points of the affirmative's case: (1) Future research could demonstrate that violence has a harmful effect in the long run (although the negative side emphasizes that the opposite possibility that there are no harmful effects is equally likely), and (2) some children who are prone to being violent children may be harmed (although such children probably would turn to violence, anyway). Everything considered, however, the negative position—as revealed in the arguments against contention III of the affirmative—represents a straightforward defense of current practices. The negative side makes two slight concessions to the affirmative. Basically, however, the negative side clings to the present policy system. As a rule, then, if the negative speakers are satisfied with their ability to refute the claims of harmful effects presented by the affirmative, they have no motive to abandon the status quo.

In a status quo defense case, the negative side also may desire to attack the disparity between the real and the ideal on the basis of the inherency stock issue. In so doing the negative speakers are saying, in essence, "Even if a small amount of disparity exists, the present system is capable (without any major changes) of removing it." The negative side may then develop certain inherency lines—for example, contending that the networks are already toning down the violence levels of their programming.

Finally, remember that a negative position based on status quo defense would involve arguments against the affirmative plan. The plan would be shown to be incapable of solving the disparity. Further, it would be pictured as unworkable and disadvantageous. In sum, the negative's status quo defense position consists of a denial of the disparity, coupled with inherency arguments and plan indictments. The negative case asserts that the present system as it stands is better than the system proposed by the affirmative position.

Modified Defense of the Present System

Often, the negative side will not feel able to defend the entirety of the present system "as is," or, for reasons of *personal conviction,* they may prefer not to stand up for all aspects of the status quo. In such a situation the negative side often chooses a strategy of modified status quo defense. This position represents a defense with limits or qualifications.

In assuming the modified defense posture, the negative side concedes that a certain degree of disparity exists between the real and the ideal. However, the concession usually is implicit rather than explicit. By this I mean that the negative speakers rarely say "Yes, we agree that the harm exists." Rather, they downplay the existence of or significance of the disparity and emphasize the inherency issue. Sometimes, this strategy is termed one of minor repairs, because the negative side identifies ways that the status quo, only slightly altered, could remove the disparity. In sum, the modified defense position calls for some admission that the status quo may be inadequate. This distinguishes a defense-with-qualifications strategy from that of a total defense position.

In order to be legitimate as a minor repairs position, the changes advocated by the negative side must meet two criteria: (1) they must be far short of the change provided for by the resolution, and (2) they must be very close to the general operations of the status quo up to the present time. Ziegelmueller and Dause (1975, pp. 175–176) identify another way of gaining insight into the modified status quo defense. They argue that when the negative side modifies or qualifies its defense of the present system, it really is defending the philosophy, principles, or fundamental structure of present policies. Ziegelmueller and Dause believe that in taking a minor repairs position, the negative side concedes only that minor improvements may be needed in the present means for *implementing* the current policy.

At any rate, one thing is clear. A modified defense is just that—a defense of only part of the present system. Some concession of a disparity is made, and the main issue becomes the inherency of the disparity. The debate centers on the question: Which system will better remove the disparity, the affirmative plan or the status quo, slightly repaired?

As in the total defense approach, the modified defense strategy becomes clearer when studied by means of an example. Assume that the negative debaters desire to refute the affirmative needs case presented earlier but that they do not feel able to deny the psychic injuries related to televised violence. In such a situation the negative side might take the following approach: (1) downplay the harmful effects issue and (2) emphasize the ability of the status quo to reduce television violence with minor repairs. To be sure, the negative side might not really concede the point that violence was harmful. They might say only that the results of research were inconclusive and call for further study. However, in this hypothetical situation we are assuming that the negative speakers desire to emphasize ways that the present system could, with only minor changes, reduce the levels of violence on television.

The list below cites six possible negative inherency lines, all of which involve slight modification of existing mechanisms for controlling violence on television.

I   Voluntary network controls will reduce the amount of violence on television.
   A   The networks desire to control the level of violence.
   B   Each network has a "standards" department, which enforces guidelines dealing with the presentation of violence.
   C   The networks have in fact reduced the level of violence, proving thereby that voluntary cooperation will work. In other words, violence is not inherent because of network competition.
   D   The network standards could be tightened even more in the future, if needed.

II Strengthening the N.A.B. (National Association of Broadcasters) enforcement will reduce the amount of television violence.
   A   The N.A.B. code relates to program content and format. It could be extended to deal more specifically with violence.
   B   The N.A.B. monitors new programs, together with shows that are already on the air.
      1   The monitoring has increased since 1969.
      2   The monitoring could be further extended.

III Viewer criticism will cause networks to decrease the level of violence.
   A   Networks are sensitive to criticism.
   B   An organized antiviolence campaign by viewers would be effective.
      1   The national P.T.A. began such a campaign in 1976.
      2   Other campaigns could be organized.

IV A consumer boycott will cause networks to decrease the level of violence.
   A   Consumers are willing to boycott the sponsors of violent programming.
      1   Many have done so already on an individual basis.
      2   A boycott campaign could be organized.
   B   A boycott would bring a quick reduction in the levels of violence on television.

V   Strict parental supervision of children's viewing will reduce children's exposure to violent programming.
   A   Many parents are doing this already.
   B   The U.S. Public Health Service could begin a campaign to encourage parental supervision.

VI The schools can help reduce the effects of violent television programming.
   A   Media education courses can be developed to explain programming to children.
   B   Such courses would help children cope with violent shows.
   C   Some schools have already begun courses in media education.

Using these six lines of inherency, the negative team would be able to defend the present system as a viable means of reducing televised violence.

These six lines represent the classic "minor repairs" strategy. Each of the six is based on something already taking place in the present system: voluntary network controls, N.A.B. controls, viewer criticism, consumer boycotts, parental supervision, and media education courses. However, in each case the negative side is advocating some tightening up or strengthening of the controls. For example, the negative side points to evidence that some consumers already have boycotted the products of companies that sponsor violent television programs. The negative side then uses this as a basis for suggesting that organized boycotts could be developed in the future. Each of the inherency arguments, then, amounts to a slight extension of an existing mechanism in the present system.

Notice, further, that these six lines of inherency are far short of the change prescribed by the resolution. Admittedly, they do amount to greater controls on network programming (hence, the negative side does tread on ground defined by the resolution as "affirmative"). However, the controls are informal rather than legal and are privately initiated, not governmentally imposed. In this connection the negative speakers must be careful that their repairs do not mark either an abandonment of the present system or a de facto acceptance of the principles of change embodied in the resolution. Such care is necessary for two reasons. First, it is undeniable that in using a modified defense strategy, the negative side does take a position slightly at odds with the present system. Secondly, the negative does come close to advocating a position that is consistent with the terms of the resolution (i.e., a position that the affirmative side could assume).

These two features of the minor repairs strategy make it a dangerous one. If the negative side either takes a position that is significantly different from the present system or takes a position that is essentially an affirmative one, then the negative forfeits all claims to a presumption. Moreover, in taking a position that approaches the resolution, the negative side risks forfeiting the debate itself—for if the negative side agrees with the affirmative side, there is no reason to debate.

Let me emphasize, though, that the modified defense can be a viable negative case. If the negative side (1) defends most of—or the "essence" of—the present system and (2) maintains a clear distance from the affirmative position, then the minor repairs strategy can be beneficial. It allows the negative side to defend an improved version of the present system rather than the system as it generally is.[13]

In sum, the modified defense approach usually involves some concession (normally by implication) of the disparity and significance issues. The negative side concentrates on demonstrating an inherent capacity of the present system to eliminate the disparity (solve the problem, meet the goal, or gain the

---

[13]Remember that, as in the case of the status quo defense strategy, the modified defense position involves attacks on the affirmative plan. The negative side alleges that the plan is no real solution, that it is unworkable, and that it poses disadvantages.

advantage). The negative side normally argues for some "fine tuning" of existing elements of the status quo, but it maintains a clear distance from the change described in the proposition. Finally, of course, the modified defense strategy includes the use of the three stock issues dealing with the affirmative plan: solvency, workability, and disadvantages.

Counterplan

In constructing a case based on the counterplan approach, the negative side totally abandons the present system. The negative admits the existence of a disparity and presents an alternative plan to solve it. In assuming the counterplan position, the negative side surrenders any claim to the presumption granted in favor of the status quo. Consequently, the negative speakers undertake a burden of proof to prove that their proposal is better than the affirmative plan. This negative burden does not release the affirmative side from its own burden of proof. Rather, a counterplan debate is one in which each side possess, simultaneously, a burden to prove that its plan is a superior method of operation. However, the practical effect of this situation is to lighten somewhat the affirmative's burden of proof. This occurs because in a counterplan debate either side could win in a "tie" situation. In a "regular" debate, you will recall, the negative side prevails in the event that the arguments come to a draw. Three features of the counterplan strategy require attention: (1) the conduct of the debate on the disparity-related stock issues, (2) the form of the counterplan, and (3) the conduct of debate on the plan-oriented issues.

In taking a counterplan position, the negative side concedes that a serious and inherent disparity exists in the present system. Indeed, this is the reason that the negative abandons the existing order. However, this concession by the negative does not preclude debate on the disparity issues, because the negative side may offer a disparity analysis that differs from that of the affirmative side. Of course, it is permissible for the negative side simply to concur with the affirmative's statement of the disparity, but the negative may find it advantageous to identify disparities that (because of the limits placed by the resolution) the affirmative side cannot solve.

If a counterplan allows debate on the disparity stock issues, what is the character of this debate? An example of this situation might be a negative team's assertion that television advertising was a major evil and should be eliminated. The negative speakers could present a proposal that, in addition to curtailing violence, eliminated commercial advertising by nationalizing the commercial networks. The affirmative side would be prohibited from either doing away with commercials or nationalizing the networks (unless the affirmative speakers opted for a rather convoluted definition of terms). In such a situation the debate would continue on the disparity issue, even though both sides agreed that disparities existed. In the example just given, the negative would agree with the affirmative's indictment of violent programming but would also offer a rationale against commercial advertising. The affirmative speakers, on the other hand, would be forced to argue against the negative's contention that advertising was a harmful element. Because the affirmative speakers would be precluded from eliminating advertising on television, they would be placed in the position of denying the value of doing this.

This situation brings us to the question of the counterplan itself. What requirements apply to the constructing of such a proposal? Basically, there are only two rules for writing a counterplan: First, it must differ significantly from the present system; secondly, it must be written so as to be distinct from the change required by the proposition (as expressed in the affirmative plan). The first requirement is maintained so as to differentiate a counterplan from proposals for minor repairs. The second rule follows from common sense: If the counterplan were consistent with all terms of the resolution, then the affirmative side could merely preempt the counterplan, adding it to the affirmative plan.

The final feature of a counterplan debate is the nature of the debate on the two plans. Usually, the majority of the debate concerns the question of which plan is best. The debaters deal with issues pertaining to which plan best solves the disparity, is most workable, and is most free of undesirable side effects (disadvantages).

Traditionally, the counterplan has been seldom used in academic debate. Probably, this happens because negative speakers have had a history of success with the other two case approaches. Also, the counterplan tends to complicate the standard legal model of debate: The number of burdens is doubled; presumption is ignored; two disparity analyses may take place simultaneously; and two plans compete for attention. Therefore, even though the counterplan may gain popularity, from time to time, in contest debate circles, the beginning debater may be better served by the other case approaches. Status quo defense or modified defense are more straightforward approaches for the novice.

Topicality: A Quasi-Negative Case

The three negative positions, or case approaches, cited to this point provide the negative side with the necessary range of options to deal with most affirmative cases. However, the negative will occasionally encounter an affirmative position that requires a special negative strategy. This is the topicality approach (sometimes called the propositionality position).

The negative speakers assume a topicality position when arguing that the affirmative team has unfairly interpreted the terms of the proposition. In maintaining a topicality position, the negative side is saying, "The affirmative loses the debate because its case and/or plan deviates from the limits on debate placed by the terms of the proposition." I have labeled the topicality stance as only a "quasi case," because topicality is not a true negative position. Even when arguing from topicality, the negative side must take one of the three positions described above. Indeed, it would be unwise for the negative side to forsake the stock issues in favor of an attack based only on topicality. The topicality approach also is not a true position for a second reason. By definition, a negative (and, for that matter, an affirmative) side must take one and only one position on the resolution. In contrast, arguers can use a topicality "position" together with any of the other three negative case strategies.

There are basically three lines of topicality analysis: (1) a line that maintains that the affirmative side (in case and/or plan) has misdefined a term of the resolution, (2) a line that maintains that the affirmative side has failed (in case and/or plan) to implement all terms of the resolution, and (3) a line that maintains that the affirmative side (in case and/or plan) has gone beyond the limits allowed by the proposition. It is important to observe, nevertheless, that these three lines often overlap to a great extent. Keeping this in mind, then, let us examine each line in turn.

Misdefined Terms Occasionally, the negative side will feel that the affirmative speakers have not defined a term of the resolution in a reasonable manner. Recall that in describing a hypothetical affirmative advantages case, I included a contention to the effect that "the plan will reduce the exposure of viewers to drug advertising." This advantage resulted from a provision in the affirmative plan that the F.C.C. would "prohibit the broadcasting of advertisements for drug products during and between entertainment programs televised by national networks." As I observed then, it could be argued that such a plan provision resulted from a faulty definition of the term "content of entertainment programs." In other words, one could argue that a commercial announcement is distinct from the content of the entertainment program being sponsored.

Obviously, the key to the affirmative's definition is in the phrase "during and between entertainment programs." The affirmative speakers are defining the content of entertainment programs to include things that take place during and between the programs. It is at once apparent that the validity of the entire "advertising" advantage is dependent on whether one accepts the affirmative's definition of the content of a program. The negative speakers thus would have a major incentive to take the position that the plan provision dealing with advertising was based on a faulty definition. They could assert that the advantage-gaining portion of the plan was illegitimate. Hence, their argument would continue, any advantage resulting from this illegitimate plan provision could be dismissed.

Incomplete Implementation of the Resolution A related line of topicality deals with whether or not the affirmative side has implemented the entirety of the resolution via the affirmative case and plan. In describing the function of the affirmative case, I cited its role in defining, explaining, justifying, and implementing the terms of the resolution. In other words, the affirmative case and plan must deal with the resolution as a whole—not with a portion of it.

Let us look at an occasion in which this topicality line could be used. The full implementation requirement would preclude the affirmative speakers from building a case around a single violent television show and coupling it with a proposal that the one show be eliminated. The affirmative case and plan must justify and implement greater controls on network entertainment programs as a whole. A case and/or plan dealing with one show, or one network, or network shows presented only during "prime time" could be judged as illegitimate. The negative side would have reasonable grounds for alleging that such cases and/or plans did not justify and implement the totality of the resolution.

A Position "Beyond the Limits"   A final line of topicality deals with the occasional situation in which the case and/or plan of the affirmative side go beyond the limits set by the proposition's wording. For instance, a particular affirmative team might argue for control of the content of all network television programs. Because the resolution provides only for the control of "entertainment" programs, the negative side could allege that part of the affirmative plan and case was illegitimate. The negative side would be arguing that the extratopical elements of the affirmative case and/or plan should carry no weight in the debate.

You may have noticed that this "beyond the limits" line of topicality is closely related to the first line dealing with illegitimate definitions. In fact, the affirmative side probably would justify the controlling of all network shows by claiming that by their nature all television programs are "entertaining." Hence, the debate on propositionality would revolve around the meaning of "entertainment." As I noted above, the three lines of topicality analysis really are quite closely related.

Conditional Argument: Another Quasi-Negative Case

Like the strategy of topicality, conditional argumentation is a specialized negative case approach. When arguing conditionally, the negative side maintains, "We don't really believe that X is true, but *if* it is true, *then* we argue Y." For instance, a negative team might deny the existence of a harm but argue conditionally that if the harm did exist, then it could be solved by a given minor repair or counterplan. By making such a statement, the negative side would be using status quo defense (denying the disparity) as its primary position. The negative would maintain the conditional argument as only a hypothetical, secondary alternative.

By definition, the conditional argument is not a true position, because the negative team refuses to positively endorse the conditional argument. They argue something to this effect: "We are not really advocating that this minor repair or counterplan be put into effect; we argue only that if the affirmative side is correct that a disparity exists (which we deny), then this minor repair or counterplan would be a better way of removing it." Because the negative side does not really advocate the conditional position, the negative must maintain one of the "real" positions in the debate: defense of the status quo, modified defense, or counterplan.

Many debate theorists deny the validity of the conditional negative strategy. They argue that because the negative side must (like the affirmative) maintain only one position, the conditional position (which by definition is a secondary position) is not legitimate. These critics make a useful point and one that should be heeded by debaters. The conditional position must be subordinate. The negative side must emphasize the defense, modified defense, or counterplan posture—keeping the conditional position clearly subordinate. If the negative speakers spend a great deal of their time developing conditional positions on the issues, then they may fail to take a real position. If, for example, these speakers spend most of their time developing a conditional counterplan, then the affirmative side may be justified in demanding, "Either defend the status quo or abandon it completely." That is, the affirmative debaters would demand that their negative opponents either drop the conditional counterplan or take a strict counterplan position.

The negative "case" consists, therefore, of status quo defense, modified defense, and counterplan, together with the quasi cases based on topicality and conditional argument. Like the affirmative the negative side must carve out one position on the resolution. By knowing the range of possible positions, the negative side is able to organize its arguments into a consistent whole. This may then be compared to the case and plan offered by the affirmative speakers.

In this chapter I have presented the basics of debate analysis. Beginning with an overview of basic terms, I have explained how one goes about analyzing the proposition, gathering evidence, building the affirmative case, and taking one of the negative positions. When you acquire these analysis, research, and organization skills, you will be able to deal effectively with policy arguments.

In the following section on applications, you will have an opportunity to put policy analysis theory into practice. Many of the exercises are suitable for in-class use.

APPLICATIONS

Exercise 10-1: Writing a Policy Debate Proposition

This exercise is designed to give you experience in formulating a proposition of policy on a topic of your choice or one that is assigned to you. Your instructor may prefer that you prepare more than one such proposition.

I Choose a subject area such as education, women's rights, etc.
II Write a policy proposition on the topic area. Follow the directions for writing propositions that were explained in this chapter. When you have written out a first or second draft of your proposition, check it against these questions:
   A Does the proposition contain ambiguous or emotional terms?
   B Is the proposition stated in a declarative fashion?
   C Does the proposition deal with only one subject?
   D Does the proposition specify a change to be undertaken?
   E Does the proposition identify the agency responsible for implementing the change?

Exercise 10-2: Writing an Affirmative Case Outline

I   Choose a proposition that you have written for exercise 10-1 or write out a resolution according to the directions in exercise 10-1. Your instructor may assign you a proposition for this exercise.

II Begin to collect arguments that support the proposition—i.e., arguments that favor the change in policy provided for in the resolution. Initially, you probably will prefer to jot these down on scratch paper or on cards. Use the methods of analysis suggested in this chapter as a means for identifying as many arguments as possible. Work to elaborate each argument. Write out supporting details about each.

III Experiment now with the various case formats as a method for organizing your arguments. Determine whether the arguments would be best placed in the needs, advantages, goals, or some other format.

IV Write out a final affirmative case organization to be handed in to the instructor. (Your instructor may wish you to take the same body of arguments and place them into each of the three standard case formats or in another case format.)

V   Be sure to write the case outline according to the outlining directions presented in chapter 2. Also follow the directions and case models shown in this chapter.

VI Remember that an affirmative case also includes a plan.

Exercise 10-3: Testing an Affirmative Case Outline

This exercise will give you the opportunity to check the quality of an affirmative case outline by applying certain tests to it.

I   Use one of the following:
  A   The outline that you prepared in exercise 10-2.
  B   An outline assigned to you by your instructor.

II For the purpose of applying the tests, assume that each point in the outline is supported by analysis and evidence.

III Apply the following tests to the case outline:
  A   Does the case outline adequately define the key terms of the resolution? Remember that a case may define terms implicitly or explicitly. State an opinion as to whether the case outline constitutes an adequate or an inadequate definition of terms. Justify your opinion in a short essay.
  B   Is the case prima facie? That is, does the case overthrow presumption with respect to each of the stock issues: disparity, significance of disparity, inherency of disparity, solvency, workability, and disadvantages? For each stock issue write at least one paragraph in which you state and justify an opinion as to whether the case passes or fails the particular stock issues test.

Exercise 10-4: Preparing a Negative Case Analysis

I   Use the case that you prepared in exercise 10-2 or one that is assigned to you by your instructor.

II Following the general approach to identifying affirmative arguments (see direction II for exercise 10-2), collect a set of arguments that opposes the proposition.

III Using parallel columns, write out the negative arguments that oppose (refute) claims made in the affirmative case. Place the affirmative case outline on the left side and draw arrows across to opposing negative arguments in the left-hand column. Your paper should look something like this:

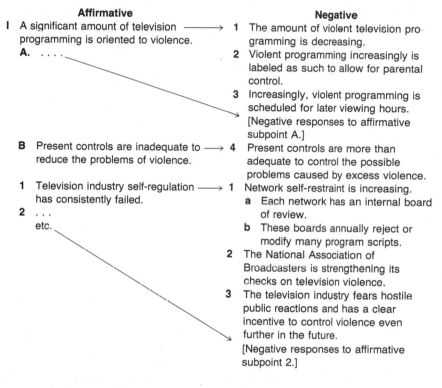

Affirmative	Negative
I A significant amount of television programming is oriented to violence.	**1** The amount of violent television programming is decreasing.
A.	**2** Violent programming increasingly is labeled as such to allow for parental control.
	3 Increasingly, violent programming is scheduled for later viewing hours. [Negative responses to affirmative subpoint A.]
B Present controls are inadequate to reduce the problems of violence.	**4** Present controls are more than adequate to control the possible problems caused by excess violence.
1 Television industry self-regulation has consistently failed.	**1** Network self-restraint is increasing.
2 ...	**a** Each network has an internal board of review.
etc.	**b** These boards annually reject or modify many program scripts.
	2 The National Association of Broadcasters is strengthening its checks on television violence.
	3 The television industry fears hostile public reactions and has a clear incentive to control violence even further in the future. [Negative responses to affirmative subpoint 2.]

Exercise 10-5: Gathering Evidence to Support a Case

I Select an affirmative or negative case outline to serve as the focus for this exercise. (Your instructor may wish you to gather both affirmative- and negative-oriented evidence.)

II Identify printed sources containing evidence that is relevant to your case.

III Using 4×6 inch index cards, write out at least twenty-five cards according to the directions for recording evidence presented in this chapter. Also, see figures 10-1, 10-2, and 10-3.

IV Using tabbed cards, organize the evidence under at least five headings according to the guidelines for organizing evidence cards that were presented in this chapter. Also see figure 10-4.

Chapter 11

Policy Advocacy Skills

By their nature, arguments are *addressed:* They are designed for presentation. Usually one does not collect or construct arguments solely for one's own private satisfaction. People prepare arguments to demonstrate to others the merits of a proposition. It follows, then, that to be fully grounded in the art of argument, you should aim to get experience in the presentation of arguments. That is what this chapter is all about. I have earlier described persuasion as an art of choosing and emphasizing arguments. This chapter on advocacy will show how one may use emphasis to deal with opposing arguments in the debate situation.

In chapter 10, I identified elements of policy analysis. I demonstrated how, given an appropriately worded proposition, one may discover arguments, gather evidence, and build a case. In this chapter I will describe methods for delivering arguments and for responding to the arguments advanced by others. The first section of this chapter will treat, in general terms, the techniques of policy advocacy. Because advocacy is the choosing and emphasizing of arguments, I will begin by describing the basic duties of each speaker in a debate. In succeeding sections of this chapter, I will explain methods for taking notes in debate, for refuting opposing arguments, and for defending your arguments against attack. Finally, I will explain parliamentary style debate as an alternative to the standard academic debate style.

STANDARD SPEAKER FORMATS AND DUTIES

There exist several standard formats for academic debate. In the next several pages, I will describe some of these formats, paying particular attention to the order of speeches and the responsibilities of each speaker. The first two formats—the traditional "10-5" approach and the cross-examination method—are team formats. That is, they are schemes providing for two affirmative and two negative debaters. The third format—the Lincoln Douglas style—is for debates involving only a single affirmative and a single negative speaker.

The Traditional "10-5" Format

For many years most college debates have taken place according to a format in which four speakers each delivered a 10-minute constructive speech and a 5-minute rebuttal speech. In this format the order of speeches is as follows:

> 1st affirmative constructive speech (1AC)—10 minutes
> 1st negative constructive speech (1NC)—10 minutes
> 2d affirmative constructive speech (2AC)—10 minutes
> 2d negative constructive speech (2NC)—10 minutes
>
> 1st negative rebuttal speech (1NR)—5 minutes
> 1st affirmative rebuttal speech (1AR)—5 minutes
> 2d negative rebuttal speech (2NR)—5 minutes
> 2d affirmative rebuttal speech (2AR)—5 minutes

Notice that according to this format the affirmative speakers have the first and last speeches. It is logical, of course, for the affirmative side to have the first speech, because in the absence of a prima facie case, the negative side has no reason to speak. However, you may ask, why the affirmative side also has the last speech. This practice has emerged because theorists generally agree that the affirmative has the more difficult task in debate. Because academic debate is a laboratory exercise that is used to improve speaker skills, the affirmative speakers are given the last speech in an effort to equalize their opportunity to win a decision.

According to the standard format, the four speakers must each have a constructive and a rebuttal speech. Also, the speakers for each team must maintain the order of speaking throughout the debate. In other words, the individual who delivers the first negative constructive speech also delivers the first negative rebuttal.[1] A final general word on the order of speeches: Each speaker has a minute or so of preparation time before a speech. Recent practice has been to allow each team a total of 10 minutes' preparation time for use during the course of the debate.

Over the years, debate practice has assigned to each speech a standard set

---

[1]The affirmative speakers usually are allowed to "switch rebuttals." In this case one individual would deliver the first affirmative constructive speech and the second affirmative rebuttal. The negative speakers usually are not permitted to do this, because the result might be one 15-minute negative speech (i.e., 2NC plus 1NR).

of speaker duties. Speaker duties are the required or customary obligations that are associated with each speech in the debate. I have made a table of the required and customary duties for each in a debate conducted according to the traditional format.

Speech	Required duty	Customary duty
1st affirmative constructive	1 State the proposition. 2 Define the terms of the proposition—explicitly or implicitly. 3 Present a prima facie case. 4 Present the affirmative plan (when using a comparative advantages case).	1 Present an overall affirmative philosophy—i.e., the affirmative side's way of looking at the resolution. 2 Establish a firm case outline to serve as the focal point for the next two speeches. 3 Make informal remarks of welcome.
1st negative constructive	1 Challenge the affirmative's definition of terms (if desired). 2 Challenge the affirmative's rationale for change by using one of the negative case approaches. (See instruction 4 in "customary duty" column.)	1 Present an overall negative philosophy. 2 Ask questions about the affirmative plan. 3 Make informal remarks of welcome. 4 Concentrate on the affirmative case (i.e., reasons for change) and leave plan analysis for 2d negative speaker.
2d affirmative constructive	1 Deal with definitional questions pertaining to the resolution (if any). 2 Answer any questions that the negative has asked relative to the affirmative plan. 3 Present the affirmative plan (if plan is not presented in 1AC). 4 Resubstantiate the affirmative case. 5 If the negative is using a counterplan, compare the affirmative and negative plans.	1 Compare the affirmative and negative philosophies. 2 If the negative is using a counterplan strategy, ask questions about the counterplan.
2d negative constructive	1 Continue negative attack on the affirmative position. (See instructions 1 and 2 in "customary duty" column.) 2 If the negative is presenting a counterplan, compare the advantages of the negative plan to those of the affirmative plan.	1 State whether speaker will treat the plan alone or whether speech will include analysis of the case (reasons for change) as well. 2 Treat only the affirmative plan, emphasizing the stock issues for solvency, workability, and disadvantages. 3 If the negative is using a counterplan, answer any affirmative questions about it.

1st negative rebuttal	1 Extend negative analysis of the affirmative's case (reasons for change). (Note: debate rules provide that no totally new lines of analysis may be introduced during the rebuttal period.) 2 Draw attention to crucial issues that have been developed relative to the affirmative case.	1 Reiterate the negative's philosophy. 2 Identify the total negative position: case and plan attacks. 3 Do not reiterate the specific plan attacks made by the 2d negative speaker in the previous speech.
1st affirmative rebuttal	1 Answer negative objections to the affirmative plan. 2 Defend the affirmative case rationale.	1 Begin with an analysis of plan attacks, devoting 3 minutes to plan defense. 2 Conclude with 2 minutes of case defense. 3 Emphasize only the most crucial arguments and issues because of severe time limitations.
2d negative rebuttal	1 Extend and conclude negative analysis of the affirmative case. 2 Extend and conclude negative objections to the affirmative plan. 3 Draw attention to crucial issues that have developed relative to both the affirmative case and the affirmative plan.	1 Summarize overall reasons that the negative analysis is superior to that of the affirmative. 2 Use the negative philosophy as a basis for comparing the negative and affirmative positions.
2d affirmative rebuttal	1 Extend and conclude affirmative analysis of the reasons for change (i.e., the affirmative case). 2 Extend and conclude affirmative defense of the plan. 3 Draw attention to crucial issues that have developed relative to both the affirmative case and the affirmative plan.	1 Summarize overall reasons that the affirmative analysis is superior to that of the negative. 2 Use the affirmative philosophy as a basis for comparing the affirmative and negative positions.

In the above summaries of speaker duties, you will notice that analysis of the affirmative rationale for change (the main part of the affirmative case—usually referred to as "the case") is customarily treated separately from the plan analysis. The case and plan analyses are separated for reasons of strategy and clarity. The 2NC and 1NR speeches are back to back. This creates a 15-minute period of negative time referred to as the negative block. Because there is no intervening affirmative speaker between the 2NC and 1NR speeches, negative teams have found it convenient to divide responsibilities: the 2NC speech being devoted to plan arguments, and the 1NR being devoted to case refutation.

You may also have cause to desire further clarification of the statement that I made about not introducing new arguments in rebuttals. The purpose of this decision rule is to preclude a surprise attack in the latter stages of the debate. If the negative team were to introduce a new line of argument in the 2NR—e.g., presenting, for the first time, an argument that the affirmative case was not topical—then the affirmative side would have only one speech in which to respond to this important challenge. More importantly, if the second affirmative rebuttalist introduced a new line, then the negative side would have no opportunity at all to respond to it. Thus, in rebuttals the two sides are limited to elaborating on lines of argument that were initiated in the constructive speeches.

The Cross-Examination Format

The cross-examination format is one that allows each speaker the opportunity to question a member of the opposing team. Correspondingly, each debater is called upon to be examined by an opponent. The usual order of speeches in a cross-examination debate is as follows:

- 1st affirmative constructive speech (1AC)—8 minutes.
(A negative speaker cross-examines the 1st affirmative speaker—3 minutes.)
- 1st negative constructive speech (1NC)—8 minutes.
(An affirmative speaker cross-examines the 1st negative speaker—3 minutes.)
- 2d affirmative constructive speech (2AC)—8 minutes.
(A negative speaker cross-examines the 2d affirmative speaker—3 minutes.)
- 2d negative constructive speech (2NC)—8 minutes.
(An affirmative speaker cross-examines the 2d negative speaker—3 minutes.)

- 1st negative rebuttal speech (1NR)—4 minutes.
- 1st affirmative rebuttal speech (1AR)—4 minutes.
- 2d negative rebuttal speech (2NR)—4 minutes.
- 2d affirmative rebuttal speech (2AR)—4 minutes.

The cross-examination format—sometimes called the "8-3-4" method—has been widely used in high school debate. In 1976 the cross-examination approach was introduced to the college National Debate Tournament, sponsored by the American Forensic Association. (A 10-3-5 format was used.) Proponents of cross-examination debating argue that this format allows for clarification of issues. They maintain that it facilitates a direct clash between the opposing affirmative and negative arguments. These claims are consistent with my earlier introduction to the dialectic method as a device for clarifying issues of definition and value.

Generally considered, speaker duties are the same for both the 10-5 and 8-3-4 formats. However, the addition of cross-examination periods does make a cross-examination debate somewhat different from a 10-5 contest. Cross-examination has several functions. I have listed some of them.

1 It allows a team to elicit necessary information. In the 10-5 format questions are answered, if at all, only in the next speech. By using cross-examination a speaker may immediately obtain needed information.

2 It sets the groundwork for refutation. By asking questions speakers may emphasize their responses to points raised by the opposing team. For instance, one could attack the inherency of the damage done by televised violence by using questions to emphasize present controls on violence. This would be a useful lead-in to one's constructive speech.

3 It may expose ambiguous aspects of an opposing team's position. Often, a team will introduce ambiguous or contradictory arguments. Ambiguities or contradictions may be highlighted through questions.

4 It tests the credibility of an opponent's evidence. Questions may be used to undermine the qualifications of a source or to cast doubt on the legitimacy of a connection between a quotation and a claim based on it.

5 It may expose assumptions underlying an opponent's arguments. As I noted in chapter 1, all arguments are supported by a host of subordinate assumptions. An arguer may weaken an argument by highlighting questionable assumptions that underlie it.

6 It can weaken the credibility of an opposing speaker. The overall effect of cross-examination should be to demonstrate that the opposing team has done an inferior job of analysis. This will weaken the overall believability and standing of the speakers themselves.

It is no easy matter to conduct one's examination period so as to reap all of the potential benefits of it, but by observing these general rules of cross-examination, the advocate may maximize his questioning period.

1 Be courteous but firm. It is tempting to take an arrogant stance as an examiner. Avoid this. Do not bully the respondent. However, feel free to cut a respondent off when the answer is wasting time, or when your opponent overqualifies an answer. Do not allow the respondent to make speeches during your examination time. Do not allow the respondent to take control of the questioning. However, you should refrain from cutting off a respondent unfairly. Try not to insist that your opponent answer yes or no to a question that cannot really be so answered.

2 Do not attempt to read quotations under the guise of presenting a question. Consider this example of evidence presented as a question: "Are you aware that Sally Smith has recently stated . . .?" Generally, such "questions" are a misuse of questioning time. Save your quotations for your speech. Remember, though, that you could "set up" the Smith quotation by asking, "Do all or even most authorities agree with your point that. . . .?"

3 Do not ask questions that allow your respondent to make lengthy interpretations. For instance, if you asked, "Why does televised violence cause antisocial behavior?" you would be giving your opponent an opportunity to make a substantive point. Instead, ask, "What is the definition of antisocial behavior used by your source, Dr. Smith?" Follow this up with related queries.

4   Avoid questions that will allow your opponent to surprise you. Do not ask questions when the response is unpredictable. Emphasize questions—often factual ones—the general answers to which you already know.

5   Attempt to develop *lines* of questioning. Rather than asking a series of miscellaneous questions, try to develop a line of interrogation. The following is an example of a line of questioning designed to set up a refutation of the harm of televised violence. Assume that a negative speaker is questioning the first affirmative speaker.

Q You have argued that violence is harmful and have offered examples and statistics to support this. Now, about your statistics—have *all* studies of television violence identified, beyond a reasonable doubt, that violence causes ill effects?

Q Have you cited any long-term studies of exposure to televised violence?

Q Moving on to the specifics of your studies, what evidence do you have to prove that children interpret violence literally?

Q Is it not true that even very young children are able to differentiate make-believe from real life?

All of these questions could be used to prepare for substantive negative refutation.

6   Drop a line of questioning when it is no longer working to your advantage. Overall, do not become locked into a rigid set of questions. Be flexible.

7   Do not ask excessively complex questions or develop excessively long lines of questioning. Your opponent may be able to avoid answering a long, involved question by confusing it. Your opponent may evade a trap that you have set if the line of questioning is too extended.

By observing the functions of questions and by following these guidelines for questioning, you may gain practical experience in the dialectical method. Cross-examination can become a valuable analytic device in policy argument.

The Lincoln-Douglas Format

The Lincoln-Douglas method is a standard academic format in which one speaker represents the affirmative side and one speaker represents the negative. Although this format is not as prevalent as the 10-5 and 8-3-4 methods, it is known by a name that antedates modern college debate. The two-person format is named for the series of debates between Abraham Lincoln and Stephen A. Douglas, who were running against each other for a seat in the U.S. Senate (Douglas was the incumbent).

Generally, a Lincoln-Douglas debate involves three speeches—two affirmative and one negative. Speaker duties vary slightly from the 10-5 format.

Speech	Speaker duty
Affirmative constructive (8 minutes)	1 Fulfill all obligations of the 1st Affirmative Constructive speech as enumerated earlier. 2 Affirmative plan must be presented in this speech.
Negative refutation (12 minutes)	1 Fulfill all obligations of the 1st and 2nd Negative Constructive speeches as enumerated earlier. 2 Speech generally is divided into separate case analysis and plan analysis sections.
Affirmative rebuttal (4 minutes)	1 Defend the affirmative rationale for change (case); summarize affirmative position on the case. 2 Defend the affirmative plan for change; summarize affirmative position on the plan.

The three formats described—the 10-5, cross-examination, and Lincoln-Douglas forms—are those that are most often used in standard academic debate. All three of these styles involve two sides debating the merits of a single proposition. In the final section of this chapter, I will describe an alternative form of debate—the parliamentary style—which operates according to a differing set of decision rules.

PRESENTING AND RECORDING ARGUMENTS

Debate speeches differ only slightly from the general principles of speech making. These differences result from the particular demands that are placed on policy advocates in the academic debate situation. Basically, the academic format places special demands of oral presentation and of written note taking. Let us consider these specifically.

Presenting Arguments

Extemporaneous Method of Speaking The debate format demands an extemporaneous method of delivery. In extemporaneous speech one works from an outline: The debaters generally speak from rough notes written out as brief points. The typical debater will take to the podium a sketch of a speech, together with a few appropriate evidence quotations or blocs. The lack of extensive preparation time precludes a written-out manuscript speech; also, because no one knows the exact course that the debate will take, it is impossible to work from a previously written manuscript. The debate participants must be ready to adapt, spontaneously and immediately, to the arguments of their opponents. The only exception to this rule is the 1st Affirmative Constructive speech, which can be written out fully in advance.

Extemporaneous speaking is a good vehicle for building analytic skills. With practice the student attains an ability to think quickly and systematically. Once acquired, these skills will be useful in later life. However, remember that "extemporaneous speaking" is not a synonym for "unprepared speaking." The good advocate leaves as little to chance as possible. Debaters engage in practice rounds to improve their extemporaneous abilities. The prepared debater tries out arguments orally and works out effective wording and arrangement alternatives.

Although debate speaking builds good delivery habits, it may also encourage bad ones. Debaters tend to speak far faster than the average speaker; gestures and movement tend to be wooden and monotonous; volume may be excessive. The debater must guard against acquiring habits that will be inappropriate for other settings. The debater should work for clear articulation and natural movement.

The question of wording the arguments is closely related to debate delivery. "Style" denotes our choice of words—the way that we verbalize ideas. The debate style is a simple one in essence. Demands of time militate against long-winded introductions, statements, and conclusions. However, the debate speaker should strive to retain necessary explanatory material. Special care must be taken to avoid excessive jargon (the particular slang of a profession or of a subject area). Instead of commenting, "Turn to the 'disads,'" the debater should say, "Now, I would like to consider the possible *disadvantages* that will most likely result from the affirmative plan." The debater should refer to the "Senate Foreign Relations Committee" rather than the "SFRC." Debaters should seek variety and should not become tied down to a few overused phrases such as "in my stand upon the floor." Debaters should look for alternatives in introductions, conclusions, and transitions.

Organization   The use of statements to partition (divide) our speech brings us to the subject of organization—the arranging of arguments. In the *Rhetoric* (III.13.1414a30), Aristotle makes the point that "a speech has two parts. Necessarily, you state your case, and you prove it."

Although contemporary speech communication theory has further refined the process of speech organization, the simplified Aristotelian pattern tends to predominate in academic debate. Debate speakers usually keep to a simple method of putting their arguments together. The debater first identifies the area of dispute—e.g., "Consider our first contention. . . ." Second, the advocate states the argument in capsule form—e.g., "We argue that a significant amount of television programming is oriented to violence." Next, the arguer proves the point by using an argument or an argument-evidence combination. Finally, the speaker concludes the point and moves on to the next one. The "state-prove" method of argument helps one to stick to the case or speech outline.

Note Keeping: The Flow Sheet

Systematic note keeping can help a debater to attain good oral delivery. Policy speakers often use flow sheets to keep track of arguments as they develop during the debate. The flow sheet is a piece of paper that is divided into a number of columns, each column corresponding to a particular speech. The typical form of the flow sheet is illustrated in figure 11-1.

The flow sheet allows the debaters to keep track of a line of argument throughout the debate. The flow sheet also aids in budgeting one's time. That is, the debater can keep track of how much of the debate has been covered in her or his speech.

Often, separate sheets are used to enter ("flow") arguments pertaining to the affirmative case and plan. Figure 11-1 would represent a typical flow sheet for case arguments. In the column on the far left, the case outline presented by the 1st affirmative speaker would be recorded in outline form. Responses by the 1st negative speaker would be recorded where they applied to the original affirmative case structure. Thus, the 1AC speech would set up the basic structure for the debate on case issues. On another sheet—or on the back of the case arguments sheet—the advocates would "flow" the plan arguments. Usually, the flow sheet for plan arguments begins with the 2NC speech, because this is normally the speech in which plan attacks are first broached.

Figure 11-2 is an example of a case and plan flow sheet. As you can see, the number of case arguments may expand rapidly after the 1st affirmative speech. Without a flow sheet the debater would be unable to keep track of the many arguments and the development of those arguments.

In figure 11-3, I present a sample flow sheet for plan arguments. Because plan arguments generally begin with the 2NC, there are only four columns in the flow sheet of plan arguments. Although it is shorter, the flow sheet of plan arguments is similar in form to that of the case.

There are some basic guidelines for using a flow sheet to record arguments in a debate.

1 Write out the key terms of the argument as it is presented by the speaker. If you compare the flow of the 1AC (figure 11-2) to the actual case outline in chapter 10, you will see that the key terms of the arguments are noted in the flow sheet. However, due to limitations in time and space, the flow sheet contains minor omissions and occasional abbreviations. For instance, in the case outline in chapter 10, the first "needs" contention stated by the affirmative is

Figure 11-1 A flow sheet.

1AC	1NC	2AC	2NC	1NR	1AR	2NR	2AR

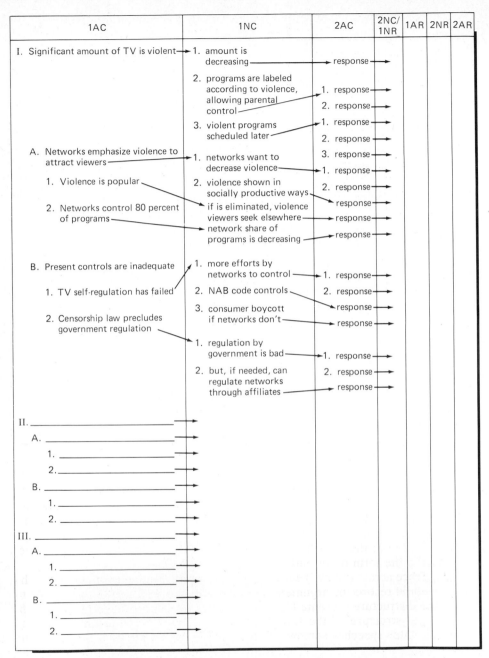

Figure 11-2   Case-arguments flow sheet.

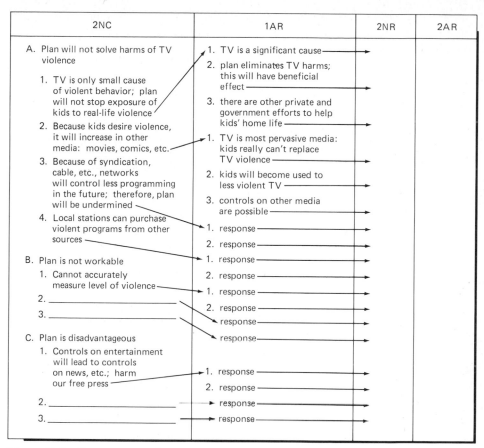

2NC	1AR	2NR	2AR

A. Plan will not solve harms of TV violence
 	
  1. TV is only small cause of violent behavior; plan will not stop exposure of kids to real-life violence
  2. Because kids desire violence, it will increase in other media: movies, comics, etc.
  3. Because of syndication, cable, etc., networks will control less programming in the future; therefore, plan will be undermined
  4. Local stations can purchase violent programs from other sources
 	
B. Plan is not workable
  1. Cannot accurately measure level of violence
  2. _____
  3. _____
 	
C. Plan is disadvantageous
  1. Controls on entertainment will lead to controls on news, etc.; harm our free press
  2. _____
  3. _____
	1. TV is a significant cause ———►
	2. plan eliminates TV harms; this will have beneficial effect ———►
	3. there are other private and government efforts to help kids' home life ———►
	
	1. TV is most pervasive media: kids really can't replace TV violence ———►
	2. kids will become used to less violent TV ———►
	3. controls on other media are possible ———►
	1. response ———►
	2. response ———►
	1. response ———►
	2. response ———►
	1. response ———►
	2. response ———►
	response ———►
	response ———►
	
	1. response ———►
	2. response ———►
	response ———►
	response ———►		

Figure 11-3 Plan-arguments flow sheet.

worded "A significant amount of television programming is oriented to violence." On the flow sheet the same argument is noted as "Significant amount of TV is violent." The flow sheet notation preserves the essential meaning of the argument but omits certain details.

    2 Write out the speeches in outline form. Each column of the flow sheet should take the form of an outline.

    3 Trace across ("flow") each horizontal line of argument with arrows. The arguer should record the arguments in each subsequent speech as they apply to the original structure presented in the 1AC or 2NC. Recording argument to fit the original structure of the flow sheet means that the debater may have to rearrange later speeches somewhat so that they fit the notation system being used.

    4 Take note whenever an evidence quotation is used to support an argument. A symbol such as an asterisk (*) may be useful for this purpose. Also, the debater should make some note of the wording of the quotation itself. This will make it easier to remember whether a piece of evidence really establishes an argument.

5 Take note whenever the opposing team makes no response to an argument. Many speakers use a "goose egg" for this purpose. Be fair, however. Do not routinely accuse an opposing speaker of having made no response when there really has been one.

Many speakers find the detailed methods of flow sheeting to be overly complex for their purposes. Indeed, several of the methods of debate presentation and note keeping differ somewhat from techniques of general speech making. However, these academic debate methods have a proven utility for the debate situation. Further, they usually are transferable to other life situations.

REFUTATION AND RESUBSTANTIATION

To refute means to attack or minimize an opponent's arguments. To resubstantiate is to defend arguments against attack—to reaffirm them. Refutation and resubstantiation are important aspects of the debate contest, because they represent the direct clash of opposing arguments. Through the clash of arguments, the issues emerge and the listeners (judges) have a basis for testing the merits of competing positions.

In earlier chapters I have identified methods for testing certain types of arguments. Now, in the next few pages, I will elaborate on the process for dealing with opposing arguments as they relate to policy claims.

Refutation

The basic task in refutation is to minimize the believability and importance of your opponent's arguments. Certain types of argument that I have treated earlier can be useful in refutation. For example, two forms of interpretive argument—the dilemma and the *reductio*—are particularly suited for weakening the force of an opponent's claim. The value-based argument of inconsistency (or contradiction) can be used both to undermine the philosophical soundness of a position and the credibility of an advocate. Finally, one may refute an argument by applying the general tests of truth, ethics, and validity. In particular, it is useful to be mindful of the forms of interpretive argument that, by definition, are invalid. (See chapter 5.) In short, the advocate who wishes to refute should be familiar with the forms of argument and the standards for testing argument.

Although successful refutation assumes a wide knowledge of the process of argument, the alert observer will notice that there are a number of specific refutation strategies. Indeed, most refutative arguments seem to take one of three approaches. The three major methods of refutation are to deny an argument, to diminish an argument, and to dismiss an argument.[2] When one uses the strategy of denial, one simply argues that a claim is incorrect. One might

---

[2]Denial, diminishment, and dismissal may be called the "three Ds" of debate. A related "fourth D," distortion, is unethical and must be avoided. Distortion is the stating of an opponent's argument in an inaccurate fashion. To be ethical in minimizing an opponent's argument, one must present it fairly. This means to present the argument in the manner in which your opponent introduced it.

assert that the major networks do not control 80 percent of total programming, (this was IA2 in the needs case presented in chapter 10) and, accordingly, supply a smaller figure. Similarly, one might deny outright the claim that the level of televised violence is decreasing.

The strategy of diminishing an argument usually takes the form of challenging the qualifier that is asserted by an opponent. One supplies counterargument and counterevidence, using these as a basis for asserting that the opponent's claim is overstated. If an arguer desired to refute the argument that "present controls are inadequate to reduce the problem of violence," the arguer could (1) identify a host of controls that are not indicted by the affirmative and (2) defend the merits of controls that had been criticized. Such a refutation would not really amount to an outright denial of the opposition's arguments. Rather, the advocate would cast doubt on the likelihood that the other side's claims were valid. When using the strategy of diminishment, the debater would argue that the other side's arguments deserved a less strongly positive qualifier. Specifically, one would challenge the high level of certainty implicitly claimed in the above example.

In contrast to the refutation strategies of denial and diminishment, the dismissal technique does not represent an assault on the argument itself. Rather, to dismiss an argument is to claim that it is irrelevant. The debater challenges the relevancy of the argument to a particular point or issue under discussion. Because the argument is not germane, the debater asserts the argument has no probative weight in the matter at hand. For instance, in a debate over televised violence, an argument about foreign policy might well prove extraneous to the controversy defined by the resolution.

The possibility that an argument may be dismissed as irrelevant draws attention to the use of issues in refutation. Simply put, refutation should be issue-centered. By this I mean that one should identify the relationship between a refutation argument and the issue to which it applies. The advocate should make clear what is the issue impact of a refutation argument. Consider a case in point. In the debate over the harm done by televised violence, the argument that "the amount of total programming time controlled by the networks is decreasing" would be relevant to the question of whether controls on networks could solve the problem. If the networks controlled less television time, then controls on network time would have less potential for decreasing the amount of violence that is telecast during the day. The plan would have less solvency potential. Solvency, of course, is one of the stock issues. In a like manner, therefore, the advocate should connect each refutation argument to at least one of the stock issues of policy debate.

A final word about refutation is appropriate now. The case strategies chosen by the affirmative and negative sides may affect the conduct of refutation. For instance, a goals case presented by the affirmative offers the negative side the opportunity to deny that the goals are truly important ones. The negative team that uses a counterplan strategy will find denial less appropriate. In such an eventuality the negative side probably would desire more to diminish the affirmative plan than to deny the affirmative need analysis. Each case format suggests lines of refutation.

Resubstantiation

Resubstantiation—the defending of arguments against attack—is closely related to refutation. Indeed, one might view resubstantiation as nothing more than the refutation of refutation. Nevertheless, there are two key principles to be observed when one desires to resubstantiate an argument. First, you (the advocate) should stay on your ground. By this I mean that you should refute attacks from the perspective of why your original argument still stands. Instead of merely denying, diminishing, or dismissing your opponent's attacks, you should use your case as the basis for the denying, diminishing, or dismissing. In doing this, the advocate's issues and major ideas are emphasized. Effective resubstantiation is marked when the speaker uses the case and overall position (or philosophy) as the basis for debate. Here the speaker sticks to his or her ground rather than debating on the opponent's ground.

A second principle of effective resubstantiation comes in the form of the traditional rule that advocates should extend rather than repeat arguments. When an argument has been refuted, one cannot merely repeat the argument. Repeating a point does not deal with the counterarguments. Extending an argument means citing a new implication of the argument. This includes (1) providing new information about the argument or (2) identifying its relationship to another argument or issue. In essence, to extend an argument is to give it new substance and force. It follows, therefore, that effective resubstantiation extends a line of argument, forcing the opposition to spend time dealing with it. When one extends a line of argument, one wins the point, pending further debate.

A Formula for Refutation and Resubstantiation

Refutation and resubstantiation can be viewed as sequential processes for presenting arguments. This means that one may sketch out certain characteristic steps for effective refutation and resubstantiation. Basically, the steps to be followed are these:

I   Identify the area of dispute. That is, state the argument, arguments, or issue that you will be treating. In following this step one might say, "Let us turn to the first affirmative contention that a significant amount of television programming is oriented to violence." Such a statement orients the listener: It tells the audience what subject will be presented in your arguments. If the listener is using a flow sheet, an orientation remark of this kind will assure that your argument will be duly noted.

II   State your argument; make your point in capsule form. When I say "capsule form," I mean a brief "headline" that gives the essence of the argument. Your argumentative headline should contain the necessary key words of your claim but should be short enough to be easily understood, noted, and remembered. The statement "A consumer boycott can force a reduction in the amount of television violence" exemplifies a short, key-word headline.

III Explain or support your argument. Provide any necessary elaboration or evidence.

IV Identify why your argument is important. Here you explain how your argument relates to the original claim that you are seeking to refute or resubstantiate. You summarize the overall implications of your claim. There are two standard ways to impress the audience with the significance of your point.

    A You may identify reasons why you have defeated the opposing argument or why you have won a general issue in view of the claim that you have presented. Here you emphasize the denial, diminishment, or dismissal effects of your point.

    B You may state how your winning of a particular argument or issue relates to the wider stock issues that determine the outcome of the debate. Such a statement makes clear to the audience the impact of your claim on the debate as a whole.

These steps of refutation and resubstantiation should not be viewed as an ironclad formula, yet they represent what is normally the best method for presenting an argument in a policy contest.

Refutation, then, is the process of minimizing opposing arguments (thus enhancing your own). Refutation provides the clash that is necessary if opposing positions are to be compared. Generally, advocates desiring to develop or improve refutation skills should study the various forms and types of argument as well as the truth, ethics, and validity standards for evaluating arguments. Specifically, students of argument should practice the denial, diminishment, and dismissal methods. Finally, refutation—and its cousin, resubstantiation—may be viewed as consisting of certain characteristic steps.

PARLIAMENTARY-STYLE DEBATE

In reading chapters 10 and 11, you may have observed that academic-style or forensic debate is heavily committed to the legal model of policy analysis and advocacy. This is clear from the organizational setup and decision rules that characterize the forensic situation. Two sides compete on a single subject, the wording of which is decided long in advance of the debate. Decision rules are enforced by a judge, who also renders an either-or decision for the affirmative or negative side. Presumption is accorded to the negative, while the affirmative speakers incur a burden of proof.

Parliamentary Debate as an Alternative to the Courtroom Model

In the real world, of course, methods of policy advocacy often differ from the special conditions of forensic debate. In many policy-making bodies, the members themselves formulate the question for debate and many different questions are debated during the course of a session. Further, it is often the arguers themselves who enforce the decision rules. Ultimately, they themselves decide to accept, reject, or modify a policy proposal. Finally, in the real world it is often the case that no one possesses a presumption and everyone shoulders a burden of proof.

It is possible that the legislative or parliamentary system of debate may better represent the actual methods of decision making that take place in organizations having a policy-setting role. The parliamentary style allows the members to control the question (motion) being debated. Further, the members decide the question. That is, they vote it up or down—or "sideways" in the case of motion to table. Each member may take a different position (expressed as a main motion or amendment) on the subject being considered. Finally, no motion enjoys a presumption. The defenders of each parliamentary motion incur a burden of proof. They must convince their peers to vote for and to pass their proposal.

Because the legislative model casts a different light on the debate process, I feel that it is worthwhile to devote some space to it. Although debate theorists probably are irrevocably committed to the legal format discussed earlier, there is room in the field, I think, for an alternative mode. Also, in the classroom parliamentary-style debate may be more universally appealing, because it involves everyone present, and not just the two or four debaters. With this in mind, I will give a brief description of the general theory of parliamentary debate, together with some specific guidelines for conducting legislative debates.

Some Features of Parliamentary-Style Debate

Motions Parliamentary debate commences when someone in a legislative body introduces a motion (also called a resolution or question) onto the floor. A motion is a declarative statement that advocates that something be done. In essence, it espouses a policy. The statement "I move that Salem Avenue be made into a northbound one-way street" would constitute a motion.

The motion serves much the same function as the proposition in forensic debate. Indeed, both can be called "resolutions." However, there are some important differences between debate on a forensic proposition and debate on a legislative motion. Whereas forensic debate proceeds on a single proposition, legislative debate may proceed on any one of a number of motions. Of course, only one motion is debated at a time, but the assembly may begin debate on a given motion and then pass on to many other differing questions.

A second difference between legal and legislative debate is that the proposition does not change during the course of a forensic debate, whereas a parliamentary motion may be amended. The proposition and motion differ also in that in forensic debate the whole proposition is either accepted or rejected, while, by contrast, the parliamentary motion may be accepted, rejected, modified, laid aside, or treated in any of a number of other ways. For instance, a parliamentary motion may be divided, with each part being debated separately.

Parliamentary theorists have classified a host of specific forms of the motion. Although these are certainly deserving of study, I will soon introduce a simplified set of motions that will suffice for most classroom debates.

The Members as Judge   Another major provision of parliamentary debate bears repeating. This is the provision that the members themselves (those present) decide the question. The members speak more to each other than to an outside audience. There is no impartial, all-powerful judge. Although the assembly may elect a presiding officer (chair or president), and although the group may elect a parliamentarian, it is the members themselves who exercise the ultimate authority over decision rules.

Positions in Parliamentary Debate   As I noted earlier, there are more than two positions in a parliamentary debate. In fact, each individual's opinion on a subject can be viewed as constituting a unique position, and a person may change a position during the debate. The fact that members must speak either for or against a stated motion does place a limitation on the number of positions that can be argued on a given motion. Nevertheless, the rules of parliamentary procedure almost guarantee that far more than two positions will be considered. This happens because any member may offer an amendment to a main motion (a main motion introduces original new business). Many amendments may be made and debated, and they may be accepted or rejected before the main motion is finally voted on. Each amendment would change the tone of the main motion and hence would represent a slightly different position.

Speaker Duties   The parliamentary situation alters, somewhat, the specific duties of speakers. Basically, each speaker who introduces a motion undertakes the burden to establish a prima facie case for that motion. Overall, speakers incur the general burden of proving what they assert. In other words, the narrowly apportioned speaker duties of academic debate do not apply to the parliamentary context. Nevertheless, the parliamentary advocate should follow the advice that was presented earlier on analysis (chapter 10) and on refutation and resubstantiation (chapter 11). Of course, note keeping is simplified in parliamentary debate: Two or three columns probably will suffice for a flow sheet.

Taken as a whole, then, parliamentary debate is a decision context in which numerous positions on a question may be debated. The advocates themselves formulate and vote on the questions. Within an overall framework of customary provisions to protect minorities, the assembly as a whole functions as the ultimate authority on rules of debate.

In my opinion, the parliamentary style is a useful educational experience, because it approximates those contexts in which many positions compete for attention. It would seem to approximate better the conduct of policy argument in small groups, business groups, legislatures, and general organizations. Used in conjunction with academic-style debate, it can provide additional skills to the student.

Guidelines for Conducting Parliamentary Debates

The rules of parliamentary procedure are many and complex. Accordingly, it is not my intention to present them here in their entirety. However, a few brief guidelines should enable students to conduct a classroom debate in which the focus is on the merits of the policy question rather than on parliamentary form.

   I   The group should choose a presiding officer. This chair (or president) will call upon individuals who wish to speak and will keep track of the time limits. The chair should remain impartial concerning the substantive issues being debated.

  II The policy debates should be held according to a general framework of debate rules. These rules should specify at least the following:

     A   The list of subjects on which motions can be made.

     B   Whether or not main motions should be circulated in advance. (I would suggest that all main resolutions be duplicated and circulated at least a week before the debates.)

     C   Whether or not all members will be required to prepare and introduce a resolution.

     D   The number and length of the debate session(s).

     E   The length of speeches. Three minutes is a good maximum.

     F   Other limitations on speakers—e.g., whether all must have spoken once before a person may give a second speech.

 III Debates should be conducted on the basis of some parliamentary format. I would suggest that the group begin with the following parliamentary principles, together with common sense and a sense of fair play. However, the group may desire to select a parliamentary manual as a reference. Alternatively, the group may decide to conduct debates entirely in accordance with a parliamentary handbook. Many different ones are available. Whatever format is used, there are some basics of parliamentary procedure that are important to know:

     A   A resolution should be patterned on the model below:

A RESOLUTION TO _____

Whereas, _____

_____ ; and

Whereas, _____

_____ ;therefore,

Be it resolved, that _____

_____

_____

_____ .

     B   The chair will call for a resolution (or will follow a schedule as to the order of main motions).

        1   The author of the resolution will read it to the group.

        2   If the resolution is seconded by a member of the assembly, then the author will present a constructive speech supporting the resolution.

C The chair will then call for speakers against the resolution and will recognize one of those desiring to speak. Speakers for and against will alternate (if possible) until debate is closed.

D Debate will close when the members indicate a desire to do so (i.e., when no one objects to closing debate on a motion) or when a motion to close debate is voted on and passed. A motion to postpone or to refer the question to a committee, when passed, will also have the effect of closing debate on a motion.

E Any main motion (and any amendment to a main motion) may be amended. However, third-level amendments are not allowed.

F Each motion will be debated and dealt with in a parliamentary manner. The types of motions (listed in figure 11-4) will be used for this purpose. The motions are listed in order of precedence, so that

Figure 11-4 Roster of basic parliamentary motions.

Parliamentary function (motions)[1]	Procedural rules (treatment of motions)				
	Interrupt business or speaker?	Second required?	Debatable?	Amendable?	Vote
1. Motion to restrict or close debate	No	Yes	No[2]	Yes[3]	two-thirds
2. Motion to appeal any decision of the chair	Yes	Yes	Yes[4]	No	Majority
3. Motion of request (a) addressed to chair: a parliamentary inquiry or point or order; a request for information (b) addressed—via the chair—to a speaker: ask the speaker to yield to question or yield time	Yes	No	No	No	Decided by chair (i.e., no vote)
4. Motion to amend	No	Yes	Yes	Yes[5]	Majority
5. Motion to postpone	No	Yes	Yes	Yes	Majority
6. Motion to refer to committee (if necessary, motion would specify details of committee formation)	No	Yes	Yes	Yes	Majority
7. Motion to terminate meeting (recess or fix time of next meeting)	No	Yes	No	Yes	Majority
8. General (main) motion: any new item of business	No	Yes	Yes	Yes	Majority

[1] listed in order of precedence

[2] some clarification of the opposing positions is permissible

[3] debate on amendment is also limited

[4] debate usually is limited

[5] an amendment may be amended only once

the motion to restrict or close debate must be acted on before any other of the motions; the motion to appeal decisions of the chair would then have priority, and so on. The rules governing each motion are noted after the motion. (The philosophy behind this simplified list of parliamentary motions is articulated by Sikkink, 1975, pp. 76–78.)

These rules do not cover all of the possible situations that may arise in the course of parliamentary debate, but when they are coupled with forbearance, fairness, preparation, and common sense, they probably are sufficient for a classroom exercise.

In sum, the philosophy and style of parliamentary debate differ somewhat from the forensic method described earlier. However, when they are used in the educational setting, both styles are means to an end. They are models that enable the student to practice skills in argument, analysis, evidence, case building, delivery, refutation, and resubstantiation.

APPLICATIONS

The following exercises will give you the opportunity to practice policy advocacy skills.

Exercise 11-1: Delivering an Affirmative Constructive Speech

You should prepare a constructive speech in support of an assigned proposition. Follow these guidelines:

I   Use the analysis and evidence that you prepared in exercises 10-2, 10-4, and 10-5.

II   Write out a final affirmative case outline on the basis of your previous work on the proposition.

   A   Prepare explanations and select evidence to support elements of your case.

   B   Review your case to make sure that it is prima facie in nature.

   C   Be sure to prepare a plan for presentation.

III   Practice delivering the speech, using your case outline and evidence quotations. Your instructor may wish you to write out the speech in manuscript form.

IV   The speech should be 10 minutes in length.

V   You should deliver your speech in accordance with the schedule of constructive speeches prepared by your instructor.

Exercise 11-2: Delivering a Negative Refutation Speech

This exercise is designed to be done in tandem with exercise 11-1. Because a negative refutation speech must necessarily follow an affirmative constructive speech, it is possible to schedule exercises 11-1 and 11-2 in such a way that each negative speech follows an affirmative one. The following are directions for the negative refutation speech:

I   Consult the guidelines for negative case analysis in chapter 10 and for refutation in chapter 11.

II   Practice using the status quo defense and modified defense positions that were discussed in chapter 10. (Of course, you must use only one of these positions in your actual speech.) The counterplan strategy is not as well suited for this exercise, because it involves less clash with the affirmative rationale for change.

III   Prepare negative evidence and blocs.

IV   Practice using the three general refutation strategies—denial, diminishment, and dismissal—against hypothetical affirmative arguments.

V   Prepare to refute both the affirmative case and plan in a 10-minute speech.

VI   Check to see that your argumentative presentation follows the general steps for treating arguments that were cited in this chapter.

VII   Deliver your refutation speech as scheduled.

Exercise 11-3: Lincoln-Douglas Debate

This exercise may be done in place of exercises 11-1 and 11-2, or it may be used as a complement. The Lincoln-Douglas debate involves a constructive and refutation speech but it also gives the affirmative speaker the opportunity to resubstantiate a given position in a rebuttal speech. Follow these guidelines:

I   The speaker assigned to the affirmative side should generally follow the directions for exercise 11-1. However, the affirmative constructive speech will be 8 minutes in length.

II   The speaker assigned to the negative side generally should follow the directions for exercise 11-2, although the negative speech will be 12 minutes in length. The negative speaker must remember to refute both the affirmative case and plan.

III   The affirmative speaker should prepare for a 4-minute rebuttal speech. Using a flow sheet, the affirmative speaker should take careful note of the negative speech. The speaker should anticipate negative attacks, practice defending the case, and practice refuting the negative plan objections. In defending the case the affirmative speaker should remember to follow the general guidelines for resubstantiation:

   A   Stay on affirmative ground.

   B   Extend arguments rather than repeat them.

Exercise 11-4: Academic-Style Debate

I   Your instructor will assign you to the affirmative or negative side of a proposition in a debate. The class may debate only one topic, or several may be selected.

II   Affirmative and negative speakers should follow the directions for speaker duties as listed in this chapter.

III All speakers should give thought to rebuttals and should practice refutation and resubstantiation.

IV Your instructor will assign either the 10-5, 8-3-4, or some other format of debate. If the 8-3-4 (cross-examination) format is used, the following examination sequence should be followed:

    A   2d negative speaker examines the 1st affirmative.

    B   2d affirmative speaker examines the 1st negative.

    C   1st negative speaker examines the 2d affirmative.

    D   1st affirmative speaker examines the 2d negative.

V   Speakers should follow the cross-examination questioning guidelines presented in this chapter.

Exercise 11-5: Practicing Cross-Examination

  I   Each student should prepare a 3-minute affirmative contention and should practice delivering a 2-minute cross-examination of an affirmative contention.

 II   Your instructor will assign class members to two-person cross-examination pairs.

III One person in the cross-examination pair should present a 3-minute affirmative contention; the second member of the pair will cross-examine the other partner for 2 minutes regarding the contention; and then the partners will switch positions.

Exercise 11-6: Writing a Debate Critique

Your instructor may assign you to do the following: prepare a short critique of each in-class debate and/or write out an extended analysis of one such debate. Here is a list of general directions for writing a critique of a debate:

  I   Rank the speakers (or the team as a whole) on a scale ranging from 1 (fair) to 5 (excellent) with relation to:

    A   Analysis of proposition

    B   Use of evidence

    C   Organization of arguments

    D   Refutation of arguments

    E   Delivery of arguments

    F   Knowledge of debate theory

  II   Explain your rankings in a short essay. Give specific reasons for your judgments.

III Make an overall judgment as to which side (affirmative or negative) won the debate. Justify and/or explain your judgment.

IV An extended debate critique should contain more explanation of both the specific rankings and the overall decision on the winner of the debate. Your instructor will inform you as to how much explanation is necessary.

V The short critiques should be submitted at the end of class. Your instructor will assign a date for the extended critique(s).

Exercise 11-7: Keeping a Debate Flow Sheet

I Observe an academic-style debate. You may use an in-class debate or one that takes place outside of class. There probably are several high schools and colleges in your area that have debate teams. Also, your instructor may supply you with a printed debate text to serve as the focus for this assignment.

II Prepare a separate flow sheet for case and plan arguments that follows the guidelines presented in this chapter.

III Use the flow sheet to keep track of the horizontal lines of argument developed in the debate. Use arrows to connect related arguments from one column to another.

Exercise 11-8: Writing a Parliamentary Resolution

The parliamentary debate format differs from the academic method in that a large number of topics may be considered in a single parliamentary session. Parliamentary debate centers around resolutions that are introduced into debate by the members. The following are guidelines for formulating a parliamentary resolution:

I The class as a whole should identify a range of topic areas for debate. Ten topic areas would be suitable for most classes.

II Each class member should prepare a resolution (main motion) relating to one of the chosen problem areas. The resolutions should be written out according to the format presented in the section on parliamentary debate in this chapter.

Exercise 11-9: Parliamentary Debate

In conducting a parliamentary debate session, the following rules should be observed:

I Each member should be prepared to introduce a parliamentary resolution. The resolutions should be written out to reduce confusion over wording. Your instructor may desire that you prepare a copy of your resolution for each member of the class or may require that you prepare copies for the parliamentary officers: chair, and secretary.

II Several students should volunteer to serve as parliamentary officers. One officer (the chair) is required, and a second officer (the secretary) is optional. In order to give all students an opportunity to debate, it is possible to rotate the officerships. Your instructor will give specific instructions to officers. If there are to be a number of parliamentary sessions, your instructor may act as chair for one or more sessions to demonstrate the procedures for presiding at a meeting.

    A The chair serves as the presiding officer, recognizes speakers, conducts the voting, reminds members of what they are debating or voting on.

    B The secretary keeps record of parliamentary business.

III Debate on the resolutions should take place as follows:

    A A member will be recognized and will introduce a motion.

    B The chair will call for speakers for and against the resolution. It is helpful to allow the author of a resolution to be the first speaker.

    C Speakers for and against the resolution will alternate until debate is closed.

    D Speeches should be from 1 to 3 minutes in length.

    E After a main motion has been introduced, other motions may be made concerning it. See the roster of motions in figure 11-4. Although subsidiary motions may be made, it is a good idea to focus on main motions and amendments to main motions. The parliamentary sessions should not become bogged down in procedural details.

    F Your instructor may intervene to straighten out a complicated parliamentary impasse.

Exercise 11-10: Advocating Policy in a Nontraditional Format

As an alternative or complement to policy debate, you may present a policy position using a nontraditional format. Follow these directions:

  I Consult chapter 9 and your instructor in order to identify a range of nontraditional methods for advancing a policy position.

  II In a paragraph or two identify your position on a topic.

    A State the topic area.

    B State your conclusion about the topic—i.e., your thesis or position.

III Identify the nontraditional format that you will be using—e.g., poem, story, song, play (skit), parable, etc.

IV Execute your nontraditional composition.

  V In a concluding essay explain the strategy of argument that you used in your nontraditional composition. Why did you construct it as you did?

CREDITS

Chapter 1

p. 8: from James J. Kilpatrick, "A Conservative View," reprinted by permission from Washington Star Syndicate, Inc.

Chapter 2

p. 32: from Lewis Carroll, *Through the Looking Glass,* reprinted by permission of W. W. Norton and Company, Inc.; p. 47: from J. Michael Sproule, "Access to the Broadcast Forum: A Rhetorical Problem," reprinted by permission from *Speaker & Gavel.*

Chapter 3

p. 60: from the Revised Standard Version of the Bible, copyright 1946, 1952, © 1971, 1973 by the National Council of Churches of Christ in the U.S.A.; p. 71: from article by David E. Rosenbaum, copyright © 1977 by the New York Times Company, reprinted by permission; p. 72: from "Dear Abby" by Abigail Van Buren, reprinted by permission from Abigail Van Buren; p. 73: from letter by Douglas Newton and Kenneth E. Scheck, reprinted by permission from *Columbia Journalism Review;* p. 74: Fenga & Freyer, "Ford's Report Card," reprinted by permission from Fenga & Freyer, Inc.; p. 76: from "Dispute Intensifies Over Nixon Role on 'Hush Money,'" copyright © 1977 by the New York Times Company, reprinted by permission; p. 81: from the *Phaedrus* of Plato, translated by W. C. Helmbold and W. G. Rabinowitz, copyright © 1956 by the Bobbs-Merrill Company, Inc.; p. 93: from *Blacks Law Dictionary,* reprinted by permission from West Publishing Co.

Chapter 4

p. 104: from letter by Joanna Komoska, reprinted by permission from the American Civil Liberties Union; p. 105: from letter by Jordan E. Kurland, reprinted by permission from the American Association of University Professors; p. 105: from news story, reprinted by permission from the Associated Press; p. 106: from news story, reprinted by permission from the Associated Press.

Chapter 5

p. 143: from *The Boys on the Bus* by Timothy Crouse, copyright © 1972, 1973 by Timothy Crouse, reprinted by permission from Random House, Inc.; p. 144: from Bernard B. Fall, *The Two Viet-Nams: A Political and Military Analysis,* 2d rev. ed., copyright © 1963, 1964, 1967 by Frederick A. Praeger, Inc., reprinted by permission of Holt, Rinehart and Winston; p. 145: from "Dear Abby" by Abigail Van Buren, reprinted by permission from Abigail Van Buren; p. 147: from James J. Kilpatrick, "A Conservative View," reprinted by permission from

Washington Star Syndicate, Inc.; p. 151; from Vincent Bugliosi with Curt Gentry, *Helter Skelter,* reprinted by permission from W. W. Norton and Company, Inc.; p. 151 from "The Row Over Offshore Energy," copyright 1975 by Newsweek, Inc., all rights reserved, reprinted by permission; p. 152: from James J. Kilpatrick, "A Conservative View," reprinted by permission from Washington Star Syndicate, Inc.; p. 152: from "How Clean is Business," copyright 1975, by Newsweek, Inc., all rights reserved, reprinted by permission; p. 157: from news story, reprinted by permission from the Associated Press; p. 157: from news story, reprinted by permission from the Associated Press; p. 158: from "An Irony of History," copyright 1975, Newsweek, Inc., all rights reserved, reprinted by permission; p. 162: from news story, reprinted by permission of the Associated Press; p. 162: from William Broyles, "Behind the Lines," reprinted with permission from the November 1975 issue of *Texas Monthly,* copyright 1975 by Mediatex Communications Corporation; p. 163: from letter to the editor by Robert J. Rafalko, copyright 1975 by Newsweek, Inc., all rights reserved, reprinted by permission; p. 164: from Theodore H. White, *The Making of the President 1960,* copyright © 1961 by Atheneum House Inc., reprinted by permission of Atheneum Publishers; p. 178: from Barbara W. Tuchman, "They Poisoned the Wells," copyright 1975 by Newsweek, Inc., all rights reserved, reprinted by permission; p. 179: from "Will There Be a Bloodbath," copyright 1975 by Newsweek, Inc., all rights reserved, reprinted by permission; p. 180: from "Numbers Game," reprinted by permission from *The Odessa American.*

Chapter 6

p. 187: from Erma Bombeck, *At Wit's End,* copyright 1977 Field Enterprises, Inc., courtesy of Field Newspaper Syndicate; p. 200: from "Can Unfair Be Fair?" reprinted with permission from Times Newspapers Limited; p. 205: from Meg Greenfield, "The Secret of Our Success," copyright 1976 by Newsweek, Inc., all rights reserved, reprinted by permission.

Chapter 8

p. 281: cartoon by Hugh Haynie, reprinted by permission from *The Courier-Journal,* Louisville, and Hugh Haynie; p. 282: from Wayne C. Booth, *Modern Dogma and the Rhetoric of Assent,* reprinted by permission from University of Notre Dame Press.

Chapter 9

p. 314: from "Firing Line," hosted by William F. Buckley, Jr., reprinted by permission of Southern Educational Communications Association, P.O. Box 5966 Columbia, South Carolina 29250; p. 325: from "A Superstar Witness," copyright 1978 by Newsweek, Inc., all rights reserved, reprinted by permission; p. 337: excerpt from Alex Haley, *Roots,* copyright © 1976 by Alex Haley, reprinted by permission of Doubleday & Company, Inc.; pp. 339ff: from Jerome Lawrence and Robert E. Lee, *The Night Thoreau Spent in Jail,* copyright © 1970 by Lawrence & Lee, Inc., copyright © 1972, revised by Lawrence & Lee, Inc., all rights reserved, reprinted by permission from Lawrence & Lee, Inc.; p. 347: cartoon and excerpt reprinted with permission of Charles Scribner's Sons from Allan Nevins and Frank Weitenkampf, *A Century of Political Cartoons,* copyright 1944 Charles Scribner's Sons; p. 350: cartoon by Hugh Haynie, reprinted by permission from *The Courier-Journal,* Louisville, and Hugh Haynie; p. 351: cartoon, *Oliphant,* © 1978, *The Washington Star,* reprinted with permission, Los Angeles Times Syndicate; p. 352: cartoon by Hugh Haynie, reprinted by permission from *The Courier-Journal,* Louisville, and Hugh Haynie.

REFERENCES CITED

Aaron, Richard I. *Knowing and the Function of Reason.* Oxford: Clarendon Press, 1971.

Anderson, Loren. "An Experimental Study of Reluctant and Biased Authority-Based Assertions." *Journal of the American Forensic Association,* 7 (1970), 79–84.

Aristotle. *Nichomachean Ethics.* I have consulted the translation by W. D. Ross, published by Random House.

———*Rhetoric.* Many translations of this work are available. I have used the translation by Lane Cooper, published by Appleton-Century-Crofts.

———*Rhetoric to Alexander* [Rhetorica ad Alexandrum]. I have consulted the translation by H. Rackham, Leob Classical Library edition, published by Harvard University Press. Although traditionally assigned to Aristotle, this work is now thought to be that of an unknown sophist who wrote it some time after Aristotle completed the *Rhetoric.*

Arnold, William E. "The Effect of Nonverbal Cues on Source Credibility." *Central States Speech Journal,* 24 (1973), 227–230.

Atkin, Charles K. "How Imbalanced Campaign Coverage Affects Audience Exposure Patterns." *Journalism Quarterly,* 47 (1971), 235–244.

Bach, George R., and Peter Wyden. *The Intimate Enemy: How to Fight Fair in Love and Marriage.* New York: Morrow, 1969.

Baird, John E. "The Effects of Speech Summaries upon Audience Comprehension of Expository Speeches of Varying Quality and Complexity." *Central States Speech Journal,* 25 (1974), 119–127.

Barnlund, Dean C. "Toward a Meaning-Centered Philosophy of Communication." *Journal of Communication,* 12 (1962), 197–211.

Beebe, Stephen A. "Eye Contact: A Nonverbal Determinant of Speaker Credibility." *Speech Teacher,* 23 (1974), 21–25.

Beisecker, Thomas D., and Donn W. Parson (eds.). *The Process of Social Influence: Readings in Persuasion.* Englewood Cliffs, N.J.: Prentice-Hall, 1972.

Bem, Daryl J. *Beliefs, Attitudes, and Human Affairs.* Belmont, Calif.: Brooks/Cole, 1970.

Berelson, Bernard R., Paul F. Lazarsfeld, and William N. McPhee. *Voting: A Study of Opinion Formulation in a Presidential Campaign.* Chicago: The University of Chicago Press, 1954.

Berlo, David K. *The Process of Communication: An Introduction to Theory and Practice.* New York: Holt, 1960.

Bitzer, Lloyd F. "Aristotle's Enthymeme Revisited." *Quarterly Journal of Speech,* 45 (1959), 399–408.

——(ed.). *The Philosophy of Rhetoric by George Campbell.* Carbondale: Southern Illinois University Press, 1963. This edition is a facsimile reprint of an 1850 edition of Campbell's *Philosophy.* The work was originally published in 1776.

Black, Henry C. *Blacks Law Dictionary.* 4th ed., revised by publisher's editorial staff. St. Paul, Minn.: West, 1968.

Boone, Pat. *A Miracle a Day Keeps the Devil Away,* Spire Books. Old Tappan, N.J.: Revell, 1975.

Booth, Wayne C. *Modern Dogma and the Rhetoric of Assent.* Notre Dame, Ind.: University of Notre Dame Press, 1974.

Bormann, Ernest G., William S. Howell, Ralph G. Nichols, and George L. Shapiro. *Interpersonal Communication in the Modern Organization.* Englewood Cliffs, N.J.: Prentice-Hall, 1969.

Bostrom, R. N., J. R. Baseheart, and C. M. Rossiter, Jr. "The Effects of Three Types of Profane Language in Persuasive Messages." *Journal of Communication,* 23 (1973), 461–475.

Boulding, Kenneth. *The Image.* Ann Arbor: The University of Michigan Press, 1956.

Bowers, John W. "Language Intensity, Social Introversion, and Attitude Change." *Speech Monographs,* 30 (1963), 345–352.

Brandt, William J. *The Rhetoric of Argumentation.* Indianapolis: Bobbs-Merrill, 1970.

Brennan, Joseph G. *A Handbook of Logic.* 2d ed. New York: Harper, 1961. Originally published in 1957.

Brock, Bernard L., James W. Chesebro, John F. Cragan, and James F. Klumpp. *Public Policy Decision-Making: Systems Analysis and Comparative Advantages Debate.* New York: Harper & Row, 1973.

Brockriede, Wayne. "Where is Argument?" *Journal of the American Forensic Association,* 9 (1975), 179–182.

Bugliosi, Vincent, and Curt Gentry. *Helter Skelter: The True Story of the Manson Murders.* New York: Bantam, 1975. Originally published in 1974.

Campbell, Donald T., and Julian Stanley. *Experimental and Quasi-Experimental Designs for Research.* Chicago: Rand McNally, 1966. This work is reprinted from a large 1963 *Handbook of Research on Teaching.*

Campbell, John A. "The Polemical Mr. Darwin." *Quarterly Journal of Speech,* 61 (1975), 375–390.

Carbone, Tamara. "Stylistic Variables As Related to Source Credibility: A Content Analysis Approach." *Speech Monographs,* 42 (1975), 99–106.

Carl, LeRoy M. "Meanings Evoked in Population Groups by Editorial Cartoons." Unpublished Ph.D. dissertation, Syracuse University, Syracuse, N.Y., 1967.

Carpenter, Ronald H., and Robert V. Seltzer, "Nixon, *Patton,* and a Silent Majority Sentiment about the Viet Nam War: The Cinematographic Bases of a Rhetorical Stance." *Central States Speech Journal,* 25, (1974), 105–110.

Carroll, Lewis [Charles L. Dodgson]. *Alice in Wonderland.* Norton Critical Edition, ed. Donald J. Gray. New York: Norton, 1971. *Alice* is a collection of works published by Carroll in the late 1860s and early 1870s.

Cicero. *De Inventione.* I have consulted the translation by H. M. Hubbell, Loeb Classical Library, published by Harvard University Press.

Clevenger, Theodore, Jr. *Audience Analysis.* Indianapolis: Bobbs-Merrill, 1966.

Copi, Irving M. *Symbolic Logic.* 3d ed. London: Macmillan, 1967. Originally published in 1954.

Corbett, Edward P. J. *Rhetorical Analyses of Literary Works.* New York: Oxford, 1969.

Crable, Richard E. *Argumentation as Communication: Reasoning with Receivers.* Columbus, Ohio: Merrill, 1976.

Cronkhite, Gary. *Persuasion: Speech and Behavioral Change.* Indianapolis: Bobbs-Merrill, 1969.

————, and Jo Liska. "A Critique of Factor Analytic Approaches to the Study of Credibility." *Communication Monographs,* 43 (1976), 91–107.

Crouse, Timothy. *The Boys on the Bus: Riding With the Campaign Press Corps.* New York: Ballantine Books, 1974. Originally published in 1973.

Darnell, Donald K. "The Relation Between Sentence Order and Comprehension." *Speech Monographs,* 30 (1963), 97–100.

Dean, John W., III. *Blind Ambition: The White House Years.* New York: Pocket Books, 1977. Originally published in 1976.

Delury, George E. (ed.). *The World Almanac and Book of Facts 1977.* New York: Newspaper Enterprise Association, 1976.

Dewey, John. *How We Think.* Lexington, Mass.: Heath, 1933. This is a revision of Dewey's original work of 1910.

Dick, Robert C. *Argumentation and Rational Debating.* Dubuque, Iowa: Wm. C. Brown, 1972.

Drabman, Ronald S., and Margaret H. Thomas. "Does TV Violence Breed Indifference?" *Journal of Communication,* 25, no. 4 (1975), 86–89.

Duker, Sam, and Charles W. Petrie. "What We Know About Listening: Continuation of a Controversy." *Journal of Communication,* 14 (1964), 245–252.

Ehninger, Douglas (ed.). *Contemporary Rhetoric: A Reader's Coursebook.* Glenview, Ill.: Scott, Foresman, 1972.

————, and Wayne Brockriede. *Decision By Debate.* New York: Dodd, Mead, 1963.

Eisenberg, Abne M., and Joseph A. Ilardo. *Argument: An Alternative to Violence.* Englewood Cliffs, N.J.: Prentice-Hall, 1972.

Fagothey, Austin, S. J. *Right and Reason: Ethics in Theory and Practice.* St. Louis: Mosby, 1972.

Fall, Bernard B. *The Two Viet-Nams: A Political and Military Analysis.* 2d rev. ed. New York: Praeger, 1967. Originally published in 1963.

Feezel, Jerry D. "A Qualified Certainty: Verbal Probability in Arguments." *Speech Monographs,* 41 (1974), 348–356.

Festinger, Leon. *A Theory of Cognitive Dissonance.* Stanford, Calif.: Stanford, 1957. This is a reissue of Festinger's book, published in 1957 by Row, Peterson.

Flynn, Lawrence J. "The Aristotelian Basis for the Ethics of Speaking." *Speech Teacher,* 6 (1957), 179–187.

Fotheringham, Wallace C. *Perspectives on Persuasion.* Boston: Allyn and Bacon, 1966.

Frankena, William K. *Ethics.* 2d ed. Englewood Cliffs, N.J.: Prentice-Hall, 1973. Originally published in 1963.

Gerbner, George, and Larry Gross. "The Scary World of TV's Heavy Viewer." *Psychology Today,* April 1976, pp. 41–45.

Giles, Howard. "Communication Effectiveness as a Function of Accented Speech." *Speech Monographs,* 40 (1973), 330–331.

Goldstein, Jeffrey, and Brenda J. Bredemeier. "Socialization: Some Basic Issues." *Journal of Communication,* 27, no. 3 (1977), 154–159.

Gorrell, Robert M., and Charlton Laird. *Modern English Handbook.* 4th ed. Englewood Cliffs, N.J.: Prentice-Hall, 1967. Originally published in 1953.

Goss, Blaine, and Lee Williams. "The Effects of Equivocation on Perceived Source Credibility." *Central States Speech Journal,* 24 (1973), 162–167.

Gunderson, D. F., and Robert Hopper. "Relationships between Speech Delivery and Speech Effectiveness." *Communication Monographs,* 43 (1976), 158–165.

Haley, Alex. *Roots.* Garden City, N.Y.: Doubleday, 1976.

Hart, Roland J., and Bruce L. Brown: "Interpersonal Information Conveyed by the Content and Vocal Aspects of Speech." *Speech Monographs,* 41 (1974), 371–380.

Hartwig, John. "The Achievement of Moral Rationality." *Philosophy and Rhetoric,* 6 (1973), 171–185.

Hayakawa, S. I. *Language in Thought and Action.* New York: Harcourt, Brace, 1949. Originally published as *Language in Action,* 1941.

Heider, Fritz. "Attitudes and Cognitive Organization." *Journal of Psychology,* 21 (1946), 107–112.

Himmelfarb, Samuel, and Alice H. Eagly (eds.). *Readings in Attitude Change.* New York: Wiley, 1974.

Hofstadter, Richard. *The Paranoid Style in American Politics and Other Essays.* Vintage Books. New York: Random House, 1967. The "Paranoid Style" essay was originally given as a lecture at Oxford University in November 1963.

Hopper, Robert, and Frederick Williams. "Speech Characteristics and Employability." *Speech Monographs,* 40 (1973), 296–302.

Hovland, Carl I., Irving L. Janis, and Harold H. Kelley. *Communication and Persuasion.* New Haven: Yale, 1953.

———, and W. Weiss. "The Influence of Source Credibility on Communication Effectiveness." *Public Opinion Quarterly,* 15 (1951), 635–650.

Hume, David. *Enquiries Concerning the Human Understanding and Concerning the Principles of Morals.* Ed. L. A. Selby-Bigge. 2d ed. Oxford: Clarendon Press, 1902. This work is an edited reprint of the posthumous 1777 edition of Hume's *Enquiry.*

Irvine, James R., and Walter G. Kirkpatrick. "The Musical Form in Rhetorical Exchange: Theoretical Considerations." *Quarterly Journal of Speech,* 58 (1972), 272–284.

Israel, Fred L. (ed.). *The State of the Union Messages of the Presidents, 1790–1966.* 3 vols. New York: Chelsea House–Robert Hector, 1966.

Johannesen, Richard L. (ed.). *Ethics and Persuasion: Selected Readings.* New York: Random House, 1967.

———, Rennard Strickland, and Ralph T. Eubanks (eds.). *Language is Sermonic: Richard M. Weaver on the Nature of Rhetoric.* Baton Rouge: Louisiana State University Press, 1970. This work is a collection of previously published essays by Weaver.

Kahane, Howard. *Logic and Contemporary Rhetoric: The Use of Reason in Everyday Life.* Belmont, Calif.: Wadsworth, 1971. Occasionally, I will refer to the 1976 second edition of this book.

Kaid, Lynda L., and Robert O. Hirsch. "Selective Exposure and Candidate Image: A Field Study Over Time." *Central States Speech Journal,* 24 (1973), 48–51.

Kelly, Charles M. "Empathic Listening." *Small Group Communication: A Reader.* Ed.

Robert S. Cathcart and Larry A. Samovar. Dubuque, Iowa: Wm. C. Brown, 1970. This essay appeared in print for the first time in this collection.

Kennedy, Robert F. *To Seek a Newer World*. Garden City, N.Y.: Doubleday, 1967.

Kerlinger, Fred N. *Foundations of Behavioral Research*. New York: Holt, 1964.

Key, Wilson B. *Media Sexploitation*. Signet Books. New York: New American Library, 1976.

———. *Subliminal Seduction*. Signet Books. New York: New American Library, 1973.

Kibler, Robert J., and Larry L. Barker (eds.). *Conceptual Frontiers in Speech-Communication*. New York: Speech Association of America, 1969.

Kimmel, Carol. "TV Violence: Are Parents Getting the Message? Children Are!" *Parents Magazine,* March 1977, p. 29.

Klapper, Joseph. *The Effects of Mass Communication*. New York: Free Press, 1960.

Klopf, Donald, and James McCroskey. "Ethical Practices in Debate." *Journal of the American Forensic Association,* 1 (1964), 13–16.

Knapp, Mark L. *Nonverbal Communication in Human Interaction*. New York: Holt, 1972.

Koestler, Arthur. *The Act of Creation*. New York: Macmillan, 1964.

Kraus, Sidney (ed.). *The Great Debates: Kennedy vs. Nixon, 1960*. Bloomington: Indiana University Press, 1977. Originally published in 1962.

———, and Dennis Davis. *The Effects of Mass Communication on Political Behavior*. University Park: Pennsylvania State University Press, 1976.

Kuhn, Thomas. *The Structure of Scientific Revolutions*. 2d ed. Chicago: The University of Chicago Press, 1970. Kuhn's book is Vol. II, no. 2, of the *International Encyclopedia of Unified Science*. It was originally published in 1962.

Lasswell, Harold D. *Propaganda Technique in World War I*. Cambridge, Mass.: M.I.T., 1971. Originally published in 1927 as *Propaganda Technique in the World War*.

Lawrence, Jerome, and Robert E. Lee. *The Night Thoreau Spent in Jail*. New York: French, 1971. This is the actors' script edition.

Lazarsfeld, Paul F., Bernard Berelson, and Hazel Gaudet. *The People's Choice: How the Voter Makes Up His Mind in a Presidential Campaign*. New York: Columbia, 1944.

Leeper, Robert. "A Study of a Neglected Portion of the Field of Learning—The Development of Sensory Organization." *Journal of Genetic Psychology,* 46 (1935), 41–75.

Lewis, George H. "Country Music Lyrics." *Journal of Communication,* 26, no. 4 (1976), 37–40.

Lippmann, Walter. *Public Opinion*. New York: Macmillan, 1960. Originally published in 1922.

Lott, Davis N. (ed.). *The Inaugural Addresses of the American Presidents: From Washington to Kennedy*. New York: Holt, 1961.

McCroskey, James C. "A Summary of Experimental Research on the Effects of Evidence in Persuasive Communication." *Quarterly Journal of Speech,* 55 (1969), 169–176.

———. *An Introduction to Rhetorical Communication*. 2d ed. Englewood Cliffs, N.J.: Prentice-Hall, 1972. Originally published in 1968.

———. "Experimental Studies of the Effects of Ethos and Evidence in Persuasive Communication." Unpublished Ed.D. dissertation, Pennsylvania State University, University Park, 1966.

———, and Walter H. Combs. "The Effects of the Use of Analogy on Attitude Change and Source Credibility." *Journal of Communication,* 19 (1969), 333–339.

————, and R. S. Mehrley. "The Effects of Disorganization and Nonfluency on Attitude Change and Source Credibility." *Speech Monographs,* 36 (1969), 13–21.

McGinniss, Joe. *The Selling of the President, 1968.* New York: Pocket Books, 1970. Originally published in 1969.

McGuckin, Henry E., Jr. "The Persuasive Force of Similarity in Cognitive Style between Advocate and Audience." *Speech Monographs,* 34 (1967), 145–151.

McKeon, Richard. "Aristotle's Conception of Language and the Arts of Language," in *Critics and Criticism: Ancient and Modern,* ed. R. S. Crane. Chicago: The University of Chicago Press, 1952. McKeon's essay originally appeared as articles in the October 1946 and January 1947 issues of *Classical Philology.*

————. "Rhetoric and Poetic in the Philosophy of Aristotle," in *Aristotle's "Poetics" and English Literature: A Collection of Critical Essays,* ed. Elder Olson. Chicago: The University of Chicago Press, 1965. McKeon's essay was specially written for this collection.

McLuhan, Marshall. *Understanding Media: The Extensions of Man.* Signet Books. New York: New American Library, 1964.

Mahoney, Michael J. "The Truth Seekers." *Psychology Today,* April 1976, pp. 60–65.

Mehrabian, Albert, and Martin Williams. "Nonverbal Concomitants of Perceived and Intended Persuasiveness." *Journal of Personality and Social Psychology,* 13 (1969), 37–58.

Mill, John Stuart. *A System of Logic: Ratiocinative and Inductive,* ed. J. M. Robson. Toronto: University of Toronto Press, 1973. This printing is based on Mill's 1872 eighth edition and includes "the substantive textual changes found in a complete collation of the eight editions and the Press-copy Manuscript" (p. ci).

————. *Utilitarianism, Liberty and Representative Government.* New York: Dutton, 1951. These essays originally were published separately as "Utilitarianism" (1861), "Liberty" (1859), and "Representative Government" (1861).

Miller, Dale T. "The Effect of Dialect and Ethnicity on Communicator Effectiveness." *Speech Monographs,* 42 (1975), 69–74.

Miller, Gerald R., and Michael Burgoon. *New Techniques of Persuasion.* New York: Harper & Row, 1973.

————, and Mark Steinberg. *Between People: A New Analysis of Interpersonal Communication.* Chicago: Science Research Associates, 1975.

Miller, Sherod, Elam W. Nunnally, and Daniel B. Wackman. *Alive and Aware: Improving Communication in Relationships.* Minneapolis: Interpersonal Communication Programs, Inc., 1975.

Minnick, Wayne C. *The Art of Persuasion.* 2d ed. Boston: Houghton Mifflin, 1968. Originally published in 1957.

Mitchell, Margaret. *Gone With the Wind.* New York: Avon, 1973. Originally published in 1936.

Moe, James D. "Listener Judgments of Status Cues in Speech: A Replication and Extension." *Speech Monographs,* 39 (1972), 144–147.

Mohrmann, G. P. and F. Eugene Scott. "Popular Music and World War II: The Rhetoric of Continuation." *Quarterly Journal of Speech,* 62 (1976), 145–156.

Monroe, Alan H., and Douglas Ehninger. *Principles and Types of Speech Communication.* 7th ed. Glenview, Ill.: Scott, Foresman, 1974. Originally published in 1935.

Montague, William P. *The Ways of Knowing Or the Methods of Philosophy.* London: G. Allen, 1936.

Mortensen, C. David. *Basic Readings in Communication Theory.* New York: Harper & Row, 1973.

Mulac, Anthony, "Effects of Obscene Language upon Three Dimensions of Listener Attitude." *Communication Monographs,* 43 (1976), 300–307.

———, and A. Robert Sherman. "Relationships among Four Parameters of Speaker Evaluation: Speech Skill, Source Credibility, Subjective Speech Anxiety and Behavioral Speech Anxiety." *Speech Monographs,* 42 (1975), 302–310.

Nevins, Allan, and Frank Weitenkampf. *A Century of Political Cartoons: Caricature in the United States from 1800–1900.* New York: Scribner, 1944.

Newcomb, Theodore M. "An Approach to the Study of Communication Acts." *Psychological Review,* 60 (1953), 393–404.

Newman, Robert P., and Dale R. Newman. *Evidence.* Boston: Houghton Mifflin, 1969.

———, and Keith R. Sanders. "A Study in the Integrity of Evidence." *Journal of the American Forensic Association,* 2 (1965), 7–13.

Nilsen, Thomas R. *Ethics of Speech Communication.* Indianapolis: Bobbs-Merrill, 1966.

Ogden, C. K., and I. A. Richards. *The Meaning of Meaning.* New York: Harcourt, Brace & World, 1923.

O'Neill, James M., Craven Laycock, and Robert Scales. *Argumentation and Debate.* New York: Macmillan, 1917.

Osgood, Charles E., George J. Suci, and Percy H. Tannenbaum. *The Measurement of Meaning.* Urbana: The University of Illinois Press, 1957.

Pace, R. Wayne, and Robert R. Boren. *Instructional Supplement to the Human Transaction.* Glenview, Ill.: Scott, Foresman, 1973.

Packard, Vance. *The Hidden Persuaders.* New York: Pocket Books, 1958. Originally published in 1957.

Paine, Albert B. *Th. Nast: His Period and His Pictures.* I have cited a facsimile, printed by the Pyne Press, of the 1904 edition.

Patton, Bobby R., and Kim Giffin. *Problem-Solving Group Interaction.* New York: Harper & Row, 1973.

Pearce, W. Barnett, and Bernard J. Brommel. "Vocalic Communication in Persuasion." *Quarterly Journal of Speech,* 58 (1972), 298–306.

Perelman, Chaim. *The Idea of Justice and the Problem of Argument.* London: Routledge, 1963.

———, and L. Olbrechts-Tyteca. *The New Rhetoric: A Treatise on Argumentation.* Trans. John Wilkinson and Purcell Weaver. Notre Dame, Ind.: University of Notre Dame Press, 1969. Originally published in 1958 in French.

Pines, Maya. "Is Sociobiology All Wet?" *Psychology Today,* May 1978, pp. 23–24.

Plato. *Gorgias.* Several translations are available.

———*Phaedrus.* Many translations of this work are available. I have used the translation by W. C. Helmbold and W. G. Rabinowitz, published by Bobbs-Merrill Co., Library of the Liberal Arts.

Plimpton, Francis, T. P. "U.S. Calls for Deeds, Not Words, in U.N. Committee on Defining Aggression." *Department of State Bulletin,* 52 (1965), 776.

Public Papers of the Presidents of the United States, Dwight D. Eisenhower, 1954. Washington: National Archives and Records Service, 1960.

Public Papers of the Presidents of the United States, Lyndon B. Johnson, 1965. 2 vols. Washington: National Archives and Records Service, 1966.

Quintilian. *Institutio Oratoria.* I have consulted the translation by H. E. Butler, Loeb Classical Library edition, published by Harvard University Press.

Report of the National Advisory Commission on Civil Disorders. New York: Bantam, 1968. An official version was published later by the U.S. Government Printing Office.

Rice, F. Edward, and Stanley C. Ratner. "Toward a Description of Language Behavior. II. The Listening Action." *Psychological Reports,* 17 (1967), 493–502.

Richards, I. A. *The Philosophy of Rhetoric.* Galaxy Books. New York: Oxford, 1965. Originally published in 1936.

Rieke, Richard D., and Malcolm O. Sillars. *Argumentation and the Decision-Making Process.* New York: Wiley, 1975.

Rights in Conflict: The Violent Confrontation of Demonstrators and Police in the Parks and Streets of Chicago During the Week of the Democratic National Convention of 1968. New York: Bantam, 1968. This work was a report submitted to the National Commission on the Causes and Prevention of Violence. It is sometimes called the "Walker Report" because its director was Daniel Walker.

Rives, Stanley G. (ed.). "1976 National Debate Tournament Final Round." *Journal of the American Forensic Association,* 13 (1976), 1–50.

Robinson, John P., Robert Pilskaln, and Paul Hirsch. "Protest Rock and Drugs." *Journal of Communication,* 26, no. 4 (1976), 125–136.

Robitscher, Jonas, and Roger Williams. "Should Psychiatrists Get Out of the Courtroom?" *Psychology Today,* December 1977, pp. 85–86, 91–92, 138, 140.

Rogers, Carl R. *On Becoming A Person.* Sentry Edition. Boston: Houghton Mifflin, 1961.

Rokeach, Milton. *Beliefs, Attitudes and Values: A Theory of Organization and Change.* San Francisco: Jossey-Bass, 1968.

———. *The Nature of Human Values.* New York: Free Press, 1973.

Roscoe, John T. *Fundamental Research Statistics for the Behavioral Sciences.* New York: Holt, 1969.

Rosenfeld, Lawrence B., and Timothy G. Plax. "The Relationship of Listener Personality to Perceptions of Three Dimensions of Credibility." *Central States Speech Journal,* 26 (1975), 274–278.

Rule, Elton. "Children's Television: The Parent's Role." *Vital Speeches,* October 15, 1976, pp. 24–26.

Rusk, Dean. "Laos and Viet-Nam—A Prescription for Peace." *Department of State Bulletin,* 50 (1964), 886–891.

Siegel, Elliot, Gerald R. Miller, and C. Edward Wotring. "Source Credibility and Credibility Proneness: A New Relationship." *Speech Monographs,* 36 (1969), 118–125.

Sikkink, Don. "Fundamental Change in Parliamentary Procedure." *Speech Teacher,* 24 (1975), 75–78.

Skinner, B. F. *Beyond Freedom and Dignity.* New York: Bantam/Vintage Books, 1971.

———. *Verbal Behavior.* Englewood Cliffs, N.J.: Prentice-Hall, 1957.

Skornia, Harry J. "The Great American Teaching Machine—of Violence." *Intellect,* April 1977, pp. 347–348.

Smith, Craig R. "Television News as Rhetoric." *Western Journal of Speech Communication,* 41 (1977), 147–159.

———, and David M. Hunsaker. *The Bases of Argument: Ideas in Conflict.* Indianapolis: Bobbs-Merrill, 1972.

Southern Educational Communications Association. *Debate: "Resolved: The Senate Should Ratify the Proposed Panama Canal Treaties,"* 1977. Southern Educational Communications Association, P.O. Box 5966 Columbia, South Carolina 29250.

Sproule, J. Michael. "The Case for A Wider War: A Study of the Administration Rationale for Commitment to Vietnam, 1964–1967." Unpublished Ph.D. dissertation, Ohio State University, Columbus, 1973.

Staff of *The New York Times* (eds.). *The Watergate Hearings: Break-In and Cover-Up.* New York: Viking Press, 1973.

Surgeon General's Report by the Scientific Advisory Committee on Television and Social Behavior, Hearings before the Subcommittee on Communications of the Committee on Commerce, U.S. Senate, 92d Cong., 2d Sess., March 21, 22, 23 and 24, 1972.

Thomas, Cheryl I. " 'Look What They've Done to My Song, Ma': The Persuasiveness of Song." *Southern Speech Communication Journal,* 39 (1974), 260–268.

Thonssen, Lester, A. Craig Baird, and Waldo W. Braden. *Speech Criticism.* 2d ed. New York: Ronald Press, 1970. Originally published in 1948.

Toulmin, Stephen E. *An Examination of the Place of Reason in Ethics.* Cambridge: University Press, 1968. Originally published in 1950.

———. *The Uses of Argument.* Cambridge: University Press, 1969. Originally published in 1958.

U.S. Department of State. *Aggression from the North: The Record of North Viet-Nam's Campaign to Conquer South Viet-Nam.* Far Eastern Series 130, Pubn, 7839 (February 1965).

Vinacke, W. Edgar. *The Philosophy of Thinking.* New York: McGraw-Hill, 1952.

Wallechinsky, David, Irving Wallace, and Amy Wallace. *The Book of Lists.* New York: Morrow, 1977.

Watzlawick, Paul, Janet H. Beavin, and Don D. Jackson. *Pragmatics of Human Communication: A Study of Interaction Patterns, Pathologies, and Paradoxes.* New York: Norton, 1967.

Weaver, Richard M. *Ideas Have Consequences.* Chicago: The University of Chicago Press, 1948.

———. *The Ethics of Rhetoric.* Gateway Edition. Chicago: Regnery, 1970. Originally published in 1953.

———. *Visions of Order: The Cultural Crisis of Our Time.* Baton Rouge: Louisiana State University Press, 1964.

Weizenbaum, Joseph. *Computer Power and Human Reason: From Judgment to Calculation.* San Francisco: Freeman, 1976.

White, Theodore H. *The Making of the President 1960.* Signet Books. New York: New American Library, 1967. Originally published in 1961.

———. *The Making of the President 1968.* New York: Pocket Books, 1970. Originally published in 1969.

Wilcox, James R. "The Argument From Analogy: A New Look." Unpublished paper presented at the Central States Speech Association Convention, Minneapolis, 1973.

Willard, Charles A. "On the Utility of Descriptive Diagrams for the Analysis and Criticism of Arguments." *Communication Monographs,* 43 (1976), 308–319.

Williams, Frederick (ed.). *Language and Poverty.* Chicago: Markham, 1970.

Young, Richard E., Alton L. Becker, and Kenneth L. Pike. *Rhetoric: Discovery and Change.* New York: Harcourt, Brace & World, 1970.

Ziegelmueller, George W., and Charles A. Dause. *Argumentation: Inquiry and Advocacy.* Englewood Cliffs, N.J.: Prentice-Hall, 1975.

Zinn, Howard. *Vietnam: The Logic of Withdrawal.* Boston: Beacon Press, 1967.

Name Index

Subject Index